BLACK
METROPOLIS

Publisher's Note to the 1993 Edition

This one-volume edition of *Black Metropolis* is a facsimile of the 1970 edition published in two volumes by Harcourt, Brace and World. While it includes everything printed in those volumes, the order of the new material has been changed so as not to interrupt the four parts of the original 1945 text.

The University of Chicago Press would like to thank Professor William Julius Wilson and Dr. James R. Grossman for help in planning and producing this edition.

ST. CLAIR DRAKE
AND HORACE R. CAYTON

BLACK
METROPOLIS

A STUDY OF NEGRO LIFE IN A
NORTHERN CITY

Revised and Enlarged Edition

With an Introduction by Richard Wright
and a new Foreword by William Julius Wilson

The University of Chicago Press

Reprinted by arrangement with Harcourt, Brace, Jovanovich, Inc.

The University of Chicago Press, Chicago 60637

Printed in the United States of America

99 98 97   6 5 4 3 2

ISBN 0-226-16234-6 (pbk.)

Library of Congress Cataloging-in-Publication Data

Drake, St. Clair.
    Black metropolis : a study of Negro life in a northern city / St. Clair Drake and
Horace R. Cayton. — Rev. and enl. ed., University of Chicago Press ed. / with an
introduction by Richard Wright and a new foreword by William Julius Wilson.
        p.   cm.
    Previously published in 2 v.: Rev. and enl. ed. New York : Harcourt, Brace & World,
[1970], in series: Harbinger book.
    Includes bibliographical references and index.
    1. Afro-Americans—Illinois—Chicago—Social conditions.   2. Afro-Americans—
Illinois—Chicago—Economic conditions.   3. Chicago (Ill.)—Social conditions.
4. Chicago (Ill.)—Economic conditions.   I. Cayton, Horace R. (Horace Roscoe),
1903–1970. II. Title.
F548.9.N4D73   1993
305.896´0730773 1—dc20

93-12615
CIP

⊗ The paper used in this publication meets the minimum requirements of the American
National Standard for Information Sciences—Permanence of Paper for Printed Library
Materials, ANSI Z39.48-1984.

Dedicated to

THE LATE PROFESSOR ROBERT E. PARK
of Tuskegee, the University
of Chicago, and Fisk;

AMERICAN SCHOLAR AND FRIEND
OF THE NEGRO PEOPLE;

who once said:

"Anthropology, the science of man, has been mainly concerned up to the present with the study of primitive peoples. But civilized man is quite as interesting an object of investigation, and at the same time his life is more open to observation and study. Urban life and culture are more varied, subtle and complicated, but the fundamental motives are in both instances the same."

Contents

List of Tables

List of Maps, Charts and Graphs

In the Appendix:

Authors' Acknowledgment

MANY YEARS OF RESEARCH AND THE EFFORTS OF A VERY LARGE NUMBER of persons have gone into the formation of this book. The original data were gathered on a series of projects financed by the Work Projects Administration, and referred to in this book as the Cayton-Warner Research. The studies began as investigations of the general social conditions surrounding the problem of juvenile delinquency on Chicago's "South Side." Employing the methods of both sociologists and social anthropologists, the research soon assumed the character of a study of the culture of the entire community, in order to determine the context within which the problem of delinquency could best be analyzed. As is evident from the book, the problem of delinquency ultimately became subordinated to the larger problem of the description and analysis of the structure and organization of the Negro community, both internally, and in relation to the metropolis of which it is a part.

In addition to the Work Projects Administration as a local and national agency, the following members of its administrative staff were particularly helpful: Miss Wilda A. Sawyer, Mrs. Amelia H. Baker, Mr. Frank J. Morris and Mr. Melvin L. Dollar. On the projects themselves, valuable assistance was rendered by Mrs. Mae C. Barnett, in charge of personnel; Mr. Lawrence Langford, who prepared most of the basic maps and charts; and Miss Juanita Simpson, who, for a time, was in charge of the statistical analyses.

Throughout the life of the research project—a period of about four years—approximately twenty research students in specialized fields participated in the collection and organization of material on various phases of Negro life. Through the assistance of the Julius Rosenwald Fund, their work, in the form of monographs, has been made available to the general public at the Parkway Community House in Chicago. The following persons were responsible for the preparation of these individual studies: Margaret Cross, St. Clair Drake, Mary Gardner, John Given, Viola Haygood, Elmer Henderson, Winifred

Ingram, Elizabeth Johns, George McCray, Mary Elaine Ogden, Lawrence Reddick, Joy Schultz, Estelle Hill Scott, Joseph Semper, Samuel Strong and Elizabeth Wimp. The Work Projects Administration has published three of these monographs in mimeographed form: St. Clair Drake, *Churches and Voluntary Associations in the Chicago Negro Community;* Mary Elaine Ogden, *The Chicago Negro Community: A Statistical Description;* and Estelle Hill Scott, *Occupational Changes Among Negroes in Chicago, 1890-1930.*

From its inception, the research was under the direction of Horace R. Cayton and W. Lloyd Warner, Professor of Sociology and Anthropology at the University of Chicago.

The various projects were sponsored by the Institute of Juvenile Research, the Illinois State Employment Service and the Cook County Bureau of Public Welfare. Individual sponsors were Dr. Earl Johnson and Dr. Louis Wirth, of the University of Chicago.

Various types of assistance were rendered to the research, also, by the Church of the Good Shepherd, the Citizens' Committee on Reemployment, the Chicago *Defender* and the University of Chicago. All of the community institutions studied, although they cannot be listed separately, were most co-operative and helpful.

A preliminary organization of the research materials was made possible by a grant from the Julius Rosenwald Fund. As originally conceived, the material was to have been presented as a research report with emphasis upon methodology in the social sciences. Later, however, the authors, wishing to reach a wider audience, developed the book in its present form. In addition to condensing, rewriting and interpreting the material from the monographs, the authors have, over a period of three years, collected new data with which to bring the book up to date. Since the monographs were used only as primary source material, neither the authors of the individual monographs, the sponsors of the projects, nor the Work Projects Administration can be held responsible for any of the interpretations and conclusions found in these pages.

The basic source materials for this book are the interview documents and newspaper excerpts collected on the Cayton-Warner Research. The most valuable secondary sources have been those publications of the University of Chicago Press referred to throughout the book. The authors wish to express their appreciation to Mr. Joseph A. Brandt,

AUTHORS' ACKNOWLEDGMENT xv

Director of the University of Chicago Press, for granting them permission to make such generous use of these sources.

The authors wish to acknowledge courtesies extended to them during various phases of the writing by the Parkway Community House, Chicago, and Dillard University, New Orleans, Louisiana. We should like also to thank Miss Arleen Wilson and Miss E. Switzer for their conscientious work in assisting in the checking of sources and the preparation of final copy.

The first six chapters of the book were read critically by Dr. Lawrence D. Reddick, historian, and Curator of the Schomburg Collection. The authors have also, from time to time, received some very valuable critical comments from Mr. Elmer W. Henderson, formerly Director of the Illinois State Commission on the Condition of the Urban Colored Population, and now Midwestern Regional Director of the Fair Employment Practices Committee. Dr. Elizabeth Johns Drake assisted throughout in the preparation of the manuscript for the press, and gave valuable technical assistance at various stages of the work.

The authors sincerely appreciate the unusual interest displayed by Mrs. Elizabeth Moore, who made editorial suggestions, and Mr. Bunji Tagawa, of Graphic Associates, who prepared the illustrations in their present form. Finally, the authors wish to express their appreciation for the sustained interest and encouragement shown by Mr. John Woodburn whose mature understanding of Negro-white relations and Negro life in America has been of great assistance.

ST. CLAIR DRAKE
HORACE R. CAYTON

Introduction by Richard Wright

IT IS WITH A SENSE OF KEEN PRIDE THAT I UNDERTAKE TO INTRODUCE
Black Metropolis, a landmark of research and scientific achievement,
to the reading public. I, in common with the authors, St. Clair
Drake and Horace R. Cayton, feel personally identified with the
material in this book. All three of us have lived some of our most
formative years in Chicago; indeed, one of the authors, Horace Cayton, still lives there. Drake and Cayton, like me, were not born there;
all three of us migrated to Chicago to seek freedom, life. . . . Drake
came from the South; Cayton from the Northwest; and I went to
Chicago as a migrant from Mississippi. And there in that great iron
city, that impersonal, mechanical city, amid the steam, the smoke, the
snowy winds, the blistering suns; there in that self-conscious city, that
city so deadly dramatic and stimulating, we caught whispers of the
meanings that life could have, and we were pushed and pounded by
facts much too big for us. Many migrants like us were driven and
pursued, in the manner of characters in a Greek play, down the paths
of defeat; but luck must have been with us, for we somehow survived; and, for those of us who did not come through, we are trying
to do the bidding of Hamlet who admonished Horatio:

> If thou didst ever hold me in thy heart,
> Absent thee from felicity awhile,
> And in this harsh world draw thy breath in pain,
> To tell my story.

Chicago is the city from which the most incisive and radical Negro
thought has come; there is an open and raw beauty about that city
that seems either to kill or endow one with the spirit of life. I felt those
extremes of possibility, death and hope, while I lived half hungry
and afraid in a city to which I had fled with the dumb yearning to
write, to tell my story. But I did not know what my story was, and
it was not until I stumbled upon science that I discovered some of
the meanings of the environment that battered and taunted me. I

encountered the work of men who were studying the Negro community, amassing facts about urban Negro life, and I found that
sincere art and honest science were not far apart, that each could enrich the other. The huge mountains of fact piled up by the Department of Sociology at the University of Chicago gave me my first
concrete vision of the forces that molded the urban Negro's body and
soul. (I was never a student at the university; it is doubtful if I could
have passed the entrance examination.)

It was from the scientific findings of men like the late Robert E.
Park, Robert Redfield, and Louis Wirth that I drew the meanings
for my documentary book, *12,000,000 Black Voices;* for my novel,
Native Son; it was from their scientific facts that I absorbed some of
that quota of inspiration necessary for me to write *Uncle Tom's Children* and *Black Boy. Black Metropolis,* Drake's and Cayton's scientific
statement about the urban Negro, pictures the environment out of
which the Bigger Thomases of our nation come; it is the environment
of the Bosses of the Buildings; and it is the environment to which
Negro boys and girls turn their eyes when they hear the word Freedom.

Chicago is the *known* city; perhaps more is known about it, how
it is run, how it kills, how it loves, steals, helps, gives, cheats, and
crushes than any other city in the world. Chicago is a new city; it
grew to be bigger in one hundred years than did Paris in two thousand. There are men now living in Chicago whose fathers saw it in
its infancy and helped it to grow. Because Chicago is so young, it is
possible to know it in a way that many other cities cannot be known.
The stages of its complex growth are living memories.

Chicago, it seems, has a way of leaving its imprint upon those
who live in it; there have been so many direct, realistic novels and
poems and plays written about Chicago by the men who have lived
in it that there rose the phrase: The Chicago School. From Chicago
have come Sandburg, Anderson, Dreiser, Farrell, Levin, Cohen,
Algren, Masters, Conroy; and even Sinclair Lewis lived there for
a while. The imaginative expressions of these men have set the tone
and pattern of literary thinking and feeling for a large part of the
nation for almost two generations.

But the spell of Chicago has invaded more than the literary terrain;
the extent to which scientists have relied upon the city for their basic
truth of America's social life is no less interesting. It is in Chicago's

school of scientific thought that one finds a close affinity among the disciplines of sociology, psychology, and anthropology, and the men most responsible for this, Louis Wirth, Robert Redfield, and the late Robert E. Park, were not afraid to urge their students to trust their feelings for a situation or an event, were not afraid to stress the role of insight, and to warn against a slavish devotion to figures, charts, graphs, and sterile scientific techniques. Scientific volumes brilliantly characterized by insight and feeling are Robert Redfield's *Tepotzlan,* Louis Wirth's *The Ghetto,* Everett V. Stonequist's *The Marginal Man,* Frederick M. Thrasher's *The Gang,* Park's and Burgess's *The City* and Harvey W. Zorbaugh's *The Gold Coast and the Slums.*

Especially has no other community in America been so intensely studied, has had brought to bear upon it so blinding a scrutiny as Chicago's South Side. It was in the University of Chicago's Department of Sociology that such men as E. Franklin Frazier who produced *The Negro Family in Chicago* and *The Negro Family in the United States,* Bertrand Doyle who produced *The Etiquette of Race Relations in the South* and Harold F. Gosnell who produced *Negro Politicians,* were trained and guided. In no other city has the differentiation between groups and races been so clearly shown; nowhere has it been revealed so vividly, for example, how birth rates, death rates, etc., vary as people move out of the center of the city to its outer edges. This, in short, constitutes some of the vast amount of research that preceded Drake's and Cayton's *Black Metropolis.*

But let me bluntly warn the reader at the outset: This is no easy book. In order to understand it, you may have to wrench your mind rather violently out of your accustomed ways of thinking. There is no attempt in *Black Metropolis* to understate, to gloss over, to doll up, or make harsh facts pleasant for the tender-minded. The facts of urban life presented here are in their starkest form, their crudest manifestation; not because the authors want to shock you, but because the environment out of which those facts spring has so wrought them. To have presented them otherwise would have been to negate the humanity of the American Negro.

Black Metropolis reveals (1) the relationship of Negroes to whites in Chicago, (2) the kind of world which Negroes have built up under their separate, subordinate status, and (3) the impact of these twin configurations upon the personalities and institutions of Chicago

Negroes. The fundamental sociological concepts employed are: industrialization, secularization, urbanization, social differentiation, the latter showing the social stratification and the development of social types.

The dominant hallmark of the book is the combination throughout of the disciplines of both sociology and anthropology. The book examines the social structure as though it were frozen at a moment of time, which is the approach of anthropology; and it examines the processes and dynamics which take place in that structure, which is the approach of sociology. In general, the book can be thought of in a phrase that Louis Wirth has used to describe the lives of people who live in cities: Urbanism As a Way of Life; but with this important exception: The Jim Crow lives that Negroes live in our crowded cities differ qualitatively from those of whites and are not fully known to whites.

If, in reading my novel, *Native Son,* you doubted the reality of Bigger Thomas, then examine the delinquency rates cited in this book; if, in reading my autobiography, *Black Boy,* you doubted the picture of family life shown there, then study the figures on family disorganization given here. *Black Metropolis* describes the processes that mold Negro life as we know it today, processes that make the majority of Negroes on Chicago's South Side sixth-graders, processes that make 65 per cent of all Negroes on Chicago's South Side earn their living by manual labor. After studying the social processes in this book, you cannot expect Negro life to be other than what it is. To expect the contrary would be like expecting to see Rolls-Royces coming off the assembly lines at Ford's River Rouge plant! The imposed conditions under which Negroes live detail the structure of their lives like an engineer outlining the blue-prints for the production of machines.

Do not hold a light attitude toward the slums of Chicago's South Side. Remember that Hitler came out of such a slum. Remember that Chicago could be the Vienna of American Fascism! Out of these mucky slums can come ideas quickening life or hastening death, giving us peace or carrying us toward another war.

Can America change these conditions? Or is it hopeless to expect an understanding of this problem? If this problem cannot be mastered, then one thing is fairly certain: The liberals, the intellectuals, the artists, the students, Communists, Socialists, New Dealers, all who hope for life and peace will lose to war. In short, what happened in Europe during the past twenty years will happen here.

I'm not naive enough to believe that many will heed such Cassandra-like warnings, for not many people really believe that any such crisis exists. Hence, at the risk of sounding didactic, I will try to show that there is a problem facing us, a bigger one than even that of the Negro, a problem of which the Negro problem is a small but a highly symbolically important part.

Lodged in the innermost heart of America is a fatal division of being, a war of impulses. America knows that a split is in her, and that that split might cause her death; but she is powerless to pull the dangling ends together. An uneasiness haunts her conscience, taints her moral preachments, lending an air of unreality to her actions, and rendering ineffectual the good deeds she feels compelled to do in the world. America is a nation of a riven consciousness. But from where did the split, the division come?

When man cast off the ancient shrouds of his feudal faith, he had supreme confidence in the natural dignity of man, and believed that reason and freedom could lead him to paradise on earth. Man of Western Europe lunged toward the future, but in the very moment of his acting he committed that error which might well spell his tragedy. Passionately ardent to make his place on earth secure, he snatched millions of black men out of Africa and enslaved them to serve him.

But the white man suffered hang-overs from a feudal morality; he could not enslave others in a confident manner. Having bid for freedom upon the assumption that all men were naturally free, that they possessed in their hearts those impulses that made dignity and nobility a given human right, he could not play the role of master with a singleness of heart. So, to keep what he had and to feel safe with it, he had to invent reasons, causes, explanations, rationalizations, all of which amounted to a declaration of the biological inferiority of the enslaved. Paradoxes and contradictions of thought and feeling became commonplace. It was claimed that white men were "helping" black men by enslaving them; it finally became right to treat black men wrong, and wrong to treat them right. The apex of white racial ideology was reached when it was assumed that white domination was a God-given right.

But another and deeper dilemma rose out of the white man's break with the feudal order, a dilemma more acidly corroding than even that of slavery, one which colored and toned every moment of his life, creating an anxiety that was never to leave him. The advent of machine production altered his relationship to the earth, to his family, to his fellow men, and even to himself. Under feudalism the family had been the unit of production, the nexus of emotional relations, a symbol of the moral order of the universe. The father was the head of the family, the king the father of the state, and God the ruler of the world, and God's priests represented Him in the mundane affairs of man. The eternal and temporal orders of existence coalesced and formed one vivid, timeless moment of meaning, justification, and redemption. Man and earth and heaven formed a unit.

Following the break with the feudal order, philosophers played the role of mediators between the old order and the new, but the facts of machine production proved, in the long run, more powerful in ordering men's lives than even the rationalizations of scientists and thinkers who sought to justify the new dispensation.

Their kinship with the soil altered, men became atoms crowding great industrial cities, bewildered as to their duties and meaning. As Robert Redfield has pointed out: Holy days became holidays; clocks replaced the sun as a symbolic measurement of time. As the authority of the family waned, the meaning of reality, emotion, experience, action, and God assumed the guise of teasing questions. These processes, of course, were realized unevenly in men's consciousness; there were violent jumps and leaps (war) and static periods, lulls (peace); many millions who were daily involved in the processes of change did not realize what was happening until a war came and destroyed some of the lingering, surviving fragments of feudal reality and made a part of the reality that they were *actually, really* living the overwhelming contemporaneous reality. (It was in this way that the fiction that war was an instrument of progress came to find shelter in men's confused minds.)

Men still cling to the emotional basis of life that the feudal order gave them, while living and striving in a world whose every turn of wheel, throb of engine, and conquest of space deny its validity. This dual aspect of living is our riven consciousness, our tension, our anxiety.

The best philosophic energy of American thought has gone into trying to "tell what time it is," how far we have strayed from the feudal home, or how close we have come to making ourselves feel secure in an arid and senseless world. The philosophies of William James and John Dewey, and all the pragmatists in between, are but intellectual labors to allay the anxieties of modern man, adjurations to the white men of the West to accept uncertainty as a way of life, to live within the vivid, present moment and let the meaning of that moment suffice as a rationale for life and death.

But man refuses to behave; having once awakened from the feudal dream and tasted of the sweet fruits of sensuality, speculation, wonder, curiosity, freedom of movement, he will accept nothing less. Stimulated by the pinch of circumstance, he acts irrationally; he won't let well enough alone; he sulks; he broods; he dreams; he revolts; his consciousness spills disdainfully over the banks of pragmatism. Everywhere in the Western world men are rejecting the life of an industrialization which has pounded their lives to meaninglessness, which has reduced them to appendages to machines. Defiantly men hoist up the old slogans of liberty, love, justice, and happiness; and no authority, civil or religious, has yet found a way to divest their minds completely of a belief and trust in these magic signs. (Even Freud, after plowing up man's pleasure-ridden unconscious, seemed to have reeled back in fear and began to babble of a "reality-principle," began to search for some way to reconcile man's inordinate desires with a world that contained no feasible promise of their fulfillment. And even Communists or Fascists, ideologically rigid though they may be, must make use of man's hope-symbols if they want to get a following. And the capitalists themselves contribute campaign funds to politicians whose sworn duty it is to stamp out of the community those very impulses whose existence makes profits possible. Modern man is afraid of himself and is at war with himself.)

Current American thought is so fastened upon trying to make what is *presently* real the only and right reality, that it has quite forgot the reality of the passion and hunger of millions of exploited workers and dissatisfied minorities; it has quite forgot the reality of the impulses that made the men of Western Europe rise and slay the feudal dragon; it has quite forgot the reality of the hot laws of feeling that gave rise to rebellions against oppressive authority. Out of the vast pools of feudal misery, men found the meaning of Revolution; but out of the vaster pools of the misery of industrialization the sons of the men who overthrew the feudal world claim that no new life can spring up, no revolutionary creation can take place. The lives of the dispossessed are not real to them.

America's attitude toward the just-finished war in Europe is an example of how the men who run our industrial world cannot see what really *is*. Locked in the stance of defending the reality they loved, but few Americans believed that the reality of a Hitler was possible; and when, belatedly, they found that he did exist, they naively thought that they could "do business with him." The very conditions of life that nurtured Hitler were not acknowledged for what they were: Seed-beds of revolution. And it is doubtful if a war—which is not yet over—costing 40,000,000 casualties, war with all of its terrible and bloody immediacy, has made what the *real* reality of our time is real for them. It may take yet another war to make them see what really *is*. The hardest thing on earth today for current thought to accept is that we are living through a series of revolutions.

But this has happened before. When the Russians, sick of their feudal prison, smashed out to freedom, the industrial magnates of the West did not believe that Russia could become industrialized, did not believe that Russian peasants had an aptitude for machinery, even when immigrant Russian peasants were operating machines under their very noses in a dozen American cities. It was comforting to believe that only the magical spirit of a God-fearing capitalism could operate machines skillfully.

Hitler saw and cynically exploited the weak spots in our society perhaps more clearly than any politician of modern times. History will no doubt dub the Hitlerites as the most devastating critics of our dis-organized industrial order, not even excepting the Bolsheviks of 1917! Hitler knew his industrial slums, knew the brutalized millions trapped in them, knew their hungers, knew their humiliations, knew the feverish longing of their hearts. Capitalists today hate Hitler for his wholesale, gratuitous murders; but they hate him for another and subtler reason: They hate him for revealing the shaky, class founda-tions of their society, for reminding them of their sundered conscious-ness, for flaunting their hypocrisy, for sneering at their hesitations, for manipulating their racial hatreds to a degree that they had never dared. Gangster of the human spirit that he was, Hitler organized into a brutal army the men who live in those areas of society that the

Western world had neglected, organized those men whose reality the Western world could not see.

Let us disentangle in our minds Hitler's deeds from what Hitler exploited. His deeds were crimes; but the hunger he exploited in the hearts of Europe's millions was a valid hunger and is still there. Indeed, the war has but deepened that hunger, made it more acute.

Today the problem of the world's dispossessed exists with great urgency, and the problem of the Negro in America is a phase of this general problem, containing and telescoping the longings in the lives of a billion colored subject colonial people into a symbol. Yes, when the Negro problem is raised, white men, for a reason which as yet they do not fully understand, feel guilt, panic, anxiety, tension; they feel the essential loneliness of their position which is built upon greed, exploitation, and a general denial of humanity; they feel the naked untenability of their split consciousness, their two-faced moral theories spun to justify their right to dominate.

But the American Negro, child of the culture that crushes him, wants to be free in a way that white men are free; for him to wish otherwise would be unnatural, unthinkable. Negroes, with but minor exceptions, still believe in the hope of economic rewards; they believe in justice, liberty, the integrity of the individual. In the heart of industrial America is a surviving remnant, perchance a saving remnant of a passion for freedom, a passion fanned by their national humiliation.

Black Metropolis is a scientific report upon the state of unrest, longing, hope among urban Negroes, and in writing it Drake and Cayton were working within the compass of the most normal ideas and moral imperatives of the West. A greater claim than that no American can make for the right to be heard.

Sometimes northern white men, seeing the misery of the northern urban Negro, exclaim: "Why do Negroes leave the sunny South to live like this?" When a white man asks such a question, he is either deliberately or conveniently forgetting that white men once left the slumberous feudal world and eagerly took the risks of, as William James phrased it, an "unguaranteed existence." So, too, when the Negro, responding to the cultural hopes of his time, leaves the South and comes to the cold, industrial North, he is acting upon the same impulses that made the men of the West great. The Negro can do no less; he shares all of the glorious hopes of the West, all of its anxieties, its corruptions, its psychological maladies. But, too, above all, like a warning, he shares those tendencies toward surrendering all hope of seeking solutions within the frame of a "free enterprise" society. To the extent that he realizes that his hopes are hopeless, he will embrace Communism or Fascism, or whatever other ideological rejection is offered.

In *Black Metropolis,* the authors have presented much more than the anatomy of Negro frustration; they have shown how *any* human beings can become mangled, how *any* personalities can become distorted when men are caught in the psychological trap of being emotionally committed to the living of a life of freedom which is denied them. The Germans had more than their share of this fundamental frustration, and it was their hopeless hope that Hitler and his murderous legions battened on.

Not long ago I saw one of the greatest documentary films ever made, *Triumph des Willens,* which showed the rise of German Fascism and the "joy" that Hitler gave (while Himmler burned the dissenters!) millions of his duped followers. What vital images flick-ered across the screen! What limpid faith, what completeness of liv-ing! But, as I watched the tragedy of men being cynically betrayed unto death, I wondered if men who love life would lead the next "wave of the future," or would haters like Hitler? I could not answer with certainty.

What would be the reaction if *Triumph des Willens* were shown to a group of American industrialists, law-makers, and college profes-sors with a commentary that said: "Here is what will happen to the millions who inhabit Chicago, New York, Pittsburgh, and Los An-geles, if you and your kind do not lead them to a life compatible with the dignity of their aspirations"? I'm convinced that the professors would say, "Prove it!" The law-makers would say, "Our police force can stop such people from taking power." Our industrialists would say, "The prospect that people will follow such paths is a romantic dream." And their answers would be sincerely given, for they simply do not see the reality of the dispossessed. Their attitude could be de-scribed by a phrase which Negroes have coined to indicate the con-tempt which whites show Negroes: "They play people cheap."

Social discontent assumes many subtle guises, and a society that recognizes only those forms of social maladjustment which are re-corded in courts, prisons, clinics, hospitals, newspapers, and bureaus of vital statistics will be missing some of the most fateful of the tell-tale clues to its destiny. What I mean is this: It is distinctly possible to know, *before it happens,* that certain forms of violence will occur. It can be known that a native-born white man, the end-product of all our strivings, educated, healthy, apparently mentally normal, having the stability of a wife and family, possessing the security of a good job with high wages, enjoying more freedom than any other country on earth accords its citizens, *but devoid of the most elementary satisfactions,* will seize upon an adolescent, zoot-suited Mexican and derive deep feelings of pleasure from stomping his hopeless guts out upon the pavements of Los Angeles. But to know that a seemingly normal, ordinary American is capable of such brutality implies making a judgment about the nature and quality of our everyday American experiences which most Americans simply cannot do. FOR, TO ADMIT THAT OUR INDIVIDUAL EXPERIENCES ARE OF SO LOW A QUALITY AND NATURE AS TO PRECLUDE THE DEEP, ORGANIC SATISFACTIONS NECESSARY FOR CIVILIZED, PEACEFUL LIVING, IS TO CONDEMN THE SYSTEM THAT PROVIDES THOSE EXPERIENCES.

Drake and Cayton, in *Black Metropolis,* do not dwell upon these imponderables; but, in writing this definitive study of Negro urbanization, they were conscious of the over-all American problem and they had to assume that white Americans know little or nothing of the Negro, that a mere statement of his problem would go against the grain of American thought and feeling; they had to assume that Negro personality, Negro conditions of life, Negro feelings, and the ardent and ofttimes bitter nature of Negro aspirations constituted an alien realm for white Americans, were unreal to them.

The authors know well that white Americans take it for granted that they know Negroes, and they understand why whites hold to their presumed knowledge with such fierceness. The authors know that the Negro has been on the American scene for some three hundred years, and has been in our society as a more or less free agent for more than seventy-five years. They know, too, that a book like *Black Metropolis* might come as a jolt to whites who assume that their knowledge of the Negro excels the knowledge of Negroes by Negroes. Some whites will feel that the authors were impertinent; others will feel that they had some special ax to grind. Yet nothing could be more erroneous.

What spurred the authors to this task was a conviction on their part that there existed a meaning in Negro life that whites do not see and do not want to see. The authors have an acute concern, not only for the welfare of the Negro, but for the nation as a whole. They willingly shouldered the risks of having gross and fantastic motives imputed to them, for they know that violent events will soon flare forth, prompted either by whites or blacks; and they know that white Americans will stand transfixed in bewilderment at the magnitude and sanguinity of these events. When those events come, the authors want you to know their relationship to you and your life, how to interpret the racial outbreaks that will plague America in the immediate postwar world. This book was written, too, so that Negroes will be able to interpret correctly the meaning of their own actions.

It will be but natural for this honest question to be asked by both whites and blacks: If the racial scene depicted here is true, if the points of view presented here are valid, if the meanings deduced here are real, then why have we not been told all this before?

An honest question merits an honest answer, and that answer lies in the hearts of the white and black readers of this book. The answer is, directly and bluntly: American whites and blacks both possess deep-seated resistances against the Negro problem being presented, even verbally, in all of its hideous fullness, in all of the totality of its meaning. The many and various groups, commissions, councils, leagues, committees, and organizations of an interracial nature have consistently diluted the problem, blurred it, injected foggy moral or sentimental notions into it. This fact is as true of the churches as of the trade unions; as true of Negro organizations as of white; as true of the political Left as of the political Right; as true of white individuals as of black.

The church in America has shied from presenting this problem to the American people from a moral point of view, for fear that it would place itself in a position of having to do something about it. On the other hand, the trade unions, which have so far done more than any other single agency on the Negro front, seek to convert the Negro problem from a complex, race, cultural, and national problem into a relatively simple one of class conflicts and interests. As a result of the trade union attitude, there now exists within the trade union movement many grave problems affecting the Negro people; but there does not exist as yet a satisfactory form of communication by which

Negro trade unionists can make their voices heard as Negroes about their problems.

The political Left often gyrates and squirms to make the Negro problem fit rigidly into a class-war frame of reference, when the roots of that problem lie in American culture as a whole; it tries to anchor the Negro problem to a patriotism of global time and space, which robs the problem of its reality and urgency, of its concreteness and tragedy. The political Right, reacting traditionally, tries to smother the Negro problem as a whole and insists upon regarding Negroes as individuals and making individual deals with individual Negroes, ignoring the inevitable race consciousness which three hundred years of Jim Crow living has burned into the Negro's heart. Both the political Left and the political Right try to change the Negro problem into something that they can control, thereby denying the humanity of the Negro, excluding his unique and historic position in American life.

The powerful Negro press, too, is somewhat afraid of stating the problem of the Negro fully; it is apprehensive lest the concentrated gravity of that problem create such anxiety in whites that they will withdraw what few paltry concessions they are now yielding.

The authors have sensitively studied all of these factors and they have come to the conclusion that any dangers inherent in speaking out boldly and honestly far outweigh adherence to traditional reticences, which strip the problem of its political, moral, spiritual, class, and economic meaning.

But *Black Metropolis* is not a volume of mere facts. The basic facts are assumed. The hour is too late to argue if there *is* a Negro problem or not. Riots have swept the nation and more riots are pending. This book assumes that the Negro's present position in the United States results from the oppression of Negroes by white people, that the Negro's conduct, his personality, his culture, his entire life flow naturally and inevitably out of the conditions imposed upon him by white America. To that extent this book supplements and endorses the conclusions arrived at by Gunnar Myrdal in his *American Dilemma,* that monumental study of race relations in the United States.

The authors have not submitted a total program of action in this book; rather, they have assumed the ultimate aspirations of the Negro, just as Negroes have always assumed them, and just as whites assume theirs. Negroes feel that they are politically and culturally Americans.

The job of the authors was not to quiet or soothe, but to aid white people in knowing the facts of urban Negro life. The authors knew well that there will be many ill-intentioned whites who will seize upon certain sections of this book, lift them out of context, and try to prove their own pet notions of Negro inferiority with them. No attempt was made to forestall such possibilities; it was assumed that the Negro is human, all-too-human.

How can any individual, group, or political party, after reading *Black Metropolis,* bring forth an organizational or ideological program for Negroes without taking into account the durable and sturdy foundation of fact presented here? The decisive and pivotal centers of Negro life in America are to be found in our northern industrial cities, and I would go so far as to say that the measure of sincerity of any individual, group, or political party seeking support among Negroes should be judged by the manner in which it effectively grapples with what Drake and Cayton have so meticulously revealed.

With the bare bones of this problem thus rendered visible, many new ideological excursions, many heretofore unimagined tangents of thought can now be contemplated. For example, what peculiar personality formations result when millions of people are forced to live lives of outward submissiveness while trying to keep intact in their hearts a sense of the worth of their humanity? What are the personality mechanisms that sublimate racial resentments which, if expressed openly, would carry penalties varying from mild censure to death? Does the Negro's tremendous fund of repression affect his speech, his walk, his dress, his music, his health? Why are the highest rates of hyper-tension (high blood-pressure) to be found among the Negro sharecroppers on the plantations of the pastoral South? Is this hypertension in any way related to their daily and dramatic rejection by the society in which they live and work and die, the society whose language they speak and whose cultural mandates they try so hard to follow and serve? Why do the personalities of American Negroes show more psychological damage than do the personalities of the Negroes of the West Indies? And is this psychological differential between British and American Negroes in any way derived from their different relationships to the two Anglo-Saxon imperialisms?

There is yet another vista now open for us, a vista of which only artists have so far availed themselves: What new values of action or experience can be revealed by looking at Negro life through alien eyes or under the lenses of new concepts? We have the testimony of a Gunnar Myrdal, but we know that that is not all. What would life on Chicago's South Side look like when seen through the eyes of a Freud, a Joyce, a Proust, a Pavlov, a Kierkegaard? It should be recalled in this connection that Gertrude Stein's *Three Lives,* which contained "Melanctha," the first long serious literary treatment of Negro life in the United States, was derived from Stein's preoccupation with Jamesian psychology.

We know how some of the facts look when seen under the lenses of Marxist concepts, but the full weight of the Western mind has yet to be brought to bear upon this forgotten jungle of black life that lies just across the street or next door or around the corner from white Americans. (How easy it is to leave Chicago and fight and die for democracy in Spain! How soothing it is to prefer to civilize the heathen in Japan when slave conditions exist in Florida! But few white Americans have found the strength to cease being victims of their culture to the extent that they can throw off their socially inherited belief in a dehumanized image of the Negro. Indeed, the whole inner landscape of American Negro life, born of repression, is so little known that when whites see it they brand it "emotionally running amuck" or "psychopathic manifestations.")

What benefits will accrue to our country if this problem is solved? Will it so unify our moral duality as to permit the flowering of our political and cultural expression? (Some politicians have estimated that the presence of rigid anti-Negro feeling in our country has retarded our political development by more than fifty years!) Or will America, when she is brought face to face with the problem of the Negro, collapse in a moral spasm, as did Europe when confronted with the problem of the Jew?

Will the Negro, in the language of André Malraux, find a meaning in his humiliation, make his slums and his sweat-shops his modern cathedrals out of which will be born a new consciousness that can guide him toward freedom? Or will he continue, as he does today, saying Job-like to the society that crushes him: Though it slays me, yet will I trust in it?

In reading those sections of *Black Metropolis* dealing with the wide prevalence of "policy playing" (lottery) among urban Negroes, we can ask with ample justification: What are the limits of individual responsibility for crime? And what is crime, anyway?

And we can ask, after reading the scandalous facts of the low level of literacy among Negro migrants in northern cities, if more education without more opportunity will solve anything. Or will more education merely render Negroes more sensitive and therefore more violently rebellious against whites whom they hold responsible for their degradation?

And, too, perhaps for the first time, we can see how the Negro has had to take Protestant religion and make it into something for his own special needs, needs born of an imposed Black Belt existence. To what extent has racial religion replaced Christian religion in thousands of Black Belt churches? And what is wrong with religion in America that it has turned its back upon the Negro and his problem? And to what degree is religion in America officially and ideologically identified with the policy of White Supremacy?

With the scientific facts of urban Negro life now given in *Black Metropolis,* the way is clear for other workers, black and white, to paint in the shadings, the background, to make three-dimensional the personalities caught in this Sargasso of racial subjugation.

William James,* in discussing the way in which the "social self" of man exists in society, says, ". . . a man has as many social selves as there are individuals who recognize him and carry an image of him in their minds." Then, in speculating upon what a man would feel if he were completely socially excluded, he says, "No more fiendish punishment could be devised, were such a thing physically possible, than that one should be turned loose in society and remain absolutely unnoticed by all the members thereof. If no one turned round when we entered, answered when we spoke, or minded what we did, but if every person we met "cut us dead," and acted as if we were non-existent things, a kind of rage and impotent despair would ere long well up in us, from which the cruelest bodily tortures would be a relief; for these would make us feel that, however bad might be our plight, we had not sunk to such a depth as to be unworthy of attention at all."

There can be, of course, no such thing as a *complete* rejection of anybody by society; for, even in rejecting him, society must notice

* *The Philosophy of William James,* Modern Library edition, page 128.

him. But the American Negro has come as near being the victim of a complete rejection as our society has been able to work out, for the dehumanized image of the Negro which white Americans carry in their minds, the anti-Negro epithets continuously on their lips, exclude the contemporary Negro as truly as though he were kept in a steel prison, and doom even those Negroes who are as yet unborn.

A casual examination of the progressive changes in one phase of Negro cultural expression is sufficient to show how a gradual estrangement has occurred in the Negro over a period of 160 years, an estrangement from complete identification with the nation to atomized and despairing rebellion.

In 1760, a black girl, Phyllis Wheatley, was brought to America from Africa and sold into slavery. By fortunate accident a Christian Boston family purchased her, treated her as an equal, educated her; she became a poet and wrote in the manner of the heroic couplets of Pope. Her *Imagination* * reads:

> Imagination! Who can sing thy force!
> Or who describe the swiftness of thy course?
> Soaring through air to find the bright abode,
> Th' empyreal palace of the thundering God,
> We on thy pinions can surpass the wind,
> And leave the rolling universe behind:
> From star to star the mental optics rove,
> Measure the skies, and range the realms above;
> There in one view we grasp the mighty whole,
> Or with new world amaze th' unbounded soul.

Whatever its qualities as poetry, the above poem records the feelings of a Negro reacting not as a Negro, but as a human being. Then, in the 1920's, when racial hate was at a hysterical pitch, and after the grinding processes of history had forged iron in the Negro's heart, we hear a new and strange cry from another Negro, Claude McKay. In his sonnet, *If We Must Die,** he seems to snarl through a sob:

> If we must die—let it not be like hogs
>   Hunted and penned in an inglorious spot,
> While round us bark the mad and hungry dogs,
>   Making their mock at our accursed lot.

* *An Anthology of American Negro Literature,* Modern Library, pages 175 and 203.

If we must die—oh, let us nobly die,
   So that our precious blood may not be shed
In vain; then even the monsters we defy
   Shall be constrained to honor us though dead!

Oh, kinsmen! We must meet the common foe;
   Though far outnumbered, let us still be brave,
And for their thousand blows deal one death-blow!
   What though before us lies the open grave?
Like men we'll face the murderous, cowardly pack
   Pressed to the wall, dying, but—fighting back!

What has America done to people who could sing out in limpid verse to make them snarl about being "pressed to the wall" and dealing "one death-blow"? Is this the result of a three-hundred-year policy of "knowing niggers and what's good for 'em"? Is this the salvation which Christian missionaries have brought to the "heathen from Africa"? That there is something wrong here only fools would deny.

White America has reduced Negro life in our great cities to a level of experience of so crude and brutal a quality that one could say of it in the words of Vachel Lindsay's *The Leaden-Eyed* that:

It is not that they starve, but they starve so dreamlessly,
It is not that they sow, but that they seldom reap,
It is not that they serve, but they have no gods to serve,
It is not that they die, but that they die like sheep.

RICHARD WRIGHT

Ile d'Orléans, Québec. July, 1945

Introduction to the 1962 Edition

BLACK METROPOLIS IS A DESCRIPTION OF ONE OF THE WORLD'S LARGER NEGRO communities, as it was during and at the end of the great depression of the 1930's. It is a history of the labor force of a great, industrially diverse city, and more especially of Negroes as part of that labor force. It is a great social survey, somewhat in the style of Charles Booth's *Life and Labour of the People of London* (17 Vols., published from 1889 to 1903. London), combining history and social statistics with first-hand observation and systematic interviewing. It is a lively monument to the *élan* which, generated by the New Deal, moved artists and intellectuals of all races and ethnic groups to common expression and action. It is, or was, a portent of the future of Negro Americans, a future in which they, like their countrymen of all varieties, would become overwhelmingly urban and would move and be moved toward a middle-class way of life.

Black Metropolis is certainly other things. Richard Wright has said it is a document of the agony of black men in a white world. It has much poetry in it. The authors, in the Appendix, "Black Metropolis 1961," give it still other dimensions. Let me enlarge on the facets I have already mentioned.

In the 1930's Chicago was already an immense gathering place for American Negroes, second only to New York. There were, and are, differences between these two black metropolises, differences which reflect those between the two cities as wholes. It is in the slaughtering houses, the steel mills and the various industries of Chicago, rather than in the light industries and services of New York, that Negro and other rural Americans and aliens get their foot on the bottom rung of the industrial ladder. Chicago's story, in this regard, may give the better clues to what is happening and will happen in other cities, both northern and southern. Some say Chicago is the most segregated city in the country; it may be so. If so, perhaps it is because Chicago is built of larger territorial blocks than many cities. Its Negro district is immense and unbroken. New York is a mosaic of smaller tiles, where the average person, although he may live in a ghetto, is not so many miles from other breeds as in Chicago. Other cities approach one pattern or the other, or lie between. But more and more of them, no matter what their geographic patterns, and especially those requiring a large industrial labor force, have large populations of newly-arrived rural people, predominantly Negro. Many of the processes, many of the institutions described in *Black Metropolis* will be found, in various stages and forms, in all of them.

Every American city has had its own industrial and labor history. To all of them—and to all industrial cities everywhere—new kinds of people have come from time to time to fill the gaps at the bottom of the occupational hierarchy. The new people are generally both rustic and poor. In some sense, then, the story of the labor force of Chicago and the role of the Negro in it is a version of the story of all industrial cities, and of all poor rustics lured to the city by the hope of prosperity or freedom, or driven to it by underemployment, landlessness or technological change. It is the story of a large part of the human race of times recent and to come. The history of every growing industrial city is one of ethnic if not of racial diversity, and of ethnic succession at the bottom of the industrial hierarchy and in the central tenements or peripheral shacks of the slums. It is not always a history of ethnic and racial discrimination, but it is so often enough for *Black Metropolis* to be more universal than the story of a single harsh new city. The themes, in various keys and combinations, are being played out in the cities of all continents.

In the meantime, the balance among the positions and occupations in industrial economies is changing. Advanced industrial economies show an increase in professional and other white collar positions, with a relative decrease in the dirtier and heavier unskilled jobs, and even in the more skilled manual trades. The slaughtering houses which brought Negroes to Chicago are but the shadow of what they were early in the century. The automated steel mill needs no large roving labor gang. As a result, rural newcomers to the city and to its industries will have to make their adjustments more rapidly than in the past; they may easily become part of the pool of permanently unemployed without ever having been fully employed. In the more recently industrialized or still-to-be-industrialized parts of the world such changes may succeed one another more rapidly and catastrophically than in North America. For North America, with its Chicago, is—

industrially speaking—an old country which had more time for its adjustments than the new ones may have.

Black Metropolis is a great social survey, as that phrase was used before the day of statistical surveys of opinion and consumers' preferences. The social survey was a study, undertaken by men who believed that social facts well presented would point the way to reform of the conditions and ways of living at or below the *poverty line*. *Black Metropolis* was produced by the techniques, and with some of the spirit of a social survey, combined with the methods of social anthropology. The anthropologist more than matches the social surveyor in closeness and intimacy of contact and observation, while achieving a far more systematic analysis of social organization than ever dreamt of by the social surveyor. In this study sociologists of the Robert E. Park tradition joined with anthropologists who had worked with W. Lloyd Warner in his series of American community studies. The result is unique; its like may not be produced again. For one thing, it took a New Deal to mobilize the small army of able young social scientists who did the footwork that made the book possible. For another, bright young Negroes do not have to be sociologists and anthropologists any more. A Cayton or a Drake might today, if he chose, become an engineer, an architect or a scientist. Even as late as the Thirties a young Negro intellectual could hardly hope to get work which did not have to do with other Negroes——as clients or as objects of study. Nowadays the social sciences have to compete with other lines of work for Negro talent. The Negro in the New Frontier is not the Negro of the WPA (although he may have been in his youth). Finally, there has been technological change in social science; we now have the survey of opinion.[1] Observation is reduced to the minimum considered necessary to developing a questionnaire yielding answers which can be "coded" or "programmed" for processing by machines. Fewer skilled observers and more standardized interviewers are used. The change is not unlike that in industry. Other styles of gathering and presenting information about various segments of American life may supplant those used in *Black Metropolis*. In the decades since they did this work, the particular people who did it and the two who wrote the book have been moved on by the times and

[1] A questionnaire survey of new migrants to Chicago is being conducted at the University of Chicago by a team of which Donald Bogue is the leader and of which I am a member. Negroes are the most numerous among the newcomers.

by the logic of their own careers to new kinds of work and study. Messrs. Cayton and Drake have become students of racial matters on the world scene; their reputations are also world-wide. They cannot go back and do the same thing over again. The business of reporting on and analyzing the world of Negro and other newcomers to Chicago and the cities of the world, must pass on to others. It is one of the major tasks and adventures before the young people of our time.

Black Metropolis when published was a portent of the future. Negro Americans were rapidly moving to cities; now they are more urban than ever. Urbanization, which used to mean movement to the North, is now proceeding rapidly in the South. In fact, the South is now at last predominantly urban. One-crop agriculture—"stoop" agriculture—is being mechanized and is declining at the same time. We are told that half the people and half the land now engaged in agriculture could be turned to other uses without reducing our national agriculture product. Rural Southerners, Negro and white alike, rapidly being replaced by machines, are streaming into the cities. In Africa, at the same time, there are mass migrations to the cities. It is possible that people of Negro ancestry may become predominantly urban sooner than the peoples of Asia, the East Indies or Latin America—peoples whose ancestors invented cities.

The forms which urbanization will take may vary; certainly the cultures and economies from which the newcomers to cities stem vary greatly. For some the adjustment to city life and industrial work is greater than for others. But the *terminus ad quem* seems much the same in all cases. There is some evidence that all urban and industrial civilizations approach a common occupational structure, require essentially the same kinds of education and technical training, make somewhat the same demands upon people, and produce men of similar mind.[2] Certainly one of the obligations upon us as social scientists is to deploy forces throughout the world to observe and compare the processes of urbanization and to use the knowledge so gained to make the way less dangerous and less costly in human life and pain.

In North America itself one of the developments described in *Black Metropolis* has proceeded so far as to seem a change in kind. We have, in our economy of abundance, become a nation of consumers.

[2] Inkeles, Alex. "Industrial Man: The Relation of Status to Experience, Perception and Value," *The American Journal of Sociology*. LXVI (July 1960), 1–31.

Negro Americans were once looked upon merely as labor. So it has often been in the early phase of industry or industrial agriculture. The consumers were to be found elsewhere. But just as other American workers eventually came to be consumers of the products they made, so also the Negroes. This is the great turning point in any economy. Negro Americans have become consumers to be reckoned with; they were only beginning to become such in the Thirties. The day of the ancient Packard flamboyantly repainted for the Negro trade has gone. In the supermarket of the Hyde Park Cooperative Society thousands of well-dressed (unless happening to choose blue jeans and wind-breaker that day) women gather daily to do the family shopping. Most come alone in the shining family car. Many of them are Negro women. Such a woman is the new Negro: the middle-class consumer. It is the Negro consumer who sits-in demanding the right to be served and to consume the products of American abundance and to use his leisure as other Americans do. And, greatest reversal of all, the middle-class Negro, militantly but without violence demanding his right to be served when he has the price, is violently set upon by whites who, by all counts except the caste-symbol of race, are his inferiors. The Chicago race riots of 1919 pitted lower class against lower class. The lynching mob usually found its victim among the poor and the ig-norant. In all cases the nice white people stayed at home. *Black Metropolis* gave us a first look at the tastes of the Negro urban middle class, which was not yet militant about its consumption.

Some years ago I cycled off westward toward State Street, Chicago, on one of the streets in the 70's, south of the old limits of the Black Belt. It was a peaceful middle-class area of one-story brick bungalows and two-flat buildings, probably built for second or third generation Irish, Czechs or Poles. Men were washing their cars, mowing the lawn, or painting the back porch on that Saturday morning. Women were coming and going from the shops, or could be seen dusting in the front room. All at once, I saw that one industrious householder had a dark complexion. Then I saw that all were brown or black. It ran counter to all stereotypes; either their faces should have been white or the district should have had a different aspect. Chicago's Negro slums have grown, but so have her Negro middle classes and the districts where they live. The forces which move people toward the middle class American ethos are tremendous among Negroes of American descent. James Conant, in *Slums and Suburbs: A Com-*

mentary on Schools in Metropolitan Areas,[3] declares that the fate of our country depends upon the speed and thoroughness with which we destroy the slum, and the chronic unemployment and unemployability, the crime, the alienation, the hopelessness, the anger which it breeds and fastens upon our body social. It depends also upon the speed with which we make it possible for all Americans to enjoy to the full the opportunities for work, for consumption of goods and services and for participation in social life in their hours of leisure which our economy of abundance makes available. The great, massive crucial case, both as concerns the slum and as concerns full consumption and participation, is with the Americans called Negro. If we do what is necessary to solve their problems, we will have of necessity done it for the rest of us.

Black Metropolis stands as the classic study of urban Negro life. It is not the last word. No living document is. But he who reads it will be well on his way to becoming an understanding and continuing observer of what is and what is to come in our cities.

EVERETT C. HUGHES

Brandeis University
April, 1962

---

[3] New York: McGraw-Hill, 1961.

Authors' Preface
to the 1962 Edition

WHEN RICHARD WRIGHT WROTE THE INTRODUCTION TO THE FIRST EDITION of *Black Metropolis* (see Volume I of the Torchbook edition), he was America's best-known Negro novelist and his most widely read work, *Native Son,* had Chicago as its locale. As Wright phrased it, "I, in common with the authors . . . feel personally identified with the material in this book."

Wright began his essay with a competent and occasionally poetic resumé of the contributions which history and social science had made to an understanding of Western man's "alienation" and the Negro's "degradation." As the essay develops, a passionate cry emerges from the heart of the man who came to Chicago as "Black Boy"—an angry and pessimistic critique of American culture pouring from the lips of a "Native Son." Here is Richard Wright at his provocative and challenging best, deliberately picking the words he knows will hurt and propounding ideas certain to shock his readers, while taking full advantage of the artist's prerogative to overstate his case. He was, undoubtedly, deriving immense satisfaction from wielding the verbal sledge-hammer and twisting the literary stiletto. He was, as all of us were in the last days of World War II, carrying a board-size chip on his shoulder and asking the question, "Have we been fighting once again for everybody else's freedom except our own?" The authors tried to discipline their feelings as they wrote (without total success, as the reader will observe). Richard Wright, as an artist, was under no such role-bound obligation and his essay pulled no punches.

Wright was always driven by a desire to escape from the limitations which systems of race prejudice and discrimination had imposed upon him. First, he made the "Flight to Freedom" from Mississippi to Chicago. Then he sought the more cosmopolitan atmosphere of New York City. During the Depression the Communist Party offered the only milieu in which ordinary Negroes could find some measure of social equality as well as a group of white people who were challenging the whole system of segregation and discrimination in the Deep South. Richard Wright joined the Party but left in disgust during the Second World War because he felt that it was trying to curb his spontaneity and intellectual freedom, and was asking Negroes to be less militant. *Black Metropolis* was written during the period of Wright's attempt to find a satisfying existence in New York. But the racism he sought to avoid pursued him even into Greenwich Village, where he had purchased a home. So he shook the dust of America from his feet and sailed to Paris, where he lived until his death in 1960. The essay in this book was written after he had broken with the Communist Party and just before he became an expatriate.

Richard Wright was not only fleeing American race prejudice when he exiled himself to Paris. He was also rejecting life in Chicago's "Bronzeville"—the Negro community described in this volume—and in all the other Bronzevilles of America. This rejection is implicit in much of what he has to say in the essay. For him, all of the segregated Negro communities were intellectually sterile ghettos into which Negroes had been driven by social forces beyond their control, and which incorporated, in exaggerated form, what Wright considered some of the worst facets of American life: conspicuous consumption, pursuit of the products of a mass culture, devotion to frivolous trivialities, and a plethora of escapist religion. Richard Wright made no pretense of being detached or even tolerant about the way of life in Bronzeville. He left that to the authors, who were trying to combine the roles of "Negro," which society imposed upon them, and social scientist, which they themselves had chosen.[1]

The "World of the Lower Class," as described in Chapters 21 and 22, was to Wright a morass from which he had extricated himself as a youth, and whose victims he had once summoned to destroy the conditions of their existence by helping to bring about the proletarian revolution. For him, the "Middle-class Way of Life" had a stultifying quality that the artist could not accept. The "Upper-class Way of Life," from which he had been barred originally by lack of a conventional education, he later rejected with scorn when its practitioners tried to make a Race Hero of him after his success as a novelist. In his view,

[1] See E. Franklin Frazier's *Black Bourgeoisie,* for an example of the work of a distinguished Negro sociologist who steps out of his professional role in order to make evaluations similar to those of Richard Wright. His earlier works on the Negro family were non-normative.

the cultural milieu of Bronzeville at all levels simply provided an "opiate" for those who should be fighting back.[2]

It is doubtful whether the people of Bronzeville shared Wright's appraisal of their "level of experience" during the mid-Forties as "crude" and "brutal." They certainly would not have seen *themselves* as those who "starve so dreamlessly" or "die like sheep" caught in a "Sargasso of racial subjugation." (They might, however, have made this appraisal of some of their kinsmen in the deep South.) But we suspect that most would have understood *why* Richard Wright reacted as he did, even though they might have felt that he did not present a rounded picture of Negro life; for Negroes, involved in the struggle for dignity and equality, often admire the "extremists" even when they themselves are conservative. They tend to operate upon the principle that "wisdom is justified of all her children."

That urban Negroes in the North have continued to accept a Job Ceiling and a Black Ghetto is due in part to the operation of factors discussed in the chapter on "Advancing the Race," and in part to the fact that the entire institutional structure of Bronzeville is providing basic satisfactions for the "reasonable expectations" shared by people at various class levels. These institutions have been able to provide such satisfactions primarily because a period of post-war prosperity supplied a level of purchasing power permitting individuals and families at each class level to broaden the base of their security and to expand the possibilities for "having fun," "serving God," and "getting ahead." *The norms and values, and the styles of living, described in this book sixteen years ago, have changed but little.* Some change there has been, of course, but it is also true that the more the values and patterns have changed, the more, in a sense, they have remained the same. The authors have attempted to assess the extent and quality of these changes in *Bronzeville 1961* (which follows p. 768 of this volume).

While there has been no drastic change in the class patterns, the proportion of people in the various classes has changed. Unfortunately, the extent of this change can only be measured by a type of detailed

---

[2] Wright never became an "escapist" despite his move to Paris. The Existentialism and Pan-Africanism which he eventually adopted as a personal philosophy, and which he blended with the Marxism he had embraced in his youth, were simply additional tools for pursuing the task he had made his life work: clarifying and restating "the race problem." See his Introduction to George Padmore's *Pan-Africanism or Communism?* and his little volume on the Bandung Conference, *Color Curtain,* as well as *Listen, White Man.*

research for which the authors have had neither the resources nor the time. For instance, one crucial question relevant to the extent and pace of change would be "Is the proportion of lower-class individuals and families being significantly reduced?", for the low social status of Negroes as a group is related to the high proportion of people who live lower-class life styles, as described in Chapters 20 and 21. There is some evidence to indicate that the number and proportion of Negroes in Chicago living "respectable" lower-class lives has been increased by the type of migrants who now come from the South. It is probable, too, that there is a growing number of young people with one or two years of high school training who have adopted some of the patterns of middle-class behavior, but who are frustrated in their desire to adopt its whole complex of values because they are not able to secure the type of employment necessary to sustain such a style of life.

Wright's essay, like the authors' concluding chapter, was preoccupied with the probable fate of the Negro American after World War II. We all assumed that post-war race riots were likely to erupt, and that perhaps Negroes were fated to become the victims of a new Depression. Happily, the fears proved groundless. New factors which none of us could have foreseen entered into the picture: full employment stimulated by the demands of a hot war in Korea and a prolonged Cold War; the rise of a vigorous national concern for civil liberties and support for integration stimulated by renewed devotion to the American Creed; competition for the Negro vote, and increased fear of Communist inroads among Negroes.

The challenge to America which, in our pessimism, Richard Wright and the two authors thought would never be taken up *was* accepted by white Americans. But, the "race problem" in Midwest Metropolis has by no means been "solved," and the searching questions raised by Wright are as relevant today as they were in 1945. We would be foolish, for instance, to ignore his query as to whether an increase in the educational level among Negroes without a corresponding expansion of opportunity will "render Negroes more sensitive and therefore violently rebellious against whites, whom they hold responsible for their degradation."

Today, social work agencies in Chicago and elsewhere constantly raise this question as did Wright in the past; and Race Leaders throughout America are continually warning that the activities of non-violent Freedom Riders must not obscure the fact that among Negro teenagers patterns of violence are prevalent and that embedded in the character structure of the Negro masses lies a deep vein of suppressed hostility. Dr. James B. Conant has recently emphasized the same point in his perceptive little book, *Slums and Suburbs.*

The family, clique, and associational structures of Negroes in Chicago have been very little affected by the trend toward "integration." Expanded contacts with white people on the job and in public places, as well as in more intimate contexts, have not altered the fact that white Chicago still forces most Negroes to marry Negroes, to have Negroes as their intimate friends, and to participate in all-colored churches and associations. *Changes have been in the direction of a more intensive elaboration of Bronzeville's separate sub-culture, not toward its disappearance.*

Richard Wright would hardly have felt that the changes occurring in Bronzeville since he wrote his essay constitute "Progress." He would not be satisfied with either the complacency of the middle and upper classes, or that hedonism of the lower class which post-War prosperity has reinforced. For Wright felt, like Arnold Toynbee (and ironically enough, like many Negro preachers), that American Negroes have a "mission." He wrote in his essay that ". . . *the American Negro, child of the culture that crushes him, wants to be free in a way that white men are free. . . . Negroes, with but minor exceptions, still believe in the hope of economic rewards; they believe in justice, liberty, the integrity of the individual. In the heart of industrial America is a surviving remnant, perchance a saving remnant, of a passion for freedom, a passion fanned by their national humiliation.*"

Amidst the prosperity of the Sixties, Wright would probably still be asking the embarrassing question: "*Will the Negro, in the language of Andre Malraux, find a meaning in his humiliation and make his slums and his sweat-shops his modern cathedrals out of which will be born a new consciousness that can guide him toward freedom?*"

The social scientist confines himself to much more prosaic questions. He is constrained to ask, for instance, "Is there any way in which Chicago can abolish the Black Ghetto and thus free the areas which surround it from the depredations of its criminals and juvenile delinquents who will probably continue to discharge their aggressions upon the surrounding white world so long as it frustrates their aspirations?" Or, "If the Black Ghetto does eventually disappear (by a process of thinning out and expanded opportunity), will a Bronzeville still remain, as a separate, but well-ordered Negro community of people who prefer to retain their own sub-culture within the larger urban setting?"

The social scientist is also led to reflect upon questions which have been taboo ever since Booker T. Washington made his Atlanta Compromise speech in the Nineties, but which the Swedish scholar, Gunnar Myrdal did raise obliquely when he wrote: "Social discrimination is powerful as a means of keeping the Negro down. . . . In reality it is not possible to isolate a sphere of life and call it 'social.' There is in fact a 'social' angle to all relations. . . . Social segregation involves a substantial element of discrimination."[3] Some questions which ought to be faced are: "Is it possible for Bronzevilles to disappear so long as *social* segregation exists?" and "Can Negroes, as individuals, ever expect to reap the full fruits of competition in American society so long as they are excluded from those 'social' situations in which so much of the nation's business is transacted and where vital contacts are made and important information communicated?" The question might even be raised as to whether it is not an abridgment of a fundamental right to deny Negroes the opportunities to make the quick jumps toward the top of society that come from "marrying into" money or influence, or to block them from marrying those who have long-term chances for unusual success. (Intermarriage is a *criminal* offense in over half of the states in the Union!)

These are questions which even the most liberal of whites and the majority of Negroes, for strategic reasons, seldom dare ask openly today. But intellectual honesty demands that they be asked, even if the hope still remains that a distinctively American kind of "equality" will evolve which will give Negroes full participation in the economic and political life of the nation without paying the price of full "*social* equality." In the meanwhile, America's Bronzevilles become the structures which "protect" white America from "social contact" with Negroes and which simultaneously provide a milieu for Negro Americans in which they can imbue their lives with meaning.

ST. CLAIR DRAKE
HORACE R. CAYTON

April, 1962

[3] Gunnar Myrdal, *An American Dilemma*, quoted in *Black Metropolis*, p. 125.

Foreword to the 1993 Edition

by William Julius Wilson

Since the early twentieth century, the city of Chicago has been a laboratory for the scientific investigation of the social, economic, and historical forces that create and perpetuate economically desolated and isolated urban communities. Much of this research has been conducted by social scientists affiliated with the University of Chicago. The most distinctive phase of this research, referred to as the Chicago School of urban sociology, was completed prior to 1950.[1] The perspectives on urban processes that guided the Chicago School's approach to the study of race and class have undergone subtle changes down through the years. For Robert E. Park and Ernest W. Burgess the immigrant slums and the social problems that characterized them were temporary conditions toward inevitable progress. Thus blacks represented the latest group of migrants involved in the "interaction cycle" that "led from conflict to accommodation to assimilation."[2]

The view that blacks fit the pattern of immigrant assimilation appeared in subsequent studies by E. Franklin Frazier. However, Frazier's awareness of the black urban condition in the 1930s led him to recognize and emphasize a problem ignored in the earlier work of Park and Burgess—namely the important link between the black family structure and the industrial economy. Frazier believed that upward mobility for African Americans and their eventual assimilation into American life would depend in large measure on the availability of employment opportunities in the industrial sector.

[1]Representative studies by those identified with the Chicago School include Robert E. Park and Ernest W. Burgess, *The City* (1925); Frederic Thrasher, *The Gang* (1927); Louis Wirth, *The Ghetto* (1928); Harvey W. Zorbaugh, *The Gold Coast and the Slum* (1929); Robert E. L. Faris and Warren Dunham, *Mental Disorder in Urban America* (1931); and E. Franklin Frazier, *The Negro Family in Chicago* (1932). (These were all published by the University of Chicago Press.)

[2]Alice O'Connor, "Race and Class in Chicago Sociology, 1920–1990," paper presented at the annual meeting of the Social Science History Association Meetings, November 8, 1992. I am indebted to O'Connor for much of the discussion to follow in this section.

In 1945 a fundamental revision in the Chicago framework appeared in the publication of St. Clair Drake and Horace Cayton's *Black Metropolis*. Drake and Cayton first examined black progress in employment, housing, and social integration, using census, survey, and archival data. Their analysis clearly revealed the existence of a color line that effectively blocked black occupational, residential, and social mobility. Thus any assumption about urban blacks duplicating the immigrant experience has to confront the issue of race. Moreover, as the historian Alice O'Connor puts it, "Drake and Cayton recognized that the racial configuration of Chicago was not the expression of an organic process of city growth but the product of human behavior, institutional practices and political decisions."[3]

Black Metropolis also deviated from the Chicago School in its inclusion of an ethnographic study of daily life in Bronzeville, based on W. Lloyd Warner's anthropological techniques. In the final analysis, the book represented an "uneasy hybrid of Chicago school and anthropological methods and, ultimately, a much less optimistic view of the prospects for black progress."[4] In the revised and enlarged edition in 1962, however, Drake and Cayton examined the changes that had occurred in Bronzeville since the publication of the first edition with a sense of optimism. They felt that America in the 1960s was "experiencing a period of prosperity" and that African Americans were "living in the Era of Integration" (p. xv). They, of course, had no way of anticipating the rapid social and economic deterioration of communities like Bronzeville since the early sixties.

THE INNER CITY TODAY

The most fundamental change in the inner city is that many neighborhoods are plagued by far greater levels of joblessness than when Drake and Cayton conducted their ethnographic research in the 1940s. As a case in point, let me take the three Chicago community areas that represent Bronzeville—Douglas, Grand Boulevard, and Washington Park. In all three areas, a majority of adults were gainfully employed in 1950, but by 1990 only four in ten in Douglas worked, one in three in Washington Park, and one in four in Grand Boulevard. These employment changes were accompanied by changes in other indicators of economic status. For example, in Grand Boulevard medium family income dropped from 62 percent of the city average in 1950 to less than 37 percent in 1980; and the

[3]Ibid., p. 22.
[4]Ibid., p. 18.

value of housing plummeted from 97 percent of the city average in 1950 to about half the city average in 1980, with the most rapid declines occurring after 1970.

When the first edition of *Black Metropolis* was published, there was much greater class integration in the black community. As Drake and Cayton pointed out, Bronzeville residents had limited success in "sorting themselves out into broad community areas which might be designated as 'lower class' and 'middle class'. . . . Instead of middle-class *areas* Bronzeville tends to have middle-class *buildings* in all areas, or a few middle-class blocks here and there" (pp. 658–660). Though they may have lived on different streets, blacks of all classes in inner-city areas such as Bronzeville lived in the same community and shopped at the same stores. Their children went to the same schools and played in the same parks. Although there was some degree of class antagonism, their neighborhoods were more stable than the inner-city neighborhoods of today.

Two factors largely account for the sharp decline in the social organization of inner-city neighborhoods.[5]

The first is the impact of changes in the economy. In the United States, historical discrimination and a migration to large metropolises that kept the urban minority population relatively young created a problem of weak labor force attachment among urban blacks and, especially after 1970, made them particularly vulnerable to the industrial and geographic changes in the economy. The shift from goods-producing to service-producing industries, the increasing polarization of the labor market into low-wage and high-wage sectors, innovations in technology, the relocation of manufacturing industries out of central cities, and periodic recessions have forced up the rate of black joblessness (unemployment and nonparticipation in the labor market), despite the passage of antidiscrimination legislation and the creation of affirmative action programs. The rise in joblessness has in turn helped trigger an increase in the concentrations of poor people, a growing number of poor single-parent families, and an increase in welfare dependency. These problems have been especially evident in the ghetto neighborhoods of large cities, not only because the most impoverished minority populations live there, but also because the neighborhoods have become less diversified in a way that has severely worsened the impact of the continuing economic changes.

This brings us to the second factor—changes in the class composition of

[5]William Julius Wilson, *The Truly Disadvantaged: The Inner City, the Underclass, and Public Policy* (Chicago: University of Chicago Press, 1987).

inner-city neighborhoods. Especially since 1970, inner-city neighborhoods have experienced an outmigration of working- and middle-class families previously confined to them by the restrictive covenants of higher-status city neighborhoods and suburbs. While Chicago lost one-fifth of its population between 1950 and 1980, Washington Park lost 44 percent, Grand Boulevard one-half, and Douglas 55 percent. And of those who departed, a disproportionate number were nonpoor. Many of these families took advantage of the housing vacancies in the rapidly racially changing city and suburban neighborhoods. The outward mobility for the black working and middle classes removed an important social buffer that could have deflected the full impact of the prolonged and high level of joblessness in these neighborhoods that has stemmed from uneven economic growth and periodic recessions.

Although these processes have had an adverse effect on all poor minorities, they have been especially devastating for the lower-class black male. For example, in 1950 in the two Bronzeville neighborhoods of Grand Boulevard and Washington Park there were 70 employed men for every 100 women.[6] That was close to the citywide figure at the time of 73 working men to every 100 women. By 1990, this proportion had plummeted to 26 working men for every 100 women inhabitants in Washington Park and 21 in Grand Boulevard.

Thirty and forty years ago, the overwhelming majority of black males were working. Most of them were poor, but they held regular jobs around which their daily family life was organized. When black men looked for work, employers were concerned about whether they had strong backs, because they would be working in a factory or in the back room of a shop doing heavy lifting and labor. The work was hard and they were hired. Now, economic restructuring has broken the figurative back of the black working class.

Data from our Urban Poverty and Family Life Study show that 51 percent of Chicago's employed inner-city black males born between 1941 and 1955 worked in manufacturing industries in 1969. By 1987 that figure fell to 29 percent. Of those born between 1956 and 1968, 45 percent worked in manufacturing industries as late as 1978. By 1987 that figure had declined to 25 percent.

These employment changes have recently accompanied the loss of tradi-

---

[6]Rates represent all males and females over fourteen years of age in 1950 and sixteen years of age in 1990.

tional manufacturing and other blue-collar jobs in Chicago. As a result, young black males have turned increasingly to the low-wage service sector and laboring jobs for employment, or have gone jobless.

Many young men in inner-city neighborhoods today have responded to these declining opportunities by resorting to crime, drugs, and violence. This in turn has fed the image of young black men as dangerous. So, when they look for work in competition with immigrants, women, or whites, employers prefer not to hire "trouble."

The employment prospects of black women in the inner city have also declined, because they have had to compete for service jobs with the growing number of white women and immigrants who have entered the labor market. All of these changes have resulted in accelerated jobless rates in the inner city.

The increase in joblessness combined with the exodus of higher-income families have resulted in declining levels of social organization in communities like Bronzeville. By "social organization" I mean the extent to which the residents of a neighborhood are able to maintain effective social control and realize their common values. The outmigration of higher-income families and increasing and prolonged joblessness make it considerably more difficult to sustain basic neighborhood institutions. In the face of increasing joblessness, stores, banks, credit institutions, restaurants, and professional services lose regular and potential patrons. Churches experience dwindling numbers of parishioners and shrinking resources; recreational facilities, block clubs, community groups, and other informal organizations also suffer. As these organizations decline, the means of formal and informal social control in the neighborhood become weaker. Levels of crime and street violence increase as a result, leading to further deterioration of the neighborhood.

In short, there has been a movement from what Allan Spear has called an institutional ghetto—in which the structure and activities of the larger society are duplicated—as portrayed in Drake and Cayton's description of Bronzeville—to a physical ghetto, which lacks the capability to provide basic opportunities and resources.[7]

For today's student of urban problems, one of the important benefits

[7]Allan Spear, *Black Chicago: The Making of a Negro Ghetto, 1890–1920* (Chicago: University of Chicago Press, 1967). Also see Loic J. D. Wacquant and William Julius Wilson, "Poverty, Joblessness, and the Social Transformation of the Inner City," in *Welfare Policy for the 1990s*, eds. Phoebe H. Cottingham and David T. Ellwood (Cambridge: Harvard University Press, 1989), pp. 70–102.

gained from reading *Black Metropolis* is that its comprehensive description and analysis of a large inner-city neighborhood at mid-twentieth century provides a good base for systematic comparisons with the inner-city ghetto today. In particular, it allows us to consider the significance of a segregated community heavily populated with *working* poor adults in contrast with a segregated community largely populated with *nonworking* poor adults.

BLACK
METROPOLIS

Introduction: Midwest Metropolis

Out of the payday songs of steam shovels,
Out of the wages of structural iron rivets,
The living lighted skyscrapers tell it now as a name,
Tell it across the miles of sea blue water, gray blue land:
I am Chicago, I am a name given out by the breaths of
    working men, laughing men, a child, a belonging.

.   .   .   .

Forgive us if we work so hard
And the muscles bunch clumsy on us
And we never know why we work so hard—
If the big houses with little families
And the little houses with big families
Sneer at each other's bars of misunderstanding;
Pity us when we shackle and kill each other
And believe at first we understand
And later say we wonder why.
                              —CARL SANDBURG, *The Windy City* *

AMERICA IS KNOWN BY HER BIG CITIES, THOSE AMAZING CONGERIES OF
people and houses, offices and factories, which constitute the nerve
centers of our civilization, the ganglia of our collective being. America
is dominated by her cities as they draw into them the brawn and brain
and wealth of the hinterland and give back not only a constant stream
of necessities and gadgets, but also a pattern for living. New York,
Chicago, San Francisco, New Orleans, Birmingham . . . the impact of
each forces itself upon an ever-widening metropolitan region and filters
into a host of tributary small towns and farms by radio and newspaper, book and magazine, and the enthusiastic tales of visitors. Each
city, too, has its distinctive reputation in the far corners of the earth,
distorted and glamorized, but with a basic element of truth beneath
the stereotype.

Put your pencil on the map near the southern tip of Lake Michigan
and you touch a metropolis (Figure 1) "Queen of the Lakes," "Capital

---

* From *Slabs of the Sunburnt West* by Carl Sandburg. Harcourt, Brace, 1922.

Figure 1

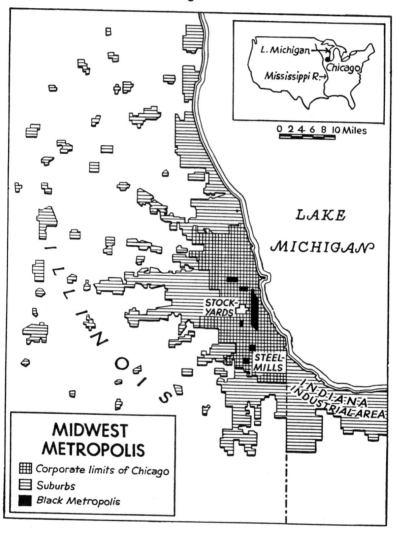

Inset map labels: L. Michigan, Chicago, Mississippi R.→

0 2 4 6 8 10 Miles

LAKE

MICHIGAN

ILLINOIS

STOCK-
YARDS

STEEL-
MILLS

INDIANA
INDUSTRIAL AREA

**MIDWEST
METROPOLIS**

Corporate limits of Chicago
Suburbs
Black Metropolis

of the Inland Empire," "Grain Center of the World"—Association of Commerce pamphlets pile encomium upon eulogy, endlessly. And the city is important—CHICAGO, America's second largest in population—MIDWEST METROPOLIS. Approach it by plane and see, sprouting from its center, a spiderweb of railroads swept by a thousand wisps of steam streaking to and fro. Ride into the red glow of steel mills turning out millions of tons of steel a year. Cruise the half-moon border of the lake and you will fly over a multitude of beaches, an impressive skyline, and a beautiful lake front. Ore-boats and cargo vessels creep in and out across the lake, linking the city with five states and Canada.

Swoop low at evening over a forest of water tanks feeding factories set upon the flatness of a prairie, and you will see Chicago's Three Million—her working men and women streaming toward their houses in the inner city, and her white-collar and professional people outward-bound to their homes on the periphery or in the suburbs. The night shift surges through the gates and the city turns into 133 square miles of lighted pin-points clustered about the lake beneath you. This is Carl Sandburg's Chicago:

> Laughing the stormy, husky, brawling laughter of
> Youth, half-naked, sweating, proud to be Hog
> Butcher, Tool Maker, Stacker of Wheat, Player
> with Railroads and Freight Handler to the Nation.*

This is what man has done in a hundred and fifty years, for when New York was over a century old and when Philadelphia numbered 70,000, this spot was still forest and prairie. Less than two hundred years ago, where grain elevators now stand by the lake front and steamers lie against the docks, the canoes of the Pottawattomie and the pirogues of the *coureur de bois* skirted the lake. Midwest Metropolis is a young city.

Chicago's civic boosters have always kept their eyes fixed in friendly rivalry upon New York, the Great Metropolis. Tradition has it that one Mayor, Carter Harrison, on the day of his death by assassination in 1893, "declared that in another half-century London would be trembling lest Chicago should surpass it, and New York would say, 'Let us go to the metropolis of America.'"[1] The fifty years have passed. Present-day local patriots worry little about overtaking the Great Me-

---

* From *Chicago Poems* by Carl Sandburg, Henry Holt, 1916.
[1] Numbers refer to the notes to be found at the end of book.

tropolis in size; rather they claim superiority through uniqueness, believing another declaration made by the same Mayor in a boastful
though less prophetic mood: ". . . second city in America in population and the first city on earth in pluck, energy, and determination."

A thousand American cities and hamlets will immediately rise to
dispute this priority in civic virtue, and will substitute a picture of
Midwest Metropolis which emphasizes the "pluck" of gangsters, the
"energy" of corrupt polticians, and the "determination" of the White
Sox and the Cubs to repeat the triumph of nearly forty years ago when
each won a pennant in the same season. Despite all that the Chamber
of Commerce and local newspapers may do to divert attention to the
University of Chicago, Northwestern University, the Field Museum,
the Chicago Art Institute, lake-front improvements, and the system of
public parks, Midwest Metropolis will no doubt continue to be a
symbol, in the popular mind, for none-too-brilliant ball teams, colorful
mayors, and gangsters. Hundreds of thousands of Americans will remember it, also, as the scene of two world's fairs and several disastrous
fires, and as the home of Sears, Roebuck and Montgomery Ward, of
Al Capone and Samuel Insull. The Second World War tossed it into
the news as the fountainhead of Midwestern isolationism; and the
antics of a mail-order magnate who defied the War Labor Board, and
of two wartime political conventions, drove even the war from the
headlines. Chicago has always been good newspaper copy.

Chicago's reputation is primarily the work of newspapermen with an
eye for the dramatic. Those indefatigable literary sleuths of a former
generation, the "muckrakers," also did their share. Upton Sinclair's
The Jungle, for instance, not only lent impetus to the passage of a
Federal meat-inspection law and resulted in a clean-up of the stockyards, but also advertised Chicago as Hog Butcher to the World. The
complexity and the contradictions, the stark contrasts of Midwest
Metropolis, have intrigued many observers as they did Rebecca West
who marveled at "an incredible city named Chicago . . . with crime
which occasionally takes spectacular and portentous forms, but also an
art gallery which alone would make the journey to these parts worth
while." And Carl Sandburg, probing it all, passes a defensive appraisal
which emphasizes traits other than culture:

> And they tell me you are crooked, and I answer: Yes, it
> is true. . . .

> . . . and I give them back the
> sneer and say to them:
> Come and show me another city with lifted head singing
> so proud to be alive and coarse and strong and cunning.*

Most observers have been impressed by the rapidity of physical growth and the constant change that characterize the city. Lewis and Smith, lively historians of Chicago's "reputation," proclaim that "The city has a daemon—Innovation . . . a passion for tearing up, improving, substituting, enlarging." † A "bareheaded," "shovelling," "wrecking," "planning," "building," "breaking," "rebuilding" city, chants Carl Sandburg as he eulogizes the City of the Big Shoulders. It is perhaps no accident that Chicago's most colorful mayor was known as "Big Bill the Builder" and that the present incumbent stresses a housing program as the keystone of the city's post-war planning.

The collective life of this city by the Lake has been organized and controlled by "The Titans"—the men of the market place, the manipulators of money and people, the fabricators and barterers of things and personalities. Chicago has become a metropolis primarily because men with money to invest discovered early that the site paid dividends. Here money and brains and skill have been conjoined to build a city.

The settling and building of a city requires money and wood and stone and steel; but above all it demands people—by the millions, and in continuous supply, for city births are not numerous enough to keep America's urban population at even a steady level. Midwest Metropolis has drawn upon that general worldwide population movement of the last two centuries which peopled the great American cities. From its birth until the First World War it tapped a seemingly inexhaustible pool of European labor, for Midwest Metropolis has been one of those spots to which people have streamed for more than a century seeking an opportunity to "get ahead," to shake off the past, to "start over." The dynamics of its rapid growth have been the pull of the American Dream and the push of hunger and discontent and restlessness.

* From *Chicago Poems* by Carl Sandburg, Henry Holt, 1916.
† For background material on the history of Chicago, the authors have drawn extensively upon Lloyd Lewis and Henry Justin Smith, *Chicago: The History of Its Reputation*, Harcourt, Brace, 1929, and Centennial Edition, Blue Ribbon Books, 1933. They are also indebted to Bessie Pierce's scholarly and readable *A History of Chicago* (Knopf, 1937). The authors have had access to a mass of primary source data collected as a part of the Cayton-Warner Research, including diaries, life-histories, and newspaper abstracts.

The first great wave of immigration in the Forties brought the Irish, fleeing from a famine brought on by the failure of the potato crop and from the heavy hand of English absentee landlords. Germans, too, in great numbers, found Chicago a welcome haven in the years after the suppression of the democratic revolutions of 1848. By 1850, over half of the inhabitants of Chicago were foreign-born. The Irish ranked first, the Germans second, while the English, Welsh, and Scotch together formed the third largest group.

By 1890, sixty years after its birth, Chicago had become a city of a million persons, and three-quarters of them were either foreign-born or children of the foreign-born. The Germans, the Irish, and the Scandinavians had been arriving by the thousands, encouraged by "runners" in New York, who met the boats and persuaded immigrants to seek their fortunes in Midwest Metropolis. The stream of Northern European immigrants diminished in the Eighties, and Eastern Europeans, particularly Poles and Jews, began to appear in increasing numbers. This "new immigration" reached floodtide between 1900 and 1910, with some 30,000 Italians, 120,000 Russians, 24,000 Hungarians, and 5,000 Greeks pouring into the city during this period.

TABLE 1

POPULATION OF CHICAGO BY ETHNIC GROUP: 1900-1944

Year	Total	Native-white	Foreign-born White and Other Races	Negro
1900	1,698,575	1,081,720	586,705	30,150
1910	2,185,283	1,357,840	783,340	44,103
1920	2,701,705	1,783,687	808,560	109,458
1930	3,376,438	2,275,674	866,861	233,903
1934	3,258,528	2,351,683	670,540	236,305
1940	3,396,808	2,441,859	677,218	277,731
1944	3,600,000	2,642,000	621,000	337,000

The outbreak of the First World War stopped the flow of European immigrants. Simultaneously, war industries in Chicago, as throughout the nation, were expanding. Midwest Metropolis needed manpower, and over 50,000 Negroes poured into the city between 1916 and 1920 from the Deep South. After the war European immigration was resumed, though now it was a mere trickle as compared with its former dimensions. It was composed mostly of small numbers of Italians, Greeks, and Mexicans.

On the eve of the Depression there were still over 800,000 persons of foreign birth in Midwest Metropolis, but the city was in the process of becoming an "American" city, peopled primarily by Negroes and native-whites. (Tables 1 and 2.) The foreign-born whites were dying

TABLE 2

PERCENTAGE OF NATIVE-WHITE, FOREIGN-BORN, NEGRO, AND OTHER RACES, IN TOTAL POPULATION, CHICAGO: 1890-1944 [2]

Year	Native-white	Foreign-born White	Negro	Other Races	Total
1890	57.8	40.9	1.3	..	100.0
1900	63.7	34.4	1.9	..	100.0
1910	62.2	35.7	2.0	.1	100.0
1920	66.0	29.8	4.1	.1	100.0
1930	67.4	24.9	6.9	.8	100.0
1934	72.1	20.1	7.3	.5	100.0
1940	71.9	19.8	8.2	.1	100.0
1944	73.1	17.1	9.3	.5	100.0

out (and leaving the city) faster than they were being replaced. During the Depression years there was a 20 per cent decrease in the foreign-born population. It was balanced by a 20 per cent increase in the Negro population. The Second World War further depressed foreign immigration, and stepped up Negro migration into the city. Between Pearl Harbor and D-Day some 60,000 more Negroes came to Chicago. As the proportion of foreign-born drops, the proportion of Negroes rises. (Figure 2.) In 1944, there were 337,000 Negroes—almost one person in every ten—living in Midwest Metropolis.

URBAN CHECKERBOARD

The various groups of immigrants who came to Midwest Metropolis tended to congregate in colonies based upon common customs, language, and national origin. Then, as individuals and families learned to speak English, as they acquired an economic stake in the new country and lost their foreign habits and manners, they steadily moved away from these areas of first settlement into more desirable areas of second settlement. Later, they or their children merged with the general population. Today, as one student of the subject has remarked: "By far the largest number of immigrants and their children . . . are no longer distinguishable from the older settlers. The longer they have been here the more widely they are dispersed in the city. Thus, there

Figure 2

PROPORTION OF NEGROES, FOREIGN-BORN AND NATIVE-WHITES IN CHICAGO: 1890-1944

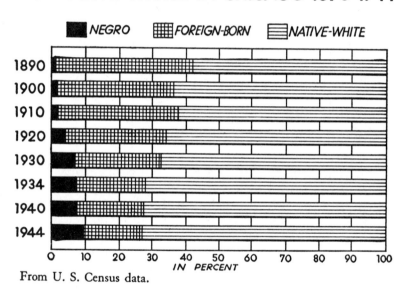

From U. S. Census data.

are practically no English and Scotch-Irish and predominantly German settlements, because these old settlers have amalgamated with the population that was already here and have lost their local and ethnic color."

Only some of the Poles and Italians now live in large, homogeneous communities. The colonies of the other national groups are being rapidly dissolved in the melting pot. (Table 3.) The communities of the foreign-born grow smaller year by year; but, as they shrink and disappear, Negro neighborhoods assume increasing importance in

TABLE 3

FOREIGN-BORN WHITE POPULATION BY COUNTRY OF BIRTH: CHICAGO, 1930 [a]

Country of Birth	Number *	Per Cent of Total Population
Poland	149,622	4.4
Germany	111,366	3.3
Russia	78,462	2.3
Italy	73,960	2.2
Sweden	65,735	2.0
Czechoslovakia	48,814	1.5
Irish Free State	47,385	1.4
Lithuania	31,430	.9
England and Wales	27,813	.8
Canada—others	25,620	.8
Austria	24,646	.7
Norway	21,740	.6
Yugoslavia	16,183	.5
Hungary	15,337	.5
Greece	14,815	.4
Scotland	14,264	.4
Denmark	12,502	.4
Rumania	11,033	.3
Netherlands	9,185	.3
Northern Ireland	7,404	.2
France	4,555	.1
Canada—French	4,211	.1
Belgium	4,106	.1
Switzerland	3,671	.1
Finland	2,261	.1
All other nationalities	15,937	.5
Total—all foreign-born	842,057	24.9

* Dr. Louis Wirth of the University of Chicago in an address before the Chicago Conference on Home Front Unity in May, 1945, called attention to the changes in foreign-born population that occurred between 1930 and 1940, "The figures showed that somewhat less than 20 per cent of Chicago's population were foreign-born in 1940. The major foreign-born groups in order of their numerical strength were those coming from Poland with 119,000, those from Germany with 83,000, those of Russian origin with 66,000, those from Italy with 66,000, of Swedish origin with 46,000 . . . and so on down the list." A comparison of these figures with those in the table reveals the gradual decline in the number of the foreign-born.

terms of size and influence. Black Metropolis emerges as a significant factor in the life of Midwest Metropolis.

BLACK METROPOLIS

Black Metropolis is the second largest Negro city in the world, only New York's Harlem exceeding it in size. It is a city within a city—a narrow tongue of land, seven miles in length and one and one-half miles in width, where more than 300,000 Negroes are packed solidly— in the heart of Midwest Metropolis. (Figure 1.) Peripheral to this Black Belt are five smaller Negro concentrations which are, in a fundamental sense, parts of Black Metropolis. Of Chicago's 337,000 Negroes a bare 10 per cent are scattered among the white population.

Walk the streets of the Black Belt and you will find no difference in language to mark its people off from others in the city. Only the black and brown and olive and tan faces of Negro Americans seem to distinguish it from any other section of Midwest Metropolis. But beneath the surface are patterns of life and thought, attitudes and customs, which make Black Metropolis a unique and distinctive city within a city. Understand Chicago's Black Belt and you will understand the Black Belts of a dozen large American cities.

Black Metropolis has appeared upon the urban checkerboard during a hundred and fifty years of city growth. The expansion of the Black Belt has been sometimes slow and sometimes rapid; today the Belt has virtually ceased to grow in area, although its population is still increasing. Until the heavy migration between 1915 and 1920, only about one-half of the Negro population in Midwest Metropolis lived in the Black Belt. Today, over 90 per cent of the city's colored population resides there, and this concentration has been taking place while foreign-born communities were disintegrating.

Midwest Metropolis seems uneasy about this Negro city growing up in its midst. In 1919, the Black Belt was the scene of a race riot, and in 1943, when race riots occurred in Detroit and New York, there were fears that a similar calamity might again befall Midwest Metropolis. The anticipated trouble did not materialize, but the fear remains. The basis for this apprehension will be revealed in these pages. Black Metropolis—how it came to be; why it persists; how its people live; what Midwest Metropolis thinks of it; what its people think of themselves and of Midwest Metropolis; whether it, too, will eventually disappear—these constitute the theme of this book.

To understand Black Metropolis, its origin, genesis, and probable destiny, it is necessary first to understand the manner in which Chicago has developed from a small prairie village into Midwest Metropolis.

THE PATTERN OF CITY GROWTH

The National Resources Committee, describing "Our Cities," has observed that "The American city is a motley of peoples and cultures forming a mosaic of little worlds which in part blend with one another but, in part, and for a time, remain segregated or come into conflict with one another."

The two basic facts about the spatial growth of Midwest Metropolis (and of most American cities) are, first, the tendency for people to move steadily outward from the center of the city as they grow more prosperous, leaving the center to business and industry, to the poor and the vicious; and second, the tendency of the foreign-born to settle originally in colonies near the center of the city, with individual families joining the outward stream as soon as they become Americanized in thought and relatively well-to-do. The competition for space among these various economic, social, and ethnic groups, and business and industry, results in strains and stresses. Group attitudes and prejudices are reflected in the rise and fall of land values in various parts of the city and in the economic and social status of neighborhoods. The extent to which these processes have gone on in Midwest Metropolis is plain if one examines a map showing the differences in the proportion of people who found it necessary to go on relief in various sections of the city during the Depression (Figure 3); poverty clusters near the center of the city. It is demonstrated also by the distribution of the foreign-born. (Figure 4.) This sifting and sorting of people through the years on the basis of affluence and social status has resulted in definite "zones of city growth." (Figure 5.) The pattern of concentric city growth is not a perfect one. It is broken by jumps and skips as new businesses or communities based on nationality or class spring up in outlying areas or along arteries of transportation, to be overtaken later by the expanding city.

Chicago began as a collection of settlements upon a prairie with a

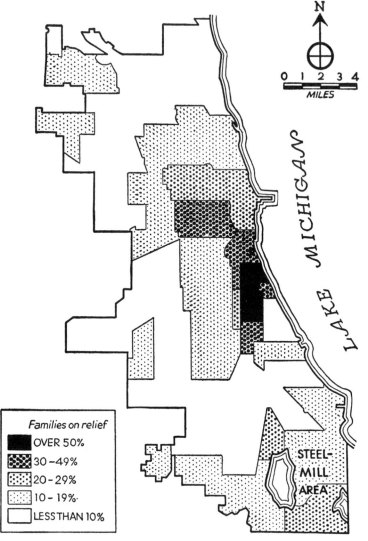

Figure 3

THE DISTRIBUTION OF POVERTY IN MIDWEST METROPOLIS

Prepared from data given in Louis Wirth and Margaret Furez (eds.), *Local Community Fact Book,* Chicago Recreation Commission, 1938. Data for 1934.

Figure 4

THE DISTRIBUTION OF THE FOREIGN-BORN

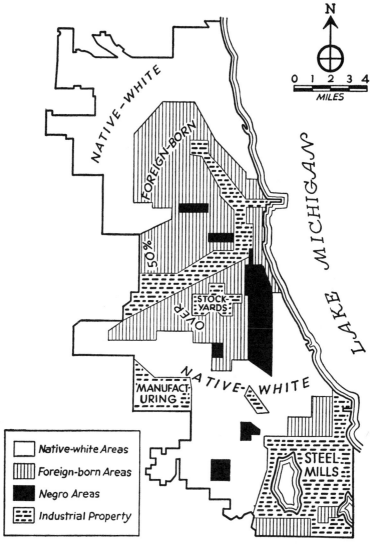

Adapted from map in Robert E. L. Faris and H. Warren Dunham, *Mental Disorders in Urban Areas*, University of Chicago Press, 1939.

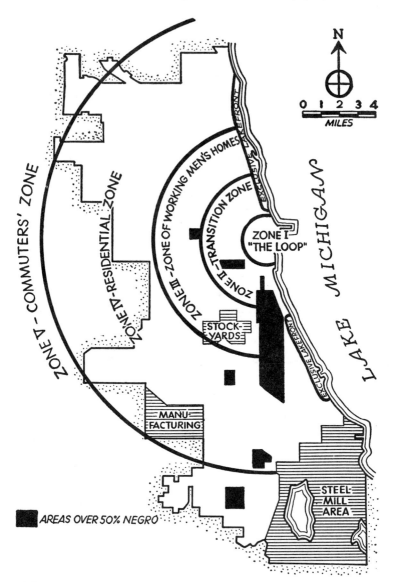

Figure 5
ZONES OF CITY GROWTH

N

0 1 2 3 4
MILES

ZONE V – COMMUTERS' ZONE

ZONE IV–RESIDENTIAL ZONE

ZONE III–ZONE OF WORKING MEN'S HOMES

ZONE II–TRANSITION ZONE

EXCLUSIVE LAKE-FRONT

ZONE I "THE LOOP"

LAKE MICHIGAN

STOCK-YARDS

EXCLUSIVE LAKE-FRONT

MANU-FACTURING

STEEL-MILL AREA

AREAS OVER 50% NEGRO

Adapted from map in R. E. Park and E. W. Burgess, *The City*, University of Chicago Press, 1921, and Cayton-Warner Research maps.

lot of room between most of them. In the Forties and Fifties these tended to be ethnic settlements—an Irish community or a German area here, a Scandinavian neighborhood or a Negro settlement there. As these expanded to touch one another they became the first clear divisions of the urban checkerboard, little groups of people each with a common language and customs. As the form of the city became set, new increments of the foreign-born tended to move into the old-established colonies until they got their bearings. Meanwhile, Americanized immigrants or their children filtered out into native-American communities, as individuals or families, and were thus dispersed through the city.

Since the Eighties the areas of first settlement for the foreign-born have been, on the whole, in or close to the so-called slums (Zones I and II of Figure 5), since rents were lowest there and the social pressure against them least. The areas of foreign second settlement were often found in the zone of workingmen's homes, where slightly more prosperous immigrants had moved.

The settlements of the Negroes have followed this pattern with one important difference: Negroes are not finally absorbed in the general population. Black Metropolis remains athwart the least desirable residential zones. Its population grows larger and larger, unable either to expand freely or to scatter. It becomes a persisting city within a city, reflecting in itself the cross-currents of life in Midwest Metropolis, but isolated from the main stream. Black Metropolis as a community is the end result of one hundred and fifty years of intense competition among native-whites, Negroes, and foreign-born for living space, economic goods, and prestige.

The entire history of Chicago from its birth to the First World War was characterized by the struggle, sometimes violent, of the first-comers and native-whites against the later immigrants—the "foreigners." In the Sixties it was everybody against the Irish and the Irish against a handful of Negroes and Hungarians; in the Seventies it was the Know-Nothing native-Americans against the Germans, Irish, Scandinavians, Bohemians, Slavs, and Frenchmen; in the Nineties, the northern Europeans and native-whites against the southern and eastern Europeans, the so-called "new immigration."

However much the native-born and older immigrant groups might dislike the "new immigration," they needed these people in order to maintain their own social and economic hegemony. In the steel mills and packing-houses, in the farm-implement factories and the railroad shops, the foreigners have done that laborious and unpleasant work which permitted the rise of an extensive native-born white-collar middle class and a small leisure class. As the immigrants arrived, the native-born were able to move up in status. By 1910 only one out of every ten native whites was engaged in unskilled labor, while three out of every ten foreigners were so employed. Only eight out of every hundred foreign-born workers did clerical work, whereas thirty out of every hundred native-born workers were doing that. Only a third of the native-born were engaged in industrial production; two-thirds of the foreign-born were so employed. In the railroad shops and on the section gangs, around the blast furnaces and rolling mills, the slaughter-and-packing-houses, the tanneries and lumber yards, wielding picks and mauls and shovels—wherever hot, heavy, or dirty work was to be done—here were the latest batches of immigrants, starting in at the bottom, but planning to get ahead themselves, or to push their children ahead. The children, once they had gone through the public schools, might be expected to move out of the slums, get better jobs, and lose themselves among the older American groups.

Since the First World War, Negroes have replaced immigrants as the primary source of unskilled and menial labor. In the mass, they rest at the bottom of the social and economic pyramid and have inherited the slums. Attracted by the American Dream the Negro residents, in numbers, have entered the city's life at a point almost a hundred years beyond its origin. They have had to compete for a place in a complex pattern already laid down, in a community where the main outlines of activity and tradition had long been set.

THE CHICAGO TRADITION

In the words of Lloyd Lewis and Henry Justin Smith, Chicago is essentially ". . . a hundred years and more of settling arguments on top of the effort to create, on a forbidding shore, a home fit to occupy." The history of the city may be viewed in terms of the continuous conflict between various economic, nationality, and racial groups. The forbidding shore was the marshy rim of Lake Michigan, its air so befouled by the stench of wild garlic that the Indians called it *Chickagou* (garlic) or *Shegagh* (skunk). The first great argument was a thirty-five-year contest to decide whether the Indians or the white men would control the spot—an argument settled by massacre, reprisal, and a shrewd, one-sided bargain just a quarter of a century before the Civil War.

"Why," we might ask, "were either the white men or the Indians interested in 'the place of the evil smell'?" A mistake made by Nature is the answer. Eight miles from Chickagou was a river down which one could sail to the Mississippi and thence to the Gulf. (Figure 1.) Had Nature let her Ice Age glacier-trowel scoop a little more, there would have been a continuous waterway from the Great Lakes to the Gulf; instead, she left a neck of land. The Indians accepted fate, lifted their canoes to their shoulders, and walked from lake to river. For them Chickagou was a convenient portage. But every white man who came there, from the time of Father Marquette and Louis Joliet, dreamed of a canal that would link the Five Lakes with the Father of Waters.

By 1830, a few pioneers had settled on the portage to trade with the Indians and those white men who were seeking farms in the West. A visiting Englishman didn't think much of the human material at the time, and described the settlement as being full of "rogues of every description, white, black, brown, and red . . . half-breeds, quarter-breeds and men of no breed at all. . . ." There was talk of a canal in the air, and a land boom was on throughout the West. In 1833, the town was incorporated—with 200 souls and 243 buildings. Wheat and corn farmers were looking for an outlet to the East, and people with an eye for business gathered in the town by the Lake. A few slaughter-houses and small farm-implement factories appeared. "Chicago was a frontier city in most respects," writes one historian. "The timid feared it; the pious prayed for it; the robust, vigorous, loud, coarse, and irreverent enjoyed it. . . . It is incontestable that a majority of the voters preferred a wide-open town."[4] Chicago had begun to develop a reputation.

During the twenty years between its incorporation and the outbreak of the Civil War, Chicago became a center of speculation in farm lands, canal rights-of-way, railroads, and farm machinery. Nature's mistake was finally rectified when in 1848 the Illinois-Michigan Canal linked the Lake with the Mississippi. Capital from eastern banks, and savings from migrants' pockets and western farmers' socks, poured into the city to finance first "plank roads" and then railroads, McCormick's reaper and George Pullman's machine shop. The town began to fill up with eastern capitalists, Irish laborers, Bohemian, Scandinavian, and German artisans, and a motley crew of sharpers and harpies, their rapid passage to the West aided by the Erie Canal. The countryside was flooded with Chicago "drummers."

In this pre-Civil War period Chicago acquired the reputation of being a "tough" town, and differences of opinion were often settled with vigorous and brutal directness. In the Fifties many of the Protestant, native-born Easterners reacted violently against the customs of their Irish Catholic and German neighbors, particularly Sunday beer-drinking. The city officials, influenced by the semi-secret anti-foreign Know-Nothing Party, eventually succeeded in placing heavy license fees upon saloons and beer gardens and in passing Sunday Blue Laws. The foreign-born responded with a full-scale riot which required a show of artillery to crush it.

This penchant for direct action was carried over into the anti-slavery struggles. Here, however, the lines were drawn in different fashion, with Easterners, Germans, and Scandinavians uniting against the Catholic, proslavery Irish. Again, amid the irritations of the Panic of 1857, the Puritan forces proceeded to clean up "the Sands"—a collection of dives—by purchasing the property and pulling down the houses of the gamblers and prostitutes upon their heads. Pre-Civil War Chicago was a gaudy, dirty, exciting small town, described by a London *Times* correspondent as ". . . an extraordinary mélange of the Broadway of New York and little shanties, of Parisian buildings mixed some way with backwoods life."

The Civil War brought a boom. Then, the war over, Chicago settled down to packing meat, shipping wheat, and making a fortune for Armour, Swift, Pullman, McCormick, Ogden, and Marshall Field. The stench of the stockyards had long since replaced the odor of garlic. "Chickagou" had become Chicago, and its fame spread so wide that Bismarck stated in 1870, "I wish I could go to America if only to see that Chicago." The next year the famous Chicago Fire burned almost the entire town to the level of the prairie.

The city was rebuilt quickly, however, and from the Fire to the turn of the century Chicago-town was busy becoming Midwest Metropolis. By 1890 it had passed the million mark in population, and the scattered collection of settlements and villages had coalesced into a city. It had acquired a national reputation for three things: rapid growth, colorful "wickedness," and frequent labor violence. The World's Fair of 1893 confirmed and advertised this appraisal. Throughout the Eighties and Nineties a few people made money and enjoyed luxuries and leisure. Others had modest security. But the vast masses of laborers were struggling for a living wage and an eight-hour day. Repeated panics periodically drew these economic class contradictions to a head, and the vigor with which labor fought gave the city an international reputation as a center of radicalism.

In the Railroad Riots of 1877, which began in the East and spread to Chicago, pitched battles were fought in the streets and wealthy families fled the city in panic. Nine years later the Haymarket Riot—dynamite, shots, at least seven dead, scores wounded, seven anarchists executed—became America's first left-wing *cause célèbre*. Even mild unionists were entranced by the words of the defiant August Spies: "If you think that by hanging us you can stamp out the labor movement, then call your hangmen. But you will tread upon the sparks. Here and there, behind you, in front of you, and everywhere, flames will spring up!" Artisans who by no means sanctioned the use of dynamite approved when Parsons, the printer, shouted through his gallows hood, "Let the voice of the People be heard!" And Samuel Fielden's words were stirring even if they came from the lips of an anarchist: "I have hated trickery, dishonesty, and injustice. . . . I trust the time will come when there will be better understanding, more intelligence; and above the mountains of iniquity, wrong, and corruption, I hope the sun of righteousness and truth and justice will come to bathe in its balmy light the emancipated world."

Much of the antagonism between capital and labor in the Eighties and Nineties was due to the fact that while the predominantly foreign-born working class fought for immediate labor legislation and talked of Socialism, the Protestant church people and the city's wealthy leaders were interested primarily in moral reform. (The politicians, meanwhile, worked both sides of the street.) The working classes consistently viewed emphasis upon reform and good government as an expression of upper-class and middle-class prejudice, a cover for sophisticated delinquencies, an attempt to beg the more urgent questions of bread and butter. Yet, in the years between the first World's Fair and the First World War, the reform forces burgeoned.

Amid the enthusiasm of the first World's Fair—the Columbian Exposition of 1893—a visiting English journalist, the eminent William T. Stead, uttered a sweeping condemnation of Chicago's municipal life

at a public meeting: "You are gigantic in your virtues and gigantic in
your vices. I don't know in which you glory the most. . . ." He implemented his criticism with a sensational, red-bound 450-page book, *If
Christ Came to Chicago,* giving names and addresses of spots where
prostitution prevailed, pilloried the sometimes wealthy owners, exposed
the tie-up between police and vice and between the city government
and powerful traction interests, and concluded with the observation
that the city needed "the application of every known device of sociology or religion to save it." He dressed up his indictment with colorful
chapter headings such as "The Boodlers and the Boodled," "The
Scarlet Woman," "Casting Out Devils," "Maggie Darling," and "The
Conscience of Chicago." On the cover was a sketch of Christ driving
the money-changers from the temple, and his last chapter painted a
Utopian picture of the future Chicago as "the ideal city of the world."
He called for united action, citing Britain as an example: "If these
things can be done in London, why cannot they be done in Chicago
by the labor unions acting together with the other moral and religious
forces of the town?" The book created a sensation.

But labor was in no mood for moral preachments. The panic of 1893
had the city in its grip. Thousands of homeless and hungry transients
who had come to the Fair were sleeping in flop-houses and saloons.
Wage slashes and unemployment were swelling their ranks. Trouble
was in the air. It broke when the workers in the Pullman sleeping-car
plant downed their tools. Eugene V. Debs's American Railway Union
interceded unsuccessfully for an arbitrament and then ordered railway
men not to handle any trains with Pullman cars attached. A paralyzing
strike spread rapidly. Violence was rife. For the first time in American
history Federal troops were used to crush a strike—on the grounds that
the mail must go through. It took artillery to disperse the angry railroad men and the unemployed mobs who fought with bricks and rifles
and even turned over a locomotive in their wrath. Eugene Debs went
to jail for six months, despite Clarence Darrow's classic defense, and
came out America's first prominent native-born Socialist.

Meanwhile a group of one hundred prominent citizens took up
Stead's challenge, organized a Civic Federation, and began a clean-up
campaign. They put through a civil service law, fought grafting
garbage-collectors, broke up a few downtown gambling places, and
organized a municipal voters' league. This organization—a coalition of
the wealthy-with-a-conscience and the civic-minded of all strata—began

a no-quarter fight against crooked politics. Within ten years they had placed ten of their men in City Hall. They trained their big guns upon vice and started a campaign (which lasted eighteen years) to abolish the Red-light District. When in the early 1900's Lincoln Steffens started out to do a "muckraking" job on the city, he was convinced that he would find a "sensationally wicked story" and planned to expose the "rough anarchistic criminality of a wild young western city." He reports that he found "evil . . . obvious, general, bold." But what he considered more significant was a group of cagy, hard-boiled reformers who through the Municipal Voters' League were able to crack the whip over ward politicians.

Another group, including some of the wealthy but spearheaded by the settlement-house workers, the "muckrakers," and the radicals, stressed the need for "trust-busting," increasing wages, shortening hours, abolishing child labor, curbing LaSalle Street and Wall Street, and fighting the traction interests. The people in this group were a part of that general midwestern movement which culminated in Theodore Roosevelt's nomination at Chicago on the Progressive ticket in 1912, with the Square Dealer shouting, "We stand at Armageddon doing battle for the Lord!"—while Jane Addams led the convention in singing *Onward, Christian Soldiers*.

The thousands of laborers in the stockyards and mechanical industries were largely unorganized, and the skilled artisans in the building trades were playing it another way. "Skinny" Madden (father of "business unionism") and his "wreckers," with bare fists, knuckles, and an occasional bullet, were "organizing" the contractors and getting slight wage increases for the workers, a neat pile for themselves, and a "cut" for the politicians. The Socialists were trying to vote in a new society and the IWW was calling for one big union to make all things new. The ward politicians, wise in their worldly wisdom, sat tight and let the winds of reform blow themselves out.

Lincoln Steffens, years later, wrote the epitaph of Chicago's early reformers. They became too interested in "representative government." Powerful interests could tolerate a "good government" movement but not a drive for "representative government." According to him, "They killed it as literally as the gunmen of Chicago now kill one another and as safely."

There have always been two reform traditions in Chicago: one concerned with stopping "vice" and petty political graft; the other with controlling "predatory big business." Sometimes these causes and their spokesmen fuse in a single campaign; sometimes they move along simultaneously; often they clash. And the "gray wolves" of City Hall have been the traditional whipping-boys of both the "good government" and the "representative government" forces.

Throughout the Nineties and early 1900's the church people, the wealthy, and the rising middle class were determined to reclaim the city's reputation and make it "clean"—on the surface, at least. On the eve of the First World War, prostitution had been scattered if not conquered—every old exclusive "resort" and historic bawdy house had been closed. The anti-vice crusaders were still hammering away fruitlessly at the saloon with Frances E. Willard leading her praying WCTU women from grogshop to grogshop.

In 1914, another depression arrived. Chicago was weary of vice crusades and disillusioned by the débâcle of the Progressive movement. War had broken out in Europe. The city turned to an exhibitionist for its mayor, the fantastic Republican playboy, "Big Bill" Thompson with his ten-gallon hat, who proclaimed that he wore no man's halter and promised to make Chicago the biggest city in the world. For the next eight years he ran the city.

The First World War altered the composition of Chicago's population. When it began, the city was two-thirds native-white and one-third foreign-born. When it ended, the proportion of foreign-born had been reduced by six per cent and over 50,000 Negroes had migrated from the South to meet the demands of an expanded industry. This sudden shift in the city's national and racial complexion was accompanied by a devastating race riot in 1919.

A series of labor disturbances occurred during the three years after the war. Neither steel nor packing was effectively organized, despite the bloody strikes of 1919 and 1921 in which Negro strike-breakers played some part. Chicago's attention was now focused on a different field. Before the war, the reformers and the civic-minded had seen their problems as VICE, IMMIGRANTS, and LABOR. Now they turned their attention to GANGSTERS, NEGROES, and LABOR. White labor, particularly, began to visualize Negro workers as a potential threat.

During the lush years between 1922 and 1929 the general population developed two consuming interests: how to share in the wave of prosperity and how to get a drink. The anti-liquor forces had won a Pyrrhic victory during the First World War like that of the vice crusaders who preceded them. They drove evil out of sight and underground, and they got the "alky mob" * as a result. The politicians waxed fat.

Perhaps the most profound change that took place in Midwest Metropolis between the First World War and the Great Depression was a gradual shift in the content of the American Dream as presented by the men of power. During the great agitation for the eight-hour day in the Eighties, the Chicago *Inter-Ocean,* financed by a wealthy restaurateur, had said of the laborers:

> The one thing that will confer upon each of them individually the greatest prosperity is to look upon the wages condition not as a necessity for life, but as a temporary stage only in life, from which the wage worker is to emerge into a worker for profits.[5]

Civic leaders emphasized thrift, the establishment of small business, and investment in large ones. But it is doubtful whether this ever represented the American Dream of the average worker. He knew that Midwest Metropolis could not become a city composed entirely of capitalists and small businessmen. To him the American Dream meant something else: a steady job at high wages, and leisure to spend with his family and cronies and in enjoying the diversified entertainment which the city offered. For many, too, it implied the ownership of a home and conveniences. (For most of the foreign-born it also meant the ability to raise a family without the need for their wives to work.) It included savings for old age and for the education of children. With the advent of mass production, automobiles, telephones, radios, plumbing, etc., it grew to include a full and ever-increasing supply of these gadgets. Businessmen of the Twenties, unlike their predecessors, began to encourage the masses to spend rather than to save.

The attitude of a large segment of Chicago's working people throughout the stormy Eighties and Nineties and into the twentieth century seems to have been: "Attain the American Dream under capitalism if we can, and by Socialism if we must." As late as 1920, Eugene Debs drew over 50,000 Socialist votes from Midwest Metropolis, and in 1919 the Chicago City Federation of Labor took the initiative in organizing a statewide labor party, one of whose "Fourteen Points" demanded "public ownership and operation of all public utilities, in-

---

* "Alky mob"—colloquial name for the gangsters who controlled the bootleg liquor business during the Prohibition Era.

cluding grain elevators, warehouses, stockyards, abattoirs, insurance, and banks." The period between the First World War and the collapse of 1929 was, however, one that made the American Dream seem attainable without drastic social change. As increasing numbers of people saw such possibilities, as an older generation of Socialists died off, Socialist tendencies withered and died, and the labor unions concentrated upon immediate demands and upon smart deals with politicians and employers.

Another trend, too, suddenly achieved visible proportions in the Twenties. As industry expanded, the tremendous increase in "paper work" opened up great perspectives that neither radicals nor capitalists of a previous epoch had visualized—a large white-collar middle class. The proportion of capitalists, large or small, had remained relatively constant throughout Chicago's period of rapid industrialization, but the proportion of people doing "clean work" steadily expanded. By 1930 only 60 per cent of the men and 40 per cent of the women in the city were engaged in manual labor or servant work. Almost half the men and over half the women were occupied in some sort of clerical work, and almost half the working population was engaged in either managerial, professional, or clerical work. The vast amount of office work in Midwest Metropolis made it possible for a young woman to work until she made a match, when she could move out and let her younger sister take her place. The native-born, the "successful" foreign-born, and the children of the immigrants left the city's heavy work and dirty work to the rapidly dwindling "new" foreign-born population and to the constantly growing Negro population.

The new middle class of the Twenties was equally unconcerned with vice reform or business reform *per se*. The system was paying off. Chicago was a big city. It had room enough for all kinds of people, and when you had accumulated enough or, if a woman, had married the right kind of man you could clear out of the crowded inner city and get a home in the residential suburbs. The members of the new middle class tried to keep their neighborhoods peopled with persons like themselves, groused about taxes, and tended to enjoy the spectacle of letting the rest of Chicago do as it damned please.

Manual workers saw hope for their children if not for themselves, and those who were organized used their unions to extract what they could without killing the goose that laid the golden egg.

Even the Negroes, last to "muscle in on the racket," weren't faring too badly.

When the crash of 1929 came the city was bewildered but considered the catastrophe just a temporary upset. Chicago's Century of Progress Exposition in 1933 was a sort of defiant gesture in the teeth of economic disaster, and people half believed that enticing enough visitors would restore prosperity. As the city woke up amidst a deepening depression it did so in a typical Chicago fashion. The unemployed took to the streets. Teachers demonstrated for their back pay. Tenants fought bailiffs to keep from being evicted. Midwest Metropolis became a New Deal town, and for the first time achieved something approaching "representative government." A tremendous upsurge of industrial unionism swept the city, with Communists playing an important part. Segments of the new white-collar middle class were drawn into the movement. The CIO organized the harvester plants, and the aged wife of a Haymarket rioter was present at the victory rally as a touch of poetic justice. The steel magnates resisted savagely. The industrialists professed fear of revolution, but the Socialist tradition had been buried with Debs and the Communists were unable to revive it. The politicians swayed this way and that, shooting down the workers in the "Memorial Day Massacre," and then running as "labor candidates" when they saw which way the wind was blowing. The Kelly-Nash machine clutched frantically at the New Deal's coattails and held on for dear life. WPA blossomed. The city limped through the last years of the Depression, a patient of "Dr. New Deal" until "Dr. Win the War" gave it a rejuvenating transfusion.

The Second World War brought new industries and new people— more than 100,000 of them; and over 60,000 of these were Negroes. Tanks, electrical equipment, airplane engines, meat, wheat, began to pour out of Midwest Metropolis in a steady stream. The labor front became quiet, but memories of the past and fears for the future stirred uneasily in the city's subconscious.

"WIDE-OPEN" TOWN

Chicago, as we have noted, has always had the reputation of being a "wide-open" town, whose citizens were never overdisturbed by graft in city government, or by alliances between politicians, the underworld, and/or big-business interests. The vast masses of the factory workers have taken corrupt government as a matter of course, the craft unions have had their own arrangements with City Hall, and the new middle classes, even when temporarily aroused, have never been able to control elections. A scandal breaks now and then, followed by a reform wave—"the heat is turned on." And then things are allowed to settle down to the old routine. The "good government forces" have never had any real strength in Midwest Metropolis. A liberal-labor coalition began to emerge during the Depression but it was closely allied with the Kelly-Nash political machine.

Numerous observers have been impressed, too, with what they call a "sporting tradition" in Chicago life. Lincoln Steffens expressed this most explicitly when he wrote in 1931: "Chicago likes audacity and is always willing to have anybody try anything once; no matter who you are, where you come from, or what you set out to do, Chicago will give you a chance. The sporting spirit is the spirit of Chicago."

A rapidly changing city, wide open, and with a sporting tradition, provides many short cuts to wealth and prestige, politics and "rackets" being the most popular. Young and old know that if you "make a pile" you can become a "big shot"—and that, conversely, if you are a "big shot" you can be expected to "cash in" on it. Sophisticated urbanites develop a cynical approach to every enterprise. "What's his racket?" is a universal Chicago query applied alike to the respectable and to the shady prosperous.

The exigencies of life in Midwest Metropolis, as in almost any rapidly changing community, put a great deal of emphasis upon "luck." Experience teaches that only a few people can get the choicest plums by hard work and frugality, so people tend to set their sights upon a goal of middle-class comfort and to admire from a distance the people who "get the breaks," who "hit the jackpot," and to become sentimental about the casualties who took a chance and lost. Even the people who play the game safe often have a sneaking admiration for the "tough guys," the "smart boys," the "smooth fellows." The tendency to view success in terms of luck is a stabilizing influence amid rapid change and frustrated ambitions; it provides a ready rationalization for those left behind.

This free and easy approach to living, this philosophy of live and let live, the "sporting spirit," is continually being checked and limited, however, by the conflicting drives toward economic security and prestige. Those who have made their pile, those who have attained a modicum of security—the new middle class and the well-organized craft workers—all represent forces of stability in Midwest Metropolis. Their own lives become ordered. Excitement becomes occasional, vicarious, and formalized—the ball game, the races, a convention, a prize fight, or reading about their "wicked city." The philosophy of such people tends to be: "Anything goes so long as it doesn't affect me directly." Let a man feel, however, that his economic security, his prestige in the eyes of his fellows, or his inner core of beliefs is being compromised and he will lash out in defense.

A more fruitful approach to Midwest Metropolis than generalizing about the "spirit of Chicago" in the abstract is to view the city as split into competing economic groups, social classes, ethnic groups, and religious and secular associations, each with its own set of traditions. The violent shifts in public sentiment and action which characterize Chicago history reflect the combination and recombination of these groups when they feel that their interests are menaced. Out of this welter of fears and loyalties and interests have exploded some of America's most bizarre and dramatic incidents—riots, strikes, colorful elections, reform movements, and reactions against reform.

As Midwest Metropolis grows up, its economic and political conflicts become somewhat more simplified in form and more disciplined in expression. There are no longer large blocs of the foreign-born to be organized by enterprising politicians and industrialists. The city gets split into three large economic groups, predominantly white American: the wealthy few, a growing new middle class, and the poorer wage-earners. Among the wage-earners are more than a third of a million Negroes, and predominantly they are the poorer wage-earners—kept apart socially, but sought as economic or political allies at one time or another by competing segments of the white society. It is these Negroes who make up Black Metropolis and who hold a pivotal position in the equilibrium of political and economic power of Midwest Metropolis. Black Metropolis did not emerge until the Twenties, but Negroes were a part of Chicago from the beginning.

PART I

CHAPTER I

Flight to Freedom

THE POTTAWATTOMIE INDIANS WHO RELINQUISHED THE CHICAGO PORTAGE to the white man in 1835 had a saying: "The first white man to settle at Chickagou was a Negro." Frenchmen—trappers, priests, and explorers—had touched this portage from time to time during the seventeenth century; and Louis Joliet and Father Marquette crossed it in 1673. But it was a French-speaking Negro, Jean Baptiste Point de Saible, described by a contemporary British army officer as "a handsome Negro well educated and settled at Eschikagou," [1] who made the first permanent settlement, some time around 1790. At "the place of the evil smell," Point de Saible erected a frontier establishment consisting of a large wooden homestead, bakehouse, smokehouse, poultry house, and dairy; a workshop and a horse mill; a barn and two stables. Here the Pottawattomie came to trade; and the English and French, exploring and fighting for dominance in the back-country, stopped to rest and replenish their stores. Reclaimed from the prairie and wrested from the wilderness, this solitary frontier settlement became the seed-bed of skyscrapers and factories. Its trading post was the progenitor of the wheat-pit and its workshop the prototype of factories and mills. The canoes and pirogues that stopped here foreshadowed the commerce of after-years.

Where he came from originally—this Father of Midwest Metropolis—we do not know. According to one tradition he was from Santo Domingo, and planned to establish a colony of free Negroes near the shores of Lake Michigan. Another story would have him the descendant of a Negro slave and a French fur-trader in the Northwest Territory. We know with certainty only that for sixteen years he and his Pottawattomie wife Catherine, his daughter Cézanne, and Jean Baptiste *fils*, lived at the present site of Chicago. In 1796, for reasons unknown he sold his establishment to one LeMai, who in turn sold it to an Englishman, John Kinzie. Point de Saible then moved to Peoria, where he spent most of the remainder of his life, dying in St. Charles, Missouri. Within the house he had built, so tradition says, Chicago's first marriage was solemnized, the first election held, and the first white child born.

Of Point de Saible one student of early Chicago, Milo Quaife, has written: "He was a true pioneer of civilization, leader of the unending procession of Chicago's swarming millions. Even in his mixed blood he truly represented the future city, for where else is a greater conglomeration of races and breeds assembled together?" [2]

With his departure, only an occasional Negro filtered into the city until the late Forties, when a steady, though small, stream began to arrive.

CHICAGO—CITY OF REFUGE

The earliest Negro migrants to Chicago, like those of later years, were refugees from the bondage of America's cotton kingdom in the South. They poured into the city by the hundreds between 1840 and 1850, fleeing slavery. Some remained; others passed through to Canada and points east.

Chicago gradually became an important terminal on that amazingly ingenious combination of secret trails, mysterious hay wagons, hideouts, and zealous people that was known as the Underground Railroad.[3] Up the Mississippi, across the Ohio River, through the Allegheny gaps, over the western prairie, nearly a hundred thousand slaves were passed from farm to farm and town to town during the seventy years' operation of "freedom's railroad." Secrecy was necessary, even in Chicago, for the Illinois Black Code required every Negro who remained in the state to post a thousand-dollar bond and to carry a certificate of freedom. The federal Fugitive Slave Law of 1793 made it a criminal offense, punishable by a $500 fine, to harbor a fugitive or to prevent his arrest. Yet throughout the Forties and Fifties a few churches and homes in Chicago served as "stations" on the Underground Railroad. The "conductors"—usually church people or political radicals—were recruited mainly from the ranks of white artisans, business people, and Negroes holding free papers. The *Western Citizen,* abolitionist journal, boasted during the Fifties: "We can run a load of slaves through from almost any part of the border states into Canada within forty-eight hours and we defy the slaveholders to beat that if they can." [4]

Furious and frustrated planters in the lower Mississippi Valley fulminated at this lawless traffic in stolen property. They derisively and indignantly dubbed Chicago a "nigger-loving town." One editor in southern Illinois, a proslavery stronghold, contemptuously dismissed Chicago as a "sink hole of abolition." [5] To the slaves, however, it was a city of refuge, and once within its boundaries they jealously guarded their own illegal freedom while helping their fellows to escape.

Chicago's small group of Underground "officials" received its first open support from a wider public when the murder of the famous abolitionist, Elijah Lovejoy, by a southern Illinois mob in 1837 drew sharp protests from a number of church groups. Several antislavery societies sprang up within the next decade. They flooded the city with pamphlets, presented antislavery dramas, sponsored lectures by eminent abolitionists from the East, and tried to organize political support for the Free Soil and the Liberty parties. Gradually the slavery controversy began to affect Chicago as it had numerous other northern communities. Churches and secular organizations alike were riven asunder as radicals and conservatives divided on points of antislavery principle and tactics.

Despite the local political contests of the Forties, however, the general public had not yet become excited over the slavery issue. It was more immediately concerned with proposals for a Galena and Chicago Union Railroad, over which wheat and corn and hogs would flow in abundance, than with the human freight of the Underground Railroad. Yet no obstacles were interposed to curb the abolitionist minority, and Chicago—with a reputation even then for colorful violence—tolerated some rather rough treatment of slave-catchers who came to ferret out fugitives. More moderate antislavery sympathizers were occasionally disturbed by the activities of the Underground; and on one occasion in 1846, when a group of Negroes, armed with clubs and led by white abolitionists, rescued a slave from his captors and "paraded in triumph," they convoked a public meeting to disavow this show of force. The editor of one influential newspaper declared: "Better even is law, enforced by the standing armies of tyrants, than for a community to be the subjects of every handful of outlaws, black or white, who may choose to combine and set the laws at defiance." [6] Just four years later, however, the Chicago city council itself was setting the law at defiance; and, as for returning fugitives to the South, an influential church newspaper was insisting that "no Christian rightly understanding his duties can engage in it." [7]

This crystallization of public sentiment was due primarily to the Compromise of 1850, which gave the southern planters a revitalized fugitive-slave act in exchange for their consent to the admission of California as a free state. The amended act raised the fine for harboring fugitives to $1,000 and added a prison term of six months. A slave-catcher's affidavit became sufficient evidence in court to identify any Negro as a fugitive. Trial by jury and the right to testify in his own defense were denied the suspected slave. Magistrates were rewarded with a ten-dollar fee for ruling in favor of the master, while only five dollars was allotted for decisions in favor of the Negro. Any bystander could be deputized to assist in a capture. Federal officials who let a slave escape from their custody were financially liable for the entire value of the lost property.

A wave of indignation swept through the North when the terms of the new fugitive-slave act were announced. In Chicago, three hundred Negroes—over half the permanent adult population—met in their Methodist Church, organized a Liberty Association, and set up vigilante groups. Seven patrols of six persons each were assigned "to keep an eye out for interlopers." The Association passed a ringing resolution explaining the Negroes' stand:

". . . We do not wish to offer violence to any person unless driven to the extreme, in which case we are determined to defend ourselves at all hazards, even should it be to the shedding of human blood, and in doing thus, will appeal to the Supreme Judge of the Social World to support us in the justness of our cause. . . . We who have tasted of *freedom* are ready to exclaim, in the language of the brave Patrick Henry, 'Give us liberty or give us death.' " [8]

White sympathizers, too, were aroused, and it became evident that some justices would refuse to enforce the law. One famous case, soon after the passage of the Compromise, involved a Mr. Hinch, who arrived in town with a devoted slave to help him catch three fugitives. One day when he and the trusty were standing near Lake Michigan, even this faithful retainer deserted to freedom, by jumping aboard a steamer pulling out for Canada. A group of abolitionists threatened to tar and feather Mr. Hinch, so he appealed to a local justice for the protection of his person and for co-operation in recapturing his property.

The justice advised him that "immediate flight would be his safest course."

Even the Chicago Common Council, the city's legislative body, took formal action condemning the fugitive-slave act as "a cruel and unjust law . . . [which] ought not be respected by an intelligent community." The city police were assured that they were under no obligation to assist in rounding up escaped slaves. At a mass meeting on the night of the Council's vote, a white lawyer made a fiery speech against the fugitive-slave act and closed by "defying the law and trampling a copy of it under his feet, to the delight and admiring cheers of his hearers." [9]

Stephen A. Douglas, Senator from Illinois, had backed the Compromise. He was now so disturbed by this smoldering in the grass roots that he rushed home from Washington to prevent it from becoming a prairie fire. His eloquent and skillful defense of the Compromise won a resolution from his audience condemning the Chicago Council for its "precipitate action." The city fathers would not retreat completely, however. They voted to "reconsider," but refused to "expunge from the record." [10]

But neither Douglas's oratory nor the desire for an orderly community restrained the aroused abolitionists. An official of the Underground Railroad commented in the late autumn of 1850: "This road is doing better business this fall than usual. The Fugitive Slave Law has given it more vitality and activity; more passengers and more opposition, which accelerates business." [11] The Chicago *Daily Journal* had insisted since the early Forties that "every man that wears the image and likeness of his Maker should be treated as a man." Now, it advocated violent action against slave-catchers with a broad, humorous hint: "We have no doubt but those interested are upon their guard and the gentlemen [i.e., slave-catchers] will return with a *flea in their ears.*" [12] The *Democratic Press,* organ of "Deacon" Bross, Chicago's most colorful civic booster of the day, declared that the Fugitive Slave Law could be enforced only "at the muzzle of a musket," and declared that "we have known of many attempts being made to take fugitives away from Chicago, but we have yet to learn the first instance in which the thing has been done." [13]

In case after case during the stormy decade between the Compromise and the Civil War, the Negroes and their abolitionist allies outwitted and outfought the slave-catchers. One of the most dramatic of these episodes involved one Eliza, an escaped slave who had found employment as a maidservant in a house of prostitution. A slave-catcher, discovering her whereabouts, came to claim his quarry, escorted by a local deputy. Eliza and a white girl companion both begged the slavecatcher not to take the girl away. They were silenced by a drawn revolver, while Eliza, kicking and screaming, was forced into a waiting hack. An angry crowd surrounded the carriage, and the captors fled into a nearby armory, dragging Eliza with them.

By this time a large group of colored men, armed with clubs and knives, descended upon the armory. The sheriff then appeared with a warrant for Eliza's arrest on a charge of disorderly conduct—a calculated stratagem to get her away from the slave-catcher. As the sheriff emerged from the armory with Eliza, the crowd wrenched her from his grasp and quickly spirited her away to a station on the Underground Railroad. The mob then proceeded to the house of assignation, threatening to level it to the ground in the belief that the owner had revealed Eliza's identity. The ringleaders were arrested but released the next day. Scant wonder that the Cairo (Ill.) *Weekly Times* was led to complain of the Chicagoans: "They are the most riotous people in the state. Mention nigger and slave-catcher in the same breath and they are up in arms." [14]

Finally, in the spring of 1861, a group of federal marshals threatened to swoop down upon Chicago and other northern cities in one last but futile gesture aimed at appeasing a South on the verge of secession. The Negro community was panic-stricken, and the Chicago *Journal,* leading antislavery daily, in a dramatic admonition advised every Negro without a certificate of freedom to "make tracks for Canada as soon as possible": [15]

Don't delay a moment. Don't let grass grow under your feet. Stand not upon the order of your going but go at once. You are not safe here and you cannot be safe until you stand on English soil where you will be free men and free women. It is folly for you to remain here an instant, for the slaveholders encouraged by their late success are making and will continue to make the most determined effort to reclaim fugitives from bondage. Strike for the North Star.

The Underground was now functioning in the open. Four freight cars were boldly chartered to carry the fugitives to an embarkation point on Lake Michigan. A *Journal* reporter was on hand to describe this exodus: [16]

All day, yesterday, the vicinity of the Michigan Southern depot was a scene of excitement and confusion. After the religious services at the Zoar Baptist Church in the morning, which was densely attended, the leave-taking commenced . . . the fugitives and their friends, going from door to door, bidding each other good-bye and mingling their congratulations and tears.—The colored clergymen of the city were also among the number, and labored ardently in extending encouragement and consolation to those about to depart. . . . In some instances, entire families were going together, in which cases there seemed to be a general jubilation; in others a few members, a wife leaving a husband, or a mother her children, amid tears. . . .

. . . All the afternoon, drays, express wagons and other vehicles were busy transporting trunks, bandboxes, valises and other various articles of household furniture to the depot. The wants of the outer man had been attended to also, and a goodly store of provisions, such as crackers, bread, beans, dried beef and apples, were packed in, and a barrel of water in each car; for the fugitives were to be stowed away in the same cars with the freight, with plenty of fresh air, but no light, and in a crowded unwholesome state.

As the hour of departure . . . drew nigh, the streets adjacent to the depot and the immediate vicinity of the four cars . . . were thronged with an excited multitude of colored people of both sexes and all ages. Large numbers of white people also gathered from motives of curiosity, and stood silent spectators of this rather unusual spectacle. The four cars were rapidly filled with the fugitives, numbering one hundred and six in all, and embracing men, women, youth and infants. In the rear car were two or three sick women, who were treated with the utmost tenderness. . . . The whole business of the transportation was supervised by two or three colored men assisted by several white people.

After all were aboard, . . . the immense crowd pressed up to the cars and commenced the last farewell. . . . Here and there was one in tears and wringing the hands, but the majority were in the best of humor, and were congratulated by their friends lingering behind, that tomorrow they would be free. "Never mind," said one, "the good Lord will save us all in the coming day." . . . [They were] bidding their friends write when they got to "the other side of Jordan," and not forget them in the new country. The minister of the neighborhood church where they had attended, also went from car to car bidding them to be men when they got to Canada.

The larger proportion of the fugitives were stout, ablebodied young men, many of them well dressed and some of them almost white. . . . The elder ones evinced no levity but acted like those who had been hardened

by troubles, and were now suffering a lot foreseen and prepared for. . . .
Quite a number of children were among the crowd, who, ignorant of
the cause of such a commotion, gave the rest constant trouble by getting
into the wrong cars and climbing round and between the wheels.

But all were finally stowed away, the bell of the engine sounded and the
train started amid lusty cheers, many-voiced good-byes and the waving
of hats and handkerchiefs as far as the eye could see. The fugitives heartily
responded and the train vanished in the distance. . . .

About one thousand fugitives have arrived in this city since last fall, a
large number of whom have left within the past few days.

The Great Canadian Exodus had become another step in the flight
to freedom.

FROM CITY STREET TO BATTLEFIELD

Street fights between slave-catchers and abolitionists or between proslavery and antislavery crowds were rather common occurrences in
northern cities between 1850 and 1860. They were the storm signals of
that great political groundswell which culminated in the organization
of the Republican party and the election of Abraham Lincoln to the
presidency. Both the sporadic violence and the humanitarian agitation
of the antislavery movement were gradually merged with and subordinated to political action. Chicago's antislavery forces had tried to elect
a mayor in 1841 and failed. Yet, less than twenty years later, the Republican party controlled the city. Migrants from the eastern seaboard,
immigrants from England, and German radical refugees from the reaction which followed the European revolutions of 1848 provided the
majority which tipped the balance in favor of the Republicans.

In 1856, "Honest Abe" and Stephen A. Douglas, the "Little Giant,"
both came to Chicago to plead for the senatorial vote. The Democrats
roared thunderous assent when Douglas declared that the government
of the United States "was made by white men for the benefit of white
men, to be administered by white men in such a manner as they should
determine."

The next night Lincoln spoke—and with a forthrightness which he
seldom assumed in other sections of Illinois. He appealed to the foreign-
born, who made up over 50 per cent of the electorate, calling them
"blood of the blood, and flesh of the flesh of the men who wrote the
Declaration of Independence and pronounced the equality of men."

He took a bold stand against the extension of slavery, declaring that "if we cannot give freedom to every creature, let us do nothing that will impose slavery upon any other creature." He made a stirring plea for national unity: "Let us discard all this quibbling about this man and the other man, this race and that race and the other race being inferior, . . . and unite as one people throughout this land, until we shall once more stand up declaring that *all* men are created equal." One eyewitness reported that as Lincoln finished his address, " 'cheers like blasts of a thousand bugles' came from the throats of his listeners." [17] Douglas won the statewide vote, but Lincoln carried the city of Chicago. He carried it again three years later when he ran for President. He carried it, too, when he sounded his call for volunteers in April, 1861.

Chicago's response to Lincoln's call for troops was immediate and enthusiastic. The native-born volunteered freely. Many of the foreign-born enrolled—in some cases under their national banners. The Hungarians, Bohemians, and Slavs organized the Lincoln Rifles. The German Turner Union Cadets, the French Battalion, and the Scottish Highland Guards marched out to defend the American Union. Even the Irish, Democratic to the core and not too enthusiastic about Republican war aims, now responded to the call of their Colonel Mulligan: "RALLY! All Irishmen. . . . For the honor of the Old Land . . . for the defense of the New!" [18] The street fights of the Forties and Fifties had been transferred to a national battlefield. The flight to freedom had been replaced by a fight for freedom. Only the Negroes were prevented from answering Lincoln's call. Not until 1863 did the Union officially permit them to shoulder arms for their own freedom.

THE COMMUNITY OF THE FREE

For many of the fugitive slaves, the flight to freedom ended in Chicago. When the Civil War began, there were about a thousand Negroes living in the city. Some were "free-born persons of color"; others had been emancipated by kindly masters or had purchased their freedom. The majority were fugitives, without legal certificates of freedom.

In the center of the city, along the banks of the Chicago River, a small community of the free had been growing since 1840. Social life centered around several small Baptist and Methodist churches which also functioned as stations on the Underground Railroad. Three years before the Civil War, the *Christian Times,* appealing to the white community for aid to one of these churches, referred to its membership in laudatory terms:

The colored Baptist church in this city is made up of very excellent and reliable material. Its leading male members are respected and successful business men, and fully capable of directing wisely the financial affairs of the church. . . . The church is small, and though, as intimated above, some of its male members are tolerably prosperous in their business, they are not able to assume the whole burden of these payments.[19]

The antislavery newspapers often referred to the small Negro community with pride, for it seemed to justify their faith in the potentialities of the slaves. On several occasions reference was made to the orderliness of the Negroes and to their interest in literary societies, religion, and education. One editor remarked, with a rhetorical flourish characteristic of the period: "Such evidences speak volumes for the enterprize of those whose fathers dwelt long ago, where the White Nile wanders through its golden sands." [20] There were even occasional hints that certain sections of the white population might do well to emulate these "well informed, and peaceable citizens [who] seldom see any of their brethren grace the police calendar." [21]

That not all the Negro settlers were quiet businessmen or devotees of church and literary societies is obvious, however, from a lurid newspaper account in 1860 of a "Negro Dive in Full Blast." [22] The "excellent and reliable material" within the colored community also had to face other threats to its reputation. Old church records reveal anxious discussion over the question: "If a slave should be separated from his spouse by the master or by escaping into a free state, and should marry another, is he guilty of bigamy?" Sometimes an embarrassing scandal broke, such as the highly publicized account of a "reverend scoundrel" who, caught *in flagrante delicto* with a parishioner's wife, fled into the street, the wrath-maddened husband in hot pursuit. Even the more friendly papers could not overlook the possibilities of such a story, although one journal softened its spicy account of the minister's plight with a sober comment: "The affair has created the most intense excitement amongst the colored population who unanimously take sides against him." [23]

Negro leaders of the period were continually urging their followers to prove that ex-slaves were worthy of the city's hospitality. Typical of those Negroes who had a stake in Chicago's future was one John Jones, spokesman for the Negro community and first colored man to win an elective political office. The *Journal* carried his business advertisement in 1860: [24]

> Go to John Jones' Clothes Cleaning and Repairing Rooms, 119 Dearborn street, and get your clothes neatly repaired and thoroughly cleaned. The oldest and best establishment in the city. Your clothes will not be drawn up by steaming, nor spoiled with chemicals. Give me a trial, my prices are reasonable.

Such men had come to the city to stay.

The antislavery forces in Chicago were united in their opposition to slavery. They were willing to make their city a haven of refuge. They were not of one mind, however, on how to treat the Negroes in their midst. At one extreme were individuals such as the anti-slavery editor who stated frankly: [25]

"I am resolutely opposed to the 'equallizing [*sic*] of the races,' and it no more necessarily follows that we should fellowship with Negroes because our policy strikes off their shackles, than it would to take felons to our embraces, because we might remonstrate against cruelty to them in our penitentiaries."

At the other extreme were a few persons who went all-out for integration and drew the denunciatory fire of southerners for being "amalgamationists" desirous of "mongrelizing" the white race by allowing intermarriage and "social equality."

Throughout the period prior to the Civil War, the laws of the state forbade intermarriage and voting by Negroes. Segregation on common carriers and in the schools and theaters was widespread. The abolitionists regarded these as side issues which should not interfere with the main fight against slavery. Indeed, many abolitionists hoped that once the Negroes were freed, the bulk of them would either remain in the South or emigrate to the West Indies and Africa.

When emancipation was proclaimed, there was considerable discussion in antislavery circles of how Chicago would meet a possible sudden influx of freedmen. The "colonizationists" were hopeful that even those Negroes already in the city would voluntarily leave. When only forty-seven Negroes accepted an invitation from the president of Haiti to emigrate to that island in 1865, and the bulk of the colored population openly declared its intention to remain, the editor of the *Northwestern Christian Advocate* was so incensed at what he called their "impolitic and ungrateful behavior" that he threatened to withdraw his support from a financial campaign of the impecunious African Methodist Episcopal Church.

Most of the former abolitionists and their sympathizers soon became reconciled to the prospect of a small permanent Negro community with its own separate social institutions. A pattern of enforced segregation conflicted with the high sentiments of equality and the brotherhood of man, and that there were some uneasy consciences is evident from the minutes of the Illinois Baptist State Convention of 1865. The impropriety of segregation is suggested in the same paragraph with a statement implying that such separation was to be naturally expected (the italics are the authors'):

". . . We ought to extend fraternal courtesy and kindness to individuals scattered among us *when their numbers are not sufficient to justify the formation of colored churches.* Let them know that all our churches offer them a home and a cordial welcome. *Let them not be tempted to organize churches on the basis of color* rather than of Christian Faith."

While there was outside pressure upon the freedmen to establish a separate institutional life, there were also internal forces at work: a community of interests, a group of educated leaders, and the existence of local Negro churches and lodges with national connections. The ex-slaves were proud to have what they called "something of our own." At the same time they insisted upon the extension of full economic and political opportunity, and access to all public accommodations.

Opposition to an increase in the Negro population was most pronounced among the white laboring classes. It was not the issue of social equality which fundamentally disturbed them, however, but the fear and suspicion that Negro freedmen would be used to depress the wage level. Most bitter in their opposition were the Irish, who, Catholic and poor, were scornfully referred to as "unwashed Dimmycrats" by the Protestant Republican businessmen and artisans who controlled the city and professed to champion the Negro. From time to time during the twenty years preceding the Civil War, Irish workingmen in Chicago rioted against fugitive slaves who secured employment as stevedores, porters, canal bargemen, and general laborers.

In 1864, the Chicago *Tribune* carried a long editorial on "Mobbing Negroes," which probably reflected the antagonism of the Protestant Germans and Easterners toward the Catholic Irish as much as it did sympathy for Negroes. A mob of four or five hundred Irish laborers had beaten a dozen Negroes on the lumber docks, allegedly because "it was degrading to them to see blacks working upon an equality with themselves, and more so, while their brothers were out of employment." The *Tribune* insisted, however, that work was not scarce, and that "if all the black people in the city should leave Chicago tomorrow it would not benefit the condition of the Irish a single dime." Calling them "mobocrats," "raw laborers," and "the most illogical people on the face of the earth," the editor proceeded to belabor the Irish for "biting off their own noses for the benefit of Copperhead demagogues." * "It is a little singular," he observed, "that no class of people in Chicago fear the competition of the handful of blacks here, except the Irish. The Germans never mob colored men for working for whoever may employ them. The English, the Scotch, the French, the Scandinavians, never molest peaceable black people. Americans never think of doing such a thing. No other nationality consider themselves 'degraded' by seeing blacks earning their own living by labor." The editor concluded with a suggestion that "if they must mob anybody, it should be the slaveholders. . . . If they must quarrel with the negroes [*sic*], it should be with the slave negroes. . . . They ought to teach the slave blacks to assert their rights; to 'strike' for wages. . . . By so doing, the Irish laborer would remove the crushing, degrading competition of unpaid labor, and open to himself vast fields of employment now shut out from him by slavery." [26]

The logic of the present was more compelling, however, than this abstract theory of long-run interests. The Irish laborers remained suspicious and resentful against people who castigated them in this fashion, and they made the Democratic party the weapon for their de-

* Chicago suffered from general war weariness during 1863 and 1864. There was widespread dissatisfaction with the draft, and on one occasion Lincoln had to rebuke some of the leading citizens for their lack of co-operation. Treason itself was not unknown, and one plot was discovered which would have resulted in a *putsch* by Confederate soldiers interned in Chicago. Yet throughout the period, except for one mayoral election, the Republicans kept control of the city, and after the war the "radical" Republicans were in the saddle.

fense. Inevitably, local policies were colored by national events, and three years after the Civil War, Irish contingents in a Democratic election parade in Chicago carried signs denouncing Republican reconstruction policies in the South: "LET THE NIGGERS PAY FOR THEIR OWN SOUP"; "NO NIGGER VOTING"; "WHITE SUPREMACY."

Chicago Republicans, their eyes focused upon the growing Irish vote, did not hesitate to openly declare their opposition to any influx of "free and untrained Negroes." There was no such influx, but by 1870 some four thousand Negroes were living in the city—one out of every hundred persons.

Five years after the Civil War the leaders of the Negro community, in conjunction with other Negroes in the state, called a Colored Convention to present grievances and "devise ways and means whereby a healthy opinion may be created . . . to secure every recognition by the laws of our state and to demand equal school privileges throughout the state." [27] The Black Code was still on the books, and, in some of the communities of southern Illinois, Negroes were as thoroughly subordinated as they were in the deeper South. Even in Chicago, as the Negro population increased, colored children were forced to attend the so-called "Black School," and when protests failed, some of the parents resorted to civil disobedience. A colored Old Settler relates the story as her mother told it to her:

"The parents—most of them—objecting to segregation sent their children right on to the nearest schools as before. The teachers declined to assign them to classes or studies.

"The children, however, attended daily, taking their seats in an orderly fashion throughout the controversy that ensued. The school board then determined that any child with no more than an eighth of Negro blood could attend the usual schools; but here again was trouble, for the wide range of complexions in the colored families soon demonstrated the impossibility in such a division. After a short time and a determined fight on the part of the colored citizens who invaded the offices of the Board of Education and the Mayor, the inglorious career of the Black School was done away with and never resumed."

It took twenty years to create a public opinion strong enough to erase all of the discriminatory laws from the state's statute book, but by 1885 this had been accomplished. Lacking political power and appealing solely within the framework of the abolitionist tradition, democratic idealism, and constitutional rights, the community of freedmen were able to mobilize enough support to establish their equality before the law, to secure the right to vote, and to erect a set of guarantees against discrimination in the use of public facilities. To lay the ghosts that stalked in proslavery southern Illinois, the Colored Convention of 1869 explicitly stated that "[we] disavow any and all imputations of, and desire to obtain, social equality." In Chicago, however, neither white persons nor Negroes had any crusading fervor either to espouse or to prevent social relations or even intermarriage. Although Negroes developed their own family and community life, there was considerable friendly social intercourse between colored and white people, and marriages across the color-line were not unknown.

Within a generation after the Civil War the community of the free was accepted as a normal part of the city's life. The tradition became set that Negroes could compete for power and prestige in the economic and political spheres. Yet the badge of color marked them as socially different. Also, the fact that no Negroes rose to the highest positions in the commercial and public life of early Chicago suggests that in a vague but nevertheless decisive sense they were thought of as having a subordinate place.

Before the Civil War the Negro was the protagonist of the abolitionist drama. After Emancipation he was no longer a hero around whom stirring battles were fought in the city streets and the courts. He and his people became just one more poverty-stricken group competing in a city where economic and political issues were being fought out behind the façade of racial, national, and religious alignments. It was a city which for the next thirty years was riven by class conflicts and seared by two disastrous fires—but which was steadily laying the foundations for industrial and commercial supremacy in the Middle West.

CHAPTER 2

Land of Promise

EMERGENCE OF THE BLACK BELT (1865-1874) [1]

AT THE OUTBREAK OF THE CIVIL WAR A HUNDRED THOUSAND PEOPLE LIVED in Chicago. Fifty years later, when the First World War began, the city boasted more than two million inhabitants. The material base for this rapid growth was laid between 1860 and 1890. The city's expanding stockyards and packing plants, farm-implement factories and railroad yards, warehouses and grain elevators attracted the hungry, the ambitious, and the foot-loose from all over the world. Fortunes sprouted in the grain pit. Millionaires were sired in the cattle pens. Reapers, made in Chicago and distributed in the wheat fields, brought prosperity to both countryside and city. George Pullman's sleeping cars, fabricated in its outskirts, carried the city's fame over America's ever-widening web of railroads. There was a magic in the names of Swift and Armour, Marshall Field and Levi Z. Leiter, Potter Palmer and Cyrus McCormick, that turned many a fortune-seeker's steps toward Chicago. Young, boisterous, and busy, the city became a symbol of the vast opportunities which the entire Middle West held for peoples of the eastern seaboard and Europe who were seeking a land of promise.

The Chicago of 1870 was a boom town, its buildings and its people new and rough. Of its sixty thousand structures, forty thousand were made of wood. It was, as one contemporary newspaper said, "a city of everlasting pine, shingles, shams, veneers, stucco and putty." [1] Fires were frequent. In 1871 the Great Chicago Fire destroyed seventeen thousand buildings and left a hundred thousand people homeless—the damage amounted to $200,000,000. The story of Mrs. O'Leary's cow that kicked over a lamp that set a fire that burned a city became an international legend. Local ministers saw the holocaust as an expression of God's judgment upon a wicked city. Southerners and former Copperheads were sure that "God had stricken the Northern city to avenge the 'wanton' destruction which the Union armies had visited upon the South during the Civil War." [2] To most Chicagoans, how ever, the fire was an unlucky but exciting accident—an unfortunate, but in no sense fatal, catastrophe.

The great Chicago fire did not destroy the Negro community, although it consumed the contiguous central business area and the world-famous Red-light District. Since the fire also spared the rows of stately mansions near Lake Michigan, many burned-out businesses were temporarily housed in their owners' fashionable residences. The bulk of the gamblers and prostitutes took refuge in the Negro neighborhood—an area three blocks long and fifteen blocks wide, with some twenty-five hundred residents. When the city was rebuilt, the former Red-light District was taken over by the wholesale trade. The gay underworld remained among the Negroes.

Chicago clergymen again professed to see the handiwork of a persistent and vigilant Deity when in 1874 another conflagration burned out gamblers, prostitutes, *and* Negroes. As a result of this second fire, almost half of the colored families were dispersed among the white residents, but a new Negro community also arose from the ashes of the old. Here, in a long, thin sliver of land, sandwiched between a well-to-do white neighborhood and that of the so-called "shanty Irish," most of Chicago's colored residents and their major institutions were concentrated during the next forty years. The "Black Belt" had emerged.

BETWEEN THE FIRE AND THE FAIR (1875-1893)

In the twenty years between the Great Fire and the first World's Fair (1893), the Negro population increased from five thousand to fifteen thousand. The Black Belt gradually expanded as Negroes took over the homes of white persons who were moving to the more desirable lake-front or to the suburbs. Most of the colored residents were employed as coachmen, butlers, cooks, and maids in the homes of the wealthy; as servants in stores, hotels, and restaurants; as porters on the increasingly popular Pullman coaches; and as maids and handymen in white houses of prostitution. A small Negro business and professional class developed, and by 1878 it had found a mouthpiece in a weekly newspaper, the *Conservator,* whose editor, reminiscing years later, described the general status of Negroes in the Seventies and early Eighties as follows: [3]

. . . There were about five thousand Negroes in Chicago. The *Conservator* was started as a means of expression for Negroes and to aid in the promotion of the welfare of the Negro group.

When the paper was started the behavior of many of the Negroes was characterized by loose living and a lack of proper standards. There were few Negroes of culture and refinement, and only a few jobs of any consequence were held by Negroes. The paper was devoted to the idea of stressing the importance of education, social uplift and correct living. Conflict between the races was not very great at the time the paper was started, consequently there was little space given to the discussion of race relations in the local community. There were, however, occasional clashes between the Irish and the Negroes. When these . . . occurred they were discussed in the paper.

The picture gleaned from the pages of this paper is that of a small, compact, but rapidly growing community divided into three broad social groups. The "respectables"—church-going, poor or moderately prosperous, and often unrestrained in their worship—were looked down upon somewhat by the "refined" people, who, because of their education or breeding, could not sanction the less decorous behavior of their racial brothers. Both of these groups were censorious of the "riffraff," the "sinners"—unchurched and undisciplined. The "refined" set conceived themselves as examples of the Negro's progress since slavery. They believed that their less disciplined fellows should be prodded with ridicule and sarcasm, and restrained by legal force when necessary. They had an almost religious faith that education would, in the long run, transform even the "riffraff" into people like themselves.

The pages of the *Conservator* expressed these attitudes by colorful words of denunciation and applause. One editorial, for instance,[4] inveighed against the seamy side of life with rhetoric and pious sentiments typical of the period:

GOING TO RUIN

We are calling attention to the fact that a number of our girls and boys are on the road to ruin. The boys rioting in the Clark and 4th Avenue dives, laying the foundations for lives of thieves, thugs and murderers, and the girls walking the streets in gaudy attire—attracting notice—exciting comment and rapidly linking their lives, with those whose "house is the gate of Hell, going down to the chambers of death."

How sad it is to see the girls we have known in their innocent childhood, change their lives, just when life's days should be the brightest;

change from piety, virtue and happiness to vice, dissipation and woe. Mothers are you blind? Fathers are you deaf? Christians are you asleep? For the sake of God and Humanity, let someone rescue these young lives from dissipation's perpetual gloom.

As opposed to this pattern of life, the paper held up [5] as pioneering models those young people who were "improving themselves," thereby "advancing the race":

Four colored students graduated last week from the University of Michigan. Two in law and two in medicine. In conversation with colored students during the past year, we were glad to hear that scarcely a vestige of the "caste" spirit is ever seen. They attend, or are free to attend, all meetings, educational and social, and are never made to feel out of place. There has never yet been a colored graduate from the collegiate course. Miss Mary H. Graham whose matriculation in '76 caused such a stir in Michigan circles will be the first to achieve this distinction. . . . Mr. C. Williams, a Sophomore and a young man of rare moral worth, is winning a golden name at the University. . . . He is held in high degree of respect by the citizens and the Faculty. . . . Would there were more such men as he—Ethiopia might well rejoice.

The "young men of rare moral worth," the "girls walking the streets in gaudy attire," as well as plain, ordinary Negroes, continued to come to Chicago throughout the Eighties. By 1890 there were enough of them to sustain twenty churches, a dozen or so lodges, three weekly newspapers, and several social and cultural clubs. Certain individuals had managed to attain some prominence and wealth, and a few possessed well-established businesses catering to a white clientele. John Jones, abolitionist leader, was still tailoring for the city's elite in a building of his own in the heart of the city. Another Negro had invested $60,000 in a downtown office building. Smiley, a caterer, was laying up a small fortune from the lavish affairs he engineered for the Gold Coast—a fortune the remnants of which he was to leave to the University of Chicago.

For these men, the land of promise had been no mirage. None of them had amassed great fortunes or secured key positions of economic control, but they had been financially successful in a modest fashion. A few Negroes of the business and professional classes had also been active in politics since the early Seventies, thus setting the precedent for Negro political representation which subsequently became a part

of the city's tradition. The first colored county commissioner, state legislator, policeman, and fireman all appeared before 1875.[6]

The twenty years between the Fire and the Fair were the turbu-
lent ones for Chicago.[7] On the heels of the post-fire boom, a six-year
stretch of "hard times" ensued, during which there were serious labor
troubles. The political antagonisms of the foreign-born and the native-
whites (evenly divided as to numbers) were organized throughout this
period around such issues as the passage of the Blue Sunday Laws and
the struggle for control of the City Hall. Then came eight years of
continuing prosperity and renewed European immigration, culminating in the panic of 1884-86, which brought in its wake a violent streetcar strike. In 1884, the Illinois State Federation of Labor passed a resolution against the "further importation of pauper labor from Europe."[8]
The Haymarket riot in 1886 resulted in considerable antiforeigner
hysteria.

The small Negro community was barely touched by these political
and economic upheavals. Having adjusted themselves to the economic
competition of the foreign-born by securing employment primarily in
the service occupations, the masses of the Negroes had little reason to
listen to the impassioned oratory of labor leaders who excoriated local
capitalists and eastern bankers. Agitation for the eight-hour day carried no appeal for a colored working population over half of which
was employed in servant capacities. It is significant that the one Negro
preacher in the Eighties who publicly espoused the cause of Socialism
quickly lost his pulpit.[9]

Although unconcerned with the violent struggles of the white workers, Negroes were persistently seeking to widen the areas of political
and economic opportunity for themselves. They found allies among
Republican politicians, civic-minded liberals, and the wealthy for
whom many of them worked. Fighters for equal rights since the days
of slavery, Chicago's Negro leaders resented any attempts to deny political and economic opportunity to themselves or their fellows. The
Illinois Black Code was repealed in 1865. By 1870 Negroes had been
guaranteed the right to vote. By 1874 segregation in the school system
had been abolished. In 1885 the leaders climaxed their efforts by securing the passage of a state civil rights bill designed to protect the liberties of Negroes in the less advanced counties of southern Illinois. They
insisted that every evidence of subordinate status should be eliminated.
They were taking the promises of democracy seriously.

Ostensibly trivial matters sometimes assumed great importance in this struggle for recognition and respect. The *Conservator* on one occasion devoted an entire editorial, humorous in tone but serious in intent, to the use of the lower-case "n" for spelling the word Negro. The editor called the practice "a mark of disrespect," "a stigma," and "a badge of inferiority," and remarked that "the French, German, Irish, Dutch, Japenese [*sic*], and other nationalities are honored with a capital letter, but the poor sons of Ham must bear the burden of a small n." [10]

Colored Chicagoans, like their foreign-born neighbors, cultivated a dual loyalty and pride—allegiance to an ethnic group as well as to America. But they did not feel that race pride should isolate them from the main streams of civic life. The editor of the *Conservator* expressed the dominant philosophy of the Negro community when he wrote in the late Eighties: "As a race let us forget the past so far as we can, and unite with other men upon issues, liberal, essential, and not dependent upon color of skin or texture of hair for its [*sic*] gravamen." [11]

The successful Negroes of the era, many of them former slaves, interpreted their own careers as proof that some day black men would be accepted as individuals and Americans. They visualized the progress of their race in terms of education, personal economic success, judicious political action, and co-operation with powerful and influential white people.

RETROSPECT AND PROSPECT (1894-1914)

In 1893 Chicago decided to show the world how it had survived panic, fire, and class war to become the second largest city in the nation—Midwest Metropolis. Its civic leaders ballyhooed, pressured, and begged until they won from Congress the privilege of playing host to the World's Columbian Exposition—the first World's Fair. For Negroes, too, this was a significant occasion. In 1891 a prominent European historian and traveler had remarked of Chicago that "the severity of the climate repels the Africans." [12] Yet, in 1893, there were fifteen thousand Negroes living in the city. It was only natural that they should wish to display what they and their co-racialists throughout the country had accomplished in the twenty-eight years since slavery. In 1892 a committee met in Quinn Chapel, once a station of the Underground Railroad, and formulated an appeal to Congress for representation at the Fair. A large Negro exhibit was eventually prepared, and colored speakers and singers appeared on various Exposition programs. For the Negroes, the occasion was a sort of silver jubilee celebrating a generation of freedom. The Prudence Crandall Club, representing the "cultured" elements, entertained the aging but still eloquent Frederick Douglass, famous Negro orator and venerable symbol of the abolition struggle. Commemoration services "in honor of the leaders in the cause of freedom and political equality" were held in historic Quinn Chapel. Frederick Douglass spoke, and when he referred to the stormy Forties and Fifties, he urged the younger generation of Negroes not to forget that "forty years ago there were always here a roof, table, and house for the most abject abolitionist."[13] The night before he left the city, he was, as one daily newspaper reported, HONORED BY BOTH RACES AT HIS LEAVE TAKING.[14]

"The church was filled with an audience of white and colored people. . . . In speaking of the prejudices against men of his race in the South, he said the people of the South had better beware as to how they aroused the strength in the black man's arm. When he made this reference he was cheered."

Before the echoes of Douglass's speech had died away a Negro was burned in effigy in the streets of Chicago. Colored laborers had been imported to break a strike in the stockyards, and the white workers had responded in a style suggestive of the South. But, significantly enough, in Chicago, the victim was burned *in effigy* rather than in person.[15]

There was nothing in the South to lend substance to Douglass's heroic warning. Booker T. Washington's philosophy of compromise was soon to become the holy scripture of southern leaders, white and black. Do not antagonize the white majority. Do not ask for the right to vote. Do not fight for civil liberties or against segregation. Go to school. Work hard. Save money. Buy property. Some day the other things may come.

For ten years after the Civil War, the Republican North had buttressed the southern Negro's franchise with federal power. By 1875, however, Republican ardor had cooled. The Party could now exist without the southern Negro vote, and northern businessmen needed the goodwill of the white South. The ex-slaves had never secured an economic base. Forty acres and a mule might have given them a sort of sturdy peasant independence. As it was, a system of sharecropping replaced slavery, and debt peonage was substituted for legal bondage. It was Booker T. Washington's hope that by hard work and thrift the Negro masses could ultimately establish their freedom by buying the land. But southern landlords, selling their cotton in a world market, had no intention of relinquishing the very source of their power. They used terror and intimidation to keep the former slaves in their place. A rigorous etiquette of race relations was enforced, in which the Negro's role was that of serf, sycophant, and buffoon, bowing and scraping at the throne of white supremacy. An effort was made to straitjacket Negroes into an American version of the caste system. The promises of freedom were harmlessly enshrined in the Emancipation Proclamation and embalmed in the Thirteenth, Fourteenth, and Fifteenth Amendments.[16]

Many ex-slaves who had tasted complete freedom during the few short years of Reconstruction could not adjust to this southern New Order. So throughout the Eighties and Nineties a constant stream of Negro migrants trickled northward to join the larger stream of immigrants from Europe. Chicago attracted a large proportion of those who left the South between 1890 and 1910 in what has been called "the Migration of the Talented Tenth."[17] Among them were prominent preachers and politicians who, for a brief spell after the Civil War, sat in southern state legislatures and in Congress; less distinguished individuals who occupied minor political posts in county and town; and all the restless educated and half-educated, who were not content to live life on southern terms. Many visitors to the first World's Fair who came to look stayed to work. By 1910 there were 40,000 Negroes among the heterogeneous two million inhabitants of Midwest Metropolis. Almost imperceptibly the Black Belt had expanded and absorbed more than 10,000 people within a period of seventeen years.

Upon the narrow economic base of domestic and personal service, Negroes in Chicago had evolved a community life gathering primarily around lodge and church. A few business and professional men, politicians, and ambitious personal and domestic servants constituted a social élite. In the years between the Fair and the First World War, these were the civic leaders, and their wives the social arbiters. A diversified institutional life taking form between 1890 and 1914 included a hospital and training school for nurses, a YMCA, branches of national organizations such as the National Negro Business League, the National Association for the Advancement of Colored People (NAACP), and the Federated Women's Clubs.

Four newspapers were started, one of which, the Chicago *Defender,* is still in existence. A sampling of front-page items from this paper in 1908 reveals the range of interests which made news during this period.

> Rev. H. E. Stewart to Preach "Great
> Sermon": "Has the Negro Any Reason
> To Expect Special Favors from God?"
> (9/12/08)

> HOPE PRESBYTERIAN CONCERT A HUGE SUCCESS. (9/17/08)

> REV. STEWART PREACHES ELKS ANNUAL SERMON;
> JUNIOR CHOIR SINGS. (9/17/08)

> SECRETARY OF LADY ELKS BREAKS LEG SKATING. (11/14/08)

> MANASSEH BALL A GREAT SUCCESS; 1,500 PERSONS—
> GRAND MARCH EIGHTH REGIMENT ORCHESTRA.
> (11/21/08)

[This club was composed of Negro men and women whose wives or husbands were white.]

> AFRO-AMERICAN HISTORICAL SOCIETY
> ORGANIZED AMONG GRACE PRESBY-
> TERIAN SUNDAY SCHOOL MEN BY MRS.
> IDA WELLS BARNETT, PRESENTING PRO-
> FESSOR R. T. GREENER, FIRST COLORED
> GRADUATE OF HARVARD UNIVERSITY.
> (11/21/08)

> CHICAGO LADY ELK COMMISSIONED TO SET UP
> LODGES IN THE SOUTH. (12/26/08)

> LADY ELLIOT CIRCLE, 199, A. D. OF
> FORRESTERS ELECT NEW OFFICERS.
> (12/26/08)

[A chatty informal article stating, "The order has done much good during the year and besides a neat bank account, they have administered to their sick and needy and have established a record of standing for high morals."]

THE GRAND LADS CLUB GIVES A SOCIAL. (12/26/08)

CHORAL STUDY GROUP ANNOUNCES SUL-
LIVAN'S ORATORIO, "THE PRODIGAL SON,"
TO BE GIVEN AT INSTITUTIONAL CHURCH.
(12/26/08)

THE BASKETBALL LEAGUE ANNOUNCES GAMES FOR 1909. (12/26/08)

"The Triangle Inner Circle Club intend giving the Old Folks' Home a
New Year's present and to make it worthwhile they have combined charity
with pleasure." Plan to hold dance at 1st Regiment Armory, 6th and
Michigan, 50 cents admission. Proceeds for "those dear old folks at 610
Garfield Boulevard." Clubs co-operating in ticket sales were:

Cornell Charity	Des Jeunes Aspirants
I. B. Wells Women's Club	Nogales Club
Centennial Club	Grendenborg Club

[This item (12/26/08) indicates one type of broad community co-operation.]

W. T. Stead's sensational exposé already mentioned, *If Christ Came
to Chicago,* started a battle between the segregationists, who believed
in a legal Red-light District, and the non-segregationists who wished to
abolish it. The struggle went on throughout this period, and engaged the attention of the entire Negro community. The Chicago
Vice Commission reported in 1909 that the growing Negro population
had never managed to keep even one jump ahead of the continuously
expanding Red-light District. It also revealed that the great majority
of the employees in the "resorts" were colored men, women, and children. In fact, some of the most exclusive "houses" were in the Black
Belt. Inevitably the Black Belt became associated in the popular mind
with "vice," and the reformers exhorted the Negro community to
clean house. Some of the conservative Negro leaders accepted the
assignment, but the more militant refused to admit complete blame
for vice in the Black Belt.

One of the most prominent colored ministers declared himself "a
firm believer in the segregation of vice," but accused a prominent white
pastor of trying to widen the boundaries of the Red-light District at the
expense of the Negro community. The white minister was charged
with a desire to push "the boundary lines of vice beyond his own bailiwick" in order to prevent "a large exodus of his parishioners to a local-

ity less honeycombed with dance halls, brothels and saloons." "So like Ajax of old," the Negro minister continued, "all through the long and bitter night, the prayer of this learned divine was for light to see his foemen's fall. And when he did, he gave them no quarter until he succeeded in driving these unfortunates to the very doors of Quinn Chapel, the Olivet Baptist and Bethel churches [colored congregations]. It will be only a matter of time before the churches mentioned will be forced to abandon their present fields. . . . The Negro, like the whites, does not care for his wife and daughter to elbow the Red-light denizens."

Chicago's "vice problem" was not solved by gerrymander, however. In 1912 the reform forces succeeded in abolishing the Red-light District, and the prostitutes were temporarily scattered from one end of the city to the other. The business finally went underground in various parts of the city, including the Black Belt. But the break-up of the segregated vice area did not remove either the reality or the stigma of vice from the Negro community.

Upon one occasion in 1912 when Booker T. Washington publicly urged Negroes in Chicago and other urban areas to wipe out vice from their communities, a colored civic leader retorted: "A good deal of the vice in the 'colored belt' is the white man's vice, thrust there by the authorities against the protest of the colored people. But the thing runs deeper than that. Vice and crime are in large measure the result of idleness, of irregular employment, and even of regular employment that is underpaid and exhausting. It would be fatuous for the white community to deny its responsibility, in very large measure, for the economic conditions under which thousands of Negro men and women struggle right here in Chicago."

The Chicago *Evening Post* supported this position, saying: "While it is a very useful thing to have Mr. Washington preaching free will and full responsibility to the colored people, it would be a very great mistake for the white community to regard this as the last word on the subject. For it is not true in any sense whatever that the colored community is wholly and entirely responsible for the vice and crime which appear now and then in its midst. . . . But these are disagreeable truths and we all shirk them when we can. . . . The colored problem cannot be solved by the colored man alone."

This emphasis upon the interrelatedness of white Chicago and the Negro community had become traditional by 1900. With the passing of the abolitionists, Chicago's wealthy merchants and industrialists had assumed a somewhat paternalistic interest in the Negro community as a part of their general pattern of philanthropy and civic responsibility. Between 1897 and 1906, five of Chicago's most prominent men died— George Pullman, P. D. Armour, Gustavus Swift, Potter Palmer, and Marshall Field I. All except the last were considered "friends of the Negro"—liberal in their contributions to Black Belt institutions and willing to employ them in servant capacities. It is reported that when Potter Palmer died a dozen Negro employees from the famous Palmer House Hotel wept at his bier.

Even after the deaths of these men, Negro leaders maintained their contact with wealthy and powerful whites, but from 1905 through to the First World War, they began to place increasing emphasis upon "racial self-reliance"—the development of political power and a strong business and professional class. They began to urge, too, a diversification of employment and assailed the bars which some labor unions had erected against colored artisans. On the eve of the First World War the pattern of Negro-white relations was one of stable equilibrium. But Negroes conceived of it as a moving equilibrium whose motive force must be "race pride" and unified political action.

Midwest Metropolis was busy absorbing immigrants from Europe between 1890 and 1910—a major "social problem." Because it was American and small, the Negro community was far less of a "problem" to native-white Chicagoans of the Nineties than were neighborhoods inhabited by the foreign-born. For their part, Negroes viewed the influx of European immigrants with mixed emotions. The foreign-born constituted a potential threat to their jobs as butlers and maids, janitors and waiters. They monopolized the skilled and semi-skilled trades. They did most of the city's common labor. Negroes feared them as economic competitors. Yet in the West Side Ghetto and among the Italians of the North Side, these recent immigrants often lived side by side with Negroes, sometimes in the same buildings with them, and fraternized freely.

On the whole, Negroes regarded foreigners with a certain amount of understandable condescension. The foreign-born, in turn, were not slow to adopt the prevailing stereotypes about Negroes. "Foreigners learn how to cuss, count and say 'nigger' as soon as they get here," grumbled the Negroes. Not until the First World War, however, were masses of Negroes thrown into direct competition with the foreign-born in industry.

CHAPTER 3

The Great Migration

BLACK DIASPORA (1914-1918)

IN 1914 THE TIDE OF EUROPEAN MIGRATION WAS SUDDENLY REVERSED.[1] AS country after country was drawn into the First World War, foreign-born men streamed home from Pittsburgh and Cleveland, Detroit and Toledo, from mills and mines, to shoulder arms. Immigration virtually ceased. Chicago, too, lost thousands of workmen.

As the war dragged on, the United States gradually transformed itself into an arsenal and granary for Europe. Farmers laid more land to the plow while industrial plants expanded production. A city whose economic life depended upon the foreign-born to handle its meat, wheat, and steel now experienced a manpower crisis at the very moment when profits were highest and production demands greatest.

Then the great mass of caste-bound Negroes in the South stirred. For several years the cotton kingdom had been ravaged by the boll weevil sweeping up from Mexico. Flood and famine, too, had continually harassed the cotton farmers of the Mississippi Valley. Prior to 1915, however, there had been little to encourage plantation laborers to risk life in the city streets. Now there were jobs to attract them. Recruiting agents traveled south, begging Negroes to come north. They sometimes carried free tickets in their pockets, and always glowing promises on their tongues. For the first time, southern Negroes were actually being invited, even urged, to come to Chicago. They came in droves—50,000 of them between 1910 and 1920. And as each wave arrived, the migrants wrote the folks back home about the wonderful North. A flood of relatives and friends followed in their wake.

A bewildered South had visions of a land left desolate for lack of labor. From every southern state the Negroes came, despite desperate attempts to halt the exodus:[2]

Up from Florida—where the city fathers in Jacksonville passed an ordinance requiring labor recruiters from the North to buy a $1,000 license or take the alternative of sixty days in jail and a $600 fine.

Up from Georgia—where the Macon city council exacted a recruiting license fee of $25,000 and demanded that the labor agent be recommended by ten local ministers, ten manufacturers, and twenty-five businessmen.

Up from Alabama—where fines and jail sentences were imposed upon any "person, firm, or corporation" guilty of "enticing, persuading, or influencing" labor to leave Montgomery.

Up from Mississippi—where agents were arrested, trains stopped, ticket agents intimidated. And at Brookhaven, a chartered car carrying fifty men and women was deliberately sidetracked for three days.

Still they came!

As coercion failed, worried businessmen and planters resorted to conciliation and persuasion in an effort to stem the tide. Leading southern white newspapers began to condemn lynching and the inequitable treatment of Negroes in the courts. Conferences were held in large cities and out-of-the-way southern towns at which Negro leaders were implored to use their good offices with the field hands. The more astute Negro negotiators began to wring promises of more schools, better treatment, higher wages, and other reforms from men who a year before would have scorned to confer with "niggers." Idealistic southern friends of the Negro found their tasks suddenly eased by these economic imperatives. The southern caste system was in the process of profound modification.[3]

The Chicago *Defender,* a Negro weekly edited by Robert S. Abbott, a native of Georgia who had come north in the Nineties and made good, played a leading role in stimulating the migration. It coaxed and challenged, denounced and applauded. It organized a "Great Northern Drive" and succeeded in getting itself banned from many a southern community. It scoffed at the Southerners' reforms under duress:[4]

Turn a deaf ear to everybody. . . . You see they are not lifting their laws to help you. Are they? Have they stopped their Jim Crow cars? Can you buy a Pullman sleeper where you wish? Will they give you a square deal in court yet? Once upon a time we permitted other people to think for us—today we are thinking and acting for ourselves with the result that our "friends" are getting alarmed at our progress. We'd like to oblige these unselfish (?) souls and remain slaves in the South, but to their section of the country we have said, as the song goes, "I hear you calling me," and have boarded the train singing, "Good-bye, Dixie Land."

Eventually America entered the war. More southern Negroes came to replace the men who were drafted. For four years the tug of war between northern industry and southern planters, northern Negro leaders and southern leaders, continued. The migrants kept streaming up the Mississippi Valley, riding the real trains of the Illinois Central over the same route their forefathers had traveled on the Underground Railroad. When the tide slackened in 1920, Chicago had over a hundred thousand Negroes among her population—an increase of 148 per cent in ten years.

Most Negroes visualized the migration as a step toward the economic emancipation of a people who had been tied to the southern soil and confined to common labor and personal service in the North. The Chicago *Defender* expressed this philosophy in an editorial shortly before the United States entered the war. Declaring that "it is an ill wind that blows no one good," Editor Abbott saw the European war not only as "bloody, tragic and deplorable" but also as "opportunity." Coldly realistic, he developed his apologia for encouraging the migration. The European war, he said,[5]

. . . has caused the people of this and other neutral countries to prosper greatly in a financial way. It has meant that the thousands who a year ago were dependent upon charity are today employed and making a comfortable living for themselves and their families. The colored man and woman are, and must be for some years to come, laborers. There is no line of endeavor that we cannot fit ourselves for. These same factories, mills and workshops that have been closed to us, through necessity are being opened to us. We are to be given a chance, not through choice but because it is expedient. Prejudice vanishes when the almighty dollar is on the wrong side of the balance sheet. . . .

Give the best that is in us when we answer the call. It is significant that the great west is calling to the southern black man to leave his old home and come out here where the prospects are bright for the future. Slowly but surely all over this country we are gradually edging in first this and then that place, getting a foothold before making a place for our brother. By this only can the so-called race problem be solved. It is merely a question of a better and a closer understanding between the races. We are Americans and must live together, so why not live in peace?

Negroes were getting the foothold, but the peace and understanding did not follow. White Chicagoans viewed the migrants with mixed feelings. As laborers they were indispensable. As neighbors they would have to be tolerated. Union men were apprehensive. Only "Big Bill" Thompson, the Republican Mayor, and his coterie of politicians truly welcomed them, as they pondered the traditional political loyalties of the Negro people and watched the First and Second Ward Black Belt precincts swell amazingly.

The attitudes of the general public were undoubtedly shaped to some extent by Chicago's newspaper headlines and stories which, day after day, commented in a none too friendly vein: [6]

HALF A MILLION DARKIES FROM DIXIE SWARM TO THE NORTH TO BETTER THEMSLEVES

NEGROES INCITED BY GERMAN SPIES
Federal Agents Confirm Reports of New Conspiracy in South; Accuse Germans for Exodus from South

2,000 SOUTHERN NEGROES ARRIVE IN LAST TWO DAYS
Stockyards Demand for Labor Cause of Influx

COMMITTEE TO DEAL WITH NEGRO INFLUX
Body Formed to Solve Problem Due to Migration to Chicago from South

WORK OUT PLANS FOR MIGRATING NEGROES
Influx from the South Cared For by the Urban League and Other Societies

Negroes were rapidly replacing foreigners as Chicago's "problem."

BLACK LEBENSRAUM

The sudden influx of Negroes into Chicago immediately resolved itself into a struggle for living space. Between 1900 and 1914, the Black Belt and its satellite areas had absorbed over ten thousand Negroes without any serious difficulty. Now the saturation point was reached, and although the migrants had jobs, there were literally no houses to accommodate them. Building construction had virtually ceased with the outbreak of the war. Doubling-up and overcrowding became inevitable. The Black Belt had to expand, and this situation aroused exaggerated fears throughout the city. Where would the black masses, still bearing the mark of the plantation upon them, find a place to live?

As in the case of immigrants, the bulk of the southern migrants during the First World War gravitated first to those areas of their "colony" where rents were cheapest and housing poorest. They took over the old, dilapidated shacks near the railroad tracks and close to the vice area. These neighborhoods had been abandoned in the previous decade by Negroes who became more prosperous and were able to move away. Now their less affluent brothers replaced them.

This tremendous demand for houses resulted in an immediate skyrocketing of rents for all available accommodations and in the opening of new residential areas to Negroes. There were tremendous profits to be made by both colored and white realtors who could provide houses. And so the spread of the Negro areas of residence began, with the whites fleeing before them. Artificial panics were sometimes created in white areas by enterprising realtors who raised the cry, "The Negroes are coming," and then proceeded to double the rents after the whites had fled.[7]

By 1920 a pincers movement of the Negro population had begun along the two boundaries of the Black Belt, a mile apart, and the pocket in between had begun to close up. (Figure 6.) As Negroes moved in, they bought the synagogues and churches, often at highly inflated prices, took over the parks and playgrounds, and transformed white and mixed communities into solidly Negro areas.

To the west of the Black Belt were the Irish, traditional enemies of the Negroes in Chicago; to the east were native-Americans and the more prosperous Jews, guarding jealously the approaches to the desirable lake front where they had made investments in residential property. The Negroes pressed against both communities, and as they swept southward, the whites in their path moved east and to the outlying areas of the city—but homes were scarce.

The impact of the expanding Black Belt on institutions in white middle-class communities has been vividly described by the pastor of Chicago's oldest white Baptist church, which was eventually sold to Negroes:[8]

... In 1915 the cry was heard, "The Negroes are coming." ... The church reported ... in 1918, "Our church has been greatly handicapped during the past year by the great influx of colored people and the removal of many Whites." ... The Negroes coming from the South by tens of thousands, lured by the promise of high wages in the packing houses, mills, and railroad yards of Chicago, swarmed to the blocks surrounding

Figure 6
EXPANSION OF THE BLACK BELT

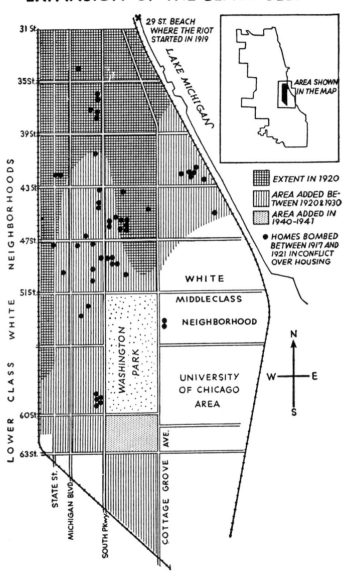

Adapted from map in *The Negro in Chicago,* Chicago Commission on Race Relations, University of Chicago Press, 1922.

the church building. Beautiful homes occupied by families belonging to the church for generations were sold for whatever price they could obtain. The membership declined to 403 and only 10 persons united with the church in that year. The church was face to face with catastrophe. No eloquent preaching, no social service, could save a church in a community that was nearly 100 per cent Negro. . . . Meanwhile the Negroes are steadily pushing down the alleys southward with their carts of furniture, but Forty-seventh Street running east and west still stands as a breakwater against the oncoming tide. If it crumbles there will be some new history for the First Church.

But the "breakwater" finally burst. Forty-seventh Street is now in the center of the Black Belt.

The expansion of the Black Belt developed so much friction that in the invaded neighborhoods bombs were occasionally thrown at Negro homes and those of real-estate men, white and colored, who sold or rented property to the newcomers. From July 1, 1917, to March 1, 1921, fifty-eight such bombs were hurled.[9] (Figure 6.)

This conflict over space often came to a head where Negroes and whites met in public places—at the beaches and playgrounds and in the public schools. Particular resentment was manifested against Negroes who frequented beaches that white people had come to think of as their own. Playground fights between Negro and white children were epidemic. Policemen, social workers, and teachers, even when they were not themselves antagonistic to Negroes, often resorted to segregation as a convenient method of keeping the peace.[10] Yet throughout this period, despite tension in the areas peripheral to the Black Belt, there were also adjusted neighborhoods in other sections of the city where Negroes and whites maintained their neighborly relations and where no hostility was evident.[11]

During the war period, civic leaders viewed the situation with some foreboding. The Chicago Urban League was founded in 1917 to deal specifically with the problem of adjusting the migrants to city life. The churches, the newspapers, the YMCA, and the YWCA had deliberately set themselves the task of training the peasant folk in the city ways and of trying to interpret them to the Negro Old Settlers and to those sections of the white community which resented their presence. Incident after incident, however, augured an eventual crisis. In 1919 it came.

CHAPTER 4

Race Riot and Aftermath

RIOT (1919)

HERE AND THERE THROUGHOUT AMERICA, THE TENSIONS OF POSTWAR RE-
adjustment flared into open violence. On the labor front and along the
color-line, deep-laid frustrations, uneasy fears, and latent suspicions
bobbed to the surface. Group antagonisms suppressed and sublimated
by the war effort now returned with doubled fury. For labor, there
were the "Palmer raids"; for the Negro, lynchings and riots. The
South, particularly, was nervous. Returning Negro soldiers, their horizons widened through travel, constituted a threat to the caste system.
They must be kept in their place. A wave of interracial conflicts swept
the country involving communities in the North as well as in the
South.

Chicago was not spared its measure of violence. The sporadic bombing of Negro homes in 1918 was but the prelude to a five-day riot in
1919 which took at least thirty-eight lives, resulted in over five hundred
injuries, destroyed $250,000 worth of property, and left over a thou-
sand persons homeless. For the first time since 1861 the Negro was the
center of a bloody drama. Then he was the hero; now he was the
villain.[1]

The generally disturbed background out of which the Chicago riot
exploded is revealed by a news item in the Chicago *Tribune* for July
4, 1917, reporting a protest meeting against a bloody riot which had
occurred in East St. Louis, Illinois. The article, headlined, "LAWYER
WARNS NEGROES HERE TO ARM SELVES," quoted one of
Chicago's most respected and conservative Negro leaders as saying,
"Arm yourselves now with guns and pistols." Another equally prominent leader was quoted as declaring that he "hoped God would demand 100,000 white lives in the War for each Negro slaughtered in
East St. Louis." [2]

The Chicago riot began on a hot July day in 1919 as the result of
an altercation at a bathing beach. A colored boy swam across the

imaginary line which was supposed to separate Negroes from whites at the Twenty-ninth Street beach. He was stoned by a group of white boys. During the ensuing argument between groups of Negro and white bathers, the boy was drowned. Colored bathers were enraged. Rumor swept the beach, "White people have killed a Negro." The resulting fight, which involved the beach police and the white and colored crowd, set off six days of rioting. (Figure 6.)

Pitched battles were fought in the Black Belt streets. Negroes were snatched from streetcars and beaten; gangs of hoodlums roamed the Negro neighborhood, shooting at random. Instead of the occasional bombings of two years before, this was a pogrom. But the Negroes fought back.

Attacks and reprisals were particularly bitter up and down the western and southern boundary between the Irish neighborhoods and the Black Belt. Here youthful white gangs—the so-called athletic clubs—functioning with the tacit approval of the ward politicians who sponsored them, raided the Negro community, attacking the people whom for years they had derided as "jigs," "shines," "dinges," "smokes," and "niggers," and who were now fair game. The rising smoke from burning homes in the white neighborhoods around the stockyards and the railroad tracks, during the next two days, was silent evidence of the embittered Negroes' reprisals.

The reaction of most colored civic leaders was ambivalent. Publicly they were constrained to be conciliatory and to curb the masses who did the actual fighting. Privately, despite a recognition of the horrors of the riot, like Negroes of all classes they justified the fighting as self-defense and as proof that Negroes would not supinely suffer mistreatment. They did not view a riot as unmitigated evil if it focused attention upon injustices. To them it held the same paradoxical elements of good emerging from evil that Wilson saw in the First World War or Lenin in the Russian Revolution.

There were some, however, particularly among Old Settlers,* who viewed the riot as the tragic end of a golden age of race relations. They were very bitter against the southern Negroes, who, they felt, had brought this catastrophe upon them. A group of representative business and professional men met to devise means for ending the disorder. Among the speakers was a lawyer who had come to Chicago

* A term used by both Negroes and whites in Chicago to designate persons who lived in Chicago prior to the First World War.

from Georgia by way of Canada in 1893, studied law, and amassed some wealth. He insisted that "a lot of the trouble is due to Negroes from the South" and called upon "some representative Negroes from the same part of the country [to] do what they can to help quiet things down."

Many Negroes expressed their resentment against one Old Settler who began his address by placing the blame for the riot on the colored population, stating that "One of the chief causes of the trouble is that the colored men have been taught they must act on the policy of an eye for an eye and a tooth for a tooth."

They condemned him as an "Uncle Tom" * when he continued:

"This starts a series of reprisals that is likely to go on until the white man will get mad, and if he does we know what will happen to the man of color. Some of us forget that the white man has given us free-dom, the right to vote, to live on terms of equality with him, to be paid well for our work, and to receive many other benefits."

They ridiculed him as a "white man's nigger" for his warning:

"If the white man should decide that the black man has proved he is not fit to have the right to vote, that right may be taken away. We might also find it difficult to receive other favors to which we have been accustomed, and then what would happen to us? We must re-member that this is a white man's country. Without his help we can do nothing. When we fight the white man we fight ourselves. We can start a riot but it takes the white man to stop it. We are not interested now in what started the riot, but how to stop it. The Germans thought these same people were so easy-going that they wouldn't fight, and they kept stirring things up until the Americans got mad. That ought to be warning enough! If this thing goes on for three days more there will be no jobs for our men to go back to."

They agreed, however, with his solution, provided it were impar-tially applied: "If the city cannot restore order then let us with the aid of the militia, have martial law, and take the arms away from the hoodlums." [3]

The bitterness felt by even the more conservative Negro leaders is

* "Uncle Tom," the hero of Harriet Beecher Stowe's famous novel of the abo-litionist era, has become for colored people a symbol of the subservient Negro. The term thus serves as a satirical condemnation of any Negro who is thought to be currying favor with white people.

plainly revealed in the tone of the annual report of Provident Hospital for 1919. Proud of the efficiency with which it handled riot casualties, the hospital board detailed its activities as follows:[4]

> . . . A crowd of young white toughs from in and near Wentworth Avenue, mainly mere boys, began raids into the colored district, destroying, wounding and killing as they went. On one of these trips the raiders shot into the hospital. That evening fifteen victims were treated at the hospital, one white, the rest colored . . . the majority stabbed or clubbed, and a few shot.
>
> As early as three o'clock in the afternoon on Monday, a mob gathered about the hospital. Feeling was running high. Many of the nurses, worn and tired by long hours of excitement and hard work, found human nature too weak to stand the hideous sights and bloodshed and begged to be taken away . . . but except for short spells of hysteria they were at their posts every minute of the time without sleep and without proper nourishment, for it was difficult from the start to get food into the hospital.
>
> During the twenty-four hours from midnight Sunday to midnight Monday, seventy-five victims were taken care of. A number were taken by friends after having received treatment and a number died. Of these patients nine were white. Cots were placed in the wards and in the emergency room until every available space was occupied; then the victims had to lie upon the floor.
>
> The demand on the hospital surgical supplies and food supplies was heavy; furnishings and equipment suffered; surgical instruments were lost and broken; mattresses were ruined, and furniture was wrecked.

The references to the treatment of white patients were a deliberate build-up for two devastating paragraphs:

> It should be borne in mind that the conditions in the colored district were exactly reversed in certain white localities where any offending colored person who appeared was ruthlessly slaughtered, whether man, woman, or baby. From these localities came the raiding parties that caused substantially all the trouble.
>
> The white doctors, of course, were not in attendance during this time and many of the colored staff doctors and the three colored house internes worked day and night; sometimes six operations were in progress at one time.

The daily newspapers headlined the Riot as big news, at the same time editorializing against it. The *New Majority,* organ of the Chicago Federation of Labor, prominently displayed an article, "FOR

WHITE UNION MEN TO READ," reminding the workers of
their "hatred of violence on the picket line" and insisting that a heavy
responsibility rested on them "not because they had anything to do
with starting the present trouble, but because of their advantageous
position to help end it." [5] The general public watched and read, but
did not participate. Probably its sympathies were divided and its loyalties confused.

The Riot was ended on its sixth day by the state militia, belatedly
called after the police had shown their inability, and in some instances
their unwillingness, to curb attacks on Negroes.

RECONCILIATION (1920-1922)

One result of the Riot was an increased tendency on the part of white
Chicagoans to view Negroes as a "problem." The rapid influx from
the South had stimulated awareness of their presence. The elections of
1915 and 1917 had indicated their growing political power in the Republican machine—a circumstance viewed with apprehension by both
the Democratic politicians and the "good government" forces. Now
the Riot, the screaming headlines in the papers, the militia patrolling
the streets with fixed bayonets, and the accompanying hysteria embedded the "Negro problem" deeply in the city's consciousness.

Civic leaders, particularly, were concerned. They decided that the
disaster demanded study, so Governor Lowden appointed the non-
partisan, interracial Chicago Commission on Race Relations to investigate the causes of the Riot and to make recommendations. For the next
twenty years its suggestions set the pattern of activity for such civic
groups as the Urban League, the YMCA, and various public agencies.
The Commission's report was the first formal codification of Negro-
white relations in Chicago since the days of the Black Code.

After a year of study the Commission reported that it could suggest
no "ready remedy," no "quick means of assuring harmony between
the races," but it did offer certain suggestions in the hope that "mutual
understanding and sympathy between the races will be followed by
harmony and co-operation." It based its faith on "the civic conscience
of the community" and opined that "progress should begin in a direction steadily away from the disgrace of 1919."

Immediately after the Riot there had been some sentiment favoring
a segregation ordinance. The alderman of one white ward introduced

a resolution in the City Council asking for an interracial commission to investigate the causes of the Riot and "to equitably fix a zone or zones . . . for the purpose of limiting within its borders the residence of only colored or white persons." Alderman Louis B. Anderson, Mayor Thompson's colored floor leader, "spoke with acerbity and resentment" [6] against the resolution, and it was referred to the judiciary committee and subsequently dropped. The Governor's Commission, too, was emphatic in its repudiation of such a solution, declaring that: "We are convinced by our inquiry . . . that measures involving or approaching deportation or segregation are illegal, impracticable and would not solve, but would accentuate, the race problem and postpone its just and orderly solution by the process of adjustment."

The Negro had come to Chicago to stay!

The Commission was very specific in its charges and did not hesitate to allocate responsibility for the conditions which produced the Riot. Even governmental agencies were asked to assume their share of the blame. To the police, militia, state's attorney, and courts, the Commission recommended the correction of "gross inequalities of protection" at beaches and playgrounds and during riots; rebuked the courts for facetiousness in dealing with Negro cases, and the police for unfair discrimination in arrests. It suggested the closing of the white adolescent "athletic clubs." It asked the authorities to "promptly rid the Negro residence areas of vice resorts, whose present exceptional prevalence in such areas is due to official laxity." The City Council and administrative boards were asked to be more vigilant in the condemnation and razing of "all houses unfit for human habitation, many of which the Commission has found to exist in the Negro residence areas." In such matters as rubbish and garbage disposal, as well as street repair, Negro communities were said to be shamefully neglected. Suggestions were made that more adequate recreational facilities be extended to Negro neighborhoods, but also that Negroes should be protected in their right to use public facilities anywhere in the city.

The Board of Education was asked to exercise special care in selecting principals and teachers in Negro communities; to alleviate overcrowding and double-shift schools; to enforce more carefully the regulations regarding truancy and work-permits for minors, and to establish adequate night schools. Restaurants, theaters, stores, and other places of public accommodation were informed that "Negroes are entitled by law to the same treatment as other persons" and were urged to govern their policies and actions accordingly. Employers and labor organizations were admonished in some detail against the use of Negroes as strike-breakers and against excluding them from unions and industries. "Deal with Negroes as workmen on the same plane as white workers," was the suggestion. Negroes were urged to join labor unions. "Self-seeking agitators, Negro or white, who use race sentiment to establish separate unions in trades where existing unions admit Negroes to equal membership" were roundly condemned.

As to the struggle for living space, a section of the report directed toward the white members of the public reiterated the statement that Negroes were entitled to live anywhere in the city. It pointed out several neighborhoods where they had lived harmoniously with white neighbors for years, insisted that property depreciation in Negro areas was often due to factors other than Negro occupancy, condemned arbitrary advance of rents, and designated the amount and quality of housing as "an all-important factor in Chicago's race problem." The final verdict was that "this situation will be made worse by methods tending toward forcible segregation or exclusion of Negroes."

Not all of the Commission's advice and criticism was directed at public agencies and white persons, however. The Negro workers who had so recently become industrialized were admonished to "abandon the practice of seeking petty advance payments on wages and the practice of laying off work without good cause." There was an implied criticism of the colored community, too, in a statement urging Negroes "to contribute more freely of their money and personal effort to the social agencies developed by public-spirited members of their group; also to contribute to the general social agencies of the community." Negroes were asked to protest "vigorously and continuously . . . against the presence in their residence areas of any vicious resort" and to assist in the prevention of vice and crime.

The Commission expressed particular concern over growing race consciousness, a phenomenon of which the riot itself was evidence. The Negro community was warned that "while we recognize the propriety and social values of race pride among Negroes . . . thinking and talking too much in terms of race alone are calculated to promote separation of race interests and thereby to interfere with racial adjustment." Negro newspapers were advised to exercise greater care and accuracy in reporting incidents involving whites and Negroes and to abandon sensational headlines and articles on racial questions. The investigation had revealed the existence of several small Negro groups, such as the Garveyites and Abyssinians, who were bitterly opposed to any interracial collaboration. The Commission rebuked them indirectly: "We recommend to Negroes the promulgation of sound racial doctrines among the uneducated members of their group, and the discouragement of propaganda and agitators seeking to inflame racial animosity and to incite Negroes to violence." There was, finally, a word of commendation for the work of "the Chicago Urban League, the Negro churches, and other organizations in facilitating the adjustment of migrant Negroes from the South to the conditions of living in Chicago."

In addition to specific recommendations of the type referred to above, the report proposed a long-range educational program grounded in the belief that "no one, white or Negro, is wholly free from an inheritance of prejudice in feeling and in thinking. . . . Mutual understanding and sympathy . . . can come completely only after the disappearance of prejudice. Thus the remedy is necessarily slow."

Social and civic organizations, labor unions and churches, were asked "to dispel false notions of each race about the other," such as "the common disposition, arising from erroneous tradition and literature, to regard all Negroes as belonging to one homogeneous group and as being inferior in mentality and morality, given to emotionalism, and having an innate tendency toward crime, especially sex crime." Prominent among the myths which the Commission sought to explode was one which drew the following comment: "We commend to the attention of employers who fear clashes or loss of white workers by taking on Negro workers the fact that in 89 per cent of the industries investigated by this Commission, Negroes were found working in close association with white employees, and that friction between these elements had rarely been manifested."

In implementing such a program, a frequent interchange of speakers between Negro and white groups was urged. Public-school principals and teachers were asked to "encourage participation by children of both races in student activities as a means of promoting mutual understanding and good race relations in such schools and in the community." The daily press, which had been excoriated by the report, was asked to tone down its sensational treatment of Negro crime and to print more news about Negro achievement. And as a concession to that touchy aspect of Negro-white relations referred to in the Eighties by the *Conservator,* the Commission recommended the capitalization of the word "Negro" in racial designations, and avoidance of the word *nigger* "as contemptuous and needlessly provocative." [7]

OLD SETTLERS AND NEW

When the Great Migration began there were about forty-four thousand Negroes in Chicago. When it ceased there were over a hundred thousand. As has been seen, the impact of this influx upon the white community resulted in a race riot. Its effect on the colored Old Settlers, while less dramatic, was nevertheless disturbing.

The southern migrants reacted enthusiastically to the economic opportunities and the freer atmosphere of the North. But the Old Settlers were far from enthusiastic over the migrants, despite the fact that many of them were eventually to profit by the organization of the expanding Negro market and the black electorate. The Riot, to them, marked a turning point in the history of Chicago. Even today, as they reconstruct the past, they look back on an era before that shattering event when all Negroes who wanted to work had jobs, when a premium was placed on refinement and gentility, and when there was no prejudice to mar the relations between Negroes and whites. As they see it, the newcomers disturbed the balance of relationships within the Negro community and with the white community. From their point of view, the migrants were people who knew nothing of the city's traditions, were unaware of the role which Negroes had played in the political and economic life of Chicago, and did not appreciate the "sacrifices of the pioneers."

Old Settlers still complain that the migrants "made it hard for all of us." Typical of such statements is that of a woman who came to Chicago as a child in the Nineties: "There was no discrimination in Chicago during my early childhood days, but as the Negroes began coming to Chicago in numbers it seems they brought discrimination with them."

Another woman, whose family arrived in 1906, insists that "There's just as much difference in Chicago now as to what it was then as night and day. Why, you could work anywhere. You could even *demand* what you wanted, but you can't do that now. The people wasn't so prejudiced then as they are now."

The theme of these denunciations is usually the idea that the migrants "didn't know how to act" or that they "spoiled things," rather than the mere fact of an increase in the number of Negroes. Occasionally, the remarks are tinged with scorn and bitterness, as in the case of a colored civil engineer who came to Chicago before the Spanish-American War:

"As far as Negroes are concerned, there were very few here then, and the ones that were here had been here for years. They were just about civilized and didn't make apes out of themselves like the ones who came here during 1917-18. We all suffer for what one fool will do."

Old Settlers sometimes cite specific areas of activity in which they insist little prejudice was shown. One of them paints a glowing picture of the "good old days":

"During that time [1912] there wasn't any difference shown in color at all. In the Loop itself they had Negro clerks in the leading stores. So far as professional and businessmen were concerned, the colored doctors had as many white customers as colored. During that time, people would get the first doctor they could, regardless of color. White people didn't pay any attention to your color. In fact, I went everywhere I wanted to go and there was no difference shown me, and you can look at my color and see that nobody'd mistake me for any other nationality. You take the restaurants—you could go into any of them downtown that you wanted to and you would be served courteously."

Another Old Settler, a son of slave parents, came to the city in 1887 from Missouri at the age of nineteen. He mentions the prevalence of miscegenation as an index to the freedom existing at the time:

"In those days Chicago was in its youth. I was a young man and soon got a job waiting table in various restaurants and working in hotels. I made eighteen dollars a month.

"Well, all the Negroes lived down round the Loop. Those were the good old days. There was some colored men that had white wives and they lived good and was respectable. My aunt lived on Twenty-second and Cottage—I lived with her. There was a white family lived there and we all got along fine."

Much of this testimony must be discounted as retrospective myth, but the fact remains that the Great Migration and the Riot profoundly altered relationships between Negroes and the white residents of Chicago and changed the basic economic and social structure of the Negro community. In 1910 Negroes formed a small, almost insignificant part of the city's life. By 1920 there were enough to attract attention, and the rapidity of the influx had excited apprehension.

The bulk of the migrants came to the city from the semifolk culture of the rural South where the daily round was timed by what one eminent anthropologist has called "the great clocks of the sky,"[8] and where the yearly rhythm of life was set by the cultivation of the cotton and the cane. Their first task was to adjust themselves to a modern industrial city. Life in the city involved the substitution of the clock for the sun and the discipline of the factory for that of the agricultural cycle. It meant, too, an adjustment to a complex world with a wide variety of associations and churches, a multitude of recreational outlets, and new opportunities in industry and politics.

When the migrants first poured into the city, social agencies and community institutions made a conscious effort to adjust them to city life. But the Negro community as it exists today is not so much the product of any conscious manipulation by social agencies and Old Settlers as it is a natural growth. The migrants were gradually absorbed into the economic, social, and political life of the city. They have influenced and modified it. The city has, in turn, changed them.

The introduction of over fifty thousand new individuals into the Black Belt within a period of ten years swelled the membership of all existing organizations to the bursting point. As groups of migrants found their congenial intellectual and social levels, old organizations accepted new members; additional units of older associations and churches were formed; new types of organizations came into being. Old social patterns, too, were often modified by the migrants who brought their southern customs. Leaders sometimes had to shift their appeals and techniques to deal with the newcomers. New leaders poured up from the South to challenge and supplement or supplant the indigenous leadership. Old Settlers could not isolate the newcomers. They were eventually swamped by them.

The migrants found a functioning political machine in the Black Belt which welcomed their participation. From the South where they were disfranchised they came into a community where the Negro vote was not only permitted but was actually cultivated. The migrants learned quickly, and they were soon incorporated into the First Ward machine in the bailiwick of the news-making bosses, "Bath-house John" Coughlin and "Hinky Dink" Kenna. In the Negro Second Ward they learned that the political life of the community was allied with the world of the saloon and the gaming house. They learned to deal with such influential figures as "Mushmouth" Johnson, the gambler, and "Teenan" Jones, the saloon-keeper, those powerful and almost legendary figures of the Negro demimonde and underworld. It was all new and exciting. The migrants accepted it with gusto and found their place in the pattern, often learning to play the game of politics with skill and daring.

In 1910 Chicago's Negroes were a relatively small group of servants. By 1920 they formed a large segment of the industrial proletariat. Between war's end in 1918 and war's beginning in 1939, over 100,000 more Negroes were absorbed by Chicago's rapidly expanding economy, and the measure of their fate was keyed to the crescendos and diminuendos of the American life during the Twenties and Thirties.

CHAPTER 5

Between Two Wars

GETTING A FOOTHOLD (1919-1924)

THE BLACK BELT BECAME THE BLACK METROPOLIS IN THE TWENTY YEARS
between the close of the First World War and the beginning of the
Second. The fifty or sixty thousand Negroes who came to the city during the Great Migration had no intention of returning to the South.
Despite bombs and riots they insisted upon a place to live within the
city, and upon room for friends and relatives who followed them
North and for the children who would be born in Midwest Metropolis.
By 1925, the city had adjusted itself to the obvious fact that a rapidly
growing Negro community was there to stay. Negroes had secured a
foothold.

Although Negroes had to fight block-by-block for houses during the
war years, they did not have any trouble getting jobs. With the close
of the war they found themselves in a precarious position. Returning
soldiers wanted their old jobs or better ones. As industries retrenched,
Negroes were either fired outright or asked to work at very low wages.
White workers became apprehensive over a large pool of unorganized
Negroes that could be used to keep wages low. Three years after the
war a minor depression wiped out most of the gains which Negro
women had made in light manufacturing and in the garment industry. The same year Negroes were used to break a stockyards strike and
although they became permanently established in that industry they
earned the bitter antagonism of Irish, Polish and Italian workers. In
1924, another recession resulted in widespread unemployment among
Negroes. By 1925, however, a boom was under way and racial conflict
in industry as well as unemployment subsided. Gangsters replaced Negroes in the civic consciousness as Social Problem No. 1.

THE FAT YEARS

"Behold now the days of super-speed, of super-brilliance, of super-power," wrote Henry Justin Smith, referring to the Twenties in Chicago; "American energy not only had survived the war, but apparently had been redoubled by it. . . . Chicago caught the pace—the amazing, dazzling, even perilous pace of the third decade." [1] This is the Chicago of popular imagination—the Chicago of Al Capone and Jim Colosimo; of Mayor Thompson and Samuel Insull; the Chicago of the great building boom, when the sound of riveting hammers alternated with the fire of sub-machine guns; of skyscrapers and factories thrusting themselves up through a subsoil of slums and speakeasies. People made money in the Twenties and they spent it freely—sometimes with calculation, often with recklessness.

The new white-collar middle class and thousands of frugal skilled and semi-skilled workers rushed to buy or build homes in the suburbs, seeking fresh air and avoiding high taxes. They left the heart of the city to the poor, the newer immigrants, the underworld, the corrupt political machine, and the Negroes. Thousands of other middle-class people stayed within the city limits to stew in bitterness over the foreign-born workers and Negroes who rented and bought the homes of their neighbors who had moved to the outskirts. Among those who stayed within the corporate limits "there arose a diverse community feeling, rather than a civic unity, all up and down the long stretch of city. . . . New centers everywhere—new groups of stores, theaters, churches, garages, and all that the ordinary man needs, with houses clustering about, neighborhood interests developing, improvement-associations, parent-teacher clubs, art and literary societies. More than a hundred Chicagos, there were, within the one Chicago." [2]

And among the "hundred" was Black Metropolis.

The five years from 1924 to 1929 were no doubt the most prosperous ones the Negro community in Chicago had ever experienced. A professional and business class arose upon the broad base of over seventy-five thousand colored wage-earners, and was able for a brief period to enjoy the fruits of its training and investment. Throughout the Twenties, additional migrants from the rural South swelled the size of the Black Belt market. The Fat Years were at hand.

The Negroes spread along the once fashionable South Parkway and

Michigan Boulevard, closing up the pocket which existed in 1920 (see Figure 6, p. 63), taking over the stone-front houses and the apartments, buying the large church edifices and opening smaller churches in houses and stores, establishing businesses, and building a political machine as they went. By 1925 the Black Belt business center had shifted two miles southward, and those who could afford to do so were trying to move from the slums into more stable residential areas. The masses flowed along persistently as the Black Belt lengthened.

Occasionally a white community resisted this expansion violently. In 1921, for instance, the Chicago *Whip,* a militant Negro newspaper, assailed Mayor Thompson for refusing to see a delegation of Negroes who wanted to protest against several bombings. "[He] has only yelped something about five-cent fares," the paper charged almost hysterically, "while our property was blown into smithereens, while our sleeping babes have been torpedoed from their mothers' arms. . . . The City Council laughs at the 'floor leader's' [a Negro] jokes while the poor black people who put him into office toss in troubled slumber with nightmares of bursting bombs." [3]

In one block on Michigan Avenue, a synagogue bought by a Negro Baptist congregation was repeatedly bombed in 1925. (The colored congregation ultimately took out an insurance policy against bombing.) But bombings became rarer and rarer, and finally ceased. To deny living space to Negroes, law-abiding white Chicagoans developed something more subtle than a "pineapple" tossed by a "gorilla" hired by a respectable "neighborhood improvement association." In the spring of 1928, the Hyde Park *Herald,* a neighborhood newspaper, reported a speech [4] proclaiming the efficacy of a new device for locking Negroes within the Black Belt (italics are the authors'):

. . . Judge —— of the Chicago Real Estate Board, before the Kiwanis Club of Hyde Park at the Windemere East, in summarizing the earnest and conscientious work of the Board for the last twelve months . . . proceeded to explain the fine network of contracts that like a marvelous delicately woven chain of armor is being raised from the northern gates of Hyde Park at 35th Street and Drexel Boulevard to Woodlawn, Park Manor, South Shore, Windsor Park, and all the far-flung white communities of the South Side. And of what does this armor consist? *It consists of a contract which the owner of the property signs not to exchange with, sell to, or lease to any member of a race not Caucasian.*

The tensions of the Riot period gradually subsided, but the migration left a residue of antagonism toward Negroes. There were definite restrictions on the activities of Negroes—restrictions due to deeply laid habit patterns which white Chicagoans shared with other Americans. Most Negroes took the matter philosophically, if not fatalistically— unless they were pushed too hard. Then they were likely to direct a storm of invective or blows at any denial of their rights. Usually they avoided trouble spots and enjoyed the city in situations where they didn't have to bother with white folks.

There were stores and restaurants that didn't like to serve Negroes. To walk into certain downtown hot-spots was unthinkable. To run for any state office higher than Senator from the Black Belt just wasn't done. To hope for a managerial or highly skilled job in industry was ridiculous. To buy or rent a house out of the Black Belt precipitated a storm. But after all, Chicago was in America, not in France or Brazil. It was certainly different from slavery sixty years ago, or from the South today. Negroes liked Midwest Metropolis.

There were evidences on every hand that "the Race was progressing." Here were colored policemen, firemen, aldermen, and precinct captains, state Representatives, doctors, lawyers, and teachers. Colored children were attending the public schools and the city's junior colleges. There were fine churches in the Negro areas, and beautiful boulevards. It seemed reasonable to assume that this development would continue with more and more Negroes getting ahead and becoming educated. There were prophets of doom in the Twenties, but a general air of optimism pervaded the Black Belt, as it did the whole city.

On eight square miles of land a Black Metropolis was growing in the womb of the white. Negro politicians and business and professional men, barred by color from competing for the highest prizes in Midwest Metropolis, saw their destiny linked with the growth of Black Metropolis. Negroes were making money in the steel mills, stockyards, and garment factories, in the hotels and kitchens, on the railroads, and in a hundred other spots. "Why," the leaders asked, "should these dollars be spent with white men or wasted in riotous living? If white men are so determined that Negroes must live separate and apart, why not beat them at their own game?"

What did it matter if white men snubbed black men socially? Negroes were building an attractive home life and "society" of their own. They did not need white intimates.

What did Negro ministers care if white Christians sealed themselves off in Jim Crow congregations? They would take the church or the synagogue that white worshipers abandoned as they fled from contact with their black brothers, and turn it into a worthy house of the Lord (when they had finished paying off the mortgage).

Why should Negro doctors and dentists give a damn that most white folks would rather die than let skilled black fingers repair their vital organs? The Negro masses were gradually learning to trust their own professional men and would some day scorn to enrich white physicians at the expense of their own.

Why beg white stores and offices to rescue educated colored girls from service in the white folks' kitchens and factories? Negroes were learning to support their own businesses, and some day colored entrepreneurs would own all the stores and offices in the Black Belt; cash registers and comptometers and typewriters would click merrily under lithe brown fingers.

If Negroes wanted to pay two cents a day for white papers that stigmatized the group as a menace, picturing them as rapists and buffoons, let them do so—but more and more of them were spending an additional dime each week for a colored paper, where they could read about themselves and their own accomplishments and applaud the verbal body-blows that colored journalists slammed at American race prejudice.

Negroes who, a few years before, had been disfranchised, were voting for Negroes to represent them in the councils of city, state and nation. In 1928, Black Metropolis won the acclaim of Negroes throughout America when it succeeded in electing a colored Congressman—the first Negro to occupy a seat in the House of Representatives since 1901. If Negroes used their political power wisely they could bargain for unlimited concessions from the two parties bidding for their votes.

This was the dream of Black Metropolis, not yet fully realized, but on the way—a hope kept alive by press and pulpit.

To some the dream was inspiring. To many it was a makeshift dream, a substitute for the real American Dream of complete integration into American life. To some who watched Negroes inherit the city's slums, crowded together amid squalor and vice, where schemers, white and black, battened on their blood, the dream seemed a fraud and a delusion. "How can we build a metropolis," they asked, "when we do not control the industries that employ the Negro masses? How can we build the good society when we can't get enough decent houses to live in?"

To others, the development of a greater Black Metropolis was a tactical maneuver within the framework of a broad strategy for complete equality. The very preacher, editors, and politicians who did the most to keep the dream of Black Metropolis alive only half believed in its ultimate realization. They knew that unless the ordinary Negro could have a steady income and could share more fully in the wave of prosperity, their own careers would always be insecure. "But," they reasoned, "if Negroes could support their own business and professional class, if they would rally about their politicians, some day their leaders might teach them how to throw their weight in such a way as to win the respect of the white world." Negroes had votes and they were ac-cumulating money. If they used both skillfully, they could force the city to grant them more room in which to live, better jobs and, some day, perhaps, *full* equality. In the meantime, successful individuals would become living examples of what all Negroes could do if they got a chance. Gradually the city would begin to accept Negroes in high places as people, and not as Negroes. The Jews had done it—why couldn't Negroes?

Symbolic of this era of optimism was a colored banker, Jesse Binga, who in 1893 had come to Chicago penniless. Within thirty-five years he had risen from Pullman porter to real-estate speculator and then to banker. A feature writer for a Chicago daily sought him out in 1928 to get his story of Black Metropolis. Binga talked of the forty million dollars which Negroes had to their credit in Chicago's banks; of the four billion dollars' worth of property on which they paid taxes; of the two million dollars they had contributed to charity that year.

He also spoke with pride of "a new generation of business and professional men, coming to the fore"; of the seven big insurance companies "managed by colored people for colored policy-holders—$1,000,000 in premiums a year." He dwelt at length upon the hope which Negro businessmen had of eventually controlling the Negro market and providing jobs for young men and women as clerks, salesmen, cashiers, and managers. He cited as examples the two colored banks, one of them his own. Five years before, these banks had been entrusted with less than a hundred and fifty thousand dollars; now, between them they handled four of the forty million dollars that Chicago Negroes had on deposit.

The Black Belt was experiencing the Fat Years. When Jesse Binga saw an unending vista of progress and profit in the Negroes' future, if only they would support their business and professional men, he was voicing the confident hope of thousands.

THE LEAN YEARS

During the Fat Years, the Negro newspapers "plugged" the dream of Black Metropolis while blasting away at the pattern of white attitudes which created and perpetuated it. Their major thrusts were reserved for those who denied Negroes equal economic opportunity. "Perhaps Negroes could turn their Black Belt into a community of which the city would be proud," they argued, "but only if they were allowed to get better jobs and thus raise their purchasing power and political power." Between 1924 and 1929 the prospects seemed bright.

Then, in 1929, the *Defender* sounded an alarm:

"Something is happening in Chicago and it should no longer go unnoticed. During the past three weeks hardly a day has ended that there has not been a report of another firm discharging its employees, many of whom have been faithful workers at these places for years." [5]

Negroes were advised to "toe the line," work hard and behave decently, in order to impress their employers. By March the paper was thoroughly aroused, and in the mood to find a scapegoat. Its headlines reverted to an old object of attack with a plea for the federal government to "ARREST FOREIGN WORKERS WITHOUT CITIZENSHIP." The paper considered it unfair for "foreigners" to hold jobs while Negroes were jobless, and further charged the foreign-born with being "apt students of segregation" who would not work side by side with Negroes.[6] The Urban League, more sober in its appraisal of the situation, called a conference of leaders in Black Metropolis, after stating that "every week we receive information regarding the discharge of additional Race workers who are being replaced by workers of other races." [7] For the first time in its history, the *Defender* began to advise Negroes to stay in the South.

White papers talked of unending prosperity and were advertising a second World's Fair to celebrate a Century of Progress. But Negroes were a barometer sensitive to the approaching storm. They had reason to fear, while most of Midwest Metropolis seemed to suspect nothing, that the Fat Years were about to end.

Chicago's banking structure broke at its weakest link—in the Black Belt. In July of 1930, Binga's bank closed its doors, while mobs cried in the streets for their savings. Within a month every bank in Black Metropolis was closed. As white housewives balanced the budget, their Negro servants were often the first casualties. When factories cut production, unskilled Negro labor was usually the first to go. Negroes buying homes in the Black Belt and its suburbs suddenly saw their life dreams dissolving. "Past calamities, the grievous incidents bound to afflict an adolescent and quarrelsome city had all been conquered," wrote Lewis and Smith of the early Thirties; "they now appeared easy to overcome compared with the slow crushing movement of a debacle which pulled down one economic edifice after the other. Poverty had spread widely." [8] The Depression had come to Midwest Metropolis and Black Metropolis reflected the general disaster. The Lean Years were at hand.

The first reaction to the Depression was a deep sense of panic and frustration, followed by unorganized demonstrations of frantic mobs. The first organized reaction within Black Metropolis was a movement directed against white men who did business in the Black Belt. A group of ragged pickets walking in front of a Black Belt chain store in the fall of 1929 signalized the beginning of a movement which stirred Black Metropolis as nothing had done since the Race Riot. The attention of Negroes all over the country fastened on Chicago's "Spend Your Money Where You Can Work" Campaign. A Negro newspaper, the *Whip,* risking reprisal from white advertisers, politicians, and mortgage holders, became the aggressive spokesman for applying a boycott against all white business in the Black Belt that would not employ Negroes. The opening shot was fired against a chain grocery which responded to the boycott by hiring three colored girls. (It had never had colored employees before.) The major attack was then leveled against the Woolworth stores, which for a time stubbornly resisted the pressure, but finally hired twenty-one girls, later raising the proportion of colored employees in all stores in Negro neighborhoods to 25 per cent.

Other minor victories convinced the Negro community that the boycott was a useful weapon, and many churches and community organizations united to pay pickets, to hire loudspeakers, to provide bail, and occasionally to supply a detail of members for the picket line.

There was only one loudly dissenting voice, that of the Communists, who insisted that [9]

The triviality of this proposal is obvious on the face of it. It is indeed possible on occasion to kick up a row big enough to force a Woolworth store in Chicago to make a promise. But what has this to do with hundreds of thousands of Negro workers in the coal, iron, steel, oil, automobile and packing industries? . . . There is no substance to the "use of our buying power" proposal; it can only be raised by those whose social vision is bounded by petty industry and petty trade, who see everything not from the viewpoint of the Negro workers—the great mass of the Negro people—but rather from that of the Negro small businessman.

Yet, some people in Black Metropolis branded the boycott campaign itself as Communistic. Others feared that picketing would lead to race riots or to reprisals in the form of more rapid firing of those Negroes who had jobs outside of the Black Belt. But the proposition that stores doing business in colored areas should be forced to hire Negroes was a very popular one.

The boycott campaign opened up a few hundred white-collar jobs. It did not solve the problem of the unemployed thousands. As Negroes watched white artisans coming into their neighborhood to work, or white laborers repairing streets and tracks in the Black Belt, their anger was aroused. On at least one occasion this simmering antagonism exploded with dramatic violence. A mob of unemployed Negroes attacked a group of white laborers who were laying a streetcar track in the Black Belt, chasing them from the site. The Negroes then refused to leave the spot until the Mayor, the colored Congressman, and several traction officials had assured them that colored workers would get a share of the track-laying jobs. Sporadic acts of individual violence against white men working in the Black Belt flared up throughout 1930 and 1931. Some people saw the hand of Communists at work; more careful observers knew that these were merely spontaneous expressions of resentment. Black Metropolis applauded such direct action.

During the first two years of the Depression, hundreds of Negroes faced eviction for nonpayment of rent. Angered by the belief that they were last-hired-first-fired, conscious of their strength since the successful boycott campaign, small groups of young unemployed Negroes formed flying squadrons to resist evictions. The Chicago *Whip* reported such an incident in the summer of 1931:[10]

Declaring their determination to defend the jobless and hungry families which abound on the south side, from eviction by landlords because of their inability to pay rent, a group of young colored radicals . . . restored seven jobless families in the community after they had been evicted by the bailiff's office and their belongings set out in the street.

The first of these cases occurred Wednesday when more than fifty of the group, most of them young men who are themselves sleeping in the Park, restored the belongings of Mrs. K—— W——, a poverty-stricken widow with two small children. . . . The woman, who had been out of work since December, is five months behind in her rent, and had no place to go when she was moved by the officers. A short while after her furniture had been set on the sidewalk, a young radical appeared, and breaking the new lock on the front door, returned her furniture piece by piece, and ordered her to return to the house.

Sometimes the flying squadrons arrived before the police, and directed the family and bystanders to sit on the furniture to prevent its removal. An old spiritual, "I shall not, I shall not be moved," became the theme song of resistance. Landlords and civic authorities again blamed the Communists—and this time they were right.

Throughout the Twenties, Black Metropolis had been hearing new voices talking to the Negro people, voices that spoke strange words: "proletarian," "bourgeoisie," "class struggle," "revolution." They heard the old-line Negro politicians castigated as "misleaders" and "reformists." They saw white men and women standing on street corners with their Negro "comrades," handing out newspapers and leaflets that denounced the "fire-traps" and "rent hogs" in northern Black Belts and painted a Utopian picture of a Negro soviet republic which would arise some day in the South. They had a slogan: BLACK AND WHITE UNITE.

Most of the Negroes in Black Metropolis were too busy enjoying the lush Twenties to pay much attention to these "Reds" or "Communists." But in the early Thirties they began to listen. The Communists' defense of the nine Scottsboro boys stirred the imagination of the Negro people, and thousands of them joined committees and participated in demonstrations. Capitalizing upon this interest, the Communists began a vigorous program of organization in the Black Belt, forming neighborhood Unemployed Councils to demand adequate relief. It was these Councils that led the fight against evictions, and hundreds of non-Communists followed their lead. When eviction notices arrived, it was not unusual for a mother to shout to the children, "Run quick and find the Reds!"

Throughout the spring and summer of 1931 small groups of Negroes under Communist leadership skirmished with the police at the scenes of evictions. Then, one August day, several thousand people decided to march *en masse* to a home in a poverty-stricken neighborhood to replace some furniture. When the police arrived there were at least five thousand people on the spot. The crowd refused to "break it up"; there was some scuffling, and then shooting. Three Negroes lay dead on the pavement when it was over and scores were wounded. Three policemen were badly injured. By nightfall, fifty thousand leaflets had been distributed throughout Black Metropolis, bearing the slogan: DEMAND DEATH PENALTY FOR THE MURDERERS OF THE WORKERS!

The bodies of the dead men were moved to the Odd Fellows' Hall in a run-down Black Belt neighborhood. A guard of honor composed of Negro and white Communists kept vigil, while over eighteen thousand persons viewed the victims. When the funeral procession started for the cemetery thousands of Negroes and white people from all over the city marched in a gigantic protest demonstration. Daily mass meetings were held for a week in a large park adjacent to the Black Belt. The three dead Negroes became the symbol of the city's unemployed masses.

Midwest Metropolis was frightened by this upheaval in the Black Belt. If it had been an out-and-out race riot it would have been understandable. But here was something new: Negroes and whites *together* rioting against the forces of law and order. The Renters' Court immediately suspended all eviction proceedings for an indefinite period. Conservative and progressive Negro leaders went into a huddle with city officials, laying the grievances of Black Metropolis before them and advising immediate action if a "Communist revolution" or a "race riot" was to be averted, and if the ground was to be cut from under the "radicals." The city and the state began to make comprehensive plans for furnishing relief. In fact, the first serious attempts to face the economic crisis in Midwest Metropolis date from this outburst. By demonstrating its discontent, Black Metropolis had set in motion a chain of actions that was to benefit the entire city.

The chaotic turbulence of the early Thirties subsided as various New Deal measures went into effect. Relief and work projects stabilized Black Metropolis. Gradually the Republican grip upon the Negro vote was broken as people began to "vote for bread and butter instead of for the memory of Abraham Lincoln." Organizations of the unemployed, under Socialist and Communist leadership, drew large masses of Negroes into various forms of disciplined petition and protest—against relief cuts, for social security; against discrimination, for housing projects. After 1935, those Negroes who remained in the mass production industries were caught up in the sweeping organizational campaigns of the CIO. The Negro peasants had become proletarians.

New increments of migrants from the South continued to come to Chicago all through the Depression. Between 1930 and 1940 the Negro population increased by more than 43,000. With the collapse of cotton tenancy in the South, and because of discrimination in the dispensing of relief and emergency employment, thousands of Negroes set out for Chicago. Occasionally the Board of Education or one of the daily newspapers would complain that this in-migration was placing a strain upon the city's finances. Negro leaders were quick to remind them that America has no laws against interstate migration, and that, with thousands of white "Okies" and "Arkies" on the road, it was unfair to single out Negroes for attack. Yet, as during the Great Migration, only the politicians really welcomed the migrants—in 1915 the Republicans; in the Thirties, the Democrats, for by 1936 Black Metropolis was a "New Deal town."

The continuous squeezing of Negroes out of industry and the tide of in-migration combined to raise the proportion of Negroes on the relief rolls, until by 1939 four out of every ten persons on relief were Negroes, and five out of every ten Negro families were dependent upon some type of government aid for their subsistence. The Illinois State Commission on the Condition of the Urban Colored Population, reviewing the experiences of the Fat Years and the Lean Years, commented in 1940 that

Given a continuously expanding economy, it is reasonable to assume that Negroes in Chicago would have been able to raise the general level of their skills and to have reduced the disparity between their distribution in industry and that of white workers. But the depression, with a devastating impact, reversed the trend of the Twenties and turned the Negro people from a group with more than its share of the gainfully employed into a population predominantly dependent upon governmental relief.

Between 1935 and 1940, the Negro proletariat seemed doomed to become a *lumpen-proletariat.*

When the first rumblings of the Second World War were heard in Midwest Metropolis, the people of Black Metropolis were living upon WPA and memories. For some, the memories were of the Fat Years. For others the memories were of the chronic southern depression they had just fled. For the former, the Depression seemed a painful, but temporary set-back. For the latter, a $55-a-month WPA check was a net gain when compared with a debt of a bale or two of cotton.

FREEDOM'S WARS

Black Metropolis became aware, long before the city as a whole did, that a Second World War was impending. Negro newspapers were quick to sense the meaning of Fascism and to impart it to their wide reader-audience. A few of the leaders in Black Metropolis were raising money for the Spanish Loyalists at a time when many Americans believed that Franco, Mussolini, and Hitler were doing a salutary police job against Bolshevism. When the Italian legions invaded Ethiopia, the barbershops and street-corners of the Black Belt buzzed with indignation. Haile Selassie became something of a hero to Negroes all over America. A resident of Black Metropolis journeyed to Addis Ababa to become the pilot of the royal family's personal airplane: his exploits were followed with interest. The failure of the Great Powers to halt Italian aggression created widespread distrust of their motives, and in a confused, semi-superstitious sort of way people in Black Metropolis were given to prophesying that those who had sold Ethiopia out would eventually find themselves menaced by the Fascists. When war broke out in Europe few Negroes were surprised, or even very much interested, except in so far as it might stimulate a wave of prosperity in the United States. Anticipation of a war boom reached fever pitch in 1939, and in the years between the inauguration of Lend-Lease and the attack at Pearl Harbor, the main interest of most Negroes was how to get some of the jobs that were opening up.

✦

During the First World War Negroes came into a labor market that needed them. When the Second World War began they were a part of a vast labor surplus. It soon became clear that Negroes were not going to get off the relief rolls until white people had secured jobs in private industry. Black Metropolis seethed with discontent as white men streamed back to work while Negroes generally were being denied employment. Here and there picket lines began to appear around factories on the margins of the Black Belt with signs reading—

HITLER MUST OWN THIS PLANT; NEGROES CAN'T WORK HERE

IF WE MUST FIGHT, WHY CAN'T WE WORK?

BULLETS KNOW NO COLOR LINE; WHY SHOULD FACTORIES?

In the forefront of these demonstrations were young people affiliated with the NAACP, churches, and social clubs. Similar demonstrations took place in other northern cities, and in 1940 a militant Negro labor leader, A. Philip Randolph, gave organized form to this widespread discontent by planning the March-on-Washington—a movement that threatened to stage a mass-demonstration in Washington with 50,000 Negroes protesting discrimination in the armed forces and the defense industries. A large contingent from Midwest Metropolis was prepared to participate. But just this threat was sufficient to force the hand of the national administration, which could ill afford such an embarrassment in the midst of a war for the Four Freedoms; and the consequence was the President's Fair Employment Practices Committee, set up as a gesture to avert the imminent March. Black Metropolis, forthwith, began to marshal its cases of discrimination for presentation to the Committee.

Pearl Harbor stimulated a tremendous expansion in the war effort and, as the industries of Midwest Metropolis stepped up production, Negroes were reintegrated into the main stream of industrial life at an accelerated pace. The Fair Employment Practices Committee (FEPC) and the War Manpower Commission took the problem out of the realm of agitation and began to plan for the use of Negro labor as a war measure. By 1944 Midwest Metropolis faced a labor shortage, and a new wave of migration from the South began.

Between 1940 and 1944, 60,000 new Negro migrants arrived in Midwest Metropolis. There were plenty of jobs, but the already trouble-some problems of inadequate housing, congestion, inferior recreational facilities, and overcrowded schools in the Black Belt were aggravated by the influx. Half-forgotten memories of the Great Migration and of the Race Riot and its aftermath were revived among both Negroes and whites. The Negro was once more becoming a "problem" and racial conflict seemed to loom in the offing.

Fear of a racial clash was intensified during the spring and summer of 1943 when serious racial disturbances occurred in Beaumont (Texas), New York, and Detroit, and incipient riots broke out in Los Angeles, Newark, and Philadelphia. In June the Chicago *Tribune,* commenting editorially on the riot of 1919 and the current racial clashes, insisted that "it must not be allowed to happen here again." Upon several occasions IT seemed about to happen. A sixteen-year-old colored boy was killed by an over-zealous white policeman and the inciting incident seemed at hand. A white streetcar conductor and a Negro passenger began to fight, and cries of "Lynch him" arose from a few white persons, almost precipitating a riot. A group of white adolescents armed with pick handles and shovels chased a colored boy out of a white neighborhood, and there were rumors that a Negro gang was preparing to march in and "clean up" the white neighbor-hood. The summer passed. Although none of these scattered incidents touched off the riot that everyone expected, the expectation remained, for many people remembered that it was *after* the war that Chicago's race riot of 1919 had occurred.

As soon as word reached Midwest Metropolis in the spring of 1943 that New York's Harlem had been the scene of a riot, Negro and white civic leaders swung into action, intent upon trying to avert a similar outbreak in Chicago. The Negro newspapers, the preachers, and various community leaders urged Black Metropolis to keep cool, to ignore rumors, and to avoid altercations with white people. Depu-tations of Negro leaders, as well as white liberals and union officials, began to petition the Mayor and the police officials to take precau-tionary measures and to assure impartial treatment to Negroes if an outbreak should occur. They also advised the Mayor to appoint a committee to study ways and means of preventing a riot. "During the last war we made a study *after* the riot," commented one Negro poli-tician; "this time let's make the study *before*." The Mayor was at first reluctant to admit the possibility of a riot. "There is no race trouble in

Chicago," he said; "talk of stopping trouble which is only a myth tends to make trouble." Nevertheless, a few weeks later, at the continued insistence of community leaders, colored and white, he appointed the Mayor's Committee on Race Relations.* With a small grant from the City Council, the Mayor's Committee opened its offices in the central business district, and a Negro economist was hired as full-time executive secretary.

Throughout the summer of 1943 the Committee concentrated its efforts upon preventing a riot. Eight private Committee meetings and two public hearings were held, as well as conferences with police officials, key newspapermen, and various influential persons. The Committee stressed the need to dispel provocative rumors, to counsel patience, and to control adolescent gangs of both races. It appealed to the police officials to lay plans for quickly squelching the first signs of a riot. It also exacted a pledge that if a riot should occur, white policemen would refrain from giving assistance, active or passive, to the whites.

When the summer passed without a riot, the Committee felt that its work had been measurably successful. But it is not easy to evaluate the real efficacy of that work. Undoubtedly the widespread knowledge that the city was prepared to act decisively against rioters had a sobering effect upon would-be disturbers of the peace. It seems less likely, however, that exhortations not to believe or circulate rumors were very effective. That there was no riot may indeed have been due entirely to fortunate accident, since no provocative incident occurred in the Negro community such as the shooting of a Negro soldier which touched off the Harlem riot. Other factors, too, were important. The migration of Negroes into the city during the Second World War did not take on the character of a mass invasion of new and strange people. During the preceding twenty years the city had become used to seeing large numbers of Negroes, and the now large Negro community absorbed

* The Committee had six white members: a banker, a prominent merchant, an outstanding industrialist, a well-known liberal minister, a representative of the Chicago Federation of Labor (AFL), and the president of the Julius Rosenwald Fund who served as chairman. Five Negroes were also selected: the only colored professor in the University of Chicago Medical School, the executive secretary of the Negro branch of the YWCA, the lone Negro member of the national executive board of the CIO, the chairman of the Chicago Housing Authority, and an eminent sociologist—the man who had directed the study of the riot of 1919 and prepared the report for the Chicago Commission on Race Relations.

migrants more easily than the small Black Belt of 1915-19 had done. Also, there was no rapid expansion of the Black Belt in the direction of neighboring white communities to excite fear and stir up violence. Most important, perhaps, were the facts that there were no bitter industrial conflicts involving the use of Negroes as strike-breakers, and that few disturbances occurred over the upgrading of Negroes such as those that took place in Detroit at various times in 1942 and 1943. In fact, the rate of upgrading was relatively slow, and although large masses of Negroes appeared in new industries, the bulk of them were employed in new plants where a tradition against Negroes had not been set and where CIO unions were deliberately preparing white workers to accept Negroes. Finally, there was no wholesale influx of white workers from the South with intense anti-Negro attitudes, as in Detroit.*

The Mayor's Committee may not have been solely responsible for preventing a riot in the summer of 1943, but its activity did focus attention upon the danger of a battle along the color-line. As an expression of the will to prevent a riot it deserves some study. The Committee was primarily concerned with police measures and with appeals to Negroes and whites for mutual forbearance. Yet, from the beginning, it accepted the premise that race riots are symptomatic of deeper-seated social maladjustments. It initiated a search for the cause and cure of racial tension—that latent uneasiness which occasionally bursts forth into violence. Early in 1944, the Committee sponsored the Mayor's Conference on Race Relations to air the underlying sources of trouble in Midwest Metropolis. A Negro sociologist, addressing the first session, suggested that "racial tensions arise when people have not been allowed to participate in the American process and where they have been slowed down in their drives to be like any other group. . . . Tensions have developed in part over the slogans of the country mobilizing itself for war, stimulating the individual to demand the Four Freedoms. . . . Tension has developed in white people who think the Negro is moving too fast or who do not want him to move at all." These were the roots of tension during the Second World War.

* Sporadic incidents involving Negroes and whites tend to snowball into a riot when there has been a period of tension raising the general level of excitability. Normally, they remain isolated conflicts between individuals or small groups. Other Negroes and whites simply view such incidents as spectators and do not pitch into the fray.

The overcrowded northern Black Belts are highly sensitized areas of discontent whose inhabitants are keenly aware of the treatment of Negroes throughout the country. The advent of the Second World War heightened this race-consciousness, for Negroes were not only segregated from whites in the armed forces, but were also Jim-Crowed at post exchanges and theaters in many camps and sometimes humiliated and attacked by civilians in the South. In the early stages of the war, the Marines barred Negroes; the Navy relegated them to the role of messmen; and the Coast Guard was not too enthusiastic about using their services. (The Waves and the Spars did not condescend to accept Negro women until the eve of the 1944 presidential election.) All of this was common knowledge, discussed in the Negro press, on street-corners, and in barbershops. Every rumor of discrimination against Negro soldiers or sailors sent a tremor through Black Metropolis.

Increasing the tension was the fact that when the country emerged from the Depression colored workers had to wait until the pool of white unemployed workers was soaked up before they could get jobs on a large scale. Even when their services were eventually utilized they had to face opposition to their use as skilled workers and foremen, or in clerical pursuits. Thus, in addition to all of the minor irritations incident to a war—rationing, long hours, crowded streetcars and buses, high prices, congested living quarters *—Negroes were confronted with discrimination on the home front and in the armed forces. Yet, at the same time, the war was advertised as a crusade for the Four Freedoms! Apathy and irritation, cynicism and resentment were widespread. The Negro's nerves were on edge.

The outburst in Harlem, the bloody melee in Detroit, and other interracial clashes here and there about the country all had their effect upon Black Metropolis. This identification with the fate of Negroes in other communities was reflected in a rumor which gained currency during the Detroit riot—that several hundred carloads of Negroes from Chicago were on the way bringing arms to aid their racial compatriots. It was against this generally disturbed national background that the Mayor's Committee set itself the task of trying to pluck up the roots of racial tension in Midwest Metropolis. The proceedings of

---

* The congestion within northern Black Belts is in itself conducive to violent outbursts, which can be rationalized in terms of *racial* protest. A rabbit-warren existence results in frayed tempers. This congestion is, as we shall see, a result of a color-line which prevents Negroes from renting houses in the open market.

the Mayor's Conference on Race Relations were published by the City of Chicago in a booklet, *City Planning in Race Relations,* and widely distributed. (The quotations and excerpts that follow are from this booklet.)

It was obvious that much of the tension originated in conditions outside of the control of anyone in Chicago, and one participant in the Mayor's Conference emphasized this point by stating that "so long as there is one single law on the statute books of any state or municipality which deprives Negroes of a single constitutional right, so long will there be racial tensions which at any time [may] lead to racial conflict. America on the national level, therefore, must move swiftly toward the abolishment [*sic*] of all forms of discrimination." Being recent migrants, it was inevitable that Negroes in Black Metropolis would be keenly interested in conditions in the South from which they came and where their friends and relatives still lived.

It was equally evident, however, that there were tension points within Midwest Metropolis itself. Negroes were accusing the city of denying them a square deal. White people were becoming alarmed at the truculent mood of the Negroes. The Mayor's Committee, aware of these circumstances, pledged itself to "work with city officials and civic groups to bring practical improvements in basic conditions that will mean a definite step toward its goal—justice and equal opportunity for all people of Chicago, regardless of race, creed or color." One white speaker posed the problem in concrete terms: "Chicago's mission is not to solve the race problem, but to do certain direct and tangible things that will insure equal access to jobs, to good housing, to health, and to welfare for all groups within the community."

The whole conference proceeded upon the assumption that doing these "direct and tangible things," making these "practical improvements in basic conditions," would reduce dangerous tensions within the Black Belt and diminish the chances of a riot. It was evident from the discussions, however, that most of the participants realized that widening the areas of Negro participation in the life of Midwest Metropolis, while reducing the tension on the Negro side, might actually excite tension among white people. Therefore, throughout the conference, the more conservative white participants placed their emphasis upon "goodwill," "education," and "gradualism." They were opposed to quick and drastic revisions of the Negro's status upward. They feared resistance from the white side. All of the Negro speakers, on the other hand, and some of the whites, called for speedy adjustments to prevent the Negro's frustrations from erupting in violence.*

The proponents of a rapid tempo of change advocated strong government action to insure equality of opportunity. The most outspoken Negro participant, a prominent attorney and former city alderman, referring to an AFL leader's plea for "goodwill" and education to erase the color-line in craft unions, said frankly: "We will not wait, but we are pressing hard to integrate the Negro into all phases of life in this and other communities. Education is not the only answer. The whites also must show some forbearance and co-operation. They must recognize that Negroes are part of America, they are giving their lives and sustenance in this great battle and they are entitled to recognition."

The Negroes were particularly annoyed at the evasions of the representative of the Board of Education who, in defending the city against the charge that Black Belt schools were neglected, had prepared a pamphlet to prove that Negroes were at least better off in Chicago than in the South. One colored speaker said flatly, "I recommend very strongly that we gather up every one of those pamphlets and burn them."

The Executive Secretary of the Mayor's Committee, a prominent young Negro economist, sounded this same note of urgency in his summary of the entire conference: "No one defined exactly how gradual gradualism is, or just exactly what this education is. Those of us who belong to minority groups, however, have been hearing about it for an awfully long time!"

One white speaker, a well-known journalist, attempted to raise the discussion to a higher plane than riot-prevention by reminding the conference that "obviously the purpose of this Committee is something far more than merely to prevent riots or to preserve the outward semblance of order. . . . Because it is right; because it is a democratic imperative; because we in Chicago share the national commitment to the total destruction of fascism in all its forms—let us then build a Chicago which is worthy of the democratic foundation on which it stands."

✦

* The riots in Detroit, New York, and Philadelphia were characterized by intensely aggressive action on the part of Negroes—particularly against white stores. In fact, these riots may be interpreted as violent mass protests by Negroes rather than as attacks upon Negroes by whites. In only one of these cities did any large number of white persons participate—Detroit.

The remaining chapters of this book constitute a study of Black Metropolis during the Depression and the early period of the Second World War. These years cover a crisis period in the history of Western Civilization. They mark the culminating point of sweeping processes set in motion centuries ago: industrialization, nationalism, imperialism, urbanization, secularization. The dominant motif of the period was the search for conscious social controls, for methods of "social planning." Politics was becoming a profession of problem-solving. An eminent Negro scholar, W. E. B. Du Bois, once remarked that "the problem of the Twentieth Century is the problem of the color-line." At first glance this seems like a very narrow, ethnocentric approach to world affairs. It contains, however, a large element of truth.

The pre-eminence of the white western European powers has been based upon the four-hundred-year-old political and economic subordination of the colored peoples of Asia and Africa. It is only within the last hundred years, however, that the color-line has become a problem. The cumulative effect of exposing millions of exploited colored people to the democratic traditions of liberty, equality, and fraternity, and to the revolutionary tradition of international socialism, while at the same time educating them, and arming them to fight in white men's wars, has begun to tell. China, Africa, India, Indonesia—within each land there are the stirrings of revolt.

The color-line in America is merely a specialized variant of this worldwide problem. For over two hundred years, Negroes were imported from Africa as slaves. But slavery never had *complete* moral sanction in America, nor were the slaves ever completely reconciled to servitude. The history of the Negro in Midwest Metropolis, like the history of the Negro in America, is the story of a conflict between the principles of American democracy and the existence of a color-line.

PART II

CHAPTER 6

Along the Color-Line

FOR OVER A HUNDRED YEARS MIDWEST METROPOLIS HAS BEEN A MAGNET drawing Negroes from the plantations of the rural South and from the streets of southern small towns and cities. Some were adventurers, carefree and curious. Others were the ambitious, burning with a desire to "get ahead." Most of them were ordinary "poor folks" who had heard that there was steady work in Chicago paying wages high enough to let them live comfortably. And when the wages failed there was adequate "relief." All were bent upon escape from a section of the United States where their freedom was limited by a rigid color-line and where equality of opportunity was denied them.

Over 80 out of every 100 Negroes in Midwest Metropolis were born in the South. Most of them came to the city as adults during the thirty years after the outbreak of the First World War. This tide of mass migration was, as we have seen, set in motion by the manpower needs of that war, and its basic impetus has remained economic. But economic drives do not tell the whole story. That there were other important motivations behind the migration from the South to Midwest Metropolis is suggested by the answers which a large and representative group of migrants gave to a question asked by the Commission on Race Relations in 1920: "Do you get more comfort and pleasure from your higher wages?" Typical of the responses were the following replies:[1] (The italics are the authors'.)

1. Yes. Living in better houses, *can go into almost any place if you have money,* and then *the schools are so much better here.*
2. Yes, I live better, save more, and *feel more like a man.*
3. Yes. I can buy more. My wife can have her clothes fitted here, she can try on a hat, and if she doesn't want it she doesn't have to keep it; *go anywhere I please on the cars after I pay my fare;* I can do any sort of work I know how to do.

4. Yes, *Go anywhere I please,* buy what I please; ain't afraid to get on cars and sit where I please.
5. Well, I make more money. I can't save anything from it. *There are so many places to go here.*
6. Yes. *More places to go,* parks and playgrounds for children, *no differences made between colored and white.*
7. Have money to get whatever is desired. Live in a better house and can go places denied at home.
8. *Don't have to look up to the white man.*
9. *Don't have to go to the buzzard roost* * *at shows.*
10. *No lynching; no fear of mobs; can express myself and defend myself.*

Such statements show exhilaration over feeling "free," over the release from subordination and fear. This sense of "freedom" was even more explicit in the answers to the question, "What do you like about the North?"

1. Freedom in voting and conditions of colored people here. . . .
2. Freedom and chance to make a living; privileges.
3. Freedom and opportunity to acquire something.
4. Freedom allowed in every way.
5. More money and more pleasure to be gotten from it; personal freedom Chicago affords, and voting.
6. Freedom and working conditions.
7. Work, can work any place; freedom.
8. The schools for the children, the better wages, and the privileges for colored people.
9. No discrimination; can express opinions and vote.
10. Freedom of speech and action. Can live without fear. No Jim Crow.
11. Liberty, better schools.
12. Like the privileges; the climate; have better health.

The subsequent experiences of the early migrants dissipated much of the élan with which they embraced their new home, for the Race Riot of 1919 and the depressions of 1921 and 1924 suggested that Midwest Metropolis was not the Utopia which many of the more naive had envisioned. The prolonged depression of 1929-39 further disillusioned them. But Negroes continued to come, and those who were there stayed.

Other factors than the economic cycle helped to disillusion the mi-

* Semi-humorous colloquial name for the Jim-Crow balcony in southern theaters.

grants. They found that though Midwest Metropolis was "less prejudiced" than the South, it, too, drew the color-line. They were freer than in the South, but not completely free. They found equality, but not complete equality. As we saw in Part I, Midwest Metropolis has always been somewhat uncertain about what place Negroes should have in the city's life. The result is a color-line which marks Negroes off as a *segregated* group deemed undesirable for free association with white people in many types of relationships. The color-line also serves to *subordinate* Negroes by denying them the right to compete, as individuals, on equal terms with white people for economic and political power.

This present chapter includes a brief discussion of the color-line in Midwest Metropolis, beginning with those situations where it is drawn least sharply and concluding with those in which it is most rigid. Throughout, an attempt is made to ascertain whether these situations are tension points or whether both Negroes and whites seem to accept the implicit segregation and subordination. The remaining chapters of Part II will analyze some of these situations in greater detail.

Why, it might be asked, do Negroes continue migrating to Chicago in the face of a color-line? The answer is simple: "That line is far less rigid than in the South." It will be seen too that although Midwest Metropolis has a color-line, the Negro masses are not deprived of an education and are actually encouraged to vote. The color-line is not static; it bends and buckles and sometimes breaks. This process results in tension; but the very existence of the tension—and even of the violence that sometimes results—is evidence of democracy at work.

FREEDOM AND EQUALITY—LIMITED

Freedom to Come and Go: In the South, Negroes are constantly reminded that they have a "place," and they are expected to stay in it. In Midwest Metropolis, they have a much wider area of "freedom to come and go." The city is not plastered with signs pointing COLORED here and WHITE there. On elevated trains and streetcars, Negroes and whites push and shove, sandwich themselves in, and scramble for seats with a common disregard of age, sex, or color.*

* At certain periods, however, crowd situations can become a source of potential conflict. During the Great Migration there was frequent friction between

At ball-parks, wrestling and boxing arenas, race tracks and basketball courts, and other spots where crowds congregate as spectators, Negroes will be found sitting where they please, booing and applauding, cheering and "razzing," with as little restraint as their white fellows. This same absence of segregation prevails in virtually all of the city's theaters and movie houses.*

The retail stores of the city, too, as a general rule, treat Negroes like any other customers with money to spend. Negroes may handle the goods, try on hats, gloves and shoes, and generally exercise the prerogatives of consumer choice. Eating in the larger chain restaurants is a mass activity as impersonal as shopping, and Negroes freely utilize these facilities, as they do most of the cheaper small restaurants throughout the city. Certain stores and restaurants discriminate against Negroes, but these are in the minority and constitute exceptions to the general rule. They will be discussed later in this chapter.

In most situations where Negroes find "freedom to come and go" without being Jim-Crowed, they are in close bodily contact with white people and are associating with them as equals. But all are essentially *public* rather than private situations, and in none is there any implication that the persons involved are friends or even acquaintances. They are simply isolated, atomized individuals who happen to be sitting, standing, looking, watching, pushing, shoving side-by-side. Each minds his own business and is under no obligation to be friendly or even courteous to others. People are lost in the crowd. This is the equality of anonymity.

Negroes in Midwest Metropolis expect free and unhampered access to all facilities operated by the municipal, state, or national government. White people in the city are not ordinarily disturbed by their

Negroes and whites on streetcars and elevated trains. Then for a period of fifteen years there was little friction on public conveyances. During the Second World War, incidents on crowded vehicles once more became fairly common.

* Access to places of amusement is guaranteed by a state Civil Rights Law, but within the last fifteen years Negroes have seldom found it necessary to invoke it. Yet, as late as 1920, the Commission on Race Relations reported with respect to theaters that "there are petty evasions of the law, disagreeable encounters, and small but insistent snobberies. . . . Reports of investigators indicate that the managers of movies are convinced that their main floors at least should be guarded against Negroes." By 1935 discrimination against Negroes in downtown theaters was virtually non-existent and only a few neighborhood houses tried to Jim-Crow Negroes. Successful prosecution of theaters during the Twenties was partly responsible for this policy.

use of libraries, museums, or the city junior colleges, but there are public situations where an attempt is sometimes made to draw the color-line. For instance, objections are frequently expressed to the presence of Negroes in certain elementary and high schools, and to their use of parks, beaches, and swimming pools in various sections of the city. These objections are usually voiced by residents in white middle-class areas. The very existence of a Black Belt leads the public to feel that Negroes should have their own schools and public recreational facilities, and should not "invade" those in other sections of the city. When Negroes do use such facilities outside of the Black Belt, attempts are sometimes made to segregate them or to limit their activities. In some areas of the city this community opposition is reflected in children's gang fights. Occasionally, too, a policeman or a park official may take the initiative in putting Negroes "in their place." Thus, the National Association for the Advancement of Colored People reports one case as follows:

At a children's party sponsored by the City Park District at Sanford Park, a park official rushed forth and tried to separate the colored children from the white. Only by the intelligent action of the group leaders was a riot averted. Protesting to the Mayor and other city officials, the NAACP was assured that no racial discrimination was intended.

Sometimes a park official finds himself in opposition to community sentiment when he tries to carry out a policy of no-discrimination. In speaking to an Irish interviewer in 1937 the director of a park in an Irish neighborhood contiguous to the Black Belt described such a situation:

"In the last few months I've noticed they [the Negroes] don't come in here so often. Well, the only reason I can give is the community just won't stand for it. In the summer there were quite a few, but the younger fellows just rebelled about them. They came to me about it and I told them that I couldn't do anything about it. One of the leaders said that *they* would see about it.

"I cannot say that we have had much trouble with the different races. The Negroes just stopped coming here. The recent outbreaks didn't happen in the park, from what I understand; they happened out on the street. If I find that any one of the people working here had anything to do with keeping them away from this park, I would do all in my power to get him fired. I don't believe in any prejudice whatsoever. In college I learned a lot about mixing with different races, and I think if they taught more about it in the lower schools there would not be any prejudice."

In Midwest Metropolis bathing beaches and swimming pools are among the primary tension points. The Race Riot of 1919 began with a bathing-beach incident, and during the subsequent quarter of a century the beach question has continued to plague Chicago authorities.* In 1931, a Negro newspaper commented editorially:

> Once again there is the threat of interracial strife emanating from the bathing beaches along the lake shore in the Hyde Park district. Several cases have been reported to this office where groups of colored bathers have been insulted, molested, or threatened by bands of white hoodlums who resented their presence at the public recreation places. In at least two cases, it is reported that South Park police officers, stationed to keep order and to protect all decent citizens from annoyance or danger, have shown a disposition to treat the complaints of the colored bathers lightly or to signify their agreement with their white annoyers.

Two years before, Negro civic leaders and politicians had expressed their determination to fight out the battle of the beaches. The Chicago *Tribune* had headlined their stand: COLORED LEADERS ASK EQUAL RIGHTS AT CITY BEACHES; SEEK POLICE PRO-TECTION FOR NEGRO BATHERS. A Negro newspaper, reminding its readers that ". . . it was just such circumstances in 1919 which resulted in race riots," went on to add that "no one wants a repetition of these outbursts and the responsibility for keeping down these interracial conflicts rests, in the final analysis, upon the shoulders of those officers of the law who are stationed at the beaches." Negroes were urged to continue using the beaches, and it was announced that "the officials of the South Park board have promised full co-operation in maintaining peace and protection of ALL citizens at the beaches which are maintained for the pleasure and benefit of all." At the same time, however, community leaders suggested the establishment of more adequate beach facilities near the Black Belt in order to relieve the "pressure" on beaches frequented by white people.

---

* There seem to have been some beach incidents even before the Riot of 1919. As early as 1913 investigators for the Juvenile Protective Association reported that "even the waters of Lake Michigan are not available for colored children. They are not welcomed by the white children at the bathing beaches, and late last summer one little colored boy who attempted to bathe at the Thirty-ninth Street beach was mobbed and treated so roughly that the police were obliged to send in a riot call."

The continued expansion of the Negro community finally brought all of the beaches along a ten-mile lake-front stretch within walking distance of some part of the Black Belt, and at some of them indirect patterns of segregation began to appear. At one park, for instance, Negroes and whites used separate sections of the beach with an imaginary line dividing them. Later a fence was erected to mark the line, and this act so enraged one prominent Negro politician that he threatened to tear it down with his own hands.

This pattern became so well known that in 1935 a group of white boys were observed chasing a Negro boy away from a *less* exclusive "white beach," telling him to "make it down to your own beach in Jackson Park"—a *more* exclusive park, but with a segregated Negro bathing area. During the same summer a conflict at this beach was reported in the Negro press: POLICE OBJECT TO MIXING OF RACES ON BEACH; ARREST 18. SAY THEY ARE TRYING TO PREVENT RACE RIOT. The paper commented cynically:

According to information given the Chicago *Defender,* the arrests came as a direct result of the efforts of a group of white youths, led by some University of Chicago students, to test the meaning of that fence which the South Park board erected during the beach season last year. At the time the fence was built, it was charged that the purpose was to separate the Race bathers from the whites on the beach. This the Commissioners denied, declaring that the fence was to enclose a "private" beach which anyone could enter by paying a small fee. But the completion of this "private" beach has been delayed, the only noticeable result being to separate the races, the whites, for the most part, going to the south of the fence while members of the Race stay on the north side.

The University of Chicago students who tested the meaning of the fence were forthwith accused by the police of being Communists.

Between 1935 and 1940, several other incidents of this type occurred. In one case a colored woman and four girls were denied a locker at a park pool; white children in the neighborhood then cut up their clothes. In another instance, at a lake-side beach, thirty Negro and Mexican children under a WPA recreation director were driven away by a group of white children. A policeman refused to make an arrest, stating that he had received orders to "put all colored off the beach." The General Park Superintendent would not admit that such an order had been given, but did blame "Communist agitators" for the presence of Negroes at a beach that they had not previously frequented.

Several liberal organizations, Negro and white, as well as the Communists, joined in the protest, and one Negro clergyman in the neighborhood was quoted as saying that "the discrimination will be met with no compromise." The trouble finally subsided, and Negroes and Mexicans continued to use the beach without further incidents.*

Most Negroes do not wish to risk drowning at the hands of an unfriendly gang. Therefore they swim at all-Negro beaches, or in the Jim-Crow sections of mixed beaches, or in one of the Black Belt parks. The NAACP, however, defends those who wish to stand upon their rights, and its files for the years 1936-38 record one "victory." In the wording of the record, the NAACP "forced the use of swimming pool for Negro youth at Armour Square Playground."

As we have pointed out earlier in this chapter, the color-line is seldom drawn in theaters or at large athletic events. But in amusement places such as roller-skating rinks, bowling alleys, and public dance halls there is a rigid line. All these are recreational situations that emphasize active participation rather than merely looking on, and in which men and women participate together. The significance of this distinction will appear after our discussion of "social equality." It is sufficient at this point to note that such centers of commercial recreation seldom become tension points, since Negroes generally avoid them.

As mentioned previously, Negroes use the city's popular-priced restaurants freely and without embarrassment. There are restaurants, however, as well as taverns, night clubs, cocktail lounges, beer parlors, and similar spots that do not welcome colored patronage. During the five years preceding the Second World War, numerous cases were verified of restaurants' and taverns' refusing to serve Negroes. Some drew the color-line openly. Others resorted to subterfuge. Some proprietors or employees, for instance, would not turn Negro customers away, but just tried to make them so uncomfortable that they would never return. They were curt to them, or they overcharged, or they made the meal unpalatable by oversalting the food or by unorthodox concoctions.

* The Chairman of the Mayor's Committee, a white man, commenting in 1944, seemed to feel that a firm stand by the city on the beach question was desirable. He complimented the Park District on "doing a good job in race relations" and said that bathing beaches "now serve the total population in a way formerly regarded as impossible. The very firmness of the interracial stand of the Park officials has quashed most of the mutterings of Nordic mothers and white youths who have tended to feel that they have the exclusive rights to such public facilities."

Such discrimination was prevalent in establishments on the margins of the Black Belt and in places where the management was anxious to maintain an "exclusive" atmosphere. A few cases will suffice to illustrate these practices: [2]

A Negro man walked into a tavern in a Polish neighborhood and was refused service by the owner. The Negro reminded him that there was a state Civil Rights Law. The owner said he didn't give a damn; he just wasn't going to serve any Negroes.

A bartender in an Irish neighborhood contiguous to the Black Belt boasted to a white interviewer of the "Mickey Finns" that he prepared in order to discourage Negroes who came in and ordered drinks.

Two colored schoolteachers and several white friends attended a luncheon at an exclusive coffee shop. The Negro women were allowed to sit down, but the waitress ignored them and served the white women. One of the colored women protested and was told that she could eat in the kitchen.

A wealthy Negro real-estate dealer, active in civic affairs, went into a downtown cocktail lounge after an evening at the theater. The waiter told him that a bottle of ginger ale would cost $10. The Negro proffered the money without complaint. The waiter, angry because his dodge had not worked, called the proprietor. The proprietor summoned a policeman. The Negro, citing the Civil Rights Law, demanded that the policeman arrest the proprietor. The officer refused on the ground that he didn't believe the Civil Rights Law made failure to serve Negroes a misdemeanor. Several city officials also subsequently refused to issue a warrant. The Negro took the case into civil court and won his suit—though the affair cost him more than the amount he received in judgment.

The city's hotel managers, by general agreement, do not sanction the use of hotel facilities by Negroes, particularly sleeping accommodations. When the issue is pressed, however, as in the case of visiting conventions or athletic teams, the barriers are sometimes relaxed. Most of the hotel cases in recent years have resulted from attempts to discriminate against Negroes who were attending meetings, or visiting guests in the hotels. A number of such cases have reached the courts in recent years. One of the most unusual was the case of a Negro labor leader who, en route to a meeting in a downtown hotel, was told to use the freight elevator. He sued the hotel. The manager settled the case out of court by paying a lump sum and giving the defendant a written promise that such incidents would not recur.

Not all hotel owners capitulate so easily. Some pay their fines and continue to draw the color-line. On the other hand a few hotels are considered "friendly to Negroes" and are frequently used by mixed groups for banquets, meetings, or dances.

Though the situations described above are possible tension points, the actual occasions upon which conflict arises are few, for Negroes tend to avoid "embarrassment." In the years immediately following the Riot, the Chicago *Tribune* actually published an editorial sanctioning violations of the Civil Rights Law and commending Negroes for not pressing more insistently for its enforcement: [3]

He [the Negro] is not Jim-Crowed by law. A line is drawn by usage. The law in fact forbids what actually is done. It is a futile law because it encounters instinct.

Legally a Negro has a right to service anywhere the public generally is served. Wisely he does not ask for it. There has been an illegal, non-legal, or extra-legal adjustment founded upon common-sense which has worked in the past, and it will work in the future.

There are many Negroes, however, who defy these "illegal," "non-legal," and "extra-legal" barriers, and who show little respect for the dictates of "instinct" and "common-sense." Others, while not seeking a show-down, sometimes bump into Jim Crow unwittingly. When confronted by such discrimination in public places, the individual Negro is likely to react with an eruption of verbal violence. (The less restrained have been known to smack a waitress or proprietor or to break up chinaware and furniture.) Persons acquainted with the Civil Rights Law, and with the functions of organizations such as the National Association for the Advancement of Colored People and the National Negro Congress, sometimes report these cases and seek legal aid. The NAACP reported, for the period 1930-40, "Judgments well over $7,000 secured from Chicago restaurants." Midwest Metropolis offers Negroes "freedom to come and go," but it is Freedom—Limited.

Equality Before the Law: To Negro migrants, fresh from the South, Midwest Metropolis presents a novel experience—a substantial measure of equality before the law. Here, they can expect a reasonably fair trial in the courts, with a choice of colored or white counsel. There are no lynchings. They can vote for those who make and administer the law. They can aspire to office. The right to cast a ballot without molestation and to vote for Negroes as well as whites is a particularly convincing evidence of freedom as Harold F. Gosnell points out in his study of "The Rise of Negro Politics in Chicago":[4]

When a Negro migrates from the South to the North, he goes through a transformation. . . . One of the badges of his changed life is the ballot-box. . . . To some of the race-conscious Negroes, the ballot-box is the symbol of emancipation, a guaranty of equality of opportunity.

Although a few prominent Negroes were active in Chicago politics before the Great Migration, the "Negro vote" did not become an important factor until there was a large Black Belt electorate. After 1915, both the Republican and the Democratic machines began to compete for the large bloc of Negro votes that could be used to swing a close election. Black Metropolis was a Republican stronghold throughout the Twenties. By 1936, however, the Depression had swung it into the New Deal ranks. Then, with the beginning of the Second World War a shift back to the Republicans became evident. But in the crucial presidential election of 1944, the Negro vote was once again in the Democratic column. The possibility that Negroes may vote as a bloc whenever they feel that their vital interests are affected means that they sometimes hold the actual balance of power.

Within a decade after the Great Migration, Black Metropolis had elected two Negro aldermen, one State Senator, four State Representatives, a city judge, and a Congressman. This political activity led Gosnell to comment in 1935 that "the Negroes in Chicago have achieved relatively more in politics . . . than have the Negroes in other cities of the United States."[5] Wielding such political power, Negro politicians have been in a position to demand appointive positions for a few hundred individuals and equitable treatment in the courts for the masses (as well as dubious "benefits" from the great Chicago enterprise of "fixing" and "rigging" everything from traffic tickets to gambling dens). They have also been able to expose and check discrimination in the administration of the civil service laws and in the enforcement of the Civil Rights Law. They have created, among influential white politicians of all parties, an awareness of the Negro's desire for

equal opportunity. The appointment of the Mayor's Committee on
Race Relations, to which we have frequently referred, was as much an
evidence of the political power of the Black Metropolis as it was an
expression of spontaneous civic foresight and virtue.

At times the political activity of Negroes can become a tension point.
There is some evidence, for instance, to indicate that the passions
aroused among Democratic politicians and the anti-Thompson faction
of the Republican party contributed to the riot of 1919. Some months
before the Riot, the Black Belt vote had accounted for three-fourths of
the plurality by which Thompson won at a time when he was fighting for his political life.* The black newcomers were accused of thwart-
ing the will of the city. The *Property Owners' Journal* called its readers' attention to the fact that there were 40,000 Negro voters in Chicago:

their solid vote is the Negroes' great weapon. . . . When both our principal political parties are split, and when each of them has two or more
candidates in the field, this solid block of 40,000 becomes a possible
power and might be able to defeat or elect a candidate. This vote situation
is the foundation of the Chicago Negro's effrontery and his evil design
against the white man's property. He feels that he holds the balance of
power. . . . He therefore becomes arrogant, insulting, threatening. . . .
The Negro should be consistent. As he segregates his vote and casts it
all together in one block, so he should live altogether in one block.

Such attacks were not confined to small neighborhood papers. The
Republican, but anti-Thompson, Chicago *Tribune* felt it necessary to
warn the Negroes in 1920: [6]

* Some of the fiercest rioting occurred along the boundary between the Black
Belt and some Irish neighborhoods. The Commission on Race Relations discovered that adolescent gangs organized as "athletic clubs" were particularly active, and that most of these athletic clubs were sponsored by precinct and ward
politicians. Interviews with "old-timers" in this area of the city suggest that politicians and policemen aided and abetted these adolescent gangs. It is perfectly
understandable why the Irish politicians saw the Negro as a "menace." Between
1840 and 1910 the Irish, as a group, had raised their socio-economic status, and
had been particularly active in Democratic politics which supplied an occupational base for a lower middle class by providing clerical jobs in the municipal
bureaus, jobs as firemen, policemen, inspectors, etc. Now, with a new ethnic
group coming into the city and voting Republican, this whole stratum of the
Irish community seemed in danger. Negroes would demand the jobs which had
traditionally gone to the Irish. This antagonism was undoubtedly a contributing
factor to the Riot. For a fictionalized version of the Irish-Negro antagonism of
the Twenties and Thirties consult James T. Farrell's *Studs Lonigan* trilogy.

The Negro has had political equality. There has been an attempt to give him a fair representation in public affairs and not to resent his presence there. . . . We admit frankly that if political equality had meant the election of Negro mayors, judges, and a majority of Negroes in the city council the whites would not have tolerated it. We do not believe that the whites of Chicago would be any different from the whites of the South in this respect.

No such blunt definitions of the Negro's "place" ever occur in party pronouncements. After the first excitement of the Great Migration wore off they also ceased to appear in the press. But a color-line in politics remains. The most ambitious Negro politician would not think of running for Mayor or Governor. He would not have a chance if he sought to represent an area outside of the Black Belt in the state legislature or in Congress. It is definitely not the custom for white voters to select Negroes to represent them, administer their affairs, or pass judgment upon them. Whites do not balk, however, when an occasional Negro, elected from the Black Belt or appointed by the Mayor or the Governor, occupies a position of considerable power and prestige. The appointment of a Negro to head the Chicago Housing Authority in 1941, for instance, excited no organized opposition and very little comment.

The color-line in politics is also reflected in the types of political plums that go to Negro politicians and their henchmen. The big contracts and the heavy graft are reserved for whites. Negroes get the petty "cuts" from gambling and vice protection. In fact, a tradition has developed that Negroes will not demand big political rewards. Also, in matters of street-cleaning, garbage disposal, and general city services, Negro areas are neglected. During the period of the Depression, however, when vast Federal funds were at the disposal of the machine in power, the Black Belt was able to secure some expansion of social services. Political leaders in Midwest Metropolis, balancing the pressures of ethnic, economic, and religious blocs, are forced to grant some of the demands of Negroes, and Negro politicians shrewdly demand all that they think the traffic will bear.

THUS FAR—NO FARTHER

Negroes in Midwest Metropolis experience a degree of "freedom to come and go" and a measure of political equality denied them in the

South. Discrimination in public places is not widespread and, being illegal, can be fought. Yet there are two areas in which the color-line is tightly drawn—employment and housing.

The Job Ceiling: Individual Negroes have never been allowed to compete on absolutely equal terms for jobs in Midwest Metropolis. Before the Great Migration, custom relegated the majority of them to servant occupations, and trade-union barriers reinforced the custom. Between the First World War and the Depression, the bulk of the Negro population became concentrated in the lower-paid, menial, hazardous, and relatively unpleasant jobs. The employment policy of individual firms, trade-union restrictions, and racial discrimination in training and promotion made it exceedingly difficult for them to secure employment in the skilled trades, in clerical or sales work, and as foremen and managers. Certain entire industries had a "lily-white" policy—notably the public utilities, the electrical manufacturing industry, and the city's banks and offices. Then, the Depression squeezed the masses of the Negroes onto the relief rolls. With the outbreak of the Second World War, they began to filter back into private industry and by 1944 they were beginning to appear in a wide variety of skilled technical and clerical jobs.

During the Second World War there was little organized opposition to the use of Negro labor, but the nightmare of postwar reconversion haunted Negroes even more insistently than it did white people. The Mayor's Subcommittee on Employment reported in 1944, after a study of Negro employment problems: "The one concrete opinion that came out of the survey was that unless maximum employment continued, the operation of seniority contracts would work heavily against Negroes, who for the most part are recent employees." The CIO representative at the Mayor's Conference prophesied that "the alternative to full employment is chaos, civil war, and a third world war." The AFL spokesman warned that "if a great crash comes after this war men will fight and die to hold or get a job. The worst of passions will be unleashed. Without jobs there will be increased racial tension." The chairman of the Mayor's Committee summed the matter up as follows: "The big question is what will happen after the present emergency is over. If we cannot keep up full employment, earlier patterns of discrimination are almost certain to return. The all-important question facing Negroes is: can they hold in industry and organized labor a fair part of the gains of the past four years?" Negroes continued to wonder whether they were fated to spend another period as beneficiaries of a WPA.

Economic competition between Negroes and whites has been, as we have seen, a source of irritation and bitterness since the days of the Flight to Freedom. The two World Wars resulted in the temporary lifting of the Job Ceiling, and raised hopes among Negroes that the gains would be permanent. There is a note of fatalism, however, in the good-humored report of a Chicago newspaperman who, discussing his meeting with some Negroes from Midwest Metropolis hauling supplies on the Western Front in the autumn of 1944, said:

Chatting with these engineers around locomotives, you hear them say what good jobs these would be back home and how it would feel to be pulling into Chicago Union Station at the throttle and whether after victory they would be driving these big engines . . . just as they drive them here in France.

Both the reporter and the men, however, know that not even a war has been able to budge the Brotherhood of Locomotive Engineers from its constitutional requirement that members must be "Caucasians of good moral character."

The Black Ghetto: The Job Ceiling *subordinates* Negroes but does not *segregate* them. Restrictive covenants do both. They confine Negroes to the Black Belt, and they limit the Black Belt to the most run-down areas of the city. There is a tendency, too, for the Negro communities to become the dumping ground for vice, poor-quality merchandise, and inferior white city officials.* Housing is allowed to deteriorate and social services are generally neglected. Unable to procure homes in other sections of the city, Negroes congregate in the Black Belt, and what the Mayor's Committee discussed as "the Problem of Congestion" arises.

Although Negroes know that residential segregation has implications of inequality and inferiority—that it implies *subordination*—they

* This is not necessarily a deliberate assignment of inferior city personnel to Negro areas. In the case of schoolteachers, for instance, it is known that white teachers begin to ask for transfers when a community is "going colored." This results in the definition of schools in Negro communities as "undesirable," and retention in such a post is interpreted as "punishment." There is also some evidence to indicate that teachers have been actually "banished" to the Black Belt as a disciplinary measure.

do not oppose residential segregation with the same vigor that they display in attacking the Job Ceiling. In fact, the insistent housing demands that arise from Black Metropolis are essentially demands for more room, for a larger Black Belt, one not confined to the deteriorated slum areas of the city. White people, however, usually interpret the attack upon restrictive covenants as the expression of a wish to scatter about the city, and they are disturbed by the prospect. But the most aggressive political leader in Black Metropolis, a man personally opposed to all forms of segregation, explained the nature of the mass pressure for the abolition of restrictive covenants, in a speech to the Mayor's Conference (the italics are the authors'): [7]

"Out in my district just a few days ago a pamphlet was passed around among the citizens. This pamphlet, signed, among others, by the Vice President of the Drexel Bank, called upon all the citizens of that section to stop the infiltration of Negroes into the community. They say, by the way, that there is a studied plan of Negroes to move one Negro family into every block in the city of Chicago. This is being circulated by white people, not by colored people, to stir up among white people throughout the South Side a feeling of resentment against Negroes. Now, everybody with common sense knows that there is no studied plan of Negroes to move one family into every block. *Negroes want a normal development in their housing problem—a normal expansion; to be able to move as they need to; to move farther and farther in extension of the area where they live.* They want restrictions put out of the way so that they can make a normal infiltration into these areas [i.e., areas contiguous to the Black Belt]."

The conflict over living space is an ever-present source of potential violence. It involves not only a struggle for houses, but also competition for school and recreational facilities, and is further complicated by the fact that Negroes of the lowest socio-economic levels are often in competition with middle-class whites for an area. Race prejudice becomes aggravated by class antagonisms, and class-feeling is often expressed in racial terms.

Residential segregation is not only supported by the attitudes of white people who object to Negro neighbors—it is also buttressed by the internal structure of the Negro community. Negro politicians and businessmen, preachers and civic leaders, all have a vested interest in maintaining a solid and homogeneous Negro community where their clientele is easily accessible. Black Metropolis, too, is an object of pride to Negroes of all social strata. It is *their* city within a city. It is something *"of our own."* It is concrete evidence of one type of freedom—freedom to erect a community in their own image. Yet they remain ambivalent about residential segregation: they see a gain in political strength and group solidarity, but they resent being compelled to live in a Black Belt.

Social Segregation: Negroes in Chicago express unqualified opposition to a Job Ceiling, and they are ambivalent about residential segregation. In the matter of "social segregation," however, they are seldom articulate. Yet, it is in the "social" realm that their segregation from white people is most complete: in voluntary associations, church congregations, and in clique relations and family life.* Black Metropolis has its own set of institutions, bound by innumerable ties to similar Negro groups all over the United States. This web of social relationships between colored people is sharply marked off from the corresponding "social" world of white people—marked off in the South by law and in the North by custom.

THE SPECTER OF SOCIAL EQUALITY

During the period of the Great Migration there was a widespread expression of fear that the color-line might not hold. While the fear applied to every aspect of Negro-white relationships, its most intense form was that of the "social-equality scare." In 1920 the Chicago *Tribune,* reflecting this general uneasiness, lashed out at "sociological transcendentalists" and "misguided sentimentalists," charging them with "spreading propaganda for *social equality."* Their activities were dubbed "even more vicious than Red propaganda among Negroes" (a reference to the activities of the IWW). Conceding that "agitation for *social equality* may have every support under the law and under what

* The term "clique," which will appear frequently in this book, is used in the specialized sense of an informal grouping of people on the basis of common interest or personal congeniality. It has here none of the sinister implications popularly associated with it, but rather is synonymous with "set," "gang," "crowd," or "bunch." In many respects, as Professor W. Lloyd Warner has demonstrated in his studies of modern communities (e.g., *Yankee City,* Yale, 1943), the clique is one of the most important social units in modern society, since it controls the behavior of its members even more rigidly than do family, church, or formal associations.

ought to be human justice," the *Tribune* vowed that social intermingling would never be sanctioned in Midwest Metropolis.[8]

The real promoters of this social-equality scare were several property owners' associations, intent upon preventing the infiltration of Negroes into middle-class white neighborhoods. Speakers at public meetings appealed to all "red-blooded, patriotic, loyal, courageous citizens" to bar Negroes from white neighborhoods, insisting that "you cannot mix oil and water. You cannot assimilate races of a different color as neighbors along *social* lines." One issue of the *Property Owners' Journal* carried the following diatribe:[9]

Keep the Negro in his place amongst his people, and he is healthy and loyal. Remove him, or allow his newly discovered importance to remove him from his proper environment, and the Negro becomes a nuisance. He develops into an overbearing, inflated, irascible individual, overburdening his brain to such an extent about social equality that he becomes dangerous to all with whom he comes in contact.

"Social equality" is a scare-phrase exciting fear and distrust of the Negro. In the North, however, nervousness about the Negro's social aspirations is sporadic—it is not the ever-present incubus that hangs over the South. A social-equality scare is sometimes fomented deliberately, as in the case of the real-estate interests mentioned above. Occasionally it will arise from excitement over the appearance of a Negro in some unusual context, as when he takes a supervisory position that no Negro has ever held before; or when a Negro man is seen talking and laughing with a white girl; or a colored family moves into an all-white neighborhood; or a Negro party enters a restaurant or night club hitherto frequented by whites only.

WHAT IS SOCIAL EQUALITY?

When a Southerner says that he is against social equality his meaning is usually clear. He doesn't believe in addressing a Negro as Mr. or Mrs. or Miss. He will not permit Negroes to call him by his first name. He doesn't approve of shaking hands with Negroes, or of eating or sharing sanitary facilities with them. He draws the line at sitting beside them in public places or allowing them to attend the same schools and churches. He definitely objects to intermarriage, and while he is not too censorious of sexual excursions across the color-line by

white men, he keeps a ready rope for any Negro male who may dare
to turn the tables.

A great deal of what the South would call "social intermingling"
takes place in Midwest Metropolis without exciting apprehension or
antagonism. In fact, lack of color-consciousness is the rule in most of
the day-by-day contacts between Negroes and whites. Members of the
two groups treat each other as individuals and react in terms of occupational roles, individual personality traits, or socio-economic and cultural attributes rather than in terms of race.

Chicago Negroes and whites are thrown together in large numbers
in work-situations where maintaining a rigid color-line would not only
be a nuisance, but would sometimes be economically unprofitable.
With no compelling tradition of separate cafeteria facilities or sanitary
arrangements, the large industrial plants of the region have maintained
a general pattern of unsegregated facilities. On the whole this pattern
has been accepted as normal.* Some "semi-social" extensions inevitably
arise from these contacts. Employees eat lunch together, call each other
by their first names, play and joke with one another, share intimacies,
gossip and news. In general both Negro and white workers, unless
facing a crisis situation, exhibit very little color-consciousness on the
job.

Color-distinctions are also minimized by the demands of economic
necessity and political expediency. The white man doing business with
Negroes, the salesman trying to close a deal, the labor leader rallying
his followers, the politician seeking votes—all such types not only extend the ordinary courtesies to Negroes, but sometimes find themselves
joking, back-slapping, dining, and otherwise fraternizing with them.

When white people in Midwest Metropolis express fear that Negroes
will demand social equality, they do not mean these semi-social acts
of courtesy, friendliness, and informal social intercourse. *They mean,
rather, the prospect of Negroes' becoming members of white cliques,
churches, and voluntary associations, or marrying into their families.*

* The Subcommittee on Employment of the Mayor's Committee on Race
Relations reported, in 1944, that unsegregated cafeteria and dressing-room facilities were the rule in the factories of the Chicago metropolitan region, but that
"in hiring and assigning new workers . . . the greatest difficulty arose from
adjustment of white workers to unsegregated facilities." Yet, "if the proper
groundwork is laid, it is the general experience in this area that a non-segregated
pattern can be followed in locker-rooms, lunchrooms, toilet facilities and work
relationships."

The last-mentioned possibility is most "frightening" because it raises the prospect that Negro men *generally* may begin to flirt and seek dates with white women.* Any gesture on a Negro's part that can be interpreted—even remotely—as a bid for such relationships will excite apprehension. Weakening of the color-line in employment or political activity is often opposed, or viewed with alarm, lest it lead to social equality as defined above.

But the pattern of social segregation, although general, is not absolute. There have always been a few church congregations with both Negro and white members. A few Negroes have always lived in "white neighborhoods." Here and there, the semi-social contacts of Negroes and whites slide over into firm and fast friendships. There are even a few whites and Negroes who are married! Midwest Metropolis not only tolerates these deviations from the general pattern, but actually seems to accept them as a normal part of city life—not enthusiastically perhaps, not without some head-shaking—but generally in a spirit of "live and let live." This tolerance of deviations is due in part to the fact that the average person is unaware of the extent to which such intermingling occurs. Being scattered and diffuse, the evidences are not general or obvious enough to excite apprehension. Isolated examples of full social equality do not seem to threaten the general pattern of segregation, and so long as they do not involve a given person's friends and relatives they do not necessarily disturb him. This acceptance of deviations is revealed in a statement which appeared in the *Property Owners' Journal* [10] in 1919 at a time when a social equality scare was being assiduously whipped up in areas contiguous to the Black Belt. Since the statement was part of a bitter attack upon Negroes,† the following excerpt is a significant index to the rather

* A social-equality scare arose during the Depression years when public attention became focused upon the activities of the Communist Party. That organization was widely accused of stirring up Negroes to demand social equality. The presence of Negroes at picnics, dances, and demonstrations sponsored by left-wing groups was cited as irrefutable evidence that the "Reds" were planting ambitions in the Negro's mind that would not stop short of the Caucasian nuptial bed.

† So widespread was the accusation that Negro leaders were advocating intermarriage that the most aggressive Negro leader of the period, Dr. W. E. B. Du Bois, editor of *Crisis,* felt it necessary to read the following statement into the record: "The *Crisis* . . . most emphatically advises against race intermarriage in America . . . because of social conditions and prejudice and not for physical reasons." The editor asserted, however, that his magazine would defend "the moral and legal right of individuals who may think otherwise." (Quoted from

wide limits of tolerance in Midwest Metropolis (italics are the authors'):

The Negro is unwilling to resume his status of other years; he is exalting himself with idiotic ideas on *social equality*. Only a few days ago Attorney General Palmer informed the Senate of the nation of the Negroes' boldest and most impudent ambition, sex equality.

From the Negro viewpoint sex equality, according to Mr. Palmer, is not seen as the equality of men and women; it is the assertion by the Negro of a right to marry any person whom he chooses regardless of color. *The dangerous portion of their outrageous idea does not consist in the accident that some black or white occasionally may forget the dignity of their race and intermarry. This has happened before; doubtless it will recur many times.* Where the trouble lies is in the fact that the Department of Justice has observed an organized tendency on the part of Negroes to regard themselves in such a light as to permit their idea to become a universal ambition of the Negro race.

As a corollary to their ambition on sex equality, it is not strange that they are attempting to force their presence as neighbors on the whites. . . .

Such tolerance of occasional "accidents" denotes a far less intense devotion to maintaining the color-line than is evident in the South. In the final analysis, the individual's tolerance of such deviations is apparently limited primarily by how close they approach, or seem to approach, his own intimate circle, his family, cliques and voluntary associations. Midwest Metropolis is a large city; it has wide social as well as spatial distances. That some Negroes and whites associate as intimate friends, or even court and marry, can be viewed with a certain amount of detachment so long as the incidents remain remote. But if a man is made to feel, by propagandists or by some personal experience, that *his* sister or *his* daughter might marry a Negro, or that Negroes might appear as members of *his* social club or church, the specter promptly arises. In the South, every white man feels impelled to protect *every* white family, clique, and church from Negro "contamination." In Midwest Metropolis, each person is concerned only with his own.

That social-equality scares are not more frequent is partly a function of greater "tolerance," but this tolerance is undoubtedly due to the small proportion of Negroes in the city, to the inconspicuous nature of

the *Crisis* in F. G. Detweiler, *The Negro Press in the United States,* University of Chicago, 1922, p. 145.)

the little social intermingling that does occur, and to the habit of interpreting much of the social contact as "not really social," but as "semi-
social" activity dictated by political or economic ends. Despite the periodic outbursts by property owners' associations, most of the white
people in Midwest Metropolis do not seem to feel that there is any
"danger" of Negroes attempting to cross the color-line *en masse* by
seeking membership in white families, cliques, voluntary associations
and churches. Sometimes, however, they seem to have their doubts.
Then the specter of social equality rises to haunt them.

DO NEGROES WANT SOCIAL EQUALITY?

Ask a Negro civic leader in Midwest Metropolis whether "his
people" want social equality, and he's likely to answer: "If you mean
the right to procure goods and services anywhere—yes, absolutely. We
don't call that social equality. If you mean the right to rent or buy a
house anywhere in the city—why, of course. Is that social equality? If
you mean a *yearning* to visit white people in their homes and to be
visited by them—nonsense! But, as for the privilege of doing even that
if both white and Negro individuals desire it—why not? This is a free
country. Intermarriage? Well, it takes two to get married, and if one
of them is white, what right has the law to interfere? But why should
Negroes seek to marry whites? They have all colors within their own
race [punctuated with a nervous laugh]. What Negroes *really* want is
equal economic opportunity and enough room to live in. If you give
us that, and just leave people alone, these social problems will work
themselves out. Why raise the question of social equality, anyhow?
Nobody's pressing that issue. You can't legislate social equality, and it's
certainly not democratic to legislate against it."

This is the "advanced view" of most northern Negro leaders. There
are many Negroes in Midwest Metropolis, however, who, as a matter
of either expediency or sincere conviction, will proclaim the philosophy
of Booker T. Washington: "In all things purely social we can be as
separate as the fingers, yet one as the hand in all things essential to
mutual progress." * These are reassuring words, and most white people

* Booker T. Washington's great popularity and influence among southern
white people was due in part to the fact that he seldom failed to lay the specter
of social equality when addressing either a Negro or a white audience. Yet a
careful reading of the very speech in which he stated the famous five-fingers-of·

seem to appreciate hearing them. In fact, many "friends of the Negro" seem to regard it as *lèse majesté* when a responsible Negro leader publicly sanctions social intermingling and intermarriage. To do so, they argue, may alienate the less emancipated whites who could be won over to support the more limited goals of political and economic equality for Negroes. White sympathizers with the Negro's struggle for status treasure any handy quotation that seems to prove that Negroes do not want social equality. Nevertheless, colored leaders today in Midwest Metropolis do not find it necessary to announce ostentatiously, as did the Colored Convention of 1869: "We explicitly disavow any and all imputations of social equality."

Yet, in so far as social equality is defined to mean intermarriage and integration into white cliques, churches, associations, and families, Negroes exert no pressure for it and manifest very little interest in it. What some people choose to interpret as a clamor for social equality— demand for equal access to public facilities, opposition to segregation in public places, and defense of the right to compete on the open market for houses—these things constitute, from the Negro's viewpoint, a demand for *civil* rights and not a bid for social acceptance. When such situations involve close contact between Negro men and white women (as in dance halls or bathing beaches) or when "exclusiveness" is an issue (as in certain hotels and restaurants), the presence of Negroes is often interpreted as a threat to the stability of the "social" color-bar. Negroes are generally indifferent to social intermingling with white people, and this indifference is closely related to the existence of a separate, parallel Negro institutional life which makes interracial activities seem unnecessary and almost "unnatural."

Since the eighteenth century, a separate Negro institutional structure has existed in America. Through the years it has been developing into an intricate web of families, cliques, churches, and voluntary associations, ordered by a system of social classes. This "Negro world" is, his-

the-hand "Atlanta Compromise" will reveal at least one sentence which sounds a little like "double-talk": "The wisest among my race understand that the *agitation* of questions of social equality is the extremest folly, and that progress in the enjoyment of *all privileges* that will come to us must be the result of severe and constant struggle rather than of artificial forcing." (Italics are the authors'.) There is just a hint in this sentence that Washington was denouncing *agitation* for social equality rather than social equality itself as an ultimate goal. In an article published posthumously, Washington attacked all forms of segregation, labeling them an insult to Negroes. In the popular mind, however, he is still thought of as the great leader who defended segregation.

torically, the direct result of social rejection by the white society. For Negroes, however, it has long since lost this connotation, and many white people never think of it as such.* It is now the familiar milieu in which Negroes live and move from birth till death. It is accepted as "natural" and is psychologically satisfying. Negroes do not usually think of their institutional life as something "inferior." In fact, they express considerable pride in it, viewing it as evidence that they, as well as whites, can create a collective life. Thus, they do not "agitate" for social equality, because they do not ordinarily experience their social separateness as oppressive or undesirable. Black Metropolis is the world of their relatives and friends. They know no other.†

Despite this almost complete adjustment to social segregation, there are situations in which resentment against the pattern is openly expressed. A Negro may have no desire to marry a white person or to make sexual excursions across the color-line; but he usually gets boiling mad at any attempts to break up mixed couples in a public place or to legislate against intermarriage. Negroes generally do not display the least interest in joining white churches, but when a white pastor preaches a "goodwill" sermon in a Negro church, there is likely to be a great deal of grumbling about "insincerity," and some biting comments about "white Christianity" with its "Jim-Crow churches."

There are certain border-line situations, too, in which Negroes feel

* This attitude toward Negro institutions is evident if we examine religious denominations. There are separate conferences, conventions, associations, and synods paralleling those among whites. Few Negroes or whites think of these as "protest" organizations. The present generation accepts them as a natural part of the social environment. Yet separate Negro churches came into being as a protest against the Jim-Crow seating of Negroes in mixed churches, against the inability of Negro leaders to rise to the top, or against being considered wards of white "home mission" boards. This process is still at work in some denominations. For instance, the African Orthodox Church was organized in the Twenties as a protest against the unwillingness of the Roman Catholic Church in America to ordain and assign Negro priests.

† This subjective acceptance of institutional segregation by most Negroes must not be confused with some important objective facts, viz., (1) that white people, in general, have a tendency to view the separate Negro institutional life with a certain amount of amused condescension and patronizing curiosity; (2) that under present conditions, segregated institutions are actually inferior in economic and social power; (3) that social isolation results in distorted perspectives and personality development. There are some gains to the total culture resulting from segregation—distinctive contributions to the arts and to literature; but against these superficial gains must be set the cost in ignorance, poverty, and resentment.

that they should be accepted for participation, but which white people often define as "social" or "private." Thus a Negro who does not interpret separate cliques, families, churches, and voluntary associations as "unfair" or "unjust" might expect to be included in a dance sponsored by a store where he works, a school that he attends, or a union to which he belongs.* In the planning of dances, picnics, or parties the question arises as to how the Negroes should be treated. Whenever Negroes in such a situation are ignored, barred, or subjected to "special arrangements" they usually resent it. Nobody likes to feel "left out" or to be regarded as a "problem." Sometimes Negroes will put up a fight for inclusion in such activities. More often they will withdraw and mask the snub by feigning a total lack of interest in the proceedings or by professing a preference for the company of Negroes. Those who elect to fight usually make it clear that they consider the issue one of "civil" or "economic" rights rather than one of *social* equality. Those who decide to withdraw accept the definition of the situation as *social* and disavow a desire to participate.

When a white person does make friendly overtures, these are often viewed with suspicion—"he must have something up his sleeve," or "she doesn't really mean it." Negroes assume *prima facie* that even the friendliest approaches are hedged about with reservations and hesitancies, if not actual insincerity. The disavowal of interest in social relations with white people is partly a protective device against actual embarrassment, since "socializing" across the color-line usually takes place in an atmosphere of constraint and uneasiness. Both Negroes and whites in such situations are constantly exposed to expressions of disapproval by both races, and it seems much simpler for each to stay on his own side of the color-line.

* The authors have had access to several hundred interviews with Negro students of Chicago's high schools, junior colleges, and universities. Many colored students, although attending mixed schools, reported a preference for all-Negro schools because they offer a more satisfying social life. In some of the mixed high schools, Negroes were not welcomed at school dances, and therefore had organized their own clubs to sponsor proms. In a few cases, discrimination against Negroes was practiced in extracurricular activities, especially dramatics and swimming. Negroes on athletic teams stated that they felt uncomfortable because they never knew when the whole team might be embarrassed by opponents who would refuse to accommodate them when they were on tour. It is difficult to make any generalizations about the dominant attitudes. A large proportion of the students were aggressively determined to demand complete integration. A very few colored students preferred to transfer to all-Negro schools. The majority seemed resigned to a certain amount of Jim-Crowism.

The vigor with which many Negroes deny any interest in being friendly with white people, any desire for social relations with them, also reflects annoyance at the widespread charge that Negroes are "pushing" for full social equality. The average Negro does not give social intermingling a second thought unless he is brought face to face with a gratuitous snub, or until he sees the specter being used to limit his civil rights, his economic opportunity, or the expansion of Black Metropolis. Negroes may not agitate for social equality, but they certainly express resentment at being reminded that they can't have it.*

Whether there is some suppressed *active* desire for social acceptance on the part of Negroes is a question that cannot be answered by sociological analysis.† There is certainly no *overt* pressure in that direction. Nevertheless, some psychologists suspect that, beneath the surface, all Negroes desire to be completely accepted and integrated into American life with no barriers of segregation—social or other—erected against them. Such drives, however, must be deeply repressed.‡ An eloquent expression of this view was made in 1944 by Lillian Smith, distinguished white southern novelist and educator, in an article in *The New Republic*, "Addressed to White Liberals." She states:

* In order to preserve their sense of self-respect, whether or not they personally desire association with white people, Negro leaders feel impelled to defend the abstract right of Negroes to be accepted as social equals. Thus the editors of the Baltimore *Afro-American* make their position clear: "Anybody who says he doesn't believe in social equality is an advocate of the Hitler theory of superior and inferior races." A well-known colored lawyer from Midwest Metropolis, writing in the Pittsburgh *Courier*, was caustic in his attack upon conservative Negro leaders: "Shrewd diplomatic colored folks do not always desire to make definite commitments as to their views on this subject. . . . They indulge in double talk. . . . Whatever the indefinable and illusory thing is that we style 'social equality,' all other enlightened people on earth desire it. . . . How can the colored American expect to be a first-class citizen as long as he is regarded as a social leper and an American untouchable?"

† Perhaps the most adequate answer to this question would come from the discipline of psychoanalysis. However, relatively few Negroes have been analyzed and there is no published body of literature to which one can refer. However, a recent article by Dr. Helen V. McLean, "Racial Prejudice," published in the *American Journal of Ortho-psychiatry*, Vol. XIV, No. 34, October, 1944, indicates that author's belief that Negroes are resentful of their humiliation and frustration at the hands of white people. The implication of the article is that Negroes do desire social acceptance and are resentful at not receiving it.

‡ Horace R. Cayton, in an article prepared for the magazine *Twice A Year*, "Frightened Children of Frightened Parents," suggests the manner in which ordinary childhood fears are deepened and intensified in the case of Negro children.

I understand the desperate fear that causes certain Negroes to deny their hunger for things that make men human. I understand also the fear in the white man's heart that makes him more willing to work for specific, short-range goals such as the vote, better jobs for Negroes, than to change his own attitude about himself and the white race. . . . We must break the conspiracy of silence which has held us in a grip so strong that it has become a taboo. We must say why segregation is unendurable to the human spirit. We must somehow find the courage to say it aloud. For, however we rationalize our silence, it is fear that is holding our tongues today.

Since there is no mass demand for social equality defined in terms of segregated cliques, families, clubs, and churches, many conservative Negroes and white people decry any tendency to discuss the issue. There is, however, a growing awareness in Black Metropolis of a fact which thoughtful students have long recognized, and which has been stated clearly by the Swedish economist, Gunnar Myrdal, whose monumental study of Negro-white relations in the United States, *An American Dilemma,* is accepted as definitive: [11]

Social discrimination is powerful as a means of keeping the Negro down in all other respects. In reality it is not possible to isolate a sphere of life and call it "social." There is in fact a "social" angle to all relations. . . . The interrelationships between social status and economic activity are particularly important. . . . As long as Negroes, solely because of their color, are forcibly held in a lower social status, they will be shut out from all middle-class occupations except in their own segregated social world. . . . Social segregation involves a substantial element of discrimination.*

The specter of social equality will no doubt continue to haunt the scene so long as social segregation is forcibly imposed upon Negroes. It becomes a source of tension, however, only when it is actively evoked by white interest groups, or when there is a wide difference of opinion as to what constitutes social equality. An examination of the analysis

* The South has organized Negro-white relations upon the juridical fiction of "separate but equal" accommodations for Negroes. It has been repeatedly demonstrated that segregation in the South is accompanied by inequality of school facilities, of accommodations in public places and on common carriers, and in the areas of the cities where Negroes predominate. Despite this fact, the Supreme Court of the United States has consistently refused to rule that segregation of Negroes is a form of discrimination. In cases involving this question, the Supreme Court never goes beyond a demand that separate accommodations must be "substantially" equal. In the North, too, although in less pronounced form, segregation of Negroes tends to be associated with a high degree of inequality.

below will reveal that there are some things which whites call social equality, but which Negroes do not think of as such. Around these critical foci tension arises. (Note situations marked by asterisk.)

AREAS OF AGREEMENT AND DISAGREEMENT BETWEEN NEGROES AND WHITES AS TO THE MEANING OF SOCIAL EQUALITY

Area of Agreement Between Negroes and Whites	Area of Uncertainty	Area of Disagreement
(No pressure from Negroes against the color-line.)	(Some Negroes exert pressure against the color-line. Some whites resist. Others accept situation as semi-social.)	(General pressure from Negroes who do not interpret these situations as "social," although white people have a tendency to do so.)
1. Intermarriage	* 1. Negro residence throughout the city.	* 1. White-collar employment outside of Black Belt.
2. Membership in white cliques, churches, and social clubs.	* 1. Use of commercial recreational facilities outside of Black Belt.	2. Membership in business and professional associations.
3. Visiting and entertaining across the color-line.	3. Use of sanitary facilities, elevators, etc., in hotels and apartment houses outside of Black Belt.	3. Use of hospital facilities outside of Black Belt and in all city hospitals.
	4. Attendance at social affairs of unions, professional and technical societies, or at place of employment.	* 5. Unrestricted use of beaches and parks throughout the city.
	5. Interracial dancing at affairs listed in (4).	

There is continuous pressure from the Negro side to have white people accept a more restricted definition of social equality—to include only intermarriage, and familial, church, and associational relationships.* Some of the relations that Negroes would define as "non-

* Occasionally a Negro leader will approach the problem the other way around. He will say, "Yes, we *believe* in social equality, but we exclude intermarriage

social," however, are those in which racial attitudes of white people are reinforced by considerations of economic interest or social prestige (as in the situations marked with asterisks). Tension will continue so long as disagreement in the evaluation of these contacts exists.

The next three chapters constitute brief case studies of the forces that keep Negroes segregated and subordinated in Midwest Metropolis. Segregation, as we have pointed out, is fundamentally a reaction against the specter of social equality. It is the way Midwest Metropolis has of saying: "We do not wish to have Negroes in our families, cliques, associations, and churches. They are not our *social* equals."

Social segregation is maintained, in the final analysis, by endogamy—the rule that Negroes must marry Negroes, and whites must marry whites—and by its corollary that when an intermarriage does "accidentally" occur, the child must be automatically classed as a Negro no matter how white his skin color. Chapter 7, "Crossing the Color-Line," describes what happens to that small minority of persons who do intermarry. It suggests the strength of those *informal* social controls among both Negroes and whites which keep the number of such marriages small despite the fact that there are no legal prohibitions against them. The chapter also deals briefly with "passing," a practice by which a few Negroes with white skin and Caucasoid features and hair do cross the color-line.

Almost as rigid as the taboo on intermarriage is the practice of resi-

and intimate social relations from the definition of the term." Thus, when Dr. W. E. B. Du Bois of the NAACP was under fire during the Twenties for advocating social equality, he answered as follows: "We believe that social equality . . . means moral, mental and physical fitness to associate with one's fellowmen. In this sense the *Crisis* believes absolutely in the Social Equality [*sic*] of the Black and White and Yellow races, and it believes, too, that any attempt to deny this equality by law or custom is a blow at Humanity, Religion and Democracy. No sooner is this incontestable statement made, however, than many minds immediately adduce further implications; they say that such a statement and belief implies the right of black folks to force themselves into the private social life of whites and to intermarry with them. This is a forced and illogical definition of social equality. . . . Social equals, even in the narrowest sense of the term, do not have the right to be invited to or attend private receptions or to marry persons who do not wish to marry them. . . . On the other hand every self-respecting person does claim the right to mingle with his fellows if he is invited and to be free from insult or hindrance because of his presence." Dr. Du Bois was thus able to *advocate* social equality without becoming an advocate of intermarriage or of acceptance of Negroes into white cliques, associations, and churches.

dential segregation. In Chapter 8, "The Black Ghetto," an attempt is made to trace the tie-up between the specter of social equality and economic interest that results in the concentration of Negroes within the Black Belt. An understanding of the forces that result in a separate Negro community is essential to an understanding of Part III of this book.

Chapter 9, "The Job Ceiling," examines the mechanisms by which Negroes are subordinated in the economic life of the city, for while segregation is not the rule in industry and commerce, Negroes are prevented from rising, in the mass, above a certain occupational level. Job discrimination, like residential segregation, reflects the specter of social equality as well as fear of the economic competition of Negroes.

It is significant that Negroes exert pressure against the color-line in the reverse order from our presentation. They feel most resentful about the Job Ceiling, are ambivalent about residential segregation, and are generally indifferent to the taboo on intermarriage. These attitudes emerge in the following chapters from materials gathered by participant-observers during the Depression when the economic insecurity of Negroes had intensified their race-consciousness. The Second World War made no change in the order of these demands for equality but increased race-consciousness even more than did the Depression.

CHAPTER 7

Crossing the Color-Line

WHEN A WHITE MAN IN THE SOUTH CASTS A ROVING EYE UPON A LIKELY colored girl, the culture permits him to engage in any type of affair that stops short of marriage, be it flirting, discreet consummation, or concubinage.* For the Negro man who might be foolhardy enough to display a similar interest in women-folk across the color-line there is a standing prescription—the noose. For the white woman, there is social ostracism. The preservation of "the honor and purity of southern womanhood" is the most sacred duty of the white gentleman. Just to make sure that there shall be no accidents, all intermarriage of Negroes and whites is made a criminal offense. Sexual excursions across the color-line must proceed in one direction only, and even these must not be dignified with benefit of clergy or of law.

In Midwest Metropolis, marriage between Negroes and whites is not illegal. Also, clandestine relations occur in both directions. In general, however, both Negroes and whites frown upon those who venture across the color-line. While some defenders of "white supremacy" might welcome the aid of the rope in keeping things straight, violence is rarely visited upon those who do cross the line. Yet Midwest Metropolis most definitely does not approve of intermarriage.

The fear of intermarriage plays a dominant role in keeping Negroes "in their place." † It may be the justification for not hiring Negro men

---

* One of the most popular novels published in 1944, *Strange Fruit,* by Lillian Smith, dealt with some of the complications arising from this old southern custom.

† Closely associated with the fear of intermarriage is fear of "passing." Because some Negroes have enough Caucasian traits to make them look like white, there is always the "danger" that they may cross over into the white society. Both types of situation involve overt acts of crossing the color-line, and are generally resented by the white society. The difference between intermarriage and passing lies in the fact that in the former case it is immediately obvious to the general public that the color-line is being crossed, whereas "passing" is, in its very nature, a surreptitious act.

Curiously, the white community in Midwest Metropolis does not seem to fear

as elevator operators or busboys, or an excuse for residential segregation. The ultimate appeal for the maintenance of the color-line is always the simple, though usually irrelevant question, "Would you want your daughter to marry a Negro?" To many white persons this is the core of the entire race problem.

SEX AND COLOR

Any discussion of intermarriage should be placed within a wider framework of general sex relations. Pre-marital and extra-marital affairs between colored and white people not only are much more frequent than intermarriage, but may be the first steps leading to it.

Lord Bryce, in his famous study of America, remarked, "Whoever examines the records of the past will find that the continued juxtaposition of two races has always been followed either by the disappearance of the weaker or by the intermixture of the two." * Race mixture takes place in Midwest Metropolis—just as it does in Mississippi. In Midwest Metropolis, the forms of miscegenation vary along a continuum ranging from the most casual sexual relations to permanent marriage unions, and from commercial relations devoid of any sentiment to those of great emotional involvement.

It is difficult—in fact, almost impossible—to estimate the amount of miscegenation in a city like Midwest Metropolis. Yet from the interviews conducted for this study it would seem that there was hardly a colored man who did not claim knowledge of some Negro male who

or resent "passing" so much as it does intermarriage, although the former is much more common and involves many more persons. Perhaps this is because passing leaves intact the fundamental principle of segregation, and at the same time provides a method of escape for those who have arrived at a state of biological whiteness which to some extent actually embarrasses the maintenance of racial barriers. Intermarriage, on the other hand, represents a flagrant and obvious breach of those barriers. The fact that it involves relatively few persons does not mitigate the tensions to which its occurrence may give rise.

* James Bryce, *The American Commonwealth,* New York, 1911, p. 532. For concrete data on racial intermixture consult J. A. Rogers, *Sex and Race,* volumes 1-3, Rogers Historical Researches, New York, 1943. Rogers, an industrious free-lance Negro journalist, has compiled three volumes of anecdotes, travelers' tales, excerpts from diaries, abstracts of laws, newspaper items, and pictures dealing with racial mixing throughout the world. Some of his interpretations seem forced, and his use of the sources is often uncritical, but since he presents his documentation, these books form an invaluable source of information on a subject about which there has been a conspiracy of silence.

had had sexual relations with a white woman. Interracial sex experiences were much less frequently reported by Negro women and varied greatly according to social class.* Negro women of the lower class sometimes boasted of "having white men," while middle-class and upper-class women were almost unanimous in denying any such experiences. Thus, a lower-class Negro girl, a semi-prostitute, related her early experiences in the South and her current escapades in Chicago as follows:

"I hadn't had nothing but white men until the Depression came, outside of my husband. I have usually worked around doctors' offices, and as a rule you 'go' with them. When I was in the South, that is all I had. They were the best that the city had, such as judges, justices of the peace, presidents of different railroads, and rich farmers. I wouldn't think of letting a poor sap 'go' with me, for that is when you ruin your reputation, but as long as you deal with rich white men, a soul will never know it. Up here it is hard to find a white man that is in love with you.† I suppose I am lucky, at that [referring to a northern white man with whom she was having an affair], for I didn't know, myself, this would end up like it did; but to my surprise he fell for me in a big way. The only thing I hate is he is not a rich guy. I could even take him away from his wife if I wanted to, but I feel like it would be too much of a sin to take him away from his children. If it was just his wife, I wouldn't care. I would just figure, let the best lady win."

The attitudes expressed by this girl are typical of a fairly large number of women of the disorganized lower class. Although a middle-class girl might be rather promiscuous, only in rare cases would she indulge in, and almost never would she admit to having had, sex relations with white men. Such an admission would disgrace her in the eyes of her associates. It would also seriously depreciate her value in the Negro marriage market; and, of course, there is almost no chance for her to marry a white man.

* Complete descriptions of the various social classes within the Negro community are given in Chapters 19, 20, 21, and 22.

† This expression implies that it is easy to find white men in the South who *are* in love with their Negro paramours. The extent of "permanent sexual relationships involving white men and Negro women" in a Mississippi town has been discussed at some length by Allison Davis and Burleigh and Mary Gardner in *Deep South*, University of Chicago Press, 1941, pp. 33-38. They report and describe several such unions, on a common-law basis, in a state where intermarriage is prohibited by law.

Negro men of all classes were open in discussing their affairs with white women. In Midwest Metropolis, as in most northern cities, there is much more sexual freedom across racial lines than many persons suspect. Flirting on the job between workers—colored and white—is not at all unusual.* Frequently, a white girl will flirt, play, and banter with a Negro lad without self-consciousness, or a second thought, even when she refuses to accept a date. A young packing-house worker relates some of his experiences with white girls on the job:

"I've been working at the stockyards. I was the only colored in a group of white girls. They treated me the same as if I was white. One gave me ice cream and candy. I says to her, 'Why don't you let me take you out sometime and show you around?' She says that she is told that policemen will beat her up if she is caught with colored.† I told her there ain't nothing to that. People would see us together and stare at us. But they wouldn't know who we were. This girl was not prejudiced. She was just afraid. There are a lot of people like that.

---

* Colored men, when they are sure of their ground, will often initiate such flirtations. In general, however, Negro men, even in a northern urban community, are hesitant about flirting with or dating white girls. Men recently from the South sometimes express fear that white women will "trick" them, i.e., voluntarily indulge in flirtation, and then, if observed by other white persons, accuse the Negro men of being the aggressors, or even charge them with attempted rape. Youngsters raised in the North are less likely to exhibit this particular type of fear, but are more apt to be afraid of losing their jobs should a white employer or fellow employees become aware of the flirtations. It is widely believed in Black Metropolis that Negroes have been dropped from employment in several large Chicago hotels and restaurants because they were too friendly with white girl employees. Negro men also occasionally have the experience of misinterpreting the gestures of a white woman, who is simply being playful without any thought of dating, and who draws the color-line sharply if the man takes her behavior too seriously.

† The fear of molestation by the police may have a basis in actual experiences. Between 1938 and 1944, in Chicago, there was ample evidence to indicate that individual policemen sometimes considered it their civic duty to break up mixed couples appearing in public. The authors know of half a dozen cases in which policemen intimidated mixed couples on the street or in cabarets, both within the Black Belt and in white neighborhoods. In one case, a policeman forced the white girl into a squad car, lectured her for "going out with a nigger," and called her a Communist. In another case, the Negro man was threatened with arrest on the charge of contributing to the delinquency of a minor although the girl was 22. These seem to be the acts of individual policemen, undertaken on their own initiative, but they reflect two widespread beliefs about Negro-white couples: (1) the parties are probably Communists, or (2) the white woman is either a prostitute or an innocent victim of a rapacious Negro.

"At the yards, me and another colored boy was coming down a dark hall with a colored and a white girl. He put his arms around the colored girl and I put mine around the white girl. The door opened and the foreman saw us. He didn't say anything. But the matron told the white girl not to have too much to do with Negroes."

Deterrents to Intermarriage: Although there is considerable interracial sexual play, actual sex relations are most frequently either commercial or casual. Only a small proportion of these contacts finally leads to intermarriage. A number of instances were known in which white girls had sexual relations with Negroes but would not appear with them publicly or marry them. And, of course, this pattern of secrecy is the rule when white men have relations with Negro women.*

When flirtation arises between a Negro and a white person in Midwest Metropolis—as it easily does, especially where the individuals are working together—the casual play may grow into romantic love. There then comes a time when the couple must face the necessity either of marrying, with all of the disadvantages which might accrue to both parties, or of breaking off the affair. This may involve an emotional crisis, for there are pressures in the Negro as well as the white society against intermarriage. The Negro community, in response to the prejudices of whites and with the rise of "race pride," has developed a reciprocal feeling of disapproval which in its extreme form borders on abhorrence. Negro women, for reasons which will be made clear later, are likely to be particularly caustic, as in the following interview statements:

"I don't think that people should intermarry. I feel that there are enough people in our own race to marry without going out of the race for husbands and wives. People get along better when they marry their own race."

* The clandestine nature of most interracial sex relations in both the North and the South indicates the strength of social controls over individual behavior. There are undoubtedly scores of individuals on both sides of the color-line who have no feelings of revulsion against such relations, and who in varying degrees are attracted toward one another. But if they are to maintain the social approval of their associates, they cannot be seen publicly associating with a person of the opposite sex and race in a situation that carries sexual overtones. Few white girls in Midwest Metropolis would be willing to risk the contumely or actual ostracism that might be visited upon them if they were accused of having intimate relations with Negro men.

"I think intermarriage is degrading to both races. If a white girl marries a colored man, her people won't open their door to him, like his people will accept her. Then, too, a white woman who is married to a Negro will never be accepted by all of his friends. In fact, the man himself will lose some of his friends."

"Why should Negro men marry white women? White men don't want to marry us. They just *use* us when they can."

There is also a widespread tendency for Negroes to deny any opposition to intermarriage on principle, but to express skepticism of the motive of a white person who marries a Negro. Thus, another woman states:

"I'm not against intermarriages, and I think everyone should satisfy themselves. But here is the thing I can't understand. Why, if they look down on us as inferior, will they come out of their race with all the superior advantages and marry one of us? I don't think the better class of white people and the better class of Negroes will seek inter-marriage."

A few—a very few—Negro women, and a larger proportion of men, will make comments like the following:

"I think it is all right, because social equality will exist some day. This old idea must be done away with that people should just marry their own race."

Certainly the thought of the antagonisms they will meet from members of both groups plays an important role in preventing many inter-racial marriages and makes very apprehensive those who do decide to marry. A young Negro factory worker related this story, replete with rationalizations of his fears, and revealing the normal reactions of a young fellow who didn't want to "get hooked."

"I went with a white girl for five years. She was Polish, and very nice; she was really a swell kid. She wanted me to marry her, but I like brown-skinned girls. Her name was Mamie. We were both working at the same factory on Halsted Street, and she worked right across from me. The first week I was there I noticed her staring at me every time I looked up. I looked off whenever I saw her looking at me. One day after I had been there about two weeks she said that she liked the materials I gave her to work on because they were fixed so well. Then later that day she asked if I ever went any place for pleasure, and if so, she would like for me to take her out sometime, if I would. Just like that, no stammering or anything. One thing I can say about white girls is that they are outspoken.* Then we began to go out together all the time.

"But one night when we were alone, she asked me if I would marry a girl if the girl was in love with me. I told her, 'Yes, if I was in love with the girl.' Then she waited a long time and asked me if I would marry her if something should happen to her. So I said, 'Yes—if it should.' She asked me if I wanted her to be a girl of bad reputation, and I told her, 'No,' and that if I had to marry her I would. She told me she loved me and wanted to marry me, and wanted me to come and tell her father that we were to be married. Now, I knew that would only start trouble, and anyway, I didn't care enough for her to marry her.

"Well, for about two weeks I didn't go out with her, and avoided her as much as possible. Then, as things happened, my part of the work was discontinued. So I didn't go back out there. The other fellows who went with the other two white girls still worked there, and Mamie used to send me messages by them. She continued it for about two weeks, and then she came over to my house. She 'pitched a fog' (made a scene). She raved about the fact that I didn't love her and that I played a dirty trick on her. I finally quieted her down and explained things to her.

"I didn't tell her that I wouldn't marry her because she was white. I just said I didn't go around her any more because I didn't think we should get married; because sometimes she would want to go places I couldn't go, and that after a while she would get tired of my company, and that I thought after a few months she would find someone she really cared for and would marry him and it would be better for

* There is a widespread folk belief among Negro men that if white women are interested in a Negro man they will be both direct and persistent about the matter. This is partly a sort of defensive reaction, an unconscious assertion by Negro men that they do not pursue white women; that the women are always the aggressors. There are other widespread beliefs, too—that if a white woman really loves a Negro man, she will exhibit an unusual intensity of passion; that "opposites attract"; that foreign white women prefer Negroes to American white men. That at least one of these myths is occasionally shared by white women is suggested by a note which a young white man showed one of the authors, from a girl he was courting. The girl, apparently teasing him, wrote, "A nice colored fellow sat across from me on the 'El,' and winked at me. What would you say if I'd dated him? Opposites attract each other, you know."

her future. She said she was willing to go any place that I wanted to and would work with me, if I would only marry her. But I couldn't do that. We finally drifted apart, and although that has been over six years ago, she was still asking about me the first of this year. This is the way I feel about it. If anyone else wants to marry out of their race—that is, if they are really in love—I say go ahead and follow your love. But personally, I wouldn't marry a white girl because I can't forget what the white people have done to my race. I was born in the South and I have seen them do awful things to women and men of our race." *

The most important deterrent and cause for apprehension, however, is the attitude of close friends and relatives. A white woman who was a domestic in a white family recalled the pressure that was put on her by her employers when it was discovered that she was going to marry a Negro who worked for the same family:

"My employer saw the notice about the marriage license in the *Daily News*. He told me he had seen it and asked if it was true. I was feeling nervous and told him it was true. He said, 'You are new here. You don't know what it is like here. Do you know what will happen if you marry this man? You will be ostracized. No one will want to have anything to do with you.' I said, 'I'm going to do it.' He said, 'You have a friend in Texas. I'll get you a ticket and you can go there till it blows over.' He tried to get me to go, but I didn't."

During the period of courtship it is difficult for mixed couples to meet openly, and although the validity of Negro-white marriage is established by state law in Illinois, couples sometimes encounter difficulty both in obtaining a marriage license and in finding a person to perform the marriage ceremony.†

It Does Happen Here: In spite of the fact that intermarriages are relatively infrequent, and that in all probability the rate has been de-

---

* The authors were acquainted with a Negro man, married to a Polish girl, who occasionally beat her when drunk. Both partners reported that when this happened, he would also curse her for all of the ills which whites had visited upon Negroes, implying that this justified his behavior in beating her.

† Some couples report that they were refused licenses in Chicago. But the authors know of at least one case within the last three years in which both partners appeared at the City Hall, and were granted a license without question. The judge who performs marriages there, however, refused to marry the couple, and expressed disapproval in a very obvious manner.

clining since the beginning of the present century, a student at the University of Chicago who made a study of Negro-white marriages in Midwest Metropolis in 1938 was able to locate 188 mixed families. He reported that he knew of an equal number of couples who either could not be located, or refused to grant interviews.*

In 147 of these 188 cases of intermarriage, the Negro partner was the husband. That so few white men marry Negro women may be partly accounted for by the fact that such marriages endanger the economic position of the white wage-earner even more than that of the Negro. Furthermore, the Negro women most likely to attract white men are at a premium in the Negro community. Also, since it is the male partner who plays the more aggressive role in contracting marriage, and since white women are "forbidden fruit" to Negro men, it is not surprising that more Negro men than white marry across the color-line. It is this one-sided aspect of intermarriage that irks Negro women.†

* This study, "Negro-White Marriages in Chicago," by Robert Roberts, was prepared as a master's thesis from materials gathered for the Cayton-Warner Research. Roberts's field notes and interviews indicate that in many cases where he had conclusive evidence that he had found an intermarried couple, the white partner insisted upon being called a Negro, and denied any identity with the white race. In other situations, the door was simply slammed in his face by couples who refused to be interviewed. It was his opinion that there were perhaps several hundred other couples who were living in common-law. Almost all of the 188 families included in this study granted extensive interviews and talked freely about the circumstances leading up to their marriage, as well as their experiences since marriage. The authors have supplemented the Roberts interviews with first-hand knowledge of eight or nine cases of intermarriage. No statistics by race of applicants for marriage licenses are kept in Chicago. Roberts interviewed officials at the marriage license bureau, and it was the impression there that less than three per cent of the colored bridegrooms married white women, and that an even smaller percentage of colored women married white men. There was general agreement that the proportion had declined during the last thirty years. Two students of interracial marriages, George Schuyler and J. A. Rogers, reported over a thousand mixed couples in Chicago during the Twenties.

† One of the authors overheard a discussion in 1939 among some Negro Communists in which the whole question of intermarriage was being aired. A young colored Communist woman was protesting because a prominent Negro artist had married a white woman. She was rebuked by her husband for uttering sentiments unbecoming to a Communist Party member, and was threatened with "party discipline" for giving vent to "nationalistic deviations." In self-defense, she flashed back with the charge that the white men in the Communist Party seldom married colored women, and that they should therefore be accused of "white chauvinism." Her critics were disconcerted, for no one could name a single male Communist in Midwest Metropolis who was married to a colored

Proportionately fewer Negroes of high social status, except intellectuals and "Bohemians," marry white persons. Both the social controls of the Negro community, which make it difficult for a person occupying a responsible position to make such a break, and the satisfactions that come with being at the apex of a social group (even though it is a subordinate one) deter such persons. Among "Bohemians" and intellectuals, however, intermarriages are tolerated by the Negro group just as eccentric behavior by their white counterparts is tolerated by the general society. But a Negro professional man, businessman, or politician would, under ordinary circumstances, endanger his position of leadership and responsibility by marrying a white woman, regardless of her status.*

There is practically no intermarriage within the present-day Negro

girl, although there were a number of cases in which Negro men had married white women. The general community pattern prevailed even within this radical sect. A very intelligent white Communist man sought to explain the matter privately to one of the authors by observing that attractive colored girls, on the whole, steered clear of the Party, and moreover, white men hesitated to make overtures to colored girls in the Party, because all colored girls seemed distrustful of any white man's sincerity.

George Schuyler, in a Haldeman-Julius Little Blue Book, *Racial Intermarriage in the United States,* claims that of 1,100 mixed marriages reported in Cleveland, 60 per cent were of white men to Negro women, while in New York and Chicago only a fifth of the intermarriages were of this type. It is probable that a surplus of foreign-born men at some period of Cleveland's history accounts for the difference.

* Prominent Negroes married to white women are always open to the charge that they have "deserted the race." There are no "respectable" Negro leaders in Midwest Metropolis who have white wives. One very prominent man was married to a very light woman and it was widely believed that she was white; but the couple always denied this.

Communist leaders report that within their circles, although intermarriages are not frowned upon, they have observed Negro women, upon some occasions, voting against measures proposed by certain Negroes who had white wives. It was difficult not to suspect that this behavior was either a conscious or unconscious expression of disapproval of interracial marriage. In northern urban areas other than Midwest Metropolis, there are isolated Negro community leaders who have not forfeited their position of leadership by acquiring white wives, but such cases are very rare. Frederick Douglass, the famous abolitionist leader, married a prominent and wealthy white woman after the death of his first wife, who was colored. He was widely criticized but answered his critics with a jocular reference to his own illegitimate infusion of white blood: "I spent the first half of my life with my mother's people. I'm spending the second half with my father's people." In general, it may be observed that when Negro leaders married to white women have found it possible to retain their positions of influence, it has been in spite of their marriage; a white wife never strengthens their position *vis-à-vis* Negroes.

middle class, which is even more conservative than its white counterpart. Members of the Negro middle class have fewer social contacts with, and opportunities for meeting, white people than do lower-class or upper-class Negroes. In most instances their self-contained world gives them enough satisfaction so that they have scant interest in the world of white society, and little tolerance for those who have. The same is true, though to a lesser degree, of the respectable lower class. Before the Great Migration, however, intermarriages were more frequent among ordinary, relatively stable, working-class individuals, particularly servants. Some of these families are still intact, and most of their children and grandchildren, now adults, have merged with the general Negro community.

There are, however, two groups in the general society which not only tolerate but, by their social philosophies, tend to encourage intermarriage. One is the Bahai movement, a religious group, while the other is made up of "left-wingers"—various groups of Communists, Socialists and other political radicals.

If not identified with one of these deviant groups, the white partner in a Negro-white marriage is not infrequently a foreign-born person, who is not completely assimilated into American culture and does not fully realize the implications of intermarriage or did not at the time that the marriage occurred. A case in point is that of an Italian, whose Negro wife described their courtship as follows:

"The white people I worked for were Italian and I met my husband through them. He hadn't been here in this country very long and didn't speak very good English. We started going out together, and in a short time he asked me if I would marry him. He said he wanted me to meet his family. I was surprised! My parents were dead, so I wrote and asked my uncle what to do. He said it was okay, and for me to quit worrying.

"Then I went over to my husband's house to meet his family. They were drinking wine and eating spaghetti, and everybody was talking in Italian. His dad told me that he didn't care what color I was so long as I was a good woman. He then told me that he wanted me to marry his son. Al, my husband, said we could get married in the City Hall; we didn't need to be married in the Catholic Church. So we were."

Statistical data on the occupations of Negroes and white people who intermarry are very scarce. There are none for Chicago, and only for Boston is such information available over a period of years. The Boston data, however, may provide some insight into the situation in Midwest Metropolis. The record shows that, in Boston, Negro-white marriages, more frequently than others, take place between persons of differing occupational levels. The white partners, both men and women, are, on the average, in lower occupational levels than the white population as a whole. Negro husbands of white women, on the other hand, are generally higher in the scale than the average Negro and often higher than their wives. Among the Negro brides of interracial marriages, however, unskilled workers (including domestic servants) predominate.

In Midwest Metropolis, the most common initial contacts leading to intermarriage were found to be of an occupational character. Often couples met while serving as chauffeur and maid for the same household, as cook and waitress in a restaurant, or as fellow-workers in a factory. Others became acquainted as neighbors, living in the same district, or met through a common friend. Very few mixed marriages resulted from contacts made in schools or religious organizations. Even the Bahai movement brought together only two of the intermarried couples interviewed, although it is the authors' belief that there have been additional marriages among the Bahai group, and certainly there have been couples who, after marriage, have turned to this movement to find the fellowship denied them by the society in general. Association in "left-wing" political groups has been somewhat more productive of interracial marriage, but most intermarried couples now living in Midwest Metropolis, despite popular belief, are not affiliated with radical groups.

The Trials of the Intermarried: Intermarried couples have their problems. One of the primary difficulties is keeping a job, and here both partners usually find (or feel) it necessary to conceal their marriage from white employers. Most of the intermarried couples interviewed talked rather freely about themselves, but when the subject of their employment arose, they did not like to give any information. "That's one subject we're both reticent about, because he would lose his job as soon as I would lose mine if they found out that his wife is white," a wife remarked. "Yes," the husband said, "I am sure of that." The wife continued:

"I stayed home from May to August when he was sick. I couldn't let it be known that I was his wife. I was supposed to be in New York.

I had to be careful that nobody from the office saw me while I was supposed to be away. I had to step about the house quietly, because the people from his [railroad] line came to visit him. I had a colored woman here and I went to the kitchen when visitors came. We have to be careful because we're buying our home and can't afford to lose our jobs. If we had enough money to be independent, we wouldn't care who knew we were married."

Another white office worker, asked if she associated with the girls from her office since her marriage to a Negro, answered: "I go out with them all the time. They don't come here because they think I'm rooming. Occasionally I entertain people from the office on the North Side, at the home of a white friend."

Fear of economic reprisal seems least pronounced among civil service employees, and within recent years a few interracial couples seem to have worked out a satisfactory adjustment in this type of employment without the necessity of concealing their marriages. In one of these cases, both partners (a white man and a colored girl) had previously been fired from the same private social agency when they were married, but the husband subsequently acquired a good Federal civil service appointment. If one of the partners to an interracial marriage has an independent business, there is even more security. Perhaps the two Chicago interracial couples most secure financially were one in which the white husband of a Negro girl was a wealthy real estate operator, and another in which the Negro husband of a white wife was a labor leader with a firm grip on his union. In some northern communities, Negro physicians seem to be among those best able to escape economic reprisals for a mixed marriage.

Mixed couples also often experience great difficulty in securing a place to live. In most cases, except where the Negro partner is light enough to pass, it is necessary for them to live in a Negro community. The exceptions to this rule seem to be rather old, established mixed couples who have been living in mixed Negro-white neighborhoods for many years. Such families report little opposition from neighbors who have known them over a long period of time. They may experience difficulty, however, if the composition of the community changes. Within the Negro community, many of the better apartment houses and hotels will not rent to intermarried couples for fear that they are not really married, and therefore are not "respectable." Certain hotels within the Negro community have the reputation of catering to common-law mixed couples and to white prostitutes and their Negro pimps. "Respectable" couples are continually complaining that the existence of such establishments makes it hard for them to convince rental agents and neighbors that they are legally wedded and law-abiding.* One wife reported that when she first moved into the Black Belt, she found notes in her mailbox saying, "We don't want poor white trash in this neighborhood." She remarked, "At first I was worried, but then I thought that I wasn't trash and shouldn't be concerned. I ignored the notes after that."

(Of course, housing is at a premium in the Negro community and any family has difficulty in obtaining living quarters. At most, intermarried couples are only especially disadvantaged.)

Even when they are able to keep their jobs and find suitable homes, intermarried couples suffer in a greater or lesser degree from social ostracism. Not only society in general but also their close friends and relatives usually disapprove of their marriage. To avoid injuring the feelings and social standing of his family, the white partner often commits "sociological suicide" and buries himself in the black community. In other cases, it is only years after the marriage that he or she will inform parents or other close relatives. One woman said: "I may tell the family some day. I'm not in a hurry. I have two sisters working in Chicago. They don't know about it. They don't know where I am." Another woman told her relatives:

"Some of my sisters and some of my brothers disapproved, but they still wrote and visited me. My other relatives don't approve at all. I have a brother in St. Louis who is very good to me. However, he doesn't approve of my marriage and is ashamed for people to know that his sister is married to a colored man."

On the other hand, a Negro who met his white wife at a university

---

* A recently married mixed couple experienced some trouble in finding accommodations. Yet their experience reveals the contradictory and unpredictable nature of attitudes in Midwest Metropolis. They went to the rental office of an exclusive apartment in the Black Belt and apologetically announced that they were "mixed but respectable." The rental agent, a white woman, said: "Oh, that's all right. We have five mixed couples in here and they're all fine people. At first the owner didn't want mixed couples because he thought it would ruin the reputation of the building. But I've picked some fine people." Since accommodations in this building were not suitable, they finally rented an apartment from a white Latvian couple marooned in a Negro neighborhood, and subsequently sustained neighborly relations both with this couple and with Negroes living in the building.

in Midwest Metropolis reported that he sustains friendly relations with the girl's six sisters and brothers (and the sisters- and brothers-in-law), all of whom were college students, and natives of a Midwestern city. One of the sisters, although friendly, at first seemed embarrassed by her sister's choice of a husband. The source of her difficulty, as she frankly stated, was her own boy-friend, concerning whose attitudes on race she was very uncertain. She subsequently married another man (an easterner) who apparently was without racial prejudice, and the former embarrassment seemed to disappear. The parents, in this case, were moderately well-to-do, and "liberal" in their general socio-political orientation. But the father, in addition to whatever personal objections he may have had, was probably irritated by his daughter's marriage to a Negro because his job depended somewhat upon the goodwill of numerous white southerners. The mother, however, took the marriage in her stride, accepted the Negro man as a son-in-law (although she had not seen him), and indicated by her letters that she intended to play the role of "approving parent." About two years after the marriage, she met the Negro who had married her daughter, and surprised him by the matter-of-fact manner in which she acted. This is an atypical case, but indicates the flexibility of the social structure in Midwest Metropolis. The ironic twist to this story is that the Negro man's mother, who lived in a small southern town, was seriously per-turbed by the marriage, because she feared the social disapproval of acquaintances who might accuse her son of "deserting the race," and the possible hostility of local whites should they discover what her son had done.

The reaction to intermarriage in lower-class white families is some-times very violent. The following conversation took place between two white men who knew of two white girls who had married Negroes:

"Are the girls' people still living?"

"Sure, but they are barred from their parents' home. Last summer one of the relations died and Willie [the girls' brother] said he would kill the nigger-lovers if they dared show their faces around. They didn't show up at the wake or at the funeral, neither."

"Do you think Willie would really start trouble if they wanted to pay their parents a visit?"

"Christ, yes. Whenever he gets a couple of shots under his belt he goes out looking for any nigger. As soon as he spots one it means trouble. He got cut up about fifteen different times, but he just keeps on looking for trouble. Some day he will get a good cutting and he will learn his lesson."

"I wonder if the parents are the same way about the thing that Willie is?"

"I don't know, but they are ashamed for what the girls done. Once the father was going to get them arrested, but he figured that if one of the newspapers got hold of the story it would be in print and everybody would know about it then, so he just disowned them and let it go at that.

"Ethel was quiet and good-looking and she was well built. She could of got herself some nice white fellow if she wanted to, but I suppose that after she got in with her sister's crowd, they went on parties with colored people, and then she teamed up with one of them. You know, that thing called love is great. But I don't think I ever could marry a boogie [Negro]."

It is ordinarily difficult for the white partner in an interracial marriage to maintain steady friendships with other white people. A white woman married to a Negro related this:

"I still have a dear friend that works downtown. She doesn't ever come to see me since I was married, but she always calls me and whenever I am downtown I go in and see her. You know how they feel toward me. They look at my husband as some kind of beast. He has made me a better husband than most of theirs have."

"Interracial couples have to watch out for themselves," commented another woman. "If they are in trouble, they can't count on help from anybody but themselves."

One of the most annoying problems that intermarried couples must face is that the white woman (for the white partner is usually a woman) will not be considered respectable by Negroes or whites. Nearly all couples interviewed expressed fear of such censure. Even women who had been married for years and had raised families still felt defensive about this prevalent attitude.* One woman, quite ad-

---

* In one case, a white mother had raised her three colored children in a mixed neighborhood without difficulty. One day she was walking down the street with her teen-age son, and passed a drugstore, before which a white crowd was congregated. Someone in the crowd yelled, "Now just look at that nigger walking down the street with that old beat-out whore." The woman was so shocked that she went home and cried. It was the first time, so she reports, that she became really aware of the "vice" label sometimes placed upon mixed couples who appear on the streets of Midwest Metropolis.

vanced in years, stated: "The colored don't like white women married to colored men. They say they are white trash. My sons won't let anybody say that about their mother." A young Negro girl coming to the defense of the white wife in an interracial marriage, whom she knew, revealed this general opinion:

"I knew a white lady who was married to a colored man. They owned their own home and he had a business. They had three girls and one of the girls and I were pals. I was in their home a great deal. I called her 'Mother,' and she was a wonderful woman. It makes me mad when I hear anyone say, 'When you see a white person marry in the Negro race, they are poor white trash.' I know 'Mother' wasn't any trash."

The widespread feeling that a white person who marries a Negro is necessarily of lower social status has some basis in reality. It also reflects the fact that Negroes (unconsciously) accept their assigned status as "inferiors." They find it hard to conceive of a "sane" or "decent" white person giving up higher status to marry a Negro. It indicates, too, a reciprocal and defensive "racial prejudice" on the part of Negroes.

Compensations of the Intermarried: In the face of so many disadvantages, how then do intermarried couples find their existence endurable? How do they justify their behavior to themselves and others? In what social milieu do they move?

The peculiar social position of intermarried couples in Chicago at one time led to their banding together to form the Manasseh Club. This club had a motto—"Equal Rights for All"—which suggests that the members sought a supporting ideology. The original Manasseh Club seems to have been founded in Milwaukee some time after the turn of the century, and shortly thereafter a branch was established in Midwest Metropolis. The members of the Manasseh Club were stable, working-class couples, who scrutinized all new candidates for membership carefully, in order to bar common-law unions and shady characters. The group was organized as a fraternal benefit society, owned a cemetery plot and had elaborate initiation and burial rituals. The organization engaged in many social activities, including an annual picnic and dance. By 1910 it had become an established part of the associational complex in the Negro community. Its annual ball, presented at the Eighth Regiment Armory, was one of the high spots of the social season. The club disintegrated in the late Twenties, but the surviving members still retain a measure of informal solidarity.*

The existence of such a club indicates that before the Great Migration, mixed couples, although not ostracized by Negroes, felt themselves to be sufficiently unusual to need some sort of mutual psychological reinforcement. They elevated intermarriage into a virtue, and the Negro community, while not accepting this valuation of their behavior, definitely did not consider them an undesirable group. One Old Settler, when asked why such a club existed, remarked: "As for the Manasseh Club, I don't know why, but they kept to themselves. I don't know if it was them or us. Our family, I know, had no prejudice. But they had their own affairs and dances."

A former member described certain service activities of the club:

"The men looked out to see if there were any Manasseh couples who needed help. The men looked up interracial couples to see if they were in any kind of need. During this Depression, sometimes we helped them get on relief. If any baby needed milk, we'd see that it got milk. If any children needed clothes to go to school, we'd see that they were clothed. We took up a collection and turned it over to families in need. I was secretary when the club broke up."

The Manasseh Club is no longer in existence; perhaps, indeed, its potential role has become less important. In recent years there has been a greater tolerance of interracial association among intellectuals, artists, and professional persons in the field of civil service, both Negro and white. Intermarried couples can find a circle of friends among these tolerant groups. Within recent years, too, the Bahai and Communist movements, advocating complete racial equality, including intermarriage, have attained some slight, though appreciable, influence. By identifying themselves with such groups and embracing their doctrines, intermarried couples not only find a suitable social milieu, but also

---

* The club took its name from Manasseh, who, according to a Biblical story, was the son of Joseph, the Hebrew, and Asenath, the daughter of an Egyptian priest, Poti-pherah (Genesis 41:44-52). Manasseh members were especially solicitous about their reputations during the period of the Great Migration when illicit miscegenation was apparently widespread and all mixed couples were suspect. (See Rogers, *op. cit.*, volume II, p. 288. The author claims that "a great wave of miscegenation swept that town [Chicago] in the early fall of 1917." He made first-hand investigations of many black and tan cabarets, buffet flats and resorts in order to document this claim.)

gain a *raison d'être* and a philosophic justification for their behavior. In fact, the social pressures against intermarriage are so severe that those who have violated the taboo invariably seem to find it necessary to develop counter-rationalizations to those contained within the dominant mores, even when they do not embrace philosophies that justify or exalt their position. For instance, a rather unsophisticated white wife of an interracial marriage said:

"I don't see why people should make any distinction between white and colored. A black and a white horse together look plenty good to me. I don't see any difference with people. It's just an opinion that has been handed down. A lot of people think in their hearts that intermarriage is all right, but they haven't the courage to express themselves before the public."

"No," declared another white wife, appealing to religion for her justification, "color doesn't mean a hill of beans to me. God made us all. I don't care about color. Some people think I'm crazy, but when they get to glory, they'll see there's no color there."

A third said, defensively: "My child looks about as good as any child on the street, black or white. So what's wrong if a person chooses a colored man as a husband? Had I married a Jew, a Dago, or some other nationality, not a word would have been said. But as soon as you take on a colored man, the world begins to think you're insane, or else low-class."

Some Negroes justify intermarriages on the basis of the sexual behavior of white men toward Negro women:

"A white man doesn't want colored to have his woman, but he will go with anybody he wants to. I am speaking of the South now. It was the white man who broke the colored race. He was the first to mix with colored women." (I.e., "turn about is fair-play.")

Some intermarried persons think of themselves as crusaders in solving a social problem or in working toward a new society. A woman who was deeply religious said:

"I think that interracial marriage will solve a lot of our problems. I think the relations between the races will be improved by interracial marriages. The right sort of marriages, I mean, because if they are interracially married, people learn to live better than other couples."

The World of the Intermarried: Many of the older intermarried couples live in the past, romanticizing the pre-Migration days when the Manasseh Club was a respected institution and when "the inter-racials" cut quite a figure in the community. Most of them have raised their families in an atmosphere of middle-class respectability, and are now spending their declining years quietly among a small circle of friends from the defunct Manasseh society, their immediate neighbors, or the members of their churches.

The new crop of mixed couples falls into four broad groups: (1) the intellectuals and "Bohemians," (2) the religious and political radicals, (3) the "sporting world," and (4) the stable middle class. In the last group are fewer than a dozen couples, who live a rather normal exist-ence. Typical of these is a Negro woman married to a white man, both of whom attend fraternity and sorority dances in the Negro community, have a small circle of friends (of equivalent social status), and are rais-ing a family. The husband is a civil service employee in the profes-sional category. Within the "sporting world" are one or two well-known, moderately wealthy couples, and a larger number of rather "shady" individuals. Stresses and strains are perhaps least pronounced within this group, which exists upon the fringes of "respectable" society anyway, and whose members derive their prestige from within their own closed circle. The intellectuals and "Bohemians," too, exist in a milieu in which people who are different and individualistic often gain prestige rather than win disapproval. The status of mixed couples within Communist circles fluctuates somewhat with the shifts of the party line. In the early days of the Depression, there was probably encouragement of intermarriage, for then the Communist Party was emphasizing revolutionary action. With the elaboration of the Popular Front ideology, more stress was placed upon conformity to the general mores. Mixed couples still find a congenial atmosphere within left-wing circles, but there is a definite feeling that prominent Communists would do well for political reasons to avoid intermarriage, since it might reduce their influence among both those Negroes and those whites whose confidence has yet to be won. The Bahai religious move-ment, however, not only sanctions but encourages intermarriage, to the end that amalgamation may occur, and, in time, a "cosmic race" emerge.*

* Miscegenation among musicians and stage people is perhaps as widespread as among any social types in Midwest Metropolis (as in other northern communi-ties). Formal intermarriage is virtually non-existent, however. People with their careers on stage or screen at stake cannot afford to risk alienating the

The following case has been selected as illustrating how a mixed couple which begins as an ordinary middle-class family may be attracted to a group such as Bahai, to obtain social reassurance amid the vicissitudes of a world that can be rather rough on the intermarried.

Mr. and Mrs. Brown live in a new two-story brick building in one of the better Negro residential districts. Their house is very attractively furnished, and the whole atmosphere is one of middle-class respectability. Mrs. Brown works in a downtown office in a supervisory position. Her husband is a railroad waiter. Their combined income makes it possible for them to maintain a standard of living comparable to that of most middle-class white couples. They are about forty years of age, and have been married for about twenty years.

Mr. Brown was born in Kentucky, the son of one of the wealthiest farmers in that section of the state. Both of his parents had been slaves. He has Negroid hair and light brown skin. Probably he has as much white as colored blood. He went through prep school, and then attended a small Negro college for a time. Later he came to Chicago, and there met his future wife. They became acquainted through a Negro girl who was passing for white in the office in which Mrs. Brown worked. After the two young women had been intimate friends for some time, the Negro girl told Mrs. Brown her secret, and invited her to her home. At that time, Mrs. Brown was engaged to a white man who lived on the North Side in Chicago. Mrs. Brown said: "When I went to this girl's home, Mr. Brown was often there. I don't know what attracted us to each other, but music was one common bond. After I had seen Mr. Brown for some time at this girl's house, we became very fond of each other. We decided not to see each other any more, and didn't for four months. But after my brother left town, we did see each other again and finally married."

One of the first problems that faced Mrs. Brown was informing her relatives of her marriage. "I was married three months before I decided to tell my sister," she recalled. "On that day we saw a hard-looking blonde woman with a dark Negro. My sister remarked, 'Isn't that terrible?' I didn't tell her of my marriage then, as I had planned, but I told her a week later. She said, 'Sis, are you happy with him?'

public by having a mixed "affair" formalized. Persons in the theatrical world have stated that they feel the American public will tolerate rumors and gossip about the interracial "affairs" of their stars, but couldn't "take" a bona fide marriage.

I told her that we were very happy together, and she said, 'That's all that matters.' "

Mrs. Brown did not, however, tell her other relatives of her marriage for a long time—not until it became necessary for her to support them:

"I rented an apartment for them on University Avenue [in a white neighborhood]. That's when I told my mother about my marriage. But I didn't tell my brother, even then. For a while I was the only one that was working in the family, and it became necessary for my mother, sister, and her three children to live with us. My sister didn't like it because the baby used to climb all over Mr. Brown, but she got over it after she had gotten to know him. My brother, who was in the Army, disapproved strongly of my marriage when he found out about it. He was in the Philippines and I know that while he was there he lived with a Filipino woman. Yet he thought it was terrible that I married a Negro. He said it was terrible, but he sent my husband and me cards on Christmas and on our birthdays. I told my sister that if she saw him, she should tell him I thought it was terrible that he lived with a native woman without marrying her, and then left her heartbroken when he returned to America. He said later that he would like to see me six feet underground. I wrote him a letter and told him that I still loved him, no matter what he thought. Then I told Mother never to mention me to him, as if I were dead.

"About two years later my brother 'phoned. I asked him to come over and he came. I put him and Mr. Brown together in the parlor. They talked and became acquainted. Mr. Brown told him that I was not supporting him, that he had always worked, and that I was working because I wanted to. My brother saw that my husband was not a bad fellow. For a year and a half after that, until he left town, he didn't miss a Sunday with us."

A major problem which Mrs. Brown faced from the first was the problem of keeping her job. She did not tell any of the office people about her marriage, and was constantly in fear of being discovered. A number of embarrassing incidents occurred, and she tells how she handled them:

"One day my husband called to drive me home from work. Just as he was about to start the car, I saw my boss. I told my husband to stop and asked my boss if he was going to the station I was going to. I was in the back seat and Mr. Brown was in the front. I introduced Mr. Brown to my boss, but didn't say who he was.

"Another time my husband was teaching me how to drive the car. I must have been talking about something intimate because we were both laughing. We were both sitting in the front seat. One of our salesmen drove right up next to our car and saw me. I told Mr. Brown to stop. I talked with the salesman and told him I was trying to learn to drive, but wasn't having much success. I always make it a point to stop and talk whenever I am with my husband and someone I know from the office sees us, else they might wonder what we are doing together and tell others what they have seen."

The Browns assert that this subterfuge is carried on only for economic reasons, for both feel that they would lose their positions if it were known that they were married. "We have to be very careful in going out," they said. "We have a car and go together often. The only thing that bothers us is that we can't introduce each other as husband and wife." Outside of Chicago, where there is no fear of detection, they have made many trips, including several cross-country expeditions, and while on these, they ate in white restaurants and stayed in white hotels. "If Mr. Brown's skin were a little lighter," remarked his wife, "we could go anywhere together."

In summarizing her attitude toward interracial marriage Mrs. Brown said:

"I think that anyone is foolish to plunge headlong into an interracial marriage without careful consideration. My sister married a Negro she had met in our home. We were all opposed to it for it was a foolish marriage. I wouldn't have wanted my sister to marry that man if he had been white, because he wasn't at all worth while, but it makes it even worse to marry a man like that who is colored. If I weren't married to a Negro and had a daughter, I wouldn't like her to make a point of intermarriage. I wouldn't want her to marry just *any* colored man."

Although the Browns have no children, they have these observations to offer about the offspring of intermarriage:

"Don't you think the children of interracial marriages are finer people than most people? I think they are generally more intelligent than either white or colored. I think the white race needs a little mixture of the Negro. The Negro is more carefree and easy-going than the white person, and the whites can use some of this characteristic."

Mrs. Brown continued:

"Don't you think that, if a good friend of a white person married a Negro, that person would think more of colored people? They would think that some colored people would be worth while or their friend would not have married one. I know one girl at the office whom I finally told of my marriage. She didn't like colored people and thought interracial marriage was terrible. Since then she has come to my house and met Mr. Brown, and she thinks he is a fine man."

Mrs. Brown does not, however, minimize the difficulties involved in interracial marriage:

"If you do make an interracial marriage, you have to think a lot of each other. We like each other enough to forget the world. The high-class colored person doesn't care to mix with white. Many people have the idea that any colored man would like to marry a white woman. That isn't true."

The majority of the Browns' friends are white and are connected with the Bahai group. It is with these people that they spend most of their leisure time:

"We go to the Bahai meeting as often as we can. I'd say we go three or four times a month. We drive to the temple in Winnetka every Sunday in the summer and go to the downtown meeting twice a month. We go to their homes and they come to ours. We have white and colored friends here together."

Their membership in the Bahai church seems to be the great stabilizing force in the lives of the Browns. It gives them a circle of associates which allows them to defy the mores of the general society and helps them to circumvent some of the difficulties of their marriage. In talking about her religion, Mrs. Brown contrasts the attitude of the Episcopal Church, to which she formerly belonged, with that of Bahai:

"I used to belong to the Episcopal Church. One day I met a bishop whom I used to know well. He asked me why he didn't see me at church any more. I told him that I went to the Bahai Temple on Sundays. He said that I was getting away from the Christian church. I said that it is simply the Christian religion brought up to date. Then the bishop said, 'There is something in your life that you are not telling me.' I said, 'Yes, there is. I'm married.' 'There is nothing unusual about that,' the bishop said. I said, 'No, but my husband is colored.' I asked him what he thought about it, and he said, 'I'm shocked.' Then he asked me if I was happy, and I said that I was. Then I asked the

Bishop if I could go to his church with my husband. He said that as an individual he would have no objections, but that the congregation would object. I told him that was the difference between his church and the Bahai."

Mrs. Brown's religion has not only acted as a means of justifying her behavior, but has fired her with a sort of crusading zeal to think of intermarriage as the solution to the problem of color. "I think interracial marriage will do a lot to break down prejudice," she said. "I can truthfully say we've been very happy. Other interracial couples that I I know have also."

Like most of the wives of interracial marriages interviewed in this study, Mrs. Brown was sensitive about her respectability:

"I think that the truth is what will help us interracial people. Of course there are some we can't speak highly of. They are the ones that get in the news. Everyone knows about Jack Johnson's wives. But if you see an interracial woman like Mrs. Sampson, who has raised a family and has always led a quiet, decent life, it never gets in the newspaper." *

It Doesn't Always Work: Intermarriage—like marriage—does not always work. Few data are available concerning interracial couples who subsequently secured divorces.† There is, however, no evidence to in-

---

* Perhaps the most highly publicized case of a Negro man's interracial "affairs," in the history of American journalism, was that of Jack Johnson, the pugilist, who married and divorced two American white women, and then married a French woman. Interracial "affairs" and marriages make the daily press when they are sensational enough to be "news" or have some human interest twist. In 1930, for instance, several Chicago papers carried the story of a millionaire who had married his colored housekeeper in 1927. The man's sister had haled him into court on the charge that he was demented and that "a scheming Negro woman" was after his fortune. Three years later a similar story appeared involving another very wealthy Chicagoan. In 1934, the biggest "interracial" story involved the daughter of a former National Commander of the American Legion who had married a Negro Communist, and whose father attempted to have her declared psychopathic. In 1938, the marriage of Mary Dawes, wealthy Boston socialite, to a prominent Negro social worker, Julian Steele, was carried as straight news.

† It is not easy to trace persons who were formerly partners in interracial marriages after the marriages are dissolved. Nor are such persons likely, even when they can be traced, to be willing to grant interviews. Rumors circulate in the Negro community about many interracial couples who have "busted up," but the difficulty is in knowing whether they were ever really (i.e., legally) married in the first place. It has not been possible to secure much information on commonlaw marriages—even when such unions are permanent—because the persons in-

dicate that the divorce rate is higher among the intermarried than in the population as a whole; indeed there is reason to think that the reverse may be true. The fact that they have violated a taboo together may well act as an additional bond between interracial couples. There is also, of course, another factor that would operate in the same direction: the difficulty which the white partner faces in securing another spouse.

Furthermore, when intermarriages do not go smoothly, it is almost impossible to ascertain whether the racial factor is ever directly or even indirectly involved, except very superficially. If a white wife quarrels with a Negro husband over his drinking, and in the process calls him "good for nothing," he may interpret the insult as a "racial" slur, and react accordingly. In fact, some interracial couples report the use of terms such as "nigger" and "poor-white trash" in family arguments. But such derogatory jousting implies a desire to "hurt" rather than any basic racial prejudice. One elderly white woman who regarded her marriage as a failure (although she had no intention of ever leaving her Negro husband) remarked: "Color hasn't nothing to do with it. He'd be just as no-good if he was white."

WHAT ABOUT THE CHILDREN?

"Broad-minded" white persons sometimes say, "I don't disapprove of intermarriage, but what about the fate of the children? For their sake, perhaps, intermarriage is unwise." Although there have been cases in which intermarried couples have refrained from having children for fear they would prove embarrassing to the white partner, or would not find a comfortable existence either in the white or in the Negro community, these are exceptions. While interracial parents may worry, particularly about how their children will be received by relatives, an examination of a large number of cases indicated that intermarriage is not a very serious deterrent to raising a family. Most of the interracial couples studied in Black Metropolis have children. They are, of course, *Negro* children.

It is difficult, but not impossible, for the children of interracial marriage to make a social adjustment. Nor are such persons invariably

volved are not likely to grant interviews. More common-law marriages in the lower class than on other social levels may explain the apparent low incidence of legal intermarriages in this group.

unhappy. The child of an intermarried couple is usually not accepted by the white community unless he passes. In the Negro community, on the other hand, while there is some stigma attached to having a white parent, it is not very strong. Some of the most popular "leading" young matrons of a generation ago in the Negro community were children of interracial marriages. Often the community completely forgets the interracial background. Some children of intermarried couples are even slightly boastful of the fact. Any stigma arising from white ancestry which may exist among Negroes can extend only one generation back. *No* light-complexioned Negro can trace his ancestry far without running into white blood. The product of an interracial marriage is always in the position to insinuate that at least *his* white blood was acquired *legally*. The usual light color of the offspring of an intermarried couple actually places the child among the preferred physical group in the Negro community.*

There are instances, however, in which parents have worried about the possible color of the children. One woman said:

"The thing that worries me is that the baby is so white. I'm afraid it will not get brown. Do you think it will? The doctor said it would be the color of its ears. If that's true, he will be white, and his hair is very light. My husband is a dark brown-skinned man. He says the baby looks like me and took everything from me. I'm worried too, on the other hand, that if the baby grows dark, he may resent the Negro blood. The social worker told me that. I don't care; he's my baby and I love him, and I'll never let no one take him from me."

The presence of a child in an intermarriage does, however, create a number of problems. One of these is the attitude of the parents and relatives of the white partner. To them, the Negro spouse is a difficult enough problem to adjust to, but still is not a blood relative. The child of the intermarriage, however, is a blood relative, and must be either accepted or rejected. This can be a real emotional crisis. Some couples reported that they had not informed white relatives of the existence of children for this reason.

A woman who had recently had a child by her Negro husband was asked if she were going to tell her family. "Maybe some day," she replied; "but I am not in a hurry." This fear on the part of the white spouse is usually well founded, for it is seldom that the relatives, even though somewhat tolerant of the intermarriage, will welcome the

* (See pp. 495-506.)

natural products of it. The white wife of a Negro commented, "One of my sisters visited me one day and she knew that Joe Junior was my child, but she just couldn't kiss him." * In another case, the Negro husband had died, leaving his wife with a number of children. It was necessary for her to return to her father's home. Although he accepted her, he had reservations about the children:

"My dad's crazy about my children, since we've been living here at home with him. Of course, whenever he gets drunk, he argues with me about having married a colored man. He doesn't like for me to have anything to do with colored people now. I tell him he married who he wanted and I married who I wanted. He objects mildly to my naming my son after my husband, but he's pretty good most of the time. You know—so far as you would expect a white father to be after his daughter had married a colored man."

How the Children Adjust: Most interracial couples realize that their children will be classified as Negroes and must adjust to life in the Negro world. One white mother, not only accepted this fact, but claimed to be proud that her children would have nothing to do with white people:

"One of my boys can pass for white, but he prefers colored. My boys wouldn't marry a white woman. They all married colored. No, they never went out with white girls."

Another white mother did all that she could to strengthen her son's position in the Negro world:

"My boy is recognized and belongs to all the best colored societies and organizations. He is a member of a tennis club composed of lawyers, doctors, and such men. It costs us a lot to keep him in these organizations, but we want him to be in with the best people."

A third white woman, however, could not quite see how her chil-

* On the other hand, a Negro serviceman from Chicago who is married to a white woman relates the following episode: "My wife's sister came to New York with her baby to visit her husband, who was in an embarkation camp. When they left, my wife and I accompanied them and my mother-in-law, who had come with them, to the station. The baby kissed my wife good-bye. I wondered what would happen next, but did nothing. Finally my sister-in-law said, 'Your niece wants to kiss you good-bye. See how she's wrinkling up her nose?' The station was crowded. Curious stares were already being focused in our direction. I reached over and pecked at the baby, acutely self-conscious. It was interesting to note that apparently it was only I, the Negro, who was self-conscious—and not my sister-in-law, my mother-in-law, my wife—or the baby."

dren would be able to adjust to either the white or Negro community. She observed: "I hope by the time they are grown up, America will not be so prejudiced. I think in ten years this country will be something like Russia."

Usually if the child of an intermarried couple tries—either owing to encouragement from the white parent or on his own volition—to associate with white people, he encounters many difficulties. (This, of course, is true only where the family cannot or does not pass for white.) The story of two very light-skinned girls who attended mixed high schools, reveals the special problems of such children. A neighbor of one of the girls related one incident:

"Her mother was very kind to her and they were a high type of family. But in some ways the mother was brutal, too, because she didn't have any real insight into the situation. The girl didn't want to go to school and said that the other kids were mean to her. When the mother left the room, I had a chance to talk to the girl alone. She said that she was neither white nor black, and got to crying. She tried to make friends with white children at school and succeeded very well. When she was alone with them after school and wasn't afraid they would discover about her home, she was much happier. She was fifteen years old, and very well developed. The white boys liked her and she went out with them quite a bit. But she had difficulties because, as she said, they fell in love with her and after a while she'd tell them she was a Negro. She was going to run away as soon as she finished high school. There had been occasions when she stayed away from home for a week end. She said she was just staying at the home of white girls, and I think she really was. She was planning to get a job as soon as she could when she ran away. I couldn't talk her out of it, but I didn't really try, because that would probably be the best adjustment for her." In this instance, the white mother encouraged her daughter to be white, and apparently the girl intended to be—by leaving her family and passing permanently into the white group.

In the other case, the girl "identified" closely with her colored mother, but could not work out an adjustment in a mixed high school, where she was thrown into contact with both white and Negro students. She said:

"I live in a colored neighborhood and I feel closer to the colored teachers because of the fact that my mother has colored blood. I would prefer associating with whites, but I have found that it is difficult to do so. They are all right until they find out that I am colored, and then they show prejudice. It is very hard to be friendly with whites and not be invited to their homes. Of course, I could never invite them to my house.

"The colored students accept me until I act as if I am interested in becoming friendly with a white girl. Then they act funny with me. I guess that I feel that I am colored, but when I tell white people that I am, they don't believe me. I think that I have an advantage that most people don't have in being able to associate freely with both races. There are some colored that are just like white, but there are some that are lowering their race. I don't tell the white students that I'm colored—but some colored students here know I am because I live around them, and they make it their business to tell the others. Some of the colored students have a funny attitude toward me when I am with whites, and I guess they think I feel myself superior to them."

Most children of this type usually solve their problem ultimately by passing over into the white group. Some leave their parents while they are very young; others wait until their education is completed, or even until their parents die. With no strong family ties, and with few roots in the Negro community, "passing" is the logical way out of a difficult situation for the very light children of a mixed marriage.

If the child of an interracial marriage wishes to be white but cannot "pass," he may suffer severe maladjustment. He does not feel at home with either group, and often considers himself neither Negro nor white. Robert, the sixteen-year-old son of a white woman and a Negro man, represents a case of this type. He is light brown in color, with black, very wavy hair and regular features. He is just too dark to be able to pass under ordinary circumstances. When questioned about whom he associated with, he answered: "I don't go out with any colored people at all. Around here they don't like me so much. But I get along all right. Once in a while I have an argument and then they say, 'You think you're smart because you're half white.' I play ball with colored, but I never pal around with colored fellows." Asked what race he thought he belonged to, he replied, "I never thought of it. I like to get along with one as well as the other, but that is kind of hard to do. Colored people don't like people who are mixed; but that's just the lower class of colored people. I know a lot who are educated and they are not like that." To the direct question, "Do you consider yourself colored?", Robert answered in the negative. In explaining the fact that he attended a certain white Catholic school, however, he remarked, "They don't allow colored in that school. But, you see, the nuns there knew my mother."

Robert also maintained that he had never gone out with a colored girl, but that he went with lots of white girls, and was going to marry one; that he would not consider marrying a Negro. "I think intermarriage is all right if they can get along together," he said. "But to tell you the truth, I don't like to see it very much. It's all right with me —I don't care about it—but I don't like to see it. No, I can't give you any reason for not liking intermarriage. I just don't like it, that's all."

But such "in-betweens" constitute a very small proportion of the children of mixed parents. The majority make a successful adjustment in the Negro community, as Negroes—or they pass completely over into the white group. It should be emphasized, also, that only a negligibly small proportion of the Negroes who can pass for white are the offspring of intermarriage. The problems of the children of interracial couples in the Negro community are, from an objective standpoint, exactly the same as those of the children of two Negro parents who look as though they were white. A child of an intermarried couple may, however, have a different attitude toward his color. If his parents are isolated, the child may identify with the white parent, and consequently find it more difficult to become completely integrated into the Negro community.

A ROSE BY ANY OTHER NAME

"Passing" is one of the most prevalent practices that has arisen out of the American pattern of race relations. It grows from the fact that one known drop of "colored" blood is sufficient to make an otherwise completely white person a Negro. As there are thousands of Negroes whom neither colored nor white people can distinguish from full-blooded whites, it is understandable that in the anonymity of the city many Negroes "pass for white" daily, both intentionally and unintentionally. But, should white people become aware of their remote colored ancestors they would, in all probability, treat them as Negroes.*

* The authors have interviews which suggest that some white people in the North are willing to overlook a small infusion of Negro blood provided the person who is passing has no social ties with Negroes. Several persons when questioned on this matter said that they knew of white people who were

There are few figures on the amount of passing which takes place in the United States. Estimates of the number of people who permanently leave the Negro group and are assimilated into white society each year vary from 25,000 to 300,000. These are only estimates, and no conclusive body of statistical data is or ever could be available, especially on those who pass only temporarily or occasionally. There is not, however, a single Negro family known to the authors that has not been aware of instances, sometimes of scores of instances, in which friends, acquaintances, or relatives have crossed the color-line and become white—"gone over to the other side," as Negroes phrase it.

There are various degrees of passing, accompanied by different degrees of estrangement from the Negro group and emotional identification with the white community. Thousands of Negroes pass unintentionally daily. In a large city such as Midwest Metropolis, light-skinned Negroes who go into restaurants, who seek choice seats at a theater, or who are hired in certain jobs are mistaken for white without their being aware of it. A very light woman recently went to an exclusive photographer to have her picture taken. She returned at a later date with her daughter, who was obviously a Negro. The photographer refused to take the daughter's picture and told the mother that he did not care for colored patronage. Only then did she realize that she had been unconsciously passing for white.

Often, when caught in a situation in which he or she is taken for white, a Negro will carry through the bluff even when challenged, in order to avoid embarrassment. A young lady who did not approve of passing related the following incident:

"Speaking of passing—a strange thing happened to me this summer. When I went down to visit my father in Kentucky, I had to change trains at a station on the other side of the Mason-Dixon line. The porter took my bags and escorted me to the coach. I wasn't paying any attention to him. I just took it for granted that he was taking me to the correct coach. When I stepped into the coach, I immediately knew that he had made a mistake. All of these white people were seated and there I was! I said, 'Listen, porter—' and that's all the further I got. He said, 'That's all right, miss, the conductor will call your stop.' He

suspected of having Negro blood and that it was a joking matter. In one case everybody, including the suspect, saved face by saying it was perhaps *Indian* blood.

passed my bags overhead and tipped his hat and walked away. So I sat down and was so ill at ease.

"I noticed several of the white people glancing at me and then after the second look, they looked off. I had had my hair freshly done, and when it is fresh it looks dark brown and wavy, and I did look decent because I was wearing my best. I took a magazine and began reading. After a bit, the conductor came up and after removing his hat and apologetically clearing his throat said, 'I know this is highly irregular, miss, but—uh—pardon me—may I ask you what nationality you are? Uh—are you Jewish?' I could have kissed the conductor for giving me that lead, because as soon as he started talking, I knew what he was going to say. I knew that if I said I was a Negro and tried to explain that I wasn't trying to pass, he wouldn't believe it. Also, to have to go back into the Negro coach with the conductor leading the way would be quite embarrassing to me. The Negroes would think I was trying to pass and got caught. So I decided to play up to the situation. 'After all,' I said, 'this is highly ridiculous. Yes, I am a Jewess, and I consider this a grand insult.' I wore my haughtiest expression, and I was scared to death. By this time several of the white people had turned around and were listening to us.

"The conductor flushed and was very much embarrassed. I just know how he must have felt. He apologized again and then walked away. I was scared. I didn't enjoy the ride at all, and but for the company of a little eight-year-old white child, I talked to no one. It was lucky for me that I hadn't told Father I was coming. Suppose he had been at the station to meet me—then I would have been in a mess. I told Daddy about it and he just laughed. He thought it was a joke! And that's why I couldn't be bothered with trying to pass. I'd rather be colored and not be bothered. That's why I hate the South."

As the above incident suggests, passing in the South can often lead to serious trouble—it violates both custom and law. There are numerous stories about the dashing young man who comes to a southern town, cuts quite a figure, perhaps becomes engaged to a socially prominent local girl, and then suddenly and mysteriously disappears, never to be spoken of again. It is discovered by accident in such instances, so the tales go, that the man, though he appeared to be white, had Negro blood. In the North, however, where the population is not so sensitized, and in the crowded and impersonal atmosphere of the big cities, little thought is given to the possibility that someone might be passing, and no punitive action is taken by the society even when a person who is passing is discovered. In Midwest Metropolis, many Negroes pass merely for convenience. A light-complexioned girl remarked to one of the authors, "Whenever I am downtown alone I always go to one of the better restaurants. They think I am white, I guess; I never ask them. I wouldn't think of going with my husband, who is dark, for they might refuse us and we would be humiliated. Of course I never speak about this to him, as he is so sensitive about his color." It is common practice for very light women to patronize white beauty parlors where, according to them, they can get better service cheaper and without waiting. Often, too, a light person will purchase theater tickets for darker persons so that the latter will not be Jim-Crowed with other Negroes in the theater, or refused seats on the main floor.

From the initial state of passing unintentionally or passing for convenience, there often develops, in more adventurous persons, a practice of passing for fun. This behavior, too, can be engaged in without any feeling of guilt or disloyalty to the race; it is looked upon as having fun at the white folks' expense. Couples, and sometimes parties, will go to white cabarets and exclusive dancing places just to see what they are like and to get a thrill. Even in these cases, however, the persons involved are rather careful about relating these escapades to their friends for fear of censure from the darker persons. "I wouldn't tell everyone this, but you get around and would understand," said a light-complexioned girl. "The other night I was out with Harry—you know he can pass for white—and after we had seen a show in the Loop he said, 'Let's go over to the Pump Room.' We did and had a glorious time and it wasn't any more expensive than the Rhumboogie. No, I wasn't in the least nervous. How could they tell we were colored? There were no colored waiters who might have recognized us. After this I am going to places like that any time I am out with him." Light-complexioned people who go out with white persons of the opposite sex frequently prefer to go to white places, for there is less fear of detection on the part of the Negro community, which in the case of a woman is a matter of some concern.

A fourth type of passing arises out of economic necessity or advantage. Negro girls have had difficulty in obtaining employment in white-collar jobs. Positions as stenographers, telephone operators, receptionists, and clerks are usually closed to anyone who is known to be colored. As there are many Negro girls of superior ability and training who wish such jobs, it is not unusual for some of them to pass, if they can, in order to obtain such work. There is no way of knowing how frequently such passing occurs, but there are few upper- or middle-class Negroes who do not claim knowledge of persons who have passed for economic reasons. Men in this category usually pass to obtain technical positions, and there are verifiable instances where eminent positions as scientists, physicians, and public administrators are held by these "white Negroes."

Usually the individual returns to the Negro community for all of his social contacts and uses his light skin color simply as a method of circumventing economic discrimination. Friendships with whites are generally avoided, as they would lead to complications. One girl reported:

"My mother is very fair and passes for white on most of the jobs she has had, but she doesn't like to do it. It always brings about so much trouble. She makes friends and soon they want her to come to see them and they want to come to see her. One friend that she had had for over a year used to invite Mother to her apartment. This woman knew Mother had two children, and she would say, 'You'll just have to bring those children over so I can see them.' We would have fun talking about it. Well, she finally had to quit; the girl was becoming too chummy."

The final stage of passing—crossing over completely to the other side of the color-line—involves passing in order to associate socially with white people. For a Negro to pass socially means sociological death and rebirth. It is extremely difficult, as one loses in the process his educational standing (if he has gone to a Negro school), intimate friends, family, and work references. People well established in the Negro world and older people seldom pass socially and completely. There is too much to lose and too little to be gained.

Who Can Pass? Scholars have speculated about the amount of Negro blood which a person must have to pass. One concludes that persons with an eighth or less of Negro blood are frequently able to pass as white in a society that is not highly discriminating. Another believes that individuals with one-sixteenth colored ancestry are always able to pass as white. In Midwest Metropolis, a person with still a greater amount of Negro blood can no doubt pass. In other parts of the country, where there are many Mexicans, Puerto Ricans, and

South Americans, it is even more difficult to detect persons with considerable Negro blood.

Passing is dependent on many factors other than skin color. Many fairly dark persons with sharp features are taken for Indians, East Indians, Egyptians, or members of other dark groups. The texture of the hair in many borderline cases plays an important role. But no single factor is so important as the general configuration of skin coloring, texture of hair, and facial characteristics in determining whether a person may be "taken for white." Because of the large admixture of Indian blood among Negroes, many have a Mongolian cast to their features. These individuals, if they have straight hair, can pass for non-Negro, even if quite dark. Then there are many subtle characteristics such as dress, general deportment, mannerisms, and degree of self-assurance which all play their parts.

Quite apart from all these factors and from any objective analysis of the individual's physical make-up is the factor of the social situation. In instances where Negroes are out of the conventional role, whites who have stereotyped notions of what Negroes should do, where they might be found, and how they should act are led to mistake obvious Negroes for white or other racial stock. A young Negro student entered a cab at the railroad station and asked to be taken to the University of Chicago. Although he was brown-skinned and had woolly hair, the cab driver asked if he was not Argentinian. A prominent Negro went to an exclusive night club with a white party, and even though he was introduced to the manager as a Negro, the manager refused to believe his eyes or the statement of the white members of the party. This sort of mistake is also sometimes made by Negroes. At a high school where all the students were colored, but it was the custom to have a white speaker for the commencement exercises, a light brown-skinned Negro addressed the audience and was thought by the majority of the student body to be white. Americans, white and black, see with their emotions as well as with their eyes, and actualities are colored by stereotyped expectations.

On the other hand, any white person—including the lightest blond can, if he wishes, pass for colored. Dr. Robert Park, the eminent sociologist, on two occasions passed for a Negro in order to obtain a room in a Negro hotel. A white girl who worked at a social agency in the Black Belt found out to her amazement, after working with Negro people for a year, that almost all of them not only thought she was a Negro, but refused to believe that she wasn't joking when she said she was white. Some white persons married to Negroes habitually pass for Negro in order to gain some advantage or to avoid embarrassment. The white wife of a Negro railroad waiter related the following incident:

"I have an annual pass with the railroad company my husband is with. I used it a couple of times. Yes, I was questioned when I used the pass and I said that although you might not think so, I have colored blood. I was telling the truth because I have red blood in my veins, and that's colored. The man who questioned me was a southerner and I told him that if he doubted my identity he could wire my husband at my expense."

Many persons, especially white southerners and Negroes, believe that they are so sensitized to Negro racial characteristics that they can detect persons who are attempting to pass for either white or Negro. The following incident illustrates a belief in this special ability. Speaking of her mother, who was passing for white for economic reasons, an informant said:

"She used to hold a nice position at a hotel here. One day a man called her name and said, 'You remind me of a little colored girl.' She thought the most suitable answer was, 'You remind me of a little colored boy.' He said, 'Maybe I am.' It turned out that he was colored and lived on the South Side. It is kind of funny how colored people know one another almost ten times out of ten."

The authors found, however, that among the staff of the Cayton-Warner research, one dark-complexioned white girl was constantly mistaken for colored and one very light Negro girl was identified by most visitors, both white and Negro, as not being colored. Mixed parties have been held in the Negro community where white girls have passed for Negro and Negro girls for white, to the utter confusion of all of the guests. Although persons particularly sensitized to racial differences may be a bit more astute in identifying racial characteristics, a point is reached where it is impossible with even the most refined anthropological measurements to distinguish Negroes from whites. The racial identification of such marginal persons is sociological rather than biological; and what really determines their "race" is how much the public knows about their ancestry.

✦

Passing as a Process: Few people, regardless of how light they may be, grow up as Negroes and then suddenly make an intellectual decision to pass for white. Those who pass over the color-line do so step by step until the emotional ties which bind them to Negroes are severed, on the one hand, and new relationships with members of the white community achieved, on the other hand. The first step, as has been indicated, is usually unintentional passing, where a Negro with a light skin suddenly realizes that in going about the city, outside of the Negro community, he is taken for white. Later the individual becomes more adventurous and begins to pass for some minor convenience, such as obtaining a Pullman when traveling in the South. The individual then may find a subtle pleasure in fooling white people and going places where he knows he would not be welcomed as a Negro. Still later he may seek employment in the white community with every intention of keeping all social relations among Negroes. But as intimate friendships are established with white fellow-workers, in many cases the individual is gradually drawn farther and farther away from his emotional attachment to members of the black community. For such an individual the final break comes when the irritations of trying to remain colored and the attractiveness of the white world outweigh his trepidation.

For one who is not firmly anchored in the Negro community emotionally, there is much temptation to take such a step. At first he finds that the color-line in Midwest Metropolis seems to disappear for him. There is no close scrutiny by his new-found white working companions and friends. There is no fear of any more reprisal than being fired from a job or losing some new acquaintances. Then more and more difficulties begin to arise. He begins to dread meeting old Negro friends while out with the new white ones. There are cases where daughters have refused to speak to their mothers on the street and sons have looked the other way, when accompanied by whites, upon encountering their Negro fathers. As the new job and the new friends become of more emotional importance, the individual has a constant, haunting fear of being discovered. There is the possibility that an old Negro enemy may turn him in, or that some white person may accidentally discover him and work vengeance on him.

Then there arises a moral crisis. On the one hand, it is hard to continue to live in two worlds; but on the other hand, there is a sense of guilt over being unfaithful to the Negro world with which he and his family have been identified. Then it is that many an individual either announces to a startled office manager, foreman, or fiancée that he is a Negro and would prefer to be known as such, or commits sociological suicide, to be reborn on the white side of the color-line.

An individual who makes the latter choice is not operating in a vacuum. There is the constant and disturbing pressure of the Negro community which both pushes and pulls him. Many very light men, especially, feel uncomfortable in the Negro community. They are very conspicuous when out with Negro groups except when all are as light as they. This is the push which exerts itself on them from birth. They are always suspect—the community feels that in most cases they are only looking for a chance to escape the confines of color. Passing episodes are carefully concealed from most of their Negro friends, for the community would in most cases censure them; and even when they pass solely for economic reasons, only a partial and begrudging sanction is given them. Finally, the condemnation of the Negro group itself operates in the same way as the attractiveness of moving freely in white society, to allow them to make a moral decision to cross over the line. Although there is far from unanimity on the subject, many Negroes would agree with a young woman who said:

"Well, I don't see anything wrong with it, if the person can get something out of it. But personally, I don't like it. I think if for commercial reasons it is done as Mary Malone is doing [she named a well-known Negro girl who passes for white on the stage], that's not so bad; but I wouldn't want to deny my race otherwise. And then I would associate with colored people after I was finished work. What I mean is that I would pass only for business purposes and not because I didn't want to be colored."

There is a widespread belief in the community that Negroes protect other Negroes who are passing. One white woman married to a Negro stated:

"Some people would try to prevent a person from holding a job if they knew he wasn't entitled to it because of color. My husband knows a man who is colored and who is working as a white man, but my husband never recognizes him. There is a sort of code of honor among colored people not to reveal the identity of a person who is working as white."

Although there are occasional instances of Negroes exposing others who are passing, in general there is great tolerance on the part of

Negroes if they know they are not being slighted or are being slighted for economic reasons only. The difference in attitude of two colored girls who worked in a downtown department store illustrates this point:

"Mary and I got a job working at Field's one Christmas. Mary had had much more practice at passing than I. But she was scared to death that someone—some colored person—would see her and recognize her. They put her in the costume jewelry section right on the first floor. Negroes would come in and she would try to avoid them and turn her back. Then they made a point of trying to speak to her. Finally she became a nervous wreck and had to quit. They put me in the hand-kerchief section on State Street, and people were coming in all the time that I knew; but I always spoke to them and would wait on them if they came to my counter. So I got along all right. Lots of people who sensed that I was going to speak to them would just nod and move away quickly. They weren't resentful. I really needed the money; but it wasn't a life-and-death matter, so I couldn't think of not speaking to someone that I knew."

The practice of passing for economic reasons is so frequent and the Negro's economic position is so desperate that some years ago the Chicago *Defender* gave partial sanction to this behavior in an editorial [1] mainly slanted toward poking fun at the attitude of whites:

In our big department stores in the Loop can be found many sons and daughters who come back "home" at the close of the day, and by the same token would come back home to stay if their identity was found out. They are not as fair as lilies but the fact that most of the stores are "manned" by Jewish girls whose complexion and hair is swarthy helps the situation out materially. It is a shame and a disgrace that we must be forced in order to make a livelihood, to live this life each day, but there is not another way. We pour thousands of dollars, hard earned, into the coffers of the storekeepers and yet we are denied recognition or a chance to earn some of it back except we apply for some menial position like running an elevator or janitorship, and in many places we are even denied this class of employment. That our men and women are superior in every way to the average wage-earner found in these stores is without question, but worth doesn't count when prejudice creeps in, so we must fight fire with fire, and those that are able to "get by" peace be with them and it is our duty not to hinder them in any way. Last Monday was the Jewish New Year and all of that faith were given a holiday—without pay—by the store managers. This, of course, made a number of our young ladies who were Jewish pro tem take two days off. "There are tricks to all trades," said one of them laughingly, "and we had it to do to allay suspicion." So even with the serious side of it there comes something in the lighter vein. But it does seem with a concerted effort this situation could in a measure be changed for the better, patronize the store that offers the most to you and yours and you will be aiding materially in the movement.

A Rose Is a Rose Is a Rose: Although thousands of Negroes are lost to the Negro race each year by passing, scores of thousands have passed for a while only to return to the—for them—warmer and more comfortable milieu of the Negro community.

A prominent colored physician reported that for some years after he left college he passed for white in practicing medicine. He could never feel quite comfortable and was particularly concerned about his relationships with his family. After having established a successful practice, he suddenly decided to return to the Negro group and there achieved a position of prominence which he could never have attained in the larger society. Another well-known Negro businessman for a number of years lived on the North Shore, but he too returned to the Black Belt and, with the capital he had accumulated and the insight into white business practices he had obtained, was able to establish one of the most successful enterprises in the community.

In both of these instances, as in many others, passing was profitable at one period of the individual's life, when he had no money and little experience, but it was equally profitable later on to return to the Negro community. Usually the fact that he has passed is a guarded secret, for it would indicate that at one time he had severed his emotional identification with the community and he would be suspected of demonstrating a similar disloyalty again. Men pass for noneconomic reasons more frequently than women; it is also more common for men to return to the Negro group. Once a light girl has passed, she would be considered disloyal—sullied, and not to be trusted—and would not be able to make such an advantageous marriage were she to return to the Negro group. While it is common knowledge that thousands of Negroes pass, cases of those who return are relatively infrequent. In the lives of many prominent Negroes, however, are gaps which can be explained only in terms of a temporary passing over the color-line.

Passing has been described as a process where one gradually relinquishes his social relationships and emotional identification with the Negro community. It should not be thought, however, that every person who passes completely goes through each step of this process; it is merely the pattern generally followed. Many people are never successful in breaking their ties completely with either group, and severe maladjustment often results.

Passing is one way of crossing the color-line. It does not challenge the mores of the society, for it is surreptitious. It does, however, bring with it miscegenation, introducing a constant stream of Negro blood into the white population. In fact, as Louis Wirth and Herbert Goldhamer state, "One southern state legislator, in speaking against an especially severe bill restricting Negro-white intermarriage, is reported as saying that if the definition of Negro incorporated in the bill were accepted there would not be enough white people in the state to pass it." [2]

Midwest Metropolis is not aware of the volume of passing nor disturbed enough about it to take punitive action. Nevertheless anyone discovered is usually considered a Negro. If such an individual has attained a position of great importance, however, the episode is often hushed up. Negroes claim to be aware of many cases of this kind, and numerous stories on the subject circulate throughout the community.* It is even widely believed that there has been at least one "Negro" president of the United States.†

A Two-way Passage: In Chicago people do occasionally cross the color-line. And when they do, they may encounter difficulties. But hundreds of Negroes have lived and are living as white, and a small group of whites have become sociological Negroes. It can and does happen here—but not with the frequency which would warrant the irrational fear of "amalgamation" held by many white people.

What does this race crossing mean? More Negro blood than most suspect finds its way into the white population—not enough, however,

---

* Such stories are hard to verify. Occasionally, however, an incident becomes a matter of public record. Just before the First World War, for instance, a wealthy Chicago publisher, always considered white, was found to be a "Negro" when his darker relatives showed up at his funeral. A similar case appeared in the neighboring state of Indiana in 1940 when a leading businessman and philanthropist was revealed as colored at his funeral.

† J. A. Rogers marshals an impressive array of evidence to substantiate this claim, including a statement from S. H. Adams, *The Incredible Era,* to the effect that the President in question not only did not deny his Negro ancestry but simply said, "How do I know? One of my ancestors might have jumped the fence." (See J. A. Rogers, *op. cit.,* pp. 254-258.)

to change the physical characteristics of that group at all. Passing is of much more serious import to Negroes. Yearly a number of "white Negroes" pass over the line. This perhaps robs the Negro group of possible leaders and well-trained persons who could add immeasurably to the welfare of the group. But it should be noted that a relatively small proportion of those who can pass really do cross over completely, and there are some who have passed completely but who "return to their race" with capital and experience which allows them to become leaders. It's a two-way passage in many instances.

Intermarriage, on the other hand, operates to introduce more white blood into the Negro group, modifying to an extent that physical type. The study of the "American Negro" is not merely the study of Negroes so designated because they are culturally distinct from the Negroes of Africa, but is also the study of the formation of a relatively distinct physical type."[3] Intermarriage (though nonlegal miscegenation is much more important in this connection) is one of the means by which this new type—the brown American—has come into existence.

THE "BLACK BABY" BUGABOO

Mixed couples usually express a desire for either light brown-skinned children or children who can pass for white. People who oppose passing often cite the "danger" of a "black baby"—a "throwback"—sometime cropping up should the Negro who has passed, or his descendants, marry a white person. Negroes who are passing occasionally hesitate to get married or to have children for fear that "Negro blood will out." This emphasis upon the "black baby" arriving to embarrass its parents has a dual significance. On one hand it reflects the general attitude of the dominant white American culture toward "typical" Negro physical traits—the definition of black skin, thick lips, and kinky hair as "ugly." On the other hand, it expresses a desire that children shall not look so different from the parents as to excite embarrassing stares or malicious gossip.*

* Esthetic standards vary from culture to culture. Many Central African groups think that thin lips, white skin and straight hair are ugly. And among white people there are many who can recognize "black" beauty or "yellow" beauty as well as white. There are people, too, who in choosing a mate do not put such standards in the primary place. Students of Latin American countries have frequently called attention to the fact that the marriage of whites to very Negroid types is not unusual, and that the white partners feel no shame in such

The "black baby" bugaboo is often cited as the primary objection to passing. Edward M. East, the geneticist, has discussed the probable origin of such black babies as do appear in the following passage:

"A favorite short-story plot with which melodramatic artists seek to harrow the feelings of their readers is one where the distinguished scion of an aristocratic family marries the beautiful girl with telltale shadows on the half-moons of her nails, and in due time is presented with a coal-black son. It is a good framework, and carries a thrill. One waits shiveringly, even breathlessly, for the first squeal of the dingy infant. There is only this slight imperfection—or is it an advantage?— it could not possibly happen on the stage as set by the author. The most casual examination of the genetic formulae given above demonstrates its absurdity. If there ever was a basis for the plot in real life, the explanation lies in a fracture of the seventh commandment, or in a tinge of negro [*sic*] blood in the aristocrat as dark as that in his wife." [4]

The genetic formulae referred to by East, and generally accepted by geneticists and anthropologists, support the following conclusions: *

1. In the case of two persons both theoretically white but having, whether they know it or not, some Negro blood, an accentuation of some Negro characteristics may occur in their offspring, but in all probability the offspring of such unions will be able to pass for white.

2. It is impossible for the offspring of a recognizable Negro and a *pure* white person to be any darker than the Negro partner, and in all probability it will be lighter.

3. The offspring of two mixed-bloods (e.g., mulattoes or quadroons) may be darker than either, but in all probability would not be black.

Even a widespread knowledge of these facts will not dispel the "black baby" bugaboo, for what white person can be sure that he has no Negro blood, or what Negro who is passing that he will not

cases. Yet, often, very devoted couples of this type want children who are blends and consider a dark child unfortunate. (See Donald Pierson's *Negroes in Brazil*, University of Chicago Press, pp. 111-76, for an interesting discussion of these patterns as he observed them in Bahia where intermarriage is not frowned upon, and in many ways is actually encouraged.)

* In detailing these conclusions we have used the expression "Negro blood" instead of the more precise formulation in terms of genes that govern characteristics such as skin-color, hair form, shape of nose, etc. Obviously, however, blood has nothing to do with heredity, but it is probable that the colloquial use of the term "Negro blood" will remain long after the general public is aware that it really refers to "genes for Negro traits."

marry a "white" person who has a few drops from way back? The chances of such marriages producing a "black baby" are extremely remote—but it could happen. "In all probability" is not a very reassuring phrase. So long as "blackness" of skin is considered a misfortune, the bugaboo will remain. Even if the habit of stigmatizing people because of their skin-color were to disappear, a "black baby" would still be considered a misfortune until everyone knew that an occasional dark child born to lighter parents did not constitute *prima facie* evidence of interracial adultery.

WHAT OF THE FUTURE?

The specter of social equality is enough to seriously limit the competition of Negroes economically, politically, and socially in Midwest Metropolis. But it is unlikely that, given our present form of government and the Negro's present political strength in Chicago, any stringent legal action will be taken to keep people from crossing the color-line. The majority of the people in Midwest Metropolis may not like intermarriage, but it is not a burning issue and therefore does not evoke formal legal action. Such action would, of course, be fought by the Negro citizens of Chicago. Although their feeling of race pride leads most of them to disapprove of intermarriage, its legality is important to them as one manifestation of their equal civil rights.

Many whites will continue to exploit the fear of intermarriage as a means of retaining economic dominance, and as a devastating question to be raised in connection with any concessions, no matter how small, which the Negro community requests. A few intermarriages will no doubt continue to take place, as well as clandestine "affairs," but "crossing the line" is not uppermost in the minds of the Negroes. Relaxation of the taboos against intermarriage is something white people are most reluctant to grant. It is also the "concession" which Negroes, as a group, are least likely to request. That it looms so large in the white mind is the irony of race relations in Midwest Metropolis.

CHAPTER 8

The Black Ghetto

THE STRONGEST VISUAL EVIDENCE OF A COLOR-LINE IN MIDWEST METROPOLIS is the existence of a Black Belt. Of the city's 337,000 Negroes, over ninety out of every hundred live in areas predominantly Negro.

It is not unusual for a language, nationality, or racial group to begin life in the city as a "colony." The distinctive thing about the Black Belt is that while other such "colonies" tend to break up with the passage of time, the Negro area becomes increasingly more concentrated. By 1940, this area in Chicago had virtually ceased to expand in size, but new migrants to the city were pouring into it, and very few Negroes were trickling out into other parts of the city.

The persistence of a Black Belt, whose inhabitants can neither scatter as individuals nor expand as a group, is no accident. It is primarily the result of white people's attitudes toward having Negroes as neighbors. Because some white Chicagoans do not wish colored neighbors, formal and informal social controls are used to isolate the latter within congested all-Negro neighborhoods.

The native-born, middle-class, white population is the group that sets the standards by which various people are designated as desirable or undesirable. The attitudes of this middle-class group are probably decisive in restricting Negroes and other groups to special areas of the city. These attitudes become translated into economic terms, and though the kinds of people the white middle class desires as neighbors do not affect property values adversely, their dislike and fear of other groups is reflected by a decline in the sales value of residential property when such people begin to penetrate a neighborhood. In Midwest Metropolis, such ethnic groups as the English, Germans, Scotch, Irish, and Scandinavians have little adverse effect on property values. Northern Italians are considered less desirable, followed by Bohemians and Czechs, Poles, Lithuanians, Greeks, and Russian Jews of the lower class. Southern Italians, along with Negroes and Mexicans, are at the bottom of the scale of middle-class white "desirability." *

The areas in which these groups are concentrated become stigmatized as "slum neighborhoods," and there is a tendency to blame the group for the condition of the area. One factor that complicates this whole matter of land-values—for the areas in question *are* predominantly slums—is the fact that the "undesirable" groups usually inherit sections of the city that the older, more well-to-do inhabitants have abandoned and thus "the undesirable racial factor is so merged with other unattractive features, such as proximity to factories, poor transportation, old and obsolete buildings, poor street improvements, and the presence of criminal or vice elements, that the separate effect of race cannot be disentangled." [1]

Given the definition of an area and the people in it as "undesirable," the expansion of the area will be resisted. If, however, individuals within it are able to change the telltale marks of poverty, name, foreign language, or distinctive customs, they may move out and lose themselves in middle-class, native-born white neighborhoods. This, Negroes wearing the badge of color, cannot do. Negro areas must either expand as parts of a constantly growing Black Belt, or stagnate as deteriorating slums.

EVOLUTION OF A BLACK BELT

The Negro area of Midwest Metropolis has been expanding for almost a hundred years—sometimes slowly, sometimes rapidly; occasionally with serious disturbances, but usually as a peaceful process. The expansion has taken two forms—a gradual filtering-in of Negroes among the white population, and mass invasion. Before the Great Migration, the usual process of filtering-in seems to have been one in which a few Negroes would move out of the Negro colony into surrounding areas. As others followed them, small nuclei of Negroes were formed. Then, when the proportion of Negroes to whites became large, the white population would move, leaving the areas all-Negro.

Before the Great Migration, over half of the Negro population lived

* Most social-distance scales indicate that native-born Americans tend to arrange people in a rank-order of desirability as neighbors which places Northern Europeans at the top, and Negroes, Mexicans, and similar colored groups near the bottom.

outside of the then small Black Belt.* Some of these were servants living near the white families for whom they worked. Others were families who had bought property on the outskirts of a city that eventually grew out to meet them. Still others were moderately prosperous people following the general residential trend away from the center of the city.

Old Settlers have a tendency to romanticize this period, but it is evident from their comments that sporadic, unorganized resistance to Negro neighbors was sometimes encountered. One woman, referring to her experience in the Eighties, indicates that antagonism toward Negroes was strong enough to permit a person to annoy a neighbor by renting a house to a Negro:

"There has always been race prejudice here, but not so strong as it is now. The owner of this house was a German and he was mad at his neighbor. He was tickled to death to rent it to colored, just in order to spite Mrs. Richmond. Later I bought the house."

Occasionally a light-skinned Negro would move into a neighborhood and it might be some time before he was "discovered." One very light Negro, reporting such an episode, said:

"In 1904 or 1905, I moved in here. I bought in 1907. There were white neighbors on both sides at first. I rented the house the first time I moved in it. The man I rented the house from talked to me about the place, and rented it to me, and he thought I was a white man. The neighbors made complaints about it. He said, 'The man has a lease and he'll keep it until it is up.' After the lease was up, I bought the house for a price reasonable at that time. The fellow was a Scotchman."

The experiences of individual Negroes during this filtering-in process depended on many factors, including the social-class and ethnic composition of the area, as well as the class and skin-color of the Negro. When only a few Negroes were involved, and they were of equivalent social status to the whites, or when the whites were of lower class position than the colored people, initial hostility usually gave way to toler-

* In 1910 there were no communities in which Negroes were over 61 per cent of the population. More than two-thirds of the Negroes lived in areas less than 50 per cent Negro, and a third lived in areas less than 10 per cent Negro. By 1920, 87 per cent of the Negroes lived in areas over half Negro in composition. A decade later 90 per cent were in districts of 50 per cent or more Negro concentration. Almost two-thirds (63.0 per cent) lived where the concentration was from 90 to 99 per cent Negro!

ance or even friendliness. But when large numbers of Negroes followed, antagonisms were aroused, and eventually the white population would move away. Old Settlers frequently refer to the relative ease with which they made adjustments, once they had filtered into some types of white neighborhoods. The following two statements summarize the experiences of scores of pre-migration Negro families. One woman states:

"I came to Chicago in 1903. I lived on Lincoln Street—there were foreigners there. My children used to go to white kids' parties, for where we lived there was nothing much but foreigners. There was only one other colored family in that block. The white people never used to call my children names."

Another woman suggested that while relations between children and adults in such areas were often friendly, the social barrier stiffened during the critical adolescent period:

"I was raised on the Near North Side and at that time we were the only Negro family over there. I didn't know so much about color until I was about eleven or twelve years old. In fact, I hadn't given it a second thought. My playmates were all white. I used to go to their parties and they would come to mine; but after I was old enough to go into high school, that was where the trouble started. I never did have any serious trouble, but it wasn't so pleasant as it had been when I was a child."

This woman also blamed an increase in the *number* of Negroes for changes in white neighborhood sentiment:

"As long as there was just one colored family over there it was all right, but after the neighborhood began to have an increase in the number of colored families, the children started to making trouble among themselves, and, of course, that brought the older people into it."

Concurrently with the filtering-in process, the Black Belt itself was expanding in these pre-Migration years. As whites moved out of areas adjacent to the Black Belt to seek better homes farther from the center of the city, Negroes moved in. So long as Negroes were but a minute percentage of the population, they were easily accommodated. It was only after 1915, when 65,000 migrants came into the city within five years, that resistance became organized. Negro migrants were then compelled to spill over the margins of the Black Belt, and their search for homes in other parts of the city was eventually interpreted as a "mass invasion." Yet even the Negroes who streamed into the city during the first three years of the Great Migration had little difficulty in renting or buying property near the small Black Belt, for middle-class white residents were abandoning these areas. Real-estate agents and property owners of both races promoted the expansion of the Black Belt, and there was little friction.

But when the United States entered the World War in 1917 building operations were suspended and a housing shortage quickly resulted. Property owners' associations began to talk of re-establishing neighborhoods adjacent to the Black Belt as exclusively white. This meant that the Negroes who had already moved in must be forced out if possible, and that no others must be allowed to enter. Before the housing shortage, these adjacent white communities had been willing to absorb a few Negroes and then to relinquish the community to them as they became too numerous. Now they were disposed to stay and fight.

Several property owners' associations which had been originally organized for neighborhood improvement, now began to focus their attention upon keeping out Negroes. They sponsored numerous mass meetings to arouse the citizens to the peril of "invasion." They published scathing denunciations of Negroes branding them arrogant, ignorant, diseased, bumptious, destructive of property and generally undesirable. A wave of violence flared up and between July, 1917, and March, 1921, fifty-eight homes were bombed—an average of one every twenty days. Two Negroes were killed, a number of white and colored persons were injured, and property damage amounted to over a hundred thousand dollars. The victims of the bombings were Negro families that had moved into white neighborhoods, as well as Negro and white real-estate men who sold or rented property to them. Feeling was particularly strong against real-estate men who were suspected of renting to one or two Negroes in a block in order to frighten the white residents away so that the realtors could move Negroes in at higher rents.

The most widely publicized bombing case was that of Jesse Binga, the Negro banker and real-estate dealer mentioned earlier. Binga was of relatively high social and economic status, and could hardly be accused of not knowing how to care for property. In fact, the property owners' associations attacked him precisely because he *did* represent a higher-status Negro. When he bought a home in a white middle-class area, the *Property Owners' Journal* denounced him for having "wormed his way into a white neighborhood," characterizing him as one of the "misleaders of the Negro, those flamboyant, noisy, witless individuals, who by power of superior gall and gumption have blustered their way into positions of prominence amongst their people." [2] Since verbal threats failed to dislodge him, bombs were tried. These also failed.

The property owners' association never admitted complicity in these bombings, and responsibility was never definitely placed by the police. Indeed, individual groups of property owners warned against violence, one such group declaring that the *moral* onus rested on the associations if the bombings continued, even though the associations were not actively involved.

By 1925, the wave of bombings had ceased. Since that time the major device for controlling the expansion of the Negro community has been the restrictive covenant—an agreement between property owners within a certain district not to rent or sell to Negroes. Although their constitutionality is being questioned, the covenants have been recognized as legal by the courts, and property owners' associations continue to use the pressure of public opinion to secure signatures from white owners who may be reluctant to enter into them.

As early as January, 1920, the Chicago *Tribune* reported [3] under the caption, "United Action Keeps Negroes Out of 57 Homes," that

The Chicago Real Estate Board extended felicitations to the Grand Boulevard branch of the Kenwood and Hyde Park Property Owners' Associations yesterday, when the association proclaimed that in sixty days it had forestalled Negro occupancy of fifty-seven houses south of Thirty-ninth Street.

In May of the following year, the same paper noted that the Chicago Real Estate Board was as ready to penalize those who sold to Negroes as to felicitate those who would not: [4]

Immediate expulsion from the Chicago Real Estate Board will be the penalty paid by any member who sells a Negro property in a block where there are only white owners. This was voted unanimously at a meeting of the board yesterday, following an appeal by Col. V—— H. S——, a former president of the organization, that the board take a definite stand on the Negro question. He called the Chicago Real Estate Board cowardly, and declared it had always sidestepped the issue. His motion followed a plea by the Grand Boulevard Property Owners' Association for co-operation of the realtors in settling the property ownership problem.

PATTERNS OF ADJUSTMENT

As a result of competition for space, four main types of neighborhoods have developed: (1) mixed, unadjusted neighborhoods; (2) mixed, adjusted neighborhoods; (3) contested areas; and (4) neighborhoods that are entirely white or Negro.*

There are certain mixed, lower-class neighborhoods which have a tradition of hostility toward Negroes; in others, hostility arises only occasionally. In most of these, Negroes are living among the foreign-born. The equilibrium is easily disturbed in these areas, and a trivial incident may precipitate a crisis. In recent years the problem has arisen whether Negroes and whites are to be segregated in Federal housing projects in these areas. This, in turn, has repercussions on the larger community.†

There are other low-status areas where Negroes and whites live side by side as neighbors in proportions of from one-fourth to two-thirds Negro. In such situations Negroes are in intimate contact with foreign-born groups. Relations seem to be most harmonious with Italians, Mexicans, and Jews, and least with the Irish and Poles. Although there are occasional fights among the children, there is on the whole little friction. The social life is generally separate, and Negroes in such areas often look down on the foreign-born. One colored woman, for instance, said: "We're not segregated here. Who are these 'hunkies' to segregate you? Most of them are as black as I am." ‡

Other Negroes who live in mixed areas not only tolerate their neighbors but sometimes become friendly with them:

* This system of classification was used originally in the study of the Riot, by the Chicago Commission on Race Relations.

† There are three Federal housing projects in which Negroes and whites live without any official segregation. In each of them there have been minor racial difficulties, but, on the whole, the various ethnic groups sustain neighborly relations with one another.

‡ Another woman, who does not live in a mixed neighborhood, expressed the same feeling: "Being a southerner, I've always lived in a Negro community, and I didn't come this far to live among the Polacks, Dagoes, and other low-class white trash. I prefer living among my own group."

"I have been in this neighborhood twenty years. I think Italians get along better with colored than other whites."

"I went to a mixed school. Two of my closest friends were Japanese, fully Americanized and friendly. We visited in each other's homes. We were friendly with Jews and Italians, mostly Italians."

"Over here there are only seventeen or twenty colored families. Most of the people are Jewish, some are Polish. The Polish are rather prejudiced. Our next-door neighbors are Irish. They visit me, but I have an excuse and never visit them."

"All of the old white settlers of this community are dead. But most of the children I went to school with still live in the community. All of the girls I grew up with are still my friends. This might seem a funny statement to make, but really I know nothing about Negroes, but I know all about white people. These white people in this community are all my friends. A Polish family moved just a few doors from me. They weren't here a week before they started trying to get my neighbors to sign petitions to get me out of the community, but they refused to sign against me and next month I saw a sign for rent in the flat the Polish people rented."

Because of the general difference in cultural background, Negroes and foreign ethnic groups have little in common, and some mutual suspicions and occasional antagonisms are inevitable, as revealed in the following statements by residents in mixed areas:

"I remember how I used to fight with the white children, especially the Dago children. They would call out to us colored children, 'Nigger, nigger, never die, black face and China eye,' and when I would catch one and get through with him he would think *he* was black."

"The Italian boys were so low morally. They made several attempts to rape some of the girls . . . used to gang us . . . We were always able to have a good fight and have some blood shed. The intense feeling lasted till now. The friendships were not lasting."

"I used to live on the North Side as a school kid. Two colored boys went to school with me. An Italian girl liked one of these boys.

Her family sent Bill one of their famous black hand warnings. All us colored fellows were scared to death."

"Over here, there is not much mixing among the grown-ups. Small children play together at times all right. Dagoes call the children 'niggers' once in a while. These Dagoes over here is rotten. They think they is better than you, especially the young women. On Clark in some of the restaurants they are not particular about serving you."

"This place is ruined. Nothing is around here but these old Italians from New Orleans. You will hear one telling his neighbor, 'Don't visit niggers in their houses.' I would send them all back to Italy where they belong. I hate them folks."

There are a few areas in which lower middle-class Negro and white families have lived harmoniously over a long period of time. A few Negroes are scattered among white families, and there is some adult family visiting and friendly contact between children below teen-age. Negroes in such neighborhoods usually go into the Black Belt for church services and recreation. Public schools and neighborhood movies in such areas seldom discriminate against the Negroes they know. This equilibrium is disturbed when the number of Negroes begins to increase appreciably or when larger numbers of lower-status Negroes filter in. Signs of trouble usually appear first in school situations. Tension between white teachers and the new Negro students arises. The older colored population is torn between "race loyalty" and antagonism toward the newcomers. Conversations between parents are reflected in the playground squabbles of the children. And the adjusted area becomes a "contested area" if the proportion of Negroes continues to mount.

RESTRICTIVE COVENANTS AND CONTESTED AREAS

It is in middle-class white neighborhoods adjacent to Negro communities, when a mass invasion is feared, that antagonisms become most highly organized. Such spots become "contested areas." There were several such areas in Midwest Metropolis on the eve of the Second World War. (Note the areas east and south of the Black Belt in Figure 7.)

Figure 7

TYPES OF RESIDENTIAL AREAS:1934

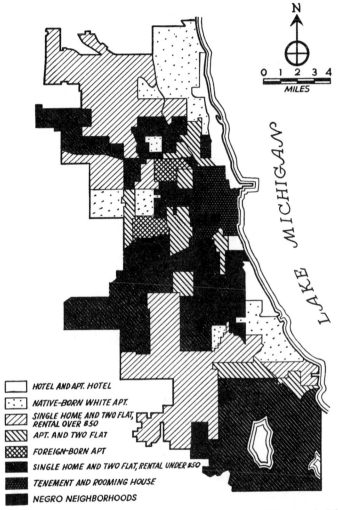

HOTEL AND APT. HOTEL

NATIVE-BORN WHITE APT.

SINGLE HOME AND TWO FLAT,
RENTAL OVER $50

APT. AND TWO FLAT

FOREIGN-BORN APT.

SINGLE HOME AND TWO FLAT, RENTAL UNDER $50

TENEMENT AND ROOMING HOUSE

NEGRO NEIGHBORHOODS

Prepared by combining a group of maps in Faris and Dunham's *Mental Disorders in Urban Areas*. The "hotel and apartment hotel" and the "native-born white apartment" areas east of the Black Belt, and the "single home and two flat" areas to the south are "middle-class" white neighborhoods.

The Commission on Race Relations had warned in 1920 against the enforced segregation of Negroes, By 1930, such measures had become so widespread, however, that three-fourths of all the residential property in the city was bound by restrictive covenants. It could not be rented or sold to Negroes. Negroes have attacked the validity of these covenants in the courts and attempted to have state laws passed declaring them against the public policy, but without success.

Tension over competition for living space since 1925 reached its highest point in 1938 in the form of a court battle to break the restrictive covenants in an area adjacent to the Black Belt—the Washington Park Subdivision. The story is revealing.

By 1937 the Negro population had so expanded as to leave one square mile—the Washington Park district—surrounded on three sides by Negroes; this district was referred to as "the white island." Most of the owners of one- and two-family dwellings in the area had joined the Woodlawn Property Owners' League, which encouraged them to sign covenants barring Negroes from renting or buying their property. It was a point of pride with the community that it served as a bastion against the Negro influx into areas adjacent to the middle-class residential neighborhoods surrounding the University of Chicago. Over 95 per cent of the frontage was reported covered by restrictive covenants.

This bastion was first breached when several well-to-do Negroes managed to persuade one or two white property owners to sell. The owners who sold contended that by the terms of the covenant it was valid only if 95 per cent of the frontage was covered, and that not enough owners had signed to make the instrument binding. The property owners' association then filed an injunction restraining one of the Negroes from occupying the property he had bought. The Chicago Title and Trust Company refused to give him a clear title. When the Negro purchaser carried the matter to the courts, the state Supreme Court upheld the property owners' association. By this time the case was becoming a national *cause célèbre* among Negroes. The NAACP prepared to present the case to the United States Supreme Court. The lines were tightly drawn. National real-estate magazines declared the case would set a precedent for all northern communities and called on member organizations to watch it with care. Money-raising campaigns were opened in the Negro community, and Negro newspapers all over the country began to comment on the significance of the case.

Meantime some of the larger white real-estate companies with an eye for business began to break the covenants. They moved Negroes into one or two apartment buildings, immediately raising the rents by from 20 to 50 per cent. In 1940 there were many cases of whites and Negroes living in the same building, the latter paying—for equivalent accommodations—rentals much higher than those paid by the whites; in such cases the realtors were urging the white families to leave so that their apartments could be rented to Negroes at a higher rate.

The smaller property owners were then pressed to sell their property to the realtors because "the neighborhood was going colored and the value of their investments would fall anyhow." Some owners, seeing the economic advantage, preferred to sell or rent to Negroes directly. But these owners were in a dilemma: If they sold to Negroes and broke the covenants, the property owners' associations would challenge the transactions; whereas, if they did not sell to Negroes, either they would find themselves stranded in all-Negro communities, unable because of the covenants to rent any portion of their property to Negroes, or they would have to sell at a loss to the larger real-estate companies.

As they became aware of this dilemma, the Small Property Owners, Associated, Inc., came into being.[5] The organization described itself as "a mutually incorporated body . . . organized solely for the express object of seeking immediate relief from the present existing impractical and now highly injurious exactions of the so-called 'Restrictive Covenant.'" It did not attack restrictive covenants on principle, nor indicate that the members wished to live in Negro neighborhoods. Covenants were now considered economically disadvantageous, and their espousal was simply called "blind loyalty" to a losing cause. In fact, the officers hastened to assure reluctant owners that the organization was

. . . composed entirely by WHITE property holders . . . and was instituted for the purpose of legally petitioning by exhaustive court procedure, relief from the glaring inequity of this existing "restrictive agreement" upon the undeniable grounds of repeatedly proven Abandonment, Impracticability [sic] to further Enforce, Public Policy and to reassure our members the restoration of their inherent American right to again freely exercise, within their discretion, adequate safeguards toward the vital protection of their financial investments herein.

Antagonism was focused on "high-priced East End attorneys" (a reference to the University of Chicago area) sponsored by funds from a "non-resident property owners' league" which allegedly

> . . . during the past several years has been actuated solely by a motive to assure the maintenance of white residential supremacy . . . regardless of the great financial detriment, mental anguish and impracticability of those owners within said subdivision to further withstand the devastating losses sustained through the vainly impotent racial rental restrictions exacted by that non-residential body.

The shoe was pinching!

The NAACP, which had been preparing the case for the United States Supreme Court, enlisted the aid of this white small-property owners' group. A brief filed by the white lawyer reveals how the white supremacy dogmas disintegrated under the pressure of economic necessity: [6]

> Your plaintiffs further allege that in view of the large Negro occupancy in said area . . . there are only a certain class of the poorer white people that desire to remain there; that they are poor rent payers; careless with the upkeep and care of property; and will pay only very low rentals, and that said property cannot be operated at a profit.
>
> Your plaintiffs further allege that the Negro tenants pay substantially larger rentals and permit the buildings to be maintained from the income of said property; that the buildings now classed as white properties are not maintaining themselves and will result in ultimate financial ruin and loss of property.

When the case was carried to the Supreme Court, a ruling was handed down which, in effect, constituted a victory for the Negroes. The court did not rule that restrictive covenants were invalid, but it did state that each parcel of property in the area constituted a specific, individual case and that no decision against one owner for renting or selling to a Negro constituted a precedent binding others. The cost of fighting several hundred cases through the courts every time a violation occurred would have bankrupted the Woodlawn Property Owners' League.

The editors of national real-estate journals were quick to point out that this was no clear-cut victory for opponents of restrictive covenants. The business manager of the Woodlawn association, in an article in one of these magazines, commented[7] (the italics are the authors'):

The Lee versus Hansberry case and the decision in connection with it are so important to Chicago real estate that they deserve a correct and complete discussion, free from racial prejudice and mysterious legal technicalities and phrases—with emphasis on the import to the city, to realtors, and owners of real estate. The United States Supreme Court *did not touch upon the constitutionality or legality of restriction agreements originally upheld by it in previous cases, nor did it rule upon the validity or sufficiency of the particular Washington Park restriction agreement before it in this case.*

The validity and sufficiency of this restrictive agreement is yet to be determined and the Woodlawn Property Owners' League stands back of a number of cases which have been filed in the courts which will determine the validity and sufficiency of the agreement not passed upon by the United States Supreme Court in the Lee versus Hansberry case.

Before such "a number of cases" were heard, however, the bastion collapsed. In 1940 the area was 80 per cent Negro. By 1945 there were practically no white families in the area.

The first "official" attitude of property owners in such a contested area is one of unqualified opposition to Negro residents, and this view is usually voiced by the property owners' associations on behalf of its members. It has been shown, however, that the divergent economic interests of small and large property owners may cause a new organization to develop, stressing the economic interests of the smaller owners. When such a crisis has arisen and Negro invasion is imminent, the residents must face the choice of remaining in the area with Negroes, of selling at a low rate to the larger real estate companies, of selling to Negroes in violation of the covenant, or of fighting the covenants.

During the period of tension, a white interviewer talked with a representative group of *property owners* living in the "white island." (Absentee owners and tenants were not interviewed.) It was found that a few of these people were very bitter toward Negroes, and a few were apparently willing to live beside Negroes as neighbors, while the largest number expressed no hostility toward Negroes as such, but wanted to sell to them at a profit and move. These attitudes may be summarized in relation to what the persons who made them planned to do in relation to their own property—i.e., whether they planned to move, or to remain in the area, or were undecided.

Most of the extreme antagonism toward Negroes was expressed by people who definitely planned to leave. But the anti-Negro die-hards were a minority, even within this group. The following statements are typical of those made by persons planning to move:

"I'm not prejudiced, but I'd burn this building down before I'd sell it to any damned nigger."

"I don't want to bring my children up among Negroes, but where can people go in this city to keep away from Negroes?"

"There are just too many colored people here now."

The last quotation represents the reason most frequently given by persons planning to leave the neighborhood. The comments of the few individuals who planned to remain in the area were more varied:

"Why move? Negroes will be in all neighborhoods after a while."

"I don't mind some colored neighbors so long as the neighborhood isn't *all* colored."

"We've owned this house for years. I think the Negroes in here should be allowed to stay, but no more should come in."

"The people in here just fear intermarriage, that's all. And they're crazy! We need more government housing for Negroes."

The largest group—the "undecided"—provided an even greater variety of reactions:

"The rich Negroes get along all right in this neighborhood."

"Before the mob started coming, the Negroes in here were good neighbors. I'm not prejudiced against them, but a Negro man held me up the other day. I'm scared to stay here."

"I don't know about covenants. It doesn't seem worth all our time and money to fight for them. We can make good money by dealing with Negroes."

"We struggled hard to get this home. I'm going to stay as long as I can, but if Negroes move in all over the place, everything we worked for will be lost."

"It isn't logical to keep restrictive covenants if the only way some people can make money is to rent to Negroes. There's nothing to do but stay here and face the problem. I think real estate is a better investment here than in the suburbs."

"I'd rather have good Negro neighbors than some of the white trash that's coming in as the Negroes come. But I feel lost in this neighborhood now."

The last quotation is of particular interest because it contains two sentiments that were widely prevalent among the white residents of the neighborhood. The first was the feeling (and it seemed to be a fact) that the area was deteriorating irrespective of the influx of Negroes—i.e., in terms of new, undesirable white residents, and of the physical appearance of the community, The second sentiment, even more universal, and present among persons who were going to move out of the neighborhood as well as those who planned to remain or were undecided as to their course of action, seems extremely significant. Most of the white people did not object to the presence of a few Negroes, but they were very much afraid that they, as individual white families, would become completely isolated in a Negro area.

Gunnar Myrdal, Swedish social scientist previously referred to, has analyzed the way in which the fear of becoming isolated in an all-Negro neighborhood operates to reinforce other aspects of the struggle for living space: [8]

". . . [the] situation creates a vicious circle, in which race prejudice, economic interests, and residential segregation mutually reinforce one another. When a few Negro families do come into a neighborhood, some more white families move away. Other Negroes hasten to take their places, because the existing Negro neighborhoods are overcrowded due to segregation. This constant movement of Negroes into white neighborhoods makes the bulk of the white residents feel that their neighborhood is doomed to be predominantly Negro, and they move out—with their attitudes against the Negro reinforced. Yet, if there were no segregation, this wholesale invasion would not have occurred. But because it does occur, segregational attitudes are increased, and the vigilant pressure to stall the Negroes at the borderline is kept up."

As to how much objection white people would have to living in neighborhoods with a few Negroes of similar socio-economic status there is no certain evidence. As we have seen, there are such mixed neighborhoods in Midwest Metropolis. Yet in an opinion poll taken by *Fortune* magazine for the Carnegie-Myrdal study of "The Negro in America," from 77 to 87 per cent of the informants in various sections of the country declared themselves in favor of residential segregation. Such uniform expression of opinion throughout the country suggests that the *thought* of having Negroes as neighbors is very distasteful—though experience shows that many people, who in answer to a direct question will oppose Negro neighbors, would not use violence to evict them, and might ultimately come to accept them.

RACIAL NO MAN'S LAND

One consequence of the pattern of residential segregation is that an area of potential conflict has been created all around the boundaries of the Black Belt. Even during a period when the Belt is not expanding there is always the possibility that an invasion may begin, and this is reflected in periodic "scares," as well as in the policy of business places on the margins of the Black Belt. Proprietors of taverns, drugstores, restaurants, and neighborhood theaters are keenly sensitive to the moods of their clientele, and business places close to the Black Belt are likely to disapprove of colored patronage. This, in turn, antagonizes the Negroes and creates an additional source of friction. From 1936 through 1940 the NAACP handled a number of court cases involving establishments on the edge of the Black Belt. As restaurants and taverns became conversant with the demands of the state Civil Rights Law, they sometimes resorted to the strategem of declaring their establishments to be "clubs." White patrons were given "membership cards," and when Negroes sought service they were asked to produce their cards. This was particularly infuriating to Black Belt residents when the enterprise was on the *Negro* side of the residential dividing line.

The intensity of feeling about Negro patronage, and the manner in which a white businessman can help to crystallize anti-Negro sentiment, are revealed by the following conversation between a white interviewer, working incognito, and a white man who had run a tavern for fifteen years on a corner now marginal to the Black Belt.

Interviewer: "Do you have much Negro trade in here?"

Owner: "No, and I don't want any of the black bastards hanging around here. All they can do is to cheapen the tavern's name."

Interviewer: "Supposing a few colored people came in right now, how would you act towards them?"

Owner: "The way I feel right now I could grab one by the ass of the pants and throw him out on the street. I hate them all, all of them."

Interviewer: "But after all, you are in this place for business, regardless of the color of people, aren't you?"

Owner: "I am in it for a living, but if I have to depend on a black son-of-a-bitch for it, I'll turn the key in the door first."

Interviewer: "Why is it that you feel that way about the Negro people?"

Owner: "I'm from the South, and I'm telling you, when I came to Chicago and saw the way some of them acted I thought I was in a different world."

Interviewer: "Do you mean to say that there was that much difference in them?"

Owner: "As much difference as between day and night."

Interviewer: "But if one or two came in, wouldn't you serve them?"

Owner: "Yes, I would, but that is not saying *how* I would serve them. I don't even like to ride on the same streetcar with them."

When the neighborhood actually seems to be "going colored," white merchants and owners of restaurants, drugstores, and taverns must face the problem of Negro patronage. As has been explained, restaurants and taverns resort to a number of devices if they feel they do not want or need Negro patronage, or that they will lose more white patrons than will be replaced by Negroes. One tavern-keeper in a marginal area, who has run his business for thirty years without Negro patronage, revealed some methods of discouraging such patronage. He indicated "how" *he* would serve them:

Interviewer: "Do you have much Negro trade?"

Owner: "No, and to tell you the truth I don't want any of it."

Interviewer: "Do you refuse to serve any of them?"

Owner: "No, I serve them all right. You see, if I have any white customers I wait on them first, and I might clean the bar and fool around for five minutes or so, then I'll go up to the Negroes and ask, 'What can I do for you?' If they call for a beer, I give them a snit [a four-ounce glass]. They might look at me and grumble to themselves and pick up their change and walk out. Most of them will bang the door. If any of them ask for a shot of whiskey, I give them this [showing a bottle of very cheap whiskey]. If they put down a quarter, I ring it up and walk away from them [the price of a "shot" of whiskey being ten cents]."

Interviewer: "Did any of them ever call you on it?"

Owner: "Some of them said something and I told them that that is what it costs and if they don't like it, stay out of here."

Interviewer: "Do you think that by coming in they spoil your trade?"

Owner: "I don't think it—I know it, and I don't want any part of them. Why, two years ago I was down South, and I'm telling you it did my heart good to see them being put in their place. They run wild in Chicago as compared to down there."

Interviewer: "You have a colored porter, haven't you?"

Owner: "You mean Bill? Sure, he's a nigger, but a good worker. Of course, I keep him in his place, though. I believe in keeping them in their places, and Chicago lets them go too damn far."

Some proprietors in these marginal areas adjust themselves to a changing clientele and occasionally reinforce their decision with myths about the *superiority* of Negroes as customers. Thus an Irish bartender who had been asked point-blank for an opinion, said:

"My experience with colored people has been that they're easier to get along with than the majority of other people. It wouldn't bother me any if our whole trade were colored. Working people and some clerks make up most of our colored trade now; a few, a very few, of the top guys—insurance men and those running the policy games. I'd a lot sooner have the workers; the top guys are just smart enough to think they own the world. No, I never made any particular friends with any of the colored people; just business, that's all.

"We never have had anything anyone could call trouble in here. White and colored fellows in here drinking every night and never a fight or a serious argument in all that time. You know, yourself, that's a lot more than most of these clubs and hotel bars in the Loop can say. You just have to let the fellows know who's running the place, that's all; no need to get tough.

"You say none of this will be used for anything? Well, by God, buddy, it better hadn't! If my name comes out, you'd better skip town. I'll be out looking for you."

In the "dives," too, the problem of a mixed clientele arises. The proprietor of a "joint" located on the dividing street between an Irish-Polish and a Negro area, detailed his contribution to harmonious race relations as follows:

Owner: "You won't see any trouble. You see, most of these girls are hustlers, and if they start any trouble they get put in jail, and you know they don't like that at all."

Interviewer: "I've been in some taverns where a mixed group causes trouble. Can you give me a lead?"

Owner: "Sure, I've been around here for six years and I've never had any trouble yet. I am not in the 'game' any more. You see, all I do now is rent rooms to the girls, and if they cause trouble here, I don't let them rent any rooms."

Interviewer: "Do you rent rooms to the white girls here, too?"

Owner: "Sure, some of the colored boys want to give a white girl a play. It's all right with me, and sometimes a white boy wants a colored girl. It's just the same thing. I'm here for money, and if they want to pay me, I'm satisfied."

Interviewer: "Do the police ever bother you or your rooming house?"

Owner: "No, I get along all right with them. You see, Sergeant —— is a silent partner in this place, and him and I get along all right, and it helps all of us. You know the old saying, 'Don't bite the hand that's feeding you'?"

Interviewer: "That's a good motto if you live up to it."

Owner: "Well, in our business we make it a point to make everyone live up to it, and if they don't we just shun them in the tavern."

The following conversation with a Jewish tavern-keeper indicates the reactions which can be expected when a proprietor decides to cater primarily to colored trade:

Interviewer: "All your trade is Negro, isn't it?"

Owner: "Yes, and I dare say the colored people are the best-natured crowd in the city."

Interviewer: "Do you have any white trade at all?"

Owner: "Yes, I have a few fellows that I made friends with over at 39th and Wentworth."

Interviewer: "Do you ever have any trouble when there are the two races together?"

Owner: "No, I am over here quite a while and I haven't had a fight in this place since I've been here."

Interviewer: "Are your bartenders white or Negro?"

Owner: "They are colored. I have to have them, because all of my trade is colored."

Interviewer: "Do your white friends that come in ever complain to you about the bartenders?"

Owner: "No, and if they did it wouldn't get them anywhere at all. I feel that if they come in this place I accept them as my friends, and I show my feeling that way. In business you've got to cater to everybody, and if Negroes spend money with me, I am their friend."

Interviewer: "Supposing your tavern was in a different location in the city, would you feel the same way about them?"

Owner: "I wouldn't even care if I owned a tavern across from the City Hall. If they wanted to spend a dime with me I would give them the same consideration that I would give you, and I know you for about five years, don't I?"

Interviewer: "Yes. Would you feel the same way about your help?"

Owner: "That would be different. If you are in a Jewish neighborhood, naturally you would have to have some Jewish people working for you."

Interviewer: "Well, Harry, it looks as if you weren't prejudiced at all."

Owner: "No, I'm not. I'll tell you one thing—if you ever make friends with a colored person you can always depend on him. One night this place was broken into and the door window was all broke.

One of my colored friends called me up on the 'phone and stood guard at the door until I came. When I got here I couldn't find a thing missing. Now I ask you how many of my white friends would do a thing like that? When you got friends like that you don't care what color they are, just as long as they are true. That's what I think about the colored people. I don't think I can say that I have one of them what I could call an enemy of mine."

RESIDENTIAL SEGREGATION AND NEGRO-WHITE CONTACTS

The dominant type of community is the "all-white" or "all-Negro" neighborhood. (The term "all-white" is less precise than "all-Negro," for there are proportionately more Negroes scattered about in white communities than there are white people living in Negro communities.) This results in a pattern of relations which reduces to a minimum any neighborly contacts, school contacts, or chance meetings in stores, taverns, and movie houses between Negroes and whites of approximately the same socio-economic status. Yet Negroes and white people are not completely isolated within their respective neighborhoods.

Negroes in White Communities: Hundreds of Negroes find it necessary to go into white communities daily in order to earn a living. Midwest Metropolis is used to seeing Negroes all over the city in the roles of domestic and personal servants, of unskilled workers in restaurants and stores, and of mechanics and car-washers in garages. They are accepted as a normal part of the workaday population, and sustain friendly occupational relations with white employees and employers.*

An occasional Negro may be found occupying some position of minor importance in a white community. Negro postmen work all

---

* Some of the craft unions have made attempts to bar Negroes from working outside of the Black Belt. In 1940, testimony before the Illinois State Commission on the Condition of the Urban Colored Population indicated that the steamfitters' and plumbers' union had made the Negro craftsmen sign a pact not to work outside of the Black Belt. When they crossed the line they were subjected to violence, their work was damaged "mysteriously," and other unions were called out on sympathetic strikes against them. The musicians' union (an AFL affiliate) has also attempted to dictate the specific spots in the city at which colored musicians may play. While restricting Negro competition in this fashion, the white craftsmen reserve the right to work in the Black Belt!

over the city, as do social workers. Colored schoolteachers, firemen, librarians, and policemen are usually assigned to Negro areas, but here and there Negroes hold these types of jobs in white neighborhoods. In 1934 there were 803 teachers in areas 95 per cent Negro and over. Of these, only 272 were colored (33.9 per cent). These 272 colored teachers made up 88 per cent of all colored teachers in the city, only 12 per cent being in more mixed neighborhoods. Harold Gosnell, who presents these figures, reports that he found 31 Negro teachers in some twenty schools which were almost entirely white.[9] Some of these were no doubt "passing" either by design or accident, as in the case of a teacher who said:

"I have been at a near West Side school for all the ten years that I have been a regular teacher. I have never been particularly race conscious. . . . I have never had any trouble with the pupils or the parents.

"There was just one colored substitute during the time that I have been there. I remember her because she proved something that I have been thinking a long time, namely, that the children don't think of a teacher as colored unless she has a black skin. I remember one of my children came in late and when I asked him the reason he said that he had been showing the 'nigger' teacher her room."

There seems to be little opposition to Negro teachers in foreign-born neighborhoods, but Gosnell reports that "in the more prosperous neighborhoods inhabited largely by native whites we did not find Negro teachers who were recognized as such." Interviews with city employees and Federal employees working in white neighborhoods reveal that most of them met initial hostility but were subsequently accepted.

Negroes make little use of the educational, religious, and recreational facilities in white residential areas. The few who do move about the city to theaters and churches or who attend neighborhood institutions meet with little discrimination. Most Negroes who attend churches outside of the Negro areas do so in rather specialized relationships— for example, a visiting group of singers, a special speaker, or a Negro preacher exchanging a pulpit with a white pastor.* These "good-will" activities are not extensive, however, and involve very few Negroes.

* The one exception would be Catholic churches. At the present time, Negroes are allowed to join the nearest parish church and to send their children to the parochial school. This is a recent development, however. In 1940, one of the authors made a study of the Catholic Church in Chicago and found that three Black Belt Catholic churches had been set aside as "Negro" churches and that

In general, the pattern of residential segregation results in habits of thought which characterize certain parts of the city as "white" and others as "Negro." Negroes are expected to remain in their areas unless they have "legitimate" business outside of them. Thus, when Negroes visit friends in some white neighborhoods they are viewed with hostility or suspicion, and may be asked to use back doors and freight elevators. In areas close to the Black Belt, when tension is high because of a threatened invasion or some alleged crime, the police have been known to adopt a policy of stopping Negroes at night and questioning them. Sometimes children's gangs will chase Negroes out of such neighborhoods. These waves of suspicion and antagonism tend to appear and disappear and seldom become set as traditional.

White People in Negro Communities: As an area is "taken over" by Negroes, only those white people remain who have sentimental associations or economic interests. Janitors of apartment houses, businessmen living on their commercial property, prostitutes, priests and nuns at Catholic churches, a few partners in mixed marriages—these are the types of white persons who reside permanently in the Black Belt. Their presence is not considered unusual and they are generally not resented by their Negro neighbors.

Although few white people reside in the Black Belt a host of them come into the area daily—merchants, laborers, social workers, schoolteachers, salesmen, agents and collectors, policemen—and all are the objects of considerable resentment. They are competing with Negroes and exercising some degree of dominance and control over them. The Negro rationalizes his antagonism to such occupational types on the ground that it is unfair for them to hold such positions in Negro communities when Negroes are not allowed to exercise similar functions in most white communities. Expressions of antagonism are usually confined to grumbling or individual discourteous acts. Occasionally, however, a movement arises designed to focus attention upon the "exploiters" in the Black Belt. The two most dramatic of these within recent years are treated elsewhere in this book: the "Spend Your Money Where You Can Work" Campaign of the early 30's, and a

colored Catholics, no matter where they lived in the city, were forced to hold membership in one or the other of these churches. They could attend Mass at other churches, but deaths and marriages were to be solemnized in the Jim-Crow churches. There were several cases of Negro children who were refused enrollment in the nearest parochial school, although this was a violation of canon law.

violent anti-Semitic campaign in 1938. Antagonism is always latent toward "white people who take money out of the Black Belt."

Not all of the white people who come into the area "take money out," however. The cabarets and other "hot spots" have become famous, and many white people come into Black Metropolis for entertainment of varying degrees of respectability. Negroes who profit by this trade naturally do not display resentment toward the "good-timers" and the "slummers." But Negro civic leaders and many middle-class people protest against the tendency to regard Black Metropolis as an exotic rendezvous for white pleasure-seekers.

The pattern of residential segregation inevitably gives rise to an intense community consciousness among Negroes. They begin to think in terms of gaining control of their own areas, and the struggle for this control is the dominant motif of economic and political action within Black Metropolis.

BLACK BELT—BLACK GHETTO

The deep-seated feeling that Negroes are, in the final analysis, somehow fundamentally different from Poles, Italians, Greeks, and other white ethnic groups finds its expression in the persistence of a Black Belt. Midwest Metropolis seems to say: "Negroes have a right to live in the city, to compete for certain types of jobs, to vote, to use public accommodations—but they should have a community of their own. Perhaps they should not be segregated by law, but the city should make sure that most of them remain within a Black Belt." As we have suggested previously, Negroes do not accept this definition of their "place," and while it is probably true that, if allowed free choice, the great majority would live as a compact unit for many years to come, they believe that *enforced* segregation is unjust. They do not always clearly see the full implications and consequences of residential segregation, but they are generally resentful. A sampling of comments made at a time when discussion was widespread about restrictive covenants in Hyde Park will reveal the nature of this resentment. Thus, one prominent Old Settler, the daughter of a German father and a Negro mother, was vitriolic in her denunciation of residential segregation:

"I don't think we would need any housing projects on the South Side if Chicago wasn't so full of this silly old race prejudice. We ought to be able to live anywhere in the city we want to. What the government should do, or somebody with money, is to fight these restrictive covenants and let our people move where they want to. It's a dirty shame that all types of foreigners can move anywhere in the city they want to, and a colored man who has been a soldier and a citizen for his country can live only in a Black Belt. What's the use of fighting for a country that treats you that way?"

A colored "wringer man" in a laundry came to Chicago in 1921 because he had heard of "the good wages and grand opportunities." Now, having become well-adjusted, he resents residential segregation:

"Residential segregation is a big mistake. When I came here, there were white and colored living in the same neighborhood and the people seemed to understand each other. But since this neighborhood is colored only, everything is different. There are less jobs, and the neighborhood is not kept as clean as it used to be. I cannot offer any way to break down segregation. When I was married, I tried to rent houses out of the district, and the real-estate agents wouldn't rent to me. Yes, if Negroes can get houses in Hyde Park, or anywhere else, they ought to take them—for the housing condition for colored on the South Side is rotten."

Another laborer from Georgia who has been in the city nearly thirty years was also heated in his denunciation:

"Racial segregation is rotten. When white and colored both lived in this section, the rents were not so high and there seemed to be a better understanding. I have often wondered if segregation has not had a lot to do with the lack of employment, for there are certain white people that try to prove that all Negroes are bad. When they come over here, they go to the worst part of the section to prove their point."

Somewhat more moderate in his disapproval is a colored chauffeur who came to Chicago in 1912 as a Pullman porter:

"Racial segregation is something that I am not sure is a blessing. The housing proposition is serious, for the rents are very high, and the houses are not kept up as they are in white neighborhoods. On the other hand, if we were scattered among the white people there would be far less work, for by being close together we get a lot of work from the stores owned by white people that are doing business in our neighborhood. I have thought of ways to break down this segregation, but when I think that anything you do makes you a lawbreaker, you then cease to fight individuals, for then it becomes a war with the law. Remember that the police, the judges, and the strongest lawyer groups are all white and they stick together. I have seen one case of a fight between the police and the colored citizens and know that it was far from being an equal fight."

Many other Negroes, however, express a willingness to risk trouble in attacking this form of segregation. A skilled worker, a respectable church member, was very emphatic on this point:

"Hyde Park is no more than any other place in Chicago. The Negroes ought to move into Hyde Park or any other park they want to move into. I don't know of anything on earth that would keep me out of Hyde Park if I really wanted to move into it. Personally, I don't care anything about the good-will of white people if it means keeping me and my people down or in restricted neighborhoods."

A minority defends the existence of enforced residential segregation. This is done not on principle, but as a matter of expediency, or for fear of racial clashes, or because such persons feel that the time to attack segregation has not yet come. Thus, a colored waiter who blames most of the discrimination against Negroes on the Great Migration, partly defends segregation:

"I myself believe segregation is good, for if the white and colored lived together there would be fights constantly. About the only business benefit we derive from a Black Belt region is from a political standpoint, for there are a lot of people working that have gotten their appointments from their power as a voting factor. I think segregation is caused by the Negro's failure to try to get out of the district. In fact, I have never tried to live out of the district. There is no reason—I just have not thought of it."

Occasionally the opinion is expressed that Negroes are not "ready" to move into better neighborhoods, that they must first prove their worth by making the Black Belt a cleaner, more orderly, better-kept area. Thus one man states:

"Our duty to ourselves and to those with whom we come in contact is to show the world that we are an advanced people, that we are law-abiding and respectable and that we are able to care for the property we control or occupy. You can bet your bottom dollar that when we do this, we will be welcome wherever we care to live."

This theory that individual Negroes must wait until the whole group improves itself before they can get out of the Black Belt is not at all popular with ambitious Negroes.

Most Chicago Negroes feel that the right to rent or buy a house offered to the public should be inalienable. Yet Negro businessmen and politicians will sometimes state privately that they prefer keeping the Negro population concentrated. During a campaign against restrictive covenants, one prominent Negro leader confided to an interviewer:

"Sure, I'm against covenants. They are criminal. But I don't want Negroes moving about all over town. I just want to add little pieces to the Black Belt. I'd never get re-elected if Negroes were all scattered about. The white people wouldn't vote for me."

Most Negroes probably have a similar goal—the establishment of the *right* to move where they wish, but the preservation of some sort of large Negro community by voluntary choice. But they wish a community much larger than the eight square miles upon which Black Metropolis now stands.

At one session of the Mayor's Conference on Race Relations in 1944, the Chairman of the Chicago Housing Authority stated [10] of the Black Belt that

"In 1939 there was an excess population of 87,300 persons, measured by citywide standards of density. Since then an estimated 60,000 or more persons have moved into the area to accentuate an already bad condition.

"The race relations problem of Chicago resolves itself around the question of living space for Negro citizens. A major revision in public opinion on race relations must be effected before private or public agencies can make any substantial contribution to the solution of this problem."

Negro newspapers and civic leaders unanimously oppose enforced residential segregation and bitterly attack the forces that have created an overcrowded Black Belt. To them, the area is a Black Ghetto, and they insist that "new areas should be opened to break the iron ring which now restricts most Negro families to intolerable, unsanitary conditions. Restrictive-covenant agreements and the iron ring creating a Negro ghetto must be smashed." [11]

Even the Chairman of the Mayor's Committee accepted the characterization of the Black Belt as a "ghetto," and there was general agreement among the participants in the Mayor's Conference in 1944 that most of the social problems within the Black Belt were fundamentally related to the operation of restrictive covenants. (Only the spokesman for the Chicago Real Estate Board disagreed.*) The conference listed among the "ghetto conditions" high sickness and death rates; † a heavy relief load during the Depression; inadequate recreational facilities; lack of building repairs; neglect of garbage disposal and street cleaning; overcrowded schools; ‡ high rates of crime and juvenile delinquency; and rough treatment by the police.

The ghetto characteristics of the Black Belt are related, in the first instance, to the poverty of its people. Here, the proportion of families on relief during the Depression was the highest for the entire city. (Figure 8.) The restricted economic base of the community was also

* The real-estate interests in Midwest Metropolis insist that a general scarcity of houses is the primary problem, and that, if there were enough houses or a building program in process, middle-class white families would move away from areas close to the Black Belt and Negroes could then take over the abandoned houses. They blame New Deal restrictions and the Federal housing program for the housing shortage, charging that private capital has been made reluctant to invest. The Chicago Real Estate Board refuses, unequivocally, to sanction the abolition of restrictive covenants. Yet plenty of houses would not solve the basic question of the *quality* of housing available for Negro occupancy. Negroes would still be concentrated in areas of the city that have begun to deteriorate.

† In 1925, Chicago had the lowest death rate for any American city of 1,000,000 and over, but the Negro death rate was twice that for whites. (H. L. Harris, Jr., "Negro Mortality Rates in Chicago," *Social Service Review*, v. 1, no. 1, 1927.) The average standard death rate for the years 1928-1932 was 9.2 for native-whites, 10.4 for foreign-whites, and 20.0 for Negroes. (Elaine Ogden, *Chicago Negro Community*, WPA, 1939, p. 201.) Differences in infant mortality are reflected in the fact that 3 Negro babies die before their first birthday to every 2 white babies. Social disorganization in the Black Ghetto is reflected in deaths from homicide—six Negroes die from violent assaults for every white person who is killed.

The striking differentials in morbidity rates are those for tuberculosis (see Figure 9) and venereal diseases. The Negro tuberculosis rate is five times the white rate and the venereal disease rate is reported as 25 times that for whites. Both diseases are closely related to a low material standard of living and widespread ignorance of hygiene. *It should be borne in mind, however, that we are dealing with rates, not absolute numbers.* The actual number of Negroes who have venereal disease does not warrant the common belief that "the Negro race is eaten up with syphilis and gonorrhea." About 75 venereal disease cases were reported among every thousand Negroes in 1942, and 3 among whites.

‡ Civic leaders are most bitter about the double- and triple-shift schools in the Black Belt. In 1938, thirteen of the fifteen schools running on "shifts" were in Negro neighborhoods. Pupils spent half of the day in school and were "on the streets" for the rest of the day. In 1944, the School Board alleged that this system had been abolished, but Negro leaders disputed the claim. The Board of Education consistently refused to give the authors any data on overcrowding in the schools. A building program has been projected which may relieve the situation in the future.

Figure 8

POVERTY AND SOCIAL DISORGANIZATION

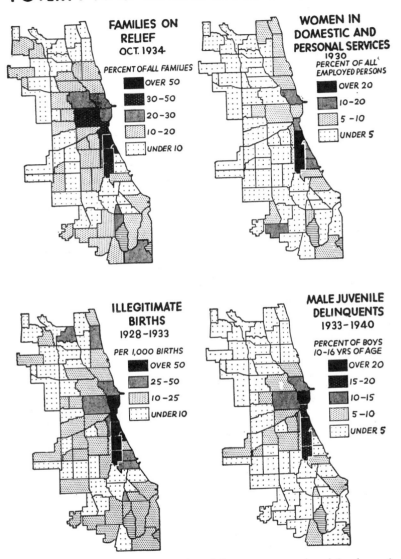

FAMILIES ON RELIEF
OCT. 1934
PERCENT OF ALL FAMILIES
- OVER 50
- 30-50
- 20-30
- 10-20
- UNDER 10

WOMEN IN DOMESTIC AND PERSONAL SERVICES
1930
PERCENT OF ALL EMPLOYED PERSONS
- OVER 20
- 10-20
- 5-10
- UNDER 5

ILLEGITIMATE BIRTHS
1928-1933
PER 1,000 BIRTHS
- OVER 50
- 25-50
- 10-25
- UNDER 10

MALE JUVENILE DELINQUENTS
1933-1940
PERCENT OF BOYS 10-16 YRS OF AGE
- OVER 20
- 15-20
- 10-15
- 5-10
- UNDER 5

The rates for families on relief and for women employed in domestic service are from Wirth and Furez, *Local Community Fact Book*. Insanity rates are from Faris and Dunham, *Mental Disorders in Urban Areas* and juvenile delinquency rates were compiled by the Institute for Juvenile Research. (The Black Belt community areas are those outlined in white.)

evident in the high proportion of women doing domestic service. As a low-income area, the community was unable to maintain a high material standard of living. This poverty was aggravated by the housing problem which caused overcrowding. Given these factors, and the lack of widespread health education among Negroes, it is not surprising that the tuberculosis death rate is five times higher than it is for whites, and that the Negro areas have the highest sickness and death rates from tuberculosis. Chicago has the highest Negro death rate from tuberculosis of any metropolitan city in the United States.*

The Black Ghetto also suffers from a type of social disorganization which is reflected in high illegitimacy and juvenile delinquency rates † and a high incidence of insanity. (Figures 8 and 9.)

Restrictions upon free competition for housing, and the inability of the Black Belt to expand fast enough to accommodate the Negro population, have resulted in such a state of congestion that Negroes are living 90,000 to the square mile as compared with 20,000 to the square mile in adjacent white apartment-house areas. Since they entered the city last and are a low-income group, Negroes, in the aggregate, have inherited the worst sections of Midwest Metropolis. They have been able to "take over" some fairly decent housing in neighborhoods that were being abandoned by white residents, but these were no longer prized as residential neighborhoods. Negroes have thus become congested in undesirable residential areas.

---

* These high tuberculosis morbidity and mortality rates among Negroes may reflect the fact that Negroes as a recently urbanized group have not developed immunity to the disease. But the wide differentials also reflect the well-known fact that the care of tuberculosis demands bed rest with plenty of nutritious food. (Rates from Dorothy J. Liveright, "Tuberculosis Mortality Among Residents of 92 Cities of 100,000 or More Population: United States, 1939-41," U. S. Public Health Reports, July 21, 1944, pp. 942-955.)

Cities of 1,000,000 and Over Population	Tuberculosis Death Rates: 1939-41	
	For Whites	For Negroes
Chicago, Illinois	45.4	250.1
New York, New York	40.4	213.0
Philadelphia, Pennsylvania	44.3	203.5
Detroit, Michigan	36.5	189.0
Los Angeles, California	49.7	137.3

† In 1944, the Superintendent of the State Training School for Girls at Geneva, Ill., reported that Negro girls made up 36 per cent of all girls at the institution. Frazier has noted a steady rise between 1919 and 1930 in the proportion of Negro boys brought before the juvenile court. In the latter year 21.7 per cent of the boys brought before the court were Negroes.

Figure 9

DISEASE AND DEATH

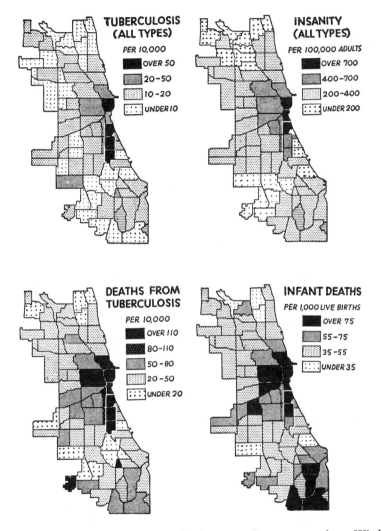

Tuberculosis morbidity rates and infant mortality rates are from Wirth and Furez, *Local Community Fact Book*. Tuberculosis mortality rates are from the records of the Municipal Tuberculosis Sanitarium. Map showing insanity rates adapted from Faris and Dunham, *op. cit.* (The Black Belt community areas are those outlined in white.)

Over half of Black Metropolis lies in that area which the city planners and real-estate interests have designated as "blighted." The "blighted areas" have come into being as a part of the process of uncontrolled city growth, for as Midwest Metropolis has grown, spontaneously and in response to economic utility, its center has become a citadel of imposing office buildings surrounded by an ever-widening belt of slums. As the city expands, this slum land becomes valuable as the site of future wholesale establishments, warehouses, transportation terminals, and light industries. No one wishes to invest in new housing upon these potentially valuable spots. Housing already there is allowed to deteriorate and is then torn down. From the standpoint of residential desirability, this entire area is "blighted."

The superficial observer believes that these areas are "blighted" because large numbers of Negroes and Jews, Italians and Mexicans, homeless men and "vice" gravitate there. But real-estate boards, city planners, and ecologists know that the Negro, the foreign-born, the transients, pimps, and prostitutes are located there because the area has already been written off as blighted. The city's outcasts of every type have no choice but to huddle together where nobody else wants to live and where rents are relatively low.

Black Metropolis has become a seemingly permanent enclave within the city's blighted area. The impecunious immigrant, once he gets on his feet, may—as we have mentioned several times—move into an area of second-settlement. Even the vice-lord or gangster, after he makes his pile, may lose himself in a respectable neighborhood. Negroes, regardless of their affluence or respectability, wear the badge of color. They are expected to stay in the Black Belt.

During the last twenty years the Negro's demand for housing has always exceeded the supply. The rental value of residential property in the Black Belt is thus abnormally high. The speculative value of the land on which the property stands is also high, and—even more than the restriction of supply—this has a tendency to drive rents up. A prominent real-estate operator, during the Depression, said frankly to a Negro social worker: "There are two ways to handle residential property in the Black Belt. Figure on amortizing the investment in twenty years and scale the rent accordingly. Plan to amortize your investment in ten years and double the rent. If this section is doomed for residential purposes anyhow, the latter is a better business practice

for us." Houses in Black Metropolis pay off now. The land they occupy will do so in the future.

Midwest Metropolis does not intend to keep on growing haphaz-
ardly. City planners and the larger real-estate interests hope some day
to control its growth, and Chicago's master plan calls for the eventual
reclamation of the inner city, with a garden belt of privately financed,
medium-rental apartments replacing the slums. Here, it is hoped,
members of the new middle class will make their homes, close to the
Loop where they work, and well within the city limits. The blighted
areas will thus be reclaimed. Low-cost housing nearer steel mills and
industrial plants in the suburbs will be constructed (also, for the most
part, with private funds) to attract the skilled and semi-skilled
workers. But some question marks remain.

"What," asked an official of a Negro civic agency, "do the Chicago
Real Estate Board, and the city, plan to do with the Negroes who now
live in the blighted areas? Will restrictive covenants be relaxed so
they, too, can move to the suburbs and near-suburbs?" This was during the Depression, when Negro labor was not in demand, and the
answer of a member of the Real Estate Board was crisp: "We have
no plans for them. Perhaps they can return to the South."

The realtor's remark reflected the rather general antagonism of Chicago taxpayers toward the 40,000 Negroes who migrated to Black
Metropolis during the Depression. There was a tendency during this
period to feel that Midwest Metropolis had no responsibilities toward
an unwanted population which was crowding into the already satu-
rated Black Belt. Vacancy rates for the entire city were low, and no
new areas of occupancy were opened to Negroes until near the eve of
the Second World War, when one square mile was added to Black
Metropolis. It is ironic that the lone Federal housing project within the
Black Belt actually displaced sixteen more families than it accommodated. The Second World War brought 60,000 more Negroes to the
city—this time a welcome addition to the labor market. Over 1,500
units of war housing were made available, but at least 10,000 more
were needed. Wartime controls froze Black Belt rents at their already
high levels, and overcrowding mounted to an almost intolerable point.

Some private real-estate groups have become interested in the possibilities of investing in Negro housing, but the question still remains:
"Where shall it be situated?"

Negro civic leaders in Chicago were quite pleased when Newton

Farr, a former president of the National Association of Real Estate Boards and one of Chicago's most intransigent defenders of restrictive covenants, conducted a survey of "hundreds of the best posted real estate men in eighteen large cities" on their opinion of Negroes as renters and potential home owners. The questions and replies are summarized below: *

(1) Does the Negro make a good home buyer and carry through his purchase to completion? . . . . . . 17 of the 18 cities reported YES.

(2) Does he take as good care of property as other tenants of a comparable status? . . . . . . 11 of the 18 cities reported YES.

(3) Do you know of any reason why insurance companies should not purchase mortgages on property occupied by Negroes? . . . . . . 14 of the 18 cities reported NO.

(4) Do you think there is a good opportunity for realtors in the Negro housing field in your city? . . . . . . 12 of the 18 cities reported YES.

To a double-barreled question, "Is the Negro good pay as a tenant or are more frequent collections necessary and losses greater?" six cities said the Negro tenant is "good pay," seven said "no," and two reported conflicting experiences. On the second half of the question ten cities reported more frequent collections are necessary, while two disclaimed this.

A majority of cities commented that Negroes maintain neatness and repairs on new property as well as whites, but underscored that relatively few properties in good condition are sold to Negroes.

Some weeks later, Newton Farr, as determined as ever to "hold the line," reiterated to Negro leaders that he was interested in providing *Negro* housing, not in mixing whites and Negroes within neighborhoods. He felt that *Negro* housing might be a paying investment in the post-War world, but segregation must be maintained.

The city faces a dilemma—a sort of social paralysis. Midwest Metropolis doesn't want to let Negroes stay where they are, and it doesn't want them to scatter freely about the city. It doesn't want to rebuild the inner city to house them, nor does it wish to provide homes elsewhere. And all the time Black Metropolis—a big, stubborn, eight-square-mile fact crammed with over 300,000 people—grows more and more congested.†

* The quoted material and summary are from the New York *Herald Tribune,* November 19, 1944.

† The Chicago Plan Commission has divided all residential areas into five types, as of 1942, and made plans for the future status of each. Thus, "blighted

These Negroes, upon whom the city depends for much of its unskilled and semi-skilled labor and for a large part of its domestic service, continue to pile up upon one another within these congested areas. As they do so, morbidity and mortality rates rise out of all proportion to those in the rest of the city. Crime and juvenile delinquency rates, too, indicate that serious maladjustments are present in the Black Belt. Black Metropolis acquires the reputation of being a "slum area," and the bare statistical record and surface impressions seem convincing evidence that Negroes make undesirable neighbors. This estimate of Negroes is reinforced deliberately by the real-estate interests and incidentally by the press and radio. Rumor and chance impressions further confirm the reputation of Black Metropolis as a "rough" neighborhood.

During the fifteen years between the Great Migration and the Depression, the Black Belt gained the reputation of being a colorful community, "wide-open" and rough. It was also considered "easy picking" for the Republican machine. Yet most of the city paid little attention to Black Metropolis for ten years after the Race Riot of 1919, except during the excitement of an election campaign or an occasional "vice crusade." Its immediate neighbors, however, feared it because it was steadily expanding and pressing upon them.

The Depression made the entire city conscious of Black Metropolis. In the first place, the area became the scene of the eviction riots and the "Spend Your Money Where You Can Work" Campaign. Then it

and near blighted" areas are to be eliminated, becoming *rebuilt* areas; "conservation" areas are those which will, in the future, become *ripe for rebuilding;* those which are, at present, "stable" are expected to become *conservation* property; present areas of "arrested" or "progressive" development and "new growth" will some day be *stable.* "Vacant" areas will gradually become ripe for *new growth.*

Two-thirds of the main Black Belt area has been classified as "blighted" or "near-blighted" and a third as "conservation" property.

Of the 250,000 people in the Black Belt, the Commission estimated that at least 87,000 persons should be moved out in order to thin the population down to the optimum in conservation areas and to a level of health and decency upon rebuilding the blighted areas with a combination of walk-up apartments and rowhouses. At least 16,000 should move even if three-story walk-up apartments replaced all the present housing in the blighted areas.

The Commission favored intensive new building within two small Negro communities outside of the Black Belt and the creation of a new segregated community on the edge of the city limits. These three Jim-Crow communities could accommodate 30,000 or 40,000 people from the main Black Belt.

(Cf. booklet *Design for Public Improvements,* by the Chicago Plan Commission and mimeographed memorandum, "Population in South Side Negro Areas.")

reversed its political tradition of fifteen years and went Democratic. Throughout the Depression period Black Metropolis was good copy for the white press. The Chicago *Tribune,* for instance, professing alarm at the high proportion of Negroes on the WPA, occasionally made snide comments on the waste of the taxpayers' money. The militant demands which Negroes raised for better housing and more relief were sometimes hysterically interpreted as evidence that Black Metropolis was turning "Red," and on at least one occasion a Hearst paper headlined a revolution in progress. (The incident was merely a tenant strike in a single building.) All the daily papers rediscovered the presence of a widespread gambling syndicate, and devoted columns to the life and works of Negro racketeers. Though the *Times,* a liberal tabloid, tried to be helpful and ran several feature stories with appropriate pictures emphasizing the dirt and squalor and ramshackle housing in the area, it rounded off the series with a sensational exposé of Black Belt "rackets."

Whenever an institution in the Negro community launched a drive for funds, the evidences of community disorganization were emphasized in the press in order to stimulate charity. On one occasion, a city-wide drive against syphilis involved the uncritical publication of statistics and maps which suggested that the Black Belt was a "cesspool of disease" (the actual words of one newspaper).* Such publicity

* Negro civic leaders are very ambivalent about the matter of publicizing health statistics on Negro communities. They point out that persons unfamiliar with statistics confuse high *proportions* with high *absolute* figures. For instance, only 5 Negroes in a 100 may have syphilis, but if the fact is publicized that the Negro *rate* is 40 times that for white people, the public will begin to view every Negro as a potential paretic. Yet, in order to focus the attention of the larger white world upon the Negro's plight, it is necessary to emphasize poverty and disorganization, to display the sores of Black Metropolis like a beggar seeking alms. One civic leader pointed out that this approach sometimes boomerangs and quoted the words of an industrialist that he had approached about hiring some Negroes: "Mr. Smith was over here recently soliciting money for that Negro hospital. He showed me a lot of charts and graphs on tuberculosis and syphilis. I can't put your people in my factory using the same rest-rooms and cafeterias that the other workers use."

The following sampling of editorial appeals in daily papers during a money-raising drive for a hospital in Black Metropolis suggests the manner in which the white public's fears are aroused and the unsavory reputation of Black Metropolis reinforced, in order to stimulate charity. The editorials of three daily newspapers, in addition to presenting factual material, stressed the imminence of some disaster originating in the Black Belt. The *Times* stated: "We must at once remedy our dereliction or, with the growing consciousness of the Negro of his political

helped to fix the reputation of Midwest Metropolis during the Depression. A new liberal daily, the *Sun,* appearing in 1941, inaugurated a less sensational approach to Black Belt problems, but the reputation of the area was already fixed.

The existence of these conditions has become a convenient rationalization for keeping Negroes segregated. The University of Chicago (with properties tangential to the Black Belt), neighborhood property owners' associations all around it, and the Chicago Real Estate Board have visualized restrictive covenants as a permanent *cordon sanitaire.*

Community leaders in Black Metropolis, as well as professional and businessmen generally, are worried about the area's reputation in the larger white world—a world which identifies each of them with the Black Ghetto. Throughout 1938, one Negro weekly newspaper ran a symposium, "Is the South Side Doomed?", encouraging discussion of community improvement. The series of articles revealed general agreement on the necessity for abolishing restrictive covenants if doom was to be averted. Community leaders devote much of their time and attention to petition, protest, and legal action designed to abolish restrictive covenants. (They have been doing this for twenty years, without success.) While aware of the economic and social forces which create the ghetto, they also cling tenaciously to the possibility of reducing life within the area to order and neatness. This hope has resulted in "clean-up campaigns," drives for increased police protection and health facilities, and the constant stimulation of community morale. These efforts are frustrated, however, by the necessity for trying to improve living conditions within an area too small to accommodate the population, given the present amount and quality of housing.

As it becomes increasingly crowded—and "blighted"—Black Metropolis's reputation becomes ever more unsavory. The city assumes that *any* Negroes who move *anywhere* will become a focal point for another little Black Belt with a similar reputation. To allow the Black Belt to disintegrate would scatter the Negro population. To allow it

and collective power, find it remedied in ways we may not care for." (June 26, 1938.) The *Daily News* suggested that "protection of health in the Negro area means health protection to every citizen of Chicago. . . . Quite aside from the humanitarian reasons, the rest of Chicago cannot afford to let this institution stop or even to curtail its activities." (July 5, 1938.) According to the *Tribune,* "Failure to raise the money will mean a vast amount of needless suffering and it may not be confined to the Negroes." (July 8, 1938.)

to expand will tread on the toes of vested interests, large and small, in the contiguous areas. To let it remain the same size means the continuous worsening of slum conditions there. To renovate it requires capital, but this is a poor investment. It is better business to hold the land for future business structures, or for the long-talked-of rebuilding of the Black Belt as a white office-workers' neighborhood. The real-estate interests consistently oppose public housing within the Black Belt, which would drive rents down and interfere with the ultimate plan to make the Black Belt middle-class and white.

The Race Relations Director of the regional office of the Federal Housing Authority suggested to the Mayor's Committee in 1944 that it "request the Real Estate Board, the Chamber of Commerce, the banks, the City Plan Commission, the Chicago Housing Authority, Chicago Housing Council, and labor organizations to develop a program to house the citizens of Chicago, including Negro families of the South Side, in the immediate postwar period. Request them to join with efforts to abolish restrictive covenants. Point out to them that the abolition of restrictive covenants will not involve the influx of any large number of Negro families to any predominantly white neighborhood, any more than free access to the purchase of automobiles will encourage all Negroes to purchase Cadillac or Ford cars. Request these groups to support public housing for the rental market which cannot be served by private enterprise." [12]

The Mayor's Committee itself went on record as being opposed to restrictive covenants and pledged to "continue to work earnestly with other effective agencies to rid the city of arbitrary restrictions on the living space of any group." The Committee chairman stated: "No people can live decently unless they can live freely. The ghetto is a feature of medieval Europe that has no place in America. . . . At present Negroes are confined to restricted areas with bad houses and exorbitant rents. They are confined to these districts by an atmosphere of prejudice and specifically by conspiracies known as restrictive covenants. This Committee has by formal vote declared itself categorically opposed to restrictions of race, creed, or color on the place where any of Chicago's citizens may live." Black Metropolis, remembering similar statements twenty years before by another Commission on Race Relations, remains skeptical.

On June 23, 1945, the *Defender* published an editorial, DANGER: DYNAMITE AT LARGE, which said, in part:

Hate-crazed incendiaries carrying the faggots of intolerance have in the past several months attacked some 30 homes occupied by Negroes on the fringes of the black belt, solely because these colored citizens have desperately crossed the unwritten boundary in their search for a hovel to live in. Buildings have been set afire, bombed, stoned and razed. Their occupants have been shot and slugged.

To date the Chicago Police Department has done virtually nothing to apprehend the guilty.

With the hot summer days ahead, there is dire danger in continued inaction.

Today racial dynamite is scattered about the South side. It needs but a spark to explode.

The *Defender* spoke scornfully of "studies and surveys . . . promises and pledges." * It demanded that the City suspend restrictive covenants by a war emergency order and "post full and complete police protection" for Negroes moving into houses.

The inhabitants of the Black Ghetto grow restless in their frustration, penned in, isolated, overcrowded. During a depression or a war (the periods covered by this account), the consciousness of their exclusion and subordination is tremendously heightened. Within this spatial and social framework morale tends to be low and tempers taut. Anti-Semitic sentiments are latent. Demands for the economic and political control of the Black Belt arise. Resentments assume various organizational forms. The people marshal their economic and political power and make demands for improvements within the Black Belt and for its ultimate dissolution as an enforced state of existence. For, while it is conceivable that many Negroes would prefer to live in an all-Negro community, they resent being forced to live there.

---

* After declaring its opposition to restrictive covenants, the Mayor's Committee seemed to avoid any further discussion of the abolition of covenants. Evidently the Committee soon realized that it had no power or authority to attack them legally and was hesitant to antagonize the political machine and powerful real estate interests. As in other fields when up against entrenched interests, the Mayor's Committee found itself powerless to act and seemingly reluctant to continue any agitation.

CHAPTER 9

The Job Ceiling

DURING THE WEEK OF MARCH 24, 1940, A BRIGADE OF FEDERAL DOORBELL-
ringers descended upon Chicago's 800,000 households to extract the
bits of information from which the Sixteenth United States Census
was to be compiled. The industries of Midwest Metropolis were just
beginning to hum again after limping along for ten Depression years.
For the second time within a generation, a war in Europe had caused
a stir upon the Midwestern plains. Hope was in the air as the unemployed dreamed of work and pay-checks. But optimism was al-
loyed with skepticism. Everybody remembered the previous cycle of
War—Boom—Collapse. Negroes, particularly, kept their fingers
crossed, repeating their widespread aphorism, "Negroes are always
the last to be hired and the first to be fired."

Negroes had originally come to Chicago in large numbers to meet
a wartime labor demand. Now, after twenty-five years, on this day
of enumeration, in the year 1940, their economic plight was not en-
viable. A new war boom had begun, but they had not begun to share
in the upswing. Here was manpower waiting for a chance. The First
World War began with a labor shortage; the Second World War
began with a labor surplus of ten years' standing—and Negroes made
up a large part of this surplus. A fourth of all Negro males above 14
years of age, and over a tenth of the females, were "seeking work" in
private industry (Figure 10). They were on relief and WPA or were
being supported by friends and relatives.

The Census of 1940 revealed some startling things about these
Negroes "in the labor market"—the able-bodied adults who wanted to
work—the "available workers." (Figure 11.)

19 out of every 100 Negro men were on Emergency Work Projects.
17 out of every 100 Negro men were seeking work.

12 out of every 100 Negro women were on Emergency Work Projects.
23 out of every 100 Negro women were seeking work.

It was evident that Negroes were suffering at least three times more severely from unemployment than the white population. (Figure 11.)

Figure 10

PROPORTION OF AVAILABLE WORKERS: March 1940

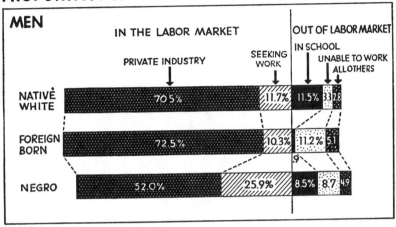

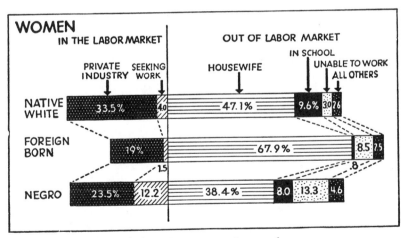

"Seeking work" includes emergency project workers.

The 1940 pattern was nothing new. Five years before, the picture had been even more bleak. The first five years of the Depression had piled up a backlog of over 150,000 unemployed workers of

Figure 11

AVAILABLE WORKERS WHO DID NOT HAVE JOBS IN PRIVATE INDUSTRY IN MARCH 1940

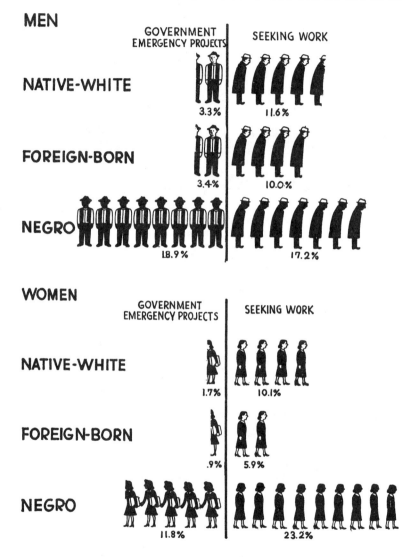

MEN

	GOVERNMENT EMERGENCY PROJECTS	SEEKING WORK
NATIVE-WHITE	3.3%	11.6%
FOREIGN-BORN	3.4%	10.0%
NEGRO	18.9%	17.2%

WOMEN

	GOVERNMENT EMERGENCY PROJECTS	SEEKING WORK
NATIVE-WHITE	1.7%	10.1%
FOREIGN-BORN	.9%	5.9%
NEGRO	11.8%	23.2%

Percentages based on total persons "in the labor market" for each ethnic group. "Seeking work" refers to persons without regular *or* emergency jobs.

whom about 35,000 were Negroes.* *While Negroes made up only eight per cent of the available workers, they constituted twenty-two per cent of the unemployed.* All along the line, Negroes had been displaced in a ratio of roughly three to one. Almost half of the Negro domestic servants, a third of the semi-skilled workers, and a fourth of the unskilled were unemployed in 1935. (Table 4.)

TABLE 4

UNEMPLOYMENT AMONG NEGROES IN MIDWEST METROPOLIS, FIVE YEARS AFTER
THE DEPRESSION BEGAN, COMPARED WITH UNEMPLOYMENT OF THE
WHITE POPULATION

(Estimates in Round Numbers) †

Occupation	Race	Number of Persons at Work in 1930	Number of Persons Still at Work in 1935	Number of Persons Displaced	Per Cent Displaced	Excess of Negroes Displaced
Professional, proprietary, and managerial	W	229,000	223,000	6,000	3.0	5×
	N	7,000	5,900	1,100	15.0	
Clerical	W	245,000	230,000	15,000	6.0	
	N	5,000	4,000	1,000	20.0	3×
Skilled	W	236,000	216,000	20,000	9.0	
	N	9,000	7,000	2,000	30.0	3×
Clerical semi-skilled	W	273,000	247,000	26,000	10.0	3×
	N	27,000	18,000	9,000	33.0	
Unskilled	W	134,000	116,000	18,000	14.0	
	N	29,000	22,000	7,000	24.0	2×
Service	W	89,000	78,000	11,000	12.0	2×
	N	46,000	34,000	12,000	26.0	

† Estimates based on tabulations in Estelle Hill Scott, "Occupational Changes Among Negroes in Chicago, 1890-1930," Cayton-Warner Research, and Chicago Housing Authority, "Memorandum on Unemployment in Chicago," 1935. Estimates are based upon the assumption that the major increases in Negro population between 1930 and 1940 began after 1935. This assumption seems to be borne out by the population census of 1934.

* The high-water mark of unemployment among Negroes was probably reached in 1930 and 1931. In January of 1931, the Unemployment Census

Why were Negroes so disproportionately represented in the ranks of the unemployed? The answer is threefold:

1. They were concentrated in the occupations which are the first to feel the results of an economic crisis.
2. As a minority group, they were likely to be dropped first, with white workers retaining their jobs longer.
3. Negroes continued to migrate to Chicago—40,000 of them between 1930 and 1940—fleeing the collapse of the southern cotton economy and discrimination in the administering of relief in the South. There were no jobs for them.

NEGRO WORKERS ON DEPRESSION EVE

To understand the intense feeling within Black Metropolis about job discrimination, it is important to visualize the economic position of Negroes in Chicago on the eve of the Depression, at the end of a ten-year wave of "prosperity." It is obvious from an examination of Figure 12 that Negroes were doing a disproportionately large amount of the city's servant work, a disproportionately small amount of the "clean work," and a little above their "proportionate share" of the "manual labor." The term "proportionate share" as used throughout this chapter is simply a device for comparing the occupational status of Negroes and whites by assuming: (1) that Negroes and whites have the same conception of what constitutes a "good job"; (2) that Negroes, if permitted, would compete for these good jobs; (3) that there are no inherited mental differences between the races; (4) that if competition were absolutely unfettered by racial discrimination, Negroes, being approximately 8 per cent of the workers in 1930, would tend to approximate 8 per cent of *each* occupational group.*

✦

revealed that over half of the Negro employable women (58.5 per cent) and nearly half of the employable men (43.5) were without jobs. These data are summarized in Richard Sterner, *The Negro's Share*, Harper, 1944, p. 362.

* This method of analysis is, of course, open to the criticism that it does not take into account the time factor—that the fifteen years between 1915 and 1930 may not have constituted a sufficiently long period of time for such a distribution to take place. At the rate of speed with which industry was expanding during the Twenties, and with the amount of turnover in personnel which seems to have been involved in the crucial fields of skilled labor and white-collar employment, it seems reasonable to assume that the differentials between the actual proportions

The "Clean Work": Professional, proprietary, managerial, and clerical work was almost a white monopoly on the eve of the Depres-

Figure 12

DISTRIBUTION OF THE CITY'S WORK

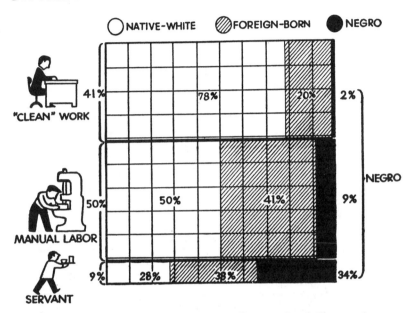

Prepared from tables in Estelle Hill Scott, "Occupational Changes Among Negroes in Chicago: 1890-1930," WPA, 1940. Data for 1930.

sion. Negro representation in Chicago's large white-collar class was very small. Those few Negroes who did "clean work" were almost entirely confined to the Black Ghetto and were dependent upon the

and the theoretical "proportionate share" would not have been so great if barriers had not been placed against the use of Negroes.

The concept of the "proportionate share" has more than theoretical interest, however. During the Depression several Federal agencies reserved a certain quota of jobs for Negroes based on their numbers in the population. Thus, on a job in area where Negro carpenters were 3 per cent of all carpenters in 1930, this percentage of Negroes was hired. In the autumn of 1944, the Communist Party raised the issue sharply within a number of unions as to whether seniority provisions should not be waived during postwar cut-backs in order to let Negro workers retain the same proportion of jobs in the plant which they had gained during the War period. This tendency to think in terms of "quotas" and "pro-

wage-earning masses for a livelihood, or upon the ability of white people to pay for their services as entertainers. (See Table 5.)

TABLE 5 *

THE TEN "CLEAN" OCCUPATIONS IN WHICH NEGROES WERE MOST HEAVILY REPRESENTED: 1930

Negro Men			Negro Women		
Occupation	Number of Men	Share of Work (Per Cent)	Occupation	Number of Women	Share of Work (Per Cent)
Mail carriers.....	630	16	Restaurateurs.....	235	19
Clergymen.......	390	15	Physicians' attend-		
Undertakers......	120	12	ants	55	12
Musicians........	525	10	Actresses	145	10
Actors..........	215	9	Messenger girls...	30	6
Messengers and of-			Musicians........	205	7
fice boys.......	385	6	Religious workers.	45	6
Taxicab owners...	110	8	Social workers....	50	5
Government offi-		5	Designers........	25	5
cials...........	40	5	Physicians........	17	4
Physicians........	265	5	Photographers....	10	4
Dentists..........	130	5	Decorators.......	20	4

* The number of people in each occupational group in Tables 3, 4, 5, and 6 is given in round numbers, and is based on data from Tables 110, 111, 112 in Estelle Hill Scott, *Occupational Changes Among Negroes in Chicago* (mimeographed), Work Projects Administration, 1939.

Servant Work: Over twenty-five out of every hundred employed Negro men and fifty-six out of every hundred Negro women were doing some kind of servant work on the eve of the Depression. This was at least four times their "proportionate share," for Negroes did over a third of all the servant work performed by women, and a fourth of that done by men. *While only twelve out of every hundred white women were in service occupations, over half of the colored women did such work.* The Negro woman's share of the various types of service work is indicated in Table 6.

portions" of Negro workers is admittedly an unsatisfactory approach to the problem of integrating Negroes into the economic life of the country, but some people feel that it is the only method of making sure that Negroes will secure broadened economic opportunity.

TABLE 6

SERVICE OCCUPATIONS WITH HIGHEST PROPORTION OF NEGRO WOMEN: 1930

Occupation	Number of Negro Women	Share of Work (Per Cent)
Laundry work done in homes..................	1,600	55.9
Elevator service...............................	200	42.7
General domestic and personal service...........	20,000	42.5
Charwomen and cleaners.......................	450	20.4
Janitors......................................	180	9.6
Waitresses...................................	1,100	9.5

Negro men had a virtual monopoly of some types of service jobs—jobs that depended upon an affluent white population, traveling, spending freely, and passing out tips.

TABLE 7

SERVANT OCCUPATIONS WITH HIGHEST PROPORTION OF NEGRO MEN: 1930

Occupation	Number of Negro Men	Share of Work (Per Cent)
Railroad porters........	3,600	94.9
Other types of portering.......................	2,100	82.5
Domestic and personal service..................	3,500	82.2
Waiting table on trains, in hotels, etc...........	3,000	31.4
General service...............................	5,000	26.6
Janitors......................................	4,000	19.1
Elevator men.................................	5,000	10.6

Manual Labor: Negroes were not overrepresented among the people who did the city's manual labor, but if we go behind the bare figure of nine per cent we find that they were doing a disproportionately large share of the poorly paid and less desirable work. They were concentrated in the unskilled labor categories which suffered heaviest from unemployment. Over half of all the Negro men who earned their living by manual labor were employed in the jobs listed in Table 8.

TABLE 8

Occupation	Negro's Share of Work (Per Cent)	Number of Negroes	Desirable Aspects of Job	Undesirable Aspects of Job
Garage labor...	58.5	1,860	Easy to get, not monotonous	Low pay, exposure, very dirty
Coal yard labor	40.5	1,525	Easy to get	Low pay, exposure, very dirty
Stockyard labor	34.2	1,640	Relatively good pay	Very heavy and dirty
Labor in stores..	31.8	3,360	Relatively clean	Low pay
Packing and slaughter labor	28.7	1,960	....	Very dirty
Laundry operatives	26.3	1,470	Easy to get	Low pay, extreme heat and dampness
General labor...	25.0	7,500	Easy to get	Low pay, insecurity, exposure
Steel mill labor	15.0	4,000	Relatively good pay	Heavy work, often very hot and hazardous
Railroad labor..	14.0	1,815	Easy to get	Low pay, exposure
Building labor..	13.3	2,850	Fairly well paid	Insecurity and intense competition of foreign-born
Road and street labor	13.0	567	Easy to get	Low pay and intense competition of foreign-born

Total number of Negro men employed.........28,547

About 100,000 women were doing manual labor when the Depression began. Of these about 15,000 were colored women—twice their proportionate share. Some three out of four of the Negro women doing manual labor were employed in the occupations listed in Table 9. All of these were marginal occupations, and the dress industry in which Negro semi-skilled women were concentrated was one of the industries hardest hit by the Depression.

TABLE 9

MANUAL LABOR JOBS WITH HIGHEST PROPORTION OF NEGRO WOMEN: 1930

Occupation	Negro's Share of Work (Per Cent)	Number of Negroes
Laundry operatives...........................	55.4	5,000
Railroad labor...............................	44.3	140
Labor in steel...............................	20.2	80
Clothing factory operatives..................	20.0	3,000
Slaughter and packing operatives..............	21.5	300
Labor in packing............................	17.0	130
Semi-skilled in boarding houses...............	16.2	1,000
General labor...............................	11.5	360

Total number Negro women employed.........10,010

THE JOB CEILING

The Depression began fifteen years after the Great Migration and at the halfway mark between the two World Wars. Despite fifteen years of urbanization during a period of industrial expansion, Negroes had not attained a proportionate share of the skilled and clerical jobs or of the professional and business occupations. They were clinging precariously to the margins of the economy. As former sharecroppers and underpaid southern city workers, they had "bettered their condition"; but they had not made the type of rapid progress which white European immigrants had made in an equal period between 1895 and 1910. This was due primarily to the fact that they had not been allowed to compete freely, *as individuals,* for any types of jobs to which they aspired and for which they were qualified. The result of these limitations was the crystallization of a "JOB CEILING."

The nature of this ceiling in terms of the "proportionate share" is indicated in Figure 13. All other things being equal, Negroes might have been expected by 1930 to approximate eight per cent of each occupational category.

The Job Ceiling also has its reflection in the internal structure of the white and the colored communities. These differences are depicted in Figures 15 and 16. Out of these differences in occupational distribution arise many of the peculiarities of social life within Black Metropolis. Over half of the white workers were doing skilled labor or "clean work." Over two-thirds of the Negroes were doing semi-skilled, unskilled, or servant work.

Figure 13

NEGRO'S SHARE IN SELECTED WORK GROUPS

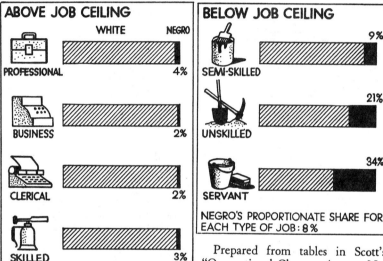

ABOVE JOB CEILING

WHITE   NEGRO

PROFESSIONAL   4%

BUSINESS   2%

CLERICAL   2%

SKILLED   3%

BELOW JOB CEILING

SEMI-SKILLED   9%

UNSKILLED   21%

SERVANT   34%

NEGRO'S PROPORTIONATE SHARE FOR EACH TYPE OF JOB: 8%

Prepared from tables in Scott's "Occupational Changes Among Negroes in Chicago: 1890-1930." Data for 1930.

EVOLUTION OF THE JOB CEILING

Between the first World's Fair and the Great Migration, Negroes constituted only a minute proportion of the city's workers. (See Figure 14.) As late as 1910 only three out of every hundred workers in Chicago were colored and at no time during this period did these few thousand Negroes offer any significant competition to the foreign-born who did the city's industrial work. Although they occasionally complained of discrimination in the building trades, Negroes, on the whole, tended to bypass skilled and semi-skilled work for employ-

Figure 14

TRENDS IN JOB DISTRIBUTION: 1890-1930

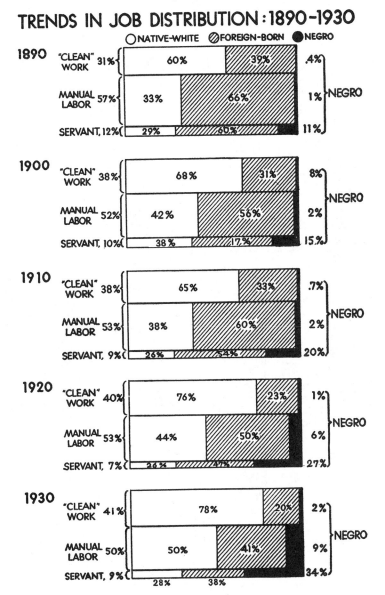

From tables in Scott, "Occupational Changes Among Negroes in Chicago: 1890-1930."

Figure 15

DIFFERENCES IN THE OCCUPATIONAL DISTRIBUTION OF NEGRO AND WHITE WORKERS: 1930

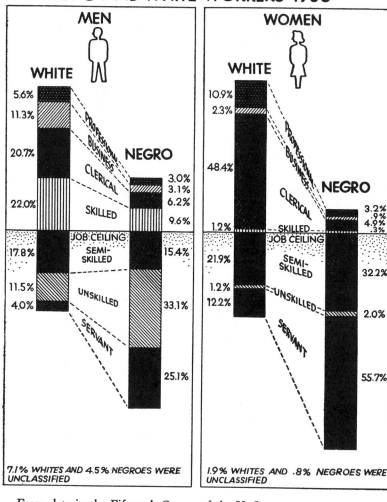

From data in the Fifteenth Census of the U. S., 1930.

Figure 16

DIFFERENCES IN THE OCCUPATIONAL DISTRIBUTION OF NEGRO AND WHITE WORKERS: 1940

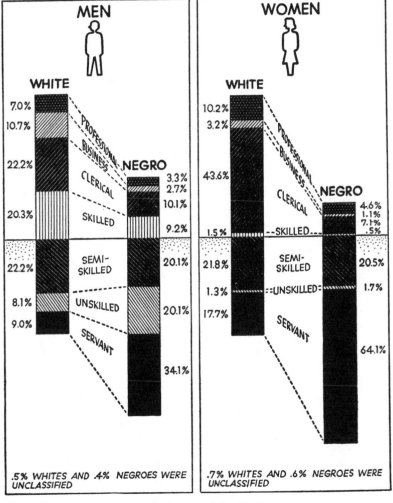

From data in the Sixteenth Census of the U. S., 1940.

ment in domestic and personal service.* The unskilled jobs which they held were largely in stores and transportation. A very small business and professional class existed, and a few Negroes held responsible political posts. But neither in the "clean work" nor in the industrial sphere had Negroes yet raised an insistent claim for a "proportionate share" of the jobs.

The First World War brought over 50,000 southern Negro workers into the city within eight years. Most of them went into unskilled labor and domestic service, but at least 10,000 took semi-skilled jobs. There were also sizable gains in the clerical field. When the war was over, however, there was a wholesale displacement of Negro workers from both industry and clerical work and a sharp increase in the proportion of Negroes doing domestic and personal service. They held what they could and took what they could get. But Negro women in the garment factories had won a permanent place as semi-skilled industrial workers, and Negro men had become an integral part of the steel and packing industry as unskilled and semi-skilled laborers.

The ten years between the First World War and the Depression witnessed a tremendous expansion of Chicago's industries. The city's share of America's total industrial production rose to fifteen per cent, and this expansion required nearly 328,000 new workers. During this ten-year period, 64,000 additional Negro workers filtered in from the South. Two-thirds of the women and a fourth of the men became servants. Over a half of all the men went into either unskilled labor or service. Nearly all of the Negro women went into either servant or semi-skilled occupations. *During this period, forty per cent of the*

---

* Old Settlers, with a tendency to romanticize the pre-Migration period, consistently minimize the extent of the Job Ceiling prior to 1914. That it was a reality, however, is evident from an examination of the few careful studies that are available for that period. The Juvenile Protective Association sponsored an investigation in 1913 which was released in the form of a pamphlet, *The Colored People of Chicago*, by Louise De Koven Bowen. There are references to "the tendency of the employers who use colored persons at all in their business to assign them to the most menial labor." It was asserted that "the colored laborer is continually driven to lower kinds of occupation which are gradually being discarded by the white man." The larger corporations were accused of refusing to employ Negroes. It was stated that while most labor unions did not refuse to accept Negro members, some consistently denied work opportunities to Negroes after they had accepted their initiation fees and dues. These charges were thoroughly documented and the conclusion was drawn that Negroes were gradually being "crowded into undesirable and underpaid occupations." (Bowen, *op. cit.*, pp. 1-10.)

new white women workers went into "clean work," but only five per cent of the Negro women secured such jobs. While few of the migrant Negro women were trained for such occupations it is probable that very few of the trained Negro women already in the city were "upgraded" to such jobs. (See Tables 10 and 11.) *

TABLE 10

HOW THE BOOM NEEDS OF MIDWEST METROPOLIS WERE MET BETWEEN 1920 AND
1930: JOBS BELOW THE CEILING

Type of Employment	Number of Workers Absorbed	How Negro Labor Was Utilized
Unskilled labor in stock-yards, packing plants, steel mills, stores, warehouses, and wharves	10,000 men 2,670 women	Negroes supplied virtually the whole demand as whites moved up. Virtually no Negro women used.
Servants	28,000 men 14,000 women	10,000 Negro men supplied about one-third of the demand for men. Negro women supplied almost all of the demand. Two-thirds of the Negro women migrants became servants.
Semi-skilled factory workers	36,000 men 11,000 women	8,000 Negro men used: 500 in the stockyards; 2,000 in garages; 1,100 in laundries; others general. 8,000 Negro women used, supplying three fourths of the demand: 5,000 to laundries; 1,100 to garment factories; others general.

In fact, Negroes who were already in the city, as well as the newcomers, found it impossible to secure a "proportionate share" of the good jobs even when they were qualified for them. They were not permitted to "advance on the job" or to secure apprenticeship opportunities. Instead, white male workers moved up, and white women either moved up or left industry to become housewives. Those Negroes who had entered industry during the Great Migration tended to ad-

* The estimates in Tables 7 and 8 are based on an analysis by Estelle Hill Scott, *op. cit.,* pp. 217-228.

TABLE 11

HOW THE BOOM NEEDS OF MIDWEST METROPOLIS WERE MET BETWEEN 1920 AND
1930: JOBS ABOVE THE CEILING

Type of Employment	Number of Workers Absorbed	How Negro Labor Was Utilized
Clerical work	35,800 men	Only 2,500 Negro men used, largely within Black Metropolis. A proportionate increase, but not enough to "catch up." At least 7,000 jobs were needed to give Negro men 8.0 per cent of clerical jobs.
	42,000 women	Only 300 Negro women secured such jobs. Ten times as many jobs —at least 3,000—would have been necessary to give Negroes their 8.0 per cent of the new workers.
Skilled labor	19,400 men	4,000 Negro men secured jobs in the building trades, but few in industry.
	2,700 women	Less than a hundred Negro women.
Professional, proprietary, and managerial	53,000 men	3,000 Negroes.
	16,000 women	1,800 Negroes.

vance to the level of semi-skilled workers, but no farther. The 64,000 new Negro workers found their place as servants and unskilled workers. (Tables 10 and 11.)

Had competition been entirely free, with advancement upon individual merit; had Negroes been integrated and promoted in accordance with principles of seniority and at the same rate as white workers, the difference between the jobs the Negroes secured between 1920 and 1930, and the approximate number of jobs they might have been expected to get is illustrated in Figure 17.

A continuously expanding economy might conceivably have operated to give Negroes their share of jobs above the ceiling, although this could have happened in the skilled and clerical fields only if there had been such a phenomenal increase in available positions as to create an actual shortage of white labor. There were signs, however,

Figure 17

NEGRO'S "PROPORTIONATE SHARE" OF JOBS

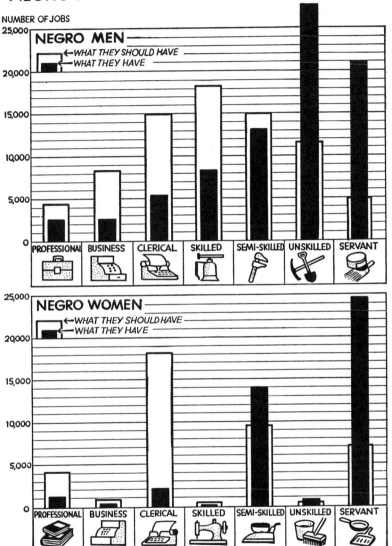

From tables in Scott, "Occupational Changes Among Negroes in Chicago: 1890-1930." Data for 1930.

that a Negro business and professional group catering to Negroes was taking root within the Black Belt, thus providing a few more jobs in the "clean work" categories. The Depression halted the entire process and froze the ceiling. At the same time, Negroes were squeezed out of the industrial machine and onto the relief rolls at a rapid rate —semi-skilled and servant groups suffering most severely.

But it is significant that there was never any suggestion that Negroes should be entirely eliminated from the industrial life of the city. This was due partly to the general temper of public opinion in Midwest Metropolis, and partly to the fact that by 1934 the WPA had stabilized the system so that everybody could at least eat and get some clothing. By 1940, there were 20,000 Negroes on direct relief and 40,000 on various emergency projects.*

THE NEGRO AS SERVANT

Negro Men as Servants: During the twenty-year period from 1890 to 1910, Negroes gradually increased their share of the city's personal and domestic service from eleven to twenty per cent—over six times their proportionate share. (See Figure 16.) In 1910 about one-half of the Negro men were servants and a third of all male servants were Negroes. One observer has stated[1] that by the time of the Great Migration:

Negro men had acquired the traditional right to be waiters in hotels, restaurants and on the trains. They were regarded as the rightful holders of positions as butlers and coachmen for the wealthy. The Negro footman and houseman were expected figures around the mansions of the moneyed class. The Negro community recognized the favored position of the waiter, butler and chauffeur. . . . They had close contacts with the wealthy whites and were able to acquire the manners, polish and social graces attendant to upper class behavior. . . . The headwaiters were at the top of society. . . . A man prided himself on being Mr. So-and-So's valet. Next to the headwaiters were the porters, and then came the barbers.

During this period, Negro men and foreign-born women were the backbone of the city's servant class.

The First World War tripled the proportion of Negro workers in

* The Illinois Emergency Relief Commission reported in 1939 that 44.9 per cent of all "general relief" cases were Negro—a term embracing families without a wage-earner and all "problem" families.

industry. Enough migrants poured into the city, however, to allow for an increase in the proportion of servants at the same time. The migrant men tended to go into industry while the women streamed into domestic service. This is dramatically illustrated by the 1920 Census returns. The proportion of all Negro men doing servant work fell from 45 per cent to 25 per cent and remained down. The proportion of Negro men in industry rose from 40 to 65 per cent and stayed up. (See Figure 18.)

Women as Servants: The proportion of all Negro women who were servants had been gradually falling from 1890 through 1910. The First World War added a large number of semi-skilled women workers who further reduced the proportion. Although the number of Negro women in industry increased from 1920-1930, female migrants from the South continued to supply the servant demand. Postwar cut-backs also eliminated large numbers of both Negro and white women from industry; by the time of the Depression, therefore, the proportion of all Negro women doing servant work had begun to rise again. (See Figure 18.) It fell again with the outbreak of the Second World War, as Negro women left domestic service for war work.

Despite the industrialization of Negroes in Chicago, 21,000 men and 24,000 women were working as servants when the Depression began. The servant situation was virtually the same in 1940 on the eve of the Second World War. The Negro's share of the servant work, too, has been continuously increasing. (See Figure 16.)

"NEGRO JOBS"

In the remaining sections of this chapter we shall examine first those jobs in which Negroes predominate (the so-called "Negro Jobs"), then those in which they make up a very high proportion but are not dominant, and finally the "White Men's Jobs." In discussing the first two types of jobs—predominantly servant occupations and semi-skilled occupations—we shall examine briefly the part played by labor unions in restricting or expanding economic opportunity.

Very few occupations in Chicago can be called "Negro Jobs," although the concept of "Negro Jobs" is not new. As early as 1885, a

Figure 18

TREND IN NEGRO EMPLOYMENT TOWARD INDUSTRIALIZATION: 1890-1930

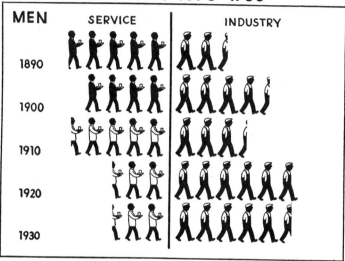

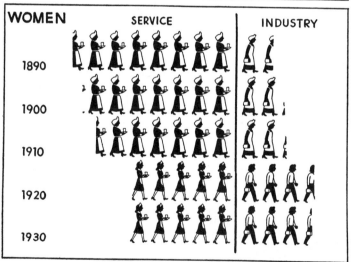

EACH FIGURE REPRESENTS 10% OF TOTAL EMPLOYMENT INCLUDING WHITE-COLLAR OCCUPATIONS. WHITE-COLLAR WORKERS ARE NOT SHOWN IN PICTURE.

From tables in Scott, "Occupational Changes Among Negroes in Chicago: 1890-1930." (Percentage of Negroes in white-collar occupations not shown.)

prominent colored woman was deploring the fact that Negroes were beginning to lose their monopoly in certain fields: [2]

It is quite safe to say that in the last fifteen years, the colored people have lost about every occupation that was regarded as peculiarly their own. Among the occupations that seem to be permanently lost are *barbering, bootblacking, janitors in office buildings, elevator service,* and *calcimining.* White men wanted these places and were strong enough to displace the unorganized, thoughtless and easy-going occupants of them. When the hordes of Greeks, Italians, Swedes, and foreign folk began to pour into Chicago, the demand for the Negro's places began. One occupation after another that the colored people thought was theirs forever, by a sort of divine right, fell into the hands of these foreign invaders.

By 1930, there were only three servant fields in which Negro men had a monopoly and none in which Negro women had a monopoly.

The two most important "Negro Jobs" are the occupations of Pullman porter and Red Cap, in which 94 and 85 per cent respectively of all the workers employed are Negroes. Both of these groups reveal the manner in which relatively well-educated Negroes, forced by the Job Ceiling to accept such positions, have tried to organize the workers in these occupations for immediate and long-range ends.

PULLMAN SERVICE

"George," the Negro Pullman porter, is an American institution. In 1930, there were 9,000 porters in America, of whom about 4,000 lived in Chicago. Since the days when the enterprising George Pullman began building sleeping cars in Chicago, Negroes have had a monopoly of these jobs. In 1925, an editorial appeared in a Chicago Negro weekly [3] expressing disapproval of such a monopoly (the italics are the authors'):

DANGERS OF MONOPOLIES

Much has been said about the Pullman porters and the fact that our Race has maintained an unquestioned monopoly in that particular field of labor. Efforts are now being made by the porters and outsiders to perfect an organization whereby this monopoly will become permanent. And in this step lie great dangers, not only to the Pullman porters themselves, but to laborers in every other branch of American industry.

For years we have fought against just such steps as this. We do not believe we should have a monopoly on Pullman porter service any more than that white people should have a monopoly on Pullman conductor service, or that Irishmen should have a monopoly on police and fire departments. We cannot hope to break down the bars that keep us from other fields of endeavor if we are going to start movements that will automatically bar others. We believe there should be black and white porters, and that there should be black and white conductors, all employed according to their abilities and not according to their race. We believe that they should all work together along all lines and not in separate contingents. . . .

We want all workers of all races to start at the same place together and work up together with only their ability determining their progress. Monopolies are dangerous if formed along race lines.

Ten years later, however, Pullman portering was still a Negro monopoly, but after a strenuous fight, the Brotherhood of Sleeping Car Porters (AFL), under the leadership of A. Philip Randolph, had secured a contract which placed porters upon a "living wage." Prior to this they had existed largely on tips. The organizational campaign which centered in Chicago was a bitter one involving frequent charges that civic leaders and ministers were being bribed by the Pullman Company to oppose union organization.

The leaders of the Pullman porters have used their all-Negro union as a nucleus around which to organize pressure against the Job Ceiling both within and without the railroad industry. The broader philosophy of this leadership was revealed in a statement by the national president in 1931:

We hold that union organization is desirable from the point of view of workers of both races, as a low-paid, unorganized group of one race is inimical to keeping up the standards of workers in another race.

Preachers, lawyers, social workers of our race are co-operating and meeting with us for discussion of such problems as unemployment. We believe we discern a change in the attitude, formerly hostile, of Negro thinkers and professional people toward labor organizations.

Randolph has carried the fight against discrimination within the AFL to the floor of the national conventions annually, though without any marked success.

Using his union as a base, this same leader emerged in 1941 as the outstanding fighter against racial discrimination in war industries and the army and navy. As has been said earlier, the March-on-Washington Movement which he fostered was primarily responsible for the institution of the FEPC.

THE RED CAPS

Tradition has it that on Labor Day in 1890 a Negro porter at the Grand Central Station in New York tied a bit of red flannel around his black uniform cap so that he could be more easily identified in the crowd. As a consequence of this strategy he "cleaned up," and set a style which became the emblem of an entire occupational group —America's Red Caps.

In 1940 there were about 600 Red Caps carrying luggage and otherwise assisting passengers to board and leave trains, buses, and airplanes in Chicago's various depots and stations. Of these 600, over 400 were Negroes.

Red-Capping has been a typical service occupation, in which both the earnings and the prospects of advancement are dependent upon cheerful and, if necessary, ingratiating service. Until 1935 most Red Caps were entirely dependent upon tips for their income. They were not recognized as railroad employees, although some stations paid nominal wages of from $10 to $40 a month. Yet, in prosperous years, an enterprising Red Cap who had advanced to servicing Pullman cars on crack express trains could average as much as $150 a month. Even very well-educated Negroes did not scorn such jobs.

Organizing the Red Caps: During the Depression an income from tips became an extremely precarious one. Stations, moreover, that had formerly paid a nominal wage now ceased to do so. Chicago's station porters turned to union organization in order to demand recognition as "bona fide employees" of the railroad stations. They sought a minimum wage and bargaining rights under the Railway Labor Act, and within two years, after a series of bitterly contested hearings before the Interstate Commerce Commission, they were so classified. In 1944 they were receiving a basic wage of $4.56 a day. The railroads charge travelers a fixed sum for each item of luggage handled, and the money is pooled. Any amount in excess of the basic wage is prorated among the men. If the pool does not meet the basic wage, the railroad company makes up the difference.

The organization of the Red Caps was begun in 1936, during the period of the nationwide union organizational drives conducted under the sanctions of Section 7-A of the National Recovery Act. Officials of the union report that some of the railroads maintained spy systems and occasionally utilized older employees with a "big banker" complex to intimidate younger porters. Reprisals against men who would not join company unions consisted in depriving them of choice trains or penalizing them for attending union meetings. One railroad company even offered its men a salaried status if they would abandon union organization. Despite these difficulties, a union official reported that, after several months of organizational activity, "at one station 60 of the 80 Negro Red Caps were organized; at another, 67 out of 90; and at one station, 103 white Red Caps. One company was threatening to replace the Negroes with whites if they joined a union."

The Chicago Red Caps began as a Federal local of the AFL. Later the Brotherhood of Sleeping Car Porters (Negro) and the Union of the American Railway Clerks (white) both claimed jurisdiction over this young union. The Red Caps eventually broke their ties with the AFL and functioned as an independent union for five years. Finally, in 1942, the organization brought its 12,000 members into the CIO.

White Men in a Negro Job: At the Red Caps' first national convention, held in a downtown hotel in Chicago, a Negro was elected president; a white man, treasurer; a Negro, secretary; and another white man as general organizer. (The Negro president, Willard S. Townsend, who has remained head of the organization to the present time, is a graduate of the Royal College of Science in Toronto.) A reporter of the Chicago *Daily News,* writing of this first convention, observed that "it's Bill and Joe and Harry among the white and Negro porters. . . . The color-line in labor relations was smashed." One of the Negro officials was also enthusiastic over the prospects of Negro-white unity at the time, and said:

"This is a mixed union. There is no discernible difference between the white and the Negro Red Caps. There is no advantage in separate locals. Lack of association between racial groups isn't conducive to solving the race problem. This ticklish question will best be solved by association and the resultant understanding of their common problems. They will discover that prejudice is based on ignorance. Together they will find that prejudice is absolutely unfounded.

"All of our social affairs have been 'smokers.' Both whites and Negroes attend. Last month we held one at the Century Club here on the South Side and it was well attended by both groups. We plan to have a big dance at the Savoy. All of the locals in the international plan to hold big dances in other cities on the same night."

But this official added that some of the Negro Red Caps in other cities had refused to affiliate with the international if the white minority controlled the General Executive Board.

The honeymoon period of Negro-white relations was short. Even at the first national convention, disagreements crystallized along racial lines in relation to every controversial issue that arose. In one argument, the president of a white local in the organization was accused of double-crossing the Negroes by appealing to the Railway Mediation Board in the following terms: "The assistance we ask of you is only for the white boys at our depot." He defended himself on the ground that he thought this good strategy in establishing a test case, since the Board was more likely to render a favorable decision if it thought only white workers would benefit.

The struggle for racial control which arose almost immediately within the union was made more bitter by the difference in educational status between the Negro and the white Red Caps. One Negro official commented on this situation at the time:

"The Negroes in our union are the best informed on parliamentary procedure. Whites lack this knowledge because the economic condition of the white man doesn't usually make for an educated man becoming a Red Cap. The educational status of the whites in the union is lower than that of the Negroes."

The official of another local insisted that 72 of the 90 Negroes at his station were college men, including two practicing physicians! It was his impression that "in the last fifteen years, there hasn't been a Red Cap there who hasn't finished high school." He was equally sure that at least half of the white Red Caps had never been to high school.

Because of the Job Ceiling, an educated Negro suffers no disastrous loss in social status within his own community by working as a Red Cap, although a white employee of similar status in such a job is likely to be insecure and "on the defensive." This is suggested in the remarks of a white union official to a white investigator:

"You may wonder why I went into this kind of work. You know, I'm a college graduate. One of my brothers studied neurology for three years, and another one studied psychology for two years, and another one is a doctor. I could teach high school in Pennsylvania if I wanted to—I've got the political pull. You might wonder why I'm a Red Cap. Well, when I got out of college, I decided that I wanted to help the masses."

Trouble between white and colored union members continued, and finally, after a conflict involving charges that a white union official had made dishonest use of union funds, the white minority in the union withdrew and went back into the AFL. The white group then adopted a constitution which prohibited Negroes from holding office in their union, but providing for the organization of Negro Red Caps in a separate local! An official of the new white union defended this action as follows:

"Us and the colored fellows used to be one organization. Now there are two separate organizations. We've made a rule that no colored person can hold office in our organization. The trouble with colored men is that they want to run things. They just want to boss the whole show. White people ain't like that, but the minute a colored man gets into the organization, he wants to be an officer and run things. Now you've got to have white people running things if you want to get anywhere. I ain't like some. I don't see no difference between a colored man and myself, except that he's black and I'm white; but all the same you have to have white people for officers. Look at that union what's all colored fellows—the Pullman Porters' Union or something like that. They're right where they were eight or nine years ago. Oh, they did get something or other, I forget what, a little while ago. But look at the union at our station—they've got everything they want. I ain't got no objection to colored people. I like them all right, and I've got a lot of Negro friends that I think a lot of . . . [but] they have been trod down so long that when they get a little power, it goes to their heads."

Another member of this white union voiced similar sentiments:

"At the beginning, when we first planned to form an organization with the Negroes, the rest of the boys didn't like the idea of teaming with Negroes, but they trusted my judgment because I have so much more education. It doesn't do for white and black to be in the same organization. The whites have no respect for the Negroes and the Negroes have no respect for the whites. And a lot of employers refuse to negotiate with a Negro at all. When we formed this organization, we had our officers—

first a black one, then a white one, then black, then white, and so on. That was all wrong. If you had real equality, you wouldn't take special care to see that Negroes were elected, you would simply elect the men who were the best qualified for an office."

The comments of these white workers indicate that they felt out of place in a predominantly Negro union. One man was far less calm about the matter than the men quoted above. His remarks included the following diatribe:

"I know what Negroes are like. I spent seven years, the best years of my life, down South and I know. Give a nigger a finger and he will take a whole hand. I suppose Jack has told you the trick Tom pulled on us?

"Tom won't show his black face around here. He's afraid of me. He knows I'd break his neck if I saw him. There's only one good one around here and that's Hank. He knows his place. He's all right. There's one way a Negro is all right—that's in his place.

"Employers don't want to deal with Negroes; a lot of them refuse to do it. When Hank wants anything, he sends for me and I go over and talk to the management. The boss has told me that he wouldn't *have* a Negro sit down in his office. It would drive him wild."

Other white Red Caps felt that Negroes were *too* influential. The blending of social and economic insecurity which gave rise to these contradictory sentiments was further revealed in a conversation between two white Red Caps seated in the rear of a union hall.

Harry: "Tom [a Negro] gets pretty nearly everything *he* wants over at the station. He is real sirupy to the bosses, always yesses them. He's a regular stooge, that's what he is. He gets what he wants. And you know, there are some people who are just naturally *nigger-lovers.* You know what that is? They just naturally love niggers. There used to be white Red Caps, too, at that station, but they're all Negro now. Some official in the railroad was a nigger-lover, and he done it."

Jack: "Yeah, that's right. The Court Street station is the only one we've got left." (This was not true—white Red Caps were employed in three stations at the time.)

Harry: "The railroad I work for doesn't like us, either. If they had a chance, they'd throw us out just like that [snapping his finger]. They'd rather see *niggers* there than us."

Jack: "So you see we've got to watch our step. We can't antagonize them too much." (I.e., the Negroes in the union.)

Negro Job—Negro Union: After the white members withdrew from the union, it became for all practical purposes a Negro organization, although it continued to include a few white persons and Japanese-Americans. As early as 1937, the president of one of the locals stated:

"Personally, I think the condition of the white Red Cap is worse than that of the Negro. The Negro takes pride in his job and feels no 'let-down' because he is performing what is considered menial labor, whereas the white considers himself above such 'menial' labor; and thus when they are forced into this occupation, they feel they are working under pressure. They make little effort to *dignify their jobs.*

"The average Negro Red Cap stays in the service a lifetime, because it is fairly lucrative and a fairly steady occupation, and somehow it 'gets' you. Come down some time and wear a uniform and cap for a week, and you'll understand what I mean. We Red Caps actually take great pride in our work and *have brought more dignity to it than you probably think."*

Eventually the union began to consider organizing all unorganized Negroes in the railroad industry into this new union, as well as those in Jim-Crow auxiliaries of lily-white railroad unions. These interests resulted in a change of name from the International Brotherhood of Red Caps to the United Transport Service Employees of America.

Two years after the union became an affiliate of the CIO, its president, Willard S. Townsend, was elected to the national executive committee of that organization. In this capacity he has been able to use his union as a pressure bloc against discrimination within all CIO unions and to stimulate the formation of a CIO Committee Against Discrimination within that body. In the eyes of Negroes he ultimately became a prominent *Negro* Leader, as well as a bona-fide labor leader. And the Red Caps' union, like the Pullman porters' union before it, has become a weapon for fighting the Job Ceiling.

IN THE WHITE FOLKS' HOUSES

In 1940, almost half of the women who did domestic service in Chicago were Negroes. Many of the Negro women who came to Chicago between the First and the Second World Wars were accustomed to working in the homes of white people as cooks, maids, nurses, and laundresses. It was inevitable that they would tend to replace the foreign-born, who were securing better jobs, and the Negro men who were leaving service for industry. (See Figure 18.) With some 40,000 white women entering industry and commerce between 1920 and 1930, it was not surprising that 10,000 additional Negro women were utilized as domestic servants.

Domestic service is not a money-making job.* During the Boom Years, wages for "day's work" tended to hover around $2 and for "week's work" at $20. The impact of the Depression on the white family budget was reflected in the widespread dismissal of Negro servants and in the drastic lowering of wages for those who remained. Yet, throughout the Depression, Negro women continued to supplement their relief checks by surreptitious "day's work." The State Employment Service reported its largest volume of Negro placements (and its highest turnover) throughout this period as temporary assignments for domestic work. Competing with these Negro women for such jobs were some 10,000 white women.

Hard Folks to Work For: Out of the servant-employer relations of the Depression period grew bitter and caustic expressions of antagonism toward white employers, often tinged with anti-Semitic and anti-foreign sentiments. The following diatribe is typical of the frustrated Negro domestic's complaints:

"You see, I am only employed regularly half-days, so in order to meet expenses, I have to find other work.

"I am supposed to work for Mrs. Carter from 2:00 P.M. on, do all the work. Both she and her husband are employed—that is, they have their own business.

"They only have three and one-half rooms in a large apartment building, yet I find plenty to do. I do all the laundry, which is plenty, and cleaning and cooking. I get so disgusted, for she always waits until she gets home before telling me what she planned for dinner and then sends me to the store.

"Tonight she made me real mad. After I had finished dinner dishes, she asked me to wash the woodwork around the windows, as she wanted to put up new drapes. She could have told me the night before, but they

* Of course, during a war, when servants become scarce, the wages for such work begin to approach those in industry. This is a temporary situation, however.

never think of your time, and too, I was so tired. I had done a day's work.

"Once a week I do all the cleaning for a Jewish couple. It is supposed to be half-day work but I never get through until 8:30 and 9 P.M. I have to get on my knees and scrub up every floor. Since I only go once a week, the house gets very dirty, and the kitchen is terrible. They have money but are too stingy and she doesn't like to work either; in fact, she doesn't do anything, only cook. She has a daughter thirteen years old and you would think she would have her clean the bathtub and bowl, but I always find a dirty rim around both, and foodstuffs that have been dropped on the floor have been walked on.*

"I never eat anything there either, for she spits in the sink if she happens to be in the kitchen. I just get $1.50 and she tries to get a week's work done, but since I only make five dollars and carfare on my regular job, I have to do it.

"I also have another place where I clean in the mornings weekly for $1.50, but her floors are all carpeted and it isn't so hard. I can't say Mrs. C. isn't nice to work for. She doesn't bother me, yet there just isn't enough money; I prefer working all day. I have been trying to leave her for some time, but some little while ago she loaned me money and I have been making so little that I haven't been able to pay her. Sometimes I just think I will leave and send it back to her. No, she doesn't even ask me for it, I guess she realizes I have had such a time. This is the fourth time I have lost my furniture. I am trying to pay out my radio and I sold some of my furniture for little or nothing."

Most domestic servants, like the woman just quoted, drew a distinction between "nice people to work for"—who pay over the usual wage or do not overwork them—and "hard people to work for."

Nice Folks to Work For: Most Negro domestic servants work for ordinary middle-class white families and do not have the intimate personal ties which characterize the few situations where the white family can afford a permanent retainer who lives on the premises and is almost a member of the family.

"Staying on the premises" is not the rule in Chicago. Most domestic

---

* The statements of Negro servants about middle-class Jewish employers reflect all the derogatory anti-Semitic stereotypes which exist among white people. Yet, many of these same servants will praise Jewish employers for being "less prejudiced" than other white employers. At least two-thirds of some 150 domestic servants who spoke of Jews thought that they treated Negroes "more like equals" than other employers but "paid less."

servants travel to and from the Black Ghetto and their work places outside of the Negro community. Yet there are Negro women who express a great deal of loyalty to specific families. These are either women who have considerate employers, or those who have not abandoned the southern Negro attitude toward white employers. One fairly well-educated Negro woman describes a "nice family."

"The Bradleys are lovely people. He being a minister and she working in the church keeps them away from home all day Sunday.

"They have two darling little girls; Baby is seven and Milly is four. That is the only confining thing about this job—they expect you to stay with the children; in fact, I almost take charge of everything. Mrs. Bradley is in her early twenties and evidently has never been used to much. She is on the go all the time. She is more particular about caring for the children than the cleaning of her house. I do all the housework except the window-washing. Neither do I take care of the laundry; that is sent out."

Another servant's comments indicate what Negro domestics consider "nice" working conditions:

"At the Darnells' I have a very nice room and bath, well furnished and cozy. I like the job very much. Of course I knew before accepting that it would be confining.

"When I went on my vacation last year, they presented me with a beautiful leather traveling bag. I imagine I will be with them the rest of my life.

"I was born in Cleveland, Ohio, and completed a high school course there. Then I finished college, later taking up musical work. Jobs seemed hard to get at this time, and not having any close relatives to whom to turn, I had to take the first job I could get, which was housework.

"I started working with the Van Lorns when they lived in New York. I had only worked for one other family. I didn't like them at all. No one could get along with her; she was so very crabby. Nothing ever pleased her, I don't care how well it was done. A friend who had formerly worked for the Darnells was leaving town and recommended me. I took the job and have been with them ever since. I began at twelve dollars per week, now I get fourteen.

"Each year I have gotten a two weeks' vacation with pay, but not until they have visited her mother for two months. She stays there until I have returned and cleaned the apartment."

Such cases of Negro servants as a "part of the family" were exceptional. Many Negro women were so desperate for employment during the Depression that they actually offered their services at the so-called "slave markets"—street corners where Negro women congregated to await white housewives who came daily to take their pick and bid wages down. One experienced stenographer who was forced to offer her services for $3 a week at the West Side "slave market" described her situation as follows:

"It is an area on the West Side of 12th St. near Halsted. A large number of girls go there daily and hire themselves by the day to the highest bidder. The more enterprising would solicit—others would wait to be approached. Many days I worked for 50 cents a day and no carfare—one meal was given. I then applied for relief. After suffering more embarrassment and humiliation I was refused relief because I could now and then get jobs at the 'slave market.' Having no references it was hard for me to get a good job."

Domestic workers often expressed the hope that their children would be able to find other types of work. Typical of the attitudes of many domestic servants with daughters were those expressed by one woman:

"I have not told you much about the life of my two daughters for, as you know, each of them has a work life of her own. My life as a maid had been brief—until I married I did office work. Only after my second husband and I separated did I begin work as a maid. My oldest daughter is quite bitter against what she calls the American social system and our financial insecurity. I hope they may be able to escape a life as a domestic worker for I know too well the things that make a girl desperate on these jobs."

Colored girls are often bitter in their comments about a society which condemns them to "the white folks' kitchen." Girls who have had high school training, especially, look upon domestic service as the most undesirable form of employment. It is not surprising that with the outbreak of the Second World War, middle-class white housewives in Midwest Metropolis began to complain about "the servant problem." Negro women had headed for the war plants or were staying at home.

During the Depression, several sporadic attempts were made to unionize domestic servants. The very nature of the occupation makes organization overwhelmingly difficult. If the domestic servant is not a casual worker, the relations between employer and employee are so personal as to form a psychological barrier against organization. If the domestic servant is not emotionally involved with the family it seems much easier to find someone else to work for or to find another type of work than to join a union. The physical conditions under which domestic servants work—each in a separate household—does not generate the kind of social solidarity that arises among a factory group. It is almost impossible to use the strike as a bargaining weapon. And most important, there was always a surplus of women seeking a few pennies to supplement their relief checks. All efforts to organize domestic servants in Chicago during the Depression failed.

The organizers of domestic workers were themselves caught between a desire to organize all domestics to fight for higher wages and better working conditions, and a desire to train a small group of women so that they could demand higher wages on the basis of more efficient work. One of the most experienced and energetic organizers stated in 1938:

"Our organization has grown but the membership fluctuates. At present the association is at a standstill as far as actual organization work is concerned, but the encouraging thing about it is that a Citizens' Committee has been organized, composed of Negro and white members who have pledged their financial and moral support in carrying out our training school project. I am primarily interested in union organization but in order to maintain it there must be a program. The training school will be that program. It will establish standards in this field, which are sadly needed, and will have an appeal to employers. It is a necessity. Maids *do* need training, and on this basis, financial backers may be interested."

A young colored Communist criticized this woman's efforts, as well as her own, in the following terms:

"I started a domestic workers' group of about 125 members who we picked up in the park. First, I think our discussions were wrong. We didn't take up the problems of the girls. We took up the problem of inefficiency and would criticize the girls for untidy appearance, dirty nails, and such things. This antagonized the girls. You've got to talk to workers about how mean the boss is, if you want to keep them interested. Such problems as long hours should have been talked about more, rather than runs in the girls' stockings. Second, I think girls should be taught that domestic work is an occupation and not a profession.

WHISK-BROOM, MOP, AND SERVING TRAY

Much of the personal service done by Negro men and women in the city is not in private homes, but in the hotels, lodging houses, houses of prostitution, athletic clubs, and similar institutions. In these situations where Negroes and whites often work side by side, labor unions have arisen that include both Negro and white members. One of these, the Miscellaneous local of the Hotel Employees' Union has 4,000 white members and 5,000 colored. The white business manager states that, on the whole, the Negro women take an active part and that both Negroes and whites attend the occasional social functions given by the union.

Before the Great Migration, Negroes had a virtual monopoly as maids at houses of prostitution. With the closing of the Red-light District in 1912, they have still maintained a large share of these jobs. One woman now in the less lucrative field of domestic service looks back with nostalgia at her employment in a North Side "resort" as she talks with a union organizer:

"Ever since the death of my husband, eight years ago, I acted as personal maid to a couple of prostitutes who lived in a hotel. I made good money then, for I had a chance to make tips. I never made less than $25 a week for they catered to the rich men, bankers, and other high-class people.

"This hotel was full of those women, and it ran wide open until party politics was changed. It was soon after a clean-up drive was begun that they were raided, so naturally I lost my job. Then the Cohens, through my mother, asked me to come and work for them. They both have nice personalities, and seem to think a great deal of me, but I am still a maid to them. I only make seven dollars a week. That is clear money but I can't do much with it.

"No, I haven't heard of the union, but I imagine it is a good thing. Maids really need helping, for those white people will certainly take advantage of you. When you first start with them you are only supposed to do so much, but the longer you remain with them, the more they expect and the longer the hours. I am so tired in the evening. I don't feel like reading—in fact, not doing anything but getting away from the house, even if it is only across the street. I have to wash all the little girl's clothes too. If I leave, I shall have more time. Then I will be able to learn more about this organization and perhaps attend a meeting. I have become rusty in everything. I don't even get to see my friends often.

Today is the first time I have visited in months and then I didn't get here until after 3 P.M. I had to prepare something for dinner before I left.

"I don't have to get back for dinner, but I must be there for seven o'clock breakfast, and the ride is quite long. I have to leave here early, for it is quite dark out there. I am disgusted with the job, yet I know I have to work for my living."

Negro men and women also serve in a variety of personal-service positions, as valets, personal maids, hotel maids, washroom attendants. Negroes and whites are thus thrown together in large numbers in this rather specialized relationship of menial service. Such contacts contribute to the confirming of stereotypes about the characteristics and "place" of Negroes. They also tend to produce, within the Negro servant's personality structure, a mixed attitude of obsequiousness and hostility.

WASHING CLOTHES—OLD STYLE AND NEW

In the South, the colored "washwoman" is a familiar figure; but in Chicago in 1930, there were only about 3,000 women who earned their living by washing clothes in the homes of their employers or by taking laundry to their own homes. Of these over half were Negro women. The average wage for such work near the end of the Depression period was $2.50 a day. Charges of exploitation were frequent, and often contained an anti-Semitic note, as in the case cited below:

"The Jewish woman that I work for tries to get a colored woman to do all of her work for as little as $2 a day and pay her own carfare.

"She is expected to do all the washing, including the linen and towels as well as all the clothes for the five members of the family. She is supposed to finish the work—that is iron the entire wash—and then clean the house thoroughly—all for $2. Because there are some women who will do all of the work for that amount, this Jewish woman feels that a colored woman who demands more is silly to think that she can get it. She says that she doesn't understand why, if some colored people can get along on that amount, all can't do the same. I know one woman who does all this work. This woman is an 'Uncle Tom' type of person who says, 'Yes, ma-a-am!' and grins broadly whenever the woman speaks to her. The woman prefers this type of servant to the more intelligent type."

Most of Chicago's laundry is done in large commercial enterprises. It takes about 15,000 workers to keep the city's clothing clean, and the mechanical laundry has replaced the "washwoman." This type of work still has menial implications, however, and wages have tended to be low. Negroes have been hired in large numbers, and in 1930, 55.4 per cent of all the women working in laundries were colored, as were 26.3 per cent of the men working as semi-skilled operatives in the industry. The nature of the work has been such as to make it more favorable for union organization than domestic service, and the laundry workers' union affiliated with the AFL, in the late Depression years, included about 2,000 white members and 8,000 Negroes.

In a union of this type, Negroes have become familiar with the processes of collective bargaining and union participation with white workers. The more personal servant-employer relationships are absent. The brief observations at a union meeting cited below indicate the manner in which Negroes and whites co-operate in a laundry union, with Negroes, in some instances, displaying leadership:

The meeting was very orderly. The crowd was made up of Negroes and whites. Negroes comprised about one-third of the total. There was no discrimination, workers from the same laundry sitting together in groups in some instances and carrying on conversations. It was clear at the outset that the rank-and-file members were gathered in order to hear a report on the negotiations that had been carried on by the union officials.

The business agent had just presented a contract which did not seem to satisfy the members. A Negro laundry operative wanted to know why they couldn't "tell the laundry owners to take it or leave it." He slowly walked to the front of the room [he was seated in the front row] and rubbing his hand over his head began in a slow drawl:

"I ain't satisfied with that contract there. Why is it that we let them bring us a contract and tell us to sign it? [Cheers.] Why don't we take *our* contract to *them* and tell *them* to sign what *we* want? For three years I've been working like a dog and I don't even make a living for dogs. I had greens last night for supper—I had greens today for lunch—and tonight I had greens for supper! Why? 'Cause I can't afford anything else."

The audience was laughing loudly because of the humorous picture that he was presenting, and the manner in which he spoke and gestured. He began again:

"Don't laugh now. Listen to what I'm saying. If you want to make a thief out of a man you just give him nothin'. I've got a wife to take care of, and how ya goin' to do it on $15 a week? [More cheers and laughter.] You tell those birds to *hell* with that contract. I don't want nothing those birds got in it, and if they don't take ours, they kin git out of business."

He took his seat amid long and loud applause, accompanied by laughter. The chair next recognized a young colored girl about twenty-two years of age.

"Mr. Chairman," she said, "you made no mention of wages for curtain stretchers. In my laundry I am the one who watches the curtain stretcher. It stretches and then finishes them. What about curtain stretchers, Mr. Chairman? I notice no mention was made of them. We got thirty cents by our own efforts. We asked the boss for a raise and when he refused, we struck by ourselves. He gave us thirty cents an hour. We joined the union because we don't think thirty cents is enough and want to get more. If the union can't get us more than thirty cents we might just as well get out and fight our battle alone." [She sat down amidst thundering applause.]

Another colored girl was given the floor.

"In my factory we already get thirty cents an hour. We struck ourselves and our employer said sure he'd give us that. Now thirty cents an hour is all right for them [gesticulating with her thumb to some girls back of her], but we don't work for nothing less than thirty cents an hour in our place now and thirty cents isn't doing us any good. We're already getting that. We want more and *we're going to get more!*" [Applause and cheers.]

She sat down and said softly, so that just those around her could hear.

"Yes, we are going to get it—thirty cents ain't nothing for us—we don't want to take it." Then she lighted a cigarette and gradually calmed down, only to rise up two more times and say about the same thing in different words. On the row in front of her were seated white girls who worked in the laundry with her. Behind was a white woman co-worker. They would tell her to "go ahead get up and tell them" and remind her of things to say. Then they would just laugh, and applaud her. Finally she asked, "Why is it that we've got to dicker and dicker and dicker with the employers? Why can't we just let them take it or leave it!"

The new Negro "washwoman" and "washman" are industrial workers, quite different from the older social types, and unlike domestic workers they have been drawn into the typical urban pattern of relationships with white employers and workers.

NEGROES AS UNSKILLED WORKERS

Until the Great Migration, Negro men and women seemed on the whole to prefer personal service in an atmosphere of relative cleanliness to the backbreaking and dirty labor of the stockyards. They preferred the heat of kitchens (where one could at least be sure of a meal) to the heat of the steel mills. There were always some Negroes in Chicago, however, who did unskilled and semi-skilled labor. (See Figure 16.)

Since the First World War, Negroes have found little trouble in securing more than their share of the jobs which expose them to dirt, grease, grime, and low pay. In the last year of prosperity, Chicago used about 170,000 workers to do the heavy lifting and heaving, the sweeping, tinkering, and furnace-tending. At least 35,000—twenty in every hundred—of these workers were Negroes. (Tables 8 and 9.)

JOBS ABOVE THE CEILING

As has been said, there are very few jobs in Chicago that can be called "Negro Jobs." There are numerous pursuits, however, which for all practical purposes are "White Men's Jobs." Custom has operated through a long period of years to restrict most Negro workers to the level of servants and unskilled laborers, although the years between the two wars witnessed the wide use of Negroes as semi-skilled operatives. On the eve of the Second World War the presence of Negroes was extremely rare on five occupational levels: (1) Control and Policy-Forming Groups in finance and industry; (2) Higher Supervisory and Technical Personnel; (3) Lower Supervisory and Technical Personnel; (4) Clerical Workers and Salespeople; (5) Skilled Labor. There are wide differences in the proportions of Negroes employed in these various types of jobs within the following fields: (1) Transportation and Communication; (2) Commerce and Trade; (3) Manufacturing; (4) Government. In general, the ceiling is "highest" in Government and "lowest" in Transportation and Communication. (Figure 19.) This is illustrated, for instance, by the fact that while no Negroes serve on the boards of directors of major public utility corporations,,

Figure 19

THE JOB CEILING IN GOVERNMENT AND PRIVATE INDUSTRY

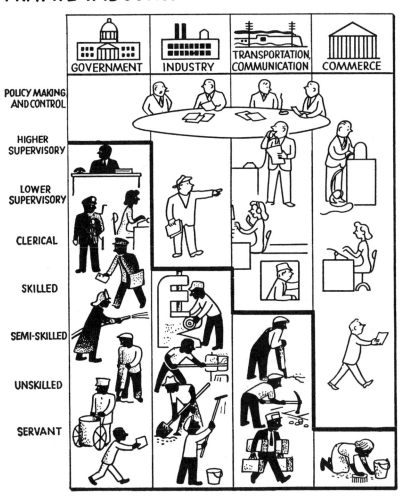

there have been Negroes on the Illinois State Commerce Commission, which has supervision over public utilities.

Control and Policy-Forming Groups: One of the most striking evidences of the Job Ceiling is the fact that there have never been any Negroes on the boards of directors of major corporations, no members of the stock exchange and grain pit, no industrial magnates. Yet there are a few Negroes in governmental positions who help to shape general policies, such as the two aldermen, two Illinois state senators, five state representatives, one county commissioner, and representatives on the state Commerce Commission, the Chicago Housing Authority, the Chicago Library Board, and the Chicago Board of Education.

During the Depression, and with the advent of the Second World War, a number of Negroes were drawn into governmental supervisory positions both through civil service examinations and by appointment. In many cases they function only as "experts" on Negro affairs, but a few of them are also engaged in the broader aspects of social planning and administration. For instance, the head of the Chicago Housing Authority is a well-trained and experienced Negro who received his position through appointment by the present Mayor. The influence of these few Negroes on *general* governmental affairs is so small that they have not been included in Figure 19 where *decisive* control is indicated. The *top* positions in government as in private industry are still invariably held by white persons. It is difficult to envision a Negro as Mayor of Midwest Metropolis or as president of the First National Bank.

Higher Supervisory and Technical Personnel: All the more lucrative supervisory and technical positions in the economic system, and those carrying a high degree of responsibility, are "White Men's Jobs." Negroes do not serve as plant superintendents, personnel men, departmental heads, etc. Where men exercise industry-wide authority and execute the policies laid down by boards of directors, bankers, and industrialists, the color-line is tightly drawn. The "lines of promotion" operate to eliminate Negroes from competition far down the line, and the knowledge of the difficulties involved in placement deters Negroes from securing the kind of business training in academic institutions that would qualify them for such positions if these were, by chance, made available. Even the free courses which were inaugurated during the early war period for training higher supervisory and technical workers had few Negro applicants. This was due partly to the fact that, lacking previous experience, few Negroes could meet the entrance requirements, and partly to the reluctance of institutions to train personnel which might be a "drug on the market."

The governmental structure is flexible enough to allow Negroes to serve as supervisors of some local social agencies, as principals of schools (in Negro neighborhoods), and as functionaries in the United States Employment Service, the Office of Price Administration, and similar agencies. But there are frequent attempts to bar them from such positions, even when they have passed civil service examinations. In one recent case, for example, a Negro passed an examination with a grade that would have made him the logical appointee for heading a major governmental office in the heart of the city. He was persuaded, finally, to remain in a less prominent position in a Negro neighborhood.

There are individual cases in which Negro technicians have been hired by private concerns. A colored man was for some years the chief air-conditioning engineer for the Pullman Company; another is an industrial chemist for a paint company; one is head chemist at a large commercial establishment; a few are mechanical and civil engineers. The general lack of opportunity for Negro technical workers in industry, however, has been reflected in the reluctance of Negro students to take technical training at public schools and in private institutions, since they feel that they would be wasting their time. The Second World War resulted in a marked increase in the employment of Negro technicians, but their use is by no means considered a permanent change of policy.

Negro accountants, architects, or civil engineers are employed from time to time by governmental agencies, but they are rarities. Certain other types of technical workers occasionally fill governmental positions, as in the case of one or two lawyers, who are experts on the traction problem, or the Negro who is considered the outstanding authority on the Illinois election laws.

Lower Supervisory and Technical Personnel: Negroes have an even smaller proportionate representation among lower supervisory-personnel and technical workers in private industry than in the group just discussed. Higher supervisory-personnel and technical workers are recruited from technical and business schools as well as from the ranks of the working class. A Negro may therefore take a short cut *via* education and thus make himself available. The lower supervisory-personnel and technical workers are largely recruited through promotions based on seniority and performance in skilled labor and clerical positions. Competition is very keen, favoritism plays a large part in promotions, and the individual prejudices of foremen are often decisive. The road up is tortuous even for white workers. Since a tight bottleneck on the skilled labor and clerical levels has prevented Negroes from securing such positions in private industry, they are usually not in strategic spots for promotion into the next highest brackets of employment.

Even in the Black Belt it is unusual for a colored man to be placed in a managerial position in a store owned by white persons, and the first Negro who secured such a position (in 1928) was widely publicized among Negroes, and thought of himself as a "pioneer." There were more than 10,000 foremen "bossing" Chicago's industry in 1930. Of these, only 140 were Negroes, and this figure included those persons in public and quasi-public employment. Even the Second World War did not open the ranks of foremen and supervisors, set-up men and minor technicians, to Negroes to any important extent.

The number and proportion of Negroes employed in minor supervisory capacities by governmental agencies fluctuates. In 1930, there were 161 colored policemen, 120 schoolteachers, and some 400 colored social workers and their activities were confined largely to the Negro community.

In general it may be stated that it is definitely not the policy in industry to place Negroes in positions where they give orders to white persons, hire and fire them, recommend them for promotions, or function as expert technicians. Competition for such positions is rigidly limited by those who do the hiring, by white competitors, and, to some extent at least, by the attitudes of the general public.

Clerical and Sales: An industrial city such as Chicago employs a host of white-collar workers—the backbone of the so-called "new middle class." These are the functionaries who do that mass of paper work upon which the complex commercial and industrial structure rests. They make out and collect the bills; they write and distribute the copy that persuades the public to buy this or that product; or they personally present the merits of rival companies and their wares to customers in stores, to retail outlets, and to housekeepers wherever they can effect an entrance by persuasion or guile.

In 1930 almost 100,000 people in Chicago were involved in "selling," and nearly 60,000 were serving the needs of commerce and industry with notebook and typewriter. *Negroes were employed in these capacities in a proportion of less than one in a hundred!* Wherever Negro members of this small group were found, if they were not in government positions they were usually working in Negro neighborhoods.

The political system has operated to place a relatively large number of Negroes in white collar and clerical positions in local government. During the Thompson administration Chicago's City Hall was dubbed "Uncle Tom's Cabin" because of the large number of Negroes employed there. The civil service lists and the payment of political obligations have spotted Negroes about in the city's libraries and governmental offices in increasing numbers, as did the shortage of clerical help during the Second World War.

Clerical and sales positions in Midwest Metropolis have been held, in the main, by people "on the make"—girls temporarily employed until they find a husband, men and women who hope to make a career in business and to advance on the job, and individuals of both sexes from working-class families who have made the first step away from back-breaking, menial or dirty work. Competition for advancement and raises, and for the personal attention of employers and personnel officials, is always keen.

Such positions, even when the pay is low, have been glamorized, and are surrounded with an aura of folklore. The myths surrounding secretary and boss, and the popular stories of the intimate activities of traveling salesmen and the escapades of "the Fuller Brush man," have invested such work with overtones of sexual as well as economic competition. Also, the large number of young women employed in clerical and sales work results in the elaboration of cliques on the job, oriented around the sharing of gossip about "boy friends," and a sort of ritualized primping and mutual admiration of clothes and physical attractiveness. Moreover, since an enterprise tends to be judged by its white-collar personnel, businessmen are reluctant to risk "goodwill" and profits by experimenting with types of workers with whom they feel the public is not familiar. The color-line, consequently, is very rigid in this area. Until the Second World War, Negroes found it almost impossible to secure acceptance, or even trial, in private white-collar employment, because it had become associated by custom with so many goals other than merely earning a living.

Figure 20

HIGH SCHOOL AND COLLEGE ENROLLMENT AMONG CHICAGO NEGROES : 1930 AND 1940

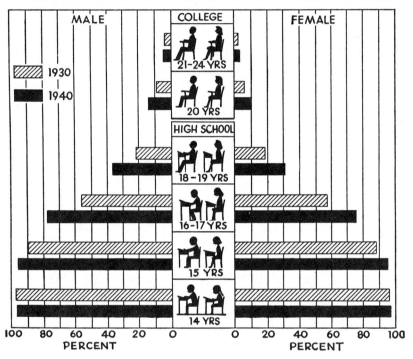

From tables in Fifteenth and Sixteenth Census of the U. S., 1930 and 1940.

Most of the colored women in clerical and sales work, prior to the Second World War were employed in the Black Belt and there were less than 1,500 of them. Clerical work elsewhere (except in Civil Service) has become the preserve of native-born white women. Negro girls, however, in increasing numbers during the last twenty years, have been attending high school and college. (Figure 20.) But the outlook for permanent white-collar employment has remained extremely bleak, despite temporary war gains. Figure 21 lends eloquence to a colored

Figure 21

ECONOMIC OPPORTUNITY FOR WOMEN

OF EVERY 10 TEEN-AGE WHITE GIRLS 5 ARE IN HIGH SCHOOL

OF THESE 6 CAN EXPECT WHITE-COLLAR JOBS

OF EVERY 10 TEEN-AGE NEGRO GIRLS 5 ARE IN HIGH SCHOOL

OF THESE ONLY 1 CAN EXPECT A WHITE-COLLAR JOB

Estimates based on data from the Sixteenth Census of the U. S., 1940.

school girl's mournful statement: "Teacher said not to take a commercial course because there were no jobs opening up for colored. So there's nothing but housework and cleaning left for you to do." *

✦

* The estimate of "economic opportunity for women" in Figure 21 is based on an analysis of 1930 and 1940 Census data, and on the assumption that most of the war-time clerical jobs held by Negro women are only temporary. Not more than 3 per cent of the Negro women held bona fide clerical and sales jobs in 1940. The saturation point for employment had been reached in Black Belt stores and offices. Yet, the high schools were continuing to turn out girls with "white-collar   rations."

Skilled Labor: Prior to 1943, Negro skilled workers operated at a very great competitive disadvantage. Skilled workers have been ordinarily recruited largely from the ranks of the semi-skilled through apprenticeship service. A few were trained from trade schools and by plant-training programs. Until the outbreak of the Second World War all of these doors were closed to Negroes. In only one skilled labor category—as foundry men—did Negroes make up any appreciable number of the workers. Here the work is heavy and hot, and Negroes secured a priority on these jobs.

Craft unions, particularly those of the carpenters, steamfitters and plumbers, machinists, electricians, motion-picture operators, and street car employees have even restricted the competition of whites by constitutional provisions, high initiation fees, and demands for sponsors who were already members of the unions. Special barriers were erected against Negroes. The closed shop contracts and the political influence of the American Federation of Labor, have reinforced this closed circle, and even extended the influence of craft unions into the public trade schools and government employment.

Until the advent of the war, some unions, such as the machinists' brotherhoods, barred Negroes either by constitutional provision or sections of the ritual which stipulated that initiates were to be "white men of good moral character." Other unions used devices such as the refusal by members to "sponsor" Negroes. Where Negroes were permitted to work they were sometimes organized into separate locals without full membership privileges and were assigned specific areas of the city outside of which they were not permitted to work. Other unions used somewhat more subtle, but equally effective methods of barring Negroes.

Open shop employers who utilized Negro labor, or closed shop employers who wished to use them, were at a definite disadvantage. In the former case they ran the risk of actual intimidation and violence; in the latter case they had no influence over union rules with respect to race. Also, those employers who did not wish to employ Negroes could justify themselves by citing union restrictions. During hearings held in Chicago by the Illinois State Commission on the Condition of the Urban Colored Population in 1940, and by the Fair Employment Practices Committee in 1943, representatives of several unions and firms that refused to hire Negroes were summoned to testify. In a few cases they definitely defended a policy of discrimination. More typically, there was considerable "buck passing" backward and forward between the unions and management as to the responsibility for the Job Ceiling with a general admission that discrimination against Negroes was "un-American."

Unlike the other areas of government employment, Negroes have not penetrated the Job Ceiling in the skilled trades. This has been due primarily to the fact that the craft unions wield considerable political power and in some cases actually give the civil service examinations. One case was verified in which a Negro who had finished an engineering course in steamfitting and plumbing at a midwestern university and who had passed two state examinations with high marks, failed several times to pass an examination prepared by the Chicago Civil Service Commission. The union gave the examination!

Even within industrial plants in which there are no unions, it has traditionally been very difficult for Negroes to advance upward in the hierarchy beyond the semi-skilled level, since the foremen are the key men for rating workers, and as a general rule, they do not recomment Negroes.

THE UPS AND DOWNS OF COMPETITION

Losing Out: Between the Depression and the Second World War, there were a number of fields in which Negroes felt they were "losing out." These were occupations, which, although not Negro Jobs, had once been freely open to Negroes. With increased white competition, their hold upon them was being broken. Among these were jobs as cooks, waiters, maids and servants in institutions such as restaurants and hotels.

At one time it was traditional in Chicago for Negroes to hold a variety of jobs in most of the major hotels. Before the Great Migration, there were frequent complaints that Negroes were being "pushed out" of these fields by the foreign-born, and the labor unions were accused of aiding in the process. In 1930, colored men made up less than 30 per cent of the waiters in hotels and restaurants, and they were meeting strong competition from white men and girls. During the Depression years, several large hotels replaced Negro waiters with white girls, and there was bitter editorial comment about the matter in Negro newspapers.

✦

Holding Their Own: Between the First and the Second World Wars, Negro men held their own as common laborers and semi-skilled operatives in the mass production industries and commercial establishments. Negro women held their own as semi-skilled workers in canning factories, paper and pulp mills and cleaning and pressing establishments, and in the garment industry.

Breaking the Job Ceiling: By way of summary, it can be said that the competitive process has become organized in such a way that the Job Ceiling for Negroes tends to be drawn just above the level of semi-skilled jobs, with the skilled, clerical, managerial and supervisory positions reserved for white workers. There has been considerable conflict for jobs between white and Negro workers for semi-skilled and skilled jobs throughout Chicago's post-Migration history, and it is only within the last ten years that Negroes have become an integral part of the labor movement in the mass production industries, accepted as individuals subject to promotion on the basis of seniority.

The perpetuation of the Job Ceiling is basically related to the "lines of promotion" during "normal" years. It is expected that a certain proportion of individuals will "advance on the job." Advancement usually comes as a result of recommendations by minor supervisory personnel, or through the operation of union seniority rules. Insofar as Negroes have not been able to secure such recommendations, or have been refused admittance to unions, the Job Ceiling is reinforced. But the Job Ceiling is occasionally broken. Chapter 11 deals with the major factors that cause rifts in the Job Ceiling, but before analyzing that process we should understand the general forces which cause shifts in the color-line.

CHAPTER 10

The Shifting Line of Color

THE COLOR-LINE IN MIDWEST METROPOLIS FLOUTS THE BASIC TENETS OF American democracy, Christian brotherhood, and the "Chicago Spirit." Most Chicagoans, if pressed, would probably admit this. They are acquainted with the lofty declaration that "all men are created equal." Most of them, as children, have pledged allegiance to the flag—"with liberty and justice for all." Abraham Lincoln is an Illinois hero, praised frequently and loudly because he "freed the slaves." Nearly everyone, too, has been exposed to the words of priest, minister, or rabbi preaching the doctrine of "the Fatherhood of God and the Brotherhood of Man." And Chicago's civic boosters never tire of presenting the city as "the land of opportunity." These ideas are conserved and transmitted by churches and schools, press and radio, as well as by organized labor and various political parties and sects.

The most important agencies molding public opinion in Midwest Metropolis have supported the Negro's claim for democratic rights ever since the Flight to Freedom. There has always been, too, a small minority within the city that has militantly espoused the rights of Negroes, and a much larger number of people who, for reasons of political expediency or economic necessity, have welcomed the participation of Negroes in various sectors of city life. The majority of the residents of Midwest Metropolis have probably had no strong feelings one way or another about the place of Negroes. Except in crisis situations, they seldom think of Negroes. They have a policy of "live and let live." *

An analysis of the speeches made at the Mayor's Conference on Race

* No adequate statistical studies of the opinions and attitudes of white people in Midwest Metropolis toward Negroes are available. This chapter is based upon miscellaneous reports of interviewer-observers connected with the Cayton-Warner Research; the report of the 1919 Commission on Race Relations; a mass of data collected by the Illinois State Commission on the Condition of the Urban Colored Population (1940); and the memoranda and published reports of the Carnegie-Myrdal study, "The Negro in America." A poll conducted by *Fortune* for the Myrdal study also contains breakdowns of attitudes by section of the country, and some tentative generalizations may be drawn from its findings for the East North Central States including Illinois.

Relations in 1944 indicates the manner in which the status-bearers of the city—the political leaders, the industrialists, the labor leaders, the higher clergy, college professors, and administrators of private and public social agencies—are verbally committed to the ideal of equality of opportunity for Negroes. The first meeting was opened with an address by the Mayor, a man with a national reputation as the boss of a reputedly corrupt political machine. Practical and hard-boiled, he announced that this was "not a meeting of idealists and dreamers to sketch a panacea." Yet, proud of anything that makes Midwest Metropolis a "first," he boasted for the record: "I appointed, last July, with the approval of the City Council, a Committee on Race Relations. Chicago's pioneering in this realm started a widespread movement. I am informed that since last July, 137 similar committees have been appointed by Mayors, Governors, or civic and religious bodies from one end of the country to the other." Out of the Mayor's address emerged the main outlines of the official, public doctrines about the rights of man, which, along with the demands of economic necessity and political expediency, help to shape events as well as rationalize them. All of the speakers echoed these basic ideas.

The Mayor emphasized the *virtue in variety*—"Our people trace their origin from almost every country on the globe, representing more than thirty-two different nationalities and sixty-two dialects. . . ." He stressed the *fact of interdependence* with an epigram: "Benefits to any one group can result in advantages to all." The *primacy of civic harmony* was driven home: ". . . to avoid friction and to promote cooperation among the many great groups that make up this city. . . ." The Mayor also revealed his *faith in planning:* "Only recently have we begun to realize that it is as important to plan for human relations as for material needs."

Belief in the *primacy of civic harmony* and *faith in planning* led most of the speakers to emphasize education and "good-will" as the desirable mechanisms of social change. *Tolerance* was constantly emphasized as the cardinal civic virtue, ideological trimmings being thus given to the more mundane imperatives of city life—a state of affairs in which bankers and pickpockets, preachers and prostitutes, artists and gangsters not only inhabit the same city, but are inextricably tied together in a web of political and economic relationships which is real although usually hidden and denied.

The Negro is automatically included within this framework of optimistic dogmas based on the realities of urban life. One speaker, a member of the editorial staff of the liberal daily, the Chicago *Sun,* reminded the conference, however, of the *moral* imperatives which should guide their deliberations: "There are many reasons why the community cannot shirk this responsibility—reasons of expediency, reasons of fair-play, reasons of long-range social prudence—what we might call self-interested social insurance for the future. But in the end none of these surpasses the basic reason that underlies them all. To act against discrimination is right, morally right; we know in our hearts it is right. We know that equality is indivisible and cannot be split by a color-line."

Equality was the master-slogan of the Mayor's Conference. The head of the city health department boasted proudly that, in the venereal disease clinics, "there is no distinction because of race, sex, creed, or nationality." The Commissioner of Relief testified that in his department, "the needs of all persons have been treated alike without regard to race, color, or creed." A district police captain, solicitous for equality before the bar as well as at the relief station and the VD clinic, stated that "men who will judge others by merit and not by the yardstick of color, creed, or nationalities should be the only persons placed in executive positions." The Subcommittee on Employment, composed of sixteen leading industrialists, went on record as being opposed to the Job Ceiling by suggesting that employers "regard each Negro employee as an individual, with potentialities and limitations, who takes his or her place in your firm on the basis of merit as a worker and not on the basis of belonging to any special racial grouping." The AFL spokesman, in a contrite mood, referred to "race and sometimes religious barriers that all of us know are contrary to the spirit of our country." The CIO representative proclaimed "the moral righteousness of treating all Americans with complete equality regardless of the pigment of their skins." The Chairman closed the conference with a reminder that "full victory will come only if we put aside our petty prejudices and, in the Chicago spirit of 'I will' make up our minds that regardless of race, creed, or color, we are going to treat all people on the democratic basis of individual merits."

These profuse expressions of belief in equality led the president of a YMCA college to admonish the conference: "We have all the ideals we need to solve this problem. We know what democracy is and we all know what the Christian ideals for human associations are. We all know them, whether we live by them or not."

BELIEFS MEN LIVE BY

With nearly everyone in Midwest Metropolis verbally committed to a belief in democracy, freedom, equality, fair play, and similar civic ideals, why does a color-line persist? The answer lies partly in the fact that these are not the ideals men live by, however much they may believe in them. Side by side with the official doctrines about men's relationships to their fellows are the "folk-beliefs" that influence human behavior far more profoundly than do any political or religious dogmas. These folk-beliefs and attitudes become set at a very early age within family and play groups, where they are acquired by imitation and unconscious absorption long before the other institutions get to work on the child's mind. Adult associations and cliques preserve them. The folk-beliefs and the behavior pattern associated with them are difficult to change.

The most basic of these reaction-patterns is the habit of reacting to people in terms of *inequalities*. Children learn early that social differences *are* important—that income, education, language, eating habits, skin-color, and a hundred and one other things must all be weighed in determining a man's intrinsic worth or his acceptability as an associate. In our Western European culture the basic categories of invidious distinction are *group* differences—of religion, nationality, and socio-economic status. In countries with an Anglo-American tradition, "race" —as denoted by skin-color—is an additional marker. We have already seen how the competition between such groups has been the thread upon which the history of Midwest Metropolis is strung.

Since the early days of the slave trade, dark skin-color has been considered a mark of inferiority—social, economic, and political—in the Anglo-American world. Africa has become the master-symbol of benightedness and savagery, its people being thought of as lowest in the scale of culture and civilization—perhaps even not fully human. A vague belief permeates the society that Negroes are "closer to the apes." Folk-thought invests them—the descendants of African slaves—with an aura of "primitiveness." They are considered impulsive, childlike, overemotional, oversexed, and short on brains and initiative. They are thought to be docile, easily frightened, incredibly superstitious, but gifted with a sure sense of rhythm (perhaps in compensation for lack of gray matter). These basic beliefs are reinforced by the objective fact that, the world around, the darker peoples are predominantly "backward" when judged by Western European standards.

The low cultural and economic status of Negroes in America seems to confirm this estimate. Quick judgments arising from limited contacts with Negroes, and from the picture of Negro life presented by the press, radio, and screen, perpetuate the stereotype. Epithets like "nigger," "darky," "shine," "smoke," "spade," "dingy," exist in the culture and may be used as short-cut symbols to express all the contempt concentrated in the popular estimate of the Negro. Kinky hair, thick lips, and dark skin become the esthetic antithesis of straight hair, small lips, white skin, and these physical traits are thought to be correlated with all of the unsavory characteristics indicated above.

Negroes in America are only eighty years out of slavery. As described in the early part of this book, less than a hundred years ago, the slave-catchers were chasing fugitives through the streets of Midwest Metropolis. In the South, Negroes are still living in the backwash of slavery—floundering in a morass of poverty, ignorance, and disease. Periodically, the South debouches a flood of these "backward" people into the northern city streets, and always there is some seepage through the ramparts of the Mason and Dixon's Line.

As the center for the formation of attitudes about the Negro, the South keeps alive the belief in the Negro's differentness and inferiority and, in doing so, depends not only upon derogatory propaganda, but also upon a caste system which effectively limits the chances for Negroes to change their status. The situation thus becomes circular: Negroes are deemed unfit for citizenship or full equality; they must be kept in their place; through being kept in their place they cannot show whether they are fit for citizenship and equality. These southern attitudes exist in a watered-down form in Midwest Metropolis, as they do throughout the North.* Negroes in the mass are poor and still display

* Eugene L. Horowitz, discussing "Attitudes and Sectional Differences in the United States" (*Characteristics of the American Negro*, Otto Kleinberg, *ed.*, Harper, 1944), presents the results of a poll which included small samples

many of the rough edges of conduct that come from their southern background and their social isolation. They are quarantined behind the color-line. But—and this is the crux of the matter—this quarantine intensifies their differentness and curtails their chances for improvement. Negroes become the victims of circular reinforcement.

Not only does folk-thought deal with Negroes as a separate and inferior group. It also brings to bear upon the Negro problem all of the superstitions about "blood," and the half-truths about heredity, which are a part of our general culture. It is assumed that "Negro character traits" are passed on from generation to generation, that somehow "blood will tell." The smallest drop of colored blood will "taint" the white stock. As Negroes sometimes jocularly phrase it: "Negro blood is powerful. One drop will make you whole." It is necessary, therefore, in order to preserve the "purity" of the white race to see to it that persons with Negro blood will mate with Negroes only and not "infect" the white race. The obverse side of this argument is that any Negro with white blood has had his undesirable traits diluted and thus becomes a little more civilized than a pure black. Such people must stay on their side of the fence and breed with "their kind." It will take centuries to submerge the Negro traits; meanwhile mulattoes, octoroons, quadroons serve as a leavening force for the black people. This theory of blood magic, in a general way, is a widespread feature of folk-thought.

But nowhere in America have caste tendencies ever been so strong—even during slavery—that *some* Negroes did not find an opportunity to exercise intelligence and skill and to display talent and initiative.

from various sections of the United States. It suggests some of the sectional differences in folk-thinking about Negroes:

	East South Central and South Atlantic States (Per Cent)	East North Central States (Per Cent)
1. Belief in intellectual inferiority of Negroes	72.5	70.4
2. Heredity alone accounts for this inferiority	52.5	38.0
3. Environment alone accounts for inferiority	20.3	40.2
4. Some Negroes surpass white average of intelligence	75.3	90.7
5. Negroes are "improving"	29.2	25.9

The Christian-humanitarian tradition and the demands of economic necessity and political expediency have consistently weakened the will, wherever it existed, to keep *all* Negroes, everywhere, in a subordinate economic, political, and social status. The beliefs in the inherent intellectual inferiority of all Negroes were contradicted by the facts long before the mental-testers ever got the statistics down on paper.* The dictum that Negroes were animal-like and incapable of assimilating Christian morality was challenged by the growth of stable family elements even before the bonds of chattel slavery fell. The early emergence of a class system among Negroes made it impossible for anyone to miss the fact that *some* Negroes were interested in "getting ahead" just like their white neighbors.† Faced with these facts, it was necessary to take refuge in certain dodges: "Of course, there are exceptional Negroes"; "Most exceptional Negroes have some white blood"; "The best of them are niggers underneath; culture and education are just a veneer"; "Education spoils the simple Negro and makes him restless and unhappy"; "If they get too far ahead they'll start wanting social equality."

These racial doctrines are not taught in any systematic fashion in Midwest Metropolis, nor do they form an integrated ideological framework. Rather, they are picked up by children from adult conversation and are mediated through play groups. They are strengthened through contact with southerners who come to Chicago and northerners who travel in the South. In a very unorganized fashion they get reinforcement from caricatures and cartoons, newspaper stories and movies, and statements here and there in textbooks. When the Great Migration began it is doubtful whether the masses of foreign-born workers and their children had any clear beliefs about Negroes such as they had about Jews and Poles and Italians and other European ethnic groups. Confronted by thousands of Negro migrants they were forced to

* A Public Affairs Committee pamphlet by Ruth Benedict and Gene Weltfish, *The Races of Mankind,* summarizes the results of intelligence tests given to whites and Negroes as a part of a general discussion of the conflict between the folk-ideas about race and scientific findings.

† Social and economic stratification among Negroes in the United States began very early. One Anthony Johnson, member of the first group of Negroes imported at Jamestown in 1619, had obtained his freedom and become the master of indentured servants within twenty years after he landed. Colonies of free Negroes existed in all southern cities throughout the late seventeenth century and subsequent years. In Chapter 2 we have described the emergence of the class system among Negroes in Midwest Metropolis.

hammer together a set of attitudes and opinions from a disjointed mass of folk-prejudices. And groups with axes to grind helped them.

THE ROLE OF ECONOMIC INTEREST

The frequently heard statement that "the race problem is economic," has become a platitude. Although this is only a half-truth, color-caste did have its origin in economic interest. Plantation owners in the West Indies and North America needed labor to grow the cane and cotton, indigo and tobacco, upon which the fortunes of the New World were built. They first tried the Indians, and then turned to a vast reservoir of indentured servants from Europe and Negroes from Africa. The early traffickers in slaves often justified their business because it "brought the heathen to Christ" as well as in terms of economic necessity. The doctrine of inherent biological and racial inferiority grew slowly throughout the seventeenth century, and seems to have been partly due to the Puritan streak in English thought. How could Christians enslave their fellowmen? Only if they were not *really* men. (As one scholar has phrased it, "Negroes suffered because of the white man's virtues as well as because of his vices.") But the circumstances that finally riveted the chains upon Negroes sprang from the conflict of interest between white landlords in the southern United States and white indentured servants. So long as there was free land to the West, no English workers, with the traditions of relatively unlimited freedom behind them, could be bound permanently to the soil of the plantation. Planters, unable to hold white labor tied to the soil, were forced to keep Negroes in a position of chattel slavery bound in perpetuity to labor. Every resource of religion, propaganda, and violence was utilized to justify this enslavement of millions of Africans.[1]

White indentured servants, having the advantage of cultural kinship with the overlords, sharply dissociated themselves from the African slaves and buttressed their privileged position by stressing the importance of the color of their skins. By keeping the Negro bound to the plantation, the lowly white man protected his claim to the free lands of the West and his opportunity to rise from indentured servant to apprentice to journeyman to master artisan in the South and East. (Further, he accepted the doctrines of inherent biological inferiority in order to square things with his Puritan conscience and his democratic idealism.)

By the turn of the nineteenth century, however, it was becoming evident that the southern landed aristocracy was ambitious to extend its system of slavery even to the free lands of the West, and thousands of southerners and ex-southerners in the border states began to turn against the planter class. Northern capitalists and artisans became the spearhead of an attack upon a slave system that threatened to hamper the growth of an industrial society, and menaced the free yeomen farmers in the West. The result was civil war. By this time the racial doctrines had become a part of the folk-thought, and, although the white workers in North and South alike hated slavery, they did not love the slave. In fact, the freeing of the slaves threw millions of potential competitors into the struggle for jobs and the scramble for western lands. This competition did not become serious, however, until the period of the First World War, for the southern landlords had no intention of letting their labor supply walk off to the North and West. Whatever interracial stability existed in the North between the Civil War and the First World War was directly related to the southern caste system which "protected" the North and West against an influx of Negroes.

Once the folk-beliefs about Negroes had come into being to justify the privileges of southern white laborers and to rationalize the economic interests of the planters, they kept going under their own power. Today, they often exist independently of economic interest. But in Midwest Metropolis, as elsewhere, there are still many situations in which the folk-beliefs about Negroes and economic interest reinforce each other. Among industrial laborers, for instance, there has been, since the days of the Flight to Freedom, the fear that employers would use poverty-stricken Negro labor from the South to keep wages down and to break strikes. This fear has been frequently justified. The traditional reaction of white workers has been to lash out blindly at the Negro as the source of the trouble, and to seek to limit his competition by refusing to admit him to membership in unions, by stressing his alleged incompetence and unreliability, and by attacking him physically when he got in the way. Even today two of the strongholds of anti-Negro sentiment in Midwest Metropolis are a group of AFL unions in the skilled trades and a group of railroad brotherhoods.

The main focal point of anti-Negro sentiment in Midwest Metropolis, and by far the most important one, is a loose association of neighborhood property owners' associations aided and abetted by the Chicago Real Estate Board and the Chicago Title and Trust Company. In Chapter 8 we have seen how the generally low cultural status of Negroes and the folk-prejudices against them, excite fear of a decline in property values when Negroes move near, or into, middle-class neighborhoods. Even middle-class Negroes are thought of as a "taint" or "blight" in a middle-class white area. When these propertied interests fight to preserve the residential color-line no holds are barred.*

The small property owners, as we have seen, are aided and abetted by the large real-estate interests and the banks. This is due partly to concern about their mortgages in middle-class white neighborhoods, but it is also a reflection of the fact that these larger interests stand to make quick profits from the high rents which they can charge in Negro areas since the Negroes can't get out. When a high official of the Chicago Real Estate Board can say at a public hearing, "I know that restrictive covenants are undemocratic; but my first duty is to the property holders I represent," we can understand the power of economic interest in holding the color-line tight.

Much of the incidental discrimination in public places is directly related to economic interest. An individual proprietor may, himself, have no objections to Negro patronage, but if even one customer objects, or if he thinks one will object, he is likely to become panic-stricken and discourage Negro patronage if he can. An employer may honestly mean it when he says, "I'd like to employ that attractive Negro girl in the office, or that aggressive colored salesman, but what can I do when some customer says, 'I don't want to do business with a nigger'?" The economic argument can always work the other way around, too. An employer or proprietor who has strong feelings against Negroes can cover his prejudice, salve his conscience, or hoodwink Negroes— as the occasion demands—by pleading that consideration for Negroes may hurt his pocketbook.

In a northern city like Midwest Metropolis, if only a tiny fraction of the white population is aggressively anti-Negro, the color-line may be reinforced. A proprietor or an employer can never be sure that a preju-

---

* The influence of the real estate interests in buttressing and extending segregation extends far beyond the Negro community. In 1945, some officials of the larger real estate associations who were also members of the board of the Chicago Y.M.C.A. demanded that a study be made of the proportion of Negroes and Jews attending the Central Y.M.C.A. College with an eye to restricting their attendance. The President of the College and over half of the faculty resigned in protest.

diced client will not close his account, cease his patronage, or create a scene. Whenever there is the possibility that a black face will drive business away, a hitch is taken in the color-line.

THE ROLE OF SOCIAL STATUS

Economic considerations, while extremely important, alone cannot account for the persistence of the color-line. One of the most powerful factors implementing it is the concern for the preservation and enhancement of social status. In the life-history of the individual he is constantly seeking approval and psychological support from various groups. First, the immediate family circle dominates; later, teachers, fellow-pupils, and the play-group; still later, courting cliques and various types of formal associations. Adults are responsive to the pressures of their work-associates, recreational groups, formal associations, and to the standards of any higher social stratum to which they aspire. These groups (or one's conception of them) act as controls upon individual behavior. In addition to these primary groups, the individual is also under the constant scrutiny of the larger public which he meets on the street and in public places. Whatever "private" attitudes an individual may have are influenced by public opinion.

There is considerable evidence to indicate that very young children react to differences in skin-color mainly in terms of curiosity. They have to be taught the facts of social life. They learn quickly, however, under the impact of a restraining hand here, a little heart-to-heart talk there, a lifted eyebrow, a stare, a frown, and gossip.* During the critical period of adolescence, if white youngsters are in contact with Negroes of the same age-group, sensitiveness to the color-line becomes sharpened, and behavior toward Negroes tends to crystallize into an

---

* Eugene L. Horowitz, in an article "Attitudes in Children" (*op. cit.*), summarizes the research findings on the development of race attitudes in children and presents case materials to illustrate the force of social pressure. The following is a typical response: "There is like a wall preventing the Negro and white people from being sociable. If you even try to be sociable with Negroes the rest of the people lift their eyebrows and say, 'Aw—that's awful.' When I meet them in the hall I say hello to them. All the other children look at me like it would be a crime to be sociable with them." (From a sixth-grade white boy in Cincinnati, Ohio.) A young Jewish child said: "I wouldn't want a Negro for a chum either. It wouldn't seem right. Everybody would be talking about me if they saw me going around with a colored person."

action-pattern for adult life. Many white persons in Midwest Metropolis, however, grow up without any close contact with Negroes. The problem of how to react toward Negroes confronts the average white person in a piecemeal, disjointed fashion. Usually he acts toward them as he would toward white persons of equivalent socio-economic status, unless his economic interests or his personal prestige seem menaced. In fact, it seems likely that there are hundreds of people in Midwest Metropolis who have very little strong race-consciousness and no particular aversion to social relations with Negroes of a similar socio-economic status. Social pressure, however, effectively keeps them in line.

The doctor in suburban Glencoe may actually wish to invite to his home for dinner the brilliant young surgeon that he met at the Negro hospital; but he is effectively deterred by the thought of what the neighbors will say when a black man and his mulatto wife get out of a Packard and go up his front steps.

The businessman in a Loop office may have no objections to a colored stenographer referred to him by the U. S. Employment Service; but could he stand the jokes that his cronies might level at him? His fear of a ribbing keeps the Negro girl taking care of his children instead of pounding his typewriter.

The white stockyards laborer at a union dance may have no aversion to dancing with that attractive brown-skinned girl who works in the smoked ham department; in fact he'd like to learn a little "rug-cutting" the way they do it in Black Metropolis. But none of the other white fellows are dancing with colored girls, and one of his buddies just can't stand these "smokes"—even ridicules him for going to a place where they let them dance on the same floor with white people.

The waitress at the restaurant thinks the colored bus-boy is a swell guy. They are always joking together in the pantry. But to walk into the Oriental Theater with him (as he half-jokingly suggested once), with all the white people staring and with the chance that some of her crowd might see her—that just isn't worth the risk. She wouldn't marry a Negro, and no white fellow would marry her if he knew she had dated a colored boy. Over to Club DeLisa in the Black Belt? Well, she'd gone with him once, but her heart was in her mouth all the time. And she couldn't let him escort her all the way home. Never again!

THE NEXUS OF SOCIAL CONTROLS

The intimate tie-up between strong folk-prejudices, economic interest, and social status is so intricate that it is difficult to unravel the threads. Negroes and whites seldom marry, not because it is illegal, but primarily because of strong folk-prejudices. Yet people without strong folk-prejudices don't do it either. Social pressure is too great and they might jeopardize their jobs. Negroes are confined to a Black Ghetto primarily because of the economic interests of property owners; but land values wouldn't be affected if folk-prejudices did not exist. And the whole problem is complicated by middle-class emphasis upon maintaining a relatively high social status. The Job Ceiling is primarily an economic device, but it reflects the reluctance of white people to lose prestige by working under the supervision of, or beside, Negroes in certain situations. It also reflects some deep-seated beliefs about the incapacity of the Negro to hold down certain jobs.

If we take a situation in which the law supports the Negro's demand for the abolition of the color-line, we can see how all these factors operate to produce incidental examples of discrimination here and there. Any given case of refusal to serve a Negro in a public place may have any or all of the following elements in it:

a. Traditional neighborhood hostility toward Negroes.
b. Fear of a Negro "invasion" by a neighborhood or establishment.
c. Fear of economic loss if customers object.*
d. Expression of an individual proprietor's own attitudes.
e. Expression of an individual functionary's or employee's attitude, sometimes in violation of established policy of the enterprise.
f. The assumption on the part of an employee that his employer wishes him to discriminate even though policy has not been defined. (Often a carry-over from previous work situations.)

* The fear of customer objection does not seem to have so much basis in reality as most proprietors assume. The Committee on Racial Equality, a group of young Negro and white people connected with churches and Socialist organizations has for three years been systematically visiting establishments that discriminate against Negroes. It reports that the general attitude of customers seems to be one of indifference. Even when an argument arises between a proprietor and the group asking to be waited on, other customers rarely join the dispute. The experimenters have never been beaten or otherwise attacked, and occasionally a white patron has sided with them.

g. Interpretation of the situation as "private" or "social" and of the Negro's demand for service as an unwarranted invasion of an "exclusive" situation.

The net result of this loose system of social controls is to make white behavior almost unpredictable, and to create a feeling of insecurity and tension among Negroes in their dealings with white people. In contrast with the South where the racial etiquette is rigidly defined, the Negroes of Midwest Metropolis can never be quite sure what will happen. It has been noted by some observers that Negroes experience a "gain" in psychological security in the South. Most of the Negroes in Midwest Metropolis would probably say that they prefer "insecurity." Within this loose nexus of controls lie the seeds of social change.

THE SEEDS OF SOCIAL CHANGE

The color-line in Midwest Metropolis is not static. The Job Ceiling is sometimes pierced and broken. Negroes occasionally find homes outside of the Black Belt, and the Black Belt does expand. In fact, Negroes are continually expressing surprise at some new "gain" made by The Race. Despite the Negro's impatience and the white man's fears, there is enough change to generate a vast amount of optimism among Negroes and progressive whites. This optimism was evident throughout the discussions at the Mayor's Conference on Race Relations. The participants, all interested in some relaxation of the color-line, seemed to define the problem in the following terms:

1. Creating a favorable public opinion toward the aspirations of Negroes.
2. Reducing the cultural difference between Negroes and whites.
3. Securing a larger measure of equality of opportunity without abolishing segregation in clique, church, and associational life, exciting a social-equality scare, or precipitating a race riot.
4. Ignoring the long-time perspective, thus avoiding commitments on intermarriage or amalgamation.

In pursuing these ends everyone seemed agreed that education and counterpropaganda were necessary to combat folk-prejudices; that increased friendly and co-operative contacts between Negroes and white people were desirable; and that considerations of economic necessity and political expediency should be exploited to set new social situations in which the status of Negroes could be changed. The summary of the conference (*City Planning in Race Relations*) assumed that social change in race relations could be controlled.

The Place of Education and Counterpropaganda: There is widespread belief among many Americans that "prejudice comes from ignorance." It is assumed that if both Negroes and whites can be educated they will learn to co-exist harmoniously (education usually meaning the verbal reiteration of certain ideas). Those who stress education start out with certain things in their favor. In the first place, Midwest Metropolis is already half educated. The absence of a slave tradition and the widespread profession of the ideals of democracy mean that most people are willing to concede at the outset that Negroes have rights which should be respected and that they are entitled to increased opportunity. Side by side with the belief in the inherent inferiority of Negroes there exists a tendency to accept the proposition that Negroes are "evolving" and that education will speed up the process. The following comment by a white drugstore owner during the Great Migration illustrates a mishmash of ideas [2] incorporating both folk-prejudices and democratic idealism:

"I have nothing against the black man as a black man. He comes into my place of business and I sell him. Not many come in, as there aren't a lot of colored people around Sixty-third and Woodlawn or Dorchester. But I don't want to live with niggers any more than you or any other white person does. People who say, 'I like the colored people and don't see why others can't get along with them' don't talk practical common sense. Theoretically, all this talk is all right, but you get a white man of this sort to come right down and live with a nigger and he won't do it.

"Niggers are different from whites and always will be, and that is why white people don't want them around. But the only thing we can do, it seems to me, is make the best of it and live peaceably with them. The North can never do what the South does—down there it is pure autocracy, I might say like Russia. That might have worked here in the North from the start, but it can't be started now, and we wouldn't want such autocracy anyway. They are citizens and it is up to us to teach them to be good ones. How it can be done, I don't know—it will have to come slow and no one can give an offhand solution. Everybody says, 'We don't want the niggers with us.' Well, here they are and we can't do anything. Must let them live where they want to and go to school where they want to, and we don't want to force their rights away."

This co-existence of folk-prejudices with a belief that Negroes should have a chance to develop (if they can) was expressed, during the same period, by a number of white community leaders. The pattern of responses is indicated in the following analysis of the opinions of four persons who wrote out their attitudes toward Negroes:[3]

Beliefs About Negroes	Attitude Toward Extension of Opportunity	Attitude Toward Negroes' Demands
1. Distinctly inferior mentality. 2. Deficient moral sense. 3. Shiftless. 4. Good-natured and happy disposition. 5. So different from whites that the two races can never be amalgamated.	"If surrounded by good living conditions and given a proper education they would be good citizens."	"I believe in educating Negroes, although I am not sure what it will lead to. . . . Probably many of their demands should be granted." (Believes in segregation only if Negroes consent.)
1. "Evolutionally" handicapped. 2. Childlike qualities: carelessness, improvidence, loyalty, imitativeness, affection, receptiveness.	"As a race have never had a fair chance for their finest development." "Their education should not be curtailed but enlarged." "Have the right to expect and demand justice in opportunity to develop industrial, social, and spiritual growth."	"Their demands should be granted if not incompatible with the common good."
1. Sluggish mentality. 2. Somewhat low moral character. 3. Seem to have more of the animal in them.	"They need education and the help that comes from association with those who are farther along in the polite amenities." "Deportation unchristian and unwise." "Complete segregation unjust and impractical."	"Regrettable that a minority cannot expect complete justice." (Thinks they should be settled in a separate state in the South, but not by force.)
1. "I have a strong prejudice."	"All Negroes should be educated as highly as possible. They have a right to it because they are Americans."	"If demands follow this education, it is right they should be granted." (Prefers colonization of Negroes in Africa.)

One of the main sources of racial tension in Midwest Metropolis is confusion and apprehension about what social change will mean. A very small minority probably feel that the ultimate result of the Negro's rise in status will be amalgamation.* A larger number feel that Negroes and whites will continue to remain socially separate. Very few people think that it is possible to deport Negroes, or that they will voluntarily leave the country.† *The general hope seems to be that Negroes will remain segregated socially and in separate neighborhoods, and will be content therewith; that they will not force the pace of breaking the Job Ceiling to the point of precipitating violence; and that they will use their political power "wisely."* Few people have consciously thought out any such position, but when the Negro issue is raised, or when

---

* Liberals and progressives try to avoid discussion of amalgamation as a possible outcome of their efforts to secure equal opportunity for Negroes. At the same time, however, they propagate the *myth of the melting pot.* For instance, the Mayor's Conference on Race Relations accepted *difference as a fact,* emphasize the *virtue in variety,* but also espoused the *myth of the melting pot.* The Mayor stated proudly, "Of all communities in the world Chicago perhaps can be most appropriately termed the melting pot." Another speaker grew almost lyrical in his reference to "this wonderful melting pot." The President of the Council of Social Agencies referred to Midwest Metropolis as the "melting pot of melting pots." The *myth of the melting pot* implies the eventual disappearance of all ethnic divisions and the substitution of social-class lines for divisions of nationality and race. It also implies the fusing of diverse physical strains into some future American type. The latter implication is found in a speech by one prominent white civic leader who told the conference: "It is highly appropriate that the first permanent resident of this city which is the melting pot of melting pots should be a sort of one-man melting pot himself. Jean Baptiste Point de Saible, who came here shortly after the Revolution, was half Negro and half French. As he had as his consort an Indian woman, he included in his immediate family the three principal races of the world." The Chairman of the Conference prefaced his summary of the findings with this statement: "Chicago has been built by many different kinds of people. The first settler in the trading post that became Chicago was Jean Baptiste Point de Saible, half French, half Negro, and married to an Indian. This cosmopolitan character has continued all through the city's history. . . ." The story of Chicago's Negro founder and his family is taught in Chicago's public schools with the same emphasis upon its symbolic foreshadowing of Midwest Metropolis, the cosmopolitan city.

Superficially it would seem that the men quoted above were advocating amalgamation, or at least sanctioning it. It is probable, however, that the use of the Point de Saible story has a totally different function. By idealizing the past it permits contemporary individuals to feel very liberal. The very fact that it can be used by an official body like the Mayor's Committee is testimony to the confidence which Chicago's civic leaders have that the present-day taboo on intermarriage will not break down.

† These generalizations are based upon interview documents, newspaper analyses, and inferences from the overt behavior of white people in Midwest

some incident focuses attention upon Negroes as "a problem," this is the type of "solution" that seems to crystallize in the popular mind.* Events, however, are continually forcing white people in Midwest Metropolis to face up to their relations with Negroes. When the problem arises, either in actuality or in conversation, they must choose sides, and the tension between democratic idealism and actual practice demands resolution. When in the throes of such an intellectual and moral crisis, people are susceptible to education and counterpropaganda.† During a strike or a war or a depression, education and counterpropaganda can be very effectively used to point up the necessity for integrating Negroes more fully into American life.

Most of the social engineers in Midwest Metropolis are primarily interested in a long-time program of education and counterpropaganda as a means of changing the folk-prejudices. They see their problem as one of gradually changing the tone of the press, radio, and screen.

Metropolis. The *Fortune* poll confirms these general observations. Horowitz (*op. cit.*) gives the following percentages for the East North Central States in response to a query on what the solution of the race problem was likely to be.

		Per Cent
1.	Believe that things will remain "about as they are"	37.5
2.	Believe that Negroes will remain socially separate but will be treated as equals in all other respects	22.8
3.	Don't know	29.8
4.	Believe that amalgamation will ultimately result	2.6
5.	Believe that deportation is feasible	1.3
6.	Believe that Negroes will secure full equality	.5

* It is perhaps significant that only 8.4% of the East North Central people queried in the *Fortune* poll thought of the Negro as a "problem."

† Such a moral crisis can also be resolved through an *anti*-Negro action-pattern. Men can strike very brutally when goaded by an uneasy conscience. People can be very stubborn if they feel their efforts to be "fair" are not appreciated. A large number of people seem to consider that Negroes are "on trial"; that they must "prove themselves"; that America has given them a fine chance to do so; that "after all, they've come a long way since slavery." When Negroes dissent from this view, a white person who holds it can become righteously indignant. There is some evidence to suggest that this attitude is widespread. Several surveys of public opinion made in 1944 by the National Institute of Public Opinion Research, Denver, Colorado, indicate that at least half of the white public professes to believe that "Negroes are getting a square deal in this country." Over two-thirds, however, think that "Negroes do not believe they are getting a square deal." In other words, well over half the population seems to feel that Negroes are being unreasonable in raising demands for the abolition of the Job Ceiling and for the relaxation of the color-bar. It could be that these verbal responses conceal an uneasy conscience arising from the knowledge that democratic profession and practice are at variance in America.

They recognize the fundamental necessity of utilizing the schools for incidental intercultural education and the churches for direct indoctrination. But the liberal and progressive forces have only scratched the surface when it comes to using the resources at hand for a planned attack upon the false ideas about ethnic groups in general and Negroes in particular.* This is due partly to a shortage of personnel and funds, but it is also directly related to considerations of social prestige and economic interest. There are individuals and institutions in Midwest Metropolis that definitely do not wish to see any basic changes in the status of Negroes. Yet an awareness of the Negro's aspirations and of the disabilities from which he suffers seeps throughout the city year by year, and increasingly large numbers of people are forced to face the issue, or experience a change of attitude so subtly that they hardly notice it.

The Role of Contact: One Negro speaker at the Mayor's Conference, after admitting the need for education, said, "The education we need most is the education of association." Another speaker, deploring the fact that residential segregation tends to separate Negro and white school children, stated:

"It is tragic that American boys and girls in the most impressionable period of their lives are prevented from having the natural and normal contacts which a mixed school system provides. The separate school system develops hatreds, suspicions, and disrespect which are carried over into our work and play life as we reach adulthood. It is significant that persons who have been taught by both white and colored teachers are more willing to work and play side by side with each other than those who have not had this broadening experience."

This almost mystical faith in "getting to know one another" as a solvent of racial tensions is very widespread. It is undoubtedly true that mere contact is likely to result in some degree of understanding and friendliness. It is equally true, however, that contact can produce ten-

---

* The Chicago Board of Education has recommended a set of carefully prepared booklets on the Negro for use as supplementary materials in the public schools. There is no adequate check, however, on the extent to which individual teachers make use of these data in the classroom. Officials of both the Mayor's Committee on Race Relations and the American Council on Race Relations have criticized the school board for not introducing a planned program of "intercultural education." Teaching "racial tolerance" is one of the stated aims of the State Board of Education.

sion and reinforcement of folk-prejudices. On the adult level this is especially true if the contact is between Negroes and whites of very different socio-economic levels.* Dr. Charles S. Johnson, the sociologist who directed the study of the Race Riot in 1919 and served as consultant for the Mayor's Committee in 1944, called attention to this fact when he observed concerning migrants that:

"The attention of the public may become focused upon the strangeness of the newcomers, upon the mannerisms and folkways that were developed in their social isolation from the best examples of public decorum. These are given high visibility by the conspicuous features of the Negroes, as well as by their strangeness. Almost invariably this reinforces racial stereotypes which carry unpleasant and even threatening implications.

"The areas of contact and racial intercommunication are wider and still widening in labor groups, in some industrial establishments, in some public conveniences outside the 'black belt'; and in unsegregated transportation. These broadened contacts, while they accelerate the accommodation and assimilation, also create new temporary problems." [4]

If contact is to play any direct part in breaking the color-line it must be accompanied by a "meeting of minds" and must involve people of similar tastes and interests. It is a significant trend of the last fifteen years that an increasingly large number of higher-status Negroes and whites have been getting to know one another, while, concurrently, thousands of Negroes and whites at the working-class level have become organized into the same unions. As we shall see in Chapter 12, this latter development has brought with it wide social and semi-social contacts between Negroes and whites. (Increasing residential segregation has reduced the amount of friendly contact between Negroes and whites of the middle classes who once shared certain neighborhoods together.)

These close contacts result in various types of co-operative action and in the multiplication of individual friendships. It is doubtful, however, whether they play a dominant part in shifting the line of color.

---

* Contact between employers and servants, for instance, may result in close bonds of friendships so long as the servant remains in her place. The stereotype of "the Negro's place" is thus reinforced. If the servant or her relatives become presumptuous enough to seek treatment as equals, tension may result. The same thing would be true if the servant were white, but in the case of a Negro the servant's behavior would be generalized in racial terms. Some studies have indicated that even contacts of Negroes and whites as equals can mean an increase in tension rather than a favorable change in attitude.

There are, for instance, perhaps a score of highly trained Negroes in Midwest Metropolis who have close and friendly relations with the city's influential and wealthy. These relations, although primarily those between philanthropist and civic leader, often have semi-social extensions. While such contacts have undoubtedly done much to influence the tone of the press and to secure some mitigation of the Negro's subordinate status, they cannot effect a major break in the Job Ceiling or the abolition of residential segregation. Economic interest again!

As we have mentioned, the members of the white middle class set the tone of Negro-white relations in Midwest Metropolis. Immigrants and their children see in them a model for imitation as they strive to become Americanized. The basic type of contact that the Negro has with members of the white middle class is economic. He has to do with them as employers, managers, and officials; he is the customer buying from white merchants and salespeople; the debtor facing creditors and collection agents; the client of lawyers, and the patient of doctors and dentists. Large numbers of Negroes are also in competition with the white lower middle class for jobs in skilled labor or clerical pursuits. Even when the Negro confronts middle-class white people in noneconomic relations, he usually does so as a subordinate—as a student under white teachers, a client dependent upon relief workers, a black criminal facing the white law. Such contacts do little to create goodwill among white people, but they do leave a residue of resentment among Negroes. The Negro middle class views the white middle class as its competitor, and the Negro lower class sees it as an exploiter.

The highly charged relations between the white middle class and the Negroes is a force for social change, though in a negative sort of way. Negroes are stimulated to organize their opposition. They fight to break the Job Ceiling, to smash restrictive covenants, to dislodge white people from the economic and political control of the Black Belt. Such activities may disturb the racial peace, but they develop self-confidence among Negroes and play an important part in shifting the color-line.

The almost complete isolation of the Negro middle class from the white middle class, and the organization of their relations in terms of antagonism, will no doubt continue so long as residential segregation and the Job Ceiling remain. Feeble attempts have been made by some of the churches and YWCA groups to sponsor teas, meetings, forums, discussion groups, etc., for bringing Negroes and whites together, but these tend to be artificial and both sides are usually under strain.*

Any major shifts in the social evaluation of Negroes will have to come from their being accepted as equals in a wide range of semi-social situations, and by a break in the Job Ceiling so that a much larger number of Negroes can function permanently in white-collar and supervisory positions. When major shifts in the Negro's status have occurred, it has usually not been as the result of education and counterpropaganda, or of engineered contacts operating in a vacuum; they have come in response to the demands of economic necessity and political expediency.

Economic Necessity: The dictates of economic necessity are primarily responsible for the presence of large numbers of Negroes in Midwest Metropolis. During the First World War the city needed labor. Southern Negroes supplied it. Once in the city they were thrown into competition with white workers, who, themselves insecure, did not hesitate to erect barriers against colored competitors. To white labor, organized and unorganized, Negroes constituted a pool of unorganized, potential strike-breakers. It could not drive them from the city—neither labor's allegiance to the democratic ideology nor the industrialists would permit that. It could not welcome them as individuals, for the folk-habits kept them in a separate category. Time after time, the Negroes broke strikes, and ultimately won a permanent place in the basic industries. They were used, for instance, to break the strikes of stockyard workers in 1904 and 1921; of the teamsters in 1905; and of the workers in the steel and clothing industries during the period of the First World War. When the CIO movement swept the city, Negroes could not be ignored. Once in the unions, they became accepted as "brothers" and were able to utilize seniority rules for an attack upon the Job Ceiling.

Any white men who wish to sell goods or service to Negroes must reckon with the fact that Black Metropolis has been experimenting

* The few Negroes who have contact with whites of equivalent status—such as social workers, politicians, lawyers, teachers, and policemen (and during the war skilled laborers and clerical workers)—sometimes form close friendships across the color-line. Such social intermingling is not general, however, and is due partly to the fact that in many cases Negroes consider themselves of higher *social* status than the whites who have the same type of job. This attitude can be fully understood only after an examination of the Negro class system.

with the application of an old political tactic to the economic field, "Reward your friends and punish your enemies." The "Spend Your Money Where You Can Work" Campaign was, as we have seen, a dramatic expression of this tendency. Yet, Negroes have not been able to organize their purchasing power in such a way as to break the Ceiling in stores outside of the Black Belt.

Political Expediency: The demands of political expediency have operated to modify the subordination of Negroes. Politicians need votes and are willing to pay for them with patronage and favors. An astute political leadership in Black Metropolis has been able to bargain for representation and to place Negroes in a number of responsible posts. This concentrated political power has also been used to demand legislation against the Job Ceiling and to provide public sounding boards for the Negro's grievances.

The existence of a political machine based upon the Black Belt reinforces residential segregation, but it also provides a powerful weapon for struggle against subordination. The political process, on the whole, acts as a stabilizing force in Negro-white relations, since it is accepted by white people as a legitimate medium for Negroes to use in seeking changes in their status. Negroes, for their part, since they can see political results, are restrained from more precipitate forms of action.

The pattern of Negro-white relations in Midwest Metropolis since the days of the Flight to Freedom has been characterized by constant, sometimes rapid, social change. The general tone of relationships has varied from period to period in response to the dictates of economic necessity, the imperatives of political expediency, and the fluctuating divergence and coincidence between these factors and the American tradition of Christian-democratic idealism.

Specific economic and political groups within the white population tend to view "the Negro" as a competitor for the rewards and privileges of the city, since it is the custom in our society to organize such competition along ethnic lines. In the fear of economic loss and in the effort to protect their privileged position, such groups have sought to maintain a Job Ceiling and a Black Ghetto. The overwhelming majority of the white residents, whether directly affected by Negro competition or not, have drawn the color-line rigidly at the point of social intermingling and intermarriage. Competition is a constant source of tension.

But employers need labor; white labor needs allies; politicians need votes. Negroes have something to offer. So the color-line bends and breaks here and there as these demands weld blocs of Negroes and whites together temporarily for common action. In those alliances there is usually a certain amount of semi-social contact. Always, too, a spiritual community of interest bridges the color-line—a small but influential fraternity of rebels and dreamers, of individualists and thinkers, and of plain, ordinary people who work or live side by side. Unconsciously, Negroes and whites maintain a moving equilibrium of peaceful interrelationships with conflict muted and competition controlled and ritualized. Sometimes, though, the pattern breaks: both groups become restless, tensions arise—and the color-line becomes a battle-line.

Actual physical conflicts between large groups of Negroes and white people in Midwest Metropolis have been rare. Occasionally, however, when small groups feel that their economic security or their social prestige is threatened, or when groups of Negroes have become aroused to the point of defending themselves or launching an attack against the color-line, violence occurs. Such violence usually breaks out in periods of *general* social unrest as during a war or a depression. Then things settle down and change proceeds at a slower pace.

In the long run, the economic and political factors are probably decisive in effecting major shifts in the color-line. The operation of these factors continuously presents Midwest Metropolis with new situations that cannot be ignored. These processes confront the ordinary white person with changes in the status of Negroes—*faits accomplis*—and he adjusts *mutatis mutandis*. These changes take place within a confused context of attitudes and opinions, of democratic idealism mixed with folk-prejudices, and the white individual is often unaware that he is experiencing a readjustment of attitude.

The last two chapters of this section are devoted to an examination of the manner in which economic necessity and political expediency operate to change the Negro's status.

Democracy and Economic Necessity: Breaking the Job Ceiling

THE PRECEDING CHAPTER OPENED WITH THE STATEMENT THAT THE ACTUAL position of the Negro in the life of Chicago contradicts the democratic principles of American society. This is true in many respects. Yet the status of the Negro is not rigidly fixed. Negroes, to use their own terminology, are "advancing," and this "advance" has assumed the form of a separate social and community life resting upon a continually broadening economic base in the larger society. The belief is widespread among Negroes that any further progress is contingent upon breaking the Job Ceiling.

PIERCING THE JOB CEILING

American society places a premium upon individual initiative—that happy combination of skill and nerve which, coupled with "lucky breaks" and a "good personality," is supposed to lift a large number of people from the level of poverty to that of a decent standard of living, and a small number to wealth and fame. Theoretically, all are supposed to have an equal chance in the combined lottery and proving ground of school, industry, and commerce. They are led to expect that, through preparing themselves in school and by showing their mettle in the world of practical affairs, they will receive rewards in the form of a "good living," the approval of their fellows, and "advancement." The hindmost, who cannot stand the pace or who "do not have it in them," have traditionally been left to the tender mercies of these social devils: poverty, charity, the jail, the potter's field.

Some individual Negroes have been able to play the game and rise in the world. Personal skill, luck, and nerve do, on occasion, pierce the Job Ceiling. In Midwest Metropolis there are Negroes who, for instance, function as industrial chemists, physicists, and civil engineers; several Negroes are even employed as professors by the larger universities. But the instances are few; the rule is that Negroes find it much more difficult than whites to rise through individual initiative, although a small professional group is supported exclusively by the Negro community itself.

THE NECESSITIES OF PRODUCTION

During a period of labor shortage, the necessities of production sometimes demand the use of Negroes as workers in jobs that are customarily above the Job Ceiling. This has happened only twice on a large scale in Chicago—during the First and the Second World Wars. The demand for Negro labor during the First World War resulted in the Great Migration and broke the ceiling that had previously confined Negroes to unskilled and service jobs. A similar demand occurred in the early Forties, with the induction of many workers into the armed forces, and the concomitant increase in the total number of employees required for the booming war industries. Shortages in housing, transportation, and other community facilities kept at a minimum the influx of white workers from out of the city. Negroes already in the city were gradually drawn from the relief rolls into industry.

The Second World War broke the ceiling at the level of semi-skilled work and integrated thousands of Negroes as skilled laborers in the electrical and light manufacturing industries, from which they had formerly been barred by custom, and in the vast new airplane-engine factories established in the area. They also began to filter into minor managerial and clerical positions in increasing numbers. Negroes in Chicago have kept their fingers crossed, suspecting that when wartime production slackens they would be rapidly displaced. Even if this happens, however, a residue of workers will probably remain in types of positions which Negroes had not held previously.

PROFIT AS A PROD

Employers customarily hire labor at the lowest possible wage level. If the members of any ethnic group are willing to work for less pay than other people, it is good business to employ them. At the present time, there are probably no large industries in Chicago in which Negroes are paid less than whites doing the same job within a given plant. There were, however, some small plants, on the eve of the Second World War, which employed all-Negro personnel at wages lower than those paid whites for similar work in other plants of similar size. During the first days of the 1939-40 war boom many incidents came to the attention of the authors that involved the use of Negroes as semi-skilled, skilled, and even technical workers at wages considerably lower than those paid whites. Such differential payment was sometimes defended by white employers on the ground that Negro workers were not so productive as white workers, though there is no reliable evidence supporting this contention.* Officials of the FEPC and the War Manpower Commission reported, in 1944, that they knew of no such differentials still existing, and that employers were no longer claiming that Negro labor was unproductive.

That profit is a prod which frequently motivates white employers to hire Negro workers or otherwise break the Job Ceiling becomes especially evident during strikes, when colored workers are used as strike-breakers. Under such circumstances Negroes may for the first time enter a specific type of job or an entire industry previously barred to them. In Chicago this was true in the packing, steel, and garment industries. As the number of Negro employees increased, unions in these industries were forced to accept Negroes in order to prevent their being continuously used as strike-breakers.

In the Twenties, some Negro leaders advised Negroes to underbid white labor systematically in order to secure jobs, and justified strike-breaking where unions refused Negroes admission. Today, few leaders take this position. Moreover, it has grown harder to use Negroes as strike-breakers since their employment in large numbers has made them an integral part of Chicago's mass-production industries, and since they have been effectively incorporated into the CIO unions operating in these industries.

The profit motive sometimes works to the advantage of Negroes in unusual ways. An interesting situation arose in 1939 when many private employment agencies having a backlog of applications, for the first time, began actively to try to place Negroes in war industries.

---

* Both the Chicago Commission on Race Relations in 1919 and the Mayor's Committee on Race Relations in 1944 report that the majority of the leading private employers agree, also, that Negro labor is as efficient as that of white workers when their training is equal. (See *The Negro in Chicago,* pp. 374-88, and *City Planning in Race Relations,* p. 36.)

As one agent told an applicant: "I get $10 a throw when I get a man a job. What the hell do I care whether he's white or black? I want the ten bucks. And I can't get it with a boxful of cards sittin' up here on my desk. I call these people up and tell them I've got some good Negro boys—why not try 'em?"

THE LAW AS A LEVER

The right to a job has never been established as a civil right in America. Employers have jealously guarded their right to hire and fire on any grounds they chose to cite. Even under New Deal legislation, an employer's right to hire and fire was curtailed only with respect to dismissal of employees for union activities. Despite this fact, Negro leaders have constantly sought legal grounds which could be used to force a break in the Job Ceiling.

The first successful use of the law as a lever arose in connection with Federal and state civil service. The purpose of any merit system is to safeguard the prospective employee from the prejudiced judgments of an employing agent. Ordinarily, civil service rules limit the range of choice to from one to three persons. But Negroes insist—and in the past there has been evidence to support the contention—that their names are often passed over; though in Illinois there is probably a minimum of racial discrimination in the civil service system, particularly in Federal jobs.

Negro legislators have sought to have riders attached to various appropriation bills making it illegal for unions that discriminate against Negroes to work on state jobs. In some cases their attempts have been successful. Another approach has involved the demand for legislation which will make it illegal to use public funds or to grant franchises to institutions that do not extend equal employment opportunities to Negroes. No bills of the latter kind have as yet become law, but their mere presentation has had a salutary warning effect upon the institutions involved.

On the basis of recommendations made by a state commission, and following the lead of New York and Indiana, the Illinois State Legislature in 1941 passed a bill making it a misdemeanor for an industry engaged in war production to discriminate, in hiring, against an applicant on the basis of race, color, or creed. Through May of 1945 there had been no convictions under this act.

The Second World War brought into being a number of Federal agencies bound by law not to discriminate against Negroes in their employment policy, and obligated to see that private employers with whom they work do not do so, among them being the War Manpower Commission and the President's Committee on Fair Employment Practices. The United States Employment Service, too, in filling manpower needs has been officially committed to a policy of "no discrimination." There have been no cancellations of war contracts, however, for the failure of an industry to hire Negroes.

In March of 1945, Senate Bill 254 was introduced in the Illinois General Assembly "to prohibit discrimination in employment because of race, religion, color or national origin; to make equal opportunity to seek employment a civil right; to declare certain employment and labor practices as discriminatory and unfair; to establish a Board of Fair Employment Practice; to prescribe its functions, powers and duties; to prescribe penalties for violation and to make an appropriation for administrative expenses." The Bill provided for an appropriation of $250,000 for "ordinary and contingent expenses incident to the administration of this Act."

The bill provides for a five-man board to receive complaints, hold hearings, and to hand down orders requiring employers or labor unions "to cease and desist from such discriminatory practices and to take such affirmative or other action as will effectuate the policies of this Act." If its orders are defied the Board is empowered to petition the circuit court in the county where the discrimination occurred to see that the order is enforced. The bill has teeth—"Any person, employer or labor organization who, or which, shall wilfully resist, prevent, impede or interfere with any member of the Board or any of its agents or agencies in the performance of duties pursuant to this act, or shall wilfully violate any order of the Board, shall be guilty of a misdemeanor, and upon conviction therefor, shall be punishable by a fine of not more than $500.00, or by imprisonment in the county jail for not more than one year, or by both; but procedure for a review of any order of Board shall not be deemed to be such wilful conduct." The Bill does not depend entirely upon punitive measures, however, but provides for "a comprehensive educational program" utilizing the public school system and private agencies to educate the public to the importance of establishing and maintaining a truly democratic form of government free from discrimination against any citizen because of race, religion, color or national origin."

Civic leaders in Chicago were mobilizing public opinion throughout the spring of 1945 to secure passage of the Bill, but were not too sure that the forces of democratic idealism could be mobilized in those parts of Illinois where Negroes wield little political power. In Midwest Metropolis political expediency and the efforts of liberals, the CIO and various church groups assured the support of the Chicago legislators.

GOVERNMENT AS AN EXAMPLE

Throughout the history of Chicago, Negroes have been able to use the political machinery to lift the Job Ceiling. They have occupied civil service, elective, and appointive positions, both high and low, and the city has become accustomed to seeing colored people in such situations.* Negro leaders are able to point to such positions as proof that Negroes are competent employees and acceptable to their white fellow-workers. Government policy in some respects sets a pattern.

According to the results of one careful investigation, approximately 6½ per cent of all employees in the classified service in the city of Chicago in 1932 were Negro—which was almost their proportion of the total population. But less than a quarter of the 1,908 Negroes constituting this group were in the clerical, professional or commissioned personnel; more than three-quarters were janitors, laborers or temporary employees. An examination of the kinds of jobs held by Negroes employed by the city reveals that the Job Ceiling, although less rigid and probably higher than in general, exists in this area, too. Only in the Department of Health, the Bureau of Parks and Recreation and the Bureau of Water and the library services did Negroes come near to their population ratio in positions which are largely clerical and professional. (Negro city employees were concentrated in these departments; they tend to be under-represented in most other city departments.) The proportion of Negroes in jobs as janitors, laborers, etc.,

---

* In the investigation for The Juvenile Protective Association made in 1913, Louise Bowen reported that over ten per cent of all the Federal employees in the city were Negroes although they were only three per cent of the population. She stated also that "the negroes [sic], however, do not fare so well in local government." They were less than two per cent of the total workers. The growth in the Negro vote within the next five years greatly increased their representation in city government.

considerably exceeded their representation in the population in all city departments.[1]

The same situation is clearly evident from a consideration of the Negro's share of governmental jobs of all types, as shown in Table 12. Negroes are somewhat over-represented in certain relatively choice jobs—as social and welfare workers, probation and truant officers, and chemists on the professional level, as firemen (except locomotive and fire department) and as mechanics. But still two-thirds of all porters and cooks are Negroes, as compared with two or three per cent of the policemen and lawyers, and one per cent of the firemen in the Fire Department and officials and inspectors.

The postal service is frequently cited as an example of what Negroes, given an opportunity, can do by way of proving their ability. In this service, positions are secured through competitive Federal civil service examinations, and reputedly without political influence. Consequently, Negroes have flocked into postal jobs, and in 1930 Negroes comprised one-quarter of all of the postal employees in Chicago. But even in this case, where Negroes are considerably over-represented in many relatively desirable types of positions, traces of the Job Ceiling remain. Contrast, for example, the types of positions—porters, elevator tenders, janitors—in which Negroes hold eight or nine out of every ten jobs, with such positions as foremen and overseers, of which Negroes are only five per cent; stenographers and typists, of which they are four per cent, and managers and officials, of which they are but one per cent. (See Table 13 on p. 295.)

Despite the existence of a Job Ceiling in government employment the fact remains that, until the Second World War, it was only in government offices that Negro men and women were given a chance to show what they could do as clerical workers, and Negroes were able to use these government white-collar Negroes as examples in educating white employers.

MASS PRESSURE

The Depression and the Second World War both created much restlessness and dissatisfaction among Negroes, each emphasizing sharply their subordinate position in the economic system. Applications for employment during these periods sometimes revealed discriminatory hiring policies. Reports of refusal to hire Negroes circulated widely in the community. At first there was grumbling; there were spontaneous and

TABLE 12

THE NEGRO'S SHARE OF SELECTED PUBLIC SERVICE JOBS, CHICAGO, 1930 *

	Number of Negro Workers	Per Cent Which Negroes Were of All Workers
Porters and cooks	16	66.1
Janitors and sextons	116	27.0
Mail carriers	631	16.0
Messengers, errand and office boys	8	17.4
Social and welfare workers	5	11.9
Garbage men and scavengers	42	11.7
Mechanics	10	11.5
Charwomen and cleaners	3	10.7
Firemen (except locomotive, Fire Dept.)	20	9.5
Other laborers	384	9.5
Probation and truant officers	17	8.8
Chemists, assayers and metallurgists	6	8.5
Elevator tenders	5	8.2
Trained nurses	8	7.5
Marshals and constables	3	7.1
Agents (not elsewhere classified)	14	6.9
Chauffeurs and truck and tractor drivers	35	5.7
Draymen, teamsters and carriage drivers	13	5.3
Officials and inspectors (U. S.)	43	5.2
Clerks	185	4.9
Plumbers and gas steamfitters	8	4.4
Advertising agents and others	43	3.9
Guards, watchmen and door keepers	20	3.8
Lawyers, judges and justices	9	3.6
Cranemen, deckmen and hoistmen, etc.	1	3.3
Housekeepers and stewards	2	3.3
Sheriffs	14	3.1
Bookkeepers and cashiers	7	2.9
Stenographers and typists	29	2.7
Officials and inspectors (city)	48	2.5
Office appliance operators	1	2.4
School teachers	452	2.3
Officials and inspectors (state)	6	2.2
Policemen	152	2.1
Oilers of machinery	1	2.0
Detectives	13	1.9
Engineers (stationary)	9	1.7
Soldiers, sailors, marines	4	1.6
Accountants and auditors	3	1.4
Street cleaners	8	1.2
Civil engineers and surveyors	5	1.0
Firemen (Fire Dept.)	27	1.0
Officials and inspectors (county)	3	.8
Carpenters	1	.8
Electricians	3	.6
Total	2,433	4.5

* Taken from H. F. Gosnell, *op. cit.*, Table XIX, p. 377. There were no Negroes in 621 public service occupations.

TABLE 13

NEGRO WORKERS IN THE POSTAL SERVICE IN CHICAGO, 1930 *

	Number of Negro Workers	Per Cent Which Negroes Were of All Workers
Porters	23	95.8
Janitors	35	87.5
Elevator tenders	12	85.7
Laborers	369	69.5
Charwomen and cleaners	9	69.2
Chauffeurs and truck and tractor drivers	42	41.6
Other occupations	28	46.0
Clerks	1,825	28.0
Compositors, linotypers and typesetters	3	27.3
Mail carriers	631	16.0
Mechanics	7	13.7
Messenger, errand and office boys	10	12.3
Machinists	1	8.3
Foremen and overseers	6	4.5
Stenographers and typists	2	4.3
Guards, watchmen and doorkeepers	1	4.3
Inspectors	1	3.7
Managers and officials	2	1.2
	3,008	25.2

* From H. F. Gosnell, *op. cit.*, Table XV, p. 304. Not listed in the above table are some 69 skilled, clerical and supervisory jobs in which Negroes were not represented at all. An examination of these jobs showed that most included only two or three workers, and, therefore, Negroes would naturally be under-represented, or they were types of jobs in which the political influence of certain craft unions was undoubtedly manifesting itself.

violent verbal outbursts against employers or employees. The net effect of such unorganized restlessness is to make the larger community aware that "something is wrong" with the Negro population. Then Negro leaders and the leaders of white liberal and political groups together appeal for increased recognition of the Negro's claim for equal job opportunities. When these appeals are not immediately successful in some measure, organized mass protests often follow.

Organized mass pressure usually follows from spontaneous mass pressures. Sometimes, however, it is deliberately planned by organizations devoted to advancing the interests of Negroes. In 1931-32, for instance, the "Spend Your Money Where You Can Work" Campaign, was started in a fairly deliberate and organized fashion, as were various picketing and boycott episodes that occurred throughout the Depression and in the early years of the Second World War.

During periods of sudden or rapid social change, the Job Ceiling, like everything else, is altered. A war or a depression, a devastating fire or a flood, may so disturb organized social relations that, for a time at least, new patterns are permitted to arise. Catastrophe acts as a catalytic agent in social change. The First World War attracted thousands of Negroes into industry and significantly altered the social composition and occupational distribution of the Negro population. The Depression of 1929-40 worked in two directions. On the one hand, large numbers of Negroes in marginal positions were pushed out of industry; on the other hand, white-collar workers found employment in clerical and minor supervisory positions on relief projects and in the relief administration. The Depression also resulted in mass action to force white business people in the Black Belt to employ Negroes. The industrial union movement, gathering momentum during this period, swept thousands of Negroes into organizations that accepted them as equals and actively sought to enforce seniority rules and promotion on merit, without reference to color.

The Second World War not only brought the demand for the full utilization of man power, but also resulted in the training of thousands of Negroes for semi-skilled and skilled jobs. Where difficulties in securing employment were experienced, Negroes, operating within the framework of the stated goals of the war, demanded jobs. Mass pressure forced the establishment of the FEPC, and the "law" became a very useful lever in raising the Job Ceiling after President Roosevelt issued his Fair Employment Practices order. Government set an increasingly strong example as Negroes flocked into Civil Service. More important still, the needs of war industries and government bureaus exhausted the supply of trained white-collar and clerical personnel and opened opportunities in these and other fields hitherto barred to Negroes. Colored girls, for instance, became salespeople in a few Loop stores, and colored Western Union messengers appeared on the streets of Midwest Metropolis for the first time. Negroes cropped up in many unusual spots.

EDUCATING THE WHITE FOLKS

All of these processes, seen in the widest perspective, result in what Negroes call "educating the white folks"—the white employer and the white worker, as well as the public. A part of this educational process is unconscious and beyond the effective control of individuals or organizations. The necessities of production, the desire for profits, the coming of catastrophe—all upset the established order and make men act as they have not previously acted. But a part of the process is deliberate, as when an individual sets his eye upon a position and achieves it, when the law is used as a lever, or when mass pressure is organized. Negro leaders and friendly whites try to manipulate the impersonal forces to the deliberate end of lifting the Job Ceiling.

Educating the Employers: One of the most important aspects of the educational process concerns employers. Employers in Chicago give a number of reasons for their failure to extend full job opportunity to Negroes. A few employers (these seem to be a minority) have stereotyped conceptions of what the Negro can and cannot do. A larger number do not question the Negro's capacity, but still feel that he should permanently occupy a subordinate place in the economic life of the society. Most employers, however, do not seem to have any clear-cut, articulate convictions on the matter one way or another. They are simply hesitant to make innovations that might curtail production, cause trouble in the plant, or otherwise jeopardize their profits or prestige. Under normal conditions the hold of custom is heavy everywhere.

But when employers have been successful in integrating Negroes in a plant, they are often very proud of their feat and sometimes wonder why they had not thought of the idea before. The following case is not at all atypical. A nationally known company that manufactures electrical equipment had never employed Negroes. A personnel official told an investigator from the War Manpower Commission that it would be impossible even to hire Negro matrons for washrooms, because, if this were done, the white girl employees would refuse to use the facilities. In 1942, this firm was persuaded to employ several hundred Negro workers of both sexes and at all levels of skill. Not only has there been no significant friction between white and colored workers at any time, but the work of the Negro employees has been highly satisfactory. The plant management is now very much pleased with this record.

Employers in general maintain that they are not responsible for discrimination against Negro labor—almost always they tend to assign responsibility for the policy to their employees. Some employers contend further that the education of white workers to accept the upgrading of Negroes is primarily a job for the unions. This was the tone of the responses reported by the Mayor's Subcommittee on Employment, and also, apparently, the official attitude of the Committee itself. This same committee, however, recommended to management that before Negro workers are first hired, a company should be sure that its *supervisory personnel* is completely won over to the new policy. Incidentally, it is to be inferred from the contents of this report that probably the principal reason why many establishments that had never before hired Negroes began to hire them relatively early during the Second World War was fear of, or at least a strong wish to avoid, investigation by government agencies on charges of discrimination. Government, too, can be a most effective prod. Employers are educable—but such education in Chicago has included mass picket lines, petitions and protests, public hearings and legislation, as well as sweet reasonableness on the part of Negroes.

Educating White Workers: Negroes are often irritated at what they feel is conscious "buck passing" between employers and labor. Employers say, "We would hire Negroes if employees did not object." Labor unions say, "Not us—the employers." The truth is complex. Doubtless there are situations in which employers honestly fear that white workers would cause trouble if Negroes were hired, but in which actually nothing at all would happen. There are other situations in which white workers are absolutely and bitterly opposed to the employment of Negroes. In Midwest Metropolis, as we have said previously, the center of such opposition is in the AFL craft unions and among the railroad brotherhoods. Though there is less evidence of organized opposition on the higher technical and supervisory levels, there is enough to indicate that the prestige concern of many white employees in these positions operates to exclude Negroes from them.

The education of the white worker has often proceeded in a very blunt fashion. Negroes have simply broken strikes and underbid white labor. White employees in the packing, steel, and garment industries have apparently learned their lesson, for Negroes are now included in their unions.

A marked difference prevails in the attitudes of the AFL and the CIO toward the incorporation of Negroes into both industry and unions. The industrial unions of the CIO, since their appearance in 1935, have uniformly and actively tried to recruit Negroes into the unions and to have them admitted into industry on an equal basis with white workers. The leaders have fought prejudice wherever it has existed: among employers, among employees, and upon occasion, among members of their own unions. The older AFL craft unions, on the other hand, have traditionally excluded Negroes. Where Negroes have been admitted to unions, they have frequently been organized into Jim-Crow locals and denied full membership privileges. This is still the general situation, despite some recent moves in the direction of liberalization, stimulated on the one hand by competition from the CIO and on the other by pressure from government agencies, particularly the FEPC.

The difference of attitude between the two organizations was evident even in the official remarks of the representatives of the AFL and the CIO unions at the Employment Session of the Mayor's 1944 Conference. The AFL representative stated that there was no justification for discrimination by unions against Negroes, but that the problem could only be solved through a long term program of education. Laws would do no good, and the AFL could not force member unions to reform because part of the "democratic" tradition of the AFL was the "autonomy" of local unions, which would refuse to accept "dictation" from above. The position of the CIO representative, who favored law as well as education, is apparent in the following statement (quoted from the report): "The CIO has been, is now, and always will be committed to a policy of complete equality for all workers, regardless of race, color, or creed, and always will militantly champion a fight to realize that complete equality. The record, too long and too extensive to cite now, will testify to the truth of the existence of that policy."

Despite these efforts to have Negroes upgraded strictly in accordance with seniority considerations, much remains to be done, even in the most advanced CIO unions and the industries where they have contracts, before the Job Ceiling will be completely removed.

✦

Educating the Public: Employers often "pass the buck" (consciously or unconsciously) to the public, instead of, or as well as, to their employees: "Educate the public to accept Negroes in the better jobs and we'll hire them," they say. "We can't risk losing our customers." It is, however, virtually impossible to predict accurately the public reaction to the widespread employment of Negroes in unfamiliar fields.

The manpower shortage produced by the Second World War resulted in the use of Negroes (at least temporarily) as bus drivers, operators, and motormen on the surface and elevated transportation lines, as clerks in stores, waitresses in restaurants and at soda fountains, and in a variety of other situations where they had not been seen previously. Before the war, it would have been considered impossible to employ Negroes in some of these spots. Yet these colored employees have apparently been accepted, without serious incident, by both their white fellow-workers and the public. A concerted campaign to have Negroes employed as saleswomen in the downtown department stores was conducted during 1943 and 1944, but met with little success.

It seems probable that the public's reaction to Negroes in new or unusual job situations goes through three phases. First, there is surprise—perhaps shock. Second comes curiosity, and "definition of the situation" (either acceptance or criticism), with or without further overt action. Third and last, there is complete acceptance.

Little effort is made to help the public over the first and the second hurdles toward acceptance. A sporadic editorial or occasional radio comment may stress the necessity of treating minorities justly or the need to utilize our manpower fully—but that is all.

EDUCATING THE NEGROES

The process of lifting the Job Ceiling is not entirely one of educating the white folks. It involves also the problem of educating the Negro—educating him to want the job, to get it, and to keep it.

Negroes have for so long had a subordinate "place" in American life that many find it hard to conceive of themselves or other Negroes except in that place. The initial reaction of many Negroes to a Negro locomotive engineer or a colored streetcar conductor is one of surprise, coupled with expressions of doubt—made jokingly, yet half-serious—as to whether the Negro is capable of holding the job. This attitude is soon replaced, ordinarily, by intense pride that "one of our boys made it."

A low ceiling results in low horizons. Social workers and vocational counselors report a real problem in encouraging Negro youth to "raise their sights." They have to fight always against a legacy of self-doubt and the acceptance of "place."

Almost all Negroes think that they and other Negroes should be given any job for which they qualify. But many of them have no idea how to prepare for and secure the better jobs. Social agencies, therefore, are continually urging Negroes to prepare themselves even when there are no jobs open to them, so that they will be ready if opportunities are created. Thus it is probable that, during the Second World War, more colored girls could have secured skilled office jobs had more possessed the training for such positions when the war commenced. There is also the problem of selling oneself to an employer. Negroes have to acquire a technique in such matters. In particular, colored job applicants have the special problem of learning how to "go back for more" when they have been rebuffed.

Many Negroes, especially recent migrants to Chicago from the South, not only are untrained for any specific job, but are often completely without previous experience in any kind of business or industrial work. They are unfamiliar with the discipline of a steady job in an urban factory or office. According to the Mayor's Committee survey, most firms stated that the Negro worker produces fully as well as the white when selected on the basis of equivalent training and experience; and that, although most of the Negroes lack a background of training for skilled work, they respond to training as well as white workers do when it is given to them.

Negro leaders in Midwest Metropolis are greatly concerned over whether Negroes will be able to hold any of the economic gains secured during the Second World War. The advice of these leaders includes everything from urging Negroes to mind their manners, to advising them to join the union. A nationwide movement, the "Hold Your Job" Committee, has been sponsored by both the Urban League and the National Council of Negro Women. The committee conducts educational campaigns in factories and in the Negro community to urge Negroes to so work and act that employers will have no legitimate excuses for discharging them after the war. Negro newspapers carry articles urging Negroes to be quiet, clean, orderly, and reliable, so that

The Race will not acquire an unfavorable reputation. This preaching sometimes irks the Negro. A packing-house worker remarked to a union official: "Why 'n the hell do these big Negroes have to always tell us how to act? I'll admit that we hurt ourselves sometimes. But the thing that burns me up is how the white man lets one Negro break all our necks. Why don't they let us break our necks for ourselves, individual?"

It is generally agreed that the problem of training Negroes both for specific jobs and for urban industrial life in general (including the problem of proper "conduct" in the urban setting) can be solved only through training, experience, and—above all—equal opportunity.

The processes through which the Job Ceiling is lifted and broken in places could be illustrated in the history of any industry in which Negroes are now employed in large numbers. Since, in Midwest Metropolis, meat packing is an industry with a long history of employing Negroes, it is perhaps most appropriate to select it as a case in point.

NEGROES AS HOG BUTCHERS FOR THE WORLD

The story of the integration of Negroes into Chicago's slaughtering and meat-packing industry provides a dramatic illustration of the interplay between the forces of democratic idealism and the economic and political forces outlined above.

According to local tradition, the first Negroes to work in the packing industry in Chicago were a beef-boner and a butcher, who secured jobs in 1881. Although Negroes and whites are today organized together in a union affiliated with the CIO, where Negroes share positions of leadership with white workers, the slaughtering and packing industry was once a racial battleground.

Between 1881 and 1894, a few Negroes filtered into the stockyards and packing plants without any apparent opposition from the foreign-born white workers who predominated in the industry. During the Pullman Strike of 1894, when the stockyard workers walked out in sympathy with the American Railway Union, a large group of Poles were employed as strike-breakers. A few days later, Negroes came into the yards in a similar capacity, and union resentment was focused on them to such a degree that a Negro was burned in effigy. After the strike a few Negroes retained their positions, and although they were numerically unimportant, their presence in the yards was interpreted as a threat to the labor unions. In employing Negroes, management had tapped an almost inexhaustible supply of cheap labor from the South and simultaneously secured a labor force that seemed very resistant to union organization.

The next large influx of Negroes into the yards occurred during the strike of 1904. When the strike began, Negroes constituted about five per cent of the labor force. Their numbers were immediately increased, and hundreds of Negroes were smuggled into the plants on the same day that the white workers downed their tools. So large a number were employed that for a time it was thought that Negroes would predominate in the packing industry. The more extravagant estimates placed the number employed as high as ten thousand.

In this dispute, the role of the Negro worker differed from his role as strike-breaker in the 1894 strike. In the earlier dispute, Poles had been numerically more important, and, in spite of the publicity which attended their activities, Negroes played only an incidental part. But in 1904 their importance as strike-breakers was immediately recognized and an even more intense resentment by union men resulted.* After the strike had been settled, a small number of colored men retained their positions. The rest were discharged or displaced by returning union men. The packers were no longer in need of Negro workers, so they were loaded into special trains and sent back to the South.

Four years later, there were about 500 Negroes in the industry, and a small but steady stream of black workers continued to flow into the yards. Then, in 1917, because of the war labor shortage, the packers again tapped the southern labor pool, sending their agents into the Deep South to recruit Negro workers by the hundreds and even thousands. By 1920, one packing plant employed over 5,000 Negroes, more than a quarter of its total labor force. The peak of Negro employment was reached in 1923, when 34 out of every 100 workers in the two largest packing establishments were colored. From 1922 until the De-

---

* "To the striking union men no scabs were as loathsome as the Negroes who took their jobs. Easily distinguishable, they were conspicuous among the strike-breakers and suffered the animus which is vented upon all scabs. They were jeered if they emerged from the plants under police escort; chased and attacked if alone. Pistol shots invariably brought the assaults to a close. Among the first of the strike-breakers to be hired, they were among the first to be asked to leave at the conclusion of hostilities." (Alma Herbst, *The Negro in the Slaughtering and Meat Packing Industry in Chicago*, Houghton Mifflin, 1932, p. 28.)

pression, the proportion of Negroes among all packing-house workers remained about 30 per cent.

Negroes and the Old Unions: After the strike of 1904, the packing-house union was so weakened that its membership dropped from 34,400 in 1904 to 6,200 in 1910. With the sudden increase in the number and proportion of Negroes in the industry, the Amalgamated Meat Cutters and Butcher Workmen (AFL) began an organizational drive in 1916-17. The packers granted an increase of twenty cents an hour to unskilled workers, but the union continued to grow, and in 1917 the Stock Yards Labor Council was formed by the united action of all the craft unions with jurisdiction in the stockyards.

The problem of establishing a policy with respect to Negroes in the union organizations soon became pressing. Twenty of the various craft unions in the council drew the color-line sharply. The union officials appreciated the importance of organizing Negroes, and realized that a union organization could not succeed without them. Nevertheless, unanimity of opinion regarding a solution of the racial problem could not be achieved. Some union leaders urged that colored men be admitted to all the unions, but in some cases this was prohibited by constitutional provisions; in others, the racial prejudice of union officials had the same effect. A typical AFL solution was suggested—the organization of Negroes into separate locals. The Amalgamated Meat Cutters and Butcher Workmen, one of the craft unions involved, followed its traditional policy and admitted Negroes, but complications over racial matters soon developed.

Many Negroes joined unions, but on the whole the organizers were disappointed in the response of the colored workers. It was estimated that among northern-born Negroes 90 per cent became union members. Few southern-born Negroes joined, however, and at the height of the drive only about a third of the Negroes employed in the yards became affiliated with any union organization.*

At the beginning of the 1917 campaign, approximately 12,000 Negroes worked in the stockyards in Chicago. The number increased in direct ratio to the success of the unions in organizing the white labor-

---

* Perhaps it should be pointed out explicitly that no one union existed in the yards at this time. There were as many different AFL craft unions represented as there were crafts in the packing industry. The largest union was the Amalgamated Meat Cutters and Butcher Workmen.

ers. Not only were the colored workmen regarded by management as almost immune to organization, and unreliable union members when they did join, but also the unions had no consistent policy toward Negroes.

The packers, realizing that their hope of defeating unionism depended upon holding the allegiance of colored workmen, inaugurated a policy of increasing the number of Negroes in their plants, at the same time influencing them against unionism. In this connection, packing-house management made use of a colorful Negro promoter, Richard Parker, who was hired to organize a Negro union. A most enterprising person, Mr. Parker started his activities by distributing about 20,000 handbills warning Negroes not to join the "white man's union" but, instead, to affiliate themselves with his organization, the American Unity Labor Union. The argument was twofold: Negroes should not join white unions because the unions would not admit them on a basis of equality, and, secondly, white employers preferred non-union help. The following is a typical advertisement[2] appearing in the Negro press at the time:

GET A SQUARE DEAL WITH YOUR OWN RACE

Time has come for Negroes to do now or never. Get together and stick together is the call of the Negro. Like all other races, make your own way; other races have made their unions for themselves. They are not going to give it to you just because you join his union. Make a union of your own race; union is strength. Join the American Unity Packers Union of the Stock Yards, this will give you a card to work at any trade or a common laborer, as a steamfitter, electrician, fireman, merchants, engineers, carpenters, butchers, helpers, and chauffeurs to drive trucks down town, delivering meat as white chauffeurs do for Armour's and Swift's or other Packers. A card from this Union will let you work in Kansas City, Omaha and St. Louis, or any other city where the five Packers have packing houses.

This union does not *believe in strikes*. We believe all differences between laborers and capitalists can be arbitrated. Strike is our last motive if any at all.

Get in line for a good job. *You are next. . . .*

It was this Negro leader's proud boast that he had brought more Negroes to the city from the South than had any other man in Chicago. Parker's organization introduced considerable confusion into the union situation in the stockyards, and thus further weakened the AFL unions.

When a strike seemed imminent in 1917, a Federal arbitrator was appointed. The Stock Yards Council enjoyed some temporary success in recruiting Negro workers by telling them that the government would see that they got a raise if they joined the union. The Council planned a special drive to attract Negroes: [3]

To this end a "giant stockyards union celebration" was planned for July 6. A workers' parade which was to include both races was scheduled. . . . On the morning of the event, the packers asked the police to revoke the parade permit lest a race riot be precipitated. As the workers were not permitted to march together, two parades formed, a white and a colored, and marched to the Beutner playgrounds, where a Negro and white audience was assembled. The marchers were greeted by cheers from the colored workers who lined the streets. . . . One of the placards which dotted the procession read:

"The bosses think that because we are of different color and different nationalities we should fight each other. We're going to fool them and fight for a common cause—a square deal for all."

In addressing the meeting, the secretary of the Stock Yards Labor Council [who some years later became the state chairman of the Communist Party] said:

"It does me good to see such a checkerboard crowd—by that I mean all of the workers here are not standing apart in groups, one race huddled in one bunch, one nationality in another. You are all standing shoulder to shoulder as men, regardless of whether your face is white or black."

But this attempt to develop solidarity among the packing-house workers was abortive, partly because of the outbreak of the Chicago Race Riot in 1919. Probably one of the underlying causes of the Riot was the conflict between union members and packing-house employers for the allegiance of Negro workers.

Each group laid the responsibility for the riot upon the other. The riot resulted in a barrier to further union organization among Negroes and brought to an abrupt end the drive to enlist Negro packing-house workers.

On the Sunday afternoon when the Race Riot started, and throughout the week, there were sporadic clashes between whites and Negroes in the packing-house area. On Monday, union members were notified by management that arrangements had been made for the militia to protect the workers in the yards. A militant colored unionist proposed that rather than send for troops, the employers should recognize the closed-shop plan, and that the union would then assume responsibility for the conduct of all workers in the yards. Needless to say, the proposal was turned down by the employers. The employees refused to work under the guns of the soldiers, and thousands of them struck. After a few days the troops were withdrawn, and the workers were notified to return to the yards. Approximately 600 laborers, both white and colored, delayed a day and were dismissed.

The union organizations connected with the stockyards labored incessantly to maintain order during the two weeks of the riot. Editorials in union papers expressed not only sympathy for Negroes, but also a concern for the future existence of the union. One editorial observed: [4]

Right now it is going to be decided whether the colored workers are to continue to come into the labor movement or whether they are to feel that they have been abandoned by it and lose confidence in it.

The friendly attitude of union officials apparently brought some of the colored workers closer to the union. It was reported that "the white and colored union men sustained each other in the main and ministered to the stricken. The financial aid and moral support which the union colored men received during the riot and immediately following it served to bring them to the headquarters of their organizations and to keep them 'out of the packers' bread line.' " It is to be remarked that both the packers and the union tried to aid the Negro workers—by feeding them and in other ways.

Under the circumstances, however, it was extremely difficult for Negroes to remain loyal to the union. The employers had replaced many staunch Negro union men with non-union Negroes, first when they refused to work without protection during the riot, and later when they refused to work under the guns of the militia. Negroes returning to work in the yards after the riot were glad to obtain employment under any terms and rapidly abandoned the union organizations.

Two years after the riot, another strike was called and lost in the yards, and the Amalgamated Meat Cutters and Butcher Workmen became a completely feeble organization. While the 1921 strike was brewing, Negro leaders expressed fear that the unorganized Negroes in the yards might become the target of another race riot. Thus the Chicago *Defender* wrote: [5]

There is a phase to the situation which cannot be overlooked, and that is the possibility of recurring race troubles. Many of our people are employed at the yards. They are not members of the union and will not be inclined to leave their employment. The fear of being supplanted by white workers will hold them at work. Naturally, they will become the targets of pickets and strike sympathizers while going to and from their employment. Clashes under such circumstances are inevitable.

Negroes and the New Union: Between 1921 and the Depression, the so-called company unions were dominant in the stockyards and packing plants. With the advent of the Depression, the AFL unions were revived, and a new union, the Packing-house Workers Industrial Union, also appeared on the scene. The latter union called several strikes in 1933 and 1934, but none of them were successful. Before the NRA, there had been fewer than 200 Negro members in the entire international organization of the AFL packing unions; but in the campaign that followed the passage of the blanket code, Negroes came into the union with the rest of the packing-house workers in large numbers. By January of 1935, there were more than 5,000 Negroes enrolled in Chicago locals alone.

Most of the Negro members, however, were highly suspicious both of the wisdom of defying the packers' will and of the white workers' good intentions. When the union showed the first sign of weakness, many colored workers dropped out. Because of the half-hearted way in which the Amalgamated dealt with the problems arising out of Negro participation in the union's social, political, and economic affairs, Negro workers became increasingly suspicious of this AFL union, but the Packing-house Industrial Workers Union, which was Communist-affiliated, never succeeded in making significant inroads among the workers, either colored or white.

When the CIO was formed in 1935, it immediately set itself the task of organizing the packing industry and breaking the hold of the company unions. Negroes responded enthusiastically to its appeal. Plant after plant was organized, until contracts had been negotiated with all of the major packers. Negroes and whites were organized together in the locals, and many Negroes were elected as officers. White workers under CIO leadership gave a convincing demonstration of solidarity with their colored fellow-workers, and Negroes responded by giving the union their confidence and loyalty.

A prominent Negro labor leader in 1937 described the relations of Negroes to the new union as follows:

"In the yards, the dominant group is the Poles. They constitute 40 per cent of the workers. Negroes are 38 per cent. The rest are Lithuanians, Germans, Italians, and Croatians. The Negro is best informed on union procedure and is most articulate. The foreign groups understand, but aren't articulate because of language difficulties. We have our union literature printed in several languages so they will understand even though they can't speak English.

"The best proof that the Negro is the best union member is that we have more Negro stewards and officers in our locals than any other group. And these were elected in mixed locals. In one local we have a Negro president. Local #6 is completely organized and a Negro is president of that local, too. The other officers are almost evenly distributed between Negroes and whites. The president of the local is white. The secretary is a Negro.

"Negroes and whites in the same departments get practically the same pay. Of course, cleaner jobs go to white workers. There are more Negroes in the wool, glue, and sausage departments because this is dirtier work. Negro women are in the dirtier departments, too. These things will have to be ironed out after the union has agreements in all packing houses."

Testimony to the effectiveness of the union in improving Negro-white relations in the industry was offered by a rank-and-file Negro member, a stockyards laborer, who said to an interviewer in 1938: "Now the union come and we has a friendlier feeling 'mongst us—we feels all together, 'stead of working 'gainst each other. That's a long ways from the time we was all fighting each other back in 1919 during the race riots. Then we was afraid to go to work for fear we would be kilt."

CAN THE CEILING DISAPPEAR?

The Job Ceiling has been rising, although slowly, in recent years. This has been especially true since the Second World War began. Perhaps the best way to give some idea of the extent to which Negroes have been incorporated into the industrial life of Chicago, to date, is to present a brief summary of the findings of the Subcommittee on Employment of the Mayor's Conference on Race Relations, in February, 1944.* The findings were as follows:

* The survey on which these findings are based covered 94 firms, employing half a million workers, of which one-tenth were Negroes, and included all types

1. By January of 1944, only an insignificant number of manufacturing and business establishments in Chicago did not employ Negroes in any capacity. A majority of the firms, however, had employed Negroes only during the last two to four years—i.e., only since the beginning of the Second World War.

2. Most of the rather large number of firms that had employed Negroes for from ten to thirty years stated that they first employed Negroes during the First World War, and because of the labor shortage. But most of the firms that had employed Negroes only since the coming of the Second World War gave the requirements of government contracts as the reason for first hiring colored workers. The labor shortage and "pressure from organized groups" were the other important reasons indicated.

3. Most of the firms that hired Negroes during the First World War employed them only in the capacity of unskilled laborers. On the other hand, plants that first engaged Negro labor during the Second World War claimed to have originally hired them in semi-skilled as well as unskilled jobs, and also maintained that Negro employees on all levels were constantly being upgraded. Virtually all colored girl employees in offices, however,* held unskilled jobs.

4. As for continuing Negro employment after the Second World War, we quote: "The one concrete opinion that came out of the survey was that, unless maximum employment continued, the operation of seniority contracts would work heavily against Negroes, who for the most part are recent employees." [6]

Gains during the Second World War would appear to be substantial, *if* Negroes can hold them. But even before this war—indeed, throughout the period since the First World War—Negroes have composed an integral part of the labor force of mass-production industries in Chicago. Although extremely limited, some occupational mobility did occur between 1920 and 1940. The occupational status of Negroes was not purely static even during the Depression. The advent of the CIO represented a gain in and of itself. The CIO has pledged itself to fight to attain equal rights on the job in all industries—which in its most significant aspect means an equal opportunity for occupational

---

of industries and businesses. There can be little doubt that the sample was representative—with the possible exception of very small plants.

* In private industry, that is, since civil service positions were of course not included in the survey.

advancement. Not only have most CIO unions fought for the upgrading of Negro workers on the same basis as white workers, but some have addressed themselves to the special problem of post-war Negro employment. One possible solution that has already been tried, at least once, is described thus: [7]

The United Electrical Workers, CIO, in one instance where a cutback took place, proposed that the proportion of Negro and white workers that had been achieved in the industry be retained and that there be a proportionate layoff in order that seniority would not adversely affect those who had been denied opportunity of employment in industry heretofore. This was the proposal of the union and it was carried into effect.

In the past, the Job Ceiling has been significantly raised only during periods in which a labor shortage existed. But, even given economic necessity, this has occurred only after white employers and workers, in some sense or another, were educated to accepting colored workers in higher jobs. Were that education to become a part of a permanent outlook—if democracy in the realm of occupational opportunity were completely extended to Negroes—the Job Ceiling might not only become independent of the undulations of the business cycle, but disappear completely.

CHAPTER 12

Democracy and Economic Necessity: Black Workers and the New Unions *

THE STRUGGLE BETWEEN CAPITAL AND LABOR HAS BEEN A DOMINANT MOTIF in the life of Midwest Metropolis since the Eighties; some of its more dramatic episodes have been described in the Introduction. By the time of the First World War, the building trades and various other crafts were strongly organized, and the Chicago Federation of Labor included some twenty-nine autonomous AFL unions. All attempts at organizing the basic mass-production industries, however, had been unsuccessful. When the great steel strike of 1919 was broken, and the packing-house and stockyards strikes of the early Twenties failed, the union movement in these industries was effectively scotched for a decade to follow. But, as we saw in the preceding chapter, the craft unions remained strong during the Twenties and wielded considerable political power. The mass-production industries, with the exception of the garment industry, remained unorganized until the CIO appeared on the scene in 1935, and swept the majority of the workers in these industries into the new industrial unions.

During the five years preceding the Second World War, the workers in the mass-production industries—steel, packing, farm equipment—selected CIO unions as their bargaining agents. The organization of these unions took place within the legal framework provided by New Deal legislation, but the process of actually building the unions has required strenuous effort on the part of union leaders. Between 1935 and 1938, the dominant organizational tactic for union recognition was the strike. After the establishment of the National Labor Relations Board, machinery was available for choosing or rejecting a bargaining agent without recourse to conflict. Unions, however, still found it neces-

* The title of this chapter is taken from a study of Negroes and the CIO movement made by Horace R. Cayton and George S. Mitchell, *Black Workers and the New Unions* (University of North Carolina Press, 1939). The chapter is based on some materials in this book and on additional data gathered in the Cayton-Warner Research.

312

sary in some cases to call strikes in order to force an election or to put themselves in a favorable bargaining position. Strike activity continued, therefore, until the outbreak of the Second World War, when a no-strike pledge was adopted generally throughout industry.

From the outset, the leaders of the new unions made a deliberate effort to win the allegiance of Negroes, for economic necessity demanded their inclusion in any industrial union movement. The approach to the Negro was not dictated solely by expediency, however, for the CIO was, in a sense, a crusading movement also—in the tradition of the old Knights of Labor. Belief in racial equality was a component part of its ideology, and was kept constantly before the membership by a vigorous left-wing minority within the CIO. Formerly skeptical of "the white man's union," both the Negro workers and the Negro community became pro-CIO. Even conservative Negro leaders who professed shock at the "radicalism" and deplored the "violence" of the new unions, praised them for their stand on race relations. An analysis of Negro participation in the new union movement during the stormy organizational period reveals the interplay of democratic idealism and economic necessity—an interplay that resulted in making the Negro an integral part of the CIO movement.

ORGANIZING THE NEGRO WORKER

In view of the long history of conflict between Negro and white workers in the basic industries of Chicago, it has been necessary for the new unions to employ special tactics in recruiting Negroes during organizational campaigns, and in educating white workers to accept them. The appeal of the CIO was both idealistic and practical. The approach was often carefully planned and executed, with the leaders stressing equality between black and white workers in addition to class solidarity.

Negro organizers who have been employed have sometimes attained important positions of national leadership. CIO leaders have usually insisted upon the election of Negro officials to responsible positions in local unions. Negro stewards and members of grievance committees, often in unions with an overwhelming majority of white workers, discuss wages, hours, and working conditions with the representatives of powerful industrial concerns. Attempts have been made to break the Job Ceiling by utilizing seniority rules.

The techniques used by CIO unions to attract Negro members throughout the organizational campaigns that were conducted from 1935 until the advent of the Second World War may be summarized as follows:

1. to employ Negro organizers who could talk to Negro workers in terms of their group experiences, special apprehensions, and general attitudes;

2. to see that Negro workers in unions with a large Negro membership were represented on grievance committees and in the official hierarchy of the unions;

3. to treat Negroes as equals at all social affairs and to avoid scheduling meetings or social affairs at places where they are barred or might be embarrassed;

4. to fight consciously for the rights of Negro workers, in relation to promotions, seniority, pay, working hours, etc.;

5. to protest against segregated washrooms and eating places;

6. to respect the special sensibilities and grievances of Negro workers; and

7. to support community drives for better housing, etc., and the broad fight against discrimination.

Probably none of these approaches would have been successful, however, had not Negroes, as well as the white workers, been assured by union leaders and the course of events that the Wagner Act provided protection against reprisals by employers.

The CIO organizing campaigns in packing, steel, and related industries had by 1940 been successful in organizing the majority of both the colored and white workers employed in these industries. One stockyard laborer expressed the basic argument for interracial co-operation which appeared during the organizational campaigns:

"Colored people has woke up to unionism now. He won't accept the boss-man's telling him, 'You don't want to be with the white man—even if you're not making as much now, you'll get more soon.' And then this same boss will tell the white people, 'Don't get together with the colored people—they'll work for less than you get.' That's how he separates the white from the Negro and the Negro from the white. The average Negro makes a good union man. 'Course, one of them told me when I asked him to join: 'What do I want to belong to a CIO union for? It's a white man's union.' But I told him, 'It's a poor man's union.'"

Another Negro laborer described the tactical approaches to packing-house workers in 1938 as follows:

"One of the men got together about twelve or thirteen men all working at the Bruno Beef Company one Sunday at a friend's house. About half of the people present was white men and we had a good discussion and all of us wanted to have the CIO.

"The reason that we did not want the AFL is because they would separate us—put the whites in one local and the colored in another. We all wanted to be in the same local. After that meeting we all pledged that by the time of the next meeting, which would be held two weeks from that Sunday, we would bring one or two with us. So we all went to work on our friends working beside us in the plant. It so happened that I was working with a foreign-born Polish man and he did not know much English. I had a hard time, but he agreed to go with me to that meeting."

The effect of these assemblies at homes and of the recruiting in factories was strengthened by frequent mass meetings that tended to generate intense enthusiasm and high morale among the newly unionized workers, and to inspire in them a feeling of identity with their fellow-workers. Something of the élan that characterized these new recruits is revealed in the statement of one Negro worker:

"Our whole gang went into the union—every one of us. Now there's Joe who lives on South Parkway; he was the first to join. We all saw that if we wanted to protect our interests we would have to join. Then there's Lupe, the Mexican; that guy is one of the fightenest guys you ever saw. He put his button on the first day he got it. Yes, all our gang is a good bunch of union men, and will stick together. If we could get the whole plant to stick together half as well, we would have a strong union and things would be better for us."

Sometimes the CIO unions were competing with an old-established company union or with a recently organized independent union—organizations likely to appeal strongly to Negroes who distrusted white workers. Also, no doubt many Negro workers, accustomed to the paternalism of employers in the South, felt more secure in a company union. One Negro defended such unions with these observations:

"It protects us against any other union because when you are a member of the Security League that shows that you are satisfied with your employer—that you don't want any other union to come in and make trouble for you. Fifteen cents a week guarantees you the right to have your own spokesman for your group. That means that every six months you elect a representative."

Another packing-house worker described the advantages of belonging to a company union in terms of the welfare program:

"The members pay ten cents weekly as dues; this was put into the general fund and was used for the benefit of the group. For instance, we could borrow money in case of sickness, and if there was a death in the family we received $3 death benefits; this could not do much good as a burial fund, but at least we were assured of flowers. Two years ago we, through the main club, started a Christmas Saving Fund, and last year the members cashed checks amounting to $7,000. This year the amount is expected to reach around $35,000. The members of the various clubs have also been given the opportunity to buy shares in the business."

The rise of the CIO weakened the company unions, and by 1938 these had ceased to constitute an important force in the mass-production industries. Negroes followed the trend into CIO unions. The following are typical of the objections to company unions voiced by Negro workers:

"It is just something in name, but it don't mean a thing to the men working there because the way things are run there, it can't do any good."

"We have our own representatives from the different departments and they meet together and work out something and take it up with the manager, but they don't get anything but promises."

"We did not get a raise until the Wagner Act went into effect, and we have the same speed-up we have always had. In brief, the company union is no good. All the men are hollering about it."

"It is no good to the men who have to work because the representatives are so afraid to say anything about conditions that they let anything happen, and they don't say anything unless the men don't be working fast enough for them when the big boss is around. Then they come around and tell you that if you don't work faster you will never get a raise. That makes the men go as fast as they can, so they can get a raise, but that don't help at all."

The active participation of Negroes in the labor movement broke the stereotype of Negroes as strike-breakers and a source of cheap labor. Once Negroes become unionized, they must depend on the union to protect their rights through seniority rules and active opposition to the Job Ceiling. They can no longer rely on personal contacts with the employer for security. It is natural for some who have previously secured advancement, or favors, to view the union with suspicion, and to generalize that unions are detrimental to racial interests. Some Negro workers, like their white fellows, felt that their chances for advancement were better if they were not "mixed up with unions." For instance, a steel chipper who had worked for one company for seventeen years, said:

"The New Deal is linked up with the CIO. I don't believe in the CIO. Organized labor is against the Negro. I believe each plant or company should have its own independent union. That is the way we have it at the Crux Steel Plant. I worked all the time during the last strike. The colored and white are treated alike in my plant. There is no discrimination—no segregation in washrooms or restaurant."

On the other hand, there were "successful" workers who, although they would not join the new union, were not hostile to the CIO. An assistant foreman in a steel plant, for instance, first cited reasons why he had preferred not to join the CIO.

"I was approached by men from both unions, but as I felt fairly secure in my position, I saw no need to join. I've worked for the company long enough so that I have a right to my job as long as the company operates. . . . I wouldn't join the union before the contract was signed, and there was no need after it was signed." But he added, "I am not opposed to unions."

Moreover this man, despite his non-union status, seemed proud of the fact that "before the contract was signed, in my department we had the strongest union representation of any unit in the plant. . . . After the contract didn't force all men to join the union, the men began to drop out because they couldn't see any advantage in paying for the same things that non-union men got."

Still other Negroes who have acquired preferred positions in industry have nevertheless embraced the union. Sometimes the action resulted from recognizing that unions can "make the way hard" for a person who has the reputation of being timid or of being a stool pigeon. More commonly, however, the men in question had been nursing grievances of long standing against the establishments for which they worked, and the union provided a means of expression for such grievances. One worker, for example, felt that he had a "lifetime job" at the mill where he worked, but he nevertheless entertained numerous grievances against the company. He joined the union, and at the time that the following interview was taken, he was a leader in a predominantly white union. He explained his union affiliation thus:

"Let me tell you a thing or two about the plant. I know, too; I've worked there thirteen years—since I was twenty years old. You know, I'm doing highly skilled work. It took me a year to learn every part, its number, where it is to be sent, where these parts are kept, how much is to be sent out each month. But what is my occupational classification? I'm assigned as a 'porter.' They can't stand the idea of a Negro being classified as a skilled worker.

"Let me tell you a thing. There are only six of us colored men. We're all classified as porters, and all of us are doing some kind of skilled work. You see how they get us this way. When we ask for a raise according to the work we are doing, the boss says, 'Why, you're getting more than most porters now.'

"Of course, I've been there so long, and it would be so hard to train another person to do what I'm doing, that they pay me more than most white workers, $27, but they'd fire me in a minute if they thought anyone else could do my job.

"Let me tell you something. I was called into the office and the boss said to me, 'Bobby, it grieves us very much to see you a member of this harebrained outfit. Haven't we always treated you fair? That outfit isn't doing anything for you.'

"I told him that I worked hard and well; that what I did off the job was *my* business; that I had worked thirteen years for them, and it took the CIO to get a vacation for me. They kind of threatened me, but I wasn't bluffed so easy, and I'm still working. What's more, I'm shop steward; I'm on the Grievance Committee; I'm the sergeant-at-arms at my lodge, too."

When an organizing campaign begins, or a strike is imminent, Negro workers must face the possibility of running afoul of management on the one hand, or of their fellow-workers on the other. Undoubtedly, in such situations, many individual workers would prefer not to join a union, but they operate in a social milieu which forces them to choose sides and to assume the consequent risks. Many persons who first "choose" the union under such circumstances subsequently become deeply interested in union activities and wish to be members.

One of the most significant aspects of the contact between Negroes and whites in the labor movement has been the emergence of Negro leaders who have won the loyalty and respect of both colored and white workers. During an organizing campaign, both Negro and white leaders are used. Appeals are made to Negroes on the basis of their individual economic interest, opportunities for "racial advancement," and the broader philosophy of class solidarity. As the union becomes more highly integrated, the appeal to class solidarity becomes more pronounced and effective. The organizing campaign, especially in initial stages, may make use of special appeals to Negroes as Negroes, but fundamentally and ultimately the appeal is to economic self-interest and the doctrine of working-class solidarity.

THE STRIKE

A strike is a crisis situation in which the state of Negro-white relations may constitute a decisive element. Negroes, as a consequence of the fact that they have been used as strike-breakers in the past in Chicago, have been stereotyped as potential "scabs." It is relatively easy, therefore, for antagonism toward "scabs" to be focused with double intensity upon Negro strike-breakers. On the other hand, where Negroes have been organized into unions with white persons, class solidarity is likely to soften racial antagonism even when other Negroes are used as strike-breakers. The symbols and slogans of the class struggle serve as doctrinal support for Negro-white co-operation against the "bosses." A strike is a conflict—a conflict often freighted with emotion and meaning for those who participate in it. A strike serves to weld workers into a class-conscious and temporarily unified action group. The following speech by a Negro strike leader, delivered during the "Little Steel" strike in 1937, illustrates the manner in which class solidarity is stimulated:

"Two thousand marching CIO miners will lay down their picks, and Girdler needs coal to blast his furnaces! Thousands of auto workers from the CIO will stop using any steel made in Republic, and Girdler must fill his contracts with the auto companies. Thousands of longshoremen will stand idle, and Girdler needs their help in transporting steel. Thousands of railway employees will let Girdler's steel sit on the tracks, and Girdler needs the railroads to carry on any business. Girdler needs them all. Girdler needs them all, and John L. Lewis knows it. They say they'll make steel anyhow. Where will they send it? When it piles so high that Girdler can't see over it, he'll sign. He'll sign."

The picket line drew Negroes and whites together in common and dangerous activity. Struggle gave real content to the doctrine that union men must "stick together as brothers." Between 1935 and 1940, a number of important strikes involving both Negro and white workers occurred. The Republic Steel Strike of 1937—one of the most dramatic of these disturbances—illustrates to an unusual degree the operation of factors that create solidarity between Negro and white workers—as well as certain other factors which impede this development.

The Republic Steel Strike: In May, 1937, approximately 20,000 workers of the Republic Steel Company, situated in South Chicago, walked out on strike. The principal demands of the workers were for union recognition and a wage increase. The strike was effectively broken in a relatively short time, though it dragged along for many months. This strike is significant because it was the setting within which the nationally famous "Memorial Day Massacre" occurred.

On Sunday, May 30, 1937, a crowd of some 5,000 people—strikers, their wives and children, and union sympathizers—were assembled near the plant for purposes of mass picketing and demonstration. During the afternoon a disturbance occurred and the police fired into the crowd. Ten workers were killed, and nine more persons were injured. The police were severely and widely denounced for unprovoked and excessive brutality. They claimed that they were "attacked," but impartial evidence assembled at the time contained nothing to justify their conduct.

When the Steel Workers' Organizing Committee (SWOC) called the strike at Republic Steel, more than half of the Negroes in the plant were union members, and these walked out with the white workers. (At the time, about 25,000 men were employed in the plant, of whom 17,000 were white and 8,000 were colored.) Some Negroes did not leave work, however. A striker interviewed at the time reported:

"Since the strike there are about twenty-five or thirty Negroes who stayed in. . . . I think those guys would come out, but they are ashamed. They don't even come around to any of the places where strikers hang out."

A Negro striker reported on his efforts to bring out all of the colored workers:

"We went around and talked to the men that stayed in because it put Negroes in a bad light. Even though many whites stayed in, we colored men felt that those staying in would give Negroes a black eye in the union. You know the first thing white union men think is that Negroes will scab and break strikes. We didn't have any success. The men said they needed the money. Most of them were scared of losing their jobs, and some are just ignorant."

At one point in the strike, strike-breakers—both white and Negro— were imported by the company. Since most of the colored employees had come out on strike, the union was able to handle the situation in a highly effective manner. One observer told this story:

"The Republic Company had hired a lot of Negroes as strike-breakers, and in order to create racial friction these Negroes had been sent out to break up the picket line—but only when there were all white workers on the picket line. The situation got pretty tense at strike headquarters. There were murmurings of 'Niggers are always scabs'; there were little tussles among some of the men.

"However, the situation was cleared up in a clever way. All of the Negro strikers stayed near the picket line and waited for a skirmish. When the Negro scabs came out to beat up the pickets, the Negro strikers were let out and gave them such a beating there was never a recurrence of the trouble."

Strike leaders exerted every effort to draw Negroes into full participation at public meetings. The emphasis thus placed upon Negro-white solidarity served to counteract the unfavorable impression created by the Negroes who were acting as strike-breakers. An observer described one of these meetings in terms of Negro participation:

"At 2:30, 'Spike' Smith, the Negro organizer, announced that a brother from the United Mine Workers of America was there to speak. Another report was made by Jack Ross, a Negro molder. . . . His appearance was greeted with cheers and applause. He has been very active in the South Chicago area. He owns an automobile, which is placed at the disposal of the strikers at all times.

"After the speeches, the Negro organizer announced that they had just received a call for a blood transfusion to aid a brother who was in the

hospital in a serious condition. [He had been hurt on the picket line.]
He asked for volunteers. At least ten men, two of whom were Negroes,
went up to the table without hesitation. They were all sent to the hospital.
Later Spike announced that a group of children were going to present a
little program. Twelve Negro children marched in, carrying violins and
banjos. . . . Another announcement was made concerning relief for strikers. The men were told to report to the organizer, Spike."

Other methods, too, were used to checkmate racial antagonisms. At
one meeting Spike addressed a mixed audience, and denounced "the
ignorant Negro who held a gun on the workers," citing this as "an old
company technique to incite racial prejudice." He cried out, "A scab
is a scab, black or white, and should be scorned by all union members,
black and white!" He insisted that today "workers refuse to bite at
the racial bait-line." Whistles and cheers followed his speech.

A special effort was made to involve Negro women in strike activities, and one observer noted: "Several of the wives of the Negro members went to the strike headquarters and worked in the kitchen where
meals were prepared for the pickets. It was felt that this pleased the
union members because the general opinion was that the Negroes
could not be depended upon in a crisis."

The climax of the Republic strike came with the "Memorial Day
Massacre." Of this affair, one Negro participant commented: "I have
been in three strikes. I was in the 'Memorial Day Massacre' and I can't
find words to express the horror of it. In the World War, both sides
at least had an equal chance."

Another Negro striker, who subsequently testified before the La
Follette Committee during that committee's investigation of the "massacre," gave a dramatic account of the police attack:

"On that Sunday we marched out of the plant with signs. Lots of us
were singing songs and laughing. I was in the front line. All of a sudden
the cops started shooting. When they started, I ran to my extreme right,
then west, then I made an 'L' turn to the south. All the time, bullets
were going right past my face.

"When I looked up I saw a guy right on top of the plant training his
gun on us. I couldn't tell whether it was a machine gun, 'cause I was
anxious to get out of the line of fire. I could see the police in my path,
the way I was running, so I turned around toward Sam's Place. I ran
to a car and started to duck in it. A bullet whizzed by and lodged right
above the right fender. Boy, I shake now when I think that if I hadn't

ducked I'd have been shot in the head. I finally made it into the car and was driven to Sam's Place."

The CIO regards the men who died that day as martyrs to the union cause. Among the ten men killed was one Negro. After being shot, he was beaten by the police and taken to jail. Later his wife had him removed to a private hospital, where he died. She seemed bewildered by this outburst of violence resulting in her husband's death. This is how she talked about it:

"He was told to go to the meeting that Sunday. He was on the front line and was one of the first to get hurt. I have his clothes here. You can see where he was shot in the back. His hat is bloody. He sure was beat terrible. His life was really lost for the CIO, whether he understood it or not. I do hope his loss will help others who live."

Her feelings toward the union were mixed, uncertain:

"He never said nothing much about it. He just told me he was joining a new union. He did say he was joining because it was beneficial. We didn't talk about those things much. I don't think he understood it either.

"I ain't never thought much about it before. I guess a union's all right, but when people have to lose their life it ain't so good. 'Course, in war, men lose their lives for freedom, but this is a little different. The union caused me to lose a very good husband. They seem to want to drop me so soon. I don't expect them to take care of me forever, but I do feel they should help till I can see my way out."

Toward the police, however, her attitude was one of unmitigated bitterness:

"They wouldn't let me in to see him until the Saturday before I had him moved to St. Luke's. They treated me all right, but they wouldn't let me see him. I saw others going in, but I couldn't tell whether they were visiting in the hospital or in the jail.

"I was let in on June 13. He'd been in since May 30. They thought he was dying that Saturday night, so they sent two policemen to my home to bring me to see him. He was so glad to see me he could hardly talk. He kept asking why I hadn't been there to see him. He cried and I cried and told him they wouldn't let me in. He said they hadn't taken the bullet out and infection had set in. He was so sick! I wouldn't let him talk, but he kept saying over and over, 'Police sure treat a man dirty; they kicks 'em and beats 'em.' He almost screamed at times.

"I thought they [the police] would tell him how I came out two and three times a day, and how I called every day, but he didn't know nothing about it. Every time I'd call, they told me he was getting along fine, until they was scared he was dying. Then they sent for me."

Those Negro members who continued to support the union after the "Memorial Day Massacre" felt that the CIO was fair to them as Negroes, and that the strike was justified. The following interview is typical of this view:

"Though Republic Steel paid all workers the same wages for the same kind of work, they did not treat the white and colored employees alike in other respects. The Negro employee was restricted to certain departments. There were no colored foremen, and no possibilities of promotion for the colored employees.

"The AFL did not attempt to organize the workers at Republic Steel. The AFL did not organize many Negro workers. I think the AFL should kick into the CIO. I feel the CIO is far the better organization for Negroes. I like the union fine. The union is 100 per cent for the colored man. There is no discrimination in the CIO."

In November, some six months after the Memorial Day affair, an observer visited the union headquarters. The strike had been broken. Men were trickling back to work. Gone were the morale and enthusiasm of former days, though some residue of the solidarity created by the strike between Negro and white workers seemed to remain.

And, through the strike, the union had gained new and loyal members, Negro as well as white. At union headquarters, one such recruit told his story to the interviewer—in the presence of a Mexican and five white unionists.

"I came to Chicago in 1922. I started working in Republic Steel in April, 1923, and was there steady until the strike was called on May 26, 1937.

"I have four boys . . . so you see it was pretty hard to walk off from my job not knowing how I'd make a living for them. I didn't know anything about unions before, but I did know that I wanted organization and a contract to stop the company from pushing the men around and to stop the speed-up. You know the company could tell you if you didn't like it you could take it or get the hell out.

"Negroes only had certain places to work in Republic. Even in the washroom, Negroes were told to use one side and whites the other side. The washroom is just one big room, yet Negroes had to stay on their side of it. I believe, from the way they talk, that there is no prejudice in the CIO.

"Negroes spend ten or fifteen years in Republic and can't get higher than chippers. They never get to be on the cranes, never get jobs as engineers or firemen. That's why I wanted organization. I understand that without organization a person can't get any place.

"While we were organizing our department, the company gave us shorter hours and only two or three days a week, and let the other departments do steady work. That was the company's way of bringing pressure on us union men.

"Once the boss said to me: 'You fellows are nothing but a bunch of Bolsheviks.' I asked him what the hell that was and he walked away. I realized that I spoke too quick. I might have got more out of him if I had waited.

"I saw some of the preparations for the strike. While I was in the storeroom one day, I saw a big delivery truck back up to the door. It had a lot of big packages on it. One of them had a hole in it where the clubs had punched through, and I could see several club handles about the size of a kid's baseball bat. I didn't say anything about it, but I certainly remembered it that Sunday in May." (Here a white union member added that he, too, had seen clubs stacked in the back room of the credit union office.)

General discussion of the strike followed; then the Negro worker concluded: "I'm a union man, from now on. There isn't no way out for us, except the union. Maybe we'll lose this time. But the day will come when we will win."

The Republic Steel strike demonstrated that in a time of crisis white workers would not only struggle side by side with Negroes, but would also follow them as leaders and honor them as martyrs. As it became a part of the traditions of the area, the incident strengthened the position of Negroes in unions, as well as the hold of unions over colored workers. The strike had shown that some Negroes, acting on the basis of their class alignments, would subordinate racial loyalty even to the point of criticizing and fighting Negro strike-breakers. It was also evident, however, that such behavior was not yet common enough to be accepted as entirely normal by many workers—white and colored.

DAY-BY-DAY RELATIONSHIPS

During the excitement of an organizational campaign or a strike, both racial antagonisms and class solidarity across race lines are at their height. Once a contract has been signed, the day-by-day routine of workers is broken only by occasional elections and grievances. Those unions in which the leaders are concerned with improving race relationships make use of these situations for further impressing upon Negro and white workers the necessity for fairness, co-operation, etc. Such interim periods bear dividends when crises arise.

Labor unionists contend that membership in a progressive union is reflected in the day-by-day relationships of Negro and white workers. The colored shop chairman in a small plant with fewer than a dozen workers described the improved atmosphere in his plant: "Well, I'll tell you what the CIO has done. Before, everyone used to make remarks about 'that dirty Jew,' 'that stinkin' black bastard,' 'that lowlife Bohunk,' but you know I never hear that kind of stuff any more."

Both white and colored workers who take their labor unionism seriously are in a position to remind the less zealous that they must not jeopardize class solidarity by exhibiting racial antagonism. One colored steel-worker cited an incident involving another colored worker: " 'Course, not all prejudices are wiped out right away. The other day I was working on a gang with another colored man and two white men. The colored man tried to get me to give the white men the hardest part to do, but I told him off on that, and later he came back and told me he realized we must *all* do the same amount of work."

Such incidents as those just cited may be exceptional, but it seems that organization of Negroes and whites together in the mass-production industries has resolved many of the antagonisms and suspicions that in the past contributed to widespread insecurity on the part of both white and colored workers.

SHARING POSITIONS OF CONTROL

Some of the AFL locals have separate colored locals in which Negroes occupy all of the positions of leadership. The CIO, on the other hand, does not sanction separate locals, but seeks to integrate Negroes and whites together in the same plant and local organization. The philosophy underlying this practice was outlined by a steel worker:

"In 1921, company stooges split the union by advising Negroes to meet in their own section and whites in theirs. This worked up destruction on both sides. Negroes met on 43rd Street some place—I believe it was at Forum Hall. This plot was quite successful. The packers were clever in bringing the proposal. Their agents told the Negroes it would be more convenient for them to meet close to home, and the plan sounded feasible. The whites met on Loomis Boulevard. This set-up made it easy to play one group against the other and built up animosity. Insidious propaganda was injected at the meetings by telling each group that the other was not to be trusted."

Where Negroes and whites are organized in the same locals, it has been customary for Negroes to insist upon some representation among the officers, executive committees, etc. White workers have become accustomed to following the leadership of Negroes.*

Out of the ranks of the workers have arisen individual Negroes who function on grievance committees, serve as shop chairmen, and act in other capacities that throw them into contact with management as spokesmen for the union. Here the personal nexus with the employer has been entirely broken and the Negro individual abandons any semblance of currying favor or depending on his relations with management.

All lodges of the CIO steel unions with Negro members have some Negro officials. There are a number of Negro shop stewards in the locals who direct grievance committees, collect dues, and deal with the management. They also appear before the NLRB when necessary. A middle-aged Negro migrant from Georgia, in answer to a question about how Negroes and whites get along in his local, replied: "Fine, as far as I know. We have both Negro and white officers in our union and nobody seems to mind."

Labor leaders believe that Negroes have a distinct advantage over the foreign workers, since the first-generation immigrants have lan-

---

* It is not to be inferred that all AFL unions, by any means, organize Negroes into separate locals, or that Negroes have never attained positions of leadership in mixed AFL locals. As a matter of fact, the pattern of organization characteristic of the CIO emerged first in certain AFL unions. In Chicago in 1920-21, this pattern—including Negro officers in mixed locals—was well developed in several Chicago unions, most notably perhaps, in the International Ladies' Garment Workers' Union, the Hod Carriers' Union and the Flat Janitors' Union. The last-named organization had Negro officers from the time it was first organized, and in 1920, 1,000 of the 5,000 members of the union were Negro. (See *The Negro in Chicago*, pp. 412-416.)

guage difficulties. Negroes are more vocal and can become leaders easily.

In the ranks of lesser leaders, both in the unions proper and in the women's auxiliaries, there are many Negro officers. One Negro president stated: "I was elected by unanimous vote. The fellows had been telling me that they wanted me as president when they held the election, and I had told that I didn't want the presidency. I resigned after they elected me, but they ignored my resignation and re-elected me, so I've been serving ever since."

The president of one local in the packing industry thus described the situation in his plant just before the war boom:

"The CIO is the greatest thing that could have happened to Negroes in packing. Before that they were outside the labor movement, mostly, and could be used as strike-breakers by the bosses. I'm happy to be president of the local, and I work hard at it to bring in as many Negroes as well as whites as I can into the union.

"The shop stewards are 50-50, white and Negro among the men; there is no friction—the white workers are willing to have a Negro shop steward head the Grievance Committee. In the meetings of the local, the Negro members feel free to go up on the floor—they make good speeches and usually talk to the point."

Stimulating Participation by Negroes: Because Negroes do not have a long tradition of union participation there are frequent complaints from both white and Negro officials that they do not participate so actively in union affairs as they might. The Negro financial secretary of a local, in a plant about one-third Negro, described relationships in his plant as follows:

"We have 621 members; 198 are Negroes. Only about fifteen Negroes come out to meetings, and we're doing good to get that many out. The whole department has only about 1,500 men. Fifty per cent of the Negroes pay dues but are not so good in attendance. Those Negroes who come out are very active and pay good. One thing, it has been easier to collect from Negroes than other races. The Negro realizes that he has a real chance to join an organization with the rights of other races. I think they're all faithful union men, though for the time being it's hard to get them out. Especially with the CIO leaders, the Negro has a chance to fill any position where he's capable. I believe the policy of the CIO is against discrimination."

Occasionally, a Negro labor leader will voice a complaint similar to that of an organizer in the fur workers union:

"There is no Negro on the Executive Board now. This is not the fault of the union. One Negro woman was nominated at the last election. There are fifty-five Negroes in the local, thirty-two of whom are eligible to vote. Only nine came out to vote, yet this woman lost by only seven votes, which proved that she was more acceptable to the white workers than to the Negro workers who didn't even come out."

The colored shop chairman of a steel local reported:

"Attendance isn't as good as it should be. Most of the boys are young; they don't really have the union at heart. They saw what the union did for them, and so they pay up their dues, but it's hard to get them out to the meetings. I notice that the men who have family responsibilities like myself are the most active members."

Labor leaders continually emphasize the fact that when Negroes are active participants in the day-by-day affairs of the union, and when they attend meetings regularly, it is possible for them to secure positions of control within the local union organization. One steel worker made the following comment:

"One thing that I have tried to get the Negro to understand and do is to join in such large numbers that they will be a power from a voting standpoint so that when the union has an election of officers they can vote some of their own into office. If the Negro would learn to pick the person best fitted for office, and quit putting a dumb person in simply because of friendship, then we should be able to meet, plan, and scheme with the other fellows and would not only be a floor member."

The very realistic attitude of the more astute Negro union leaders is revealed in the comment of a packing-house worker during the organizational drive of 1937:

"I am chairman of the —— local and Secretary of the Industrial Council. I was given one of the fourteen offices in the local. Negroes are taking a leading part. When some of them say the Negro will get a dirty deal from the CIO like they do in the AFL, I preach to them to get in when the policies are being formed and help form them. I tell them that workers themselves form union policies when they have enough sense to get in on the ground floor and take part in shaping policy.

"They seem to understand better now and they are getting in on the ground floor in the CIO. We have ten locals in the yards. Four have Negro presidents. At one plant only about ten per cent of the employees are Negroes. But a Negro has one of the elective positions out there; this is encouraging."

Protecting the Rights of Negroes: Negro workers share in whatever economic gains a union brings, but they also expect their union to protect their rights to promotion, office holding, and treatment as union brothers. The day-by-day problems arising in the plant and at union meetings provide union officials with an opportunity to use both persuasion and pressure for enforcing the union program of equality. The Negro president of a steel local explained the procedure in his shop as follows: "The person in question would be called before the executive board where the disadvantage of prejudice would be explained to him. He would then be given another chance, and if the difficulty arose again he would be expelled."

The colored trustee of a local in the meat-packing industry said, "There's no prejudice at all," and then explained: "We have by-laws and constitutions, but there is no rule covering prejudice. I'm pretty sure if a case occurred, everyone would embarrass the person to death."

SOCIAL EXTENSIONS OF ECONOMIC CONTACT

Labor unions are not concerned entirely with economic problems. They depend on dances, picnics, parties, and similar social events to raise money and to maintain *esprit de corps*. Such social and quasi-social events often involve the attendance of Negro members. During the organizational drives in the mass-production industries in 1937 and 1938, such affairs were very frequent, and the more enthusiastic union members reported their experiences in glowing terms:

"Our lodge gave a dance in September. It was a free social to try and encourage men to come out. It was very successful, and quite a few Negroes came out. They socialized with the others and seemed to feel that we're all one race."

"At the social events, one sees mixing of the groups. Both Negro and white drink beer together. More and more there is an intermixing between both races and sexes in the dancing."

"One thing can be said for the SWOC staff and lodge officers: They stress Negro participation in social affairs. This gives a sort of education in race relations."

After the first novelty of the new CIO movement had worn off, social participation, while less frequent, was also less commented on. Today, the presence of Negroes at a union dance or party is not a matter for remark except in certain special situations.

A crucial point in this social participation has been interracial dancing. A young Polish Communist commented during the organizational drives of 1937: "If everybody felt like me, we wouldn't have any trouble running dances and other affairs. That's the struggle we got to fight now, so that Negroes won't be scared away from our affairs." The common pattern was described by a trustee in a predominantly Negro shop: "There was a large attendance of both white and colored. There were no colored and whites dancing together. Some stayed in groups by themselves, mostly whites. There was no friction, they just didn't dance together. They all talked and laughed together." At one dance on the South Side attended by more than 1,000 persons, only ten or fifteen white men and women came, though the manager said, "A lot of tickets were sold to whites who didn't come."

That many Negroes do not adjust easily to interracial dancing is suggested by the complaint of an organizer who said: "Certain indications point to the strong influence of the idea of not mixing, in the form of Negroes' limiting themselves. I was the only one who danced at this affair. The rest of them drank and talked with the whites, but they didn't dance."

Many Negro workers use the test of social participation as one measure of the white worker's sincerity. This attitude was illustrated by an incident in which a Negro member came to the local headquarters to report a rumor which, as he phrased it, "was causing some confusion in his lodge." It seems that a white official, in referring to a dance which had been planned, stated that it was being held in a neighborhood unfriendly to Negroes. Some of the Negroes interpreted this as a gentle hint that they were not wanted, and the Negro union member said: "I felt that I should come right to you so that the rumor can be stopped. The men are kinda touchy and if it gets around it will have a bad effect on the colored members of the union." The union official was quite anxious to straighten out the matter, assured the member that he would bring the grievance up at the council meeting that night, and stated that he could "easily see how they might have felt that it was intended to discourage Negro attendance because that's the approach used by persons who actually don't want Negro attendance. I think I made a mistake when I apologized for having the dance at a place inconvenient for Negroes. I should have told the members that if they disapproved of the place, we'd get another where Negroes wouldn't be molested. We'll make it clear tonight."

The more conservative Negro members take the position of a colored worker who said: "We work together and we understand each other better when we socialize and find out that we're all alike, and especially the white ones find out that the Negroes don't bite. I like to dance but I prefer dancing with colored girls. I think we can show solidarity without dancing together."

The strength of the general social taboos against dancing with Negroes is indicated by the comment of an Italian president of a steel workers' women's auxiliary to another white woman:

"We used to have a lot of colored fellows in the lodge, but they're all gone now, every one. We even had two of them officers. But they've all left now. When they were in, we used to try to get their wives to join, but now they've gone.

"Of course, as my husband and I have said to each other, you give them a foot and they'll take a yard. If you ask them to your dances, they'll come and they don't just dance with each other but some of them will try to dance with white people. If they do, the white women will just stop going to the dances. There's something about colored men that just makes you *afraid*. I don't know what it is, but you have a certain *fear*. I don't feel that way at all about the girls, but the men are different —I don't know what it is, exactly, but it's fear. At a dance we had here a while ago, a Negro man actually came up to me and asked me if I would dance with him. I didn't know what to say, but I wasn't going to dance with him, so I told him that I had promised that one to someone. With a colored man, I just feel afraid. I don't know what it is. The girls are different, but I don't feel that way about them. A Negro woman has been a good friend of mine for years, but the men are different.

"I know that Negroes *are* workers, and I suppose that, really, they *are* human, but there's just something about them—that black skin— I guess the trouble with us is really that we're not liberal enough. You know, the thing is that you would like to be nice to them yourself personally, but other people don't feel that way. Perhaps if you were just with a colored person away from the eyes of everyone, you would act quite different; but with the eyes of everyone on you, you don't feel that way."

On the level of informal social participation, friendships sometimes arise between Negroes and whites which involve taking a beer together, visiting in the home, and participation in private parties. Such behavior is not widespread, but it has undoubtedly been made more general by the union movement. The president of one SWOC local related an incident which occurred in the South Chicago area which indicates the type of relationships that develops:

"This community was not neighborly. A year and a half ago Negroes could not walk in some of the streets out here. The change is due to the union and the intelligent part the Negro has played out here. Since the union campaign, I have been there on many occasions to different union members' homes. I knew these same people before the campaign started, but I was never invited to their homes. It is much different now. On June 11, my wife's birthday, the white women of the East Side gave her a surprise party at a white woman's home. It was a fine party. There were about thirty people present, and only four of us were Negroes. There were so many flowers, I thought someone had died. They called me to come over and we didn't know what it was all about. The party was at the home of Joe Petronio. He's an Italian. He's financial secretary of the union."

The secretary of one steel local, a white Virginian, said: "We occasionally have just a few cases of objections to the colored members in the union. And there is some partiality. The colored members attend the union's social affairs and dance the same as the whites. There is a complete intermingling at our social affairs. Of course, some conflicts are to be expected. Workers as a whole are still uneducated."

UNIONS AND THE JOB CEILING

The Job Ceiling in the mass-production industries has been maintained by a combination of factors. In the first place, Negroes entered industry as untrained workers at the bottom of the occupational hierarchy. But this consideration is not sufficient to account for the fact that twenty years later Negro workers have not risen in appreciable numbers into the ranks of the skilled, white-collar clerical and supervisory occupational categories. Before the advent of industrial unionism in these industries, the exclusive policy of the craft unions and the reluctance of employers in both union and non-union plants to advance colored workers were the principal factors in the lack of occupational mobility among Negroes.

The interplay of these two factors is revealed in the testimony of experienced and reliable workers, both colored and white. A highly skilled Negro worker in a packing plant who was a member of the CIO union blamed the company for discrimination existing in 1938:

"In the plant Negroes work in most departments but are definitely excluded from the bacon department. This work is done by women and is the cleanest department in the whole plant, being the one that is most often shown visitors. No Negro women are allowed here, it being said that the public objects to black hands touching the bacon. The union does not approve of this and fights against it."

There is a tendency among union members to blame the corporations for the absence of colored workers in the better jobs in the plants, while Negro non-union workers blame white workers.

The lack of opportunity for occupational advancement is the most prevalent grievance expressed by Negro workers.

A union trustee in a plant in which Negroes have exceptional opportunities said: "Negroes can advance up to supervisor and timekeeper. We got a new timekeeper the other day—a Negro. Of course, Negroes don't advance as fast as whites and they don't intend to give Negroes proportional representation on boss jobs."

A Negro steel-worker blamed management: "I never had any boss trouble, but they never promotes us Negroes."

Another steel-worker said: "Most Negroes does common labor. They ain't no Negro bosses and no Negro electricians. Only white men has them jobs. . . . The company keeps the Negro down."

Another colored worker remarked in the same vein: "Though the company paid all workers the same wage for the same kind of work, they did not treat the Negro the same in other respects. The Negro employees were restricted to certain departments. There were no colored foremen, and no possibilities of promotion for the colored employees."

A Negro skilled worker who had been able to advance within his plant said:

"Mexicans and Negroes don't get breaks like whites get. I haven't seen any Mexicans or Negroes on cranes or in the electrical department. We have one Negro craneman now in plate mill yards. He's been there since 1919. You know why—he stayed in during the strike. . . . Plenty of us coulda done skilled work after the strike, since many of us did it during the strike. The whites say Negroes can't do skilled work. We can do anything we get a chance to do—and sometimes better than whites, because Negroes know they have to be twice as good as anyone else to get and keep a job."

A colored worker in an open-shop steel mill maintained that the company was responsible for the exclusion of Negroes from the electric department:

"The company definitely excludes Negroes from the electric department. At one time the white workers circulated a petition to get a Negro electrician who was an expert on a job in the electric department. It was signed by all the workers in the department, yet the company turned it down."

A white chemist in a packing plant confirmed the role of company policy in maintaining the Job Ceiling, and incidentally revealed the dilemma of a friendly white worker who objects to discrimination in industry:

"They just don't hire them, but I don't see any reason for it. I have been friends with the colored people a long time and I find them just as capable as the whites. The company could get some colored to do that job if they wanted to, but I haven't heard any discussion on the question at all. I have wanted to raise it, but I was afraid that they would take the wrong attitude towards me and I wouldn't get my promotion. Although I have many friends among the colored people there is one thing I do not understand about them. They take anything or whatever condition is imposed upon them and will not put up a fight for their rights; that is, I have seen one at a time try to stop something, but it's never effective that way. And another thing, in our own shop some of the whites try to be friendly with the colored, but they seem to keep away from them as much as they can, although one or two visit me and I visit them. But on the whole there is a lot of room for improvement on the part of all."

A left-wing Polish worker was equally insistent that the company was responsible for not promoting Negroes: "Generally the management considers the Negro less able than the white. I don't understand why they permit them to do skilled work in someone else's place if they consider Negroes so dumb. They won't promote Negroes as rapidly as whites."

It is very difficult to secure expressions from employers as to why the Job Ceiling exists. The prevailing tendency is to blame the unions or to allege that advancing the Negroes would cause trouble in the plant. Occasionally, however, an employer will reveal personal attitudes that operate to reinforce the Job Ceiling. Thus one steel executive observed:

"Negroes are nice, simple people. I don't approve of using them for skilled work—not that they couldn't do it, but we have enough competition within the skilled groups. Let the Negroes scramble for the unskilled jobs. It used to be possible for Negroes to be used as strikebreakers. The CIO has lots of them now, and sometimes it's harder to get them. The CIO fools them with parties and social gatherings so that they get the idea they're as good as white people."

In general it can be said that plant policy is formulated with a view to uninterrupted production. Anything that might cause trouble is avoided. Minor supervisory personnel is undoubtedly a decisive factor in the promotion policy of many plants. The tendency in many large industrial organizations is to put into foremen's hands such personnel questions as the employment policy toward Negroes. There is a widespread feeling among Negro workers that foremen are largely responsible for the failure of colored workers to advance. Since many foremen are first- or second-generation Americans, of foreign ancestry, the Negro's verbal attacks on foremen are likely to be tinged with anti-foreign sentiments. A colored Baptist minister, working in a steel mill, gave vent to his feelings in the following words:

"Of course there's discrimination. . . . A couple of times I know that my foreman has given me some raw deals. He's a lousy Polack. They're the worst."

So long as the skilled jobs in the basic industries were under the jurisdiction of AFL craft unions, it was difficult to judge accurately whether management or the unions were primarily responsible for maintaining the Job Ceiling. With the advent of industrial unions, the situation has changed. All of the CIO unions have been and are committed to a non-discriminatory policy and union contracts embody clauses calling for the promotion of workers strictly on the basis of seniority. In such situations it is possible to determine clearly whether management or labor is at fault. If a union does not "go to bat" for a Negro, the blame can be squarely placed. If the union does support the colored worker's claim to advancement, and management balks, the situation is equally clear.

The policy of the CIO on this issue is clear cut and has forced many AFL unions to change their attitude toward Negro workers. One AFL organizer said: "My union does not practice discrimination against Negroes. I will admit that some time ago that was a practice, but this union don't carry any of that policy now."

Another AFL organizer recognized that the CIO was responsible for this change of policy: "We make special efforts to recruit the Negroes, because we know how they feel toward the AFL, but we try to explain to them that this is not the old AFL, [that] we have a policy to organize the unorganized. Whenever they join we make them feel at home where they belong. This was not the policy of the union until the CIO was started. Then the International saw that the workers wanted the CIO because of its method of organizing. Since our locals have adopted a militant program, now the workers will join the AFL."

The official position of all unions, then, is increasingly in the direction of demanding equal rights for Negroes. But whether or not a specific union local actually breaks the Job Ceiling in a given plant depends on several factors. First, a new position (or positions) must be open. Secondly, a Negro whose skill or seniority qualifies him for the position must be available in the plant. Given these, the local union must be willing to fight for the advancement of the colored worker, if management or individual white workers oppose the move. The union's weapons in such a situation are persuasion and economic pressure.

The three Depression years between 1937 and 1940 did not offer a favorable situation for measuring the power of unions to break the Job Ceiling. New jobs were few; labor turnover was slow. The period 1940 to 1942 did not provide too good a test situation either, because the labor shortage that attended the coming of war resulted in increased employment opportunities for Negroes without pressure from the unions. However, the Job Ceiling has been rising, and the CIO unions have certainly hastened the process. The question is whether the unions could not have been even more aggressive with respect to this issue.

Both Negro and white labor leaders continually point out that unions are only a tool which Negroes may use, and that colored workers must raise the issues within their own locals. One colored international organizer for a CIO smelters' union said: "Our people don't push hard enough for their rights under the union contracts. They've got to make the union abide by its contracts. They've got to speak up for jobs that belong to them."

Union strategists are now inclined to advise progressive white workers to initiate action in the matter of promotions of Negroes. In this way, they contend, Negro workers will not feel isolated, but will be encouraged by the presence of white allies. In locals in which white unionists do take the initiative, a friendlier feeling than usual seems to prevail between white and colored workers. Negroes in such unions frequently make comments similar to that of the steel worker who said:

"Of course there is the problem of removing the prejudice of bosses, or perhaps I should say, the technique of keeping the Negro out of certain jobs by playing on the prejudice of the white workers. Little by little white workers are learning that they must include the Negro and demand his promotion on the basis of merit. They are not being fooled so easily as in the past."

In the final analysis, white workers must become habituated to working with Negroes in skilled pursuits, and accepting them in supervisory capacities if the Negro Job Ceiling is to be broken. Even the more thoughtful and progressive workers may face an adjustment problem in this connection. A white steel worker, who said that he believed white and colored workers should have the right to work at the same jobs, answered when asked if he would work under a Negro foreman: "I tell you the truth, at first I wouldn't like a Negro boss even if he was smarter than anybody in the plant. Maybe later on, I would get used to him. Then I wouldn't care. I think the CIO will get us away from thinking so much about color."

Any sober estimate of the influence of the labor movement on Negro-white relations must avoid the overenthusiastic claims of partisans, or the disillusionment exemplified in the comment of an elderly steel worker, who said bitterly: "The white men get up and talk about unity, about how a black man is just as good as a white . . . but I never notice any of the colored men, CIO or not, go to any of the white brothers' homes."

A white CIO leader gave that organization's answer: "People seem to forget that the CIO didn't just come along and wipe out prejudice like a wet sponge on a plate. It is doing much toward establishing better race relations and some day prejudice will be brought to a minimum."

Union members, themselves, frequently size up the situation accurately. One white union member—though his explanation of the roots of prejudice is too simple—nevertheless senses the operation of processes that may overcome it: "A union doesn't eradicate prejudices the minute it makes its appearance, but successful negotiations through a union of Negroes and whites working together against a common enemy cannot but result in breaking down prejudices built up by employers."

Negro union leaders also view changing Negro-white relations as a long-term process. One organizer of packing-house workers, after commenting on the former role of Negroes as strike-breakers, said: "Race prejudice will only be overcome through a sustained campaign of education. It will take years to do this. We need the universities, the radio, the press to help us."

That the attitudes of individual white workers are affected by contact with colored workers in the union is suggested by frequent remarks like those of the steel-worker who stated:

"I learned a lot from that fellow [a Negro organizer]. He woke a lot of us up by showing how the company built up race hatred by playing on our sense of superiority. It'll be a lot different when steel is organized one hundred per cent. I never thought much about colored men before I joined the union. Of course, I knew there was discrimination against Negroes, but I just didn't think about it in my department. There were no Negroes there when I got the job, and I never gave it any thought until I began attending union meetings."

Labor union activity in Chicago during the Depression resulted in an increasing propensity on the part of white workers to accept Negroes as equals in the competitive process, and as joint participants in conflicts with employers. With this acceptance of Negroes as *economic* equals, there has developed a rather general acceptance of them as social equals in such semi-public situations as union dances and picnics. But there is little evidence, thus far, that the basic patterns of separate Negro and white family, clique, and associational relationships, other than union relationships, have been much affected by these developments.

The demands of a war economy broke the Job Ceiling at various points, though it is a matter of conjecture how extensive and permanent these changes will prove to be. In this process of breaking the Job Ceiling, the new labor unions have played a perhaps subsidiary, but nevertheless very important, role.

Within the new labor movement, a new Negro leadership has emerged which speaks not only for Negroes but often for white workers as well. The Communists have played an important part in promoting this leadership, as well as in developing the general favorable policy toward Negroes within the CIO—but these developments are now a part of the official policy of the organization.

With the appearance of this new union leadership, other Negro leaders of all class levels (including the preachers) began to lose their skepticism and fear of labor and to praise the CIO. For the first time Negroes seemed to have found a large mass of white people who not only welcomed them as allies in a struggle but also accepted them as friends; who added *fraternity* to liberty and equality.

A Bronzeville Negro—Willard S. Townsend—became the first colored man to sit on the national executive board of the CIO and soon after his appointment, he helped to persuade the organization to establish a committee for the investigation of possible discrimination within CIO unions.

The AFL, faced with CIO competition, has been forced to face the Negro issue more squarely. This was apparent in certain events of the 1944 AFL convention, held in New Orleans. At this convention the spot-light was turned on the race issue in a manner unprecedented in the history of the organization. Three spokesmen for the Negro attended the convention—two in addition to A. Philip Randolph who at previous conventions had carried the ball alone. Twenty other accredited Negro representatives were present. Eleven sweeping resolutions against racial discrimination were introduced during the course of the meetings. Although only the traditional, weak resolution was passed, the extensive discussion of the subject indicated that certain elements within the AFL were increasingly aware of the issue. Almost unprecedented also was the lack of segregation in the seating of white and colored members at an AFL meeting in the South.

At the same time that the AFL met in New Orleans, the CIO convened in Chicago. Numerous resolutions against race discrimination were presented and the strong anti-discrimination resolution unanimously passed by the convention delegates pledged the CIO to a cease-less fight against racial inequalities and recommended that all affiliated unions include non-discriminatory clauses in their contracts. In supporting this resolution, President Philip Murray stated, in part:[1]

"I think that this . . . provides an opportunity to invite, through the medium of this convention, all Negro workers eligible for membership in trade unions to promptly seek affiliation with CIO organizations. . . . I do really believe that the eventual economic emancipation and political emancipation of the colored people lies in their willingness to associate themselves with organizations such as are affiliated with the CIO. . . . God help the Negro in America, and God help the minority groups of America, were it not for the splendid work that is being done by this great institution of yours and mine. We don't confine ourselves to the mere adoption of resolutions in meetings of this kind; we make those resolutions effective and workable. . . .

"I regard this work, this particular work of protecting and advancing the cause of the Negro, as a holy and a noble work, the kind of a work that all right-thinking citizens, regardless of their status in life or their affiliation with other groups, should dedicate themselves to."

It is this kind of talk that has made most Negroes in Chicago, regardless of social class, look toward the labor movement with some hope. But while they accept the overtures of the labor movement they still do not dismantle their *racial* organizations. Rather they increase their demands for racial solidarity. They believe that their bargaining power *within* the labor movement will be strengthened if they stick together. Many feel that they have been wooed by the labor movement primarily because in the past they have demonstrated their strength.

CHAPTER 13

Democracy and Political Expediency

THE SOUTHERN NEGRO COMING TO MIDWEST METROPOLIS DURING THE Great Migration was not welcomed by white Chicagoans either as a neighbor or as a fellow worker. But there was one group which, if it did not welcome him, at least did not disdain to work with him and even assist him in adjusting to northern urban life—the politicians.

Politicians, especially those connected with the political machines of our great cities, are realists. The politicians of Midwest Metropolis may have had their own private deprecatory attitudes toward Negroes and may have resented their coming to the city, but they realized that the Negro had a commodity in which they were interested—the vote. Politicians are concerned with winning elections, and they were therefore willing to organize Negroes into the political machine, as they had done before with the Poles, the Irish and the Germans. It was necessary to learn new methods of appeal and, to some extent, a new vocabulary, but this presented no great difficulty to a group of worldly-wise persons who knew intimately the polyglot peoples of Midwest Metropolis. So the Negro vote was organized. The peasants from Mississippi and Alabama became a part of the body politic of the city.

The Negro entered the struggle for political power in Chicago with many disadvantages. As one student has observed, individual success in politics depends on access to large campaign funds, on the support of the daily newspapers, on a certain measure of social prestige, and on political experience and insight. The Negro had none of these advantages. The southern migrants who came streaming into Chicago during and after the First World War were poor and without property. They were a minority—and an unpopular and disliked minority. Not only did the press fail to present a sympathetic picture of their struggle for status and power, but as a rule it reported the most unfavorable aspects of their behavior. Moreover, the Negro migrants were totally inexperienced in the jungle politics of the city slum.

But the stakes for which the Negro was playing were high, and not even a background of frustration and failure, such as many brought with them, could daunt them as they faced the challenge of political emancipation. Through politics the Negro hoped to obtain justice in the courts; police protection and protection against the persecution of the police; the chance to get administrative jobs through civil service; and a fair share in playgrounds, libraries, sewers, and street lights. To win these and the many other benefits which political action offers to a socially subordinated group, the Negro overcame many of his difficulties with remarkable ingenuity. If he did not have enough money to finance his own campaigns, he made connections with rich white people—whether real-estate barons, bootleggers, or utility magnates. When he did not get support from the daily press, he utilized his own weeklies to foster community solidarity and political awareness. Though Negroes lacked experience, the more alert of them soon found their way around in the maze of city politics. They took over, and even improvised upon and improved, the techniques for getting out the vote, for organizing and controlling a political machine, and for trading and bargaining with candidates.

Politics became an important, perhaps the most important, method by which the Negro sought to change his status. It was often the only avenue open for struggle against caste tendencies. This struggle invested his political behavior, even when corrupt, with an importance and a dignity that similar behavior could not command in any other portion of the population. To paraphrase Lincoln Steffens, the Negro favored *representative* government, even if it was not always *clean* government.

EARLY NEGRO POLITICIANS

The political history of the Negro in Midwest Metropolis did not begin with the Great Migration. As far back as 1837, one George White, a Negro, served as the town-crier, doubtless by political appointment. As fugitive slaves began to gather in the city they were immediately caught up in the political whirligig. John Jones was elected county commissioner in the Forties. In 1876, J. W. E. Thomas, a native of Alabama who had come to Chicago at the age of twenty-six and started a grocery business, became the first Negro to sit in the State legislature.

While Negroes have traditionally supported the party of Abraham Lincoln, the colored vote of Midwest Metropolis was sought by the Democrats throughout the pre-Migration period. The famous Mayor

Carter H. Harrison I, a Democrat, was one of the first white politicians to win the support of a large percentage of the Negro electorate. Indeed, it was his administration which first attracted some Negroes to the Democratic party, and during his period of tenure the Colored Democratic League of Cook County was formed.*

Not until 1894, however, did the first powerful Negro politician emerge—Edward H. ("Ed") Wright. In that year, at a meeting of the First Ward voters, he urged his hearers to support the straight Republican ticket. The response was surprisingly favorable. The ward's support of the Republican candidate for mayor, George B. Swift, contributed greatly to his election. Since the delivery of Negro votes from Wright's ward was directly attributable to him, he became an important political figure over night. He managed to have a Negro, Theodore W. Jones, nominated for county commissioner at the Cook County Republican convention of 1894. As Gosnell has stated, "These were the days of the caucus, the convention, rough-and-tumble politics, 'boodle' aldermen, and public utility scandals." (In the 1896 Cook County Republican convention over one-third of the delegates were saloon-keepers.) Wright, with a capacity for hard work and keen insight into traction problems, not only played the rough-and-tumble game, but also became an expert on city problems extending far beyond the confines of the Negro community. In 1896, having dictated the appointment of other Negroes to important jobs, he now engineered his own election as county commissioner, and thus became the third colored man to hold that office. With his election he was established as the most forceful leader of the Negro electorate.

Wright's political shrewdness is illustrated by the method he used

* One of Harrison's biographers points out that although there were only 3,000 Negro voters in Chicago in 1890, Harrison carefully cultivated them. He was "one of the few Democrats who could make any headway with this race. . . . In one of his campaigns he sent out a circular in which his love for the dark-skinned race was painted in highly tinted colors, and the 'man and brother' was exhorted to cast his ballot for Harrison. In the election which followed, the *Inter-Ocean* estimated that at least half of the colored vote went for the former Kentucky planter [Harrison]." On one occasion when Harrison had been claiming that the blood of a half-dozen ethnic groups flowed in his veins, everyone was eager "to see whether he would slight the Negroes by neglecting to claim kin with them or scandalize his family by claiming such kinship. He did neither. He said that he was a southern gentleman, born in Kentucky, and that he was proud to state that he had been nursed by a Negro 'mammy,' and that (quickly twisting a bit of hair on his finger) he had a little kink in his hair." (Claudius O. Johnson, *op. cit.*, pp. 98, 196.)

to win the presidency of the county board. He told each member of the board, privately, that he would appreciate a vote for the presidency as a mark of recognition for his people. All the votes except two were cast for Wright; each man thought that he was just giving a token vote to Wright. Another instance of his political skill was manifested when he refused to authorize an appropriation for the office of State's Attorney Charles S. Deneen until that official fulfilled an earlier promise to appoint a Negro as assistant state's attorney. Deneen appointed Ferdinand L. Barnett, and the appropriation was granted.

In 1897 Carter H. Harrison II was a candidate for mayor. Capitalizing upon the reputation of the elder Harrison as the source from which Negro Democrats had received their first inspiration, his son won considerable Negro support. Shortly after his election, Harrison appointed S. A. T. Watkins assistant city prosecuting attorney, and Robert M. Mitchell was given an appointment of like importance. In spite of the Negro's Republican tradition, young Harrison expressed the belief that "the Negro will divide his vote if the proper intelligence is displayed in seeking it." Harrison continued in office until 1905 and was supported by a large portion of the Negro vote.

Throughout this period Negroes were active in the Republican party also. In 1894 John C. Buckner, a Republican, was elected to the Illinois House of Representatives. Little is known of his background before his election except that he had worked as headwaiter at private parties and had participated in the establishment of the Ninth Battalion, a Negro unit of the State Militia. In 1895 Governor Altgeld accepted the application of this body for transformation into the Eighth Regiment of the Illinois National Guard, with Buckner commanding it as major. He served a second term in the legislature from 1896 to 1898, representing the Fifth Senatorial District.

Following Buckner, William L. Martin, a lawyer, was elected to the legislature in 1898. Martin has been characterized as "just a half-wit wonderfully bright along some lines." His record in the legislature was undistinguished.

The continuity of Negro representation in the Illinois House of Representatives, unbroken since 1882, was maintained in 1900 by the election of John G. Jones. The next Negro member, Edward H. Morris, was so vigorous a personality that the Republicans made him floor leader, "to keep the Speaker out of trouble."

By 1904, the Black Belt's most colorful politician had emerged—Oscar DePriest, later to become a Congressman. He was then holding office as county commissioner. The Chicago *Tribune* smugly charged that DePriest was "a low-grade Negro politician" with no standing in the community; but DePriest, along with Buckner, was a main assistant to Martin B. Madden, the powerful white political boss on the South Side. DePriest's ability as an organizer had attracted the attention of Congressman Madden, and he was placed on the Republican ticket for the office of alderman in the spring of 1904, when the question of representation of the Third Ward came up for discussion in the Republican caucus. DePriest lost, but at least he had been allowed to run.

In 1906 the first Negro made a bid for the office of judge of the Municipal Court. Ferdinand L. Barnett, previously mentioned as editor of the *Conservator,* who had been appointed assistant state's attorney by Deneen, was endorsed by the Chicago Bar Association. Barnett was defeated by white Republicans, who stated openly that they would not support a Negro candidate for judge. He was the only Republican candidate defeated at the polls, losing by 304 votes. Twenty years went by before a Negro secured a judgeship.

In 1910 Edward H. Wright ran against a field of white candidates for alderman of the Second Ward. He, like DePriest, was defeated; but he had demonstrated that a militant Negro leader could attract Negro votes in an area that was rapidly becoming race-conscious. Thus ended the first chapter of the Negro in politics in Chicago.

"BIG BILL"—LITTLE LINCOLN

As we have mentioned in Chapter 6, Negroes became a powerful political force in Midwest Metropolis during the first administration of William Hale Thompson ("Big Bill, the Builder"). Thompson was elected for his first term in 1915, served until 1923, was voted out of office and then returned for a four-year period, 1927-31. The Republican party was riven with factionalism and Thompson needed a solid bloc of votes on which he could depend. The thousands of Negro migrants pouring into the city—poor, feared and despised by large sections of the white community—were welcomed by Thompson as a potential source of votes. He cultivated them, and thus drew the fire of a wide circle of enemies. Of Thompson, Gosnell has said:[1]

As mayor of the city . . . , he was hailed as "Big Bill, the Builder," Chicago's greatest booster, the defender of the weak, the champion of the people, while at the same time in certain newspapers the word "Thompsonism" came to be a symbol for spoils politics, police scandals, school-board scandals, padded pay-rolls, gangster alliances, betrayal of the public trust, bizarre campaign methods, and buffoonery in public office.

But this was not important to the Negro voters, for in Thompson they had at last found someone who valued their friendship and gave them jobs, protection, and, above all, the recognition for which they hungered. In the four primary elections at which Thompson was a candidate for mayor, he received over 80 per cent of the total Republican primary vote cast in the Second Ward, the ward with the largest proportion of Negro votes. In fact, he obtained such a hold over the Negro voters that in 1923, when he was not a candidate, he was able to deliver to William E. Dever, a Democratic candidate, 60 per cent of the Negro vote in the rock-ribbed Republican Second Ward, as a gesture to spite the Republican faction which had dropped him from the ticket.

What was the secret of Thompson's popularity among the Negro voters? [asks Gosnell, who then proceeds to analyze the appeal of "Big Bill."] Thompson's showmanship, bombastic style of oratory, ready platform wit, geniality, and practical ethics appealed to many Negroes as well as to many whites. . . . He was "Big Bill," the mayor, who did not hesitate to stand up for their rights. . . . His opponent was a southern "cracker"; he discriminated against Negroes; he was supported by "the dirty lying sheet, the Chicago *Tribune.*" . . . There was clearly a friendly feeling between the chief executive of the city and his listeners. To have a friend in the powerful position who could wrest benefits from a hostile community. That was something worth having. Who else was more deserving of their support? [2]

Another factor that helped Thompson to hold the Negro voters during the postwar period was the hostility of the Democrats. When Thompson promised Negroes jobs and protection, the Democrats used the promise as a means of stirring up race feeling among whites. Calliopes playing "Bye, Bye, Blackbird" were sent through the streets, and leaflets were circulated displaying a trainload of Negroes en route from Georgia with Thompson as pilot of the train, and the caption: "This train will start for Chicago, April 6, if Thompson is elected."

The answer of Negro leaders was: "Elect Big Bill or it's going to be 'Bye, Bye, Blackbird' in Chicago."

But Thompson's popularity was based not alone on his satisfying the Negro community's need for recognition and even for protection. His Honor also gave out jobs. He gave out so many jobs to Negroes that some of his opponents called the City Hall "Uncle Tom's Cabin." Moreover, the Mayor gave Negroes responsible and conspicuous positions. Two of the most important appointments were that of E. H. Wright as assistant corporation counsel and of the Reverend Mr. Archibald Carey to an equally prominent post.

Thompson's rise to political power was coincident with and perhaps partially due to the Great Migration, which lasted from 1915 to 1925. The 1910-20 increase in the Negro population of Midwest Metropolis (from 44,103 to 109,458) amounted to 148 per cent. The following decade it rose by an additional 114 per cent—to 233,903. Most significant politically, however, was the *distribution* of the Negro population in Midwest Metropolis. The trend toward the greater concentration of Negroes in a single area was evident by 1910. At that time the areas with the greatest colored population were about 50 per cent Negro. These were located in wards one to four, the heaviest concentration being in wards two and three. The Black Belt spread till two wards became nearly completely Negro, and in three others the colored group was an important factor. Although the community had always contained persons of widely divergent interests and backgrounds, its compactness had facilitated economic, social, and political solidarity. Because of this, Negroes were able to elect two aldermen to the City Council, two representatives and a senator to the state legislature, and finally a congressman. While Negroes have generally been able to elect colored candidates on citywide tickets, without such rigid residential segregation few of these could have been elected, except in cases where the candidate was not known to be colored or had the staunch backing of the machine in power. As a prominent newspaperman stated in connection with a movement to break down segregation: "It's okay to break it down in principle and get a few Negroes over the line. But we want the majority to stay here so they can vote in a bloc."

This increase in the colored population of the city and the movement to force Negroes into a Black Ghetto were accompanied by much friction and even open violence, as witness the race riot of

1919. All was grist to the mill of Thompson, who with each new difficulty proved to his most consistent supporters that he was "a friend of The Race."

Each new wave of Negro migrants was recruited by the precinct captains, who were diligent about introducing them to the process of voting. Most of the migrants were closely attached to the Republican party, or, because of their southern background, were at least predisposed toward the party of Lincoln and Frederick Douglass. The dramatic appeals of the leaders knitted the community into an almost homogeneous political unit.

During the ten years that followed Thompson's rise to power Negroes made a number of gains. Oscar DePriest was elected to the city council, thus becoming the first Negro alderman. Because of an indictment just before the primary in 1917, DePriest refused to run for re-election, and Louis B. Anderson was nominated and elected with little opposition. Anderson served successive terms in the council for the next sixteen years. In 1918 Major R. R. Jackson, who had served three terms in the General Assembly, was elected alderman of the Second Ward; and when the ward lines were redrawn in 1921 he became the alderman of the Third Ward, in which capacity he served for twenty years. The number of Negroes in the state legislature rose to a peak of five in the lower house in 1928. In the state senate, the first Negro was elected in 1924—Adelbert H. Roberts. Finally, as the acme of achievement through Thompson's assistance, Oscar DePriest was elected to Congress, representing the First Congressional District. An even more difficult achievement, since it necessitated citywide support of a Negro candidate, was the election of Albert B. George as municipal court judge.

In appointive offices, too, Negroes advanced. They were well represented in the law departments of the city and state—in the offices of the city prosecutor, state's attorney, and corporation counsel. The peak of recognition of Negro lawyers came in Thompson's last administration, when six assistant corporation counsels, five assistant city prosecutors, and one assistant state's attorney were appointed. This recognition was due in part to the strategic position of Negroes in the Republican primaries, a factor employed to great advantage by the Negro political leaders in bargaining for places on the ticket and for organizational support. These favorable circumstances also allowed the Negro community to build up one of the smoothest-functioning machines in the city. It was during Thompson's regime that the machines in the Second and Third Wards were taken over by Negroes.

The first evidence that Negroes were strong enough and experienced enough to take over the ward machines was the election of Edward H. Wright as committeeman of the Second Ward in the primary of 1920. This was also the first indication that they had been really admitted into the inner councils of the Republican party, for the ward committeeman was the party's ward representative who distributed the patronage and had the power to nominate certain judges and to send representatives to party conventions. Already the recipient of several appointments at the hands of Mayor Thompson, Wright, although temporarily eclipsed by Alderman DePriest, was the outstanding Negro Republican. When he received the backing of Thompson for ward committeeman his election was assured. He remained the recognized spokesman of the dominant Republican faction for a period of six years.

In the next few years Wright built up one of the strongest ward organizations in the city. He kept a card index of his followers, whom he rewarded with positions or money in accordance with their delivery at the polls. He was able to wrest important jobs and favors from white politicians, and by threatening to vote for white candidates forced other ward committeemen to support his candidate. It was thus that he engineered the election of Judge Albert George in 1924. Later he was able to say, with substantial accuracy, "Every conspicuous political appointment of a colored man or woman in Chicago and Illinois from industrial commissioner and Illinois commerce commissioner down has been brought about by the Second Ward Republican organization under my leadership." Further, through his organization Wright was able to influence legislation. (He even won from the state legislature an act placing a statue in honor of Negro soldiers on one of the boulevards.) When testifying at the hearing of the Senate committee investigating campaign expenditures in 1926, Wright was asked about the Crowe-Barrett group in his ward. He answered: "Well, there isn't any Crowe-Barrett group in my ward . . . I am the group."

Through a factional fight, Wright lost control over the Second Ward soon after this, but the ward organization continued under the leadership of Daniel Jackson, who, it is alleged, was the head of a gambling syndicate. He was never the forceful leader that Wright had been, but he too kept the Second Ward organization a powerful factor in city politics with which all ward leaders had to deal.

In 1923 Mayor Thompson decided not to be a candidate to succeed himself, and William E. Dever, a Democrat, was elected Mayor. (During the "closed town" administration that followed in 1928, Dan Jackson was indicted for protecting gambling.) In 1927, however, Thompson again ran for mayor, receiving 94 per cent of the Republican primary vote and 91 per cent of the general election vote. The end of this term closed the reign of Big Bill Thompson.

If Thompson was not a "second Lincoln," as enthusiastic supporters sometimes called him, at least he had treated his Negro followers more fairly than they had ever been treated before. If he had allowed the community to be corrupted and had put into power Negroes connected with the underworld, he had nevertheless given recognition to the entire Negro population and offered it a hope for the future. If for the entire city he had been a buffoon and a corrupt politician, for Negroes he had made possible their own organization into ward machines which could and did demand concessions in return for support.

THE DEMOCRATS COME INTO POWER

In the mayoralty contest of 1931 Negroes again lined up behind their patron saint, Bill Thompson. Charges and invectives were hurled by Thompson against his opponent, Anton Cermak: "Your mayor is building playgrounds, Cermak is building jails." "Thompson is a public servant; Cermak is a public master." "Cermak fights for the multimillionaires." And Thompson's friends echoed: "Thompson is much poorer now than when he went into politics. Cermak has held public office twenty-eight years, starting as a poor boy, and is now worth seven million dollars." "I earned my money," answered Cermak; "Thompson was born with millions." He further accused Thompson of inciting race prejudice.

Other Republicans on the ticket promised more and better jobs to Negroes: "I will do everything in my power to appoint a Negro to the school board." "If elected I will appoint a colored man deputy coroner." "I will give colored people jobs of responsibility." Still other Republicans promised fair treatment in the courts. One judge said, "If elected judge I will ask to be placed at the Forty-eighth Street Station [in the heart of the Black Belt]. Anyone brought there will get justice." Another suggested: "If any one of you gets into trouble, see me or one of the boys here." Still others made straight party appeals: "This election means more than the election of Thompson. It means the salvation of the Republican party. When it's sunk, you're sunk." In great enthusiasm another white candidate, closing a speech endorsing a Jewish candidate, exclaimed: "With the Jews, Irish, and Negroes together we are going to give them a good licking."

This vigorous campaign with its not too subtly injected race issues succeeded in giving Thompson an overwhelming lead in the Negro wards. Cermak received his lowest relative vote in these wards. But Cermak was elected; and, not having received the support of the Negro community, he was under no obligation to reward it. Numbers of Negroes in important positions and any number who held temporary civil service appointments were dismissed. Although Negroes did not know it, they were facing a national change in political parties which would last for twelve years before the Republicans could make even local inroads.

In 1932 the presidential election was before the community. Again the majority of the Negro voters supported the Republican ticket. Hoover had not altogether pleased them, but they felt that they could take no chance with a Democratic candidate such as Roosevelt, who had served in the Wilson administration, especially as his running mate was "Cactus Jack" Garner of Texas. "Hoover," declared one orator, "is like Booker T. Washington, a man of God who has borne the sorrows of the world." Perhaps a more telling argument was, "If Roosevelt should die you would have 'Cactus Jack' Garner for president." Roosevelt received only an estimated 23 per cent of the Negro vote.

With that election there was a temporary eclipse in the influence of the Negro vote in Chicago. The power of the Second and Third Ward machines was no longer felt, as they were in the wrong column. Without patronage the ward machines began to disintegrate. On the other hand, without patronage—for that matter, without leadership—Negroes could not immediately build up a Democratic machine. The ward committeemanship in the Second Ward was in the control of a white man through a "rotten borough" system. However, one group —the policy men—were quick to shift their allegiance to the new party. Political protection was necessary for them to carry on their business.* By 1933, after a series of raids by the police, the "Jones Boys," who were among the largest operators, found it expedient to join the Democratic party.

Many Negroes were offered jobs and other favors to leave the Republican party. This led to demands for colored candidates on the Democratic ticket in 1934. "Mike" Sneed, who had won the committeemanship in the Third Ward in 1932, began to build a Negro Democratic machine in that ward. In the Second Ward Joe Tittinger, a white man, began to organize his area. With the election of Arthur W. Mitchell to Congress on the Democratic ticket in 1934, the shift to the Democrats was well on its way.

After Cermak's death Edward J. Kelly became mayor. He adopted a conciliatory attitude toward the Negro community. Not only did Mayor Kelly appoint Negroes to positions which had been given them by Mayor Thompson but in addition placed a Negro on the school board, made a Negro captain of the police, and gave still another the chairmanship of the Chicago Housing Authority. Kelly also had a Negro put on the ticket and elected as judge of the municipal court. With the election of William Dawson, a former Republican, as committeeman of the Second Ward to displace Tittinger, the transformation was complete. With less ballyhoo and bombast, Kelly had performed the same feat that Thompson had once performed. The Negro community was as strongly Democratic as it had previously been Republican. However, it remained for the national election to give the final blow to the old saying, "The Republican party is the ship, all else the sea."

WHAT THE NEW DEAL DEALT

Although for years the choice between the Republican and the Democratic parties was for the Negro largely a choice between Tweedledum and Tweedledee, with the coming of the New Deal some very definite issues arose on which Negro and white Democratic candidates could capitalize. The popularity of President Roosevelt is shown by the fact that he performed the miracle of transforming a large proportion of Negro voters from staunch Republicans to zealous supporters of the Democratic ticket. While in 1932 only an estimated 23 per cent of Chicago's Negro vote went to Roosevelt, 49 per cent

* See Chapter 17.

supported him in 1936, and 52 per cent in 1940. Perhaps one of the most important factors in that shift was the WPA. One of the "blues" recorded during that period eulogized this Federal agency:

> Please, Mr. President, listen to what I've got to say:
> You can take away all of the alphabet, but please leave that WPA.
> Now I went to the poll and voted, I know I voted the right way—
> So I'm asking you, Mr. President, don't take away that WPA!

One Negro preacher is reputed to have told his flock, "Let Jesus lead you and Roosevelt feed you!"

The Democrats were not slow in learning to use this appeal to Negro voters. "I want the WPA to stay—this is a fight for your jobs," stated one white candidate. Another argued: "Prosperity is here now. A living is what we all want. If the government spends millions, why should we worry? Riches come from the toilers—what does it matter if it is taken from those who accumulated it from the sweat and toil of the masses?" Against these powerful and persuasive arguments the Republicans had but a feeble answer to their job-hungry constituency: "The present administration is trying to make rich men poor and poor men poorer. The New Deal takes from those who have and gives to those who have not. There is no brotherhood in the present relief set-up." But who was looking for brotherhood when he could get a good WPA job?

One realistic Negro candidate was more adroit in attacking the Democrats. He said: "Fifty per cent of Negroes are out of work. We are the last to get jobs, and we have inadequate relief. Some Negroes who get on WPA are removed for white men. My platform is: jobs, security, better housing, higher wages, cash relief, old-age assistance— thirty dollars or more per month." This candidate decided to steal the Democrats' thunder by ignoring the fundamental differences between the two parties and outbidding the New Deal. Negro Democrats, too, were direct and realistic in exploiting the gains of the New Deal. "I hope," explained an ardent colored Democrat, "that if you are a WPA worker or a relief client, and vote against Roosevelt, the food you get will give you indigestion!"

Thus the policies of the national administration aided Mayor Kelly in his successful attempt to pry loose the Negro vote from the hold which the Republican party had had on it since Emancipation. Roosevelt, Kelly, and the WPA accomplished more with the Negro vote than had Thompson in spite of all the odds in his favor.

DR. WIN-THE-WAR AND HIS BLACK PATIENTS

In the spring of 1942, the President of the United States, in an effort to unify the country behind the war program, held out an olive branch to the conservatives and announced that Dr. New Deal was dead and that Dr. Win-the-War had taken his place. Negro Republicans were jubilant. They had found a chink in the Hero's armor and they let the arrows fly. The remnants of the once powerful Second Ward Republican machine, dreaming of the days of Thompson and Oscar DePriest, launched an attack upon the Democrats which seemed to make sense. "If the New Deal is dead," they argued, "it means that Roosevelt has sold out to Rankin and Bilbo and his gang of lynchers." Precinct workers and Republican leaders began to amass the evidence to document their case. Has the President spoken out against segregation in the army and navy? Has he supported the anti-lynching bill? Has he rebuked southerners who abuse Negro soldiers in uniform? Has he forced factories to employ Negroes on an equal basis with white people? Can Negro women become Lady Marines, Waves, Spars? In 1942 they were able to answer every one of these questions with a resounding NO! Meanwhile a champion arose on the national scene—Wendell Willkie. Without compromise, in straightforward language, and with a vigor that a man out of office could easily afford, Willkie supported a straight frontal attack on army Jim-Crow and on undemocratic practices wherever they existed. Black Metropolis began to listen to the Republicans with renewed interest.

During the four years preceding the presidential election of 1944, Republican hopes were high. Negroes were drifting back into steady jobs. They didn't have to vote for WPA any more. Time after time, southern Democratic Congressmen spewed forth their contempt for Negroes on the floors of Congress. It seemed likely that Negro voters would soon feel that it was time for a change. Republican hopes were raised tremendously by a perceptible drift away from the Democrats in the Illinois congressional elections of 1942 and 1943, and by the city aldermanic and mayoral elections of 1943. It looked as if the good old days of Negro Republican regularity might return. Many

Race Leaders felt that this was a good sign. If Democrats wanted to keep the Negro vote, let them show it by making some wartime concessions.

The first evidences of a swing away from the Democrats came in the congressional elections of 1942. Dawson, Negro Democratic incumbent from Black Metropolis, was fighting to retain the seat in Congress first captured by Republican Oscar DePriest. The Black Belt Republicans had a weak candidate opposing him, but they decided to campaign on the issue of "Why support a party dominated by Rankin and Bilbo?" Then, while the campaign was on, a lynching occurred in Duck Hill, Mississippi. It was one of those particularly horrible episodes in which two Negroes were not only hanged but were also fried to a crisp with blow-torches applied by white hands. Immediately thousands of leaflets flooded the Black Belt depicting the two Negroes hanging from a railroad trestle. Over the picture was a caption to the effect that "if you vote Democratic, you help pull the rope." In addition to this racial appeal, Dawson was bitterly attacked as a "Republican renegade" and a "tin-horn Hitler" who was trying to be a dictator in the Black Belt. Congressman Dawson weathered the storm, but his plurality was several thousand less than it had been before. A white senatorial candidate running on the Democratic ticket with him lost the Black Belt. The swing-back had begun.

In the winter and spring of 1943, the Democratic grip on the Black Belt was further weakened. There were two colored aldermen in the city council. One was a popular lawyer with a citywide reputation as a progressive leader. The Kelly-Nash machine feared him, however, because he was hard to handle. The other colored alderman was a "regular" Democrat, but he had been displaying an alarming amount of independence and was actively seeking CIO support. The regular Democratic machine was not anxious to see either of these men returned to the city council. In a bitterly fought primary campaign the "progressive" lost the nomination to an intelligent but pedestrian organization man. The other alderman managed to squeeze through. The Republicans, aware of this factionalism within the Democratic party, saw an opening and skillfully exploited it in the period between the primaries and the general election. They assailed the Democrats for "dictating the election of a man the Negroes don't want." They invited the defeated liberal to return to his "original home—the Republican party." They hinted that they might run him for Congress eventually. In the other ward, they played a trump card by prevailing upon the old warrior, Oscar DePriest, to emerge from his retirement to run again for alderman as he had first done in 1915. The magic of the DePriest name bowled over the Democratic opponent. Thus, on the local scene, the Republicans succeeded in defeating one Democratic alderman and in destroying the confidence of many Negroes in the sincerity of the Kelly-Nash Democratic machine. All through the campaign they hammered home the fact that southern Negrophobes dominated the national Democratic party.

In the spring of 1943 Midwest Metropolis prepared to elect a mayor. Kelly was very popular and Democrats appealed to Negroes to support their "best friend since Big Bill Thompson." They spent hundreds of dollars reminding the Black Belt of the housing project he had sponsored, the scores of persons he had appointed to various jobs, and his friendly, democratic, unprejudiced attitude toward Negroes. The Mayor himself stressed the fact that he was making plans for plenty of jobs when the Negro soldiers should come home. The Regular organization plugged the straight racial line.

For the first time a new political movement appeared in the Black Belt. Anticipating the organization of the National Citizens Political Action Committee and the CIO Political Action Committee by over a year, the liberal and labor forces in Midwest Metropolis began to experiment with independent political action. The liberals called off their traditional fight against "corrupt machine politics" and supported Mayor Kelly in order to checkmate the isolationist Republicans. The labor unions agreed to forget such incidents as the "Memorial Day Massacre" and to support the pro-Roosevelt Kelly as against the anti-labor Chicago *Tribune* Republicans. Both groups appealed to the Negroes on a broad basis of patriotism and progressivism. Though suspicious of these new allies, the Democrats needed them, and for the first time in Midwest Metropolis a broad coalition of liberal-labor leaders began to appeal to Negroes as political allies.* Black Metropolis be-

* In the light of the charges made a year later that labor political action was dominated by Communists, it is interesting to examine their role in this election. The Democratic party and the CIO frankly accepted the aid of Communists in organizing the electorate for this campaign and depended upon them for much of the onerous detail work, of canvassing and getting out the vote. It would be inaccurate, however, to say that the Communists "dominated" this political activity.

came a sort of experimental laboratory, and the labor action groups set up a headquarters with their card files and canvass books ready to prove that they could swing some of the Negro precincts behind the Democratic candidates.

Mayor Kelly carried the Negro vote, but by the narrowest margin he had ever received in the Black Belt. Without the labor action groups he might have lost it. But local political analysts are inclined to attribute the victory to a piece of clever work by the Regular organization. On the Saturday before the election, the Chicago *Defender* hit the streets with an enormous front-page facsimile of a restrictive covenant which the Republican candidate for mayor had signed barring Negroes from residence in his neighborhood. The exposé was a bombshell. The next day, Sunday, the Republicans sent several hundred thousand copies of a leaflet into the Black Belt implicating Kelly in a restrictive-covenant mess. They entrusted these to a white real-estate man who was a known defender of restrictive covenants, and asked him to deliver them to Oscar DePriest. As he walked up the steps of DePriest's home a strong-arm squad grabbed him and hustled him off to the police station, demanding that he be arraigned on a charge of bringing leaflets into the Black Belt designed to incite a riot. The Monday dailies carried front-page stories reciting the episode in detail and deploring the fact that one of the city's most respected white citizens had been "kidnapped by a band of Negro Democrats." But, in carrying the story, they naturally revealed the contents of the pamphlets and thus advertised the issue—RESTRICTIVE COVENANTS. Hardly a Negro voter could escape reading or hearing about the "kidnapping" of a white real-estate man by Negro Democrats. The Democratic machine denied complicity and dutifully denounced this lawless act. But, on Tuesday when the Negroes went to the polls, many Republican precincts voted against the candidate who had signed a restrictive covenant against Negroes. Kelly was in again, but he knew that his hold on the Black Belt was weakened.

The Democratic machine came out of these three elections somewhat battered. Meanwhile a national election was in the air. The Republicans began to oil up the machine for the great contest. The fact that the Republican convention was to meet in Midwest Metropolis lent added zest. But the Negro Republicans' ardor cooled considerably when it became evident that their champion Wendell Willkie would not be the party standard-bearer. They set to work, however, to build up Dewey as a friend of the Negro and to wait for a Democratic blunder.

Before the Republican hullabaloo had died down, the Democrats were in town for their convention. The Negro Democrats, too, had a champion, the vice-presidential candidate for nomination, Henry A. Wallace. For years the Negro press had reported his every speech and move, admiring him for his forthright defense of Negro rights. They were demoralized when Wallace was sacrificed in the interests of party harmony to Missouri-born Harry Truman. The Republicans immediately threw them on the defensive, with the query "What will happen to Negroes if Roosevelt dies and Truman of Missouri becomes president?"

Throughout the campaign period, both Republicans and Democrats vied in pinning the anti-Negro label on their opponents' candidates, or at least upon the party. The Democrats warned the party bigwigs that the northern Negro vote was in danger. Congressman Dawson of Black Metropolis was ultimately appointed to the Democratic National Committee to help deliver the vote to Roosevelt, and the fight was on.

The break in Roosevelt's favor probably came during the summer of 1944 when a group of transit workers in Philadelphia struck against the upgrading of Negroes. Roosevelt faced a showdown. His own FEPC had been defied. What would he do? The fate of Negro votes in a half-dozen northern cities hung on this episode. Negro Democrats breathed a sigh of relief when the army was ordered into Philadelphia and the Negroes' right to the jobs was upheld. From then on, Negroes throughout the country began to feel that, in a showdown, Dr. Win-the-War would write the effective prescription for his Negro patients. The clincher came a week before the election at a political rally in Chicago.

President Roosevelt came to Chicago on November 4, and the Kelly-Nash machine and the CIO Political Action Committee had 200,000 cheering spectators out to hear him, one of the largest political gatherings in American history. Negroes waited to see if the President would speak the Word. They were not disappointed. Four times within the speech, he struck the blow they were waiting for: He assailed the poll tax; he came out for a *permanent* FEPC; and twice he said that he believed in equal opportunity for all men regardless of race, creed, or *color*. Black Metropolis was jubilant. Roosevelt had waited until he came to the political capital of Negro America to make his pledge.

The next day, Henry Wallace, the repudiated hero, came to Black Metropolis and told a cheering audience that they could depend on the President to buck the Rankins and the Bilbos. Two days later, Black Metropolis gave the Democrats 65 per cent of its vote—the highest percentage Roosevelt had ever gained there.*

In a sense Chicago Negroes were voting to give the Democrats another chance before continuing their swing-back to the Republicans. But they did so only after Roosevelt had said in effect that he had resurrected Dr. New Deal. It is doubtful whether they would ever have extracted such an explicit pledge if the Republicans had not threatened to capture the Negro vote. Negroes in Midwest Metropolis had displayed unusual political maturity.

BLACK METROPOLIS VINDICATES "THE RACE" †

On January 29, 1901, George H. White of North Carolina, last of the Negro Congressmen elected during Reconstruction, made his farewell speech:

This, Mr. Chairman, is perhaps the Negro's temporary farewell to the American Congress; but let me say, Phoenix-like, he will rise up some day and come again. These parting words are in behalf of an outraged, heart-broken, bruised and bleeding, but God-fearing people, faithful, industrious and loyal people—full of potential force.

Negroes in the South had been disfranchised and there were not enough of them concentrated at any one spot in the North to elect a Congressman.

On December 18, 1929, a tall, rugged man, with snow-white hair, raised his six-foot frame from a seat in Congress to make his maiden speech. It was a plea for the passage of a bill to investigate American imperialism in Haiti, a measure supported by a number of southern Democratic legislators. His words dripped with sarcasm:

* Some political analysts feel that the Negro vote was won on patriotic and progressive economic issues rather than political issues. It is difficult to prove or disprove this thesis. The vigor with which both parties stressed *racial* issues would suggest that they were decisive, although Roosevelt's post-war economic program undoubtedly had an important appeal.

† This section is based on H. F. Gosnell's *Negro Politicians,* Chapters 4 and 9 (University of Chicago, 1935), from which comes all the quoted material on the Negro Congressmen.

I am very glad to see the gentlemen on the minority side of the House so very solicitous about the conditions of the black people in Haiti. I wish to God they were equally solicitous about the black people in America.

The speaker's skin was almost white, but he was a "colored" man—Oscar DePriest. A Negro had come again to Congress—after twenty-eight years—and Black Metropolis had sent him.

The story of how the black migrants from the South gathered their strength to fulfill George White's prophecy is a story of machine politics—Chicago style. It is the story of the way in which the "God-fearing people, faithful, industrious, and loyal people" are yoked with the gamblers, the prostitutes, and the demimonde and are led by forceful personalities to the conquest of political power. It is a typical story of politics in the "slum wards" of Midwest Metropolis, but it involves the destinies of thousands who shudder at the thought of "machine politics." It reveals the relationship between democracy and political expediency.

Oscar DePriest was born in Alabama six years after the Civil War closed. His father was a teamster, his mother a part-time laundress. Members of his family were so active in Reconstruction politics that when Negroes were disfranchised after 1875, they had to emigrate to save their lives. They moved to Kansas where young Oscar attended grammar school and took two years of bookkeeping and business at a normal school. Then, at the age of seventeen he struck out on his own and arrived in Chicago four years before the first World's Fair. He earned a living by painting and decorating, a trade he had picked up from his uncles. Since it was difficult for Negro craftsmen to secure steady work he sometimes passed for white. Eventually he met one white employer who not only gave him steady work in spite of his color, but also encouraged him to enter business for himself.

Soon after the turn of the century, DePriest was introduced to the intricacies of Chicago machine politics. He tells the story himself as follows:

A friend of mine came by one evening and said, "Come go to a meeting with me." I had nothing to do, so I went. It was a precinct meeting and they were electing precinct captains. The vote was 20-20 for rival candidates and I saw right away that a deal could be made. So I went to one of the candidates and said: "Now you're the man who ought to be captain—I'll give you two additional votes if you'll make me secretary."

The man refused. I went to his rival and made the same proposition. He accepted. I was made secretary. I kept at it because it was recreation to me. I always like a good fight; the chance, the suspense, interest me. I never gambled nor played cards so it was fun to me.

DePriest caught on quickly. He learned that each of the major parties had its "machine"—a tightly knit, hierarchical organization extending into every city block. At the bottom are the precincts, each with its captain dealing directly with a few hundred voters. The precinct captains owe their allegiance to a ward committeeman who dispenses the campaign funds provided by the city and county party organization, and who directs the campaign in the ward and is responsible to his superiors for delivering the vote. He is the real "boss" of the local area. All the ward committeemen, sitting as a body, make up the county central committee, whose chairman is the recognized head of the "organization." This body dictates policies, raises and supplies campaign funds, and carries out the line laid down by the State party organization. As secretary to a precinct captain, DePriest soon realized that a "machine" rises or falls according to the ability of individual captains to "deliver the vote." And he drew the conclusion that a group of precinct captains who stuck together could bargain with the higher-ups.

Working in the old Second Ward in the period before the First World War, DePriest became familiar with another political fact— that every community institution is dependent upon the machine in power. For instance, a man wishes to open a small business at a spot where the zoning ordinances forbid it. The precinct captain can arrange with the ward committeeman to "fix" it. Or a man may need to do a little "private business" with the Bureau of Licenses. Payment for services rendered or as "insurance" for future service is made through votes as well as actual cash.* "Donations" in cash and kind

---

* The proprietor of a small grocery described to an interviewer on the Cayton-Warner researches how pressure is sometimes applied to get out the vote:

"The precinct workers didn't know what party I belonged to, and I was determined to let it remain that way, because although I have a small business I find it profitable to be in the good graces of both parties. I have many Republican customers as well as Democratic, and of course these small-fry politicians take their politics very seriously. If it got around I was voting a Democratic ticket, the Republican precinct captain would tell his people not to trade with me. So I didn't want to vote and I told him he was wasting his time arguing with me

are also given for the machine's Christmas basket fund or for picnics and parties.

Within the ward, too, are various types of "protected" businesses—some illegal and some on the borderline. If they are to exist without continual molestation by the police, they must make their peace with the powers that be. Midwest Metropolis has always been a wide-open town, and the political machines have had rather close connections with these institutions of the underworld.*

Every family in a low-income area finds it expedient to "stay in" with the machine. When someone is in trouble, or if there is a problem of getting a bed in the county hospital or the sanitarium, the precinct captain can be depended upon to "fix" the matter. During a depression the machine is helpful in getting immediate relief. A church may have mortgage problems or need some free baptismal water—the committeeman can lend a hand. A social club may want to use a public park for an outing—the ward organization can arrange it. There is no pay-off connected with these favors. Good politics is the art of laying the

because I wasn't going to vote in the primary. I told him I liked —— and would give him a vote but I was very busy.

"He waited around a while then said, 'I see you are operating without any license.' I told him, 'Well, you are going to force me to vote, huh?' 'No,' he said; 'I am not going to force you to vote, but we need your vote and you have just about half an hour to vote, and we would like to have your vote. You would be wise to vote.'

"I went to the polls and voted. I had no alternative. I knew he was smart to discover my not having a license, and he was trying hard to carry his precinct, and the consequences would be much more damaging than voting; so I voted."

* See Chapter 17 for a detailed discussion of the tie-up between the policy racket and politics. One operator of a small gambling set-up described the political connections with the machine in 1939 as follows:

"If you have any idea of entering any sort of racket your best move is to first get in the good graces of the organization [political] and the syndicate [gambling organization]. Let's take this district as an example. You know, C—— is the head of it. He is the first man to see. Then he goes to L—— [ward committeeman], and it's so adjusted up the line except the police. Down at the City Hall they have a list of all the places the organization protects. If a place opens and the organization knows nothing of it, when it's reported to them they do not immediately raid it or close it down. The organization notifies the police captain, who goes to the place in operation. He asks for the operator and when he finds him he tells him only one thing and that is, 'You can't operate this place like this. It is unlawful; you had better get yourself straight.' The operator knows exactly what he means and proceeds to 'straighten' himself with the organization by paying off, and when that is done he has nothing else to fear from the police. Every week he pays off for the operation of his place and feels safe and secure."

voters under obligation so that they will deliver at the polls—the art of creating good-will.

For those who wish to be active in politics, however, there are rewards other than favors. People are paid for working the polls on election day; they are given a few dollars to use for drinks and carfare in getting out the vote. If they are intelligent and ambitious there are minor jobs for them at City Hall. And for the favored few there is the chance to win elective office.

DePriest became an expert in handling these intricate community relations and in organizing the energies of the people to support his own political advancement. His first independent political action was to organize a group of precinct captains for bargaining with Martin B. Madden, the white committeeman of the Second Ward. In 1904 DePriest got the nomination for county commissioner by assuring the ward committeeman of a bloc of votes he needed at the county convention. DePriest then won the election and served for four years, during which time "he helped educate the Negro poor to avail themselves of the relief resources of the county, and as a member of the building committee he secured some important contracts." In 1908 he got caught on the wrong side of a factional fight between his ward committeeman and a state senator; he was punished by being dropped from the ticket.

For the next six years DePriest concentrated upon making some money from his decorating business. He also began to dabble in real estate and "would take a long lease on a building that had been occupied exclusively by whites and then fill it with colored people. Since Negroes were charged higher rents than the whites, this business was profitable. In this way DePriest built up a private fortune which enabled him to become an investor in real estate, stocks and bonds." One observer justified these deals by saying that "if DePriest hadn't gotten it [money from the high rentals], someone else would have." Although he was not too active in politics, DePriest maintained friendly relations with the powerful ward boss, Madden. Three times when Negroes ran for alderman in the City Council during these years, DePriest supported the white candidate backed by Madden. Meanwhile, on the strength of his role as a leading businessman, DePriest was quietly preparing to make his own bid for the City Council.

By 1914 he felt strong enough to try for the aldermanic post. He solicited endorsements, arranged mass meetings, and built up such a large personal following that he was able to present the white Committeeman of the Second Ward with "the endorsements of thirty-eight precinct captains, the Hotel Waiters' Association, the Chicago Colored Barbers' Association, ministers of the Chicago Baptist Churches, ministers of the Chicago Methodist Churches, women's church clubs, the Physicians', Dentists' and Pharmaceutical Club, and many individual party workers." Madden, impressed by his genius for organization, also endorsed him, and thus he was able to run in the primaries as a "regular" candidate. Using his own money, DePriest put up such an effective campaign that he won by a plurality of 11,000 in a field of four candidates competing for 20,000 votes. His victory electrified the Negro community. The *Defender,* which had not supported him enthusiastically at first, now wrote:

In the Second Ward, where the voters of the Afro-American race in large numbers reside, the excitement was at fever heat. The race had one of its own on the ticket for alderman. . . . They came to the front 11,000 strong for Oscar DePriest, and for the first time in the history of Chicago a member of this race will sit in that august body.

DePriest represented the Negro Second Ward adjacent to the notorious First Ward—the city's leading white "vice area." It was impossible to "represent" such a ward without dealing with hundreds of voters who made their living by shady pursuits. It was almost inevitable that Alderman DePriest would be swept up along with others when the Democratic State's Attorney decided to lift the lid on the activities of the Chicago Republican machine. DePriest, along with several others, was indicted in 1917 for "conspiracy to allow gambling houses and houses of prostitution to operate and for bribery of police officers in connection with the protection of these houses." He was defended by none other than Clarence Darrow, who contended that while there had been a passage of money it was not for "protection" but was merely a campaign contribution for Mayor Thompson's Republican machine. He warned the jury against showing race prejudice when they judged DePriest. The verdict was "not guilty," but the machine suggested that Oscar get out of the limelight for a while, and not run again for the City Council.

DePriest had no intention of committing political suicide. The Black Belt was growing by leaps and bounds. There were votes in those precincts. With the odor of machine "corruption" about him and six indictments still hanging over his head, DePriest made a test run for the Republican nomination in the primaries and lost. He then proceeded to organize a "People's Movement" to sponsor him as an independent candidate, and so vigorous was his campaign that even without any patronage to dispense he polled 6,000 of the 15,000 votes that were cast. Hundreds of people saw him as the victim of a plot to defame a hard-hitting leader. On the strength of his 6,000 followers, DePriest in 1919 went over to the *anti-Thompson* faction of the party and secured its endorsement for the City Council post. But, although he delivered his 6,000 votes at the polls, they were not enough to pull him through. The Race Riot that year unified all the competing Negro Republican politicians around Mayor Thompson, "the friend of the Negro." De-Priest, too, came back into the fold, where he remained quietly for two years. *But he did not disband his People's Movement*—his personal following of at least 6,000 voters.

The Black Belt was growing fast, and after the Race Riot an adjustment was made in ward lines to make more homogeneous Negro political units. DePriest moved the headquarters of his People's Movement into the new Third Ward and began to gather together a personal following there. In 1923, Mayor Thompson did not run, but in order to show his strength in the Negro community he called upon his followers to deliver the Negro vote to the Democrats. That the delivery was made is testimony to the hold of both Thompson and De-Priest on the imagination of the Black Belt voters. DePriest then quickly made his peace with the very anti-Thompson faction he had fought—Senator McCormick's group. He delivered the vote to them.

Confident of his growing power, DePriest decided to run two of his independents against the Republican "regular" candidates for aldermen of the Second and Third Wards. He dramatized the battle as one of "the Outs" against "the Ins." He charged the incumbents with responsibility for "dirty streets and alleys, the growth of vice, the misery brought upon the families of the discharged officeholders, the lack of adequate police protection, the lack of bathing beaches and recreational facilities." The People's Movement polled about 6,000 votes in each ward, but its candidates lost. Four times now the DePriest forces had been routed, but Oscar kept at it.

At this point DePriest began a "crusade" for the restoration of Big Bill Thompson to power. Ringing doorbells, visiting gambling dens, speaking at churches, saying the good word to neighbors, the People's Movement preached the Gospel of the Good Old Days when Big Bill, the "Little Lincoln," ran the City Hall. Patiently, one by one, the De-Priest forces gathered Thompson pledge cards. And DePriest paid for much of this activity out of his own pocket. In 1928 Big Bill was again swept into power on a wave of reaction against the closed-town Democratic administration; but he could never have turned the trick without the Black Belt vote. He rewarded DePriest with the coveted prize of the Third Ward—the post of Ward Committeeman. With all the precinct machinery now in his hands and with plenty of patronage to dispense, Oscar immediately used his power to rally the Negroes behind his political mentor, Ccngressman Madden, in his fight for re-election.

Madden was opposed in the Republican primaries by a young Negro lawyer, a college graduate, and a World War veteran, William L. Dawson. He appealed to the Negroes to send him to Congress:

Mr. Madden, the present Congressman, does not even live in the district. He is a white man. Therefore, for these two reasons if no others, he can hardly voice the hopes, ideals, and sentiments of the majority of the district.

Thompson came into the Black Belt to support Madden, declaring that

a Negro might go to Congress and after serving there for twenty years *might* become chairman of the powerful finance committee; perhaps he might—*perhaps.*

He was surprised when his hitherto loyal Negro supporters hissed and booed him. Yet DePriest supported Madden. For the time being he put party regularity above "race loyalty." He was playing for high stakes and he didn't believe in pressing his shots too hard.

Then one of those rare accidents happened which often speed up a historical trend. Madden died between his nomination in the primaries and the general election. DePriest struck fast and hard. He was out of town, but he wired all of his fellow ward committeemen (the group that would choose Madden's successor) that he expected their support for the job. He then telegraphed Mayor Thompson. As Gosnell phrases it, "DePriest had the nomination before the other aspirants woke up as to what was happening." Big Bill, who had opposed Dawson's candidacy, said a few years later to a Black Belt audience:

"I used to come to you and say to you that Bill Thompson would be the last one who would put his hand on a Negro's head to prevent him from rising higher. Yet I used to ask you to vote for a white man for Congress—the Honorable Martin B. Madden—not because I was for a white man, but because I was for Martin B. Madden, Calvin Coolidge, Len Small, Bill Thompson. Martin B. Madden was fighting to complete the waterway. Why did we keep him there? Because of the great work Madden was doing.

"When he died there came some Judas from Washington and said to me, 'We don't want a Negro Congressman. You're the man that can keep a Negro out of Congress.' I said, 'If I'm the one man who can keep a Negro out of Congress, then, by God, there'll be one there.'"

When the regular election took place DePriest carried the district by the small plurality of 4,000. Several factors helped to reduce the margin of his victory. A Negro independent ran against what he called "disreputable leadership of the gangster, gambler, grafter type." Also, before the campaign was well under way a Special Grand Jury returned an indictment against DePriest for "aiding, abetting, and inducing South Side racketeers to operate gambling houses and disorderly places and to protect them from the police." Many white voters in the Congressional district refused to vote for him. But, small though his margin was, he had the satisfaction of being elected—the first Negro Congressman from a northern state.

There was still the question whether he would ever be allowed to take his seat in Congress. The eyes of the country were on machine politics in Illinois. Only two years earlier, Senator-elect Frank L. Smith had been denied his seat after it was revealed that power-magnate Samuel Insull had put $150,000 into his campaign fund at a time when Smith was head of the state commission in control of public utilities. A few days before Congress convened, the State's Attorney announced that the evidence against DePriest was "insufficient to warrant the defendant's being brought to trial," and the case was dismissed. But the rumor was abroad that certain southern Congressmen planned to challenge DePriest when he was being sworn in. Mrs. McCormick, widow of that Senator McCormick whom DePriest had once supported in a factional fight, got to work behind the scenes in Washington. When Speaker Longworth swore-in the 1928 Congress he broke precedent and swore-in the whole body at one time. The usual procedure was to swear them in in small groups and to allow challenges from fellow Congressmen. The Party looks out for its own!

DePriest remained in Congress for two terms. Then factional quarrels within the Republican party and the Democratic shift in 1932 unseated him. The Democratic machine was now in power. It, too, ran a Negro, Arthur Mitchell, a graduate of Tuskegee. Meanwhile William L. Dawson, whom DePriest had opposed in 1928 in favor of a white man, had come over to the Democrats. He built a strong unit of the Kelly-Nash machine in his Black Belt ward and became ward committeeman. We have already mentioned the prominent part that he ultimately played in both local and national politics. DePriest, however, remained something of a legendary figure, the pioneer who was first to crash the City Hall, and then the halls of Congress.

Negroes throughout America have come to regard the Negro representative from Illinois as their lone "watchdog" in Congress—and as the symbol of their struggle for status.* DePriest defended Negroes with vigorous speeches on the floor. He fought for larger appropriations for Howard University. He defied all attempts at segregation in the Capital City. He was idolized as a fearless man who did not hesitate to travel all through the South speaking straight from the shoulder. He accepted the role of the national champion and enjoyed it. He especially relished an opportunity to pillory the South, as in following comment on certain habits of some white southern males:

I spoke in Nashville, Tennessee. Someone said I should talk on social equality of the races. But the whites of the South are not an appropriate audience for talk of social equality. The Federal census shows an increase by thousands and thousands in the birth of mulattoes, mostly in the South. They have Jim-Crow theater laws and Jim-Crow streetcar laws, but what they need is Jim-Crow bedroom laws.

Arthur W. Mitchell, the Democrat who followed DePriest, was never a popular Congressman, partly because he displayed little of the dash and vigor which DePriest had developed in the hurly-burly of Chicago machine politics. Dawson, who followed Mitchell, while less colorful than DePriest was more forceful than Mitchell. He carried on the tradition of "the fighting Congressman." Negroes, realizing that

* In 1944 New York elected a Negro to Congress, the Rev. A. Clayton Powell,

one Negro Congressman can wield but little actual power, expect him to make up in vigorous language for his inability to influence legislation decisively.

WINNING THE "NEGRO VOTE"

Political expediency is a powerful lever in obtaining some concessions for the Negro from the larger white society. Perhaps the greater part of what white candidates say on the platform before election will not be followed by appropriate action; but it is important for the community that it be said. This not only gives the Negroes some immediate satisfaction but also builds up their expectations (in spite of their cynicism) and makes them demand and expect better treatment than that they have been accorded.

The appeals that white candidates make to obtain Negro votes are varied. Nothing is too "corny" or sentimental to "pull" on the electorate —especially if this helps them to escape a discussion of actual specific problems. Here are a few examples:

"I'm Your Friend:"

When I look over the railing I don't see black or white or red—I see human souls and others to deal with.

The characteristic gratitude of your race will cause you to support those who have helped you.

I have gotten to be the father of the colored people in Chicago in every way. We are making history—your race and mine [Irish].

We must stick together and not abuse one another—the Jew and the Irish stick together.

I am proud to say that I was elected by the colored vote.

Another candidate referred several times to the fact that one of the Negro leaders had said that "he must have Negro blood in his veins." Other white candidates stated:

Thanks for having been placed on the ticket—I am one of you.

I have been a close friend of your alderman for twenty years.

Every colored man should vote for every colored candidate. If you don't vote for them, nobody will.

I am very fond of colored people. I have a Negro chauffeur and a Negro laundry woman.

I don't go around talking about my "black mammy" like my opponent.

If elected, I will work for the fair distribution of patronage.

If you elect me, I will do all I can to obtain jobs for Negroes.

"Don't Desert the Party:"
Roosevelt asks you to send a Democratic Congressman.

Do not bite the hand that feeds you.

My politics is like my religion—I never change. I am careful about serving the Lord and voting the Republican ticket.

The Republican party safeguards your liberty; Democrats don't even know the Lord's Prayer.

If Lincoln were alive today, he would be a Democrat.

The Republican party is like old-time religion—it was good enough for my father and it's good enough for me.

The Republican party is the party for all, regardless of race, color, or creed.

"Bread and Butter:"
I want the WPA to stay—this is a fight for your jobs.

Relief is leading us back into slavery.

"On My Record:"
I will continue to fight for an anti-lynch bill; I appreciate what you have done for me.

Thanks for the vote you gave me in the primary. This means that I am a good servant.

The Negro does not need a master, he needs a servant. That is what I am going to be—your servant.

I have learned a great deal during the four years I have been out of office. I will be a better judge than ever before.

The extent to which some speakers will go in their effort to court the vote is shown in the following instance. The speaker appeared on the platform with a bundle under his arm which, when unfurled, proved to be a banner about three feet square. On it an acrostic with the candidate's name was printed in large letters:

F for faithfulness
E for earnestness
L for loyalty
D for duty
O for obedience to law
T for truth
T for trustworthiness

"Damn the Democrats:"
The Democratic party is controlled by devils from below the Mason-Dixon line.

The Democrats make apologies for having Negroes working in their offices.

Negro candidates are no less dramatic in their appeal for support. They have, however, an advantage. Being colored themselves, they can criticize other Negroes more freely and be much more specific in their promises and demands. Here is what colored candidates say at election time.

Racial Appeal:
The Republicans of today have deserted the true principles of the party as interpreted by Lincoln.

Negro high-school and university graduates need an opportunity to work. If I am elected, I will work for such opportunities.

How can a Negro be a Democrat, like Mrs. Bethune? She can't even walk the sidewalks in Georgia.

My grandmother was forced to bear babies for a white master. How can I be a Democrat?

Let us purge the colored people of all the old-time, reactionary, do-nothing, handkerchief-headed Republicans.

M—— apologizes for being a Negro. I am proud to be a Negro.

When white men are wrong on the race issue, they are wrong on everything.

We want a man in Congress who will tell southern white men, "I am as good as you are."

The Negro should divide his voting strength between the major parties. Political solidarity is a myth.

When Negroes learn not to knife each other, we can hope to get somewhere.

We in the Fourth Ward are going to vote for the first man to elevate black womanhood.

We are not going to vote for any man whose home town will not allow Negroes to get off the train there.

We want the man who if he was not colored would be president of the United States—that sterling American, Oscar DePriest.

These candidates may prate of brotherly love, but to test them, try eating in the same house.

The Negro has a "place," and that "place" is where the Negro can reach.

Five hundred years from now, black men and women will sit in this Congress. It will be done without making the black race white or the white race any blacker.

They say that if you vote for me you can't play policy. That's a lie. How can I be expected to stop policy? If money should be made from Negroes, let a Negro make it and not some out-of-town outside interest.

We don't want humility—we want someone who will have courage to stand up and speak out against indignity and oppression.

Economic Appeal:
The alliance of the Negro to the Democratic party will make it a poor man's party. New blood will help rectify the evils of the party.

The Republicans' theory is to give to those at the top first. Those at the bottom get what trickles through.

Patriotic and Party Appeal:
It is not important who is on the ticket. Party is the important thing.

I am for the Democratic party and for the President, who is trying to make the country so we will be proud to say, "I am an American."

In their effort to influence the voters of the community to support them, these appeals are made by the formal political organizations and the leaders of the informal and temporary alliances which have been made with business interests, churches, voluntary organizations, and the underworld. The most spectacular method of appealing for the vote is through the political meeting.

THE POLITICAL MEETING

One writer has compared the political meetings in the Negro community to the religious revival or the camp meeting. They are, Gosnell points out,[3] charged with great emotional appeal: A Negro mass audience is attentive, enthusiastic, good-natured, and content to sit for many hours on uncomfortable seats. When a speaker says something which strikes a popular chord, people yell, clap, or wave programs, hats, or hands in the air. Politics is evidently something which is very close to their experiences and their racial aspirations. They act as if their jobs, their freedom, their right to vote, their happiness, their very lives almost are at stake unless their candidates win.

The following is an account of a meeting held at the height of the Depression before Dawson shifted to the Democratic party and displaced Mitchell as Congressman.

The meeting was in a very large room in an old, dilapidated building, probably at one time a dance hall. Between 250 and 300 persons were present, most of them workers and precinct captains in Alderman Dawson's organization. They seemed to be a rather poor, forlorn group for the most part, running from middle-aged to elderly, with a few young people scattered here and there. Apparently they were mostly southern migrants who still clung to the old traditional Republican ideology.

The first speaker was an elderly gentleman, a rock-ribbed Republican, a long-time member of the Second Ward organization. He said:

"We are worshiping a great cause. If I were a preacher I would take a text in the Psalms: 'Oh, how well it is for men to dwell together in unity!' We need prayer more than anything else on earth. A lot of our folks seem hypocrites because of the misfortune that befell them here in Illinois, the home of Lincoln, who cut the shackles from the legs of your grandparents and made it possible for us to be here above the Mason-Dixon line. We should give some credit to the Republican party. Of course you have a right to be anything—Communist, Socialist, even Democrat; but first you should consult God. We are tired of white people using us as drawers of water and hewers of wood. In this cruel world no one loves anybody. They only crave for dollars. We are not as interested in this fight as we ought to be—there are too many empty chairs.

"I was in Mitchell's [Negro congressman] office and had a talk with him for two hours. He gave me some of his speeches and told me he gave 50 white boys jobs and 50 colored boys jobs. Now I am not prejudiced, but I asked Mr. Mitchell, 'Do you think you are doing us justice?' There are 434 white Congressmen to look out for the whites. We have fifteen million Negroes in America to help. Friends, get your heart in this thing!"

Another speaker took the floor:

"We are leaders of a family. Our family has become separated in the last four or five years. A lot of us cannot stand pressure. Yet it is painful to have a lot of children and they crying for food and bread. People have left their party affiliations—many have gone Socialist, Communist; some have turned their backs on the Republican ticket and turned Democrats because of poverty, hunger, and lack of work. It reminds me of the parable of Abraham just as he was about to sacrifice his son on an altar but a hand stayed him. I thought about that today downtown in the City Hall in the Council Chamber.

"There are many people now on WPA, some making $85 and some $105. All of that money comes from Washington. Send Dawson to Washington to get us more money."

This talk was followed by music. Miss Pitts of the Ninety-ninth Precinct sang "I'll Tell It Wherever I Go."

Dawson then addressed the meeting and introduced Stanton DePriest, son of Oscar DePriest, the first Negro Congressman from Chicago. DePriest said:

"History is repeating itself.

> Lives of great men all remind us
> We can make our lives sublime,
> And departing leave behind us
> Footprints on the sands of time.

You know and I know the dire necessity of having a county commissioner. For thirty years we have been deprived of representation. You all know the slogan on which our government is founded, 'Taxation without representation is tyranny.' The same is true today, and I will be your county commissioner after November 8. The conditions are terrible at the county hospital. It is all the fault of the Democrats. The Democrats never played fair with the black man."

DePriest was followed by Representative Harewood of the state legislature (a Negro), who said:

"PWA, WPA, relief, etc., is here to stay. We need a man who can get the most for us. We need Dawson to protect us from American Fascists. We need more men like Dawson in the high councils of the Republican party."

Evangelist Essie Whitman was called on to sing two original songs she had composed about Dawson.

Dawson said: "We must have a record made of those songs. I like the part she sang about Mitchell having to grow up."

Mrs. Keller then addressed the meeting:

"It is up to us to make Mitchell moan and groan. We should give him the cramps because he has done nothing for us. Dawson is the man of the people and for the people. He is a friend of his race and the champion of his people. We need he-men of this black group to represent us. It is only seventy-five years this side of Emancipation—Lincoln would roll over in his grave. It is time we woke up our racial pride and sent Dawson to Congress. We want a fearless man to fight for the black race."

Two solos followed: "The World Is Mine Tonight," dedicated to the Republican party, and "Without a Song," dedicated to the Democratic party.

Alderman Robert R. Jackson closed the meeting with these stirring words:

"We must stick together to get somewhere as a race. Every Jew will hunt for and vote for a Jew. The same for the Irish and every other race. The Negro can't find a Negro's name to save his life. Look for his name until you find it! He's your own flesh and blood, and nobody is going to vote for him if you don't. We are going into the Second Ward to help William L. Dawson—by telephone, telegraph, and tell-a-woman, the great agencies of communication in the world."

The Republicans were not strong enough to send Dawson to Congress, despite their enthusiasm. He shifted his party and the Democrats sent him to Washington!

Much of the political history of Midwest Metropolis has involved the fight of reform groups against "machine politics." Negroes, as a low-income group, looked down upon by the white middle class and feared by white labor, have seldom supported the reformers. They have preferred to deal with hardheaded realists who are willing to trade political positions and favorable legislation for votes. A cynical realism has pervaded Black Metropolis which sees democracy as something granted to Negroes on the basis of political expediency rather than as a right. In the past this has meant dealing with "corrupt" machines, and even the clergy have not hesitated to play the game.*

Since 1930, the local Democratic machine has been tremendously influenced by the tone of national "welfare politics" and by the growing influence of the industrial unions. The "sordid" aspects of political life still remain; but, as large sections of the Negro electorate have come under the influence of labor political action groups, the general level of political life has been appreciably raised. So long, however, as Midwest Metropolis is run by a machine, Black Metropolis will reflect, in microcosm, the pattern of the city's political life—in fact, it reflects, and refracts, every aspect of the larger city's life.

* There have been one or two very prominent Negro clergymen closely associated with the Republican machine. One of these, a bishop, was appointed to the Civil Service Commission, and like DePriest became involved in bribery scandals.

PART III

CHAPTER 14

Bronzeville

Ezekiel saw a wheel—
Wheel in the middle of a wheel—
The big wheel run by faith,
An' the little wheel run by the grace of God—
Ezekiel saw a wheel.

—Negro spiritual

STAND IN THE CENTER OF THE BLACK BELT—AT CHICAGO'S 47TH ST. AND South Parkway. Around you swirls a continuous eddy of faces—black, brown, olive, yellow, and white. Soon you will realize that this is not "just another neighborhood" of Midwest Metropolis. Glance at the newsstand on the corner. You will see the Chicago dailies—the *Tribune*, the *Times*, the *Herald-American*, the *News*, the *Sun*. But you will also find a number of weeklies headlining the activities of Negroes—Chicago's *Defender*, *Bee*, *News-Ledger*, and *Metropolitan News*, the Pittsburgh *Courier*, and a number of others. In the nearby drugstore colored clerks are bustling about. (They are seldom seen in other neighborhoods.) In most of the other stores, too, there are colored salespeople, although a white proprietor or manager usually looms in the offing. In the offices around you, colored doctors, dentists, and lawyers go about their duties. And a brown-skinned policeman saunters along swinging his club and glaring sternly at the urchins who dodge in and out among the shoppers.

Two large theaters will catch your eye with their billboards featuring Negro orchestras and vaudeville troupes, and the Negro great and near-great of Hollywood—Lena Horne, Rochester, Hattie McDaniels.

On a spring or summer day this spot, "47th and South Park," is the urban equivalent of a village square. In fact, Black Metropolis has a saying, "If you're trying to find a certain Negro in Chicago, stand on the corner of 47th and South Park long enough and you're bound to see him." There is continuous and colorful movement here—shoppers streaming in and out of stores; insurance agents turning in their collections at a funeral parlor; club reporters rushing into a newspaper office with their social notes; irate tenants filing complaints with the Office of Price Administration; job-seekers moving in and out of the United States Employment Office. Today a picket line may be calling attention to the "unfair labor practices" of a merchant. Tomorrow a girl may be selling tags on the corner for a hospital or community house. The next day you will find a group of boys soliciting signatures to place a Negro on the All-Star football team. And always a beggar or two will be in the background—a blind man, cup in hand, tapping his way along, or a legless veteran propped up against the side of a building. This is Bronzeville's central shopping district, where rents are highest and Negro merchants compete fiercely with whites for the choicest commercial spots. A few steps away from the intersection is the "largest Negro-owned department store in America," attempting to challenge the older and more experienced white retail establishments across the street. At an exclusive "Eat Shoppe" just off the boulevard, you may find a Negro Congressman or ex-Congressman dining at your elbow, or former heavyweight champion Jack Johnson, beret pushed back on his head, chuckling at the next table; in the private dining-room there may be a party of civic leaders, black and white, planning reforms. A few doors away, behind the Venetian blinds of a well-appointed tavern, the "big shots" of the sporting world crowd the bar on one side of the house, while the respectable "élite" takes its beers and "sizzling steaks" in the booths on the other side.

Within a half-mile radius of "47th and South Park" are clustered the major community institutions: the Negro-staffed Provident Hospital; the George Cleveland Hall Library (named for a colored physician); the YWCA; the "largest colored Catholic church in the country"; the "largest Protestant congregation in America"; the Black Belt's Hotel Grand; Parkway Community House; and the imposing Michigan Boulevard Garden Apartments for middle-income families.

As important as any of these is the large four-square-mile green, Washington Park—playground of the South Side. Here in the summer thousands of Negroes of all ages congregate to play softball and tennis, to swim, or just lounge around. Here during the Depression, stormy crowds met to listen to leaders of the unemployed.

Within Black Metropolis, there are neighborhood centers of activity having their own drugstores, grocery stores, theaters, poolrooms, taverns, and churches, but "47th and South Park" overshadows all other business areas in size and importance.

If you wander about a bit in Black Metropolis you will note that one of the most striking features of the area is the prevalence of churches, numbering some 500. Many of these edifices still bear the marks of previous ownership—six-pointed Stars of David, Hebrew and Swedish inscriptions, or names chiseled on old cornerstones which do not tally with those on new bulletin boards. On many of the business streets in the more run-down areas there are scores of "storefront" churches. To the uninitiated, this plethora of churches is no less baffling than the bewildering variety and the colorful extravagance of the names. Nowhere else in Midwest Metropolis could one find, within a stone's throw of one another, a Hebrew Baptist Church, a Baptized Believers' Holiness Church, a Universal Union Independent, a Church of Love and Faith, Spiritual, a Holy Mt. Zion Methodist Episcopal Independent, and a United Pentecostal Holiness Church. Or a cluster such as St. John's Christian Spiritual, Park Mission African Methodist Episcopal, Philadelphia Baptist, Little Rock Baptist, and the Aryan Full Gospel Mission, Spiritualist.

Churches are conspicuous, but to those who have eyes to see they are rivaled in number by another community institution, the policy station, which is to the Negro community what the race-horse bookie is to white neighborhoods. In these mysterious little shops, tucked away in basements or behind stores, one may place a dime bet and hope to win $20 if the numbers "fall right." Definitely illegal, but tolerated by the law, the policy station is a ubiquitous institution, absent only from the more exclusive residential neighborhoods.

In addition to these more or less legitimate institutions, "tea pads" and "reefer dens," "buffet flats" and "call houses" also flourish, known only to the habitués of the underworld and to those respectable patrons, white and colored, without whose faithful support they could not exist. (Since 1912, when Chicago's Red-light District was abolished, prostitution has become a clandestine affair, though open "street-walking" does occur in isolated areas.) An occasional feature story or news article in the daily press or in a Negro weekly throws a sudden light on one of these spots—a police raid or some unexpected tragedy; and then, as in all communities, it is forgotten.

In its thinking, Black Metropolis draws a clear line between the "shady" and the "respectable," the "sporting world" and the world of churches, clubs, and polite society. In practice, however, as we shall see, the line is a continuously shifting one and is hard to maintain, in the Black Metropolis as in other parts of Midwest Metropolis.

This is a community of stark contrasts, the facets of its life as varied as the colors of its people's skins. The tiny churches in deserted and dilapidated stores, with illiterately scrawled announcements on their painted windows, are marked off sharply from the fine edifices on the boulevards with stained-glass windows and electric bulletin boards. The rickety frame dwellings, sprawled along the railroad tracks, bespeak a way of life at an opposite pole from that of the quiet and well-groomed orderliness of middle-class neighborhoods. And many of the still stately-appearing old mansions, long since abandoned by Chicago's wealthy whites, conceal interiors that are foul and decayed.

THE ANATOMY OF A BLACK GHETTO

As we have seen in Chapter 8, the Black Belt has higher rates of sickness and death than the rest of the city, and the lowest average incomes. But misery is not spread evenly over the Black Ghetto, for Black Metropolis, as a part of Midwest Metropolis, has followed the same general pattern of city growth. Those Negroes who through the years have become prosperous tend to gravitate to stable neighborhoods far from the center of the city.* They have slowly filtered southward within the Black Belt. Always, however, they hit the invisible barbed-wire fence of restrictive covenants. The fence may be moved back a little here and there, but never fast enough nor far enough.

Out of this moving about, this twenty-five-year-old search for "a better neighborhood," has arisen a spatial pattern *within* the Black Belt similar to that found in the city as a whole. E. Franklin Frazier, a Negro sociologist, was the first to demonstrate clearly this progressive differentiation statistically. His *Negro Family in Chicago* graphically

* Faris and Dunham describe Black Metropolis as ". . . in general, similar in character to the foreign-born slum area," but add: "In the parts farther to the South live the Negroes who have resided longer in the city and who have been more successful economically. These communities have much the same character as the nearby apartment house areas inhabited by native-born whites." (Robert E. L. Faris, and H. Warren Dunham, *Mental Disorders in Urban Areas*, University of Chicago, 1939, p. 20.)

portrayed the existence of "zones" based on socio-economic status within Black Metropolis. (Figure 22.) The Cayton-Warner Research, some years later, revealed what happens in a ghetto when the successful and ambitious can't get out and when the city does not provide the poor and the vicious with enough living space, or enough incentive and opportunity to modify their style of life. (Figure 22.) The "worst" areas begin to encroach upon the "more desirable areas," and large "mixed" areas result. These, in turn, become gradually "worst," and the "more desirable" areas begin to suffer from "blight" and become "mixed." [1]

A few people from time to time do manage to escape from the Black Ghetto into the city's residential and commuters' zones. (Cf. Chapter 8.) They are immediately encysted by restrictive covenants and "sealed off." (Districts 1, 2, 21, 22, 23 in Figure 22.) Such settlements—"satellite areas"—are unable to expand freely, although there is a tendency, in time, for the white people in immediate proximity to move away.

THE SPIRIT OF BRONZEVILLE

"Ghetto" is a harsh term, carrying overtones of poverty and suffering, of exclusion and subordination. In Midwest Metropolis it is used by civic leaders when they want to shock complacency into action. Most of the ordinary people in the Black Belt refer to their community as "the South Side," but everybody is also familiar with another name for the area—Bronzeville. This name seems to have been used originally by an editor of the Chicago *Bee,* who, in 1930, sponsored a contest to elect a "Mayor of Bronzeville." A year or two later, when this newspaperman joined the *Defender* staff, he took his brain-child with him. The annual election of the "Mayor of Bronzeville" grew into a community event with a significance far beyond that of a circulation stunt. Each year a Board of Directors composed of outstanding citizens of the Black Belt takes charge of the mock-election. Ballots are cast at corner stores and in barbershops and poolrooms. The "Mayor," usually a businessman, is inaugurated with a colorful ceremony and a ball. Throughout his tenure he is expected to serve as a symbol of the community's aspirations. He visits churches, files protests with the Mayor of the city, and acts as official greeter of visitors to Bronzeville. Tens of thousands of people participate in the annual election of the "Mayor." In 1944-45, a physician was elected mayor.

Figure 22

ECOLOGICAL AREAS WITHIN NEGRO COMMUNITY

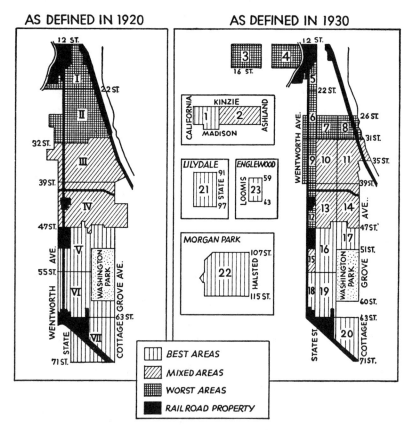

The "zones" (note Roman numerals) as defined in 1920 are from E. Franklin Frazier, *The Negro Family in Chicago,* University of Chicago Press, 1932. The "districts" (note Arabic numerals) as defined in 1930 are from Cayton-Warner Research maps. The "types of neighborhood" ("best," "mixed," and "worst") were defined by the latter group and have been superimposed on Frazier's zones. Neighborhood areas were classified on the basis of median rentals, median education, and juvenile delinquency, illegitimacy and insanity rates. Extensive demolition of substandard housing took place in the northern end of the Black Belt between 1920 and 1930.

Throughout the remainder of this book we shall use the term "Bronzeville" for Black Metropolis because it seems to express the feeling that the people have about their own community.* They *live* in the Black Belt and to them it is more than the "ghetto" revealed by statistical analysis.

The Axes of Life: What are the dominating interests, the "centers of orientation," the lines of attention, which claim the time and money of Bronzeville—the "axes of life" † around which individual and community life revolves? The most important of these are: (1) Staying Alive; (2) Having a Good Time; (3) Praising God; (4) Getting Ahead; (5) Advancing the Race.

The majority of Bronzeville's people will insist that they came to Midwest Metropolis to "better their condition." Usually they mean that they were seeking an opportunity to sell their labor for a steady supply of money to expend on food, clothing, housing, recreation, and plans for the future. They were also searching for adequate leisure time in which to enjoy themselves. Such goals are a part of the general American Dream. But when a Negro talks about "bettering his condition" he means something more: he refers also to finding an environment where exclusion and subordination by white men are not rubbed in his face—as they are in the South.

STAYING ALIVE

Before people can enjoy liberty or pursue happiness, they must maintain life. During the Fat Years the problem of earning a living was not an acute one for Negroes in Chicago. More than three-fourths of the Negro men and almost half of the women were gainfully employed, though their work tended to be heavy or menial. Wages were generally lower than for the bulk of the white working people, but they permitted a plane of living considerably higher than anything

---

* The expression "Bronze" when counterposed to "Black" reveals a tendency on the part of Negroes to avoid referring to themselves as "black." And, of course, as a descriptive term, the former is even more accurate than the latter, for most Negroes *are* brown.

† The term "axes of life" has been used by Samuel M. Strong, of the Cayton-Warner Research, to describe the dominant interests of Bronzeville. It is used here with some modifications of the original list that Strong compiled. (Cf. Samuel M. Strong, "The Social Type Method: Social Types in the Negro Community of Chicago," unpublished Ph.D. Thesis, University of Chicago, 1940.)

most parts of the South had to offer. Though the first few years of the Depression resulted in much actual suffering in Bronzeville, the WPA eventually provided a bedrock of subsistence which guaranteed food and clothing. The ministrations of social workers and wide education in the use of public health facilities seem to have actually raised the level of health in the Black Ghetto during the Depression years.* The Second World War once more incorporated Negroes into the productive economic life of Midwest Metropolis, and most of them had plenty of money to spend for the first time in a decade.

The high infant mortality and general death rates, the high incidence of disease, and the overcrowding and hazardous work, have all operated to keep the rate of natural increase for Negroes below that for whites. The man in the street is not aware of these statistical indices, but he does experience life in the Black Belt as a struggle for existence, a struggle which he consciously interprets as a fight against white people who deny Negroes the opportunity to compete for—and hold—"good jobs." Civic leaders, who see the whole picture, are also acutely aware of the role played by inadequate health and recreational facilities and poor housing. They also recognize the need for widespread adult education which will teach recent migrants how to make use of public health facilities and to protect themselves against disease. The struggle for survival proceeds on an unconscious level, except when it is highlighted by a depression, a race riot, or an economic conflict between Negroes and whites.

ENJOYING LIFE

Bronzeville's people have never let poverty, disease, and discrimination "get them down." The vigor with which they enjoy life seems to belie the gloomy observations of the statisticians and civic leaders who know the facts about the Black Ghetto. In the Lean Years as well as the Fat, Bronzeville has shared the general American interest in "having a good time." Its people like the movies and shows, athletic events, dancing, card-playing, and all the other recreational activities—commercial and noncommercial—which Midwest Metropolis offers. The

* Data concerning pre-Depression incomes assembled for this study indicate that in a significant number of cases even the bare subsistence level permitted by relief allowances and WPA wages constituted a definitely higher material standard of living for the lowest income group than did the wages earned in private industry during the Fat Years.

recreations of an industrial society reflect the need for an escape from the monotony of machine-tending and the discipline of office and factory. For the people of Bronzeville, "having a good time" also serves another function—escape from the tensions of contact with white people. Absorption in "pleasure" is, in part at least, a kind of adjustment to their separate, subordinate status in American life.

If working as servants, Negroes must be properly deferential to the white people upon whom they depend for meager wages and tips. In fact, they often have to overdo their act in order to earn a living; as they phrase it, they have to "Uncle Tom" to "Mr. Charley" a bit to survive. If working in a factory, they must take orders from a white managerial personnel and associate with white workers who, they know, do not accept them as social equals. If self-employed, they are continually frustrated by the indirect restrictions imposed upon Negro business and professional men. If civil servants, they are in continuous contact with situations that emphasize their ghetto existence and subordinate status. But, when work is over, the pressure of the white world is lifted. Within Bronzeville Negroes are at home. They find rest from white folks as well as from labor, and they make the most of it. In their homes, in lodge rooms and clubhouses, pool parlors and taverns, cabarets and movies, they can temporarily shake off the incubus of the white world. Their recreational activities parallel those of white people, but with distinctive nuances and shadings of behavior. What Bronzeville considers a good time—the pattern for enjoying life—is intimately connected with economic status, education, and social standing. A detailed discussion of recreational habits is therefore reserved for those chapters dealing with social class. Suffice it here to say that Bronzeville's people treasure their inalienable right to pursue happiness.

PRAISING THE LORD

It is a matter for continuous surprise that churches in America's large urban communities are able to compete with secular interests and to emerge even stronger than the church in rural areas.* Despite the fact that only about half of the adults in America claim church membership, the strong Protestant and Catholic tradition in the cul-

---

* "City churches, collectively speaking, are succeeding better than rural ones." (H. Paul Douglass and Edmund deS. Brunner, The Protestant Church as a Social Institution, Harper, New York, 1935, p. 44.)

ture retains its hold upon the minds of the American people. The church and religion have been displaced from the center of the average man's life, but remain an important side-interest for many people. The general trend toward secularization of interests has affected men more strongly than women, but probably the majority of Americans pay some lip-service to religion and participate occasionally in the rites and ceremonies—at least upon occasions of birth, marriage, and death.

It has become customary in America to refer to Negroes as a "religious people." The movies and the radio, by their selection of incident and dialogue, tend to reinforce this prevalent conception. A walk through Bronzeville also seems to lend confirmation to this belief, for the evidences of an interest in "praising the Lord" are everywhere— churches are omnipresent. Negroes have slightly more than their expected share of churches and twice their share of preachers; a large proportion of the people seem to enjoy "praising the Lord." The spirit of Bronzeville is tinctured with religion, but like "having a good time" the real importance of the church can be understood only by relating it to the economic and social status of the various groups in Bronzeville.

GETTING AHEAD

The dominating individual drive in American life is not "staying alive," nor "enjoying life," nor "praising the Lord"—it is "getting ahead." In its simplest terms this means progressively moving from low-paid to higher-paid jobs, acquiring a more comfortable home, laying up something for sickness and old age, and trying to make sure that the children will start out at a higher economic and cultural level than the parents. Individuals symbolize their progress by the way they spend their money—for clothes, real estate, automobiles, donations, entertaining; and the individual's choice is dictated largely in terms of the circle of society in which he moves or which he wishes to impress. These circles or groupings are myriad and complex, for not all people set their goals at the same distance. Out of the differential estimates of the meaning of success arise various social classes and "centers of orientation."

There are, of course, some small groups in Midwest Metropolis, as elsewhere, who interpret success in noneconomic terms, who prize "morality," or "culture," or talent and technical competence. In general, however, Americans believe that if a man is *really* "getting ahead," if he is *really* successful, his accomplishments will become translated into an effective increase in income. People are expected to "cash in" on brains or talent or political power.

For thousands of Negro migrants from the South, merely arriving in Bronzeville represented "getting ahead." Yet Negroes, like other Americans, share the general interest in getting ahead in more conventional terms. The Job Ceiling and the Black Ghetto limit free competition for the money and for residential symbols of success. Partly because of these limitations (which are not peculiar to Chicago) it has become customary among the masses of Negroes in America to center their interest upon living in the immediate present or upon going to heaven—upon "having a good time" or "praising the Lord." Though some derive their prestige from the respect accorded them by the white world, or by the professional and business segments of the Negro world, most Negroes seem to adopt a pattern of conspicuous behavior and conspicuous consumption. Maintaining a "front" and "showing off" become very important substitutes for getting ahead in the economic sense. Leadership in various organizations often constitutes the evidence that a man has "arrived."

Leaders in Bronzeville, like Negro leaders everywhere since the Civil War, are constantly urging the community to raise its sights above "survival," "enjoying life," and "praising the Lord." They present "getting ahead" as a *racial* duty as well as a personal gain. When a Negro saves money, buys bonds, invests in a business or in property, he is automatically "advancing The Race." * When Negroes "waste their substance," they are "setting The Race back." This appraisal of their activity is widely accepted by the rank and file, but leaders sometimes press their shots too hard. When they do so, they often get a response like that of the domestic servant who resented the attempts of a civic leader to discourage elaborate social club dances during the Depression: "We [the social club] give to the Federated Home and

---

* "Service" is a key word in American life, cherished alike by Rotarian and labor leader, politician and priest. All forms of intense individual competition are sanctified under the name of "service," and individual success is represented as "service" to the community. The struggle for prestige, too, is dressed up as "service." Bronzeville, like the rest of Midwest Metropolis, has its frequent money-raising drives for charitable institutions and its corps of enthusiastic volunteers who, under the auspices of churches, lodges, clubs, and social agencies, function as part-time civic leaders. "Service" in Bronzeville is usually interpreted as "advancing The Race."

about ten or fifteen other institutions. If we want to give a dance, I think that's our business. We poor colored people don't have much as it is, and if we sat around and thought about our sufferings we'd go crazy."

ADVANCING THE RACE

White people in Midwest Metropolis become aware of Negroes only occasionally and sporadically. Negroes, however, live in a state of intense and perpetual awareness that they are a black minority in a white man's world. The Job Ceiling and the Black Ghetto are an ever-present experience. Petty discriminations (or actions that might be interpreted as such) occur daily. Unpleasant memories of the racial and individual past are a part of every Negro's personality structure. News and rumors of injustice and terror in the South and elsewhere circulate freely through Negro communities at all times. "Race consciousness" is not the work of "agitators" or "subversive influences"—it is forced upon Negroes by the very fact of their separate-subordinate status in American life. And it is tremendously reinforced by life in a compact community such as Black Metropolis, set within the framework of a large white community.

Negroes are ill at ease in the land of their birth. They are bombarded with the slogans of democracy, liberty, freedom, equality, but they are not allowed to participate freely in American life. They develop a tormenting ambivalence toward themselves and the larger society of which they are a part. America rejects them; so they tend to hate. But it is the only land they know; so they are sentimentally attached to it. Their skin color and social origins subject them to discrimination and contumely; so they often (consciously or unconsciously) despise The Race. The people they know most intimately, however, are colored, and men cannot totally hate themselves and their friends. Thus their moods fluctuate between shame and defiance. Their conversation becomes a bewildering mixture of expressions of "racial depreciation" and "race pride."

The Cult of Race: Negroes feel impelled to prove to themselves continually that they are not the inferior creatures which their minority status implies. Thus, ever since emancipation, Negro leaders have preached the necessity for cultivating "race pride." They have assiduously repeated the half-truth that "no other race has ever made the progress that Negroes have made in an equivalent length of time." They have patiently attempted to popularize an expanding roster of Race Heroes—individuals who have attained success or prominence. "Catching up with the white folks" has been developed as the dominating theme of inspirational exhortations, and the Negro "firsts" and "onlies" are set up as Race Heroes.* "Beating the white man at his own game" becomes a powerful motivation for achievement and explains the popularity of such personalities as Joe Louis or Jesse Owens, George Washington Carver or outstanding soldier-heroes. A myth of "special gifts" has also emerged, with Negroes (and whites also) believing that American Negroes have some inborn, unusual talent as dancers, musicians, artists and athletes.

In the period between the First and the Second World Wars, this emphasis upon race pride became a mass phenomenon among the Negroes in large urban communities. Race consciousness was transformed into a positive and aggressive defensive racialism. Negroes in Black Metropolis, as in other communities, feeling the strength of their economic and political power, have become increasingly aware of the achievements of individual Negroes, and have developed an absorbing interest in every scrap of evidence that "The Race is advancing," or is "catching up with white folks," or is "beating the white man at his own game." Unable to compete freely *as individuals,* the Negro masses take intense vicarious pleasure in watching Race Heroes vindicate them in the eyes of the white world.

Race pride is a defensive reaction that can become a mere verbal escape mechanism. Negro leaders are therefore perpetually involved in an effort to make race pride more than an end in itself: to utilize it as a morale builder, as the raw material of "racial solidarity." They seek to use it for "advancing The Race." They foster race pride in order to elicit support for collective action—the support of Negro business enterprises, the organization of petition and protest, the focusing of economic and political power. The most persistent theme of speeches and editorials in Bronzeville is: "Negroes must learn to stick together." The leaders use it also to encourage individual achievement, by inter-

---

* Among Bronzeville's "firsts" are: Dr. Daniel Williams, "first man to suture a human heart"; Dr. Julian Lewis, "first Negro to serve on the faculty of the University of Chicago's medical school"; and Robert R. Taylor, "first Negro to serve as the head of the Chicago Housing Authority." Among the "onlies" are the only Negro on the schoolboard of the city, and the only Negro on the library board.

preting the success of one Negro as the success of all. Out of this inter-play between race consciousness, race pride, and race solidarity arise certain definite social types: the Race Hero, the Race Leader, the Race Man, the Race Woman.

The average person in Bronzeville is primarily interested in "staying alive," "getting ahead," "having a good time" and "praising the Lord." Conscious preoccupation with "racial advancement" is fitful and spo-radic, though always latent. The masses leave "the burden of The Race" to those individuals who are oriented around "service"—the Race Leaders. Some of these are people who devote much of their lei-sure time to charitable organizations or associations for racial advance-ment. For others solving the race problem is a full-time job. For in-stance, a score or so of individuals in Bronzeville are elected and ap-pointed politicians who "represent The Race." There are also a few civic leaders who earn their living by administering social agencies such as the Urban League, the YMCA, the YWCA, settlement houses, and similar organizations. In Bronzeville, too, there are numerous "self-appointed leaders"—men and women, often illiterate and poverty-stricken, who feel the call to "lead The Race out of bondage." They harangue their small groups of followers on the streets, in store-fronts, or in the public parks with a fanaticism that alienates them from the masses as well as from the affluent and educated.

Most of the people in Bronzeville do not hold membership in any of the organizations for "racial advancement," such as the National Association for the Advancement of Colored People (NAACP), the National Negro Congress, the Urban League, or the Council of Negro Organizations. They follow the activities of Race Leaders in the Negro press, they cheer and applaud an occasionally highly publicized victory over those who maintain the Job Ceiling and the Black Ghetto. They grumble persistently about "lack of leadership." They contribute an occasional nickel or dime to drives for funds. But when some inciting incident stirs them deeply, they close ranks and put up a scrap—for a community housing project, to remove a prejudiced policeman, to force a recalcitrant merchant to employ Negroes. And they periodically vote for Negroes to represent them in state, local, and national bodies. In general, "solving the race problem" is left in the hands of Race Lead-ers—the "racial watchdogs," as one Bronzeville preacher called them.

✦

Race Leadership: Race Leaders are expected to put up some sort of aggressive fight against the exclusion and subordination of Negroes. They must also stress "catching up with white folks," and this involves the less dramatic activity of appeals for discipline within the Black Belt, and pleas for Negroes to take advantage of opportunities to "advance." A Race Leader has to fight the Job Ceiling and Black Ghetto and at the same time needle, cajole, and denounce Negroes themselves for inertia, diffidence, and lack of race pride; and the functions sometimes conflict.

There is rather widespread agreement in Bronzeville on what an ideal Race Leader should be. When the people are asked to describe a "real Race Leader" they always stress "sincerity" as a cardinal virtue: A Race Leader, they say,

. . . knows the difficulties of the race and fights without a selfish reason;

. . . is a sincere person with some moral principle;

. . . is sincere and has a plan;

. . . has a constant, sincere interest in the race;

. . . is sincere and people know he is not after some hidden personal interest;

. . . has the interest and well-being of the Negro race uppermost in his life.

"Everybody will tell you," a young stenographer observed, "that a real Race Leader is 'square'!"

Sincerity is prized, but, as one of the persons quoted above stated, a leader must have a plan. Theories about solving the race problem range all the way from amalgamation to emigration to Africa, from sympathy with Communism to the demand for a "49th Negro state." The "accepted leaders," however, tend to be people who stress the use of political and economic pressure (without violence) and gradual advancement by slowly raising the economic and educational level of the entire group.

"An ardent racialist without ability is not a race leader," comments a clerical worker; "he must have something to contribute." A leader must be able to formulate and present the Negroes' demands and aspirations to white people. Many people insist that a real leader must be "calm, well poised, well trained." Some think he should be "an educated person who has a great deal of influence with whites and prestige with Negroes." The more conservative people feel that he should also be a person who "believes strongly in caution and patience" and who is "adept in the arts of personal and political compromise."

Bronzeville knows that the powers of its leaders are limited, that in the final analysis the white majority can break any leader who is too aggressive. It is well aware that white America makes concessions to Negroes primarily from the imperatives of economic necessity and political expediency rather than from devotion to democratic ideals. Out of this knowledge arises a kind of cynical realism which does not expect too much from leaders.

Bronzeville knows, too, that "leaders are human," that they are motivated by the desire for power and prestige as well as by the "service" ideal. The whole business of "advancing The Race" offers wide opportunities for fraud, graft, and chicanery. There are opportunities for "selling out to the white folks," diverting funds from "the cause," or making a racket out of race. People try to draw a line between "sincere Race Leaders" and those Race Men who "are always clamoring everything for The Race, just for the glory of being known." They will characterize some leaders as being "like the William Randolph Hearst variety of patriot whose Americanism means a chance to make more money." They are skeptical of those who, "when you see them, are always talking about The Race." Sincerity is hard to test, however, and Bronzeville seems to expect that its leaders will "cash in" on their positions, in terms of personal influence if not in terms of money.

The Race Man: Frustrated in their isolation from the main streams of American life, and in their impotence to control their fate decisively, Negroes tend to admire an aggressive Race Man even when his motives are suspect.* They will applaud him, because, in the face of

* The term Race Man is used in a dual sense in Bronzeville. It refers to any person who has a reputation as an uncompromising fighter against attempts to subordinate Negroes. It is also used in a derogatory sense to refer to people who pay loud lip-service to "race pride." It is interesting to note that Bronzeville is somewhat suspicious, generally, of its Race Men, but tends to be more trustful of the Race Woman. "A Race Woman is sincere," commented a prominent businessman; "she can't capitalize on her activities like a Race Man." The Race Woman is sometimes described as "forceful, outspoken, and fearless, a great advocate of race pride" . . . "devoted to the race" . . . "studies the conditions of the people" . . . "the Race is uppermost in her activities" . . . "you know her by the speeches she makes" . . . "she champions the rights of Negroes" . . . "active in civic affairs." The Race Woman is idealized as a "fighter," but her

the white world, he remains "proud of his race and always tries to uphold it whether it is good or bad, right or wrong," because he sees "only the good points of the race." One high school girl explained that "the Race Man is interested in the welfare of the people. Everybody says that they admire a Race Man, but behind the scenes they may not regard him as being sincere. The Race Man is usually a politician or a businessman. He sponsors movements for the benefit of the people. It is a way of securing honor and admiration from the people. Personally, I admire a Race Man even if he seeks his own advancement." A well-known minister interpreted the admiration for the Race Man as follows: "The people are emotionally enthusiastic about a Race Man. They know that a Race Man may not be quite as sincere as some of the more quiet leaders. Still, the very fact of his working for the race gives him prestige in their eyes." A Race Man is one type of Race Hero.

The Race Hero: If a man "fights for The Race," if he seems to be "all for The Race," if he is "fearless in his approach to white people," he becomes a Race Hero. Similarly any Negro becomes a hero if he beats the white man at his own game or forces the white world to recognize his talent or service or achievement. Racketeer or preacher, reactionary or Communist, ignoramus or savant—if a man is an aggressive, vocal, uncompromising Race Man he is everybody's hero. Even conservative Negroes admire colored radicals who buck the white world. Preachers may oppose sin, but they will also express a sneaking admiration for a Negro criminal who decisively outwits white people. Even the quiet, well-disciplined family man may get a thrill when a "bad Negro" blows his top and goes down with both guns blazing at the White Law. Such identification is usually covert and unconscious, and may even be feared and regretted by the very persons who experience it. Race pride sometimes verges upon the vindictive, but it is a direct result of the position to which white America has consigned the Negro group.

associated role of "uplifter" seems to be accepted with less antagonism than in the case of the Race Man. She is sometimes described as "continually showing the Negro people why they should better their condition economically and educationally." Cynics are apt to add: "intelligent and forceful but has little influence with whites." Certain women were repeatedly named as "good Race Women"— one or two local Bronzeville women who were active in civic organizations, and such nationally known figures as Mrs. Mary McLeod Bethune.

WORLD WITHIN A WORLD

The people of Bronzeville have, through the years, crystallized certain distinctive patterns of thought and behavior. Their tenacious clinging to life, their struggle for liberty, their quest for happiness, have resulted in the proliferation of institutions. The customs and habits of Bronzeville's people are essentially American but carry overtones of subtle difference. Bronzeville has all the major institutions found in any other Chicago neighborhood—schools and churches, a wide range of stores and shops, varied commercial amusements, segments of the city political machine, and numerous voluntary associations. And besides, as a low-income community it has had more than its share of relief stations and never enough playgrounds, clinics, and similar social services.

While Bronzeville's institutions differ little in form from those in other Midwest Metropolis communities, they differ considerably in content. The dissimilarity springs primarily from two facts: Because the community is spiritually isolated from the larger world, the development of its families, churches, schools, and voluntary associations has proceeded quite differently from the course taken by analogous white institutions; and, second, Bronzeville's "culture" is but a part of a larger, national Negro culture, its people being tied to thirteen million other Negroes by innumerable bonds of kinship, associational and church membership, and a common minority status. The customs inherited by Bronzeville have been slowly growing up among American Negroes in the eighty years since slavery.

But Bronzeville is also a part of Midwest Metropolis, and Negro life is organically bound up with American life. Negroes attend the same movies, read the same daily papers, study the same textbooks, and participate in the same political and industrial activity as other Americans. They know white America far better than white America knows them. Negroes live in two worlds and they must adjust to both. Their institutions reflect the standards of both. In so far as Midwest Metropolis is a "wide-open town," in so far as it has a "sporting tradition," to the extent that it is young and rapidly changing, Bronzeville reflects these characteristics.

In order to understand this city within a city, we shall first examine four major institutions with special reference to the manner in which they reflect the system of Negro-white relations: the Negro newspaper, the Negro church, Negro-owned business enterprises, and the "policy racket." Chapter 15 deals briefly with the over-all influence of the newspaper and the church, detailed discussion of the church being reserved for later chapters. Considerable attention is given to "Negro business" in Chapter 16, since the whole temper of Negro life is keyed to the myth of "salvation through Negro business." When Negro rioters in Harlem, Detroit, or Philadelphia demolish the stores that white men operate in the Black Belt, they dramatize this pivotal aspect of Negro-white relations. In Chapter 17, the policy racket is presented as a "protected" business rather than as a criminal activity, since both Bronzeville and the political machine in Midwest Metropolis deal with it as "big business."

Having described these major institutions, we shall then note the way in which the ideal of "getting ahead" operates to divide the community into a number of "social classes" which, in turn, set the pattern for the way in which an individual may "have a good time" or "praise the Lord." Chapters 18-23, inclusive, are primarily concerned with internal relations within Bronzeville, though even these, we shall see, are dominated by the system of Negro-white relations.

The picture of life in Bronzeville that emerges from these chapters is a candid-camera shot of the community in the final stages of the Depression and in the midst of the Second World War. Community life during those years was in flux, and all of Bronzeville's inhabitants were wondering which the post-war world would bring them—the flowering of Bronzeville, or merely a continuation of the Black Ghetto.

CHAPTER 15

The Power of Press and Pulpit

WHEN THE NEGRO FUGITIVES MADE THE "FLIGHT TO FREEDOM" IN THE pre-Civil War days, they often found refuge in one of the two small Negro churches in Chicago that served as stations on the Underground Railroad. We have already mentioned the role of these churches as stabilizing elements in early Chicago, and the approval they elicited from white abolitionists. In the years between the end of the Civil War and the beginning of the Great Migration, the Negro church was the most influential institution in the Chicago Negro community. The pastors of the larger churches were frequently consulted by white philanthropists, and were on the boards of Black Belt social agencies. With the development of a larger and more diversified community, Negro professional and businessmen, politicians and "civic leaders" emerged as the dominant Race Leaders. But the church remained the most powerful single institution in terms of wealth and mass support. It was forced to compete for its very existence, however, with other institutions, and in doing so had to emphasize its role as a "race institution" rather than as a purely "religious" institution. This involved merely a shift in emphasis, for, as we have stated previously, separate Negro churches came into being as protest organizations and have always been associated in the popular mind with "racial advancement."

The early influence of the church was based on face-to-face contact between the minister and his congregation. The pulpit was the main source of news and inspiration; the church was the town hall; the minister was publicist as well as exhorter. The Negro church stimulated its members to become literate, and in so doing it widened the horizons of the slaves and ex-slaves. Within twenty years after the Civil War, the Negro community in Chicago had enough literate people to support a weekly newspaper with a circulation of about 5,000. The church remained a center for the formation of public opinion, but the Negro press emerged as a victorious competitor.

Chicago's first Negro newspaper was founded in 1878 by a young

Negro lawyer, Ferdinand Barnett, son of a slave who had purchased his freedom and moved to Canada in the pre-Civil War years. This paper, already referred to in Chapter 2, was the prototype of some half-dozen Negro weeklies established in Chicago during the pre-Migration period. Of these only one has survived to the present, the Chicago *Defender,* founded in 1905 by Robert S. Abbott. Between the Great Migration and the Second World War a number of other papers were started, including a militant journal, the Chicago *Whip,* which sponsored the "Spend Your Money Where You Can Work Campaign." *

Just before the Second World War, five weekly newspapers were being published in Bronzeville: the Chicago *Defender* (estimated city circulation, 40,000); the Chicago *Bee* (8,000); the Chicago *World* (5,000); the *Metropolitan Post* (3,000); and the *News-Ledger,* house organ of a cosmetics-manufacturing company, distributed free (about 30,000). In addition to these local papers, the Chicago edition of the Pittsburgh *Courier* had a circulation of eight or ten thousand.

These Negro weeklies are established institutions, wielding enormous influence over Bronzeville's thinking. They are by far the most important agencies for forming and reflecting public opinion in Black Metropolis.

* Between 1880 and 1915, the following papers were founded: the Chicago *Appeal* (1885); the *Clipper* (1885); *Free Speech* (1888); the *Church Organ* (1893); the *Broad Ax* (1899), and the *Defender.* Most vigorous of these was the *Broad Ax,* whose editor stated its aim as follows:

"Our little paper will contend for the liberation of the minds of the Colored people from political slavery, and will strive to infuse a spirit of liberal independence into the minds of the Afro-American voter in the consideration of political questions.

"It is our honest opinion that it is the duty of those comprising the white race to read and support Afro-American publications. By doing so it will enable them to become familiar with the aims, the objects and the aspirations of the millions of Negroes of this country who are endeavoring to reach a higher goal."

In 1916 the *Fellowship Herald* was started, then the Chicago *Enterprise* in 1918, and the Chicago *Whip* in 1919. The *Whip's* credo was formulated thus on June 24, 1919:

"We believe that Negroes should trade with Negroes even at a personal sacrifice in order that the race might have an economic average for which they will not have to compromise. . . . Trading first with Negroes and with white people in the community who are most friendly to us next. . . . We believe that the working men and women together with the businessmen should control the politics of this ward instead of the ignorant selfish peanut-headed professional politician."

THE FACE OF THE NEGRO PRESS

Of Bronzeville's five weekly newspapers, the *Defender* is oldest and most widely known. On the eve of the Second World War, some 40,000 people in Bronzeville bought the paper every week—and it cost a dime a copy. At least 100,000 people read the paper. Nearly everybody discussed it. Employing over 150 people, and with a weekly payroll of more than $6,000, the *Defender* is a stable business enterprise as well as an organ of public opinion. For more than 35 years the name of the *Defender* was associated with that of its editor, Robert S. Abbott—an ardent Race Man, who insisted in an interview shortly before his death that he had always had only one goal in life: "complete equality of Negroes with white people." Abbott believed in "individual achievement" coupled with vigorous group action as the Negro's program for advancement. He thought of himself as an example of what Negroes could accomplish if they were given a chance—he who began the publication of his newspaper in the kitchen of a friend's home, peddled it himself, and succeeded in developing it into a $300,000 enterprise.

Throughout most of his life Editor Abbott was a Republican, but he believed that Negroes should not put all their eggs in one political basket. Though he himself was an economic conservative, anybody who fought for The Race* was his friend. During the Depression, when the Communists were very active in Bronzeville, the *Defender* on one occasion even ran a favorable editorial about the trial of a Milwaukee Communist by his Party for displaying "white chauvinism":

WHY WE CANNOT HATE REDS

. . . The cause for which he was expelled was that he had made some uncomplimentary remarks about workers of the Race. He didn't call us criminals, thugs, or rapists. . . . He said merely that we are "dumb, cowardly and can't be organized." And for those words, things which we have said about each other numbers of times, he was expelled from the organization to which he belonged and for which he had a high regard. . . .

A white man made that statement, and for it he was penalized. How,

* One of Editor Abbott's peculiarities was his dislike of the word "Negro." As long as he lived, the *Defender* always used the word "Race" instead of Negro. Stories were edited so that "Negro business" became "Race business," "Negro achievement" was dubbed "Race achievement," etc.

under such circumstances, can we go to war with the Communist Party? Is there any other political, religious, or civic organization in the country that would go to such lengths to prove itself not unfriendly to us? Is there any other group in the country that would not applaud the sentiments expressed by the man who was ousted in this instance?

We may not agree with the entire program of the Communist Party, but there is one item with which we do agree wholeheartedly and that is the zealousness with which it guards the rights of the Race.[1]

Such a policy helped to fix the reputation of the *Defender* in the popular mind as a "radical" paper. But it was a racial radicalism rather than an economic radicalism which the *Defender* espoused.

Abbott died in 1940, but the *Defender* lives and thrives on its reputation as an aggressive fighter for Negro rights. Though the present publisher is somewhat more responsive to the wider currents of general American liberal and progressive thought than was Editor Abbott, the paper itself remains an ardent "Race paper."

The *Defender's* city edition usually contains about 40 pages—reduced under wartime paper restrictions to about 26. On the surface, and in terms of the kinds of things that make news in Bronzeville, there is little difference between the *Defender* and the white dailies. (Table 14.) But all news in the *Defender* is "race-angled," and specific items on "interracial relations" account for about six per cent of the front-page space. Crime, politics, community activities become "news" when—and only when—they involve Negroes. If we examine the *Defender's* front page to learn what kinds of personalities made the headlines over a five-year period (during the Depression), we find them to be the kinds that made the front pages of the white dailies: political leaders, criminals, famous athletes, murder victims. In the Negro press, however, such personalities have a special "racial" significance. (Table 15.)

With the outbreak of the Second World War, the Negro press emerged as one of the most powerful forces among Negroes in America.* These weekly papers became the "racial watchdogs," and, with a unanimity that surprised Negroes as much as it did the rest of the country, their editors began a campaign for the complete integration of Negroes into all war-related activities. The Negro newspapers

* The *Defender* reported an increase in city circulation of about 20,000 between 1938 and 1944. The total circulation, city and national, in March, 1945, was reported as 160,000.

TABLE 14

PROPORTION OF SPACE ON THE FRONT PAGE OF THE CHICAGO "DEFENDER" ALLOTTED
TO SPECIFIC CATEGORIES OF NEWS: 1926-1937, INCLUSIVE

News Category	Percentage of Column Inches
1. Crime	22.3
2. "People"	7.7
3. Interracial relations	6.1
4. Accidents	4.7
5. Community affairs	4.6
6. Government	4.1
7. Politics and political scandal	2.6
8. Human interest	2.4
9. Law suits	2.3
10. Foreign affairs	2.3
11. Organizations	2.0
12. Suicide	1.6
13. Church news	1.6
14. Labor	1.5
15. Mass meetings	1.1
16. Education	1.1
17. Sports	1.1
18. Weather	.6
19. All other news	8.8
20. Cartoons and pictures	18.8
21. Editorials	2.7
Total	100.0

called conferences, and their representatives haunted the offices of the White House, the Congress, and the Pentagon with a set of clear-cut demands: No segregation in the armed forces; no discrimination in industry; the progressive abolition of exclusion and subordination in civilian life. The newspapers advised Negroes to support the war, commended the partial relaxation of discriminatory barriers here and there, but defined the primary function of the press as one of pressure and needling. The Negro papers drew heated denunciations from illiberal die-hards and words of caution from white liberals. (The FBI, completely off the track, sniffed about for traces of Japanese subsidies.) In spite of these attacks, most Negro papers continued to follow the policy that the Pittsburgh *Courier* dubbed "Double V"— a fight for the victory of democracy at *home* as well as abroad.

As the war developed, these papers gave increasing space to the exploits of Negro soldiers, to bond sales and other patriotic activities, and to occasional evidences of "victory at home." At no time, how-

TABLE 15

THE TEN PERSONS RECEIVING THE MOST PROMINENT FRONT-PAGE DISPLAY IN THE
CHICAGO "DEFENDER": 1933-1938 INCLUSIVE

Person	Nationality and/or Race	Significance	Incidence of Display*
Joe Louis	American Negro	*Race Hero*—first Negro to hold world heavyweight title since Jack Johnson.	80
Haile Selassie	Ethiopian	*Race Hero*—leader of nation with which Negroes felt kinship, during attack by a white nation, Italy.	24
Oscar DePriest	American Negro	*Race Hero and Race Leader*—First Negro Congressman since 1901. Elected by Bronzeville voters. Reputation for being "fearless."	20
Jesse Binga	American Negro	*Race Hero and Race Leader*—Home bombed by white persons who objected to his living outside the Black Ghetto. Banker whose bank failed during depression. Jailed for embezzlement.	16
Arthur Mitchell	American Negro	*Race Leader*—Successor to DePriest in Congress. Often charged with lack of aggressiveness.	15
Edward Kelly	American, white	Mayor of Chicago. Considered a "friend of the Negro."	15
Colonel John C. Robinson	American Negro	*Race Hero*—aviator. Served in Italo-Ethiopian war.	11
R___ J___	American Negro	*Criminal*—committed sensational crime.	9
Benito Mussolini	Italian, white	*Race Enemy*—leader of attack on Ethiopia.	9
Dr. Mercer	American Negro	*"Big Negro"*—died mysteriously.	8

* "Incidence" means the total number of times the person was mentioned in front-page headlines or appeared in a front-page picture.

ever, did they stop thundering away at every hint of discrimination —from discourteous treatment of Negro soldiers in Red Cross canteens to the diatribes of southern Congressmen. Concurrently they waged a side battle against lethargy and dirt and disorder within

America's Black Ghettos. The sample front page of the *Defender* in Figure 23 and the excerpts from the editorial pages which are superimposed upon it, suggest the run of attention in the Negro press during the war—elation at partial victories over Jim Crow, pride in the achievement of Negro soldiers, displeasure at discrimination, and an attempt to throw the American race problem into a world context.

On New Year's Day, 1944, the "World's Greatest Weekly" heralded the advent of the New Year with an announcement: 14 CHICAGO SOLDIERS WOUNDED. (Figure 23.) These casualties were headlined with scarcely less prominence than the news that OPA CRACKS DOWN ON LIQUOR STORE PRICES. Prominently displayed within a box was the "Honor Roll of 1943," * bestowing laurels upon 22 persons—Negro and white—"honest and fearless," who "have battled against the barriers of race prejudice to see that this great nation of ours truly represents the land of opportunity for Negroes as well as others." At the bottom of the page, balanced against each other, were a hopeful announcement: GEORGIA CHAIN GANGS TO VANISH WITH THE NEW YEAR, and the depressing news that the Texas state's attorney DEFENDS RIGHT OF TEXAS PRIMARY TO BAR NEGROES. A small item sandwiched in between announced that TEXANS PLANNED TO JIM CROW MERCHANT MARINES at a United Seamen's Service Club. A popular columnist raised a query: DO WE FACE A NEW BIRTH OF FREEDOM IN 1944? side by side with news of "Fourteen Chicago Negro Soldiers . . . wounded in action"—which "brought home the full force of the war to Chicago's Negro citizenry."

A victory on the home front is recorded: MAYOR NAMES MOLLISON [a Negro] TO SCHOOL BOARD POST. A fight in progress is headlined: SENGSTACKE† SPURS FIGHT FOR PLAYERS IN BIG LEAGUES. The latter article called upon "Negro publishers throughout the nation to follow up with their local organized

* The selection of an annual "honor roll" in race relations has been adopted by several Negro papers and organizations. The first and most widely publicized "honor roll" was sponsored by Dr. L. D. Reddick, Curator of the Schomburg Collection, New York City.

† Publisher of the Chicago *Defender* after the death of its founder, Robert S. Abbott. In 1944 Sengstacke was elected president of the National Negro Publishers' Association; and the importance of the *Defender* among Negro newspapers is revealed by the fact that in the same year he was chosen to head the Negro division of the National Independent Voters Committee for the Re-election of Franklin D. Roosevelt.

Figure 23

baseball club managers in seeing that the practice of excluding Negroes from organized baseball is discontinued." The lighter side of life was allotted space in the form of a large picture of an attractive New York girl who, visiting Bronzeville for the first time, duly testified, "I like Chicago and the hospitality of its people."

This is the face of Bronzeville's press, prettied up for a New Year's special. In its news selection and emphasis, however, it is typical of Bronzeville's wartime front pages.* From an examination of headlines over a five-month period (Table 16), it is obvious that Bronzeville, while interested in the war, was interested in it in a special sort of way—in the colored men who were wounded and killed; in Joe Louis, the Race Hero; or in Dorie Miller, colored messman who received an award for heroism at a time when Negroes were barred from all ratings other than messman in the navy. Bronzeville was concerned, too, about Negro soldiers who were being abused, mistreated, and even lynched, in uniform.

When 7 GET "L" TRAINMEN JOBS after years of agitation for such employment by local transit companies, the story drives the war from the headlines. (When a colored streetcar motorman is attacked and a white policeman, Sweeney, kills a white boy while protecting the motorman, it is the signal for a crusade in defense of Sweeney.) And throughout the period, the ever-present housing problem receives attention—in a war context.

The *Defender* editorials include explicit commentaries on events that are reported as news in the banner headlines and elsewhere. During this same five-month period the paper printed 68 editorials. Only about one-sixth of these pertained to the war, and actually only two or three were "war editorials" in the sense familiar to readers of daily newspapers. Of these, a New Year's editorial entitled "1943-1944" concluded: "May 1944 bring us closer to victory and peace, and nearer the ideals of justice and common humanity." Another, in connection

---

* A facsimile of a *Defender* (National Edition) front page for the week of November 18, 1944, is presented in Figure 24 for comparative purposes. The presidential election was given a big play—the *Defender* had been on the winning side. International comment ranged from a sensational article on miscegenation in London to a eulogy of Negro troops in the Philippines, written by the paper's former city editor, now a National Negro Press Association war correspondent. Two victories on the home front were recorded: NEGRO REAL ESTATE BOARDS FIND NEGRO HOUSING A GOOD RISK and NAVY SWEARS IN THREE WOMEN AS FIRST WAVES. (Negro women were not admitted to the Waves until three years after the entry of the United States into the war.)

Figure 24

TABLE 16

PRINCIPAL AND SECONDARY BANNER HEADLINES IN THE CHICAGO "DEFENDER":
NOV. 13, 1943, TO MARCH 25, 1944, INCLUSIVE

1. CHICAGO SOLDIER LYNCHED
   Cops Crack Down on Policy; Seven Jailed in New Drive (11-13-43)
2. COURT HITS HOUSING BAN
   5 War Workers Drown (11-20-43)
3. 7 GET "L" TRAINMEN JOBS
   Hubby of Blanche Calloway May Face Bigamy Charges (11-27-43)
4. Hold Dr. Gordon Jackson in Dope Case
   64 SOLDIERS JAILED FOR ARMY USE OF TRUCKS (12-4-43)
5. Charge Real Estate Agent with Fraud
   WAGE WAR ON VICE AND CRIME (12-11-43)
6. REPORT DORIE MILLER MISSING!
   Blast Telephone Company for Job Color Bar Policy (12-18-43)
7. CUBS TO SCOUT NEGRO PLAYERS
   Blame Bad Housing as Fires Hit South Side (12-25-43)
8. 14 CHICAGO SOLDIERS WOUNDED
   OPA Cracks Down on Liquor Store Prices (1-1-44)
9. Two Killed, Four Hurt in Auto-Bus Crash
   HOUSING PROJECTS TO RELIEVE SO. SIDE (1-8-44)
10. 11-Day-Old Baby Dies, 3 Hurt in Fire
    WHITE COP HALTS NEAR RIOT; JAILED ON ASSAULT
    CHARGE (1-15-44)
22. Parents Away; Children Die in Fire
    PETITION MAYOR KELLY IN SWEENEY SHOOTING (1-22-44)
12. Cite 2 Bartenders in Sweeney Shooting
    MARVA'S DEBUT HALTED! (1-29-44)
13. Mother Saves Baby from Blazing Fire Trap!
    HUNT DOCTORS USING DRUG TO "BEAT DRAFT" (2-5-44)
14. Army Orders Sgt. Joe Louis Overseas
    MOTORMAN IN SWEENEY SHOOTING TELLS STORY! (2-12-44)
15. Protest Slum Project in "Exclusive" District
    WAR ON "GOUGING" JITNEY CAB DRIVERS (2-19-44)
16. Sweeney Freed in Street Car Shooting
    DEMAND SLASH IN CAB FARES (2-26-44)
17. Cab Owners to End Fare "Gouging"
    DR. GORDON JACKSON IS SENT TO PRISON (3-4-44)
18. FBI Cracks Down on Draft Dodgers
    CHARGE LIQUOR STORES WITH FLEECING PUBLIC (3-11-44)
19. Chicago Soldier Hero as 24th Infantry Routs Japs
    BURN HOMES TO OUST TENANTS (3-18-44)
20. North Side Families Fight Evictions
    OUST ROWDY CABMEN; SET NEW TAXI RATES (3-25-44)

with the Fourth War Loan, urged Negroes to "Buy Bonds," stating that "In spite of the injustice done us [Negroes] . . . this is our war too." (It also emphasized the "good investment" angle.) More typical of the *Defender's* interest in and attitude toward the war were the sentiments expressed in an editorial entitled "The Four Freedoms," which was for the most part a denunciation of southern Congressmen: "The hypocrisy of these crusaders for freedom in other lands but not in America is beneath contempt."

About half of the "war editorials" were primarily criticisms of the Army and Navy for discrimination against, or mistreatment of, Negro soldiers.

About a sixth of the editorials dealt with foreign affairs. The interest was of the same general type as that noted in war editorials, about half of these being discussions and criticisms of British colonial administration in Africa. One of these, "How About Africa," concludes with the bitter observation that while all other peoples have been promised liberation, "Africans in particular and Negroes in general are apparently not to share in the fruits of a victorious peace." The relations between Abyssinia and Italy, and the question of the Allied attitude toward the restoration of Ethiopian independence, also received considerable attention.

By far the largest number of editorials—almost half—were concerned with those national political issues which Negroes regard as most important. About a quarter of this group dealt with the Anti-Poll-Tax Bill, which was thus defined as the biggest political issue during the period. Typical is an editorial entitled "Defeat the Confederacy!" which states that "The Confederacy, defeated in bloody battle some 80 years ago, still is riding rough-shod over the people's will." The Anti-Poll-Tax Bill, insisted the *Defender,* is the test of "our Union, our democracy." Several editorials demanded Federal bills against certain public manifestations of racial prejudice. The Republican and the Democratic parties (as well as individual Congressmen) were warned upon several occasions that neither party had the Negro vote "in the bag"—that Negroes would vote on the basis of past performance.

Remaining editorials pertained to local topics, such as housing and jobs for Negroes in Chicago, or general topics of interest to Negroes nationally—the question of Negro migration and problems of post-war employment and race relations. Not all editorials "panned" white people, however. Thus, the favorable handling of news about Negroes in Chicago's daily newspapers was hailed in "The Friendly Press." Paul Robeson's Broadway success in *Othello* was similarly an occasion for rejoicing; the Theatre Guild was complimented, and the editorial concluded, "American art is marching against the forces of reaction."

The *Defender* is no less stinting in its praise of friends or in its rejoicing at the "progress" of the Negro people—anywhere—than it is lavish in the castigation of foes, or in its alarm at "set backs"—anywhere.

But life goes on in Bronzeville, and often gaily, in spite of prejudice and discrimination, war or no war. Newspaper headlines (if not the editorials—and it is safe to assume that the *Defender's* readers, like those of all newspapers, are more familiar with the headlines than with the editorials) also reveal diversified interests of a lighter nature. Bronzeville learns the latest news about the policy racket; learns of the debut of Marva (Joe Louis's wife) as a night-club singer; the price of liquor and of a cab ride; gossip and scandal, accidents and crimes, and Bronzeville's draft-dodgers. (Table 3.) Within its 23 or 24 other wartime pages, too, there is ample evidence that Bronzeville does not spend all its waking hours brooding over war, segregation, and discrimination. Club news, church news, the sport pages, cabaret and movie ads in profusion—all indicate a vigorous attachment to life amid the stagnation of the Black Ghetto and the quick death of war.

The *Defender* has its critics as well as its warm partisans, but the wide influence of this paper, and others like it, is undeniable. Though the variety of reader reaction seems almost infinite, it is significant that people continue to read Negro papers whether they approve or disapprove of them. Thus, one elderly gentleman likes the *Defender* because it is a "good paper." "I like to read about my race, learn what they are doing and thinking about, and see what big Negroes are entertaining," he says. Another man feels that the editor should be supported because "all of the worth-while things of the Negro are in his paper and he never bites his tongue when he has anything to say, regardless of color."

One woman reader, however, doesn't approve of all the paper's policies and thinks that its editors are "a little bit too strong on the racial question. They knock the whites too much." A professional man is completely cynical in his comment: "I don't read any of the colored papers but the Chicago *Defender*. It may sound funny, but I read that paper because I get all of the dirt at once. I have noticed that anything my race does, such as cutting, fighting, or killing, the *Defender* has it." A day laborer commented: "I read the *Defender* whenever I have a dime to spare. I don't see where all that noise they make helps any, but I like to read it."

A wide sampling of reasons given for reading the *Defender* include the following, listed in order of frequency: (1) The *Defender* is published by colored people and is fighting for the interests of The Race; it is the duty of colored people to read it. (2) It reports the "doings" of Negroes. (3) It has plenty of club and social news; it reports the activities of "big Negroes." (4) It contains news from the South. (5) It "makes people think."

The *Defender*, like all other Negro weeklies, has the dual function of reporting news and stimulating race solidarity. Also, of course, as a business enterprise, it seeks to make a profit—to make race pride pay. Unlike the large white dailies, however, the *Defender* depends primarily on income from circulation rather than from advertising.* The paper, in the interests of maximizing circulation, gives the public what it wants—in news and in attitude toward the white world. The public, in turn, supports the paper by purchasing it regularly. But, having such wide circulation among the Negro masses, the paper is in a favorable position for soliciting advertising from white businesses. In 1940 it was reported that over three-fourths of the *Defender's* advertising revenue came from white sources. Most of this was from concerns doing business in the Black Belt, but a few nationally known concerns also were beginning to use its pages for touching the Negro market.

On the surface it would seem that Negro newspapers such as the *Defender* are almost completely free from white control. Certainly the tone of the editorials and the handling of the news is "militant" and even aggressive. Yet upon several occasions even the *Defender*

---

* Daily newspapers in the country as a whole receive about one-third of their income from sales and two-thirds from advertising. (In metropolitan cities the proportion of income from advertising is considerably higher.) The proportion is almost exactly reversed in the case of the *Defender* and Negro newspapers generally. In "good times" (e.g., 1940) the *Defender* receives about 40 per cent of its gross income from advertising, 60 per cent from sales. In "bad times" the proportion of revenue from sales rises to 70 per cent or even higher, as during the worst years of the Depression.

has been accused of trimming its sails with a weather eye toward white advertisers. During the "Spend Your Money Where You Can Work" Campaign, for instance, the *Defender* did not go all out for boycotting white businesses. While this may have been due to the honest conviction of the editorial board (tempered by a natural antagonism toward the *Whip,* a rival newspaper sponsoring the campaign), it was undoubtedly motivated partly by fear of losing the support of white advertisers. One staff member remarked frankly to an interviewer in 1940, "We are in a dilemma; we can't really support Negro business as such." Another said: "Nobody knows the hole we are really in. If we really fought white business we'd go under in two weeks." The *Defender* staff, viewing the demise of the *Whip* (reputedly because of reprisals by white people), steers a middle ground—encouraging Negro business enterprise but not counseling any boycott of white men doing business in the Black Belt. The larger white community exercises economic controls over Negro papers in other ways, too—through mortgage-holders, bankers who extend loans, and politicians who may grant or withhold political contributions during campaigns. Despite such controls, these papers are rarely maneuvered into a position where policy is actually dictated by these sources.

The Chicago *Defender* is typical of America's three hundred Negro weeklies in tone and format. Some may be more or less belligerent or sensational, but all conceive of themselves as "Race papers." Despite the fact that these papers are businesses, they like to define their role as did Ferdinand Barnett in the Eighties: "The *Conservator* [is a] creature born of our enthusiastic desire to benefit our people rather than any motive of self-aggrandizement or pecuniary profit." Bronzeville people know that this is only a half-truth, but they do not expect the Negro press to be Simon-pure; they merely expect it to be interesting and to put up a fight while it tries to make money.

THE GRIP OF THE NEGRO CHURCH

The Negro newspaper is a business institution which Bronzeville expects to "serve The Race." The Negro church is ostensibly a "religious" organization, but Bronzeville expects it, too, to "advance The Race." There are nearly 500 churches in Black Metropolis, claiming at least 200,000 members and distributed among over thirty denominations. (Table 17.) Almost half of the churches, and over two-thirds of the people who claim church membership, are affiliated with one of the two Negro National Baptist Conventions. These congregations and their ministers have virtually no face-to-face relationships with any of their white co-religionists. The first Negro Baptist Convention arose as a split from white organizations primarily because colored preachers felt that they were being denied an opportunity to express their talents without discrimination. Negro Baptists think of their organization as a "Race church," and their leaders concern themselves with such matters as fighting the Job Ceiling and demanding equal economic opportunity as well as "serving the Lord." There are also three Negro Methodist denominations represented in Bronzeville, and the colored Holiness, Spiritualist, and Community churches. There are also a number of small denominations indigenous to Bronzeville and such all-Negro "cults" as the African Orthodox Church, the Christian Catholics, the Temple of Moorish Science, and numerous fly-by-night groups organized around enterprising but untrained preachers.

About ten per cent of the churches and less than ten per cent of the church-goers in Bronzeville are affiliated with predominantly white denominations, such as the Methodist Episcopal Church, the Episcopal, Presbyterian, Congregational, Roman Catholic, Lutheran, Christian Scientist, Seventh-Day Adventist, and Disciples of Christ. Though in the state and national organizations of these churches Negroes wield very little influence, a number of the churches have extensive educational and social welfare projects for Negroes throughout the United States. Some people in Bronzeville who would prefer to be identified with these relatively powerful white groups have found that individual white congregations in these sects do not welcome Negro members, even though the Negro church officials and the white church officials often have very close ties. On the whole, Bronzeville sticks to the "Race churches." *

* During the last ten years an intensive drive by the Roman Catholic Church has met with considerable success in Bronzeville. There are three large Catholic Churches in the Black Belt, and the Masses are well attended. Interviews with Negro Catholics, and with non-Catholics whose children go to parochial schools, seem to indicate that one of the primary attractions of the Catholic Church is its educational institutions. With the public schools running on double shifts during those years, many parents felt that the parochial school offered a more thorough

TABLE 17

NEGRO CONGREGATIONS IN CHICAGO: 1928 * AND 1938 †

Group	Denomination	Number of Churches and Per Cent of Total			
		1928		1938	
		Number	Per Cent	Number	Per Cent
1	Baptist (No special designation)...........	98	33.2	141	29.7
	Missionary Baptist......................	30	10.2	68	14.3
	Primitive Baptist.......................	5	1.7	6	1.3
	Total...............................	133	45.1	215	45.3
2	African Methodist Episcopal..............	24	8.2	27	5.7
	African Methodist Episcopal Zion.	5	1.7	8	1.7
	Colored Methodist Episcopal.............	6	2.0	7	1.5
	Total	35	11.9	42	8.9
3	Methodist Episcopal.....................	8	2.7	6	1.3
	Episcopal..............................	3	1.0	3	.6
	Presbyterian...........................	3	1.0	4	.9
	Congregational.........................	2	.7	2	.4
	Disciples of Christ......................	2	.7	3	.6
	Seventh-Day Adventists..................	2	.7	3	.6
	Catholic (Roman).......................	1	.3	3	.6
	Lutheran...............................	1	.3	2	.4
	Church of Christ, Scientist..............	..	...	1	.2
	Total...............................	22	7.4	27	5.6
4	Community Churches, Inc.................	3	1.0	10	2.1
5	Church of God in Christ.................	24	8.2	27	5.7
	Church of Christ (Holiness USA).........	3	1.0	3	.6
	Church of Christ (No designation)........	5	1.7	1	.2
	Church of the Living God...............	2	.7	4	.9
	Church of God (Holiness).	1	.3	7	1.5
	Church of God (no designation)..........	6	2.0	10	2.1
	Church of God and Saints of Christ.......	1	.3	4	.9
	Apostolic and Pentecostal	11	3.8	27	5.7
	Pentecostal Assemblies of World..........	2	.7	3	.6
	Old-Time Methodist.....................	1	.3	1	.2
	Holiness (Miscellaneous Groups).........	..	...	20	4.2
	Total...............................	56	19.0	107	22.6
6	Spiritual and Spiritualist.................	17	5.8	47	9.8
	I.A.M.E. Spiritual......................	..	...	4	.9
	Total...............................	17	5.8	51	10.7
7	Cumberland Presbyterian.................	2	.7	1	.2
	African Orthodox.......................	1	.3	1	.2
	Christian Catholic......................	..	...	1	.2
	Liberal Catholic........................	1	.3	1	.2
	Others.................................	25	8.5	19	4.0
	Total...............................	29	9.8	23	4.8
	Grand Total...........................	295	100.0	475	100.0

* Adapted from: Robert Lee Sutherland, An Analysis of Negro Churches in Chicago (Ph.D. Dissertation, University of Chicago, 1930).
† Compiled from a field survey of the Cayton-Warner Research.

As we have noted previously, Negroes purchased the white churches and synagogues in the Black Belt area as the white population moved out. These financial deals often embittered Negroes against their white brethren, whom they accused of unloading church property on them at exorbitant rates during the Fat Years. In 1933, Chicago Negro churches were carrying the second highest per capita indebtedness among all urban Negro churches in the country. Some of these were fine buildings in good repair. Others were deteriorating. Many had formerly been maintained by well-to-do white congregations, and the Negroes found difficulty in keeping the properties in good condition. Thus during the last twenty years all the larger Negro churches have been forced to spend a great deal of their income on paying off mortgages and maintaining church property. Some have also spent a great deal upon interior decoration. All this financial activity brings Negro church trustees into contact with white businessmen and sharpens somewhat the antagonisms between Negroes and whites in Midwest Metropolis.

There are five churches in Bronzeville seating over 2,000 persons and claiming more than 10,000 members, and some fifty church buildings seating between 500 and 2,000 persons. Seventy-five per cent of Bronzeville's churches are small "store-front" or house churches, with an average membership of fewer than twenty-five persons. Many of these represent survivals from the period of the Great Migration. Others are the result of leadership conflicts within the larger churches. The proselytizing drive in certain denominations has also helped to swell the number. Although there were "missions" in the Black Belt prior to the Great Migration, the prevalence of store-front churches seems to have resulted from the lack of available edifices during the first years of the influx. Church memberships skyrocketed during this period, and competition between congregations for the abandoned white churches and synagogues resulted, on the one hand, in the payment of exorbitant prices for church property, and, on the other, in

education in a quieter atmosphere with adequate discipline and personal attention for all students. The Catholic approach to the Negroes has been aided by the establishment of a small community house, by the extensive athletic program of the Catholic Youth Organization, and by the forthright stand against race prejudice taken by an auxiliary Bishop of the Chicago diocese. In 1944, the Catholics purchased the most imposing piece of church property in Bronzeville—Sinai Temple, a wealthy Jewish synagogue—and converted it into a school and community center.

the proliferation of makeshift churches. In many cases, pastor and congregation hoped some day either to build or to move into a larger edifice. Many of them did one or the other. In other cases the congregation remained where it was, or moved into another store. Several large congregations boast of their evolution from store-fronts, and in their anniversary souvenir programs proudly display "before and after" photographs. The enterprising pastor who leads his congregation from store-front to edifice is well on his way to success in the church world. If he ever pays off the mortgage, he is a hero.

"Serving the Lord (and Man)": While about a third of Bronzeville's churches have only worship as an activity, the majority of them also sponsor some associated activities, if no more than a Sunday School and an usher board or several money-raising clubs. The key activity for all is what the people call "Sunday service." An average Sunday morning probably finds at least 65,000 of Bronzeville's 300,000 persons in some church, and many persons who do not themselves attend church hustle their children off to Sunday School as a part of their "right raising."

Sunday morning in Bronzeville is a colorful occasion. At 9 o'clock, little knots of children and adolescents, in their Sunday best, begin to gather around the doors of the store-fronts in the poorer neighborhoods to joke and play before going inside for two hours of singing, studying the lesson, and lifting the collection—all amid a great deal of friendly banter. At the larger churches the picture is similar, except that once inside the building the various groups of pupils are more likely to study the lesson in separate classrooms with teachers who boast certificates from the Interdenominational Council of Religious Education, and the teachers are likely to stray from the Bible to discuss current events, the race problem, or questions of personal adjustment. It has been estimated that an average of 60,000 Negro children attend Sunday School each week. Sunday School out, most of the youngsters are ready to spend the rest of the day in play at some park or on the streets. Many of them, too, begin to queue up for the opening of the movies. A few may "stay for church," especially those who attend the one or two congregations that have a special "junior church."

"Eleven o'clock service" is the main event of the day, and some of the larger churches are filled by 10:45 A.M., when the older members start the pre-service prayer meeting. Jitneys, streetcars, and buses do a rushing business. Rows of automobiles, freshly polished, line the streets around all the larger churches and many of the smaller ones. "Church mothers," their little gray caps perched on their heads and secured by chin straps, mingle around the door with the younger folks clad in their stylish Sunday best. On special occasions such as Easter and Christmas it is impossible, at 10:45 A.M., to secure a seat in any of the five largest Protestant churches. (These churches each seat more than 2,500 persons.) A surprisingly large number of young people attend these morning services, and special usher boards and junior choirs provide them with specific functions.

Afternoon services, though not a definite part of most church programs, are by no means rare. These are usually "special services"—lodge turnouts, rallies, "Women's Day," "Children's Day," etc. Most churches also have a young people's society, which meets late in the afternoon, though it draws comparatively few youngsters.

Some of the higher-status churches have dispensed with night services entirely, especially in the summer months. Others, in order to meet the competition of Chicago's night life, have evolved the custom of giving "special programs" in addition to, or instead of, preaching. These take the form of dramas, musical extravaganzas, or occasional movies. These Sunday night services are usually entertaining enough to appeal to a circle far wider than the membership of the church. In fact, a great deal of interchurch visiting takes place without regard to denominational lines, and many persons will attend services of this type who make no claim to being religious. It is good entertainment with no cover charge and no compulsion even to drop a nickel in the "free-will offering."

Throughout the week, most churches are centers of activity—singing and praying in the smaller, lower-status churches, and club meetings, socials, plays, concerts, movies, and mass meetings in the larger ones. Community organizations may ordinarily have access to a church building, provided the church itself has nothing scheduled for the night. Bronzeville's churches are centers of free speech, and many a bulletin board is just as likely to list a meeting of a left-wing labor union, or even of a Communist organization, as a meeting of an American Legion post.

Church *attendance,* however, is not a reliable index to church membership in Bronzeville. A careful study of the four largest churches, each averaging over a thousand Sunday morning worshipers and claiming more than 5,000 members—indicates that the actual dues-paying membership may hardly exceed 1,500 persons. Church rolls are seldom pruned, and a boasted "10,000 members" may include the dead, "backsliders," and persons who have shifted to other churches. The largest proportion of people who maintain relationships with the church probably do so, except in very small congregations, through sub-organizations. In fact, many persons have their only relationship in this indirect manner. Such associated organizations range from purely social clubs to co-operative stores. Yet were it not for the primacy of the worship service, and for the hard labor of the "sustaining members" (predominantly women), the average church could not maintain itself. As it is, all the larger churches are saddled with heavy mortgages, and much of the money raised through frequent rallies must be applied to debts. Those interested in "serving the Lord" provide an institution for "serving man."

"A Bone of Contention": Forty years ago, church news was "big news" in Negro newspapers. Today, churches and preachers seldom make the front page unless some sensational incident is involved. In total bulk, too, church news falls far behind club news. The church is not the *center* of community life as it was in Midwest Metropolis before the Great Migration or as it is today in the small towns of the South. Yet the church is the oldest and wealthiest institution in the community, and in competition with a wide range of secular organizations it has managed to remain an important element in the life of Bronzeville. The southern migrants brought to Chicago a tradition of church membership which has persisted in the metropolitan setting. The preachers have adjusted speedily to rapid changes in the urban community, and have thus been able to compete with the "worldly" organizations in an environment notorious for its secular emphasis.

For many people the church is still the center of attention. For an even larger number it is an interesting topic of conversation. Commanding the allegiance of so many people and handling such a large amount of Bronzeville's money, the church inevitably becomes a matter for public discussion. The Cayton-Warner Research staff collected thousands of random comments during the Depression years. The most striking thing about these comments was the prevalence of grumbling against preachers and the church—a habit found among

members and non-members alike. The major criticisms ran somewhat
as follows:

(1) Church is a "racket," (2) Too many churches, (3) Churches
are too emotional, (4) There's no real religion among the members,
(5) Churches are a waste of time and money, (6) Ministers don't
practice what they preach, (7) Ministers don't preach against "sin,"
(8) Church places too much emphasis upon money, (9) Negroes are
too religious.

During the Depression the charge that the church was a "racket"
was encountered everywhere in Bronzeville. This typically Chicago
reaction expressed a doubt of motives that did not necessarily mean
refusal to co-operate with the church but did indicate disapproval of
the emphasis placed upon money by the preachers. It also implied a
suspicion that funds were being used dishonestly or unproductively;
non-church members made the latter charge more frequently than
did the "faithful." The proprietor of a gambling establishment, for
instance, observed: "The church is getting to be too big a racket for
me. I'd rather support my own racket." A flat-janitor who attended
church infrequently confided to an interviewer, "You know churches
are nothing but a racket." The proprietor of a small business said:
"I just don't care anything about the churches because I think they
are rackets." An optometrist was caustic in his comment: "I was baptized in a Baptist church but I don't go regularly. . . . It's just
racketeering on people's emotions anyway." A young business woman
used the same term: "I used to be a member of the Flaming Sword
Baptist Church, but I've dropped my membership. One of my brothers
is a deacon. My other brother, like myself, thinks the church is just
a racket." A housewife in the lower income brackets states that her
husband objects to her attendance at church. He calls the church
"nothing but a racket" and insists that "nobody gets anything out
of it but the preachers." His wife is inclined to agree.

Even when Bronzeville's people do not bluntly characterize churches
as "rackets," they often make the charge by implication. Thus, a hotel
maid states: "I just haven't made up my mind to join a church. Of
course I was a Baptist at home in the South, but most of these
churches are full of graft. You pay and pay money and the church is
still in debt." A WPA worker stated that he didn't attend church
because "they don't help anybody, and all they want is money to keep
the big shots going."

Inevitably the criticisms focus on the preachers. "Blood-suckers!" snapped a skilled laborer; "they'll take the food out of your mouth and make you think they are doing you a favor."

"You take some of these preachers," observed a steel-mill worker; "they're living like kings—got great big Packard automobiles and ten or twelve suits and a bunch of sisters putting food in their pantry. Do you call that religion? Naw! It ain't nothing but a bunch of damn monkey foolishness."

Church members, too, while retaining their membership, are sometimes as caustic as the "unbelievers," making statements like the following:

"I'm a church member. I believe churches are still useful. But like everything else, there's a lot of racketeering going on in the church."

"The preachers want to line their pockets with gold. They are supposed to be the leaders of the people, but they are fake leaders."

"Ministers are not as conscientious as they used to be. They are money-mad nowadays. All they want is the almighty dollar and that is all they talk about."

"When you are making plenty of money and share it with them you are all right, you're a fine fellow. When the crash comes and you are not doing so well, they forget all about you."

Closely related to the charge that churches are a racket is the contention that there are too many churches. One businessman expresses a very general complaint when he says: "I am a churchman and I believe that the church occupies an important place in the life of any community. But I'm also positive that there are too many Negro churches in Chicago and too many false preachers."

Large numbers of people combine a belief in religion with a denunciation of the church, as in the case of the woman who said: "I thinks there's only one heaven where we all will go, but the biggest thieves are running the churches, so what can they do about saving us? Nothing!"

These criticisms express the annoyance and frustration of a group trying to survive on a subsistence level during a depression. The church, too, was trying to survive, and the ministers were forced to emphasize money-raising to keep their doors open and to gather sufficient funds to meet obligations incurred during the Fat Years.* (Figure 25.) Except for a dozen pastors of the largest churches, ministerial salaries averaged less than $2,000 a year, but most preachers, whether in charge of big churches or of small, were conspicuously better off than

Figure 25

WHERE THE CHURCH DOLLAR GOES

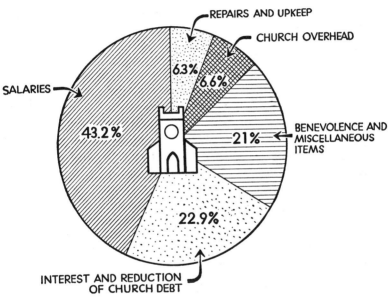

From table in Benjamin E. Mays and Joseph W. Nicholson, *The Negro's Church,* Institute for Social and Religious Research, 1933.

most of the laity, and hence served as convenient targets for attack. Few churches have adequate systems of accounting and it was virtually impossible to verify or disprove charges of stealing and misappropriation of funds. The truth of such charges is, however, largely irrelevant, since antagonism to the church seems to lie deeper than mere hostility toward preachers or concern over clerical probity.

* Frequent newspaper accounts of mortgage-burning ceremonies in the autumn and winter of 1943-44 indicated that churches in Bronzeville were taking advantage of the war boom to institute drives for clearing off their debts.

Bronzeville's loyal church members, thrown on the defensive by these criticisms, usually defend the institution in conventional terms. A "racial angle" (note the italicized passages) is sometimes added. The following expressions are typical of the "defense":

"I am a member of the Solid Rock A.M.E. Church. Churches are a necessity, for I believe that *it is through them that our people first got the idea that we must co-operate with each other.* Take the church away with its teachings and I'm afraid we would not be able to live because it is fear of the beyond that causes one to think of his fellow man and respect his feelings."

"My opinion is that the church is a good influence on the community. People seem to have a certain amount of respect for the church that no other institutions can enjoy. People who are members of churches are the ones that you find trying to accomplish something worth while and are very seldom in the clutches of the law."

"My wife and I are members of Pleasant Green Baptist Church and get a lot of pleasure out of attending services. I think the church is a great necessity, for the people get something from it that is resting and gives them a feeling of peace."

"My family and I are members of Zion's Star A.M.E. Church. I think the church is a good influence. The store-front churches are all right too, and I am sure they are able to interest some people that otherwise would not go to church at all."

"My whole family belongs to St. Simon's Baptist Church. I am of the opinion that the church fills a great need. It is hard to picture the amount of evil that would take hold of the world if the church were done away with. *I also believe that many of our folks have learned from the church that big things can be accomplished only by the joining of forces of a large group of people.*"

WHAT THE CHURCH HAS TO OFFER

"Why," it may be asked, "in the face of widespread criticisms and such apparent dissatisfaction, does the church still flourish?" Underlying the conventional reasons which the faithful give for supporting the church are more fundamental satisfactions that bind them to the institution. Churches offer a wide variety of activities, and a person may take his choice.

The collective ceremonies lend a certain rhythm to existence, and there is little emphasis upon theology. If a person has talent, is a Race Leader, or even a moderately successful business or professional man, he can believe anything he chooses, so long as he "supports the church." In the South, people are sometimes "churched" (i.e., accused publicly) when they have breached the moral code or the church rules, verbally or in their conduct. In Bronzeville this hardly ever happens. One critic commented cynically, "The only thing they might put you out of church for up here is not paying dues." One of the most striking aspects of Bronzeville's church life is a mutually shared core of religious custom that cuts across denominational lines. People "feel at home" in any of the major Protestant denominations, and interdenominational visiting and shifts in church membership are widespread. Bronzeville's churches provide a congenial environment for the thousands of people who were taught as children that they "ought to go to church."

Many people who attend church offer no "religious" reasons at all in explaining their behavior. They attend church, they say, because they "like good singing" and "good speaking," or because the services are "restful and beautiful." Bronzeville's churches are centers of entertainment as well as places of worship. Popular preachers and a wide variety of musical offerings draw large crowds both on Sundays and on week nights. It is not unusual to find a total of over 10,000 people attending Sunday evening musicales in the four largest churches, and an equal number distributed among the smaller churches. The most popular pastors in the Black Belt are excellent showmen. Their sermons are replete with humor and apt illustration, as well as pithy epigram, good jokes, and rousing flights of oratory. Preachers who can flay sin in an original manner, who can denounce iniquity with a "knowing" air and with some sexual innuendo, attract large crowds. In addition to this incidental entertainment, all of Bronzeville's churches are continually offering concerts, pageants, plays, suppers, and other similar activities. Many people without formal membership in any church might be attracted, for example, to the horse shows and fashion shows featuring Joe Louis's wife, Marva, which some Bronzeville churches have sponsored within the last few years.

It is probable, however, that the church's main attraction is **the** opportunity it gives for large masses of people to function in an organized group, to compete for prestige, to be elected to office, to exercise power and control, to win applause and acclaim. Even church fights, although dubbed "unchristian," are interesting.

The Church as a Race Institution: Much of the grumbling against the church is on the basis of "race loyalty." Both members and nonmembers expect the church to play a prominent part in "advancing The Race," and they often judge the institution from this angle alone. As we have mentioned, segregation of Negroes from whites at the congregational level is almost absolute. Negroes seldom see white people in their congregations. The great mass denominations—the Baptists and Negro Methodists—have separate state and national organizations. The relations between white and Negro ministers are rare and formalized. The larger white denominations have a tendency to look upon the Negro churches as a field for "home mission" work. Negroes, as a low-income group, are somewhat dependent upon these white groups for assistance in paying off mortgages, and whenever large community programs are contemplated, Negro churches must either approach these white boards for assistance or seek assistance from other white people.

In enlisting support for their special projects, Bronzeville's churches have had to develop a technique for extracting donations from "white friends." At one extreme is the attractive folder written by a sociologist to get money for a new church building and community center. The appeal is directed to high-status whites as

an opportunity to build a model, influential Negro church that can serve as an example and standard for institutions of similar kind throughout the country. The need of such a high example of intelligent ministry, rational religious services, adequate recreational and community social service, is imperative as the Negro gropes for an intelligent, sincere, and fearless religion.

At the other extreme is the almost illiterate plea of a Negro Pentecostal evangelist, soliciting funds and gifts over the radio each Sunday night:

"Now you white folks in my radio audience mus' have some ol' pianos an' sewin' machines up in yo' attic that yuh kin sen' me. We need 'em. Our church kin use 'em."

In between is the pastor of one of Bronzeville's largest churches who has noticed some white people at the Sunday evening musical:

"Now, Mr. —— of the —— Steel Company is here tonight. I didn't know he an' his frien's were coming, but since they're here we're gonna make them pay for it. [Laughter.] Pass those baskets, ushers! We're tryin' to build up a church here that will make good citizens out of these Negroes on the South Side. I've got 15,000 members and they're all spillin' outa the place. We need a building on that lot we've bought over there, an' if you white folks will put up the building we can save the South Side.

"Now, Deacon —— works for this steel company. Stand up over there, Deacon. He may have told these visitors to come. I didn't. But we're glad you're here. You know Negroes always did love white folks, anyhow— that is, we love the *men*. [Laughter from the audience at this daring play on a socially tabooed subject, the relations between Negro men and white women—a type of joke that could not have been used in addressing white visitors in the South.]"

Such "begging from white folks" is distasteful to many of Bronzeville's church people, but it is mixed with admiration for those preachers who can do it with finesse and without "Uncle Tomming" or sacrificing their dignity.* The following incident illustrates the mixed reactions of Negroes, dependent upon whites for financial support but desirous of preserving their independence of action. In this case the trustee board of a small school for training store-front preachers was in session. The funds for the experiment had been supplied by a white denominational board, and the Negroes were trying hard to meet a pledge they had made. They felt, however, that they would have more success if they had a concrete objective such as buying a building to house the school. They planned a large money-raising campaign around this financial project. The white co-sponsors felt that the purchase of a building was a too ambitious goal. After the

* One of the authors observed another case of flattering powerful white people. A large church was giving its annual music festival. The Chicago postmaster had been invited to attend, since many Negroes worked under his supervision, including the choir director. Near the end of the program, while the audience was expectantly awaiting the *Hallelujah Chorus,* all postmen in the audience were asked to stand. The postmaster proceeded to deliver a 45-minute harangue while the audience twisted, squirmed, and muttered in disapproval. After "honoring" the postmaster, the choir director announced that a prominent white banker was present. He explained that this man had flown to Chicago from New York especially to attend this service. Both the pastor and the choir director praised him fulsomely. The banker was the main mortgage-holder on the church property!

enthusiastic speeches of Bronzeville's ministers had all been delivered, a young white minister representing the Home Mission Board of his donomination rose. He was very blunt.

"Before you brethren start discussing the purchase of a building, I think we should pay some attention to the fact that we are running a $300 deficit on this year's budget. I am sure Dr. —— [the white president of the Home Mission Board] would want this wiped out before we make any further commitments."

The Negro ministers were incensed. It was a fact that they had fallen behind on their pledges for the year, but the white speaker had touched a raw spot: he had reminded them of their subordinate position. He had implied that they were putting nonessentials first. He had assumed the air of a missionary or a tutor lecturing his improvident wards. The chairman of the meeting, a well-educated Negro minister, rose to defend the honor of The Race.

"I think the time has come [he said] when Negroes ought to take up their own responsibilities and maintain their own organizations. There are 126 churches in our denomination on the South Side. I think we can support this institution by ourselves. White people have helped me. They gave me money to go to Harvard. They helped me pay the mortgage on my church. But I think the time has come when Negroes can handle their own affairs. Now, I feel we should pay these brethren [the whites] what we owe them, then buy our building, and run this institution by ourselves."

The atmosphere was tense. The three white board members were embarrassed and disconcerted, the Negro ministers uneasy. At this point a skillful and eloquent Bronzeville preacher took the floor and began to restore the atmosphere of "goodwill," using all the techniques of handling white folks which Negroes in the South have developed —humor, a little "stooping to conquer," playful denunciation of Negroes. At the same time he threw in some concessions to race pride to appeal to the Negroes. His approach is a striking illustration of the technique of a Race Leader handling a mixed audience in a crisis situation:

"Brother Chairman, you may be ready to cut loose from the white folks, but I'm not. I'm going to get all the money I can out of them. [Laughter from both Negroes and whites.] I'm going down *tomorrow* to see about getting some money for *my* church. You know it's the *duty* of white folks to help their colored brothers, and I'm not going to do anything to stand in the way of letting a man do his Christian duty.*

"Negroes are poor. You know the white folks have all the money. Just because Negroes ride around in fine automobiles and wear good clothes doesn't mean that they've got any money. You said that we have 126 churches. Now, you know as well as I do that if we come right down to it, there are only about 26 real churches, and every one of them is so interested in taking care of his own corner that they can't get together.

"Now, I'm tired of so much talk. Negroes can preach longer, pray louder, and make more noise than any folks on God's earth. [Both Negroes and whites laughed at this bit of racial depreciation.] I think we ought to pay that $300 deficit just to show the brethren that we are co-operating with them. I think we ought to put up or shut up. I have a check for $50 in my pocket that I was getting ready to use to pay another bill. I'm going to give that $50. Who'll match it?"

At this point the chairman was forced to pledge $25 in order to save face. Within ten minutes $125 had been pledged. The peacemaker assured the white members of the board that the Negroes would have the remainder by the next Sunday. He then turned to the subject of the building:

"Now I think that if the colored brethren want a building they ought to have it. I think that the finance committee should look the site over and report back to us. We've got a great future and, Brother Chairman, I believe we can buy that building if we want to."

Despite the dependence of Negro congregations upon the occasional friendly aid of white co-religionists, the Negro church is largely free of white control. Negro preachers have the greatest "freedom" of any Race Leaders. Politicians must fit themselves into machine politics. Most "civic" leaders are dependent upon white philanthropy. Most of Bronzeville's preachers are answerable to no one except their congregations. They can say what they please about current affairs and race relations; there are no church superiors to discipline them and no white people to take economic reprisals. Because they are so largely free of the political and economic controls of the white com-

---

* In 1939 only two or three Negro churches were receiving aid from white church boards in paying off mortgages, but the number has been much larger in the past. At a state convention of one large Negro denomination in 1939, the moderator was heard telling the delegates: "They [the whites] will help us if we help ourselves. The whites are looking at what we are doing. . . . If you need help go down and tell them. Some arrangement will be made."

munity, Bronzeville expects them to be *real* Race Men. Preachers are subjected to continuous community criticism, and to retain the allegiance of their followers they are forced to concern themselves with a wide range of secular activities—political action, protest against discrimination, advice on securing jobs and legal aid, and the encouragement of Negro business enterprises.

Yet, when a preacher responds to these demands, he immediately risks being accused of "racketeering."* For instance, most of the larger churches advertise Negro-owned businesses on the theory that successful colored businessmen are "advancing The Race." They try to throw business toward certain Negro undertakers, physicians, and retail stores. Church newspapers carry ads of colored enterprises in Bronzeville and of white stores that employ Negroes. Sometimes a pastor will appoint special agents or representatives within his church to plug specific stores or products.† Naturally, the community assumes that the ministers get "kickbacks" and special considerations from these businessmen.

* This charge is very frequently made with respect to political campaigns. The ministers are accused of promising to "deliver the vote" for a sizable financial reward or for the promise of some position. The ministers, on the other hand, are likely to insist that they accept donations for the church but no personal gifts from politicians. There have been ministers in Bronzeville who were actively engaged in politics. One of them, Bishop Archibald J. Carey, held several high appointive positions under Mayor Thompson and finally secured a post on the state Civil Service Commission. He was accused of accepting bribes, although there was widespread belief that he had been "framed." Any minister who does business with the political machines lays himself open to criticism. Yet many people in Bronzeville feel that their preachers should go into politics. The popularity of clerico-politicians in Negro communities is illustrated by the elections of 1944 in which a Negro preacher was elected from New York's Harlem to represent the area in Congress, another was made Recorder of Deeds in Washington shortly before the election, and still another was elected to the state legislature in Ohio.

† The following ads have been selected as typical of hundreds appearing in church newspapers of Bronzeville's largest churches:

> —— ELECTRIC SERVICE COMPANY—Inquire about our special plan to the members of —— Baptist Church. Miss ——, Representative. At your own authorized dealer.

> —— SHOE AND DRY GOODS STORE—Headquarters for Florsheim Shoes. Men's, Ladies', Children's Ready to Wear. We Employ Colored Salesmen.

> WHEN IN NEED OF FURNITURE SEE REV. WM. P. ——, Representative of the —— FURNITURE COMPANY.

Bronzeville is very critical of its preachers when accusing them of tying up too much money in church property or in other "noneconomic" uses. Ordinarily these sentiments are expressed in rather vague and general terms, such as one man's comment:

"I used to be active in the church; I thought we could work out our salvation that way. But I found out better. These Negro preachers are not bothered about The Race—about all they think of is themselves."

The ministers counter with the argument that the church is not *primarily* a business or political institution, and insist that if they weren't meeting the people's "needs" they couldn't survive. Often the criticisms are by no means vague—they are an insistent demand that the Negro churches should encourage the support of Negro businessmen who "make jobs for The Race."

CHAPTER 16

Negro Business: Myth and Fact

THE DOCTRINE OF THE DOUBLE-DUTY DOLLAR *

IT IS SUNDAY MORNING IN THE "BLACK BELT." THE PASTOR OF ONE OF THE largest churches has just finished his morning prayer. There is an air of quiet expectancy, and then—a most unusual discourse begins. The minister, in the homely, humorous style so often affected by Bronzeville's "educated" leaders when dealing with a mass audience, is describing a *business exposition:*

"The Business Exposition at the Armory was one of the finest achievements of our people in the history of Chicago. Are there any members of the Exposition Committee here? If so, please stand. [A man stands.] Come right down here where you belong; we've got a seat right here in front for you. This man is manager of the Apex Shoe Store—the shoes that I wear. . . . We can get anything we want to wear or eat from Negroes today. If you would do that it would not only purchase the necessities of life for you, but would open positions for your young folks. You can strut as much as you want to, and look like Miss Lizzie [an upper-class white person], but you don't know race respect if you don't buy from Negroes. As soon as these white folks get rich on the South Side, they go and live on the Gold Coast, and the only way you can get in is by washing their cuspidors. Why not go to Jackson's store, even if you don't want to buy nothin' but a gingersnap? Do that and encourage those girls workin' in there. Go in there and come out eating. Why don't you do that?"

This is the doctrine of the "Double-Duty Dollar," preached from many Bronzeville pulpits as a part of the weekly ritual. Church newspapers, too, carry advertisements of all types of business from "chicken shacks" † to corset shops. Specific businessmen are often pointed out to

---

* The term "Double-Duty Dollar" seems to have been first popularized by a Negro minister, Dr. Gordon B. Hancock, who runs a column called *Between the Lines* in several weekly Negro newspapers. In Chicago, the term is frequently used by public speakers and writers.

† Restaurants which specialize in fried chicken.

the congregations as being worthy of emulation and support, and occasional mass meetings stress the virtues of buying from Negroes—of making the dollar do "double-duty": by both purchasing a commodity and "advancing The Race." The pastor quoted above had been even more explicit in an address before the Business Exposition crowd itself:

"Tomorrow I want all of you people to go to these stores. Have your shoes repaired at a Negro shop, buy your groceries from a Negro grocer . . . and for God's sake, buy your meats, pork chops, and yes, even your chitterlings,* from a Negro butcher. On behalf of the Negro ministers of Chicago, I wish to commend these Negro businessmen for promoting such an affair, and urge upon you again to patronize your own, for that is the only way we as a race will ever get anywhere."

Residents of the Negro community rather generally approve of those churches and ministers who lend their support to Negro enterprises, and church members sometimes cite such actions as evidence that their pastors are "progressive." As one woman phrased it: "Reverend Moss is one of the progressive ministers. . . . He tells us that we are too dependent on other races for employment and that we must establish good sound business enterprises and at least give employment to the many youths that finish their education each year. His one principal subject is co-operation and racial solidarity, for in union there is strength."

Preachers who do not preach the gospel of the "Double-Duty Dollar" are liable to such caustic criticisms as this:

"God have mercy on our preachers! They are the supposed-to-be leaders of The Race. But all they are interested in is money for themselves. . . . We pay hundreds of thousands of dollars for churches, but when it comes to building Negro businesses, it seems that our people are not interested."

Some of the Holiness sects protest vigorously against this mixture of religion, business, and race pride, but they are definitely a minority voice in Bronzeville.

This endorsement of business by the church simply dramatizes, and brings the force of sacred sanctions to bear upon, slogans that the press, the civic organizations, and even the social clubs repeat incessantly, emphasizing the duty of Negroes to trade with Negroes and promising ultimate racial "salvation" if they will support racial business enterprises.

* A southern delicacy prepared from the intestines of the hog.

The efficacy of these appeals is difficult to measure. There is no way of knowing, for instance, how many of the hearers react like the person referred to in this (probably apocryphal) story told by a colored merchant:

"A Negro came in here with five dollars worth of Jew stuff * in his arms and bought ten cents' worth of salt pork from me. He said: 'Every Sunday morning the Reverend wants all who bought groceries from a colored grocer to raise their hands. Now I can hold *mine* up with a clear conscience.'"

To the Negro community, a business is more than a mere enterprise to make profit for the owner. From the standpoints of both the customer and the owner it becomes a symbol of racial progress, for better or for worse. And the preacher is expected to encourage his flock to trade with Negroes.

That these ministerial appeals do have some effect is suggested by the rather general comments of white businessmen in the Black Belt, such as that of one man who told an interviewer:

"There has been a great deal of propaganda created against the white merchants in this neighborhood, some of it coming from the ministers in the pulpits of their churches, advising the people to patronize Negro merchants whenever possible. And they are doing it!"

The elevation of the Double-Duty Dollar slogan into the realm of almost sacred dogma results primarily from the fact that Negroes participate in two worlds—the larger community of city, state, and nation, and the smaller, socially isolated, and spatially separate Negro world.

---

* In 1938, about three-fourths of the merchants in Bronzeville were Jewish. During that year an organized anti-Semitic drive arose in Bronzeville. A small newspaper, *Dynamite,* scurrilously attacked all Jews. Jewish philanthropists were accused of trying to dominate Negro institutions; Jewish merchants were dubbed exploiters. Suggestions were made that all Jews should be expelled from Bronzeville. Finally, after conferences between Negro and Jewish leaders as well as representatives of various labor unions, the editor of the paper was dissuaded from publishing further attacks. Because many of the interviews we quote were made when the campaign was at its height, the repeated references to Jews may represent an abnormal situation; in other years such references might be less frequent. Yet, as the most highly visible and most immediately available white persons in the community, Jewish merchants tend to become the symbol of the Negroes' verbal attack on all white businessmen, and anti-Semitic waves sometimes sweep through Bronzeville. In New Orleans, where Italian merchants predominate in Negro areas, "Dagoes" are the target of attack. In Bronzeville it is the Jew who is the scapegoat.

As participants in the general American culture, they are exposed to a system that places a high premium upon business success and white-collar occupations. Financial power and economic control bring those political and social rewards which have traditionally been supposed to serve as incentives to thrift, enterprise, and hard work. Negroes, using the same school textbooks as whites, reading the same papers, attending the same movies, and in constant contact with the white world, tend to incorporate the general ideals of American life. Inevitably, they measure progress since slavery partly in terms of the positions of power and prestige which Negroes attain in the business world.

Objective reality, however, is at variance with the ideal. No Negro sits on a board of directors in La Salle Street; none trades in the grain pit or has a seat on the Stock Exchange; none owns a skyscraper. Negro girls are seldom seen in the offices and stores of the Loop except as maids. Colored traveling salesmen, buyers, and jobbers are a rarity. The largest retail stores and half of the smaller business enterprises in Bronzeville are owned and operated by white persons, and until recently many of these did not voluntarily employ Negroes.

THE GROWTH OF A "NEGRO MARKET"

Chicago's first colored businessmen did not serve an exclusively Negro market. Most of the earliest colored businessmen were engaged in service enterprises catering to a white clientele. Reference has already been made to John Jones, the tailor, in the Seventies. There were also barbers, hairdressers, wigmakers, masseurs, and caterers. A few Negroes ran livery stables and served as draymen. One Isom Artis made his living in the Seventies by drawing water from Lake Michigan and selling it to the residents for eight cents a barrel. In the late Seventies, another Negro opened a large lumber yard from which he later made a small fortune. While most of these had a predominantly white clientele, there were also less lucrative restaurants, barber shops, and small stores in the small Negro area.

Between the close of the Civil War and the publication of the first *Colored Men's Professional and Business Directory of Chicago* in 1885, the participation of the Negro in the business life of the city developed to the extent of some 200 enterprises in 27 different fields. Most numerous were barber shops. Restaurants competed with "sample rooms" (combination liquor stores and saloons) for second place. Even as late as the turn of the century, however, the Negro market was relatively unimportant.

On the eve of the Great Migration, there were about 500 Negro businessmen concentrated either in the service occupations or in those enterprises calling for small amounts of capital and but little experience. Barber shops (now serving a Negro clientele) predominated, but it is significant that colored moving and storagemen (successors to the early draymen) serving both whites and Negroes were still numerous, for automobiles had not yet arrived in sufficient numbers to drive horses from the streets.

The Great Migration created the "Negro market." Both white and Negro merchants, as well as the Negro consumer, became increasingly conscious of the purchasing power of several hundred thousand people solidly massed in one compact community. The rapid growth of the Negro community between 1915 and 1929 was accompanied by expansion in all types of Negro-owned businesses, not the least lucrative of which was speculation in real estate. (Table 18 and Figure 26.)

TABLE 18

RELATIONSHIP BETWEEN GROWTH OF TOTAL NEGRO POPULATION AND TOTAL NEGRO BUSINESS: 1860-1937

(Showing Types of Business and Per Cent of Increase)

Year	Population	Per Cent Increase	Total Number Businesses	Per Cent Increase	Retail Total Number	Per Cent Increase	Total Number Services	Per Cent Increase
1860	955		33		3		30	
1885	10,376	986.5	111	236.4	46	1,433.3	64	113.3
1905	37,126	257.8	566	409.9	180	291.3	374	484.4
1908	41,312	11.3	371	−34.5	145	−19.4	214	−42.8
1912	46,480	12.5	526	41.8	132	−9.0	370	72.9
1916	83,316	79.3	727	38.2	215	62.9	479	29.5
1921	121,902	46.3	1,260	73.3	486	126.0	761	58.9
1923-24	146,791	20.4	1,385	9.9	489	.6	869	14.2
1927	196,569	33.9	1,168	−15.7	327	−33.1	816	−6.1
1930	233,903	19.0			815	149.2		
1935	236,905	1.3			724	−11.2		
1937	237,105	1	2,464	111.0	914	26.2	1,463	79.3

Figure 26

RATE OF GROWTH OF NEGRO POPULATION
AND OF NEGRO-OWNED BUSINESS: 1860-1937

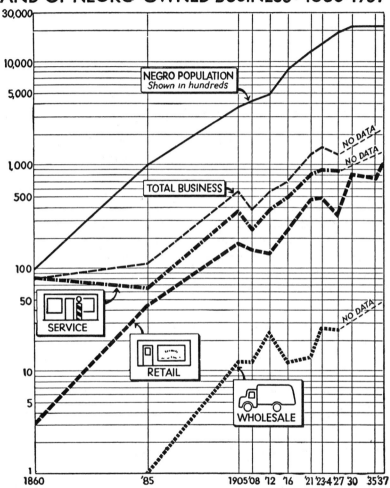

Adapted from a graph prepared by Joseph Semper and drawn by Lawrence Langford, Cayton-Warner Research.

The curve of Negro enterprise rose throughout the Twenties.* (Figure 26.) Two colored banks and three or four insurance companies began to amass capital from within the Negro community and to lend money for the purchase of homes. As the population moved southward from the Loop, the business center moved with it. But there was little tendency among long-established white businesses (especially those on the main thoroughfares) to move away from these areas newly occupied by Negroes.

The Depression of 1929 liquidated the two colored banks and wiped out many of the larger enterprises. Paradoxically, however, it stimulated an increase in the number of smaller businesses, as many people with some savings saw in the opening of a small store one means of insuring themselves against starvation. The impact of the Depression combined with the fierce competition for good locations, for credit and capital, also resulted in an accentuation of racial antagonisms, including anti-Semitic manifestations.

The Depression also revivified the dream of organizing the purchasing power of the Negro—not only for the salvation of Negro businessmen threatened with extinction, but also as a possible method of creating jobs for the thousands of persons who were going on relief and for the impecunious and unemployed white-collar class. Attempts to organize the economic power of the Negro have followed two main lines: (1) forcing white merchants to employ Negroes through the use of the boycott, and (2) urging Negroes to trade with Negroes. The latter has, of course, been the preferred objective of Negro businessmen.

That Negroes have not become fully integrated into the commercial life of the city and do not have a larger measure of economic control even within their own communities is due primarily to the fact that

* For the first five years of this period, the center of Bronzeville's commercial activities was still in the northern end of the Black Belt at State Street and 35th. Negro-owned businesses jumped from 47 to 77 within two years on 35th and State, and from 9 to 71 on 31st Street. Many migrants who had been shopkeepers in the South, or who brought ambition or savings with them, opened small retail enterprises; and, except for a short period between 1924 and 1927, there was a steady increase in retail business. In 1920, the ranking five businesses from the standpoint of number of units were: barber shops, 211; groceries and delicatessens, 119; hairdressing parlors, 108; restaurants, 87; cleaning, pressing, and dyeing, 68; express and storage, 71; tailors, 62; real estate offices, 52; notions, 25; shoe-shine parlors, 26; dressmakers, 32; drugstores, 31; shoemakers, 26; undertakers, 21.

their normal participation in the economic life of Midwest Metropolis is curtailed by traditional attitudes toward colored persons and by the vested economic interests of white occupational groups. These factors are reinforced by the subtle, but none the less powerful, tendencies toward dispersal of effort which result from the conditions of life in the Black Ghetto.

For Negro businesses to compete with white businesses in Negro communities, they must be able to "meet the price" and give equivalent service. Negro businessmen insist that they face five main competitive difficulties: (1) difficulty in procuring capital and credit, (2) difficulty in getting adequate training, (3) inability to secure choice locations on the main business streets, (4) lack of sufficient patronage to allow them to amass capital and to make improvements, (5) inability to organize for co-operative effort.

These circumstances have resulted in a situation in which Negroes have found it extremely difficult to compete with white businessmen in the same field as to prices and service. This, in turn, tends to reinforce the stereotype that Negroes are not good businessmen. In order to meet the competition, Negro businessmen and community leaders stress the dogmas of racial solidarity in an effort to amass capital and patronage. This results in a pattern of behavior in which both Negro customers and merchants are always on the defensive *vis-à-vis* one another, and often take refuge in mutual derogation. Despite these difficulties, some Negroes *have* been able to compete with whites for the Negro market, and some have even been able to develop businesses competing in the general city market.

ODDS AGAINST THE NEGRO

In the second year of the Depression, Chicago Negroes were spending about $39,000,000 annually—over $11,000,000 on groceries and vegetables; $7,000,000 on meat; a little over $4,000,000 on wearing apparel; over $2,000,000 on milk, butter, and eggs; nearly $2,500,000 on shoes and overshoes; a little less than a million dollars on millinery and haberdashery; over a quarter of a million on laundry and cleaning; and about $12,000,000 on furniture. Four years later, the Department of Commerce estimated the purchasing power of Negroes in Chicago at about $81,000,000. Today, the figure must be somewhere near

$150,000,000. This is the Negro market for which both white and Negro businessmen are competing.

In 1938, Negroes in Bronzeville owned and operated some 2,600 business enterprises.* Most of these were small retail stores and service enterprises on side streets, or in the older, less desirable communities. There were also about 2,800 white businesses within the Black Belt. *While Negro enterprises constituted almost half of all the businesses in Negro neighborhoods, they received less than a tenth of all the money spent by Negroes within these areas.*† The odds have been against Negro merchants, and their behavior reflects their plight.

TABLE 19

THE TEN MOST NUMEROUS TYPES OF NEGRO-OWNED BUSINESSES IN CHICAGO: 1938

(1,356, or 64% of All Negro-owned Businesses, Are Included in These Ten Types)

Type of Business	Number of Units
Beauty parlors............................	287
Groceries................................	257
Barber shops.............................	207
Tailors, cleaners, and pressers..........	163
Restaurants..............................	145
Coal and wood dealers....................	87
Taverns..................................	70
Undertakers..............................	50
Shoe repairing...........................	48
Dressmakers..............................	42
Total................................	1,356

* Bronzeville's merchants like to feel that Chicago leads the country in Negro business enterprise. The Nov. 27, 1937, issue of the Pittsburgh *Courier* carried an article headlined:

CHICAGO ANGERED OVER RANKING OF UNITED STATES CENSUS BUREAU

WINDY CITY BUSINESSMEN DENY THAT NEW YORK AND PHILADELPHIA LEAD THEM IN STORES AND SALES

The Negro businessmen insisted that white census-takers never enumerate Negro areas properly. New York and Philadelphia had Negro census-takers. One Bronzeville businessman was reported as saying: "If Chicago's business census was taken now by Negro enumerators, the results would show us away out in front. . . . We ought to start now and lay plans for the 1940 census of Negro business, so as to regain our lost prestige." Another man said: "Those figures just issued by the Census Bureau are all wrong. Everyone knows that Chicago has more and better business places than New York, and always will have."

† A business census of 1935 revealed that only 5 per cent of the $11,000,000 which Bronzeville spent on groceries was spent with Negroes.

Negro grocers and general retailers, matching wits and prices with the small white merchants and with the chain stores in Bronzeville and the Loop, appeal loudly to "race pride" and fulminate bitterly against white storekeepers in Negro neighborhoods. These Negro businessmen, quite naturally, dream of organizing the Negro market to corral the errant dollars. When they do not succeed in doing this, they are peeved with both competitors and potential customers. Out of this anger flow both bitter invective and a sigh of resignation. "No community can hope to thrive," insists one newspaper editor, "where people come from other communities and operate businesses in this community, and at the close of day you see the money taken out of the neighborhood never to return, except in the form of some more second- or third-grade goods to take the rest of the Negro's money." Awareness of the potentialities of the Negro market has evoked many protests such as that of the Baptist minister who commented bitterly:

"The Negro in Chicago spends billions on merchandise. All of that money goes into the white man's pocket and then out of our neighborhoods. It is used to buy white men cars and homes, and their wives mink coats and servants. Our money is being used by the white man to pay us for being his cook, his valet, and his washwoman."

In its most extreme form, the dream of controlling the Negro market visualizes a completely separate Negro economy: "The idea is to be able to support ourselves instead of being wholly dependent on the white race." Despite this dream, nine-tenths of Bronzeville's money is spent with whites, and this is why the Negro businessman complains that his own people do not support him.

BUSINESSMAN'S COMPLAINT

Bronzeville businessmen are convinced that one of the main problems facing them is the power of "the white man's psychology." "Negroes," they feel, "have never learned to patronize their own." Merchants are continually making such statements as the following (usually associated with one or two other complaints):

"I think that colored people will have to be educated to trade with each other. I notice that even now what you would call the most substantial people on this street pass my store on their way to 31st Street to trade with some Jew merchant. *Of course, the chain stores offer a deal of com-*

petition to any independent merchant, but having come in close contact with Jews, as I did, I know they feel they can 'jive' a Negro along and get his money."

The proprietress of a beauty shop, who does not herself have white competition but who has had difficulty in securing a favorable location for her shop, was very bitter, using an epithet which Negroes would resent if applied by a white person:

"I think it is a shame that these old, dumb 'darkies' will trade in those places. They [white people] only pocket the money and leave the community. They will hire a few colored girls so they can get the business, but they aren't bothered about you after they get rich. It will never be stopped because some of our people refuse to trade with a Negro."

Even a huckster, peddling vegetables in the alley, has similar views:

"The colored seem to prefer the whites. There was a white fellow that came through the alley and the colored used to bring their pans down to him. They would holler for me to come up to them, and then instead of really buying from me would wait for him."

Sometimes the rural, southern origin of the Negro is blamed for this alleged slavery to "the white man's psychology." Thus, a fairly successful grocer who felt that his customers patronized him only because they thought he "fronted for a Jew," was sure that "these people are used to living on the farm and trading with the white man. They don't know any better."

An unsuccessful cleaner and presser has this same view:

"Ninety per cent of Negroes in Chicago are from the South, and with that in mind they feel as if they must buy from a white man or that a white man's commodities are better than those of a Negro."

One woman offered an interesting variation on this southern theme:

"They want to appear important, and many of them go to a white man's place just to make him wait on them. It is like getting revenge for not having had the opportunity of going into some white places in the South. The one sad thing is the Negro does not realize that he is hurting himself in doing this, for his group needs his trade to stay in business."

Occasionally, a person reverses this argument, insisting that southern Negroes are more likely to trade with Negroes. Here is one grocery-store proprietor's opinion:

"One thing the average person does not realize is that a business in the South is entirely different from one in the North. There the southern white man does not want a Negro's trade and will tell him so. That makes the Negro patronize his own people. . . . Then, too, it teaches the Negroes to trade with each other. . . . I have often heard people say that Negroes do not patronize each other here. I have made a study of this and find that people from the South do."

Negro women, as spenders of the family income, are frequently the target of the merchants' criticisms:

"They shop for the whole house and they easily influence the men in their spending. I would say without fear of contradiction that Negro women are responsible for the success or failure of Negroes in business."

One male proprietor even added a pseudo-Freudian note:

"Negroes don't want to trade with the Negroes as they should, and I think Negro women are responsible for this situation, because two-thirds of the purchases are made for home consumption . . . and the men generally leave it to the women folks to do the shopping. I am inclined to the belief that Negro women are attracted to white men in the same proportion that Negro men are attracted to white women. Just ordinary politeness and courtesy and an occasional smile on the part of a white merchant gives the Negro woman an opportunity to release to some extent her suppressed desires. Of course, there are many exceptions to this rule, but the fact still remains that unlike objects attract."

Frequently, Negro businessmen will relate, with evident satisfaction, some incidents in which Negroes who have spurned their wares were "tricked." Thus one cobbler told his story: "The Negro has no faith in colored business. He thinks I can't fix his *good* pair of shoes. He don't know that the Jew down the street brings his work for me to do. I do all his sewing."

Some of the most bitter comments are reserved for the Negro leaders, who, as a group, are accused of not supporting Negro business enterprises. A typical complaint of this type was made by a storekeeper:

"You know the 'big shot' don't patronize his own color as much as the little fellow does. After he gets up in the world he don't need you. . . . The only colored business that the leading colored man will patronize is the barber shop, the pool hall, and the undertaker—because he has to. If one barber shop don't suit him, all he can do is go to another colored shop. He can't go to a white one."

One of the most successful insurance executives in Bronzeville cited the case of a prominent minister whom he accused of being dominated by "the white man's psychology":

"We have a reinsurance contract with a large white insurance company here in Chicago, and with a few other white companies throughout the country. Recently, Reverend Clissock took out $5,000 worth of insurance with this white company. One of the officials called me and asked me if my company would take $4,500 of the policy. Needless to say, we agreed. Now, there's a Negro who gets all his money from poor hard-working parishioners; yet, with a Negro company big and powerful enough to carry his risk, he ignored us and went to this white company. Now he has a policy with the white company's name on it, and he would probably die if he knew that a colored company had over four thousand of his five thousand dollars."

A fairly well-educated and somewhat analytical merchant summed the matter up as follows:

"Some Negroes do patronize Negro business. They are usually the laboring class, though—people who work in factories and do laboring work. The professionals and the so-called 'big Negroes' spend nearly all of their earnings with the whites. The reason for this is simple: the professional group like the school teachers, doctors, and lawyers, earn large salaries and get better fees. They have greater earning power and hence they open charge accounts and do most of their buying in the Loop. They buy not only clothes and furniture there, but also food-stuffs. They contribute very little to the success of the Negro merchants on the South Side."

Preachers are sometimes excoriated for their failure to support Negro business aggressively. One editor of a Bronzeville paper engaged in a long discussion with an interviewer about "what these no-good preachers ought to do." He insisted that they should buy all their clothing from Negroes—"every last handkerchief and necktie"—wear this clothing to church on Sunday morning, and tell their congregations to "do as they had done." "They'll get up there with Marshall Field labels all over them and tell Negroes to trade with the race," he observed scornfully. One merchant accused a very prominent pastor of "buying his daily needs from the Jew" and having the packages delivered to his home so that he wouldn't be seen coming out of the store.

One Negro merchant was so irritated by the alleged failure of Negroes to support business that he said: "Other businesses ought to force the colored man to patronize his own color by refusing to wait on him!"

With so general a feeling on the part of colored merchants that they do not receive the support of the Negro community, it might be instructive to turn to "the public" for its side of the case.

THE NEGRO CUSTOMER'S DEFENSE

Race Pride vs. Prices: Over and over, Negroes in Bronzeville reveal a conflict between the economic imperative of "making ends meet" and the social demands of "race pride." They insist that Negro merchants cannot give equivalent goods and services for the same price:

"I'd like to do all my shopping—what little I do—with colored, but I can get things cheaper at the chain stores. I buy there for that reason."

"I buy at the A & P where I can get food cheapest. I try to patronize my race, but I can't on my husband's salary [$55 per month, WPA]."

"I do all of my buying at white stores. They always seem to be a penny or two cheaper."

"My real friend is a dollar. I try to patronize my people, but when it comes to saving a penny, especially at this time, I do so, even if I have to buy from whites."

Race Pride vs. Credit: Poor people need credit. Negro merchants on the whole are unable to grant it. This forces the Negro housewife to avoid the colored grocer as well as the chain store. One woman who formerly shopped at the A & P, and who says she now goes to "the Jew," makes the following somewhat apologetic statement:

"You see, I can get credit from him and I can't from the A & P or a colored store. I like to trade at the A & P because you can pick up quite a bit of fresh vegetables and stuff, but I tried to get credit there and couldn't."

A grocer corroborates the testimony that the credit problem is a real one:

"We have the trade of young people—penny trade. People come in here begging as soon as they want charity, but they trade regular with the Jews. People we never saw before come in and ask for credit. They've been customers of the Jew all the time. They go to State Street and come back here with big bundles they bought from the Jew. Then they stop in here and buy a pound of sugar or two pickles. Five days after that they ask for credit. Our people would just rather trade with the Jew."

Race Pride vs. Quality: Colored housewives often combine with these criticisms of price and credit the charge that the quality and variety of stock in Negro stores are poor.

"I try to spend as much as I can with Negro stores, but most of them don't have what you want, or they are too high. That may be our fault for not trading with them more, but we are too poor and have to count pennies."

"There are colored businesses in the neighborhood, but they never have a good supply. The colored lady who had a store across the street is a penny or two higher than Tony."

Race Pride vs. "Service": Colored storekeepers are also accused of general inefficiency and ineptitude: "The Negro does not know how to wait on customers"; "The clerk forgets his work and tries to sweetheart with you"; "Our people are too slothful; they are behind the white man."

One of the most general criticisms of Negro merchants is the charge that "they are stuck up," or "hincty." As one customer complained: "The average Negro in business will frown and become very haughty at the least thing." One woman contrasted the Negro merchant with "the Jew" in this respect:

"Some of these colored people make you hate them when you try to trade with them. When you go into a store and try to be choicy they get mad. But a Jew tries to fool you and make you think he is pleasing you. . . . I trade at Jew stores *where Negroes work* most of the time because they appreciate what you buy from them."

One colored businessman shared this belief that "the average colored man who gets a few dollars takes an extra head-size and you can't touch him," but also blamed the customers for their lack of patience with the merchant: "Negroes rate their businessmen as the scum of the earth. They are ready to censure them for the least little mistake that they make."

A housewife summed up what many Negroes no doubt feel about the whole matter of supporting colored merchants:

"The Negro must learn to be independent and have the same type of goods the white man has for the same price. The Negro should not be expected to trade with another Negro because he is a black man. People of any race should have some respect for their people, but any people naturally want to get things where they can get the best bargains."

THE MERCHANT'S REBUTTAL

Negroes Expect Too Much: Many Negro merchants have faced these criticisms frankly, and have studied the behavior of their customers. There is a general tendency to feel that Negroes "expect more" from a colored merchant than from a white, that they are "touchy" and constantly make comparisons with the type of service offered by whites. The woman owner of a successful hosiery shop insisted that "Negroes support our business. If they didn't, we would have closed shortly after we opened." She was just as certain, however, that "one of the biggest problems we have is trying to please the customers. The women customers will get runs in their stockings and bring them back to me with a complaint and want adjustment. The Loop stores don't have this sort of thing to contend with." A florist, too, insisted that she had "to give more service and all the trimmings to induce Negroes to buy." One merchant said: "The public expects more out of a colored man than it does out of a white man. It expects a better grade and prices, and more courtesy." He felt that Negroes should try to meet the competitive disadvantage, however, and accused most colored businessmen of "lack of courtesy." "The trouble with the Negro businessman," he observed, "is laziness, lack of energy, lack of stock, and ignorance of his public." Such a blanket indictment does not give sufficient weight to other factors, however.

White Competition Is Keen: The more reflective colored businessman is likely to add that Negro businesses, on the whole, lack sufficient capital and experience to compete with the average white merchant. Thus they are often unable to provide the range of goods and services which a customer has a right to expect. As one very successful merchant phrased it:

"There is one thing that gives the white merchant the jump on the Negro. The average Negro goes into business simply because he cannot find work, and the place he opens is started with very small capital and his stock is limited. A customer does not like to go to more than one place when shopping. The people who have the money and could open large, well-stocked stores do not do so because they cannot get the locations they want."

The owner of one small sandwich shop states that he plans "to make this little place one of the best-looking stores on 47th Street" because "Negroes *do* patronize each other and they would do so to a greater extent, only we do not fix up our places to encourage them." A delicatessen owner is sure that "the Negro will patronize you if you have the money to put into your store what he wants. There are lots who would rather trade with their own people if they had what they want." From her analysis of the situation, lack of capital is "the greatest handicap of the Negro merchant."

Some merchants feel that any accumulation of adequate capital is primarily dependent upon sustained support and that Negroes should "give their merchants a break." Thus, one woman who runs what she calls a "very high-class" beauty parlor and "has no serious problem" of her own, states this view at some length:

"I think Negro business in Chicago is quite progressive, especially considering the experience our people have had in business and the small amount of money they invest in it. Negro business suffers, though, from lack of co-operation from the public."

The pooling of purchasing power is frequently mentioned as a possible competitive technique, as in the following case:

"The Negro, on the whole, will try to patronize his own merchants, but the fact that they ask higher prices and often give poor merchandise causes him to stay away from them. The reason for this is that each merchant, no matter how small his place, buys independently of other merchants. This buying in small quantities makes him pay more for his commodities wholesale than the white customer asks of his customers retail.

"We, as a group, are much more lenient with other groups than with our own. If we go into a Jewish store and ask for something and the Jew doesn't have it, we either buy something else in its place or go on without a murmur. Our own people could stock everything we want, but we fuss and carry on and say: 'You see, that's the reason we can't patronize our own people; they never have anything we want.' If they'd just buy from us, we'd stock all the things they want."

Two small merchants have the same theory:

"When we opened up, we had just as good stock as any of them whites. But then, the colored did not come in and buy so we went backward. Some of our people will always trade with the Jew. They have not been educated to trade with the colored people."

"Maybe our prices are a little higher than those of the white merchant, but that's because we buy in such small quantities. If the people would spend more with us, we could give them better prices, because we could buy at a better cost." *

One colored woman who runs a grocery detailed her woes at length, intimating that the competitive process sometimes involves skulduggery:

"The white merchants cut their prices to the bone when I took over this store, trying to force me out of business, but I stuck to my guns and made friends with the boys that came in here. They all call me Mother and respect me. I favor my customers when they are in need of a little money for food. They know I am their friend and they come to me. The Italian on the corner has given me the most trouble, but I have been so nice to the men that they spend their money here that the whites have lost trade. My neon sign has been broken and my place robbed by my enemies. My competitors had a petition circulated in the block by the agents of this property in an effort to get me out of business, and they have raised my rent each year for the past three years that I have been in business."

Some merchants also accused ward politicians of putting the squeeze on them. One man told the following story:

* Other merchants do not blame the customer for the failure to buy in larger quantities, but tend to blame themselves. Despite several abortive attempts, Negro merchants have never been able to organize for co-operative purchasing. A Jewish merchant operating in the Black Belt describes a co-operative purchasing group of which he is a member:

"My financial structure is $1,500 and $1,000 in time credit with the Progressive Store Association which is a co-operative purchasing set-up. I have $300 worth of stock and pay $5 per week service charge. This association functions efficiently and enables me and other members to meet all competition with quality merchandise. At the end of the fiscal year, the books are audited by an accredited auditing company, and the profits on hand are rebated proportionally and distributed to members and stockholders." Negro merchants insist that they are barred from membership in such white-controlled groups. One promising attempt at co-operative purchasing among Negroes, The Colored Merchants Association, failed in the early days of the Depression.

"I've had trouble here. Yesterday I was refused a license. The city says that a basement store is too unsanitary. I have been called to court several times. Through the Ward Committeeman the case has been thrown out. It's the Republicans that's doing it, and the Jews. The man that owns the building is colored. He had some political trouble. They refused me a license two years ago until I convinced them that I was not connected with him."

One owner of a small store said:

"The Jews are trying to get colored out of this basement. They have friends in the city council. They can go any place and stick. They have harassed me ever since I've been here. On Michigan Avenue a colored man had the place and had trouble. Now a Jew has the place and has no trouble."

Another store-proprietor had a similar story:

"We started here in May, 1937. We had to pay $100 for a license. We had to pay a $50 electric-light deposit. The zoning law hindered us. It was the Jew across the street. That's all. We had to get petitions to open up. I belong to the NAACP, but that didn't help.

"The Jew across the street was around here first. He's been here four or five years. He's cut prices since he has been here. He extends credit more than we do because he is able to. He has offered credit to our customers. Credit is one of my major problems."

The most frequently voiced charge is the contention that Negroes cannot lease choice business spots. All of Bronzeville believes what a grocer states:

"If we could get better locations our businesses would be better. The location I have is only fair—it is too far from the corner; but two white merchants keep the best places leased in order to prevent any Negro business from getting them. I find good locations are hard to get. I tried several months before I got this location. Several others that I tried to get rented too high."

As these typical quotations suggest, all complaints tend to assume an anti-Semitic tinge. It is hard to convince most merchants in Bronzeville that they are not victims of a "Jewish conspiracy."

The problem of securing choice locations is a very real one. Table 20 indicates that Negroes have a larger proportion of the businesses at the extremities of the Black Belt than in the choicer areas near the center. (Table 20.)

TABLE 20

DISTRIBUTION OF NEGRO AND WHITE RETAIL STORES BY DESIRABILITY OF BUSINESS
SITES: 1938

Color of Proprietor	Number			Percentage		
	North	Center	South	North	Center	South
Negro..............	401	187	407	60.4	36.1	45.3
White..............	263	331	492	39.6	63.9	54.7
Total............	664	518	899	100.0	100.0	100.0

A survey of twenty-seven blocks through the center of the Black Belt in 1938 revealed that fewer than half the Negro businesses were in the main shopping district, while over three-fourths of the white businesses were on the chief thoroughfare. Of all the Negro businesses on the main thoroughfare, half were second-floor locations. Only one white business was so located. Thirty years ago there were no Negro businesses at all on the street. Today, however, there is a wide variety. (Table 21.) This competitive struggle for locations has been interpreted in racial terms by both Negroes and whites, and has been so organized.

Negroes are emphatic in their insistence that leases are denied them on the basis of race, and the testimony of at least one prominent real-estate man seems to confirm this charge: "Stores are rented to the Negro merchant only for the purpose of opening a barber shop, a tavern, or a beauty shop." He proceeded to justify this exclusion on the ground that Negroes do not have "high-class stores." "Negro merchants do not have enough working capital. The average Negro store is small, with meager stock, which indicates purchases in small volume and dependence on small profits after a quick turnover. Because of inexperience, his credit is impaired."

Beating Whites at the Game: But even with the odds against the Negro merchant, many manage to survive. The ones who do are usually proud of it, as in the case of a merchant who recited his experiences as told on page 452.

TABLE 21

NUMBER OF BUSINESSES OPERATED BY NEGRO AND WHITE PROPRIETORS ON 47TH STREET, BETWEEN STATE STREET AND COTTAGE GROVE: 1938

Types of Businesses	Negro	White	Total
Food stores...............................	3	45	48
Bakeries................................	..	1	1
Candy shops........................	..	1	1
Fish markets........................	..	3	3
Food marts........................	..	1	1
Grocery and markets....................	2	38	40
Poultry houses.........................	1	1	2
Business services.........................	4	15	19
Currency exchanges.....................	..	2	2
Insurance companies.....................	1	1	2
Real-estate companies...................	..	7	7
Savings and loan companies..............	1	3	4
Telegraph offices.......................	..	1	1
Plumbing companies....................	..	1	1
Sign painters..........................	2	..	2
Automotive..............................	1	3	4
Tire and battery stores..................	..	2	2
Filling stations........................	..	1	1
Garages...............................	1	..	1
General merchandise......................	1	16	17
Credit clothing stores...................	..	4	4
Dry-goods stores.......................	..	9	9
Five and ten cent stores.................	1	2	3
Notion stores..........................	..	1	1
Clothing stores..........................	8	49	57
Dress shops...........................	3	13	16
Lingerie shops.........................	1	6	7
Men's dry goods and furnishings..........	1	9	10
Millinery shops........................	1	8	9
Shoe stores............................	2	11	13
Men's and women's furnishings...........	..	2	2
Furniture and household supplies	0	15	15
Sewing machine agents..................	..	1	1
Furniture stores.......................	..	14	14
Hardware stores	0	4	4

TABLE 21—*Continued*

NUMBER OF BUSINESSES OPERATED BY NEGRO AND WHITE PROPRIETORS ON 47TH
STREET, BETWEEN STATE STREET AND COTTAGE GROVE: 1938

Types of Businesses	Negro	White	Total
Prepare food	8	13	21
Chili parlors	1	1	2
Ice cream parlors	..	4	4
Lunch rooms	3	4	7
Restaurants	3	4	7
Chicken shacks	1	..	1
Drug stores	0	9	9
Other retail stores	7	22	29
Cigar stores	..	1	1
Florist shops	..	1	1
Jewelry stores	..	4	4
Liquor stores	1	8	9
Taverns	5	6	11
Paint stores	..	1	1
Window shade companies	..	1	1
Cosmetic products	1	..	1
Personal service	42	36	78
Cleaners and pressers	5	8	13
Furriers	..	2	2
Laundries	1	8	9
Photograph studios	2	2	4
Storage	..	1	1
Tailor shops	5	9	14
Shoe repair	1	6	7
Barber shops	12	..	12
Beauty parlors	11	..	11
Funeral systems	4	..	4
Old gold and silver salvage	1	..	1
Bookies	1	1	2
Repair service	2	7	9
Leather bindings	..	1	1
Radio service	2	6	8
Miscellaneous	6	2	8
Herbs and incense	1	1	2
Pool rooms	5	1	6
Totals	83	237	320

"There were nine Jewish merchants in this block when I opened. They predicted I would remain in business only one month. They sought to discourage me in many ways. When one of my customers would carry a package of merchandise purchased from me into their stores, they would open the package, criticize the merchandise, and try to get the customer to come to me for a refund. They were often seen peeping into my show windows to determine the quality and prices of my merchandise. Well, I bought as cheaply as they did and I sold at a reasonable margin of profit. So it was impossible for them to undersell me.

"I have been led many times into the discussion as to why Negroes don't patronize each other. Well, if they hadn't patronized me I would have closed many years ago, whereas I have been in this one spot thirteen years and at this time have no competitors. These favorable results have been obtained by a strict adherence to fundamental business principles. My customers are frequently advised not to buy from me merely because I am a Negro, but my merchandise and service are not excelled by any one of my competitors. Ninety-five per cent of the business I have gotten has always been from my people."

Many colored merchants are resigned to the competition of the white merchants and some think it a healthy (or at least natural) phenomenon. Thus one man observed:

"I haven't anything against Jews owning business in Negro neighborhoods. They could, of course, be eliminated if the Negro public co-operated and patronized their Negro businesses more. But the Jews come over here and open their stores. They have what we want in them, so we buy from them. Just a simple story of supply and demand."

The proprietor of a well-stocked electrical and radio shop felt that Negro businessmen themselves were frequently to blame for lack of patronage, stating that:

"The Negro is branded with having no racial understanding. Yet, when one takes into consideration the large number of small businesses that exist, one is compelled to acknowledge the fact that as a whole they do patronize each other. If they didn't, these places wouldn't be in existence. And mind you, these places are so small and the stock is so poor that the customer does not have any confidence in the person operating the business. One feels that to go into the store would be a waste of time for they wouldn't have what he wants anyway."

Another businessman echoes these same sentiments:

"The public does to a great extent patronize the Negro merchant. It is the lack of knowing how to run the business that causes the public to lose confidence in him. But even with his handicap, the Negro business-man can stay in business. The people are far more co-operative than they are given credit for."

The woman proprietor of a fairly successful grocery store has a theory of statistical realism and is quite philosophical about the whole matter: "Colored people will patronize you if you keep what they want. But there's a certain number of them that's going to trade with the Jew anyway. Some colored is going to trade with the Jew always."

THE WHITE MERCHANT'S VERDICT

White merchants in competition with Negroes will sometimes com-ment on the failure of Negroes to compete successfully with them. A few hold to stereotypes such as those of the real-estate agent who said: "The happy, carefree nature of the Negroes in seeking lines of least resistance in the conduct of their business is largely responsible for the high credit risk tabulated against them." Another white mer-chant thinks that "as long as Negroes have enough money to spend on booze and policy, they are happy," but concedes the point that "they haven't got the dough to invest in business." He is also sure that "they don't have the brains either" and "it takes brains to make a good busi-nessman." A Jewish furniture dealer with years of experience in Negro neighborhoods thinks that "most of the colored people you find in business are failures," and observes: "I don't know what causes this, whether they don't grasp the principles of the business or whether they want to start right out on top as big shots. I'll bet that about all their failures are due to this fault. I really think they've got too much ego. That's the way they impress me."

Other merchants tried to take into consideration the basic factors which place Negro businessmen at a competitive disadvantage, as did the owner of a very large department store in Bronzeville's main busi-ness area, who analyzed the situation as follows: "There is no possi-bility of the Negro merchant ever predominating in this area because of his inadequate working capital, insufficient credit extension, and lack of experience in business."

THE LURE OF THE BUSINESS GAME

Many of the more successful Negro businessmen criticize their less successful competitors on the ground that the latter do not take their business seriously, and thus give all colored enterprises a bad name. The successful ones were particularly antagonistic to "depression businesses"—the numerous small stores that between 1929 and 1938 sprang up in houses, basements, and old buildings. During those years many persons with small savings went into business. One man, typical of this group, explained to an interviewer: "When I started business in 1933, the going was tough. We were at the height of the Depression. I had just a small amount of money and could not find a job, so I decided to open a grocery. If worst came to worst, I would at least have something to eat." "If work was plentiful, these small places would not exist," commented a successful entrepreneur, and he is no doubt right. But throughout the Depression those small merchants continued to cling precariously to the margins of the business world, the owner often subsisting out of his meager stock. He preserved his sense of dignity and was sometimes successful.

Negro businessmen have "a hard way to go," but there are still the status drives and the hope of monetary rewards to stimulate them. On the whole, Bronzeville's businessmen tend to be somewhat above the average in educational attainments. Many of them often verbalize their desire to remain in business in terms of a wish to be independent. One woman tells her story as follows:

"I got tired of working for 'the other fellow' [i.e., whites] and decided to go into business for myself. I told my husband I was going to open a fish market, as I wanted to be at home days instead of off at work. He consented, so in 1935 I opened a fish market. From the start, business was good. About six months later, I installed a line of canned goods, meats, and vegetables."

Another man had "always wanted to get into business," so he saved his money and opened up. At first he believed that "business was lazy work," but he soon learned that he "had to work exceedingly hard, and that the hardest thing is trying to please the public and encourage them to buy." A garage owner, "tired of working for others," wanted to go into business for himself. The proprietor of a poolroom had "always liked billiards and spent a lot of time around poolrooms." He knew that "there was money in the business," so when the Depression set in and he was without work "and too old to get the kind of employment" he wanted, he decided to open a poolroom.

Few Negro retailers had any apprenticeship or training in business before taking the plunge. Of eighty-three grocers interviewed in 1938, almost half were from the rural South and had had some high school training. Only nine, however, had ever had any connection with grocery stores. Most of them had been laborers, domestic servants, and porters before entering business; one or two had been teachers and dentists. "We started from rock bottom" was the usual report. "I wanted to try something, so I decided to try the grocery business," was one woman's explanation of her business venture, and this was typical.

Of a larger sample of 345 Negro businessmen, about a third reported some post-high-school training, but on the whole their businesses did not differ appreciably from the general run of Negro enterprises, except that there was a tendency for them to have slightly better locations—a distinct competitive advantage. About a third of their businesses were of types that required a certain amount of advanced training, such as drugstores, insurance brokerages, or printing and publishing shops. These businessmen with post-high-school training spent an average of ten years in some other field before going into business. Only 14 out of 75, however, entered business before being out of school ten years. Their previous occupations covered a wide range, among them being six former Pullman porters, a maid or two, a secret service agent, and a football coach. To them, business was the realization of a "lifelong ambition," a chance for the individual to be his "own boss," a refuge when he got "broke and disgusted." It is probable that many of the charges leveled at Negro businessmen, accusing them of condescension and curtness, are directed at these fairly well-trained individuals whose frustrations have not developed gentleness of temper. It is among them, too, that much of the intensive propaganda for supporting Negro business originates.

Business courses are not overpopular in the Negro colleges. Negro students have been traditionally oriented toward teaching, law, medicine, and the church—a fact that has elicited a bitter comment from a columnist in a Negro paper widely circulated in Chicago:

Our people of unusual training seem to have rushed into the sheltered and safe professions and have virtually ignored those fields which dominate and control our civilization. This has left most of the business pioneering to be done by persons ill equipped to do so.

A Negro preacher, however, thinks he has an answer to the weakness of Negro business enterprises:

"These dagoes and Jews come over here and start out with a peanut stand. They'll eat stale bread and live in the back of a ol' store. They'll starve themselves and get your pennies. And then one mornin' they'll move out in front with a nice fruit stand or a restaurant. While they doin' this, the lazy Negro is jitterbuggin', an' the college Negro is either lookin' for a soft job down South or else is carryin' bags down in some railroad station."

A more objective analysis, however, would take account of the fact that the average college-trained Negro, if he is not a professional man, is more likely to go into insurance or real estate, publishing or printing, than into the hurly-burly of retail merchandising, or he prefers a civil service job where he can immediately attain the standard of living to which he has been trained.

The highly individualistic motivations for entering business are of course at variance with the much touted doctrine of doing business for racial advancement. This is partly responsible, on one hand, for the lack of enthusiasm with which the Negro public responds to the "race pride" dogmas, and on the other hand, for the extreme difficulty which Race Leaders and business promoters have in organizing trade associations and buying pools.

ODDS TO THE NEGRO

Though the odds are against the Negro in the general merchandising field, Bronzeville's undertakers, barbers, and beauticians operate within a closed market, competing only among themselves.

Burying the Dead: Between 300 and 400 Negroes die in Chicago every month. They must be "put away right," whether in a pine box with a $75 funeral or at a $20,000 ceremony complete with couch casket and Lincoln limousines. Negro undertakers have a virtual monopoly on burying the colored dead, most of the white undertakers taking the position of the one who said: "I've been here for over fifty years and have seen this area change from all white to all black.

However, I've never catered to the Negro business and at no time conducted a Negro funeral." One colored undertaker explained this present competitive situation as follows:

"Twenty-five years ago we had competition from the white undertakers. They bury very few Negroes now. When they do, competition comes mostly from Jewish and Irish undertakers. There are some few families that will not have a Negro undertaker today. I am unable to give the reason except to say that many of these Negroes work for white families."

The number of colored undertakers grew steadily from one in 1885 to nearly 70 in 1938. The greatest increase took place between 1927 and 1937. Most of the establishments are on main thoroughfares and some of them are very elaborate. A few, however, are mere deserted stores with a chapel in front and an embalming room in the rear. There is constant competition for finer cars and new wrinkles. One undertaker, for instance, who came to the city seventeen years ago proudly claims credit for the vogue of "smart funeral homes," insisting that before his time Negroes only had "undertaker shops" in old store-fronts; he boasts that "now Chicago is noted for having the smartest funeral homes in the country." At the Business Exposition referred to earlier, one undertaker displayed his large, new, spotless, white ambulance in the center of the floor. Thousands of persons crowded around it and talked with the owner personally. He was the cynosure of all eyes.

Since an undertaker's success is based upon popularity as well as upon service and efficiency, "morticians" are very careful to maintain wide connections with lodges, churches, and civic and social clubs. Many of them arrange with a few ministers to have funerals thrown their way. Some pastors advertise a special undertaker for their church and use various forms of subtle pressure to force their members to use him. In fact, the undertaker's name appears on many church bulletin boards beside that of the pastor. Various forms of advertisement are used to dramatize the "mortician" as a social benefactor, and the largest and most consistent advertisers in the Negro press are the undertakers. (The Undertakers' Wives' Charity Club also assists in perpetuating this myth.) The opening of a new funeral parlor is usually "news," and sometimes includes "a bevy of charming ladies . . . on hand to serve all in attendance to a sumptuous tea and refreshments." [1]

Bronzeville's undertakers, on the whole, are a hardy lot. A few are college men, but most of them have left menial jobs for an embalming college. The larger ones bury people of all social levels, high and low, while some of the smaller ones specialize. One undertaker near the southern tip of the Black Belt had moved there to avoid "relief funerals." Of such burials he said:

"I think I had three; then I refused to accept any more. They only paid $75. There is no kind of decent funeral you can get for that amount. With the case workers and clients demanding so much more than they can pay for, I got fed up. On one occasion, I had to cuss out a case worker. Then, too, I did not like going into some of the dirty, filthy homes. I realized that by locating here I would be among the better class."

While Bronzeville's undertakers do not suffer seriously from white competition, they are faced with competition from other Negro businessmen who are interested in profits from burying the colored dead— the managers of "burial associations," sometimes called "funeral systems." One undertaker described the nature of this competition as follows:

"I get most of my competition from the funeral systems. They are just like the chain stores. You see, they combine insurance with the funeral business, and because of the volume of business they get, the individual undertaker in some instances is put out of business. This sort of competition has been going on since 1922, and it's been keen."

The burial association represents the impact of a southern culture pattern upon the northern community. The church "burying leagues" and lodges had, by 1920, been replaced in many sections of the South with associations organized by the undertaker. Each member paid weekly or monthly dues and the undertaker guaranteed an impressive burial. When a person had a policy with an insurance company and could not keep up the payments, the burial association would take over the policy in the role of beneficiary and continue to pay the premiums. The founder of the first burial association in Chicago defended the innovation thus:

"There was a need for one here in Chicago—you know they are a common thing in the South. Since the Depression, you will find more people in funeral systems than previously carried life insurance. I suppose it's because they had to cash in the policies for what they could and didn't have any protection left."

The largest burial association in Chicago was founded in 1922 by an undertaker with an eye for increased business. At this time, the masses of the migrants were unprotected except for lodge benefits. Many who had insurance policies had let them lapse or had cashed them in. White companies were charging exorbitant premiums. Northern Negro companies had not yet attained prestige. Into the breach stepped the burial association, offering a policy which, while it had no "turn-in" or borrowing value, assured the holder of a funeral, required no medical examination, and imposed no age limit. The association buried its policy-holders from its own funeral parlors, thus seriously threatening the ordinary undertaker. The Depression made burial societies even more popular, since when a policy was turned over to the association it did not need to be listed as an asset when applying for relief. A white doctor with a large Negro clientele commented somewhat patronizingly on the funeral system as follows:

"Doug and his brother had a funeral parlor. I think he is now the owner of the Eureka Funeral Association. You pay him so much a year to get a high-class funeral—something like ten cents a week. These Negroes will do a lot to be sure of a classy funeral. You see, Doug is in the insurance end of this just as much as the funeral business. He has a $15,000 Lincoln hearse and a whole string of Lincoln limousines. He offers an 'All-Lincoln' funeral. He tells them they are getting a thousand-dollar funeral; what he really does costs him probably a hundred dollars. He uses cheap coffins with a lot of paint. The way the thing is worked, they sign over their insurance policy for maybe a thousand dollars and are promised a big funeral. So Doug gets a cut two ways because he is in the insurance company, too. You should see his funeral parlors; they are elegant."

By 1937 the undertakers were able to secure the passage of a law requiring the burial associations to pay the value of the policy in cash rather than in the form of a burial. The funeral systems, however, have simply written this section of the policy in agate type and proceeded to continue with business as usual.

Despite the combined opposition of undertaker and insurance company, burial associations have become increasingly popular. One of Bronzeville's most recently established show places is a large funeral home and dance hall built by one of these companies. In fact, about a third of all death premiums paid to Negro companies are now paid to burial associations.

The associations are aware of the antagonism toward them, but heatedly justify their existence, some even claiming that they aid the undertakers: "Before these societies were established, these undertakers were not getting their money. Now, since we pay claims in cash, they can get theirs." (Undertakers deny that claims are usually paid in cash.)

One burial association manager insists that they will eventually aid even the insurance companies:

"I think the burial association is the foundation out of which will grow stronger, stouter insurance companies. You see, as a group of people, we have not had enough business training since we got out of forced servitude. If you recall, all of our large insurance companies owned and managed by our group cracked up during a crisis. [This is not true.] We start too high and don't work up. Soon we will be given participating policies, policies which give you a loan value."

The undertakers, working as they do in a closed market, have little personal reason to react violently against white businessmen. As Negroes, however, they do share the general ideologies of race pride. One rather successful undertaker with an annual turnover of about $70,000 and a profit of 17-20 per cent on his investment is proud of the fact that he buys "fluids and quite a number of caskets from Negroes," but regrets that he is "compelled to buy from whites when better qualities are selected." He does not approve of a racial business monopoly, however, insisting that he "should have the right to operate a business anywhere in Chicago and not be confined to the Black Belt." He states that he has no objection to whites' entering business in Bronzeville. Negroes who bury the dead definitely have the odds in their favor.

Beautifying the Living: If colored undertakers have a virtual monopoly in burying the Negro dead, the colored barber and beautician have an even more exclusive monopoly in beautifying the living. In 1938, there was not a white beauty parlor or barber shop in the Negro community, a circumstance which impelled one colored beautician to comment that "they *would* have them if they knew how to work on Negroes' hair." The fact of the matter is that few white persons have had experience with the cutting of Negro hair, or with the exceedingly complicated preparations and processes used in "straightening" the hair of colored women (and some men) who have not been favored with "good hair." Negroes often jest at themselves for trying to straighten their hair while white people are curling theirs, or for using "bleaching creams" while whites are risking sunburn to get a tan. Yet the advertisements in the colored papers continue to call attention to such products as X SKIN WHITENER which promises "the thrill of lighter, fairer, brighter, younger-looking skin," or Y HAIR POMADE—"Know the Joy of Straighter, Glossier Hair—Good-bye, Hair Kinks."

The fairly large proportion of Negro women in Chicago who are listed in the Census as proprietors is due primarily to the prevalence of "beauticians," many of whom use their homes or vacant store fronts when they cannot afford a "salon." Training in beauty culture is rather easy to get, either in the public schools or in any of several "beauty colleges." In each of the latter an exclusive "system" is taught, usually involving the use of a particular brand of cosmetics. Many operators who have apprentices complain that "they are hard to keep" because they usually want shops of their own.

Despite the intense competition in the field, some of the most successful business associations in Bronzeville are those of the beauticians. Composed of beauty-shop owners, operators, and apprentices, and beauty-school owners, these organizations have as their aims the standardizing of prices and the enforcing of state health regulations. They also function as pressure groups for "racial advancement."

Closely associated with beauty parlors and barber shops are the manufacturers of beauty preparations, who, as said above, sometimes have "colleges" for training in their own systems. The full significance of these concerns is evident when we note that the first very large fortune accumulated by a Negro in America was that of Madame C. J. Walker, who sold enough of her beauty preparations to retire to a mansion at Croton-on-Hudson. Since her day, scores of such companies have mushroomed, offering a wide variety of products. There are over a dozen such companies in Chicago, constituting one-third of all manufacturing enterprises owned by Negroes.* One

* According to a survey directed by Joseph Semper as a part of the Cayton-Warner Research, there were in 1938 some 38 manufacturers distributed as follows:

Toilet goods and cosmetics	15
Clothing	5
Casket makers	3
Mattresses	2
Miscellaneous	18

of the most successful of these is a firm which was able to scoop its competitors by having Joe Louis endorse its product, and which has recently extended its business to Cuba with special agents to teach the more Negroid islanders how to get their hair to resemble that of their Spanish-type compatriots. On the manufacturing level, however, Negroes do not have a monopoly of beauty preparations, since enterprising whites have been quick to size up the potential market and to enter the field.

HIGH FINANCE

Insurance: The Negro businesses that have been most successful in direct competition with whites during the last twenty years are insurance companies. In significant contrast to entrepreneurs in the field of general merchandising, these companies have been able to amass capital, secure a trained personnel, and weather the Depression. In 1940 there were four such companies with home offices in Chicago.* They were valued at over 10,000,000 and employed over 2,000 persons.

Prior to 1912, white companies had a monopoly on the Negro insurance business in Chicago, and charged a higher premium than whites paid. They hired some Negro agents, however, and a number of these became familiar with this aspect of the insurance business. By the time of the Great Migration, a dozen young men who subsequently became prominent in Bronzeville's business life had had some office experience with a white company. In 1918 and 1919 three Negro companies were organized by this group and one of these now has the largest amount of insurance in force of any Negro company in America. Organized in 1919, by 1938 it was operating in nine states outside of Illinois. In 1944 this company reported $3,843,408.20 in assets with a "legal reserve" of $2,967,588.00 to cover $71,003,778 of insurance in force.

In 1923 another businessman, who was amassing a small fortune from the manufacture of cosmetics, organized a life insurance company, capitalized at $100,000. By 1927, this company "had the distinction of being the first and only life insurance company operated by Negroes to be licensed in the state of New York and the only Illinois company thus licensed." Its growth was phenomenal and it was able

---

* Between 1919 and 1927 several small companies were started, but after the first flashes of success most of them fell by the wayside. At present there are four companies that have survived.

to accumulate capital from all over the North. But the Depression crushed it because it was so closely interlocked with the founder's manufacturing company and his bank, the death-blow being given by the latter's collapse. In 1933, however, the concern was reorganized as a mutual insurance company.

The mushrooming of insurance companies between 1919 and 1927 was due to a number of factors, not the least important of these being the fact that Negroes were familiar with lodges and successful colored insurance companies in the South, and there was thus no initial skepticism to overcome, as was often the case in other types of business. The companies were also able to exploit the fact that the white companies charged Negroes a higher premium than they did whites.

The secretary of one of the four companies surviving the Depression said that he entered the business in 1926, after selling all of his real estate in the South, because

"we considered it a good business. We had no charitable reasons, I assure you. We were out to make money and we felt that there was a splendid opening in Chicago. . . . A large number of the persons who were coming to Chicago were accustomed to carrying insurance policies with Negro companies. Our worst competitors are the white insurance companies. A lot of Negroes have been carrying policies with the Metropolitan ever since they were babies. Then, too, we have large white companies selling industrial insurance. There's money in it, though. All you've got to do is get it out. We've learned that you can make money if you run it right. When I came here all the colored insurance men were successful. It seemed the ideal business to enter. A great many Negroes were going into business in those days. Many of them brought money with them when they came, the way I did, and were able to start up business."

During the late Twenties, the colored insurance companies, faced with the competition of burial associations and white insurance companies, began to throw their weight behind a boycott campaign ostensibly designed to make white companies employ Negro agents. This campaign began when a militant Negro newspaper directed a letter to the Metropolitan Company complaining that the company did not employ Negro agents, that white agents were discourteous, and that they refused to collect at night when it was most convenient for Negroes to pay. The company's tactless and discourteous reply was made public in the Negro community; hundreds of Negroes were angered, and a boycott resulted.

The Negro insurance companies exploited the boycott proposal to the utmost, using large billboard posters to point out that support for colored companies would "make jobs for our boys and girls." An official of one of these companies thus appraised the effect of the campaign:

"I have no statistics on the matter, but it has probably put most prospective policy-holders in a favorable mood for an unanswerable argument that the money they put in colored companies, besides providing insurance of the best class, also provides employment for colored people and an opportunity for Negroes to acquire capital through our loans to them. This kind of sales talk, when properly handled, usually works."

Another official, speaking in 1932, stated that Negroes in Bronzeville still carried the major part of their insurance with white companies, "especially the Metropolitan." It was his impression that it is virtually impossible to get Negroes to give up their policies with white companies and the agents had not attempted to do that. "But," he said, "when the issue of a *new* policy is in question, our agents use the job argument for all that it is worth, and usually with telling effect."

These insurance companies are frequently cited as proof that Negroes can successfully conduct business, run office machines, handle big money, and give employment to The Race. Such companies proudly publish the pictures of their offices and stress their function as "racial" enterprises. One company, in its twentieth-anniversary pamphlet, attributed "much of its success" to the fact that "its officials and employees never permit themselves to forget that the primary reason for being is to provide a unique service to the Negro people. . . . On its twentieth birthday, it rededicates itself to the cause of Negro progress and betterment."

The boards of directors of the largest of these companies include, in addition to businessmen, a few prominent preachers and civic leaders. Even Joe Louis is now on one insurance company board.

Banking: The largest measure of control and the greatest prestige in the American economy are associated with banking. It is therefore natural that the successful operation of a bank would have high symbolic significance for Bronzeville. In the Fat Years, Bronzeville had two colored banks, which held over one-third of all the combined deposits in Negro banks in the United States. The Depression wiped out both of them, as it wiped out the four white banks in the Black Belt and sixty-six banks in other parts of the city.

In the Twenties, the pride of Bronzeville's Rialto was Binga's State Bank, once described by an enthusiastic Chicago *Tribune* reporter as a "building of rich Ionic architecture, with such lofty reaches of marble and bronze, and such massive steel vaults and such mellow walnut panelings and such subdued hangings, as you would expect to find in the Loop, but not in the Black Belt." The story of Binga and his bank, which has been briefly touched on earlier, is a typical American success story with the unhappy dénouement of an Insull or Whitney biography. Jesse Binga came to Chicago in 1893, having begun life as a porter. He invested in real estate,* patched and repaired his own buildings, and saved his money.

In 1908 Binga founded a private bank and, with the great influx of Negroes during the migration, it prospered. He married the sister of "Mushmouth" Johnson, notorious gambler-politician, and when "Mushmouth" died much of his fortune went into the bank. In 1920, Binga's private bank became a state bank, and within four years, its deposits had increased from $300,000 to $1,181,704.15. In 1929 the banker erected the Binga Arcade, an imposing five-story edifice with banking chambers, dance hall on the roof, and extensive office space. (The *Defender* commented, after Binga's fall, "It was a dream of Jesse Binga's, and although he had been warned that such a building would not bring back sufficient returns in rentals, he insisted on erecting it at that corner.")

In 1921, Binga was made chairman of the board of a newly organized and rapidly growing life insurance company. Later that same year he was feted as a leading citizen by the Mid-Southside Chamber of Commerce, an interracial group. This was but one of the many honors heaped upon him during the next nine years. In 1929, when the Depression set in, Binga's Bank had $1,465,266.62 in deposits.

On July 31, 1930, the state examiner closed the House of Binga—

* The Chicago *Defender,* commenting on these deals years later when Binga had lost his wealth and popularity, was none too complimentary: "Binga is reported to have leased homes which rented for $20 and $25 a month and re-rented them to his own people for $10 to $15 more than the white renters had been paying. This method was followed by other real-estate dealers." (Chicago *Defender,* March 7, 1931.)

"insufficient cash and frozen assets." With banks closing throughout the country, and with rumors flying thick and fast through Bronzeville, it was not strange that the 20,000 depositors had started a run on the bank—a run which neither the friendly efforts of Samuel Insull nor those of many Race Leaders could stem. There were frantic efforts at reopening; there were charges that Binga's resignation could clear the way for reorganization; there were ugly hints that dishonesty and incompetence had played their part in the debacle.

Binga went into seclusion. On March 5, 1931, two deputies set out to arrest him on a charge of embezzlement. Two *Defender* reporters and a photographer trailed the police and reported the details of the sheriffs' mission: [2]

They were unable to gain entrance in the afternoon but returned after dark and lay in wait. When the door was opened for a doctor the deputies entered. Binga was taken to the county jail when he was unable to make the bond of $55,000. He spent the night in the jail hospital, broken in health and spirit.

The grand jury returned a true bill indicting him for the embezzlement of $300,000. According to the prosecutor: "Real estate manipulations resulted in the shortage of the financial institution's funds . . . by signing notes on mortgages and taking money from the bank. . . . The mortgage notes . . . would be turned in for cashier's checks, and when the mortgages fell due they would be renewed for long periods or replaced with other signed notes." Binga's sentence was one to ten years. Immediately Bronzeville began to take sides. To some, Binga was a thief; to others, he was a persecuted man, a victim of circumstances—perhaps of doublecrossing by his white friends.

The fall of the House of Binga had a profound effect upon Bronzeville. Guilty or innocent, Binga was a symbol of "racial advancement," and the *Defender's* account, although florid, does reflect the underlying significance of the episode:

The closing threw the South Side into turmoil. Crowds of depositors gathered in front of the bank. Two uniformed policemen were out on guard for several days. There were no disorders. Instead, there was a deathlike pall that hung over those who had entrusted their life savings to Binga, not so much that they had any love for the head of the bank, but it was pride—that pride of seeing their own Race behind the cages, that led them to 35th and State Street to do their banking. For years, the Binga Bank was pointed out to visitors as something accomplished by our group.

The *Defender* carefully pointed out that *white* banks, too, had failed.

Binga, like all successful Negro businessmen, thought of himself as a Race Leader, and of his bank as a symbol not only of the fact that Negroes could do business, but also of the larger American myth celebrating individual enterprise and thrift. Binga was proud of his booklet, *Certain Sayings of Jesse Binga,* which contained such Franklin-like advice as the following:

Learn a business and then mind it.

Learn something not so you know about it, but so you know it.

Save, Save, Save, and when you've got it, then Give, Give, Give.

Get a competency. Then the world—white or colored—will concede that you are competent.

Only business contacts with the community as a whole—white and colored—will educate the colored man in business.

Learn Business. Establish a credit. Provide for your own wants. That is the message to our group.

You can be a menial or a man of business. But to get out of the menial place requires the thrift that produces property. And property enlarges life. Work, then, not for gain alone, but for the enlarged life that honest gains create.

Life is pretty much what you make it—and making it big means using every bit of it.

Be honest.

Nothing is so easy or so wasteful as the work of hating—except hating work. And that goes for races as well as individuals.

The *Daily News* saw drama in the courtroom at Binga's trial: [3]

Practically penniless now at sixty-seven years, the sage of the near South Side believes firmly that if he's given the opportunity he can spend the twilight of his life building up another fortune.

Committees were established for his vindication, and finally, in 1940, he was paroled to the custody of a Catholic priest. He became the janitor of a Bronzeville Catholic church immediately upon his release, but subsequently secured a less menial job.

Binga once stated that "only prejudice could beat him." He had forgotten the business cycle, which licked even his friend and counselor, Samuel Insull. Binga was beaten, not by prejudice, but by too many first mortgages.

OF FAME AND FORTUNE

From the days of Point de Saible to the present, there have been some wealthy Negroes in Chicago. Individuals here and there have been able to amass property and bank accounts valued in hundreds of thousands of dollars. But there has been little continuity in these fortunes, and little combination of them into large corporate holdings. A man able enough to amass a fortune is not likely to invest it solely according to the promptings of Race Pride. During the optimistic Twenties, however, when real estate and insurance seemed profitable, they did invest in "racial ventures."

These fortunes had usually been accumulated through abstemious saving coupled with shrewd business ability. Very few wealthy Negroes ever made their money from playing the stock market. One notable exception was a prominent Old Settler who, beginning as a stenographer with a steel company in Cleveland, is reputed to have accumulated over $500,000. When the company opened its Chicago offices, he was sent as an accountant at $150 a month. Two years later, he was made Traffic Manager at $300. Living on a modest annuity during the Depression, he recounted his experiences:

"This position I held for thirty-two years, and the contact with other leading industries proved to be beneficial. My salary continued to increase, and after being associated with the firm for ten years I was receiving a salary of $10,000 a year. I had charge of directing the transportation of all their products. I was the only Negro ever hired by this company. I played the margins in the stock market, increased my money, and when I resigned in 1928 I could write a check for $100,000. I made a small fortune speculating with the market; purchased two six-flat buildings, an expensive automobile, a residence for myself, two small cottages, and land in Michigan. I was interested in various enterprises for The Race and invested $50,000 in insurance, $50,000 in a hotel at a Michigan resort, and $10,000 in a cosmetics company. Now, I'm broke."

Because of his contact with La Salle Street bankers, this man had been able to participate in the financial life of the city in a manner not possible for most Negroes.

There are today two main types of fortunes in the Negro community: those that have come from some success in the total society, such as the rise to fame of Joe Louis; and those that have come from the so-called "protected businesses," notably policy or the numbers racket. The one significant exception among Bronzeville's wealthy is a young man who inherited some Oklahoma oil property. The largest aggregations of liquid capital during the Depression were in the hands of the so-called "policy kings." Since they, without exception, also own legitimate businesses, they are "businessmen" as well as "racketeers."

CHAPTER 17

Business Under a Cloud

"POLICY": POOR MAN'S ROULETTE

ALMOST AS NUMEROUS AS THE CHURCHES (AND MORE EVENLY DISTRIBUTED) are Bronzeville's 500 odd "policy stations," in any one of which a person may place a bet that certain numbers will be announced as lucky by one of fifteen or sixteen "policy companies." Policy is a lottery game.* It is also a "protected business," operating in defiance of Illinois State Statute No. 413, but under the benevolent patronage of the city political machine. In order to keep up a semblance of respect for the law, about half the stations are "fronted" by legitimate businesses. Most of the others can be easily recognized by the initiated, sometimes by a light over a basement entrance, again by a sign on a window or door: "OPEN"—"4-11-44"—"DOING BUSINESS"—"ALL BOOKS."

A knowing observer can also spot a policy station by the constantly moving stream of customers going in and coming out carrying "drawings"—the slips on which the winning numbers are printed. (Figure

---

* The origin of the term "policy" is obscure, but at least as early as the Nineties it was applied to lottery games in which the gambler "purchased" a number and received a duplicate receipt, the original being forwarded to the headquarters of the "pool." Gosnell, in his *Negro Politicians,* states that this type of lottery was so prevalent in New York City around the turn of the century that an anti-policy law was passed by the state in 1901. Illinois passed a similar law in 1905 in an effort to break up the game in Chicago.

In the early policy games the winning numbers were selected by drawing numbered slips from a bowl. In the late Twenties, some enterprising New Yorkers hit upon the idea of taking bets on the probable last three numbers of the daily Federal Reserve Clearing House report. This variant form of "policy"—known as the "numbers game"—was very popular on the Eastern seaboard because it placed the game "on the level." No racketeer could tamper with the Clearing House figures, and anyone could read them in the newspaper. During an attempt to smash the racket, newspapers were asked to print these reports in round numbers. The resourceful racketeers then shifted to other published numbers. Throughout this period, "policy" numbers in Chicago were selected by the traditional lottery drawings. Clearing House numbers were never popular in Midwest Metropolis.

25.) These slips are distributed three times a day, and at busy stations long queues form as people come to place new bets, collect their winnings, or inquire about results. The unwary person who stands too close to the door of a policy station at certain hours is likely to be hit by the small roll of policy slips—the drawings—which are flung from a speeding car by the "pick-up men" as they hasten from shop to shop carrying the latest numbers.

Figure 27

POLICY "DRAWINGS" OR "SLIPS" *

TWO-LEGGED BOOK   ONE-LEGGED BOOK

ROYAL PALM			IOWA	
C867½ MN			C277½ MN	
40	46		72	} 1st Cap
50	7		29	
4	26	1st Six	56	
2	11		28	
7	22		30	} 2nd Cap
77 BOTH	52		38	
47	50		8	
12	44		59	} 3rd Cap
39	15	2nd Six	2	
66	61		53	
17	62		4	} 4th Cap
45	27		9	

* For explanation of the terms used in this figure, see footnote on p. 472.

Bronzeville places its bets in one or more of thirty "pools" known colloquially as "books." These pools have distinctive names, such as Monte Carlo, Bronx, Royal Palm, Harlem, Interstate, North and South, East and West. (If you're unlucky in one book today, you may shift to another tomorrow.) The policy slips in Figure 27 are announcements of the winning numbers in the Royal Palm and Iowa books for a midnight drawing. The Royal Palm, with twenty-four numbers, is known as a "two-legged book." The Iowa, with twelve numbers, is a "one-legged book."

If a policy addict had gone to a station between noon and midnight on the day of these particular drawings and said, "I want to put a dime on number 56 in the Iowa book," his lucky guess that this number might appear at midnight would have made him the winner of fifty cents. Playing a single number in this fashion is known as playing a "day number."

The most popular "play" in Bronzeville is the "gig." In this case, the player would have guessed at three numbers that might "fall"— for instance, 72-59-4. For his dime he then would have received $20. (The odds against guessing three numbers out of twelve are 76,076 to 1!) Policy players often "saddle their gigs" by investing an additional dime in a bet that at least *two* of the numbers will appear.* Then, if the whole gig is lost, the player may still salvage something. The reward for a saddle is a dollar to the dime. To guess on the appearance of four numbers is to play a "Horse." The winner receives $40, but the odds against such a winning are 1,426,425. A five-number bet—a "Jack"—pays $200 for a dime.

Winning numbers are listed three times daily, after selection at a public "drawing." The places where the drawings are made are known as the "wheels." These "wheels" are scattered about the community at strategic spots.† The drawings are made from a small drum-shaped container in which 78 capsules or balls, numbered consecutively, are placed. After each turn of the drum, a ball is pulled and its number read aloud. As they are called, a printer sets the numbers and locks them into a special printing press. As soon as the last number is drawn, the press rolls out the policy slips, which are then distributed all over Bronzeville.

In "normal" times, when the "heat is off," a wheel is a beehive of activity, day and night.‡ It is run by a corps of well-trained white-

* There are two other two-number plays: "Sides" and "Caps." A policy slip is printed in either one or two vertical rows of twelve numbers each. These twelve numbers, when divided into threes, result in sections known as "Caps." (Figure 24.) Two numbers directly beside each other and within a "cap" constitute a winning "cap." On the other hand, any two numbers in a two-legged book, beside each other but not in "caps," are known as "sides" and return $8 for a dime. A winning "cap" yields $20.

† Before the present policy syndicate had made satisfactory arrangements with the city fathers, the drawings were conducted surreptitiously in old garages, in the front rooms of apartments, in trucks, or in the open fields and woods in the suburbs of the city. During the last ten years, when the "heat was on" several times temporarily, the drawings have been made in a truck equipped with a lottery wheel and printing press.

‡ One prominent policy syndicate member told an interviewer about a period when the "heat was on"—i.e., when an attempt was being made by the police to suppress the game: "In the spring of 1929, the heat was turned on the policy game and stations as well as wheels were raided. Small fines were assessed in some cases. They were paid by operators, and business was continued the next

collar experts. Usually, several hundred persons are present to watch, and sometimes the crowd includes a co-operative policeman or two. Many of the onlookers are "walking writers," some 2,000 of whom were canvassing Bronzeville in 1938, writing up plays for a 20 per cent commission on the amount played.

Just before the wheel begins to turn, the walking writers arrive, straighten up their books, turn in duplicate slips, and fraternize with one another. Some wheels provide chairs with writing arms; a few even have a lunch counter. All have a "bouncer" or "overlook man" to keep order, to hurry the writers along so they will have the bets recorded before the drawing is made, and to enforce silence during the process. A drawing has been described by an observer as follows:

"Up and down the aisle, a large, dark man (I learned later that he was a prize-fighter) walked to and fro. He shouted continuously, 'All right, get them in, folks. Get those books in.' A large sign in front of the room read: ALL BOOKS MUST BE IN FIFTEEN MINUTES BEFORE PULLING TIME. PULLING TIME, 1:30.

"The overlook man looked in our direction and said, 'Baby, is that your chair? If not, you'll have to go downstairs. We don't want any confusion about the chairs. You know how crowded it is here.'

"By this time it was nearly 1:15 A.M. and the barker continued to prod the writers. 'Let's get them in, folks!' Everyone seemed in a jocular mood. Then suddenly there was a deep silence. At 1:40 a syndicate official stepped to the office window. A small wooden barrel fixed horizontally on an axle was placed in front of him. He set it spinning, and when it stopped a young lady put in her hand and pulled out a small pellet of paper, which she handed to the man. He opened it and, walking close to the microphone of the public address system, called out a number. A young man and the young lady pulled numbers alternately, 24 times for the North and South book and the same number of times for the East and West book.

"The people were rapt. The silence was broken by happy ejaculations or almost inaudible sighs as people saw that they had hit or just missed by a small margin. When the last number had been called, a sudden rushing noise arose, as people began to form in line at the printing press in the back of the room. In less than five minutes, the slips had been

day. The heat stayed on until about 1933, but this did not stop the wheels from operating. They continued to run and pay bonds for the writers. After the death of Mayor Cermak, the syndicate was formed and policy has run under this protection since." The heat was turned on temporarily during the winter of 1940, creating considerable excitement in Bronzeville.

printed and were being distributed in the streets. Pick-up men were speeding through the Black Belt carrying the news of the latest winning numbers."

At the policy stations throughout the community, the players reach avidly for the slips to see if they have "caught." There are intense little groups discussing the close margins by which they have missed. Occasionally one can hear the rejoicing cry of a winner. A conversation is in progress on a street corner.

"Yes, maybe the jinx is on us, huh?"

"This 9-9-29 [Death Row] is playing right well. It saddled last night and again this morning. The same with the Nigger Baby Row, too—13-32-50."

"Oh, I missed on that Death Row. I don't play it because it made me miss my mother's name once. Man, I would have had good money. You see, my mother is dead and I dreamed about her. Instead of playing her name, I played the Death Row, and missed out because her name fell out in the first sixes. Wheeee, I would have been a rich man."

Suddenly, a shout: "I caught on my son's name, 'Henry'! It's out in the last sixes in the North and South, 27-31-33. Wonder why I didn't put some *real* money on it? Well, anyway, I caught $5.75 and that's better than nothing. Then, with these saddles, I think I'll clear about $6. Not bad for a dollar. It'll help out a lot at home."

"POLICY"—A CULT

As is evident from the conversations quoted above, policy is not only a business—it is also a cult. It has a hold on its devotees which is stronger than the concrete gains from an occasional winning would warrant. It has an element of mystery and anticipation. It has developed an esoteric language. It organizes, to some extent, the daily lives of the participants. And, as in all cults, it has developed a group of functionaries and subsidiary businesses dealing in supplies.

Just any number will not do for a "gig." People want "hot" numbers. Numbers and combinations of numbers derived from "lucky' situations are much more powerful, have more of what the anthropologists call *mana,* than ordinary run-of-the-mill, garden-variety numbers. Lucky numbers may be obtained from the license plates of a car involved in an accident; from hymns announced at a church service; from streetcar transfers; from newspapers; or by asking a child. ("Children are lucky, you know, and are the best ones to give you winning gigs.")

Indispensable to the inveterate policy player is his "dream book," valuable for translating both dreams and "significant" occurrences into "gigs." The five most popular dream books in 1938 and 1939 were *The Three Witches, The Gypsy Witch, The Japanese Fate, Aunt Della's,* and *Aunt Sally's.* The gigs range from Abdomen (28-33-54) to Young (51-52-77), with a word like Accident subdivided into "to see" (4-31-50) and "to be in" (1-37-50). Boys' names range from Aaron (12-17-48) to Zephaniah (16-21-33); women's names from Ada (7-2-50) to Zenobia (46-47-53).

Many persons use the dream book not only for the interpretation of dreams, but also for the translation of personal experiences and public occurrences into numerical expressions. It is said that following the death of Will Rogers, the plays were so heavy on 7-10-11 (William) that some policy syndicate members sent out notices not to accept plays of over fifty cents. Some dream books contain numbers for the primary biological functions, and where the book does not have them, they are generally known by the initiated. (For instance, numbers for urine, dung, or copulation are not printed in books read in polite society; but everybody knows them.) One writer, advising another on how to hold down a job in a station, indicated the function of the dream-book symbolism:

"What you need to know is what each common thing and common name plays for. Sometimes a player forgets his book or can't remember. Some of the old-time writers get so good they can write poems with gigs, they know the meaning of the numbers so well. Incidentally, you mustn't bat an eye at the plays when they give 'em to you. You know some darkies think it's cute to play some of the dirty gigs when a pretty 'chick' is the writer. But a good writer doesn't let it feaze her an inch."

A middle-aged woman who has been writing policy for years said to an interviewer on the sources of gigs:

"Well, some play by hunches, dreams, or numbers on a car or transfer ticket. Some go to Spiritualists. They are obtained for the most part, though, from dreams and hunches. You watch the 'book' your dream falls in most and play in that 'book.' Some people are lucky and some are not. Some people believe in burning different incenses for luck. They claim it gives them success. My dreams are good in the Harlem and the Bronx.

The Spiritualists referred to are not, as a rule, pastors of churches (although some few Spiritualist pastors do actually give out numbers), but "spiritual advisers," who may or may not conduct actual church services. A few spiritual advisers who also conduct worship services frankly admitted that they give out gigs. One explained the matter thus:

"As far as literature is concerned, I don't believe these people read anything but policy slips. There are policy stations all around here, but you can't blame the people for trying to better their condition to the best of their knowledge. The whole thing is just this—there is so much sin that we can't be surprised at what happens.

"I have done good for a lot of people and they never forget what I do for them. When the spirit comes to me, whatever it tells me I do that. If it says pray, I do that. To give numbers is no sin because the people have to live, and to try to win a little money. That is no harm. Knowledge will have to come from God and no man can do the job if he is not in possession of that knowledge. That power I have. On many occasions God comes to me in a dream. That dream I will play in policy and catch it. Then, I invest the money wisely. That is all there is to it. But you have to live free from sin to do this."

This minister is an atypical Spiritualist preacher, however. He is on the border line between a minister and a "spiritual adviser" such as MADAM WILLIAMS, "Your Friend and Adviser," who advertises special meetings every Wednesday, Friday, and Sunday evening and who has "advised thousands in their personal problems with complete satisfaction." The Madam offers "advice on all affairs of life, love, health, domestic and financial conditions." She advertises LUCKY NUMBERS FREE —11 HITS IN 3 DAYS. She makes no charge, but lifts a silver offering announced as twenty-five cents! There are several hundred such advisers in Bronzeville.

Somewhat closer to a purely commercial enterprise is the establishment of PROFESSOR EDWARD LOWE, ASTRO-NUMEROLOGIST. The Professor, Texas born and bred, sells gigs ranging in price from ten cents to $3, the latter guaranteed or money back. Professor Lowe asserts that his "gift" came from his mother, that he has studied "the science of the Zodiac," and that "some of the most intelligent people in the city of Chicago are in sympathy with the work that I engage in." In a bookstall outside of his store, the Professor displays his own magnum opus, the *Key to Numerology*, side by side with *Albertus Magnus, The Sixth and Seventh Book of Moses, White and Black Art for Man and Beast, The Book of Forbidden Knowledge,* and others of the same general type. Displayed too are Adam and Eve Roots, Policy Player's Oil for 50 cents, Genuine Live Lodestone, and the Lucky Oil of Mystery.

Occasionally, the magico-religious and the commercial enterprise are combined, as in the case of Doctor Pryor who has his Japo Oriental Company on the first floor and King Solomon's Temple of Religious Science in the basement. The latter teaches "The Fellowship of God and the Brotherhood of Man," while the former sells adjuncts to the faith—Sacred and Lucky Powders, Holy Oriental Oil, Oriental Controlling Oil, John the Conqueror Oil, and Dr. Pryor's Holy Floor Wash and House Spray Oil. The Floor Wash and House Spray is guaranteed to "rent houses, draw crowds, and eliminate the evil works of the Devil." The Doctor insists that he is "The World's Greatest Psychoanalyst," and his gifts range from "changing love to hate" to giving out gigs.

He advises his clients to distinguish carefully between "dreams" and "visions"; and between dreams induced by "overindulgence in food, drink, unhappiness, exercise, and worry" and dreams in which "the Good Spirit appears." He also gives some advice on how to play policy:

"I've put out a book designed to give accurately the number following or pertaining to any dream one may have of any consequence. I tell them to stay on their numbers and don't change them too often. Do not play too many different gigs. Put all your energy on one set and wait. Do not be too impatient and jump from gig to gig. They're all in the wheel."

As an added impetus to buy some oil or roots, the Doctor further advises his clients:

"Why many persons are not successful in games or financial enterprises is because they are crossed with the evil influences and bad wishes of someone else. Before one can be successful this condition must be removed. Believe it or not, success cannot and will not come in unhealthy homes. The word jinx means the evil works of a would-be friend, a representative of the Devil. I advise them to search themselves, find out what the trouble is, and get rid of it. *All advice is free.*"

But the Doctor "makes his" from the sale of "jinx-removal candles" and efficacious oils. If you seek his help he leads you to the temple in the basement and places you in front of the elaborate altar, where a rack of candles burns and a colored glass bowl contains oil and water. You drop your coin into the water, letting your fingers touch the liquid. Then you light your candle and the Doctor places it in the rack. If you don't "catch" on the next gig, there is always the suspicion that you were not "purified" sufficiently or didn't burn enough "jinx-removal candles." So you return for more.

"POLICY"—A BIG BUSINESS

The Policy Station: This is simply a brokerage office for the players, having to a great extent replaced the once popular "walking writers." A steady player contrasted the two types of play:

"I don't mind giving a play to a walking writer once in a while, but you know they often keep the money, thinking your gig won't come out, and when it does fall he will be long gone and you can't collect a dime. Of course, the syndicate will make it hot enough for him, perhaps stop him from writing any more, but it's hard enough to catch policy as it is, without having some spade * mess you up by keeping your plays. Again, you know if you get a good hit with some of these walking writers, they may go home with your money. The stations won't do that because they are in business."

Station owners are allowed to keep 25 per cent of the gross business they write, and so lucrative is the business that the 500 stations employ some 2,000 porters, writers, and other employees. (See Tables 22 and 23.)

An observer has described the interior of one such station as follows:

"The station is located in the basement at ——, an apartment building. On entering the station, you notice, to the right, a pressing shop. Along the walls are three troughlike racks with signs reading A.M., P.M., and M.N. These are the receptacles for the drawings for morning, afternoon, and midnight. These troughs have a section for every wheel for which the station writes. There are small blackboards on each side of the wall where lucky or hot numbers are placed. Each week, or every two or three days, as the case may be, advertisements of all the important wheels are placed in a conspicuous place. On a table is a large scrapbook with draw-

* "Spade" is a term playfully used by Negroes to refer to a member of The Race.

ings pasted in for months past. These drawings are for reference and are often used by patrons in determining their daily plays. In the rear end of the station, behind a barred cage resembling a teller's window, the writers are stationed. A tailor's sign camouflages the entire station—the only sign in evidence on the outside of the building."

TABLE 22

FINANCIAL ANALYSIS OF THREE POLICY COMPANIES FOR ONE WEEK: 1938

Interstate Company

Income		Expenditures	
Approximate weekly "take"..............	$6,000.00	Weekly salary of checkers (and other inside employees)..............	$ 265.00
Approximate expenditures	3,085.00	Pick-up men.............	170.00
		Rent (owns building)....	......
Approximate weekly net income of owner.......	$2,915.00	Political payoff..........	250.00
		Hits, if normal, 40% of take.................	2,400.00
			$3,085.00

East & West Company

Income		Expenditures	
Approximate weekly "take"..............	$7,200.00	Weekly salary of checkers (and other inside employees)..............	$ 240.00
Approximate expenditures	3,797.00	Pick-up men.............	135.00
		Manager (said to get 10%)	372.00
Approximate weekly net income of owner.......	$3,403.00	Political payoff..........	250.00
		Hits, if normal, 40% of take.................	2,800.00
			$3,797.00

Monte Carlo Company

Income		Expenditures	
Approximate weekly "take"..............	$6,000.00	Weekly salary of checkers (and other inside employees)..............	$ 230.00
Approximate expenditures	3,250.00	Pick-up men.............	310.00
		Rent....................	60.00
Approximate weekly net income of owners......	$2,750.00	Political payoff..........	250.00
(Two owners each receive)	$1,375.00	Hits, if normal, 40% of take.................	2,400.00
			$3,250.00

TABLE 23

EMPLOYEES AND ESTIMATED WAGES IN POLICY RACKET FOR ONE WEEK: 1938 *

Number of policy stations.........................	483	
Median number of employees per station............	3.5	
Median wage per employee........................	$9.00	
Total wages paid......................................		$15,214.50
Number of pick-up men...........................	109	
Median wage..................................	$33.00	
Total wages paid......................................		3,597.00
Number of checkers or clerks......................	125	
Median wage..................................	$25.00	
Total wages paid......................................		3,125.00
Door men, floor men, janitors, stampers, and others...	118	
Median wage..................................	$15.00	
Total wages paid......................................		1,770.00
Commissions to walking writers...................	2,075	2,178.75
Grand total of wages paid............................		$25,885.25

* Research on the policy racket was done before the beginning of the Second World War. Since policy continued to thrive during the war, it is probable that these wages were tripled. It is the authors' impression that the volume of business done by the policy companies was at least tripled by the war boom.

So lucrative is the policy station that some legitimate businessmen have turned to it as their major enterprise and use their other business merely as a front. One restaurateur reported:

"Two years ago, my business was so bad that I thought I would have to close up. Then I thought of a policy station. I divided the store, and I find that I make more money from the policy than from the lunchroom."

A cigar-store proprietor hoped to open a station soon:

"I have a small turnover—about $15 a day. Money comes pretty slow in the cigarette business, but with a policy station, I ought to do pretty well. Competition has almost forced the Negro out of business."

Another fairly successful owner of a lunch stand commented that "work was hard to find, so I thought I would start in business." A friend allowed him to open a restaurant in front of his policy station.

A few months later, the friend went out of business and left him both the station and store. He reports: "I kept the station open, putting on a girl to take care of it for me. I was surprised to find that the station earned enough to pay the girl and yet make a profit."

In some cases the legitimate business is purely a front, as in the case of a laundryman who told an interviewer: "I just took the laundry business over as a front for my station. I don't really expect to make any money out of it. Yet I may start up a hand laundry. I am just an agent for a white laundry now and the percentage don't amount to much." It is often to a legitimate businessman's advantage to rent out the rear of his store to a policy station, thereby reducing his overhead. In a selected area of the Black Belt, where there were 50 policy stations (over one to a block), they were fronted with the following types of business:

No front	33
Shoeshine parlor	5
Candy store	2
Barber shop	4
Cigar store	2
Beauty parlor	2
Delicatessen store	2

In single instances stations were found behind a laundry, grocery store, lunchroom, tavern, cleaning and pressing shop, poolroom, coal and wood yard, moving and expressing store, and incense store.

The Syndicate: The station is simply the most visible expression of a complex machine employing over 5,000 persons, which in 1938 had a weekly payroll of over $25,000 and an annual gross turnover of at least $18,000,000. This business is organized as a cartel with a syndicate of fifteen men (including twelve Negroes) in control of the game. On the syndicate payroll were 125 clerks, more than 100 pick-up and delivery men, a dozen or so accountants, including several CPA's, and over 100 miscellaneous employees—doormen, floormen, janitors, stampers, bookkeepers, and "bouncers."

The syndicate was founded in 1931 because the heat was being too frequently turned on the previously unorganized individual entrepreneurs. The syndicate was designed to bring order into a tangled and extensive business and to protect the member-operators from exploitation by politicians. It provided financial aid to individual members hard pressed for money because of abnormally large hits, and

maintained a set of lawyers and bondsmen. It handled "public relations" with "downtown" political authorities, who in 1938 received at
least $7,500 a week from the syndicate.* The syndicate also helps to
deliver the vote at election time and makes special campaign contributions.

The main function of the syndicate is to make the necessary political alignments so that neither the police, a crusading state's attorney,
nor pressure from reform groups can jeopardize the smooth running
of the business. If a "set-up" raid is to be conducted as a concession
to public opinion, arrangements must be made so that no damaging
evidence will be found or the wrong persons arrested. Individual
station owners agree that they are seldom molested and do not have
to make payoffs to policemen as they once did. The syndicate now
takes care of such matters. One station owner, referring to the old pre-
syndicate days, said:

"At that time, there wasn't any syndicate to furnish protection for gambling. The payoff was made directly to the police. Squad cars with the
police from the detective bureau received the largest sums, $10 to $20 per
month."

The police today rarely try to "muscle in," although owners are usually deferential toward them. The editor of one Negro weekly, commenting on the power of the syndicate, stated: "The Mayor won't
mess with the syndicate, and the Police Commissioner doesn't dare." †
The extensive ramifications of policy are diagrammed in Figure 28.

So widespread was the conception of policy as a business that the
writers for one company actually organized in 1938 and struck for

* Estimates of the amount sent "downtown" vary. One precinct captain insisted that $40,000 a week was the sum. A policy-station owner exclaimed know-
ingly, "Why, hell, everybody knows they pay a thousand bucks a week!" An
editor in a position to know estimated $100 a week "for each turn of the
wheels." This would make a sum of nearly $30,000 a week. A well-informed
lawyer said, "One per cent of each day's take." The estimate here is based on the
conservative figure of $250 a week for each of the 16 wheels.

† One wheel owner reported a specialized type of favor by the political machine: "One Negro played the wheel consistently, $5 every day. He finally hit
for $6,000. Rather than pay his hit, the wheel owner had the state's attorney's
policemen pick him up. They did so and held him incommunicado for three
days, and they alleged a trick had been played on the wheel from the inside in
connection with this fellow. Finally he was released and given back the money
he had played in the wheel."

Figure 28

THE "POLICY RACKET"

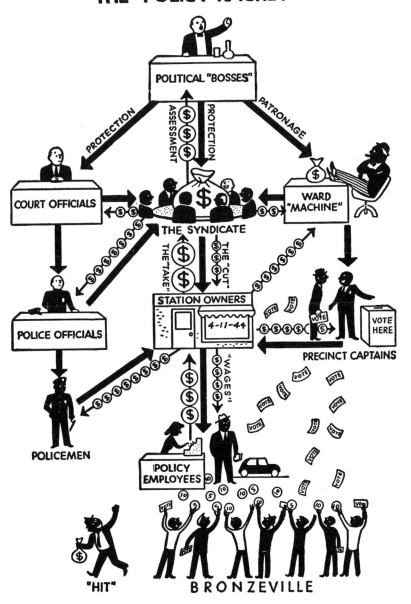

"better working conditions." The following comment by a walking writer reveals this matter-of-fact appraisal of policy as a big business:

"Well, honey, I guess you heard about the sit-down strike the writers at the Belmont and North Shore pulled, ain't you? They been picketing the place, but nuthin' definite has come of it. You know they are striking against the midnight drawing, but I don't think it will work. It's been done before. You know all of them aren't together on it. Some are striking and some ain't. I would be a happy one if they would stop those midnight drawings, because it makes it so hard on us. Policy day and night is too much. We don't get a chance to stick together long enough for that to happen, though.

"The people don't realize that policy is a syndicate, and whatever the bosses up at the head say goes. . . . And the bosses certainly ain't in favor of not having a midnight drawing because they lose that much money. And you know they don't want to do that."

POLICY: A COMMUNITY INSTITUTION

The strength of the "policy racket" in the Negro community may be due to Bronzeville's penchant for gambling, but it is perpetuated by the intricate tie-up with the "downtown" political powers, who render protection not only from the police, but also from attempts of civic leaders to interfere with the game. The historic connection between Black Belt "vice" and the political machine has already been discussed elsewhere. Suffice it to say that a "kickback" of perhaps half a million dollars a year to "downtown" makes the policy racket a lucrative one for the machine in power.*

The proximity of the Negro community to the Red-light District before 1912 had its effect on every community institution, and re-

* A prominent colored lawyer, asked to comment on policy, launched out vigorously:

"I blame gambling conditions in this city on the Mayor. He is in direct charge of the police, and they don't dare raid certain places because the people pay well for protection.

"Graft collection for policy and other kinds of racket on the South Side is here in this building. A lawyer is in charge of the collecting. If anyone wants to open up a place, they must see him. If he gives his O.K. they must pay so much every week. He notifies the police captain in the district to instruct the patrolmen not to bother. Monday and Tuesday of every week is pay-off day. A string of white and colored come into this building to make their weekly payments. Later in the day a man from downtown comes to take the money. Sometimes he has a bodyguard and sometimes a squad car comes with him."

formers often castigated the church for its inability to control the situation. One paper came forth with these headlines:

REVS. LUCAS, BRITT, AND CROSS ARE INACTIVE
OR SLEEPING WHILE VICE, CRIME, SINKHOLES
OF INIQUITY, AND SALOONS ARE FLOURISH-
ING RIGHT IN FRONT OF THEIR RESPECTIVE
CHURCHES

CRICKSMITH, ATTORNEY FOR THE GAMBLERS' TRUST,
MAY NEGOTIATE A TWENTY-YEAR LOAN ON GILEAD
CHURCH

After the abolition of the Red-light District, prostitution never again became highly organized in the Negro community. Saloons gave way to taverns after prohibition, and Negroes did not attempt to compete with the Capone beer-barons in the palmy Twenties. In fact, it is rumored that a deal was made by which Negroes were given control of gambling but ordered to stay away from liquor in the Black Belt.

The first important gambler to see the possibilities in policy was the John "Mushmouth" Johnson already mentioned. He amassed a fortune from the nickels and dimes that he "cut" from crap games at his "emporium" on State Street. It was in the late Nineties that he struck up a partnership with "King Foo," a Chinaman who, with Patsy King, a white man, had run a lottery in the old First Ward. In 1905, the state legislature passed an antipolicy law aimed primarily at Johnson; but he continued with the game and a white daily reported of Johnson's funeral in 1907 at a prominent Methodist church:

King Foo was there, a Chinaman representing his people, who at one time was a partner with Johnson in the policy game. He sat with bowed head with every indication of sorrow while the dead Negro's fellows conducted the service.

Old-timers do not forget that "Mushmouth's" sister was the wife of Jesse Binga and that the House of Binga was based partly on the fortune that Johnson derived from gambling. They remember, too, another character—"Policy Sam," who died broke in 1937, but was sometimes called the father of the game. In 1885 Sam opened a wheel of which it has been observed:

Gamblers shied away because of the huge odds against the players. The game was supported in the main by the small change of poverty-laden workers, housewives, prostitutes, and gambling-house flunkies who were lured by the 180-to-1 dividends.

Policy Sam withdrew from the game after the antipolicy law of 1905, but Johnson and others kept the game alive, and in 1931 the syndicate was formed. All the Negroes involved in the game became legendary figures who "never let a man starve," who were "honest," "big-hearted," "kind" gamblers. The present syndicate has managed to perpetuate this tradition.

Highly important in strengthening the policy racket is the fact that Negroes are spatially separated and socially isolated from the remainder of the community, and are denied full participation in the economic life of Chicago. This permits every attack on South Side gambling to be interpreted as an attack on The Race—which is to an extent true considering that vice and gambling flourish unmolested in other sections of the city also. Bronzeville's civic leaders will rally to the defense of a Negro gambler if it seems that he is being made a scapegoat. A united front cutting across political and social-class lines emerges when there is reason to doubt the motives of some ambitious state's attorney or police chief, who can be accused of making political capital by attacking "Vice in the Black Belt." The policy kings know well how to exploit this feeling and rally their defense.

Policy Kings as Race Leaders: The Depression, with its devastating impact, weakened the legitimate Negro business institutions, the symbols of financial control and stability in Bronzeville. The policy kings emerged as one group who could point to the thousands of workers still employed by The Race. They were thus able to assume the role of Race Leaders, patrons of charity, and pioneers in the establishment of legitimate business. They were able to wield some economic control over community institutions through their power to withhold or grant gifts.

In 1938, for instance, of the fifty-eight advertisements appearing in the program of a fashionable style show sponsored by a major charitable institution, four legitimate businesses owned by policy kings had taken quarter-page ads, two had half-page ads, and two bought an eighth of a page each. In addition, two known policy bankers purchased half-page ads expressing their compliments. It is interesting to note that half-page ads were the largest size sold, and that of eight of these, four were taken by policy men, three by white merchants, and one by Joe Louis.

Of a group of 87 advertisers and participants at the Negro Business Exposition referred to in the previous chapter, 14 were found to be businesses backed by policy money. Of the twenty-one full-page advertisements in the program for that affair, five were taken by businesses owned by policy kings. When in 1939 one outstanding organization was trying to raise $4,000, one policy king donated a $1,000 check. This ability to make large contributions to charity has had tremendous implications for the whole Negro community, leading to a reappraisal of the concept "respectability" and affecting profoundly the system of social classes.

The policy kings have, almost without exception, invested a portion of their "take" in legitimate businesses. Taverns, shoestores, food marts, and real estate businesses are among the enterprises based on this unorthodox form of primitive accumulation. About twenty per cent of the largest Negro business enterprises, and those most conscious of the value of public goodwill, are owned by policy people. Many ministers, civic leaders, and politicians have eschewed any discussion of policy, purely on the ground that the game is a business, employing many people, and that the policy men have also opened legitimate business places. The policy kings have been enthusiastic proponents of the myth of "racial salvation by Negro business." They have given some reality to the hope of erecting an independent economy within Black Metropolis.

The rise of the policy kings to the status of Bronzeville's respected capitalists has been made easier by the tradition of "Mushmouth" Johnson and Dan Jackson. Also, three of the present syndicated men are brothers—the sons of a minister—and are well-educated, affable fellows. One of Joe Louis's backers is also reputed to own a wheel. Finally, there have been no scandals involving murders, and few instances of hooliganism. The game is thought to be "on the level." All these factors combine to make it easy for Bronzeville to accept the policy racket as a community institution.

THE POLICY KING AS A RACE HERO

To open a successful business in Bronzeville makes any man something of a hero. For a policy king to do so also sets him on the road to respectability.

Most famous of these legitimate enterprises is the so-called "Jones Boys' Store." Situated on the main business street, in an area that Negro businessmen have found it difficult to enter, the store has become a master symbol of successful Negro enterprise. Its opening in 1937 was a major community event. Thousands of people filled the street, and a special police detail was necessary to keep the traffic moving. Participants on the program appeared at a second-story window. A popular theatrical editor was master of ceremonies and a loud speaker carried the program through the streets. First upon the program was Joe Louis who, when he appeared at the window, sent the crowd into a noisy demonstration. His wife commented to a reporter: "I am just as thrilled over this opening as I was the night my husband won the championship." Bill (Bojangles) Robinson, the Negro dancer, stepped to the mike and kept up a stream of jokes. "Really, I don't know what you, my people, want," he said. "You have everything. You have Jesse Owens, the fastest track man of all times; Joe Louis, the greatest fighter in the world. You even have God—Father Divine—Peace, it's wonderful! Now, you have the Jones Brothers with one of the finest stores in the world. Patronize them and do everything you can to be satisfied." Mrs. Bojangles sent her greetings: "The store is a marvelous project and is something we really need. We hope the public will patronize it today, tomorrow, and forever."

From time to time the owners spoke to the audience. Even a police lieutenant was on the program, flattering the crowd with a statement to the effect that "this has been one of the best-behaved crowds I have ever witnessed in my life, and I want to tell you all I thank you." A white civil service commissioner insisted that he had advised "the boys" to open the store despite the opposition of Negro leaders. "I told them I thought it would be one of the greatest things that ever happened in history. . . . I am indeed glad to have had a part in this celebration." Two other syndicate members' wives felicitated the owners on their "realization of a dream." One of the most prominent lawyers in the city dubbed the opening of the store "a milestone in the progress of our business," and expressed his faith that "with their excellent equipment and fine stock of merchandise I am sure they will be successful."

The ceremony over, the crowds streamed through the store for hours admiring what in actuality was a medium-sized variety store. To them, however, it was the Negroes' first significant challenge to the large white department stores that dominate Bronzeville's shopping district.

One or two popular preachers were there to grace the event. They prayed and spoke. One prominent Baptist minister, though not present, later claimed the credit for persuading the policy kings to open the store:

"I was severely criticized for my contact with them. It was said that I was catering to racketeers and gambling. . . . I told them [the policy men] they were men of families—men who could stand for something in the community. My next step was to interest them in a legitimate business. They knew I disapproved of policy."

One successful Negro entrepreneur on 47th Street, who had several times been threatened with the loss of his lease, offered the following comment:

"The people who represent the policy barons have done something that none of our race has done before. By buying the building here on 47th Street and opening a store, they are showing that we must have good established places of business to compete with the white people. There are many others of our race that have large sums of money but seem to think that it should be used for pleasure and will never risk it in some business venture that will give employment to our own group. I contend that we are in the condition that we are in simply because we are not in the position to supply anything for ourselves. Everything must be obtained from white people."

A restaurant owner who is among their admirers has summed up the general attitude of Negroes toward the "Jones Boys":

"They have established a store that would do credit to any race; even the building they have was purchased by them. They may come under the head of racketeers, but as long as they have done something that no other one of our group has done, they should be given a lot of credit and are entitled to the support of our people."

In the spring of 1940 the prison gates opened to release Jesse Binga, symbol of the Negro's bid for financial power *via* respectability; the business cycle had broken him. A few months later, the prison gates closed on one of the "Jones Boys." He was (reputedly) "taking the rap" for the family's alleged collective evasion of income-tax payments. Bronzeville, pondering the fate of both, is no doubt bewildered. To them, neither is a criminal; both are the victims of the white man's system.

"POLICY"—SCOURGE, BLESSING, OR NECESSARY EVIL?

A widespread, illegal institution, carrying in its train "madams," "professors," and "doctors" of the type described above, naturally has its opponents on moral, cultural, and economic grounds. In 1938 one ministers' conference lashed out with a fiery resolution: THE POLICY RACKET MUST BE STAMPED OUT. THE CHURCH CANNOT UNDER ANY CIRCUMSTANCES COUNTENANCE GAMBLING UNDER WHATEVER FORM AS HAVING MORAL OR ECONOMIC JUSTIFICATION. Church people at all levels are likely to state that policy is "immoral" (even though they play). "I did play policy and was lucky," states an almost destitute woman; "but after I joined the Church of God in Christ, I stopped that. My church is against policy and gambling." "I don't think any Christian should partake of those wicked things"; "my preacher preaches against policy," so the comments run from people who take their religion seriously.

The opponents on religious grounds are relatively few, however, and a more prevalent attack is that launched from the perspective of those slightly well-to-do persons who feel that "most of the players are poor people who can't afford to gamble; those people on relief and WPA who haven't anything and always hope they'll win more." The secretary of one Parent-Teachers Association dubs policy "an obsession with our people . . . which takes their minds away from the higher things of life." Teachers, social workers, and businessmen sometimes express concern over the way policy encourages and reinforces the idea of "getting something for nothing if you can." Thus one physician states positively: "I don't think policy should be allowed. It discourages thrift among Negroes." An Old Settler whose husband is an active civic leader says she doesn't condemn people for "trying to make money," but that "you can't get something for nothing." Such critics frequently deplore the effect on children of seeing their parents play policy. "Policy," says one woman, "is a great detriment to our people. It has ruined the minds of the young people. It tends to encourage other forms of gambling. In the alleys around here you'll find little kids shooting craps. What can you expect when their parents play policy?" One professional woman complained indignantly: "So many people send their children to put in the plays. Parents like that should be tarred and feathered." People sensitive to Bronzeville's reputation, especially home-owners, see policy as a threat to neighborhood stability, and are likely to react as did the woman who said: "I would like to see all the policy stations closed. Policy has a very bad influence in most neighborhoods where colored people live." One community worker combined these criticisms:

"There is a policy station across the street in the basement. I do not play policy and never have. I think the policy game is about the worst thing in this community. There are grown people playing policy that should be buying something to eat or buying themselves some clothes. I understand that many of them are going ragged playing policy."

This type of criticism is sometimes echoed by persons on relief or in lower-income brackets: "I don't believe in taking a chance on losing your carfare or dinner money," or "I think it's awful for people to play policy when their families need this money to try to buy bread and meat."

An objection raised more often by members of lower-income groups is the odds against the player. Statements of this type follow the general pattern of those by the relief clients mentioned above.

"Policy is hard to beat, and I don't have no money to throw away. I can't see any good it does or how 'charity-people' can play." *

"Probably one out of a hundred 'catch policy.' That's all. I'd have to know a gig was coming out before I'd play it, and I don't believe anybody knows what numbers will come out."

A rather unorthodox preacher, noted for playing a good hand of poker, combined the ethical with the calculating in his comment that "policy is demoralizing the Negro. Policy is a sucker's game!"

Some preachers feel obliged to attack policy from their pulpits, but—

---

* Persons on relief during the Depression were referred to as "charity people." Being on relief was called "being on the charity."

as one woman phrased it—"the ministers preach and preach about gambling, but they don't refuse money that comes from gambling." A policy station owner expressed this opinion: "I can tell you this much. I certainly believe that every policy station in the city of Chicago would have to close up if it were not supported by church people." One store-front pastor has given up in resignation and relates his woes:

"I went into that store one day to see why so many of my people were going in there, and I found out it was a policy station. One of my members was playing policy and she walked out as I walked in. I don't believe in vice, but I can't do anything about it."

Pastors are indeed on the defensive if they have many members such as the one who, when asked what he would do if his pastor found out he played policy, said:

"Nothing. My dollar looks as good as any other dollar to him. He knows it. He has to have money and he isn't telling us how to get it. He just says, 'Get it.' And another thing—any time he doesn't want my policy money, I know lots of nice ladies that will welcome it."

For years, the periodical and abortive crusades against policy led by ministers have been the butt of jokesters. Bronzeville is definitely pro-policy, and civic and religious leaders cannot arouse any righteous indignation against the game. In fact, the majority of the civic leaders do not think of the game as "vice," and opinion is divided as to whether it should be suppressed, licensed, segregated, or defended.

Most "respectable" people in Bronzeville, when they defend policy, do so on the basis of the achievements of men such as the "Jones Boys." For instance, one legitimate businessman said, "I'm glad to see our group go into business enterprises no matter where the money comes from." Businessmen frequently cited the "racketeers" as "the ones who have taken the lead in the business world," as persons who "give employment to a large number of people and give The Race a rating among the people of the white business world that we have not enjoyed before." One successful entrepreneur, after listing a half-dozen prominent racketeers, said, "All of these men are known as racket men, but at least they have opened places that give employment to our own people." One female tavern owner doesn't "know how to explain it, but the people who have opened the best businesses are those who have made the money from policy." Occasionally, these encomiums are associated with a criticism of the "respectable" businessmen who "always had large sums of money at their disposal, but none of them have opened anything worth mentioning."

Many defenders of policy do not base their arguments solely upon the symbolic value of the legitimate business, however. During the Depression years, they were quick to point out the beneficial effect of a $26,000 weekly payroll in the community itself. This led many persons to question the wisdom of attacking the game. One housewife observed thoughtfully:

"To be perfectly frank, I would not like to see policy stamped out, for I am of the opinion at the present time that policy is actually doing more good than it is harm. Now, if someone could suggest something to take its place, I would be in sympathy with it. Just suppose they would absolutely stamp out all policy in Chicago—what would all these people do?"

(When this study was made, few knew that less than 6,000 people were employed at any one time by the game.)

Some persons indorse the game with reservations. Two young businessmen, for instance, look on the whole policy complex as a kind of informal co-operative set-up:

"The few pennies that the public loses in policy can hardly be missed by them. Yet it amounts to thousands of dollars a day and goes to make it possible for many a family to survive."

"Yes, I have heard a number of people say that policy is a bad thing for the Negro, yet I say that the number of people it employs makes up for the little that the people who play lose. I do not know anything else those people could work at."

Business people might be expected to oppose policy as uneconomic but, surprisingly enough, a large number of them defend the game. The excerpts quoted below are typical of a large segment of businessmen.

A Bartender: "There are many hundreds of people who are working for the policy wheels, and if it were not for the wages they make from the wheels those people would be dependent upon someone for a living. Some people think that a policy writer has a soft job, but let that person get out and walk around from house to house three times a day and they will soon find out that it is nothing to laugh about."

Owner of Barbecue Stand: "Policy, I think, is doing a lot of good. Thousands of people make their living by working for the wheel, and although many people do not believe it, there are many who are lucky enough to win often enough to pay all their expenses."

Tavern Owner: "I am in favor of policy because it helps keep people employed. It is more than surprising to know the many thousands that make their living from this source."

One young man who worked for years as a coalheaver, and who was never able to get a "better" job until he went into policy, was a warm defender of the game:

"Policy was a godsend to the Negroes on the South Side, and I think most all the people who have jobs in the game will agree with me. You can make a living without slaving for it. As for me, I don't think that I would have been living if I had stayed at the coal yard. Long hours and short pay for common labor is too much for me. . . . I don't know what we'd do if the heat was turned on; I suppose we'd eventually have to go on relief. Sometimes the girls could make $20 a week. There isn't a laundry in the city or a kitchen in Hyde Park where a girl without learning could earn $20 for a week's work."

One informant tried to visualize the effects of stopping policy:

"If the heat were turned on, 5,000 people would be unemployed and business in general would be crippled, especially taverns and even groceries, shoestores, and many other business enterprises who depend on the buying power of the South Side."

One loyal church member, after stating that he wasn't enthusiastic about policy, ended with the laconic statement, "If it takes policy to keep some people eating, that's all there is to it."

CHAPTER 18

The Measure of the Man

AS WE HAVE NOTED IN THE PRECEDING CHAPTERS, BRONZEVILLE JUDGES ITS institutions and leaders in terms of "racial loyalty." To be called a Race Man is a high compliment. But "race-relations" is only one axis of life. People are also interested in "getting ahead," "having a good time," and "serving the Lord," and when people are choosing a church or social club or selecting a wife or a husband, they do not choose primarily according to how the organization or person "stands on the race question." There are other measures of the man. Yet, as we shall see, the shadow of the Job Ceiling and of the Black Ghetto falls on every activity, and all of Bronzeville's standards of appraisal are conditioned by the way Negro-white relations are organized.

COLOR OF THE SKIN

White people with an interest in "Negro progress" sometimes profess shock at the distinctions Negroes make among themselves. Most disconcerting are color distinctions—the lines that Negroes draw between black and "light," "fair" and brown-skinned. "How," they ask, "can Negroes expect white people not to draw the color-line when they do it themselves?" Negro leaders in Bronzeville usually throw the ball back to the whites by demanding in effect, "How can Negroes ignore color distinctions when the whole culture puts a premium upon being white, and when from time immemorial the lighter Negroes have been the more favored?" A Negro physician, for instance, told an interviewer:

"Any Negro who is honest will admit that he is dominated by the standards of the society he is brought up in. When we are little children we use story books in which all the characters have long blond hair. When we go to church we're taught that God is a white man. The Virgin Mary is white. What can you expect? All our early concepts of desirable physical attributes come from the white man.

"It is a sociological rule that people are pulled into the standardized

495

ways of thinking. The average Negro may say that he's proud to be black. This is more or less a defense mechanism. People in America don't black their faces and make their hair kinky. They would be laughed at; it would be too different from the American standard. The whole situation is easy enough to understand."

There is much truth in this argument. "Black" is a word loaded with derogatory implications in Anglo-Saxon linguistics. Things are "black as sin." When you don't like a person you give him a "black look." When trouble passes, you emerge "from darkness into light." Conversely, "That's damned white of you" is a compliment. To be "free, *white,* and twenty-one" is considered the ultimate in independence. White people will even sometimes compliment a Negro by unconsciously saying, "Good—you did it like a white man." Scant wonder that Negroes have picked up the idea that "black is evil."

The "Color-struck": When "fair" (i.e., light-skinned) Negroes seem inordinately proud of their skin-color, or when darker Negroes have a predilection for associating with very light ones or encouraging their children to do so, Bronzeville calls them "color-struck." One color-struck woman told an interviewer that she liked dark-skinned people "in their places. . . . I mean I like them, but not around me. Their place is with the rest of the dark-skinned folks." Another woman says much the same: "I have no ill-feeling for the 'less fortunate,' but I don't care to entertain them outside of closed doors. I really feel embarrassed when people see me with black persons. I do have a friend who is quite dark. I love her and really forget that she is black until we start outdoors. I never go very far with her, though." Of such people, a dark-brown-skinned professional man observed: "Somewhere in their early childhood these light-skinned people who think they are better than the dark Negroes are taught that the nearer they are to white the better they are. They have a superiority complex. This attitude, just like the attitude of white people toward Negroes, is the result of propaganda."

There are very few "fair" Negroes who will speak so bluntly as the two women quoted above. But there are clear indications that light people (especially women) have a tendency to form social cliques based upon skin-color. There are persistent rumors that certain formally organized voluntary associations, including one or two churches, are "blue-vein"—that is, will not accept any members whose skin is not light enough for the veins to show through. Though there is no evidence to indicate that any "blue-vein societies," as such, exist in Bronzeville, there are a few clubs like the one described by the organization's secretary:

"Don't quote me in telling this. Of course it is an unwritten law in our club that all of the members range from light-brown to yellow. I think it's positively silly, because there are so many fine people who are darker."

The member of another club insists that such homogeneity is accidental:

"The club is over sixteen years old. The color pattern, I guess, would be light-brown to fair. I am the darkest member in the club. I have never paid any attention to that in any of the groups that I have been affiliated with. The question of a person's color or how much money he had or did not have has never arisen in any discussion that I can recall."

Being "Partial to Color": When Negroes show preferences or draw invidious distinctions on the basis of skin-color, Bronzeville calls them "partial to color." And "partial to color" always means "partial to *less* color"—to light color. The outstanding example of partiality to color is seen in men's choices of female associates. It is commonly charged that successful Negro men of all colors tend to select very light-brown and fair women. One cynical young man summed up the situation by declaring that "no man, irrespective of how dark or light he is, wants a dark woman." A prominent professional man, discussing two of his fraternity brothers, began with the usual "I don't want you to put this down," and then proceeded to name two men "who have gotten themselves white-looking women." One has "two of them—little white dolls." He also called attention to "a big black bandmaster who has got himself a little white-looking doll." A lawyer (himself married to a light-brown-skinned woman) expressed his disapproval of marrying "fair" women:

"I heard a University of Chicago girl say that an educated dark girl has a hard time trying to find herself a husband. Why did she say that? Because just like Dr. ——, our educated men will go and marry some pretty little light, senseless, and dumb chick. Well, I like brown-skinned girls. I started off in high school with one, and I married one. But when most of our educated men get well off, instead of finding themselves a

woman that matches them they pick one of those little white chicks."
(I.e., very light Negro girls.)

While the charge is made that successful Negro men put a premium
on women that "look like white," it would be more accurate to say
that they seem to put a premium on marrying a woman who is not
black or very dark-brown.* Such mate-images are revealed when men
are having "bull sessions" about women. Thus one young man tells
his fellows:

"I never go out with dark women because they just don't interest me.
I prefer a light person for a sweetheart or a wife. They are more affec-
tionate, lovable, and understanding. They are usually more attractive;
they're prettier; they have good hair. They're more intelligent. I don't
look for coal mines; I look for gold mines."

These attitudes toward "marrying light" are often implanted at an
early age. One mother told an interviewer frankly: "I'm not prejudiced, but I don't want my children to marry dark people, because I
feel they're hard to understand and I want my children to be happy.
Of course, if they did marry someone dark-complexioned, I couldn't
do anything about it. But I hope they don't."

Despite talk of not preferring a dark woman, hundreds of men
do marry women darker than themselves. (There are not enough light-
browns to go around.) But it is a rare man who will say, as did one
young college fellow: "I would marry a dark girl if I loved her and
she loved me. The same about a white girl if she loved me and I loved
her. I am not prejudiced against race or color. It's the individual I'm
interested in." (It isn't fashionable to say things like this except to
interviewers.)

If male partiality to color constitutes a *social* handicap for the very
dark woman, it may also be an *economic* handicap in seeking certain
types of employment. Undoubtedly it is harder for a very dark woman
to get a position as a stenographer or physician's attendant than it is
for others. There is also some evidence to indicate that Negro restaurants and stores draw the color-line in hiring girls. The owner of
one of the best-known restaurants in Bronzeville frankly stated that
he was partial to color:

---

* Most of these color evaluations are very imprecise. What one man calls a
"dark" woman another may call "light." The important differential is between
very dark-brown women and all others.

"I have a policy of hiring only real light girls with good hair. I do this because they make a good appearance. The people of the sporting world who trade here will favor a light girl. A dark girl has no drawing power. The men who play in orchestras come here, and if I was to hire a dark girl she would be forced to stand around and do nothing while the other girls would be busy. I know this. I've even tried hiring brown-skinned girls, and they didn't make enough money to pay their carfare. Every girl who works as a waitress has got to depend to a certain degree on tips. The dark girls don't get 'em."

Another man, himself brown-skinned, said categorically, "Even the very blackest man would come into my restaurant oftener if light girls were employed." Probably any entrepreneur who is trying to be particularly "classy" feels that a bevy of light girls is desirable.*

Since very light women are a decided minority in Bronzeville, they are not always available for proprietors or professional men who would like to utilize their services. With a constantly growing pool of girls and young women with high school training, color-distinctions become less important. The proprietor of one employment agency reported in 1938:

"The Negro employer used to ask for very light-skinned or very light-brown-skinned Negro girls, but since the Depression he is getting some sense—now he is asking for 'a well-qualified young woman.' This is better both for the young people and for us as an employment agency."

Many Negroes feel that white people, by favoring lighter Negroes, make it hard for dark-skinned Negroes to secure personal-service jobs as well as other types of employment. Even men make this complaint. One light-brown-skinned boy who had no grievance of his own said:

"When it comes to finding a job with either whites or Negroes, they prefer light people. That is especially true of white people in the North. In the South it is exactly turned around: down there the blacker they are the better the white people like them."

* Some less exclusive restaurateurs feel that light women are "hard to get along with." One such employer states: "I have tried both real light girls and darker girls. I find that the darker girls give the best service. If you ask them to help keep the place clean they will do so. On the other hand the light girls will complain, and then they'll take their spite out on the customers. Light girls only serve the people that they know will tip. I hire only black girls and give them a decent salary so they don't have to depend upon tips."

There is some evidence, based on a study of newspaper advertisements and interviews, to substantiate the claim that upper-class and upper-middle-class white families and establishments in Midwest Metropolis do favor lighter-skinned servants,* despite the observation of one Bronzeville man that:

"White women don't like to have too light-colored girls working for them, or too pretty ones. It introduces an element of competition that they don't like. A light girl might look in the mirror and say, 'Well, I'm about as light as you are and maybe a lot prettier.' She'll feel just as good as her mistress. Dark women make better servants."

Escape from Shame: Two groups within the Negro community are sometimes made to feel "ashamed of their color"—the very dark and the very light. We mentioned above some common colloquial phrases derogating blackness, and cited examples of partiality to color on the part of Negroes and of whites. At the other extreme of the color-scale, the few Negroes light enough to pass for white are liable to obscene taunts about the way they acquired their white blood, or can be ridiculed as "rhinies" if they have reddish hair. It is this kind of ridicule that was referred to by a social worker in charge of placing children in foster homes when she reported: "We have the most difficulty in adjusting children at the two extremes. Brown-skinned children seldom seem to have conflicts over color." † Yet, light-skinned Negroes often learn to adjust either by "passing" or by forming élite cliques. They can get a certain amount of satisfaction from the suspicion that the darker people who criticize them are envious; also they can retaliate by imputing all sorts of undesirable characteristics to darker folk. Thus, one light-skinned woman described a newly organized club:

"We always had a lot of trouble with the darker women in clubs. We found them disagreeable—you had to be careful of every move you made.

---

* As to the charge that southern employers prefer dark servants the truth is rather complex. It does seem that there is something to the following homely explanation, however: "The southern whites prefer dark Negroes, and the Yankees prefer the light Negroes. The southern white man says that light Negroes think they are white, that they don't use the Uncle Tom language as frequently as black Negroes."

† Detailed confirmation of this observation can be found in a study by W. Lloyd Warner, Buford Junker, and Walter Adams, *Color and Human Nature* (American Youth Commission, Washington, D. C., 1940), based on materials collected in Bronzeville and dealing with personality problems arising from color differentials within the Negro community.

So we organized a club that we could enjoy. We went places and enjoyed a lot of opportunities we wouldn't have had if we had had a darker group with us.* I found that darker people don't know how to mix amiable. I don't care how cultured and educated they are, they feel they're being slighted by the lighter people."

Consciousness of having an undesirable skin-color comes very early. Hundreds of dark-skinned people in Bronzeville report experiences like that of a girl who said: "My oldest sister, Lucy, was always calling me names and telling me that the buzzards laid me and the sun hatched me. I hate to say this, but she made me hate her." A young man reports his reaction to the discovery that his mother was "partial to color":

"I knew that my light-skinned brother had always got the preference, but I accepted it because he was older. Whenever somebody went on a visit or to the store, he always went. Then one day—I must have been seven years old—I was left at home by myself. I was so lonesome that I went over next door to play. When my mother came home she was furious. She told me I was disgracing myself by playing with black children, that I was dark enough and should be satisfied. It was then that I became conscious of the reason I was never permitted to go places and do things like my brother."

Sometimes play groups drive the point home vigorously:

"I was about ten or eleven years old when I began to learn what the different colors of Negroes meant. We were playing house. Some of us were very fair children; some were light-brown; and some were very dark. We were choosing up for playing house. We made the very fair person the father, and so on down the line until we came to the darkest children. We tried to make them the servants, but they refused. We couldn't get enough co-operation to play house that day."

One of the most baffling things to a dark person is his inability to tell when he is being discriminated against because of his skin-color. He is likely to be oversensitive and suspicious—to "smell a rat" that isn't there. One young man who has never finished high school owing to lack of money was sure that "light fellows get all the breaks." He said: "I've often wished to be real light. Those people always get the

---

* Negroes in Bronzeville are continually charging that white people in exclusive downtown stores and restaurants treat the lighter Negroes with more consideration than the darker. This belief, whether true or false, puts an additional premium upon a light complexion.

better breaks." (In this case other traits than color may have contributed to the boy's lack of success.)

Most dark Negroes, however, do not sit around wishing they were light. They are much more likely to develop a kind of belligerent and aggressive affirmation of their worth.* Some fortunate children have parents who encourage them to overcome their color handicap by striving for superior achievements. One physician who reports that he had been "conscious of color" all his life told how his family handled the color problem:

"When I was a little boy—I guess about six years old—my uncle, who is very light, said to me, 'Boy, I believe you are getting blacker and blacker every day you live.' I was the darkest child in my family. My mother was brown-skinned and my father was very fair. My brothers and sisters used to call me 'tar baby.' That would hurt me, but my mother would say, 'You shouldn't mind—you have more brains than they have.' Sure enough, none of them went to school to make anything out of themselves. But it's just too bad to think that one must do extra work to be recognized just because he's a certain color."

Some parents not only spur the darker child on, but may also humor or spoil him. One woman stated: "I am about the darkest girl in my family. I was always sensitive about my color. Mother and my youngest sister are light-brown. My brother is medium-brown. Kids used to tease me about my color, and I'd come home crying. Mother would feel sorry for me and humor me." As Warner, Junker, and

---

* This affirmation sometimes takes the form of repeated references to "black people" in public speeches by darker folk. It also emerges in a tendency to decry the infusion of white strains into the Negro group and to insist that a "pure black" is better than a "half-caste." It has even assumed organized expression in the form of the "Garvey movement" during the Twenties—a mass movement among Negroes with a "Back to Africa" emphasis. Garvey, a West Indian Negro, was very hostile to what he called the "traitorous mulatto leadership" among Negroes. In general, however, this aggressiveness operates on an individual level, with people refusing to accept any estimate of their color which implies that they are inferior. On the lower cultural level derogatory remarks about blackness are a fighting matter. On the upper levels various types of compensatory behavior emerge.

Many dark-skinned Negroes develop the opposite personality traits. Dark people with a "sweet disposition" can be extremely popular in Bronzeville. The myth persists, however, that most dark people are "touchy," easily offended, and oversensitive. The very persistence of such a belief reinforces whatever tendency there is for them to be sensitive about their color.

Adams have pointed out, the way parents handle this color question in the very young child may determine the set of his or her personality.

Bronze Americans: A light-brown-skinned mother surprised one of the interviewers with the frank statement of a wish:

"I have five children, you know—all grown now—four girls and one boy. Three of the girls have decent light-brown skins, but the boy and the other girl are dark-brown-skinned. The Lord in Heaven knows that I love them all dearly, but He also knows that I wish the two dark ones were lighter."

Such a feeling is common among parents. They do not wish for "fair" children, but for "light-browns" or "smooth-browns." Men, too, often idealize the light-brown girl. A very dark-brown-skinned young man was being interviewed. At one point in the conversation he said earnestly: "To be frank with you, I am partial to light-brown-skinned girls. I don't mean yellow women. I think nothing is prettier than a good-looking brown-skinned woman." Another young man of like complexion described the kind of woman he wanted to marry: "I don't want her to be either yellow or too dark. If she is yellow, the first time she called me 'black' that would be the end. I don't want her too dark— just dark enough so she can't call me black."

Such comments are heard at all social levels in Bronzeville. There is a veritable cult of the brown-skinned woman * and a pronounced tendency to idealize "brownness" in contradistinction to "blackness." Negro journalists and publicists have popularized expressions such as "sepia artists," "The Tan Yanks," "Brown Bomber." The very name Bronzeville is, as we have mentioned, one of these euphemisms. Nowhere is the cult of the brown-skinned more vividly revealed than in newspaper advertisements for cosmetics and hair preparations. Today, the brown-skinned girl with "good hair" is the type.† A decade ago such ads featured the "white" type of Negro.

* Note the popularity of a movie actress like Lena Horne among both white people and Negroes.

† When Negroes disapprove of "blackness" they often mean a whole complex: dark-skin color, pronounced Negroid features, and kinky hair. Sometimes they do not mean color at all! Thus, it is common to hear a person say "She is a pretty black girl." Here the person (usually) means that the girl has Caucasoid features and hair that is not kinky. (Sometimes the term is used for a person with Negroid features *if* these are well proportioned.) In all such evaluations hair-type is crucial. Negroes do not like "kinky" hair, whatever the color of the

Race Leaders of all colors may orate about "the black hands that have built this country and fought for it." But in their *personal* choices of the "ideal female type" and also in many other contexts, Negroes reveal their preference for an in-between color that is neither black nor very light. The evidence from interviewer-observers is voluminous, but only a small number of illustrative examples can be presented here.*

On the level of nonverbal behavior: when a Negro artist decorates a church with colored angels and disciples, he paints *brown* ones. When a Negro storekeeper displays colored dolls, they are usually *brown* dolls. The most popular colored female movie stars are *brown*. Beauty contests and fashion shows are usually displays of *brown* beauty.

On the verbal level, comments on desirable boy-friends and girl-friends and children stress the brown-skinned type. One brown-skinned girl claimed to have been in love with a very light Negro man. She broke off the affair to marry a brown-skinned boy though he was lower in socio-economic status. Her reason? "I would rather not have the embarrassment of having to explain to folks that our children were *mine*—that I was not their nursemaid." Another brown-skinned girl states that though she doesn't want an "ashy black" or a "shiny black" husband, she would take such a man if he were a superior person. "But I'd have to be absolutely sure he was superior. My ideal type is a brown-skin, so that I could have pretty brown-skinned children. Also I'd like him to have good hair." Another said that she wouldn't have a black-skinned man, no matter what his quali-

girl's skin. A whole industry has grown up around the manufacture of "hair-straighteners." "Good hair" means straight or wavy hair. The emerging ideal type is similar to the Brazilian "moreno": brown skin, soft but not Negroid features, and "good" hair.

* A statistical study of color preferences among Negro high school students in several northern cities, including Chicago, reveals that 34.5 per cent of the boys and 35.1 per cent of the girls thought black was "the worst color to be" and 28.8 per cent of the boys and 27.9 per cent of the girls thought yellow was the worst color to be. Over half the boys and girls thought that "black is ugly." About two-thirds of them preferred a "light brown" or "brown" complexion, and nearly 70 per cent thought that "the most handsome person" of the opposite sex was "brown" or "light brown." (Cf. Charles S. Johnson, *Growing Up in the Black Belt,* American Council on Education, 1941. The Cayton-Warner Research questioned over 300 high school students in Chicago at Dr. Johnson's request.) E. Franklin Frazier, in *Negro Youth at the Crossways,* American Council on Education, 1941, reports similar color preferences among young Negroes in the border states.

fications: "To be frank with you, personally I don't even like black coats. And a black man? Honey, I just can't use one!"

That brown-skinned people should express such sentiments is natural. But the darker folks, too, seem to idealize brown skin-color. One very dark woman reveals this attitude when she related an unhappy love experience:

"I'm off of love. Some day I hope to get married, but it will be for security. You see, I don't feel there is security in love because love has its limitations. I was very close to, and loved, a boy once, but he decided that because I was dark and he was dark it would be unfair to our children for us to get married and propagate another dark generation. So he went and married a very fair girl and they have a beautiful light-brown child. In the beginning, when he intimated the difficulties of our getting married and having children, I didn't take it too seriously. But he showed me!"

Another woman who had a bitter love experience (her husband had divorced her for a light woman) rationalized the difficulty as follows:

"I feel it's my fault in a way. He always wanted children, and I am so black and ugly I just didn't want any children to look like myself. So I wouldn't have any. He is so proud now that he is going to have a child of his own. I am really proud for him. He is a good man and really deserves what he wants. He kissed me good-bye twice. We both cried. Now he is gone."

Girls sometimes consider these questions before getting married. A high school girl described her dream-children:

"I would have the boy very fair. That would be more of an advantage to him in his business or profession. I would have the girl a beautiful brown-skin, very attractive, with a million-dollar personality. It isn't essential for a girl to be fair to get along, but is essential that she have a good personality."

Another girl declares: "Well, if I had children of my own I'd want a brown-skin husband. The children would be brown, and that's the way I'd like them."

The Lessening Importance of Color: Though color is an important measure of the man in Bronzeville, it is by no means the most important one. A very dark woman may find her skin-color a handicap in getting the man she wants, but it is no bar to her being accepted by the community as a brilliant, useful, and admirable woman. A Negro man does not find his opportunity to get an education or to make money limited by his black skin. Bronzeville people sense what most sociologists agree on—that, as one doctor said: "Color-distinctions among Negroes are gradually disappearing. Some older people have told me of the time when color was the thing." He added: "I feel that ability counts more now." Another man observes that "with the older group color played an important part. With the younger generation it is different. I don't think color is as important as it used to be."

Many factors have contributed to the lessening importance of skin-color as the measure of the man within Bronzeville: the extension of education, the increase of "race pride," the accumulation of money by dark people. An additional factor of extreme importance should be mentioned—the tendency of successful dark men to marry light. Most of the children will be darker than the mother and lighter than the father. Any tendency toward the growth of a light-skinned caste is continually being defeated by the rise of the darker people into the higher-status brackets. Very dark Negroes can't do much about changing their skin-color, but they can get a favored occupation, secure a higher education, or accumulate wealth. And when they do so they win prestige and respect.*

JOB VS. "POSITION"

Emphasis upon skin-color differences within the Negro group was at one time associated with occupational differentiation. During slavery, the lighter-skinned Negroes were very often given preferred spots at "The Big House" or were favored with other posts away from the fields. With the passing of slavery, the free Negroes in both southern and northern cities became the nucleus for the formation of an upper class. Predominantly a mulatto group, they were at the pinnacle of Negro society—often the personal servants of wealthy and influential white people. They had a head start over the rest, and from their ranks emerged doctors, preachers, lawyers, and publicists. By the time of the First World War, however, the Negro servants to the wealthy

* There is some evidence to indicate that the proportion of light-brown and light Negroes is still higher among the more affluent people in Bronzeville than among the rank and file. This, of course, has nothing to do with the superiority of their "white blood." It is the result of a *social* process which has, in the past, made it easier for the lighter Negroes to get ahead, and of the tendency for the more successful men to marry women lighter than themselves.

were rapidly losing their privileged position within the Negro communities, and the professional and business men were consolidating their position at the top of the social pyramid. The Great Migration brought a mass base to the northern cities to support this top stratum. Today in Bronzeville, if we examine the occupational structure in terms of a social prestige scale, we find a small group of people holding down what the people call "positions"—professionals, proprietors, managers and officials, clerical and kindred workers—and a large mass of people who have "jobs." (Figure 29.)

Figure 29

COMPARISON OF THE NEGRO AND WHITE OCCUPATIONAL STRUCTURE : 1930

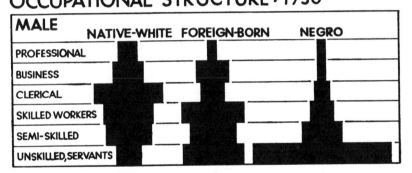

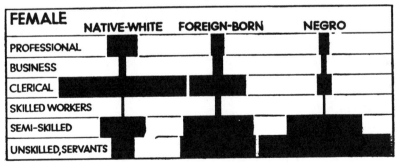

From tables in Scott, "Occupational Changes Among Negroes in Chicago: 1890-1930." The ranking of occupations is that used in Alba M. Edwards, *A Social-Economic Grouping of the Gainful Workers in the United States,* U. S. Dept. of Commerce, Bureau of the Census, 1938.

The Professions: There are over 2,000 Negroes in Midwest Metropolis practicing medicine, law, or dentistry, teaching school, or functioning as social workers. The more successful of them have incomes ranging from $5,000 to $10,000 a year. The less successful, though their salaries are smaller, still have high status by virtue of their "position," since they exercise control over the complicated processes of the human mind and body. Classified as professionals, too, are some editors, chemists, designers, architects, engineers, and librarians. These are less often in the public eye than the members of the learned professions and are often unknown to the masses. Occasionally, however, one of them becomes highly publicized as the "first" or the "only" Negro to hold such a position and thus becomes established as a Race Hero.

Businessmen and Public Officials: Bronzeville also accords very high status to successful businessmen. This is both a reflection of general American standards and a function of the weak economic position of Negroes. Virtually excluded from the general field of commerce and industry except as laborers, and looking out as they do upon a world where the industrial magnates are men of power and prestige, Negroes feel that "The Race has a body without a head," that it is truncated and incomplete. Bronzeville admires anybody who opens up a business and employs Negro white-collar workers.

Since Negroes are conspicuously absent from the decisive sectors of the city's commercial life, the first Negro who gets a place on the Stock Exchange or in the grain pit will be a *real* "hero." The absence of Negroes from the key positions in commerce has some far-reaching repercussions. The Race Leaders who are recognized by whites tend to be politicians, social workers, and professional men rather than businessmen. There are no Negroes of great wealth to sit upon the philanthropic boards and to function on the Community Fund. This means that when an influential Negro does sit with his white "peers" he is in a very insecure position because he cannot match them in wealth or influence.

Except for a small number of political appointees and elected officials, there are fewer than a dozen Negroes in key positions of public administration or in managerial posts in industry and commerce. It is understandable, therefore, why the appointment of a department store manager in the Black Belt was a community event of great importance. It is clear, too, why the Negro community jealously guards its political power. It can put a representative on the Illinois State Commerce Commission, though no Negro could hope to be president of a corporation under that body's jurisdiction.

Large numbers of Negroes in Bronzeville take the civil service examinations whenever they are posted. Sometimes a Negro receives an appointment which makes him a "first" or an "only." Sometimes, too, the Negro passes, but does not get the job for which he qualifies. Such people, too, become Race Heroes and almost Race Martyrs—they beat the white people at their own game but didn't get the job.

Membership in the learned professions, or an important supervisory or technical position in government or industry, places a man or woman at the "top" in Bronzeville.

Clerical and Kindred Workers: White clerical and kindred workers are a commonplace in Chicago. Thousands of such people are unnoticed, taken for granted. But in Bronzeville, stenographers, bookkeepers, clerks, and typists have a fairly high status. This seemingly exaggerated appraisal of white-collar work flows directly from the fact discussed in Chapter 9, that Negroes have traditionally been shut out from these fields. This exclusion has given rise to a tremendous demand for Negro businesses that can employ more white-collar Negroes and for jobs in Black Belt stores operated by white people.

The significance of the white-collar position is illustrated by what happened when the Postal Telegraph Company after years of pressure decided to employ a colored office manager. The first girl selected was from one of Bronzeville's most prominent professional families. The event was highly publicized. The girl became a symbol of the Negro's successful struggle against discrimination.

Negro leaders complain continually of the forces that bar Negro women from the commercial life of the city and often cite this type of discrimination as a factor contributing to prostitution and rackets. During the Depression, policy employed more Negro white-collar help than all the other businesses in the Black Belt combined. The Second World War relieved this situation temporarily, but it is probable that the prestige of white-collar jobs will become even higher if colored employees are dropped during the reconversion period.

Some 16,000 Negroes have carved out a niche in the city's life by securing jobs in the postal service. In the post office one will find not only colored high school graduates, but also men with advanced col-

lege degrees seeking economic security and students studying medicine
and law. In 1939, at least a half-dozen Negro postal employees were
writing books! The "postal worker" is a social type in Bronzeville
ranking lower socially than professionals and businessmen, but of definitely high status.*

During the Depression years an increasingly large number of Negroes were absorbed into the Federal and State Civil Service. It is an
ironic commentary that many of these received their first contact with
white-collar work on various WPA projects. One such project, at the
peak of WPA employment, had over 200 colored workers receiving
training on various types of office machines and in clerical procedures.
So long as Negroes are denied general white-collar employment, even
comparatively minor clerical positions will seem very important in
Bronzeville's scheme of things.

Skilled Labor: Within the Negro community there is a sharp social
break, as there is among whites, between the white-collar ("clean")
workers and manual laborers. Often a single family will incorporate
both manual and white-collar workers, but the latter are thought of
as those who have "progressed" or who are advancing the family status.
Though this is particularly true of attitudes toward women workers, it
is also true of male occupations. While there are still ethnic groups
that perpetuate a tradition of pride in craftsmanship, the development
of mass production has cut the ground from under the prestige associated with skilled labor. In the pre-Migration days white craftsmen
drew the color-line against Negroes primarily because of tradition and
pride; today, with craft work on the decline, they do so primarily out
of fear of Negro competition. The new skilled workers—factory employees—try to draw the line just as tightly, but with less success,
owing to the operation of seniority provisions in plant regulations and
union contracts.

Because Negroes have been denied an opportunity to compete freely
for skilled jobs, such occupations become invested with some prestige
value. Negro carpenters, bricklayers, or machinists are considered an

---

* Interview studies indicate that the post-office worker is associated in the
popular mind with affluence and stability. The income is steady. Postal employees
must pay their bills or lose their jobs for repeated delinquencies. Carriers wear a
uniform and therefore have an official status; clerks are white-collar. Both must
be literate.

"asset to the race." Civic leaders urge young Negroes to turn their attention from white-collar work on one hand and domestic and personal service on the other so that the gap in the Negro's occupational structure may be filled in. They have little success, however, for much of the emphasis upon skilled trades is lip service. Like their white counterparts, Negro leaders praise the "worker" but prefer white-collar work for themselves and their children.

The Alba Edwards prestige scale of occupations (see Figure 26) lists policemen and firemen as skilled workers. Bronzeville places them in a different category, rating them almost on a level with teachers and social workers. They are "officials"—symbols of authority. Among the unsophisticated they cut quite a figure. They are an ever-present evidence of the fact that Negroes in the North are "free." The traffic policeman on Bronzeville's main boulevard dresses impeccably and directs the flow of automobiles with the grace of an orchestra leader. He knows he is on display. A lifted hand—and hundreds of white men must stop at his command. A wave—and they may proceed. No policeman would get an invitation to a professional men's party, perhaps, but he has high status of a sort.

The Second World War offered an opportunity for thousands of Negroes to become skilled laborers in factories and changed the basis of popularity of this type of work from that of "race pride" to that of the "good, well-paid job." But if Negroes are displaced in great numbers in the reconversion process, skilled work will again become high-prestige work—because Negroes are shut out from it.

Semi-skilled Workers: It was during the First World War that Negroes broke the Job Ceiling at the semi-skilled level. In the succeeding years, they have come to see nothing unusual in a Negro being an operative in the steel mills, the stockyards, laundries, and numerous other industries. There is still some tendency to look down on women who work in factories, but as constantly growing numbers of Negro women have become emancipated from the more personal ties of domestic service, a shift in the evaluation of Negro female factory workers has taken place. This re-evaluation was speeded up by the Second World War. Semi-skilled jobs for both men and women are today considered nothing out of the ordinary.

Unskilled Workers vs. Servants: Although rated above servants in the Alba Edwards scale, it is probable that unskilled factory and building laborers have the lowest status in Bronzeville. Servant occupations may involve a certain amount of servility, but they are relatively clean and light compared with work in foundries and stockyards, or the digging of ditches. To call a man in Bronzeville "a ditch digger" is the height of insult. The relatively high economic status of Pullman porters and Red Caps has elevated these servant occupations above the level of unskilled labor, but domestic service and portering are very close to the bottom of the scale.

In assessing the relative status of unskilled labor and service, the age-differential is important. Older Negroes are oriented toward "service," the younger Negroes away from it. As the educational level of the Negroes rises they become more and more dissatisfied with personal service. At the same time, however, they also detest "common labor." For thousands of Negro men, however, an unskilled factory job is prized, and increasing numbers of Negro women prefer the industrial plant to the "white folks' house."

"The Relief": During the Depression years, with about half the Negro families dependent on relief or emergency work, the whole occupational status scale was askew. In Bronzeville it was no disgrace to be on WPA, even for people on the white-collar level. The WPA set-up was made parallel with the job hierarchy in private industry: there were white-collar projects and labor projects, and the former had a wage-spread of from $65 at the bottom to nearly $100 at the top.* A large number of Negroes were thus able to maintain their accustomed standard of living despite the fact that they were on WPA; some were even able to improve it. In fact, for many young people in Bronzeville the WPA offered the only opportunity to learn how to operate business machines or to use white-collar training acquired in high school. By 1940, government emergency projects had disappeared, but memories of "the Relief" did not carry the implications of shame which large sections of the white population attached to such an "occupational" status.

* A few non-relief administrative employees on WPA projects in Bronzeville earned nearly $200 per month.

MONEY TO SPEND

A job is an index to status. It is also, of course, a means of earning money. There is no one-to-one relationship between the prestige of a job and its money value, although there is a general relationship. In Bronzeville, however, job status and earning power are often far out of line, as they sometimes are within white society. A stenographer earns much less than a foundry worker, but enjoys a higher social status. A prize-fighter makes considerably more than a doctor, but does not have so much prestige. Pullman porters and mail carriers receive a larger and steadier income than some dentists and physicians, but are not ranked so high socially. In the long run, however, what a man has to spend becomes almost decisive as his measure.

A study of family income in Chicago, conducted in 1935-36 by the United States Department of Labor, provides the best available information on Bronzeville's purchasing power. The findings of this study indicate that, taken in the aggregate, Negroes were close to the poverty line. (See Table 24.)

TABLE 24

PERCENTAGE DISTRIBUTION OF FAMILY INCOME IN CHICAGO, 1935-36 *

Income Class (Dollars)	All Families	Native-born White	Foreign-born White	Negro
Under 500	13.7	12.0	13.1	30.9
500-999	18.4	14.7	19.6	37.0
1,000-1,999	39.8	39.7	42.0	25.9
2,000-2,999	18.2	21.1	16.9	4.3
3,000-4,999	8.0	9.7	7.3	1.1
Over 5,000	1.9	2.8	1.1	0.8
Total	100.0	100.0	100.0	100.0

* Adapted from *Family Income in Chicago, 1935-36*, United States Department of Labor, Bureau of Labor Statistics, Bulletin No. 642, Vol. I, Washington, D. C., 1939, Table 3, p. 8.

Almost 70 per cent of the Negro families in Chicago in 1935-36 had less than $1,000 a year ($83 a month) to spend. Their situation was just the reverse of the white population's—only a little over 30 per cent of the white families received incomes of less than $1,000 a year.

More than 30 per cent of the Negro families, as compared with about 13 per cent of the white, had annual incomes of less than $500.

Almost one-half of the Negro families—as compared with somewhat more than one-tenth of the white families—were on relief.

Out of every 100 colored families only five had more than $2,000 a year to spend; out of every 100 white families, more than 30 had over $2,000 a year to spend.

Of course, the relatively much larger proportion of Negro families on relief accounts to a considerable extent for the lower incomes. But in almost *half* the families in which at least one member had a job, the earnings were still less than $2,000 a year.*

At the very top of Bronzeville's economic pyramid is one family reputed to have inherited a fortune in Oklahoma oil property. A handful of individuals below this family probably have a few hundred thousand dollars in investments, and an annual income that runs into three figures. These are the policy kings, one prominent physician, and two small manufacturers. Far below these men, but far above the ordinary professional group, is a larger group of families with accumulated "wealth" of between $25,000 and $50,000 and a supplementary annual income of over $5,000 a year. Most of these are people who've made money through smart real-estate deals, petty manufacturing enterprises, investment in insurance companies, or earnings as artists, professionals, or athletes. Not over 30 out of Bronzeville's families could, by any objective American standards, be called "wealthy."

Underlying the small group of actually wealthy Negroes are several hundred Negro families which, even during the Depression, received incomes of from $5,000 to $15,000 a year. The men in most of these families are professionals, businessmen, or higher civil servants. *This group, middle-class by general American standards, forms the core of Bronzeville's upper class.* As we shall see in Chapter 19, this group jealously guards its social status, stressing "culture," "refine-

---

* Richard Sterner summarizes the studies which contain data on Chicago in his *The Negro's Share* (Harper, 1944). In addition to the Department of Labor study, he cites the National Health Survey, published in 1935-36 by the U. S. Public Health Service. This study revealed that while 66.9 per cent of the white families had over $1,000 a year to spend, only 31.8 per cent of the Negro families had even this much. In other words, two out of three Negro families were living on less than $85.00 a month!

ment," and "education," and erecting social barriers against the "upper shadies"—the very wealthy who have gained their wealth through "rackets." The upper class admits to its circles many whose incomes are far less than theirs, but who possess other valued attributes, such as advanced education or high standards of public decorum.

EDUCATION

A physician in Bronzeville, commenting on social status, remarked that "social position doesn't depend on the kind of work you do. There are a lot of my own fraternity brothers who 'went on the road' after they got out of school [i.e., they took jobs as Pullman porters or dining-car waiters]. And there are plenty of fellows with university degrees working in the big hotels." This remark points up a peculiarity of the Negro social-status scale in America: a heavier weighting of education than of occupation. With a very narrow occupational spread, education is used to mark off social divisions *within* the same general occupational level. Persons who wish to circulate near the "top," whatever they may lack in money or job, must have enough education to avoid grammatical blunders, and to allow them to converse intelligently. Ignorant "breaks" and inability to cite evidence of education —formal or informal—can bar a person permanently from the top. The "learned professions" have been the traditional top occupations in the Negro community, and all of these require some education beyond the high school level. Fine distinctions are drawn among the people of the uppermost stratum—between those who attended top-flight northern universities and those who went to schools of lesser rank; between those who have earned higher degrees and those with "honorary" degrees; Ph.D.'s and Phi Beta Kappa keys are prized possessions for those who have them, and a topic of conversation among those who haven't. Such people think in terms of sending their children to the best schools they can afford. There are some 4,000 adults in Bronzeville with a complete college education, and about 6,000 who have attended college. They make up about two in every 100 individuals.

This small college-trained group rests upon a broad base of people who have never been beyond the eighth grade. (In this Bronzeville does not differ greatly from the white society where 7 out of 10 persons have not been beyond high school.) (Figure 20.) Black Metropolis is essentially a community of sixth-graders. While the adults, most of them from the South, have had very limited educational opportunity, the compulsory school laws of Midwest Metropolis are keeping an ever-increasing number of Bronzeville's young citizens in school until they are 16 years old. Of these, far fewer go on through high school than among whites, but enough do so to maintain two large high schools in the area which turned out over 9,000 students between 1930 and 1940. Over 60 per cent of these were girls.

For the bulk of Bronzeville's population, finishing high school is considered a "great step upward." High school diplomas are often ostentatiously displayed in ramshackle homes, and one interviewer's comment on a girl she met is very significant: "The daughter is very proud of being a high school graduate and feels that it reflects considerable ambition and determination upon her part." It is highly probable that for a large number of girls in Bronzeville, graduation from high school means an increased chance of avoiding domestic service and factory work. It also means a greater likelihood of "marrying up." There is a tendency for girls still in high school, and for women graduated from high school, to form cliques and social clubs that draw lines tightly against "ignorant people." The following comment by a social club secretary is not unusual: "No member is allowed to bring in anyone who does not at least have a high school education."

Education is an important measure of the man (or woman). Because it reflects earning power, and more importantly because it denotes a broadening of intellectual horizons and tastes, it becomes a natural basis for clique groupings. In general, too, securing an education is the most effective short-cut to the top of the Negro social pyramid. Money and occupation are important, but an educated man without a high-status occupation or a very large income, might be admitted to circles that a wealthy policy king or prize-fighter would find it hard to enter.

STANDARD OF LIVING

Money and a job are important primarily because they offer a base upon which a "standard of living" may be erected.* In the final anal-

---

* The term "standard of living" is used here in its popular sense to apply to the actual level of living. It is customary in some academic circles to reserve this term for the level on which a family would like to live, and to use the term "plane of living" for the actual state of affairs.

ysis, the way in which people spend their money is the most important measuring rod in American life, particularly among people *within* the same general income range. In Bronzeville, where most incomes are comparatively low, a man's style of living—what he does with his money—becomes a very important index to social status. It is through the expenditure of money that his educational level and ultimate aspirations for himself and his family find expression. Stockyards Worker A may spend his $150 a month on flashy clothes and plenty of liquor, while his wife and children live in squalor. Stockyards Worker B brings his pay check home, his wife and children are well clothed and fed, and a bank account for the children's education is piling up. Bronzeville puts A and B in quite distinct *social* classes. Difference in occupation and income sets the broad lines of status division, but standard of living marks off the social strata within the broad income groups.

This emphasis upon standard of living is apparent in the two statements quoted below from interviews with Bronzeville's professional group:

"These people are just common ordinary people having no intellectual inclination whatsoever. I have known them for approximately a year, and I find they spend a large sum of money on food and don't bother so much about clothes. They are not affiliated with any club or social group. I should put them in the middle class so far as income is concerned, but socially in a class slightly lower."

"Now take that house next door. Why, for three years people lived over there who were the nastiest folks I have ever seen. The building was condemned and they didn't have to pay any rent so they just lived there like pigs or dogs. The water was cut off. The man who had the garage in back used to let them come over and get water. They brought their pails. You should have seen them go in droves after the water. They reminded me of people in the South. . . . Most of them were working, but they were just a bunch of no-good Negroes."

During the Depression, the masses of the people were operating on a "subsistence budget" which allowed little surplus for savings or "culture." * Within the community were thousands of clients on direct

---

* In 1935, the standard emergency budget as set up by the WPA for the family of a manual laborer with two children under 16 was $973 per year. At least 40 per cent of Bronzeville's families were existing on or below this level, supported by WPA or relief. Of the families with jobs in private industry or

relief, each visited periodically by a case-worker who gave him a small check for rent and food; for other commodities he went to a government depot. When he was sick he got free treatment at a public clinic. Others had WPA jobs netting an average of $55 a month. Obviously the standard of living for all such was rather rigidly limited, dependent as it was on a meager income plus what little could be gleaned from policy winnings or earned by occasional domestic service. Many people on relief had been used to something better during the Fat Years, but had been gradually reduced to "subsistence level." They lived in hope that prosperity would return. Thousands of people on relief and WPA were drawn back into productive employment by the industries of the Second World War. With plenty of money in their hands some concentrated on "getting ahead," while others devoted their time and money to a round of immediate gratification. The business of selecting a pattern of expenditure and saving became vital.

All during the Depression, at least a third of Bronzeville's families could be classified as "strainers" and "strivers." These were people who were determined to maintain what America generally regards as "the middle-class way of life." They were interested in a well-furnished home, adequate clothing, a car, and membership in a few organizations of their choice. Their ideal was to be what Bronzeville calls "good livers." Wartime jobs allowed them to realize some of these goals.

Those members of the business and professional group who weathered the Depression, and those with stable incomes from civil service jobs, formed the status bearers of Bronzeville. They were likely to look down somewhat on "strainers" and "strivers" who had accumulated money but didn't know how to spend it with taste. Thus one physician ridiculed the pretensions of the climbers:

"A person who has little or no background usually feels that it is necessary to have a high-priced car, loud in color with flashy gadgets that will single him out. Such persons seek houses and apartments in good neighborhoods, but their furnishings are not always in good taste. Yet some of the 'strivers' are smart enough to have an interior decorator when they realize that their knowledge is limited. Now a person who has education, family connections, and background will satisfy himself with a modest and comfortable home and an inexpensive car."

domestic service, only a third received an income greater than the WPA minimum.

Bronzeville's more conservative well-to-do people—"those who are used to something"—were particularly critical of the rapidly mobile, especially if the latter had got money through "shady" enterprises. One man who had a long criminal record, but who opened a successful business, managed to get into an exclusive apartment house. A resident with "education, background, and family connections" belabored him for his "crudeness":

"All individuals like J—— feel a need for elevating themselves socially, you know. Well, he's gone in for display in dress with his loud suits. He's dressing a bit better now. I think he must have started buying his things from some good clothing store downtown, and he must be taking its suggestions about his clothes because they are more conservative now."

Standard of living is decisive in measuring the status of a family, and standard of living is one aspect of that important characteristic—"front."

THE IMPORTANCE OF "FRONT"

Over and over, people in Bronzeville told interviewers that "it's not what you do that counts, but how you do it." This dictum is applied to varied aspects of behavior—dancing, liquor-drinking, wife-beating, church-going—by those who maintain a rather stable and relatively high standard of living. There is a very sharp division, as we shall see later, between those who value "front"—who stress decorous *public* behavior—and those who don't.

Because of the stress that the "dicties" place upon correct *public* behavior they are often the target of the less sophisticated people who dub them "hypocrites." They are constantly gossiped about by people who do not value front and who exult at finding a chink in the "stuck-ups" armor. But one of the most fundamental divisions in Bronzeville is that between people who stress conventional, middle-class "American" public behavior and those who ignore it. Professional men, postal workers, clerical workers and others with "position" rail constantly at the "loud," "boisterous," "uncouth" behavior of other segments of the society. The "respectable," "educated," and "refined" believe in "front," partly because it is their accustomed way of life and partly in order to impress the white world.

The decisive measure of the man is how he acts in public.

FAMILY, CLIQUE, AND CLASS

All the measures of the man that we have described are either objective traits or types of behavior. More important, however, in placing people are their social relationships. People not only ask, "What kind of person is he?" They also want to know, "What kind of family does he come from?" "Who's in his crowd?" "What kind of organizations does he belong to?" Occupation, income, education, standard of living, and public behavior ultimately find their reflection in social groupings.

Family background is not too important in Bronzeville. Three generations ago nearly all Negroes were slaves, and "getting ahead" by education and the acquisition of wealth have gone on at too fast a pace to allow any tradition of "old families" to mean much. But contemporary family *behavior* is very important in placing people.

Far more important in "placing" people than their family connections are their clique affiliations. The rough rule that "birds of a feather flock together" is used to stratify people in Bronzeville. A man takes on the reputation of his crowd. In a rapidly changing society, clique affiliations become important for social mobility also. People may change their cliques easily, and thus change their social personalities. The cliques become "selectors," and at the top of the society the small high-status cliques become the social arbiters for the community.

It has become fashionable for a broad section of Bronzeville's people to formalize their small cliques as social clubs devoted to card-playing and dancing. Between "Society" at the top and the disorganized masses at the bottom are several thousand of these social clubs. To belong to any of them a person must discipline his behavior, keep up a front, and spend his money for socially approved types of clothing, entertainment, and whatever other appurtenances the social ritual requires. These social clubs are a distinctive feature of Bronzeville's middle class and will be discussed in Chapter 23.

In a very limited sense, churches, too, are ranked in a system of social prestige. Congregational and Episcopal churches are considered high-status; Holiness and Spiritualist churches low-status. Most churches, however, include people of all status levels. Neither the question "What church does he belong to?" nor the question "Does he go to church?" is important in placing a man, except at the very top and the very bottom of the social scale.

For persons "on the make" or "on the rise," getting the proper "connections" becomes extremely important. People change their status by acquiring money and education, and then changing their "set." The dynamics of social mobility in Bronzeville can only be understood by observing individuals actually shifting from clique to clique, church to church, and club to club in the struggle to get ahead. The people who are "in" control this upward mobility by setting the standards and holding the line against those who don't make the grade. They also limit the number of persons who are "accepted." At the same time the socially ambitious are able to copy the behavior of the strata above them and to bring *new* cliques, churches and clubs into existence with the desired pattern. After a time such new increments are accepted and the ambitious rise as a group.

THE SYSTEM OF SOCIAL CLASSES

Everybody in Bronzeville recognizes the existence of social classes, whether called that or not. People with slight education, small incomes, and few of the social graces are always referring to the more affluent and successful as "dicties," "stuck-ups," "muckti-mucks," "high-toned folks," "tony people." The "strainers" and "strivers" are well-recognized social types, people whose whole lives are dominated by the drive to get ahead and who show it by conspicuous consumption and a persistent effort to be seen with the right people and in the right places. People at the top of the various pyramids that we have described are apt to characterize people below them as "low-class," "trash," "riff-raff," "shiftless." The highly sensitive professional and business classes, keenly aware of the estimate which the white world puts on Negro behavior, frequently complain that white people do not recognize the class distinctions within the Negro community.

Class-thinking is essentially a way of sizing up individuals in terms of whether they are social equals, fit for acceptance as friends, as intimate associates, and as marriage partners for one's self or one's children.* It differs from caste-thinking (which dominates Negro-white relations) in that the people in the upper strata expect some of the people below them to enter the upper levels of society once they have qualified. The individual measures of the man are weighed and com-

* See A Methodological Note, pp. 769-82, for a discussion of types of social stratification.

bined in such a way as to strike a rough average of position. According to these estimates, and out of the cliques, families, and voluntary associations that arise from them, people in Bronzeville become grouped into several broad social classes.* [1]

A Negro social worker is referring to this class system when she says to an interviewer:

"I think education gives social status. And of course money talks. After a person gets an education I think he should try to get money so as to be able to live at a certain standard. Of course there are different classes of people. The educated won't go with the ignorant and those with money won't go with poor people."

The Upper Class: At the top of the social pyramid is a scant 5 per cent of the population—an articulate social world of doctors, lawyers,

Figure 30

THE NEGRO CLASS STRUCTURE

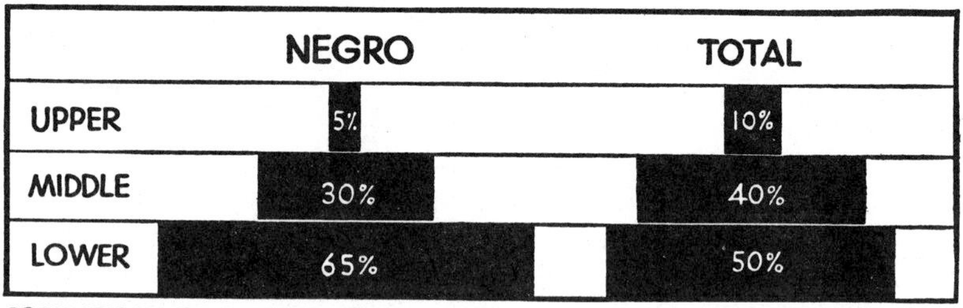

	NEGRO		TOTAL	
UPPER	5%		10%	
MIDDLE	30%		40%	
LOWER	65%		50%	

COMPARISON OF CLASS DISTRIBUTION OF NEGROES IN CHICAGO WITH TOTAL POPULATION, USING EDUCATION, RENTAL AND OCCUPATION AS CRITERIA

schoolteachers, executives, successful business people, and the frugal and fortunate of other occupational groups who have climbed with difficulty and now cling precariously to a social position consonant with what money, education, and power the city and the castelike controls allow them. They are challenged at every point, however, by the same forces that condemn the vast majority of the people to poverty and restricted opportunities (Figure 30).[2]

Carrying the responsibilities of the major Negro institutions and co-operating with sympathetic and liberal whites who give them financial and moral support, this Negro upper class becomes symbolic of racial

* The methods used in studying Bronzeville's class system are revealed indirectly throughout the next three chapters. For a more detailed analysis of methodology and techniques see pp. 769-82.

potentialities, and, despite the often caustic criticisms leveled at them from the classes below, they go their way supplying goods and services to the Negro community; seeking to maintain and extend opportunities for themselves and their children; snatching some enjoyment from the round of bridge and dancing; seeking cultural development from the arts and sciences; and displaying all of the intraclass conflicts which a highly competitive social and economic system has made characteristic of any group in an insecure position—as this upper class certainly is. Yet they have a measure of satisfactory adjustment which makes their life pattern fruitful if measured by any of the objective standards of "success," except for certain disabilities that *all* Negroes share.

The Lower Class: The Chicago adult world is predominantly a working-class world. Over 65 per cent of the Negro adults earn their bread by manual labor in stockyard and steel mill, in factory and kitchen, where they do the essential digging, sweeping, and serving which make metropolitan life tolerable. During the Depression, whether on public projects or in private industry, the bulk of the employed adult Negroes, with a minimum of education and still betraying their southern origin, were toilers, working close to the soil, the animals, and the machinery that undergird Chicago's economy. Many of them also were forced to "only stand and wait" at relief stations, on street corners, in poolrooms and taverns, in policy stations and churches, for opportunities that never came and for the work which eluded both them and their white fellow-hopers.

A part of this working class constitutes the backbone of Bronzeville's "middle" *social* class, identified by its emphasis on the symbols of "respectability" and "success." The largest part of this working class is in a "lower" *social* position, however, characterized by less restraint and without a consuming drive for the symbols of higher social prestige. Desertion and illegitimacy, juvenile delinquency, and fighting and roistering are common in lower-class circles.

Not alone by choice, but tossed by the deep economic tides of the modern world, pressed and molded by a usually indifferent and occasionally unkind white world, and hounded by an often unsympathetic Law, the lower social classes in Bronzeville have their being in a world apart from both white people and other Negroes.

The Middle Class: About a third of Bronzeville is in a social position between the "uppers" and the "lowers"—an amorphous, sandwich-like middle class. Trying with difficulty to maintain respectability, they are caught between the class above into which they (or at least their children) wish to rise and the group below into which they do not wish to fall. Some of them are in white-collar pursuits; many of them must do manual labor; a few of them are secure in civil service jobs. Released somewhat from the restraints of poverty, they have not found it necessary to emphasize the extremes of religious or recreational behavior, or to tie their lives to the rhythm of the policy drawings or the very occasional relief or WPA check as has the lower class. Life to them has some stability and order; expectations for their children and for their own future can be predominantly this-worldly; and the individual psyche is given form by the church and associations whose dues they are able to pay with some regularity and from whose functions they are not barred by inadequate clothing or by lack of education, formal or informal.

The "Shadies": But the class structure of Bronzeville is not a simple tripartite system through which individuals move by attaining the class-behavior pattern which their occupational and educational position permits and their training stimulates. Within each class there is a group, proportionately smallest in the upper class and largest in the lower class, which has secured and maintained its position by earning its income in pursuits not generally recognized by the community as "respectable." The marginal position of the Negro in the economic system and the traditional role of the Negro community as an area for exploitation and risqué recreation by the white community have brought into existence and maintained the whole complex of "protected business"—illegal enterprises winked at and preyed upon by co-operative politicians. This complex is composed of the "policy" business, prostitution, and allied pursuits, and is intimately connected with the legal but none-the-less "shady" liquor interests and cabarets. Thus a considerable proportion of each class is connected at some points with these businesses, and the more mobile individuals are able to rise even to the top where they challenge the position of the upper "respectables" who, as one student has phrased it, "find it politic to accord them some measure of social recognition." These "upper shadies," in turn, are by no means entirely scornful of the opinions of the "upper respectables." They seek to secure prestige in the eyes of this group by assuming many aspects of its behavior pattern, and by attempting to become Race Leaders even to the extent of supporting the organizations of the upper and middle classes, becoming the patrons of the arts, and entering legitimate business.

Figure 31

THE SYSTEM OF SOCIAL CLASSES IN BRONZEVILLE

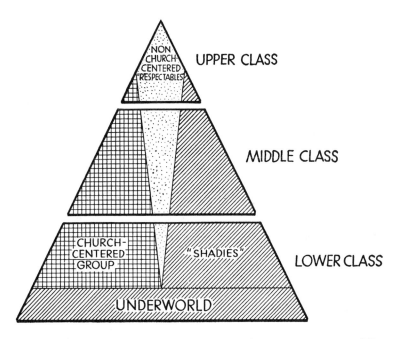

Bronzeville's upper class is oriented around a *secular* pattern of living, with emphasis on "culture" and "refinement" as well as "racial advancement." A smaller group within the upper class is church-centered, and a very small but powerful group earns its living in "shady" pursuits. As we leave the top of society, however, and move toward the bottom, the proportion of "church minded" people and of "shadies" increases, and the group of "non-church" respectables decreases. (Figure 31.) [3]

CHAPTER 19

Style of Living—Upper Class

IF ONE WISHED TO ASCERTAIN JUST WHAT PEOPLE CONSTITUTE BRONZE-
ville's upper class, it might seem practicable to group together those
persons who have the most money, those with the greatest amount of
education, those with the "best" family backgrounds, and those who
wield the greatest political power—and attach to this group the label
UPPER CLASS. But this mélange, though including everyone whom the
community calls "upper," would also include some persons not quite
"in." So far as any single attribute entitles a person to this label, it is
that he knows how to live with a certain definite "style." An income
sufficient to maintain this style is taken for granted.

The general tone of upper-class life is conveyed by phrases used
when people are explaining what they mean by "dicties," "hincties,"
"muckti-mucks"—i.e., "upper-class" people. Among such phrases are:

". . . have money, culture, influence, and surplus money in the bank
to go on . . ."

". . . dress according to the latest styles and with quality . . ."

". . . try to give their children the very best in life—education, luxuries,
and things like that—according to their money . . ."

". . . have reached their aim in life and become leaders of The
Race . . ."

". . . believe in taking life easy and taking trips wherever they want
to without thought of work . . ."

". . . secure recognition after they've made a trip abroad . . ."

". . . go to church only to be seen and run the place . . ."

". . . have received a high standing by hard work and labor or inherited a lot of money . . ."

". . . most of them are college-educated or have been up North a long
time . . ."

". . . travel a good bit . . ."

". . . have money enough to give them a lot of leisure time . . ."

". . . know the correct rules of etiquette even if they don't always
observe them . . ."

". . . the very top in the Negro neighborhood."

WHO'S WHO IN BRONZEVILLE

When asked to name upper-class individuals, people of all levels will point out certain prominent doctors and lawyers, the editors of the major Negro newspapers, outstanding civic leaders, an occasional politician, and sometimes even a policy king. These are not necessarily the wealthiest persons in Bronzeville, but they have more than average education, and usually are well known as Race Leaders.

One Dr. Cruikshank, whose name appeared very frequently in these community listings of upper-class persons, voluntarily submitted himself to study, averring that he was "pleased to be a guinea pig." Urbane and sophisticated, sure of his status, and interested in social research, he felt none of the objections to being studied that were expressed by many Bronzeville residents—perhaps quite justifiably. Dr. Cruikshank, in his early fifties, was at the top of most of Bronzeville's pyramids of power and prestige. A medical doctor, with a degree from an outstanding northern university, he was on the boards of several successful Negro-owned business enterprises and enjoyed extensive contacts with white philanthropists and wealthy "friends of the Negro."

Before the outbreak of the Second World War, the Cruikshank family lived comfortably on an income that ranged between $15,000 and $20,000 a year. The doctor owned a well-appointed house in the center of the Black Ghetto during the Fat Years and most of the Lean. Near the end of the Depression, he moved to an exclusive residential area outside of the Black Belt where a small group of well-to-do Negroes were beginning to establish homes. His children had been sent to college and graduate school; the family owned two automobiles, took an annual vacation, and had traveled abroad. As in many of Bronzeville's upper-class families, however, all of the members of his family were employed. His wife and children were schoolteachers. When the Second World War began, Dr. Cruikshank received a very high commissioned officer's rating in a Jim-Crow army unit, as befitted a man of his stature.

Dr. Cruikshank was not born to wealth. His father had been a barber in a southern town, one of that older generation which derived considerable status from catering to a white clientele. At the age of eleven young Cruikshank could wield razor, shears, and clippers, but both he and his father realized that the colored barber's social pre-eminence was a southern-small-town kind of prestige, even then on the way out. So young Cruikshank was sent to college, where he received some aid from his family, though for the most part he was expected to earn his own way. He ran "on the road" in the summers as a Pullman porter, while attending college and medical school. Even then he showed signs of becoming a Race Leader, for he organized a union among the colored porters.

Dr. Cruikshank is light enough to pass for white, and his features and hair reveal the mingling of Negro and Indian strains with those of the English Cruikshanks and the Irish Mulligans. The doctor is proud of his distinguished English ancestors, and at one time in his life considered "passing" permanently. When he finished medical school, he went to a Latin-American country, thereby "resigning" temporarily from the American Negro group. But life as an émigré from American race-prejudice did not satisfy him. His family and friends were in America; he had grown up in an atmosphere that stressed "race pride"; he felt confident that he could be successful within some Black Metropolis. So he came back to the States and finally settled down in Bronzeville. For over thirty years he has been a Race Leader in Midwest Metropolis and has gradually attained national prominence. After practicing medicine for a few years, he became even more interested in "advancing The Race." Combining a career in medical education with business, Dr. Cruikshank emerged as a "leading citizen," respected by white political and civic leaders. Within Bronzeville, he won both the respect and the caustic criticism that Black Metropolis accords all its leaders.

Dr. Cruikshank is only one of Bronzeville's 300 doctors, all of whom are upper-class or potentially so. Among them are men who have had training in the best medical schools in America and Europe. A few are distinguished practicing physicians: the city's leading dermatologist, two authorities on obstetrics and gynecology, and several widely known specialists in venereal diseases and tuberculosis. One or two are members of the medical faculties at the University of Chicago and Northwestern University—schools which, ironically enough, do not welcome Negro medical students. These physicians and their wives, along with the majority of the dentists, lawyers, and the more prominent businessmen, social workers, schoolteachers, and public administrators, make up the core of Bronzeville's upper class. With family incomes ranging from $3,000 to $50,000 a year, their prestige is based not primarily on income (though in 1936 about 97 per cent of the residents of Bronzeville had family incomes of less than $3,000 a year), but rather on education and professional status, and upon a definite way of life.

There are very few professional people in Bronzeville with an income from salaries of more than $5,000 a year, and very large incomes usually result from investments in real estate, Negro businesses, or securities to supplement salaries and fees. The following median incomes for Negro college graduates in the North are, in general, typical of Bronzeville:

TABLE 25

MEDIAN INCOMES OF NORTHERN URBAN MALE NEGRO COLLEGE
GRADUATES FOR A SELECTED GROUP OF OCCUPATIONS *

Insurance officials	$4,250.00
Elementary school principals	3,750.00
Social work executives	3,750.00
Executive secretaries	3,000.00
High school principals	3,000.00
Physicians	2,750.00
Lawyers	2,666.67
Clergymen	2,421.05
Dentists	2,391.03
High school teachers	2,285.71
College professors	2,250.00
Vocational teachers	2,166.67
Post office clerks	2,193.18
YMCA workers	1,750.00
Druggists and pharmacists	1,750.00
Teachers, unspecified	1,714.28
Social workers	1,437.50
Businessmen	1,250.00

* Charles S. Johnson, *The Negro College Graduate*, University of North Carolina Press, 1938, p. 155.

The white upper class in Midwest Metropolis is a wealthy leisure class. Bronzeville's upper class is a well-trained but only moderately well-to-do group who have more leisure than the rank and file, but who nevertheless must work for a living.

There are perhaps a thousand families in Bronzeville, probably comprising almost 5,000 individuals, who recognize each other as upper-class. They consider themselves equal to each other in social status—fit associates for social affairs, marriage partners, and intimate friendships. Within this group are fewer than a hundred couples in their late fifties and sixties who constitute the social arbiters and status-bearers for the upper class. Most of these people came to Bronzeville long before the Depression, although very few are Old Settlers. As they die off, the middle-aged professional families assume their social position.* A list of the 106 Bronzeville celebrities mentioned in *Who's Who in Colored America* was submitted to some of these older social arbiters with the request that they check the names of persons who were "really upper" and not "just prominent people" or individuals who had bought their way into *Who's Who*. After the pruning, there were only 31 Chicagoans left on whom there was unanimous agreement.† Most of these were men over forty years of age, though there were also five women. Twenty-six of the thirty-one were actively engaged in the professions and one other had had some professional training. The others were either retired professional and businessmen or active business executives. All had attended college. In church affiliation, most were Congregationalists, Episcopalians or Presbyterians. Only three were Baptists. One was a Christian Scientist, and one (who was reputed to have a white wife) belonged to the Bahai group. All were members of at least one professional association, and over half of the men were Masons. Nearly all reported membership in some social clubs or fraternities or sororities, and in the NAACP.

Interview-observation studies of these persons' families revealed extreme emphasis on maintaining "a good home," with fine furniture, linen, glassware, china, and silver much in evidence. Before the Second World War the majority kept at least a part-time maid, and a

---

* Between the time in which field work for this study was begun and the date of publication, two of the key men in this group died. One was the founder of the Chicago *Defender,* and the other was the president of an influential Negro insurance company.

† An elaborate analysis of the behavior pattern of this small group was made by the Cayton-Warner Research staff. Using newspaper material and interview-observation records, social participation charts were kept of most of the functions at which these people appeared over a two-year period. They were then thoroughly interviewed as to their attitudes toward these events and the people who were present. Having defined the various cliques and associations to which these people belonged, a study was then made of the age, occupation, education, church affiliations, and associational connections of the clique members. Thus it was possible to describe *inductively* the traits of a large group of people who constantly associated together. The same procedure was used on other groups of cliques of various age-levels within the upper class.

few had more than one servant, even during the Depression. The men dressed expensively, but conservatively; the women smartly, but in good taste. All of the families carried accounts with exclusive downtown shops. The majority owned automobiles, and one family had three cars and a chauffeur. All were interested in real estate. All thought that Negroes should develop more business enterprises.

Politically, all of these persons were conservative, but they were tolerant even of extreme radical political activity on the ground that it might shock white America into awareness of the Negro's needs. Without exception these families were training their children for business or professional pursuits, or reported that the children had already received such training.

These upper-class people took "respectability" for granted. They were concerned with "refinement," "culture," and graceful living as a class-ideal, although many of them had never had the opportunity to cultivate an appreciation for music, art, and literature, or had been so involved in the competitive struggle for professional advancement that they had ignored such interests. Twenty of the thirty-one were light-brown-skinned or very fair in color, but they all talked like ardent Race Men and Race Women.

THE SOCIAL RITUAL

Bronzeville's upper class is "home-centered," stressing an ordered and disciplined family life. Its style of living demands enough space and enough income to allow for frequent entertaining. The wives maintain the social ritual, and small cliques of women, or of women and their husbands, constitute the basic non-family social units. Social life revolves around bridge parties, and upper-class women and men of all ages are expected to know the intricacies of bidding and the associated ritual of entertaining.* Some of these cliques have been formalized into clubs, especially among the older women. For instance, one typical upper-class woman of the late-middle-aged group said to an interviewer: "I am a member of the Eureka Contract Club and the Matrons' Bridge Club. We also have another club without a name. We meet evenings, talk, play bridge, and have lots

---

* Upper-class people play bridge with people of their own class level, but serve as officers of national and regional bridge associations, the bulk of whose membership is lower in status.

of fun. There are no dues." Membership in these small intimate groups imposes a continuous claim on the time of upper-class women, who often belong to several clubs and play bridge three and four times weekly.*

Some of the bridge clubs are old established groups and act as "selectors" for people socially "on the make." Seven of the present members of the Monday Night Bridge Club, for instance, have been in the club for eighteen years. A member details the manner in which the club has been kept exclusive:

"The enrollment never exceeds sixteen. New members are admitted only upon unanimous vote. The woman in question is contacted by some one member of the club who is interested in having her enrolled. Her name is then presented individually to each member. Then it is brought before the entire club for a vote. As we wish to avoid any sort of embarrassment which group discussion of the proposed member might arouse, we approach each member privately to test attitudes."

Another club, over ten years old, was described by a lawyer. In this case the men had taken the initiative in forming the club.

"Our club is composed of men and their wives. We decided to accept women when we first organized. The wives get together and prepare dinner and we play bridge. The men submit men members' names and at the following meeting they come as visitors. We have two affairs a year, an invitational affair and a closed dance."

This club is atypical, however, for most of the older upper-class social clubs of the small intimate type do not give dances. Upper-class dances are usually sponsored by sororities and fraternities or by the younger men's social clubs.

Upper-class men tend to play their bridge in mixed groups, but they also have their all-male social clubs. These provide the occasions upon which the women of their class appear at public dances.

---

* In such cases the husband often states that his wife organizes his social behavior. One prominent physician, for instance, said: "I belong to a little bridge club—there are about fourteen of us—but I don't do much in social activities. It is mostly on account of my wife that I am as active as I am." Another physician in this clique made a similar comment: "My friends are built around professional and social-service work. My *social* friends, however, are my wife's." He then proceeded to name several doctors and businessmen, one former judge, and one important government official as members of the bridge group—"all good solid citizens."

Only one exclusive upper-class men's club is organized around cards.* There are about a dozen men's clubs of very high status, composed of men in their thirties and forties and called by such names as The Frogs, The Snakes, The Druids, The Owls. Interview-observation studies reveal that each club has a core of professional men with a fringe of nonprofessionals.† The men uniformly stress the necessity for a "good moral character" as a prerequisite for membership—a phrase that really means a reputation for not being indiscreet and open in sexual escapades or guilty of boisterousness or lack of refinement in public.

The pattern of activity which characterizes these clubs and the kind of reputation which the members like to maintain is revealed in the comments of a member who was aware that his club might be discussed in a book some day:

"We meet once a month except in the summer. Two men entertain together at a meeting. The refreshments are paid for out of the club treasury. There is always a discussion by a member or an outsider. A member is notified about a month in advance that he is expected to conduct a discussion, but we leave the subject to his discretion. He is expected to discuss something outside of his field or profession. We don't sit around and tell dirty jokes and that type of thing like so many of the men do. We are gentlemen all the way through."

Another member seemed less anxious to have the club described as a model of male virtue. He merely stated:

* The older upper-class men tend to belong to the larger and older clubs which twenty years ago were "exclusive," but which have been growing larger and less exclusive through the years. Two of these, with between 200 and 300 members, maintain club houses where upper-class men and prominent men of somewhat lower status—politicians and businessmen who are not outstanding—gather to chat, play poker, read, and argue race and politics. They also sponsor annual dances—though these are not events that are regarded as distinctively upper-class. An examination of the life history of upper-class men suggests that they are least class-conscious in youth and old age, and most class-conscious during the middle years.

† The upper-class male club with the youngest age-spread has twenty-four members, all married except two, one of whom is divorced and the other single. Seven are physicians, six are dentists, one is a very responsible official at Bronzeville's hospital, one is a schoolteacher, another is an accountant with a government agency, three are attorneys. The group also includes an embalmer, a chemist, two pharmacists, and a post-office clerk. A charter member referred to the men as "a group that works hard but wants to take time out to enjoy itself in a manner a little different from the usual social club."

"The members entertain the club at a hotel or the —— fraternity house or in their homes. A bunch of fellows get together to socialize. We play cards and often have a speaker. We give one annual affair at which from six hundred to seven hundred guests are present.* During the year we usually give a small party. It might be a supper for the members and their wives, or the members might invite another couple. In the summer we usually have a picnic."

Like the women's groups, these male clubs also make a fetish of "exclusiveness." The following comment can be duplicated whenever a club member is asked how new members are selected:

"It is necessary to weigh carefully the names of any persons submitted to the club. If there is anything whatever against a person he is black-balled. Plenty of good men have been blackballed just because they didn't quite measure up to our standards. It's no disgrace to be blackballed by our club."

The procedure for inviting guests to the large dances also involves drawing class lines. The president of one male club described the process:

"When a person is invited he must submit the name of the lady who is to accompany him. If she is approved by the club members, she in turn will be sent an invitation. Invitations must be presented at the door. The wives of the club members have quite a bit to say as to who is to be invited."

Members of other clubs, too, reported that although they "don't have the wives telling their husbands what to do" they always take into consideration the compatibility of their wives and prospective guests. Upper-class women thus serve as social arbiters through the male clubs as well as through their own.

Upper-class men repeatedly described the types of persons against whom they attempted to draw the line at large social events: racketeers, the "uncultured," and people notorious for "immorality." Within the cliques the lines are drawn much tighter, with occupa-

---

* The large dances sponsored by upper-class men's clubs are the high spots of the winter social season. They get elaborate write-ups in the weekly press with picture displays. The majority of the guests at a dance will be upper-class, but also present are business friends of the upper class, younger people of lower status who are popular or ambitious, and a scattering of popular middle-class club women. These dances bring most of the young and middle-aged upper-class people into face-to-face contact during the social season.

tion and amount of schooling as very important factors. Of ten male upper-class clubs studied, having a total of 152 members, there were no skilled or semi-skilled workers or laborers holding membership. There were only five Red Caps or Pullman porters (all with college educations). Over half the men were professional men and the rest were businessmen, civil servants, or prominent politicians. A young attorney defined the class ideal when he said of prospective members, "We like them to be ambitious and to be 'regular.' They must have some goal in life other than a purely social one."

Skin-color is not an important factor in upper-class male clubs, although at least one male club has been accused of being blue-vein.* According to upper-class gossip, this club came into being in the early Twenties and had several very dark members. They felt they were not wanted and withdrew to form a rival club. A member of the older club, in giving his version of the split, did not deny that the original club was predominantly "light":

"There were possibly twelve or fifteen members of our club who varied in color from very light to olive or Indian brown. Two or three were very dark. The rumor circulated that we were a color-conscious group because a majority of the fellows were light. That's why they put that on us. They [the founders of the younger club] organized in direct competition or contrast to us and chose a great majority of dark fellows in order to try to show that point up."

A member of the younger club would not accuse the older club of a color-complex directly but showed familiarity with the tradition:

"At the time we were organized there was a similar club called the Leonine. They have sometimes been accused of having color complexes. I don't know how true it is. I was one of the charter members of that club also.† Some dissension arose between the members. . . . Our club

* A Negro sociologist who has thoroughly studied upper-class club life in Bronzeville states that "the question of color of skin was more important apparently to the women than to the men. As a member of one of the clubs among the women stated, 'We don't discuss color of one's skin when we are considering a member, but when you think it over we don't have any dark-skinned members.'" (From Ethel Ramsey Harris, *Voluntary Social Activities Among Negro Professional People in Chicago*, Unpublished Master's Thesis, University of Chicago, 1937, p. 22.)

† Today the "light" club is by no means lily-white. Its members are brown-skinned. Thirteen of the men are married, seven single, and one divorced. The roster includes six physicians, five lawyers, one prominent official in Washington, an insurance salesman, a broker, a dentist, a schoolteacher, a real-

was then organized. There was a friendly rivalry; no open hostilities ever existed. We used to try to take their girls away from them and give better parties than they had. Just childish. . . ."

As the younger members of the upper class reach adulthood, finish college and settle down, a few are absorbed into the existing exclusive clubs. The majority, however, form new clubs on the pattern of the old. A young attorney described how one such club came into being during the first stages of the Depression:

"An informal group of hard-working businessmen, as we termed ourselves, met at my home to play bridge. There were about fourteen. We played auction bridge, had a few highballs, discussed timely topics, and planned to meet once a month on Friday to relax and spend an evening at our favorite pastime.

"Months passed, and one evening during the game a member of the crowd said, 'Let's organize a bridge club.' The idea, a splendid one, was discussed, but the name was not mentioned. Weeks passed and no name was given to the club. One evening while we were playing for money, it seemed that no one had any change, and one of the members commented that we were 'Striving Strainers.' The name fitted the group at the time and was later adopted. No new members have been added to the original group." *

The members of this club play bridge and have dinner together. Wives are occasionally invited.

Frater and Soror: Each of the six national Negro college fraternities and six sororities has a chapter in Black Metropolis. Among the middle-aged and younger members of the upper class these organizations probably have higher status than the ordinary small social clubs. Fraternities and sororities bind together some 500 individuals on the basis of school ties. They function not only as social clubs but also as organizations for "racial advancement." Each has its "service" emphasis—the Kappa Alpha Psi concentrating on vocational guidance in accordance with its slogan, "Guide Right"; the

estate agent, and a functionary in the Federal Housing Authority. Nine are active in churches.

* In 1938 the club was composed of four physicians, four attorneys, one electrical engineer, two dentists, one businessman, a clerk with a state bureau, a supervisory official of the National Youth Administration, and an insurance broker. All were college graduates except two men who had some college training but didn't graduate. All were married. Ages ranged from 38 to 47.

Alpha Phi Alpha stressing an annual "Go to College Week"; the Phi Beta Sigmas standing for "Bigger and Better Negro Business."

While a few individuals within these groups are primarily interested in "service," the majority utilize the fraternities and sororities as a source of social prestige. In fact, one student of Black Metropolis felt that they were the principal agencies in the community responsible for sustaining the idea of "exclusiveness."

Church and Religion: There are some entire denominations as well as a few individual churches that have the reputation of being upper-class. Traditionally the Episcopal Church has symbolized upper-class standards, with its high proportion of upper-class members. Congregational and Presbyterian churches have enjoyed the same reputation. Owing to the small size of the upper class, however, no congregation has a majority of upper-class members, though there are some in which such persons exercise dominance, and in which mobile individuals from the other classes look to the upper-class members to "set the pace."

One woman of moderately high social status thinks that the Congregational Church is "based on a 'solid' group of people, for if a person in that church were not socially educated, he would not enjoy it." When returning home one Sunday, she had heard a bystander remark, "The people that go to that church are all big shots." Other Congregationalists say, "Our church is simple, dignified and modern"; "People of the upper stratum come here," etc.

The oldest Negro Presbyterian church also has the reputation of being a high-status church, drawing largely upon the older members of the upper class. A former pastor of this church observed:

"On coming here I was surprised to find the majority of the members are outstanding Negroes. You would be surprised to find out how many are in *Who's Who.* Mr. Tompkins, the undertaker, made the same statement the other day, and he is a member of the A.M.E. Church. We also have some of the oldest families in Chicago among our members."

In one study involving a small sample each of upper-, middle-, and lower-class families, it was found that a high proportion of the upper stratum were members of the Presbyterian, Congregational, and Episcopal churches, and that none were Holiness or Spiritualist adherents.[1]

One Baptist church and one Methodist Episcopal church, as well as two A.M.E. churches, are considered high-status, but not upper-class though they have quite a few upper-class members, including several manufacturers and two former bankers.

The pastors of the upper-class churches are all college-trained men of wide experience. Their sermons are usually scholarly in form and devoid of the cruder emotional tricks common in many other churches. Upper-class church buildings tend to be small, but are very well cared for and artistically decorated.* Two of the churches are situated in higher-status residential neighborhoods. One has been marooned in a low-status neighborhood, but has not adapted its program to the community, preferring to draw higher-status members from a distance. One of the Episcopal and one of the Congregational churches have been planning for several years to build community houses, and their pastors have broad community interests, participating up to the point of "playing politics," but refusing to do so actively.

Many members of the Congregational Church stated that they liked their church because it was progressive and had a community program. But to the upper class, the church is not primarily a religious institution; it is rather a status attribute. Something of what people expect from churches of this type is indicated by the comment of a Presbyterian, who had once belonged to a Southern Baptist Church:

"When I first came to Chicago I was a member of the Baptist Church. But I never joined a church here because I did not like the way people exhibited their emotions. At home, in the church I belonged to, people were very quiet; but here in the Baptist churches I found people rather noisy. For that reason I tried to find a church that was different, and in visiting the various churches I came across the Presbyterian Church, which I joined. I have remained a member ever since."

In order to attend a church which has the desired social status, upper-class persons will often affiliate with churches a long distance

---

* A publication of one of these churches contains the following description:

OUR BEAUTIFUL CHURCH AUDITORIUM

SIMPLICITY AND DIGNITY

Chaste beaded glass windows; unobtrusive insets of the Cross at the interstices of the windows; beamed ceilings; dignified pilasters; finely wrought iron chandeliers; dark, substantial pews; simple pulpit; heavy, soft carpets. Paintings . . . in three panels above and behind the choir loft. "A real house of worship"—quieting the spirit, inspiring the heart. 21 Sunday School Rooms, Modern Kitchen, Dining Room, and Stage for Dramatics.

from their homes. One woman, when asked why she didn't attend a church nearer her home, answered: "Any church that doesn't have the class of people that we like to associate with would be very unpleasant. Not that we feel that the other people are not nice, but they are too poor to keep up with our kind of life. Sometimes a group of us visit some small church, but they are so backward in doing things that we feel ashamed of them. We couldn't belong to that kind of church."

Members of the Congregational Church were keenly aware of the class position which it occupied, and were sensitive to criticisms of its alleged exclusiveness. One member said:

"I so often hear nasty remarks about the membership. They will say that it is not a church for black folks; that they don't want you there unless you are nearly white, so it is of no use to try to join the church for you are not welcome. Now, not a word of that is true, for if you will go there you will find members of all colors. It just has the name of being a blue-vein church."

While none of these "upper" churches are "blue-vein," they do perhaps have a higher proportion of light members than other churches.

In general, it seems that though formal membership in some church is expected of older persons who wish to maintain status within the upper class, active participation is not required of either men or women. There is, however, a "church-centered" segment of the upper class which participates actively in the affairs of the churches mentioned. These persons not only have wide contacts with prominent Negroes, but their church relations often bring them into contact with prominent white persons.* One Negro businessman boasted that he was on the Episcopal Diocesan Council with several of the most outstanding white bankers and businessmen in America. Upper-class members tend to monopolize the handling of funds and the general planning in the churches with which they are associated, and often express themselves quite frankly as believing that it "pays" to be affiliated with a church. Membership in very low-status churches would be definitely taboo, however.

Upper-class women who are not in the most exclusive sets of "So-

---

* The proportion of men who are active in church work seems to be higher among the upper class than in other segments of the society, although the proportion of upper-class persons who are "church-centered" is very much smaller.

ciety," older women who have been widowed or suffered financial reverses, and "Old Settlers" who live in the past seem to make up the bulk of the church-oriented upper class; though even these usually combine their church life with a secular pattern of "entertaining" at home.

In summary, it may be said that the function of the church in orienting the upper class toward its world is extremely limited. For most persons church membership is merely an additional fact from which prestige may be derived—and it is not crucial. But, if one belongs to a church, it must be the right kind. For a person seeking social mobility, however, the upper-class church is an important stepping-stone, bringing him into indirect relation with the upper-class tradition and into direct contact with some upper-class individuals.

As community forces, high-status churches extend approbation to all "worthy" civic enterprises, and take some pride in participating in programs of social amelioration.

But in the words of Bronzeville's masses, they are "hifalutin'" or "high-toned." Their activities are definitely a part of upper-class social ritual.

SOCIAL RITUAL VS. CIVIC VIRTUE

Most upper-class men have a life-pattern of activity and interests which combines devotion to a career, a restrained good time, and participation in organized community "uplift" and "racial advancement." At least half of the upper-class wives are either career-women or persons who accept occasional white-collar employment. The others are "the pillars of Society." Within the upper class, too, are a number of Race Women whose lives are oriented almost entirely around Race Leadership. Such women often assail the preoccupation of "Society" with "frivolity." Thus one woman, an officer in a club which she described as "a dependable group of civic-minded women who have done the uplift work of Chicago for thirty-one years without pay," sized up the women on this level as follows:

"There is first of all the group which we might term the 'butterfly group.' What we call the 'Society' group in Chicago and most of our large urban centers is made up largely of the 'butterfly' type of person—people who play bridge four or five times a week, who belong to social clubs only, and who do not do any constructive work in the community except perhaps once or twice a year.

"The second group is made up of educated persons—the intelligentsia, you might say. In this group are many sorority and college women, vastly superior to the first group. The college-trained women have studied the community and are therefore prepared to render it a greater service because of their technical knowledge. I do not believe that this group lives up to its ideals." *

A prominent young social worker who had been interested in the placement of wayward children in foster homes was critical of both upper-class and middle-class women for their preoccupation with entertaining. Of her own associates, she said:

"No wonder some of them can play bridge so well. They play as if their lives depended on it and get indignant if you don't play just so. Then they talk to you as if you were a child: 'Why did you play that card?'— 'Didn't you know she'd do so-and-so?' And it makes them so mad when I reply, 'No, I didn't know I ought to do thus-and-so.' I've never had time to learn to play bridge well. They remember all the cards that go in, and I *don't*."

These women with a civic orientation maintain their upper-class status partly because of their occupation and education, but primarily because of their role as "leaders." They act as needlers of society women, continually urging the "frivolous" women into active civic work, encouraging them to serve as "sponsors" of fund-raising drives,

---

* This equating of "butterfly" behavior with lack of college training is not borne out by the facts. Many of the older upper-class women, though not college-trained, have taken an active part in community work, while many of the younger college-trained women take no part. Aside from the question of temperament and individual interests, the most important factor in determining whether a person will choose "Society" to the exclusion of "civic virtue" seems to be the occupational status of the upper-class woman. Those who do not work or whose work does not bring them into contact with community problems seem less likely to be aggressive reformers than women employed as teachers, social workers, etc. Age, too, is a factor, younger women, on the whole, being more concerned with society or establishing their homes and raising children. There are also more subtle factors, such as personal attractiveness, type of husband, or skill in entertaining. There is some evidence to indicate that the less attractive women—women who feel inadequate at the bridge table, or whose husbands are not "in the money"—stress civic behavior rather than society. This is only a tendency, however, and exceptions are numerous. Personal crises also seem to play some part in determining whether women become society leaders or civic leaders, a number of Bronzeville's younger civic leaders being divorcees with no family to anchor them to the upper-class social ritual.

as honorary members of committees, and as contributors to causes. The first woman quoted felt that, during the latter years of the Depression, she could detect an increased interest in civic work on the part of society women:

"The 'butterfly type,' who at one time did nothing but play bridge and serve cocktails, are now beginning to realize the uselessness of such living and are more willing to work with us. . . . This is the first time that this type of woman has sought an alliance with the civic-minded woman. . . . The latter has looked on the 'butterfly women' with contempt, regretting that they are wasting their capacities on the things they do."

(It might be added that the butterflies have sometimes looked with amusement upon their more strenuous sisters, whose whole life revolves around "advancing The Race," and have expressed skepticism of their motives.)

The civic-minded women tend to ignore the fact that the *typical* upper-class woman in Bronzeville, while not exclusively occupied with "reform" and "uplift," does include civic activity as a part of her life pattern. Dr. S——'s wife, for instance, is representative of the older upper-class women. She sketches her activities as follows:

"I am a member of the Women's Auxiliary of Provident Hospital and spend most of my leisure time as a member of the Board of Directors of the Chicago Branch of the YWCA. . . . I am a member of two social clubs which meet once a month. I also belong to another informal bridge club which has not been named yet. The doctor and myself recently became members."

A typical day in the life of a woman of this type was noted by a participant-observer as follows:

Wednesday

1. To library to return books (fiction).
2. Afternoon at board meeting in white YWCA downtown.
3. Knitted on return, while maid prepared dinner.
4. To Dr. Smith's at 8:30 for bridge. Husband came in car about 11 P.M. to take her home.

Thursday

1. Hospital Board meeting.
2. Afternoon at colored YWCA.

3. Bridge in late afternoon.

4. Friends in for formal dinner at night.

Civic virtue, for the average upper-class woman, consists in spending at least a little time in active work (usually helping to raise money) for one or several of the major conservative and liberal Negro organizations like the NAACP, the Urban League, or the Council of Negro Organizations; or for the Provident Hospital, the YWCA, or one of the various settlement houses or community centers. This does not involve abandoning the social ritual—it may indeed mean drawing civic activity into that ritual through giving a tea or a card party or getting up a fashion show for some organization. For the Race Woman, on the other hand, civic virtue often demands a turning away from "Society." Unlike society women, she comes into close contact with middle-class women in "uplift" organizations and has wide contacts with white liberals, trade unionists, and politicians. She derives prestige as well as personal satisfactions from "advancing The Race," and she is the keeper of the upper-class conscience.

THE SHIFTING BASES OF STATUS

The present upper class represents a group which rose to power during the Twenties, displacing an older status group—the pre-Migration upper class. The upper class before the First World War was composed of the house servants of the wealthy, Pullman porters, successful politicians, and a few business and professional men. Their common bond was social ritual and a concern with "culture" and getting ahead. Family background, light skin-color, and length of residence in Chicago were important class attributes. The Negro market created by the Great Migration resulted in the expansion of the business and professional classes who gradually displaced the Old Settlers as the "cream of society." Old Settlers, living in the past, still feel that they are the *real* upper class, holding the title by priority of residence. The secretary of the Old Settlers' Club stated proudly in 1938:

"I was a patient of the first Negro physician; a pupil of the first Negro public schoolteacher; a patient of the first Negro dentist. I knew the first Negro county commissioner and the first Negro legislator of Illinois."

Yet she herself was relatively unknown to most of the present upper class. Ask for the names of Bronzeville's upper class today and you will get a list of professional and business men who have come to Chicago within the last thirty years, plus a few of the most successful Old Settlers. Of their class traits, you will receive a description like the following: "men who have attained some cultural development and who by their energy have won a record of the highest accomplishments."

During the Fat Years, the new Negro upper class flowered. A former society editor of a Bronzeville weekly, writing during the Depression, described the social ritual of the period:

They gave banquets, five- to seven-course dinners, debuts, musicals, teas, and affairs for vacationists. These events were as carefully planned as were the futures of upper-class families. These families set the standards and everybody tried to follow. . . . We don't have any society today. The upper class of yesterday sits at home playing bridge and knitting, or they have died years ago. Their daughters are married or are old maids. The coming generation is a disgrace hardly worth mentioning.

The Depression of 1929-39 seriously threatened the economic base of the upper class and forced it to drastically curtail the conspicuous consumption which symbolized its pre-eminence in the Twenties. This was matter of frequent comment in Bronzeville, and one upper-class woman who herself had made a sociological study of the social ritual[2] quoted the following interview to describe the change:

"A lady was speaking the other day of the differences which have been brought about in this community within the last five years—you actually wouldn't realize it. People don't live like they did then. Why, you were invited to breakfast, bridge parties, luncheons, afternoon bridge, suppers, dances, and then after-theater parties. You could start any morning and go straight through until midnight without stopping. Everybody had you on the go . . . some of them trying to keep up with the next person.

"The bridge clubs among the women were large, and when the women entertained they always had two or three extra tables to return some of their obligations and invite friends whom they liked to have and without whom their party did not seem complete. . . . But now, instead of the large expensive parties which always brought forth a display of china, silver, and linen, for the most part they just play bridge in groups of two couples or so who are very good friends. Why, at one time Dr. V——'s wife would have to have parties on three successive days in order to include all her friends and take care of her obligations."

The Depression, too, made it possible for persons on fixed salaries to challenge the pre-eminence of doctors and lawyers who depended on a now impoverished clientele—a fact that prompted widespread discussion. One upper-class woman commented on it as follows:

"There was a time when the man in the post office did not have much social status in the community. He just wasn't in the picture. The only persons who were in 'Society' were the doctors and lawyers. The fact that post-office men and some other people had steady incomes did not mean a thing. But now it is different. Do you know that some real-estate agents will not accept a physician's signature on a lease? . . . Do you know that a whole lot of people will not give these professional persons credit? The post-office man can get credit now where the doctors and lawyers cannot, because people know that he is going to get his money, and if he does not pay his bills he can be garnisheed. . . . They tell me that a whole lot of these physicians and dentists are trying to get relief patients. Some of them have to, because they do not know how they are going to get money to live otherwise. They have a hard time getting their money because some people do not have it to pay them."

This greater economic stability for civil service employees was reflected in the figure they were able to cut at larger dances and in the competition for "girl friends."

The Depression not only weakened the established professional classes—it also interfered with the recruiting of new members into the upper class and the education of children in this group. Though most of the young people of college age were able to remain in school, they could not maintain the standard of living to which their older brothers and sisters had been accustomed. Doctors and dentists just beginning to practice were laughed at for "sleeping in their offices." Some of the children of the upper class found it necessary to seek employment on WPA white-collar projects. Here they formed clique relationships with children from families of lower status who had education but lacked an economic base. This tended to lessen the importance of occupation and income as a class trait among the younger group and to force the parental generation to acquire tolerance toward their children's impecunious associates.

In general it might be observed that the Depression, while it did not ruin many of the upper class financially, did alter their whole pattern of recreational behavior and class standards. It also laid the base for association between a heterogeneous group of young college-trained men and women who had not yet been able to establish themselves economically and a group of people who had stable incomes but were short on education. Most important, however, it brought to the upper class the almost traumatic experience of facing the implications of life in a Black Ghetto. As a result, there was a sharp increase in civic activity, a general restlessness which found expression in the support of radical and labor groups by professional and business people, and a tendency on the part of many to seek prestige through race leadership rather than through conspicuous consumption.

The social pre-eminence of the upper class was challenged from below by less prominent people living on fixed incomes. It was challenged also by the policy kings who, because they had money, were able to steal the show. In discussing the rise of the racketeers to prominence, one very well-informed newspaperman said:

"Once we had some society. Now anybody that can entertain is in society—racketeers' wives, Mrs. B——, and anybody like that. All you have to do is to have a beautiful home and serve champagne. Publicity is easy to get—everybody can get it by display or can buy it. Take the B—— family—racketeers; well, that type wants publicity. The real uppers don't want to be with them."

THE "UPPER SHADIES"

The "real uppers" may look askance at "the racketeers" and their wives, but in the decade between the beginning of the Depression and the outbreak of the Second World War, the "Gentlemen Racketeers" and their coterie emerged as the most widely publicized group in Bronzeville. Five Negro policy kings form the core of a "fast set" which has money in abundance and spends it lavishly. This group, who might be called the "upper shadies," is composed of the wealthiest policy men and their wives, a few lawyers and retired undertakers, at least one family with an inherited fortune, and a wealthy Negro manufacturer. The people in this group do not ask, "How did you make your money?" but only, "Have you got money?"

These men with money like good-looking women, and those of them who are married have wives of very light-brown or "fair" complexion. The unmarried ones are usually seen with the pick of Bronzeville's chorus girls, policy station employees, and "good timers" of attractive appearance and engaging personality. Rumor has it that there are "kept women" within this group, but there are properly married couples too. The wives of the Gentlemen Racketeers and their associates are women of leisure; unlike many wives of "respectable" uppers, none of them have to work for their living. They can spend their time at the dressmaker's and in the swank downtown shops, or in supervising the details of entertaining in their sumptuous town houses or country homes. The women's lives, like the men's, are centered on conspicuous consumption—display of the most lavish kind.

This set is organized around a cult of clothes. Nothing but the right labels and the right prices will do. Both the men and the women know how to buy and wear clothes—and with taste rather than garishness. Clothes are both an end in themselves and an adjunct to the social ritual of this *café au lait* society. The ritual can be summed up in a word—entertaining. All through the year there is a continuous round of private informal parties and formal dinners. Into the homes of the "upper shadies" stream nationally known colored theatrical figures and sportsmen. On their tables one will find wild duck and pheasant in season, chicken and turkey in season and out, and always plenty of the finest spirits and champagne. The upper respectables call themselves "good livers"; the shadies are "high livers."

In addition to entertaining, the "upper shadies" go in for attending the races, for horseback riding and cabaret parties, and for poker games where the stakes hang high. They also like to travel. They are continually shuttling between Midwest Metropolis and New York; they occasionally visit friends on the West Coast; they have their summer homes in the lake regions of Michigan and northern Illinois. Before the Second World War, the wealthiest families in this set had spent some time in France and one policy king was having his children educated there. After the war began they shifted their attention to "good neighborly" relations and began to explore Mexico and Cuba. One policy king, looking forward to really seeing the world, purchased a yacht. All these activities are reported at length in the Negro press, and on several occasions the Midwest Metropolis dailies have devoted columns to the exploits of the Gentlemen Racketeers.

Despite their wealth and their free and easy mode of life, the "upper shadies" are not unconcerned over what the upper respectables think of them. The Gentlemen Racketeers who form the core of the group have drawn into their circle a few professional men who are by no means wealthy, but who are witty and good dressers and like a good time. These men act as a link between the "shadies" and the respectable uppers, but it is significant that, although the "shadies" have been entertained at the homes of these few upper-class men, they have not been accepted socially by the broader circle of uppers. Two of the most prominent Gentlemen Racketeers are proud that they attended college and that their father was a minister. Further evidence of these two men's orientation toward respectability is furnished by the fact that they have sent their children to the best northern prep schools and some of their sons to technical colleges; the children are ambitious for the normal upper-class evidences of success and have been pledged to sororities and fraternities. At one time, so it is alleged, one clique hired social secretaries to teach them the know-how of upper-class life and were cultivating an interest in the opera, symphony, and world affairs. The respectable uppers continue to draw the social line against the parents, but not against the children.

In their striving for "respectability" the men among the "upper shady" set have also manifested an active interest in civic affairs and have, to a certain extent, become known as Race Leaders. We have already said, in our discussion of policy, that the policy kings all have legitimate businesses as well as their shady enterprises. They give regularly and generously to all fund-raising drives for Bronzeville charities. With the outbreak of the war they began to play a prominent part in bond rallies and in the sponsoring of a service men's center. Their motives appear to be highly mixed, but undoubtedly one motive is their hope that such activities will wipe away the stain of policy.

One of the wealthiest policy kings revealed certain of his experiences and his philosophy of life to an interviewer in the following statement:

"I was born in Mississippi. My father was a Baptist minister, my mother a housewife. The financial condition of our family was fair. I went to college for three years and then came to Chicago just after the last war. I went into the taxicab business first. Then I began 'running on the road' and made about a hundred dollars a month. After I quit railroading— I didn't like being a porter—I went into the gambling business—race horses. I made about a hundred dollars a week and employed six or seven people. By 1937, I had a car and a home and several gambling places.

"The reason a young man goes into policy or becomes a teacher or doctor or anything else is because he notices outstanding individuals in those fields who are successes. They attract him. So I went into policy."

Now a successful policy king, this Gentleman Racketeer insists that his heart's desire is to "advance The Race" through his large, *legitimate* business, acquired only a few years ago.

"What good is a lot of money to a man if he doesn't put it to some use? If you pile it up just for the sake of piling up money, you are selfish. Why not spread it out into business and continue to increase the possibility of employing more of your race?

"Stepping out into business was just like another gamble to me. I decided to stick my chin out, and if I got socked on it, O.K. What I want to do now is this—get into a position where I can demand that white business concerns from which I buy my supplies will employ Negroes as distributors and salesmen. We can gradually demand that Negroes be put in various jobs that are related to our business, and sooner or later white meat markets and grocery stores will get used to seeing Negroes come into their stores to deliver supplies."

This Gentleman Racketeer does not put too much confidence in mass action of the "Spend Your Money Where You Can Work" type, "because Negroes are too dependent upon white people for jobs and everything else. If we start boycotting they might start laying us off from this job and that about town." He puts his hope for the salvation of the Negro in the multiplication of legitimate businesses like his own. At the time, he was employing forty girls in his department store and it was his proud verdict that they "do their work just as well as whites." Looking toward the future, he dreamed of organizing a Negro Businessmen's League. He also hoped to organize a bank to replace the House of Binga, destroyed by the Depression.

"What I want to do is to go into banking and lending. I am not studying banking, though I realize that theory is necessary. You've got to have
men around that know their business."

Yet this Gentleman Racketeer wants to be more than a *Negro* businessman:

"I also want to open a department store in a community that's 50-50
white and Negro, because I believe that white people will buy from
Negroes if they run their businesses right."

Proud of his ability to run an efficient store, he wants to feel that
he is just a man competing with his business peers. He therefore
states with some satisfaction:

"I guess you've noticed that in my advertisements I never stress that
people should buy from me because I am a Negro. I am in business competing with other stores. I'm not trying to play upon any psychology by
calling this a 'Negro business.' "

While the "upper shadies" have been displaying some interest in
social acceptance by the upper respectables—they like to be invited
to dances given by the upper male clubs and the fraternities and
sororities—this is not their primary interest. What the "shadies" hope
ultimately to do, perhaps, is to displace the older upper class, to out-
shine it, to incorporate sections of it within their own circles, and
to emerge as the *bona fide* upper class. They have the money, but
they are keenly aware that there are some things money won't buy.
But they know that once they become known as good Race Men,
Bronzeville will forget the source of their income and accord them
honor and prestige. And in the eyes of many Bronzeville people they
are already *the* upper class.

REACTION TO RACE

The members of Bronzeville's upper class are very race-conscious.
Some of them depend upon the Negro market for a livelihood.
Another segment is in constant contact with white people of equal
educational and economic status, competing with them on unequal
terms for power and prestige in the world of politics and civil service.
All upper-class Negroes, too—most of them intelligent, well-informed
persons with some higher education—resent the inequalities of op-

portunity and status which exist throughout America. At certain periods in their lives many have worked for white people in a menial capacity, but by "getting ahead" have escaped the day-by-day subordination to whites to which ordinary laborers and servants must submit.

Some members of the upper class are northern-born, but many are migrants from the South. Their very presence in Chicago reflects an unwillingness to live life on southern terms, although many of them could certainly carve out a relatively comfortable position there, in business or the professions. Not all upper-class persons are so heated in their denunciation of the South as the young man quoted below, though most of them share his sentiments to some degree:

"The South is one place that I would not want to be taken to dead. I loathe it. I hope the day will soon come when it will be wiped off the face of the earth. I have absolutely no sympathy for Negroes who stay there, still living in servitude. Why don't they leave?"

To the upper class Midwest Metropolis is a Land of Opportunity in almost every respect, as compared with the South. Chicago shows few obvious and blatant evidences of subordination and exclusion. Yet upper-class Negroes do experience discrimination and race prejudice in the form of inconveniences, annoyances, and psychic wounding. There are exclusive shops and restaurants that discourage or refuse their patronage. They cannot buy homes in most of the better residential neighborhoods, and in others they can do so only after protest, violence, and court fights. When they travel in the South, or even only through many communities in southern Illinois and Indiana, they are barred from hotels, restaurants, and tourist camps. Many a door is still closed against their economic, educational, and professional advancement.

Despite the fact that Midwest Metropolis offers greater political and economic opportunity and less social subordination, it does not offer talented, aggressive Negroes complete freedom and equality. Within the Negro upper class are men and women who, if allowed to compete freely, would probably appear in positions of wide influence in the political and economic life of Midwest Metropolis. As it is, they may become "Big Negroes," but—with the exception of perhaps half a dozen men—they do not become "leading citizens."

Professional men are hampered by the lack of free intercourse with their peers in medical and dental societies and bar associations. They are also barred from the "contacts" that are so important in securing a clientele from among the white upper-middle class and the wealthy.* Whenever they are able to do so without sacrificing their dignity, Negro professional and businessmen seek to broaden their participation beyond the confines of race. Thus doctors question their exclusion from the American Medical Association, and lawyers assail the tradition that keeps them out of the Chicago Bar Association.† Some of the difficulties surrounding the full participation of professional men with non-Negro colleagues in Midwest Metropolis are revealed in an incident related by a prominent Negro surgeon. He had been admitted to membership in a medical society, and had gone to attend a meeting at a downtown club in 1938, when the incident occurred.

"A few weeks ago I was thrown off the elevator at the Medinah Club. I have attended these meetings for two years, but we had not met there before. Until recently, when a doctor from Provident Hospital was admitted, I was the only Negro member of the society. The two of us were on the elevator together; the elevator boy refused to budge. He said he was sorry, but that he was obeying orders. I have since received a notice to come to the meetings, that everything is all right, but I haven't had any desire to return. I didn't like the way the president went about it. He didn't seem sincere. I didn't push it because they had taken me in and I hope that they will take in other colored physicians who are eligible."

His statement reveals a very prevalent reaction of upper-class Negroes to interracial contacts: suspicion of the sincerity of white people, caution about forcing issues that may "set the race back" in some respect, and avoidance of situations that may be personally embarrassing. A young lawyer summarizes a general thought pattern when he says: "I don't have dealings with them [i.e., white persons] other than business. This doesn't entail conflicts. Socially I'm not interested in them."

* There are certain significant exceptions to this generalization—e.g., a colored dermatologist enjoys a citywide reputation and patronage, and one or two Negro lawyers have handled corporation cases.

† Among the twenty lawyers' associations functioning in Chicago, only one, the National Lawyers' Guild, admits Negroes freely. The Chicago Bar Association, the largest professional group in the city, has traditionally excluded Negroes on the grounds that the organization is "social"—although a rule of the Supreme Court of the State of Illinois has constituted the Chicago Bar Association a special commission for investigating and disciplining all lawyers in the city, white and colored. In the spring of 1945 one very light Negro was admitted, but other Negroes were refused.

Either in their professional and business capacities or as civic leaders, most upper-class Negroes in Bronzeville are from time to time drawn into meetings and conferences with white people, to discuss "racial advancement," or conditions in the Black Belt. The general skepticism with which they view such verbal activity is illustrated by the comment of a dentist who is active in civic affairs: "My only connection with whites is through civic organizations. I have no friction with them. Most of the groups that come together for the purpose of bringing about an understanding of race problems do very little. Very little comes out of the conferences. They mostly *talk* of the discrimination problem, but nothing is ever done."

College students who have been involved in such conferences at school are likely to react as did the young man who belonged to a religious interracial club which "has teas and discusses the race problem." He thinks that "all they do is talk," and accuses them of "hypocrisy." "In the club meeting everybody is brother and sister. Outside the room we don't know one another. I have absolutely no faith in these interracial clubs. Their programs don't go far enough." In their more reflective moments, however, such critics are likely to react as did a young lawyer in his late twenties who said: "Well, at least no harm is done by having interracial relations. I can't say so much for the merits of them. They are rather new and haven't been in existence long enough for us to pass fair judgment upon them. But I don't think they're going to solve the race problem. I think just those individuals who are actually participating on the committees will benefit."

The feeling is widespread that white people are either insincere or impotent when it comes to attacking the Job Ceiling or the Black Ghetto. The upper-class leaders, therefore, while they co-operate with liberal and progressive white people, are less sanguine about interracial co-operation than their public behavior would seem to indicate. So, depending on momentary mood or circumstance, any upper-class individual is likely at one time or another to swing through a gamut of "isolationist" sentiments ranging from complete disillusionment and despair to optimistic emphasis upon Negro solidarity:

"I don't see how the race problem will ever be solved. I believe that both groups are partly responsible for race prejudice."

"I'm interested in social problems but I'm tired of hearing so much discussion and argument about them. I think we can better a great many of our conditions by improving ourselves instead of complaining about what the white man does."

"The greatest need for Negroes is race pride which includes confidence in themselves and their group."

"Business is the great need of our race. We must become economically self-sufficient. Although we don't have large capital to invest, we must be willing to start on a small scale. Most of our people want to have a beautiful home and a big car first."

In moods of extreme disillusionment, their comments can be quite drastic—the expressions of people who have wearied in well-doing. For instance: "I don't think there is any solution to the race question and I don't bother myself asking a solution." One upper-class man remarked in 1938: "After each war the Negro is elevated beyond his previous status. I think a war would be a good thing now."

At the same time that they verbalize in this fashion, upper-class Negroes give financial support to and actively participate in the two basic Negro organizations: the NAACP with its militant program for fighting discrimination, and the Urban League with its social-work approach. A few upper-class people, here and there, without losing either status or influence in Bronzeville, openly support the Communist movement.

Although upper-class Negroes stress racial solidarity, this is primarily a *defensive* racialism. As a long-term proposition they oppose segregation and share the sentiments of the social worker who said emphatically: "I think that with segregation one loses freedom of contact. I don't care what anyone says—discrimination produces inferiority!"

Bronzeville's upper class believes in a continuous fight against all forms of segregation, yet it resents the implication that Negroes are primarily interested in *social* relations with white people, or that they are "trying to be white." Thus, a prominent YWCA worker, after denouncing segregation by whites, hastens to add, "But I enjoy *socializing* with my own race." This is not merely a sour-grapes mechanism. The ordered family life, the social ritual of people on this level, and the circle of friends made in college and professional life constitute a completely satisfying milieu for relaxation—"a good time."

Negroes feel no drive to seek such satisfactions among white persons of similar status. Many of them have no desire to even accept friendly overtures when the initiative comes from the other side of the color-line.

Some social and quasi-social relationships with whites inevitably arise, however. Civic activities are often accompanied by luncheons and banquets. A common interest in politics, reform, scholarship, or professional problems often takes on social extensions and some few Negro and white individuals become intimate friends, visiting one another and sharing intimacies.

Some of the more prominent upper-class Negroes and a growing number of persons in civil service have some white friends of equivalent social status. An attorney with a number of white clients is typical of this group, with his comment: "I think it is quite all right to have friends among other races. My wife and I have white friends whom we visit and they visit us, and we enjoy each other very much. I think that some white people are all right. I feel that I can appreciate people for what they are and what they strive to be, regardless of their race and how they were born."

The more general attitude toward the social overtures of white persons, however, is one of suspicion and avoidance. A young college graduate states: "I have had quite a few white acquaintances but I didn't consider them friends. We have lunched together here and in Los Angeles. I have never been to their homes to eat and I have never invited them to mine. I suppose I'd return the courtesy if they ever extended me an invitation." And from a Negro civil engineer come these remarks: "Interracial contacts are socially not of any value. I have a few white friends who visit me. A white man or woman will be friendly with one individual, but he won't accept us as a group." Upper-class persons continually stress a desire to be treated as individuals. If this eventuates in intimate social relations, many of them feel that the situation should be accepted without excitement or fanfare. Others, however, can never feel that a white person is really sincere; they prefer to be left alone.

Inevitably the subject of intermarriage occasionally arises in upper-class conversation. Both women and men, on the whole, tend to pride themselves on being "tolerant" and "broadminded," and are likely to make some such statement as, "I have nothing against it, but I think I prefer my own race because I feel that I could be happier that way," or "Intermarriage is O.K. if the people are of the same social set," or "There should be no law against it. People should marry whom they please." When an interracial marriage actually occurs, however, it becomes a choice morsel of interesting and sometimes malicious gossip. In such cases, conversation is likely to turn upon a class point. "When you find a colored man and a white woman," the argument runs, "the girl is usually white trash, after money or notoriety." Women, particularly, resent the marriage of a prominent Negro man to a white woman. Men feel duty-bound when in the presence of women (or if they think they will be quoted) to say something of this order: "Personally I haven't any use for a white woman. I prefer brown-skin women. In fact, I love colored women. They are beautiful to me." Or, "So far as I'm concerned, I'll always prefer a beautiful brown-skin girl any day to a white one." Among themselves, however, they will recount escapades with white women when they were sowing their wild oats. Such stories are considered proof of an urbane sophistication which refuses to accept white women as sancrosanct, but which also implies a final decision to settle down as a good Race Man. Occasionally one finds individuals—both men and women—with opinions like the following:

"I rather believe that intermarriage should be encouraged. I think it would be the solution of the race' problem. It can only be solved by miscegenation. When there is one group that is not absorbed it is physically isolated, and therefore easily segregated. Groups that remain 'pure' tend to deteriorate, anyhow."

"I think that intermarriage will perhaps break down barriers among the races. It's all right as far as I'm concerned."

The whole matter of interracial sex relations is often discussed in terms of differential reciprocity. Most upper-class men will have in their repertoire one or two experiences to relate similar to the following, told by a civil service employee at a fraternity smoker:

"An interne friend of mine was talking to some white physicians and they said, 'Some time we want you to take us out to meet some of your girl friends and have some fun.' My friend replied, 'Yes, sure, I'll take you out to meet some of my girl friends—and you take me out to have some fun with some of yours!' The white fellows looked shocked and said no more. But that is the general attitude of white men toward colored girls, and I think my friend did just right in taking the attitude he did."

Or in another case:

"The other night I was going to call on a lady. As I was starting up the steps, a white man asked me if I knew where he could get some nice colored girls. I asked him, 'Do you know where I can get some nice white girls?' He said, 'Don't be funny.' I gave him a swift kick out on the street. I suppose they think that because there are some women who would go around with white men, any colored woman would. I work with white women every day and I know just what *they* would do."

Upper-class colored women, when in college, are likely to have had some fleeting friendly contact with white men of their age and class level. And in their adult life they are often brought into contact with white men through travel and employment or civic activities. In general, they keep their relationships on a very impersonal level. Before marriage they are wary of any intimate relationships, for, as one woman said, citing a young man who had made overtures to her, "I knew he wouldn't have thought of marrying me, and I have more self-respect than to be intimate with a person who would only want to use me." A prominent social worker, attractive and unmarried, and having wide professional contacts with white people, related the following incident to illustrate her present attitude: "We sailed on an Italian liner. A white man, a passenger, asked me to dance, and I refused—I didn't want to dance with a white man. I was always taught at home that if white people were nice, we were to act nice to them . . . but still and all . . . they were white people."

Upper-class Negroes are not, as some superficial observers imagine, pining to be white, or to associate with whites socially. They are almost completely absorbed in the social ritual and in the struggle to "get ahead." Both these goals are inextricably bound up with "advancing The Race" and with civic leadership. In actuality, the Negro upper-class way of life is a substitute for complete integration into the general American society, but it has compensations of its own which allow individuals to gain social stability and inner satisfaction, despite conditions in the Black Ghetto and their rejection by white America.

On Top, Looking Down: At the top of the social pyramid, the members of Bronzeville's upper class find some emotional security. They can never be fully at ease, however, for both the white community and the Negroes have charged them with the responsibility of being Race Leaders. As they contemplate the Job Ceiling and the Black Ghetto, they direct a barrage of criticism at white people, on one hand, for being unjust, and at Negroes, on the other hand, for being "backward." They express impatience and irritation with Negroes of lower status. Thus, a prominent Greek-letter fraternity man spoke roughly to a girl interviewer, declaring: "Negroes just don't know how to do things as well as white men. The whites are the ones who can do things, and we copy them. You are here interviewing me because whites make it possible." He then began to belabor "The Race": "Really, our people are a mess. You can't get Negroes to work together. The only thing that they will stick together in is a church. They just think the other man [i.e., white people] ought to help you all the time, and if they see you succeed, they'll knock you every time." Sometimes this racial denigration takes the form of an emotional rejection of the Negro group as "uncultured." Thus a man who has been very successful in his professional life, and who has wide contacts with white professionals, goes so far as to say: "If I had to live among Negroes without white contact, I would feel life wasn't worth living. We are so far below the white man. I know he is my superior. I doubt if we'll ever catch up with him." And a young civil servant commented sardonically, "Nothing is exclusive about Negroes except that they live in neighborhoods that are exclusively Negro."

Such statements do not imply any admission of biological inferiority, but they may indicate a sort of drop in morale when the contrast in power and prestige between Black Metropolis and Midwest Metropolis is considered. For example, the same persons who have made the statements quoted above may on some other occasion reverse their attitudes, thus: "Negroes have an inferiority complex which they have acquired from many years of unhappy experience. This complex is passed on from generation to generation."

Since the upper class is identified with Black Metropolis by white people, and since most of them must live within the Negro community, they are sensitive to any type of behavior which will embarrass The Race and thereby reflect discredit upon them. Because they meet the Negro masses in the capacities of businessmen, lawyers, dentists, physicians, schoolteachers, social workers, and journalists, they have rather intimate knowledge of all aspects of Bronzeville's life.

They are very definite in their conception of what constitutes lower-class behavior. It is not poverty that outrages their sensibilities, but lack of public decorum—what they call "ignorance," "boisterousness," "uncouthness," "low behavior." Sometimes their estimate of undesirable behavior is tinged with moral disapproval, but more often it is couched in terms of race. Such ways of behaving are called "a drag on The Race," and those who exhibit them are considered neither a "credit to The Race" nor fit associates for intimate social relationships or potential mates for themselves or their children. There is a high degree of consensus as to what "lower-class" traits are. The following summary is a composite picture abstracted from a mass of interviews.

THE PATTERN OF LOWER-CLASS LIFE AS DEFINED BY THE UPPER CLASS

1. *Decisive Criteria for Stratification:*

    ". . . the important thing is the standard of living, which hinges upon occupation and education. These decide their associates."

    ". . . so stratified because of their lack of education, their basic character, and their mode of living."

    ". . . their aims and satisfactions in life rotate around essential things, rather than intellectual and esthetic pursuits."

    ". . . they have no decent background."

    ". . . it all centers in the absence of something."

2. *Occupations:*

    ". . . the man is a stockyards employee, semi-skilled; his wife is a domestic."

    ". . . I think of stockyards and steel mills, policy pick-up men and policy writers, pimps and prostitutes."

3. *Economic Status:*

    ". . . extreme poverty."

    ". . . more dependent than classes above them."

    ". . . low financial status."

    ". . . usually they are working in the eighteen-to-twenty-dollar wage class—when working. However, there are other characteristics which are more dominant in placing them than economic status."

4. *Educational Status:*

". . . I would put illiteracy first."

". . . one generally finds their average education grammar school or less."

". . . usually low in educational status—fourth or fifth grade."

". . . extreme ignorance."

". . . full of slang about gates, cats, and other jive talk."

5. *Housing:*

". . . house cut into three sections and only one bathroom for two or three families—that signifies lower-class behavior to me."

". . . squalid, crowded housing conditions."

". . . many of them live in kitchenettes."

". . . crowded housing conditions produce their class stigma."

". . . dirty homes—dirty children—dirty people."

6. *Family Relations:*

". . . family life very loose."

". . . ranges from the respectable individual to the rowdy who beats his wife to make her respect him."

". . . wife is a street-corner arguer who starts fights with her husband on the corner at 3:00 A.M."

". . . both of them are inconstant and run with individuals who are never superior in any sense to the legal mate."

". . . have large families and can't take care of them."

". . . children run wild, with little respect for parents."

". . . children are unmoral."

7. *Aspirations for Children:*

". . . never encourage them to secure even a high school education, but urge them to become self-supporting as soon as possible."

". . . as a group they are not ambitious, although a number of them have high hopes for their children."

". . . most of them appear to be satisfied for themselves and their children to remain as they are."

8. *Sexual Behavior:*

". . . enjoy sexual entertainment."

". . . sex behavior is loose and overt."

". . . immorality is one of the criteria of lower-class behavior."

". . . on the whole, you don't find the strict morality which exists in the middle class."

". . . immoral and hang around other immoral people. I don't think there is any such thing as amorality in the civilized state."

". . . his loud conversation runs largely to the women he was out with last night, and those he will be with tonight."

9. *Gambling:*

". . . hangs out in small, unclean taverns or gambling clubs."

". . . man is a crapshooter—wife an inveterate policy player."

". . . he's a regular patron of the cheapest gambling joints and beer taverns."

". . . both gamble."

10. *Drinking:*

". . . they drink excessively."

". . . husband a habitual drinker of moonshine."

". . . he goes behind posts and drinks whisky out of a bottle with a paper bag over it."

". . . they enjoy liquor brawls."

11. *Public Behavior:*

". . . the men stand on the corner and ogle the women that pass by."

". . . they are boisterous in public."

". . . drunkenness of both men and women on the street; I believe men who hang around on street corners and make audible remarks to and about women are lowers."

12. *Violence:*

". . . carries a knife and is apt to use it, either in offensive or defensive operations—he believes that others also carry weapons."

". . . razors and knives as weapons are always associated in my mind with lower-class persons."

13. *Religious Behavior:*

". . . some few of them go to church."

". . . the majority of them are highly religious—that is, if we give a superstitious connotation to religiousness."

". . . these people make up half the congregations of the store-front churches."

14. *Recreation:*

". . . their main recreational outlets are churches and taverns."

". . . hangs out in small, unclean taverns or gambling clubs."

". . . they don't seem to have any recreational activity."

"... taverns, policy playing, sometimes movies."

"... orgies in the home."

15. *Personality Pattern:*

"... strongly swayed by prejudices and emotions."

"... they are emotionally unstable."

"... arguments are won by loudness of voice rather than by logical thinking."

"... he doesn't try to advance himself in any way."

REASONS GIVEN BY THE UPPER CLASS FOR LOWER-CLASS BEHAVIOR

16. *Economic Status:*

"... you find dirtiness more often and more generally in the lower class; it results from extreme crowded conditions, extreme poverty, and ignorance."

"... their low income limits their standard of living."

"... as a result of poverty and environment some people don't come in contact with education, morals, and the like."

17. *Southern Background:*

"... their present position is often due to their former environment in the South."

"... in the main, their status is due to lack of education and poor environment. I am referring now to the former environment of the southern farm migrants. The theory that it all depends upon economic status doesn't hold water to me. There are people who are not lower-class who have less than many who are lower-class."

18. *Education:*

"... their educational status must be low. Otherwise they wouldn't sink permanently into this type of living."

A few of the persons interviewed brought only economic criteria to bear in defining the lower class: high income meant high status; low income, low status. The larger number, however, were thinking of a "pattern," a constellation of traits, when they considered the meaning of the term. Rowdy or indecorous behavior in public seemed to be the one trait that in these expressions emerged most consistently as an index to lower-class status. Lower-class people are those who give free rein to their emotions, whether worshiping or fighting, who "don't know how to act," or dress correctly, or spend money wisely. Yet, throughout these comments, there is also a tendency to indicate the existence of some poor and uneducated people who are more quiet and restrained.

> ". . . I would expect no home life, but I find that this isn't necessarily true."
> ". . . these neighbors of mine are respectable lower-class people."
> ". . . it is not necessary for all of them to be rowdy, although many are not genteel."

The attitude of the upper class toward the lower is ambivalent. As people whose standards of behavior approximate those of the white middle class, the members of Bronzeville's upper class resent the tendency of outsiders to "judge us all by what ignorant Negroes do." They emphasize their *differentness*. But, as Race Leaders, the upper class must identify itself psychologically with "The Race," and The Race includes a lot of people who would never be accepted socially. Upper-class Negroes, too, depend upon the Negro masses for their support if they are business or professional men. The whole orientation of the Negro upper class thus becomes one of trying to speed up the processes by which the lower class can be transformed from a poverty-stricken group, isolated from the general stream of American life, into a counterpart of middle-class America. The chapters that follow will reveal something of this process of acculturation at work, and the "problem" as Race Leaders see it.

CHAPTER 20

Lower Class: Sex and Family

IT WAS CHRISTMAS EVE, 1938. DR. MAGUIRE HAD JUST FINISHED A HARD DAY.*
Now for a highball, and then to bed. The doctor stepped back and
admired the electric star at the top of the Christmas tree and the gifts
neatly stacked beneath it. Judy would certainly be a happy girl in the
morning when she bounced downstairs to find the dolls and dishes
and baby carriage and candy that Santa Claus had brought her. The
doctor smiled, drained his glass, and headed for the bathroom. He
caught himself musing in the shower. Not so bad, not so bad. Three
years out of med school, in the middle of a depression. A pretty wife
with smooth olive skin and straight black hair. A sweet little girl,
image of her mother. And buying a home. Well, it was just the
"breaks"—lucky breaks ever since he quit picking cotton in Georgia
and went off to Howard University in Washington. Plenty of other
fellows were better students, but a lot of them were still sleeping in
their offices. One or two who were supposed to turn out as distinguished surgeons were Red Capping. He reflected a moment. Yes—
the breaks. Suppose he hadn't married a woman like Sylvia. He'd be
"on the turf," too, perhaps. Dr. Maguire sharply pulled himself to
heel. No, he didn't really believe it had been luck. He prided himself
on "having some get-up about him," enough ambition to have made
his way anyhow. If he could do it, the other fellows could have, too.
He looked at his wife, peacefully sleeping, kissed her lightly on the
forehead, and crawled into bed.

Man, what a tough day this Christmas Eve had been! Three ap-
pendectomies in the morning and a hernioplasty in the early afternoon. Making the rounds in the midafternoon. Then a few minutes

* This account of a doctor's Christmas experience is based on an actual incident witnessed by one of the authors, when he was a participant-observer in a
group of lower-class households for six months, and on interviews with the
physician involved and his wife. The principal characters' inner thoughts are
obviously fictionalized. But the other quoted material in this chapter, as throughout the book, has been selected from interview-documents gathered by trained
interviewers and has not been subjected to imaginative recasting.

out to help distribute baskets for the Christmas Fund; time out to sign some checks for the legal defense committee of the NAACP; and an emergency meeting of the YMCA executive board. That Y meeting had looked as if it were going to last all night. Negroes talk too damn much. He had hoped to be home by ten o'clock, but it was midnight before he parked his Plymouth. Three late emergency calls—TB patients who ought to be in the sanatorium. Not enough beds—Negro quota filled. Damn this country anyhow. Negroes always get the dirty end of the stick. Christmas! Peace on Earth, Goodwill . . . Bull . . . Sometimes I think the Communists are right. And those old fogies over at the hospital yell "socialized medicine" every time somebody wants to extend medical care. Aw, hell, what am I bellyaching about? I haven't had it too tough. He shrugged his shoulders and relaxed. He was just drifting off to sleep when the 'phone rang.

Sylvia bounded from the bed like a tennis ball coming up after a smash from the net. She was that way, always ready to protect him and conserve his strength. What would he do without her?

"Are you one of the doctor's regular patients? . . . Well, why don't you call your regular doctor? . . . I know, but Dr. Maguire is . . ." He snatched the 'phone from her hand in time to catch the stream of denunciation: "That's the way you dicty niggers are. You so high 'n' mighty nobody kin reach ya. We kin lay here 'n' die. White doctor'd come right away. Yore own people treat ya like dogs."

Dr. Maguire winced. He always shuddered when this happened. And it happened often. He waited until the hysterical tirade stopped, then said calmly but firmly: "Now listen, you want me to do you a favor. I'll come over there, sure. I'm a doctor. That's my business. But I'm not coming unless you have the money. Have you got five dollars?" He hung up and began to dress wearily.

"Do they have it?" queried his wife.

"I don't know," he snapped, irritated at himself for having to ask such a question, and at his wife for pressing the point. "You know I'm going whether they have it or not. I'm a doctor. I always go. But you might just as well scare them—it'll be hard enough to collect anyhow." He slammed the door and went down the snowdrifted path that led to the garage.

When he arrived at the building, the squad car was at the door. He and the police went in together. Dr. Maguire pushed his way through the ragged group of children and their excited elders who jammed the hall of the dilapidated building.

"Right this way, Doc," someone called.

"What is it?" he asked jauntily. "Shooting or cutting?"

"She stabbed him," volunteered a little girl.

"Boy, she shore put that blade in him too!" A teen-age boy spoke with obvious admiration, while a murmur of corroboration rippled through the crowd fascinated by tragedy.

For a moment, Dr. Maguire felt sick at his stomach. "Are these my people?" he thought. "What in the hell do I have in common with them? This is 'The Race' we're always spouting about being proud of." He had a little trick for getting back on an even keel when such doubts assailed him: he just let his mind run back over the "Uncle Tomming" he had to do when he was a Pullman porter; the turndown he got when he wanted to interne at the University of Chicago hospital; the letter from the American Medical Association rejecting his application for membership; the paper he wrote for a white doctor to read at a Mississippi medical conference which no Negroes could attend. Such thoughts always restored his sense of solidarity with "The Race." "Yeah, I'm just a nigger, too," he mumbled bitterly.

Then he forgot everything—squalor, race prejudice, his own little tricks of psychological adjustment. He was a doctor treating a patient, swiftly, competently, and with composure. Anger and doubt were swallowed up in pride. His glow of satisfaction didn't last long, however, for the woman who had cut the man was now blubbering hysterically. He barked at her, "Shut up. Get a pan of water, quick! He isn't dead, but he will be if you don't help me." He prepared a hypodermic, gave the shot, and dressed the wound.

"How'dja like to have to give him that needle, honey?" A teen-age girl shivered and squeezed her boy friend's hand, as she asked the question.

"Me? I ain't no doc. But, girl, he flipped that ol' needle in his shoulder sweet. Just like Baby Chile did when she put that blade in Mr. Ben. You gotta have education to be a doc. Lots of it, too."

"I'm gonna be a doctor, I am." A small, self-confident urchin spoke up. The crowd tittered and a young woman said, "That's real cute, ain't it? You be a good one too, just like Doc Maguire." Dr. Maguire smiled pleasantly. An elderly crone mumbled, "Doctor? Humph!

Wid a hophead daddy and a booze houn' mammy. How he ever gonna be any doctah? He bettah get his min' on a WPA shovel." Everybody laughed.

"The old man will be all right, now." Dr. Maguire was closing his bag. "Just let him lie quiet all day tomorrow and send him down to the Provident Hospital clinic the day after Christmas. The visit is five dollars."

Baby Chile went for her purse. There was nothing in it. She screamed a frantic accusation at the crowd. "I been robbed. You dirty bastards!" Then a little girl whispered in her ear, while the crowd tittered knowingly. Baby Chile regained her composure and explained: "Sorry, Doc. I had the money. I was gonna pay you. But them goddam policemen was gonna take me off on a 'sault and batt'ry charge. My little girl had to give 'em the ten dollars I had in this here bag, and the folks out there had to raise another ten to make 'em go away. Them policemen's got it all. I ain't even got a red cent left for Christmas tomorrow. You got anything, Ben?"

The sick man growled: "You know I ain' got nuthin'! You know I can't holp you."

The doctor didn't say a word. He just picked up his bag and left. But he ostentatiously took out a pencil and wrote down the number of the apartment before he went out. The crowd seemed pleased at his discomfiture. One woman remarked: "He got the number. Them doctors don't never disremember."

"What was it, dear?" Mrs. Maguire asked as her husband once more prepared for bed.

"Same old thing. Niggers cutting each other up over nothing. Rot-gut whisky and women, I guess. They ought to start cutting on the white folks for a change. I wonder how they got my number?"

"Did you get the five dollars?" his wife asked.

"Nope. Told me some lie about bribing the police. Maybe they did—I don't know. Let's forget it and go to sleep. Judy will have us both up before daybreak. Tomorrow's Christmas."

Mrs. Maguire turned over and sighed. The doctor went to sleep.

Baby Chile crawled into the bed with Mr. Ben. She cried and cried and stroked the bulky dressing on his shoulder. "Honey, I didn't mean to do that. I love you! I do! I do!"

Mr. Ben didn't say a word. The needle was wearing off and his shoulder hurt. But he wasn't gonna let no woman know she'd hurt him. He bit his lip and tried to sleep. He pushed her hand away from his shoulder. He cursed her.

"Hush up, dammit, shet up!" he growled. "I wanna sleep."

Baby Chile kept moaning, "Why'd I do it? Why'd I do it?"

"Shet up, you bitch," Mr. Ben bawled. "I wisht they'da let them creepers take you to the station! Cain't you let me sleep?"

Baby Chile didn't say another word. She just lay there a-thinking and a-thinking. She was trying to remember how it happened. Step by step she reconstructed the event in her mind as though the rehearsal would assuage her feeling of guilt.

She'd been living with Mr. Ben six months now. Of course he was old and he hadn't ever got the country outa him yet. But he had a good job s'long as he kept the furnace fired and the halls swept out. And he got his room free, bein' janitor. She had a relief check coming in reg'lar for herself and her little girl. They could make it all right as long as the case-worker didn't crack down on 'em. But Mr. Ben was so suspicious. He was always watching her and signifyin' she was turning tricks with Slick who helped him with the furnace and slept in the basement. She wouldn't turn no tricks with Slick. He had bad blood and wouldn't take his shots reg'lar. But you couldn't convince old Mr. Ben. Ben didn't treat her little girl right, either. 'Course, it wasn't his child. But he oughta act right. She cooked for him and slept with him and never held her relief check back on him. He could treat her child right. That was the cause of it all, anyhow.

Baby Chile had come home near dark after a day of imbibing Christmas cheer. She must have been a little slug-happy. All she remembered was chasing her little girl outa Mamie's kitchenette next door, telling her to stay outa that whorehouse. "I ain't raisin' you to be a goddammed whore! Why I send you to Sunday school? Why I try to raise you right? For you to lay up in there with them whores?" You just couldn't keep her outa that place listening to the vendor playing boogie-woogie and seein' things only grown folks oughta see. Then she remembered stretching out on the bed. Just before she lay down she'd asked her daughter, "What Ben get you for Christmas, chile?"

"Nothin', Mother Dear."

"Nothin'?"

"No, ma'am."

Her eyes fell on the sideboard covered with new, shiny bottles of whisky and beer and wine—plenty of "Christmas cheer." A turkey was cooking in the stove. "An' that no-'count bastard didn't get *you* nothin'?" She remembered throwing herself on the bed in a rage. The radio was playing Christmas carols—the kind that always made her cry because it sounded like church back down in Mississippi. She lay there half drunk, carols ringing in her ears from the radio, boogie-woogie assailing them from the juke-box across the hall, the smell of turkey emanating from the kitchen, and her little girl whimpering in the corner.

She recalled the "accident" vividly. She was dozing on the bed in the one large room which along with the kitchen made up their home. She woke up when Ben came into the room. She didn't know how long she'd been sleeping. Whisky and beer don't mix anyhow, and when you been in and outa taverns all day Christmas Eve you get enough to lay you out cold.

When Mr. Ben opened the door near midnight she was almost sober, but mad as hell. Her head ached, she was so mad. Ben grunted, walked into the kitchen, and started to baste the turkey. She challenged him:

"You buy Fanny May a present?"

"Naw," he grunted. "I spent my money for the turkey and the drinks. Tomorrow's Christmas, ain't it? What you do with yore relief check? Drink it up? Why'n you get her a present? She's yore chile, ain't she?"

Ben wouldn't have been so gruff, but he was tired and peeved. That damn furnace hadn't been acting right and everybody was stayin' up all night to see Christmas in, and pestering him for more heat. And all the time he was trying to get the turkey cooked, too. Baby Chile oughta been doing it—she had been sashayin' roun' all day drinking other men's liquor. How'd anybody expect him to think about a present for Fanny May? That girl didn't like him and respect him, nohow—always walling her eyes at him, but polite as hell to "Mother Dear." Crap! Mr. Ben didn't say any of this out very loud. He just mumbled it to himself as he bent over the stove basting the turkey.

Baby Chile stood up and stared at him. She felt her hell arising. She didn't say a word. She walked deliberately to the kitchen table and took up a paring knife, studied it for a moment, and then—with every ounce of energy that anger and frustration could pump into her muscles—she sank it between his shoulders and fled screaming into the hall. "Oh, I've killed Mr. Ben! I've killed my old man! I've killed him!"

Her little girl raced over to the noisy room next door and asked Miss Mamie to call the doctor. And Mamie interrupted her Christmas Eve business to help a neighbor.

Now Baby Chile was in bed with Mr. Ben. His shoulder was all fixed. She squeezed him tight, kissed him, and went to sleep.

Everybody had a good time on Christmas Day at Mr. Ben's. Fanny May went to church. The old folks began a whist game in the morning that ran continuously until midnight, with visitors dropping in to take a hand, eat a turkey sandwich, and drink from Mr. Ben's sideboard. The janitor sat in his rocking chair like a king holding court, as the tenants streamed in and out and Baby Chile bustled about making him comfortable. Baby Chile was "high" enough to be lively, but was careful not to get drunk. No one mentioned the tragedy of the night before. Only Slick was uncomfortable.

BRONZEVILLE'S LOWER DEPTHS

Slick felt "left out of things." He had teamed up with Mr. Ben a month before Christmas after his mother and father had evicted him from their two rooms because his drunken escapades were bringing trouble to the household. Nearly thirty, Slick was a floater with two deserted wives behind him, an insatiable appetite for liquor, and spirochetes in his veins. He was not unattractive and he liked women. But he had an ugly scar over his entire left side where wife number one, in a fit of jealous rage, had thrown a bucket of lye on him. "She tried to hit my privates, but I turned over too fast," was Slick's comment. *"Now* what girl wants me? My side's enough to turn her nature." Yet, during the Twenties, when he had a job and money, he had girls. Now, during the Depression, he was, to use his own words, "a bum."

Slick's family had migrated to Chicago from St. Louis where his mother, a lower middle-class woman who "married a no-'count

Negro," had worked as a seamstress. She had tried to make something out of her only son, but according to her, "It didn't take." With a chronic alcoholic for a husband and a delinquent for a son, Slick's mother had resigned herself to being lower-class, although she refused to take a job in domestic service. When the Depression began, she went on the relief. She kept her two rooms and her person spotlessly clean, tried to make the old man hold a WPA job, and in 1938 got a job as housekeeper in a lower-class kitchenette building. But Slick jeopardized her steady income, and she threw him out.

Slick drifted about. Now he was thinking that he'd better move again as soon as Ben's shoulder got well. Ben was beginning to give him the evil eye. Slick hadn't turned a trick with Baby Chile yet, but he was sure she did want "to be with him." He was gonna stay outa trouble. Just as soon as Ben's shoulder got well, he was gonna cut out—danger was on his trail.

Slick had already propositioned Betty Lou about living with him. He had met her at Streeter's Tavern, bought her a few beers, and "jived" her. She had agreed to live with him if one of Slick's employed friends would consent to board with them until Slick could get a WPA job. This would provide a steady income for food. So Slick wheedled ten dollars from his mother and rented a basement room in the center of the Black Belt—three-and-a-half a week for room, bed, chair, and table. Life began—with Betty Lou, though without a stove or even a hot-plate.

Betty Lou, a native of Alabama, had come north to Detroit in the early days of the Depression and entered domestic service. A rather attractive light-brown-skinned girl in her early twenties, fond of good clothes and with a great deal of personal pride, she worked for three years, went to night school intermittently, and then married a common laborer. One year of married life and they separated after a furious fight. She then came to Chicago to stay with a married sister whose husband worked in the steel mills. Later she secured a job in private family and lived "on premises" for several months. She didn't like living with white folks, but when she decided to return to her sister's home, a lodger was sleeping on the sofa in the living-room where she had formerly slept. Betty Lou had to occupy a pallet on the floor in the bedroom with her sister and husband. Slick's offer of a home provided an avenue of escape.

Slick and Betty Lou lived together in the basement for about a month. He made the rounds of various employment agencies, but spent most of his time trying to work his acquaintances for enough money to buy drinks and pay the rent. Betty Lou, faced with the problem of cooking, made a deal with the unmarried janitor who let her use his kitchen in return for a share of the food. She took a great deal of pride in her biscuits and occasional hot rolls. She was enjoying domesticity.

Here, beneath Bronzeville's surface, were a variety of living patterns. The twenty households, sharing four bathrooms, two common sinks in the hallway, and some dozen stoves and hot-plates between them, were forced into relationships of neighborliness and reciprocity. A girl might "do the hair" of a neighbor in return for permission to use her pots and pans. Another woman might trade some bread for a glass of milk. There was seldom any money to lend or borrow, but the bartering of services and utensils was general. Brawls were frequent, often resulting in intense violence. A supper interrupted by the screams of a man with an ice-pick driven into his back might be unusual—but a fight involving the destruction of the meager furniture in these households was not uncommon.

Slick's immediate neighbors were two teen-aged boys, recently discharged from a CCC camp. They were now making their way by robbing laundry trucks and peddling "hot" shirts, towels, socks, and handkerchiefs among the kitchenette dwellers. Each afternoon their room was a rendezvous for schoolgirls—truants and morning-shift pupils—who pooled their lunch money, prepared pots of steaming spaghetti and hot dogs, and spent the afternoon "rug-cutting," drinking whisky, smoking reefers, and "making love." Slick gave strict orders to Betty Lou to "stay outa that reefer den with all them hustlers and reefer smokers."

Betty Lou's best "girl friend" in the basement was Ella, whose husband, "Poke," had recently been jailed for breaking a liquor store window and stealing a pint of whisky. "I just as well not have no ol' man. Stays in jail all the time," Ella confided one day in a pensive mood. Several days later she was living with another man for the interim. "My baby's got to have some milk," she apologized, "an' that damn worker won't get me a job on the WPA 'cause I have a baby. I can run a power-machine, too!"

Down the hall was Joe, a former cook on the railroad who had been fired for stealing Pullman towels and who was now a dishwasher. Living with a waitress, he was currently much agitated because of a letter he had received from his legal wife in Detroit notifying him that she was en route to Chicago. He kept his bags packed.

Strangest of all was Lily, a tall, husky, masculine woman who was subsequently thrown out of the building and warned never to return. "A damn bull-diker * who's been messing with the women in here," was Slick's terse comment.

During this period, Slick's mother visited him several times, and professed to be very fond of her son's new common-law wife. Betty Lou's married sister came to visit them too, as did a woman friend who borrowed the room for a few hours each week on her night off so that she could entertain a boy friend. These visitors sometimes brought a little food when they came.

Slick spoke often of wishing to regularize his alliance if he could get an annulment and if Betty Lou could get a divorce. He fantasied too (usually when drunk) about getting on his feet, taking a civil service examination for a post-office job, and showing the world, his boarder, and his mother that he wasn't a derelict.

After two months in the basement, the couple decided to raise their standard of living. Slick had got a $55-a-month WPA job, so they decided to move into a first-floor kitchenette † with a stove and an ice-box. Thus began the second phase of their joint life.

From Kitchenette to Penitentiary: The three months in the kitchenette started on a note of confidence and ended in tragedy. During this period Betty Lou's sister and her brother-in-law visited occasionally, made the acquaintance of Slick's family, tried to mediate quarrels, and in general functioned as approving relatives. Betty Lou's conception of her role was that Slick should work and support her. Slick, however, insisted that she too should get a job, and often charged her with running around during the day "turning tricks." Such "signifying" became the focal point for continuous quarrels and occasional fights; it eventually resulted in separation.

Betty Lou was anxious to join a church and a social club, and, as

* "Bull-diker"—homosexual woman reputed to have male genitalia.

† Bronzeville's kitchenettes are single rooms, rented furnished and without a lease. Sometimes a hot-plate is included for cooking, but often there are no cooking facilities despite the name. Hundreds of large apartment buildings have been cut up into kitchenettes to meet the chronic housing shortage in the Black Belt. See p. 576.

soon as she could, became a member of an usher board at a lower-middle-class church. Slick resented this attempt at mobility, especially since he had neither the personal organization nor the money and clothes to maintain such social connections. He was often torn with doubts about her motives, and on one occasion said, "I think Betty Lou is just tryin' to work me till she gets another man or gets on her feet."

For a month, Slick worked steadily on the WPA labor project, drank far less than usual, and seemed to achieve a moderate amount of emotional stability. He cashed his first check and allowed Betty Lou to purchase groceries and pay the rent. As for the second check, he spent at least half of it on a "good time." After the first month of fairly steady employment, Slick began to miss work frequently, and it was soon evident that he was spending his time watching Betty Lou in an attempt to catch her with other men. This behavior resulted in some serious fights and a threat on the part of her sister to take Betty Lou back home. In one drunken fit, Slick chased her through the building with a butcher knife, and the housekeeper was forced to call a policeman. On another occasion an argument, which began with the passing of mutual insults, ended in Slick's tearing up Betty Lou's clothing and breaking some cherished china souvenirs which she had patiently gathered at a neighboring tavern over a period of several months.

With the approach of Easter, Slick worked steadily in order to make a down payment on some clothing for himself and Betty Lou. On Easter day both were "togged down." * Within two days, however, all of Slick's clothes were in a pawn shop and he was again in rags. This contributed to the ultimate breakup of the alliance, since Betty Lou was now able to go to church and to dances, while Slick, lacking clothes, was never able to participate in any public social activities with her except at taverns.

The fights continued. Then one night Betty Lou stormed out, vowing never to return. Slick was in a disorganized and drunken state for several days, plotting vengeance one moment and crying the next. His mother, who had been friendly toward Betty Lou, now insisted that she had always known she was no good, and that she was probably a prostitute anyway. Betty Lou decided a few days later to return to Slick, but what she saw when she entered their apartment perma-

---

* Exceptionally well-dressed.

nently estranged her. There in the room was a white girl ensconced in her bed! Betty Lou snatched her clothing from the closet, cursed the woman roundly, reported the incident to the housekeeper, and left. Slick insisted to the housekeeper that he had met the white woman wandering in the cold and like a gentleman had invited her in. To his cronies he proudly told a different story. The woman, he said, was a "hustling woman" he had known when he worked at a North Side "resort." She had befriended him and given him money. Now she was down and out, and when he met her at a Black Belt tavern he decided to bring her in, sleep with her, and to play the role of pimp for a day or two in order to make some extra change. Slick was given three hours to vacate the room under threat of arrest. He moved into a liquor joint for several days and then rented a single room.

One morning several weeks later, a WPA research project in the basement of a church near Slick's lodging place was thrown into an uproar when he rushed through the premises followed by "Two-Gun Dick" and another officer with drawn revolvers. Having met Betty Lou on the street walking with another man, Slick had followed her until her escort left her, and then stabbed her in the breast. His first impulse was to flee to the WPA project, where he had acquaintances who had befriended him in the past. He did not tarry, however, for the police were close behind. He hurried to his mother's home and hid there for the rest of the day. Returning in the evening to the area in which he had committed the crime, he was arrested. His mother borrowed money on her insurance policies for bail and a lawyer. Her only comment on the girl was: "She ought to be glad my boy didn't mark her in the face. She kin get another man since she ain't marked in the face." When it became evident that Betty Lou would recover, the judge sentenced Slick to a mere six months in the Bridewell Prison.

On his release Slick was at the peak of physical condition; regular treatment for his various bodily ailments, disciplined labor, and regular food had made him almost a different person. But within two months he was once more thoroughly disorganized. Another two months and he was back in prison, this time on a charge of stealing. On his release he departed for St. Louis, whence he had originally come to Black Metropolis.

Slick and Betty Lou—Baby Chile and Mr. Ben: there were hundreds of them in Bronzeville during the Lean Years.

HERE TODAY—GONE TOMORROW

Flophouse and Kitchenette: During the Depression years, thousands of homeless men and women floated from room to room in the cheap lodging houses and hotels sandwiched in among the junk yards, factories, and warehouses of the rundown Black Belt areas near the Loop. The most disorganized individuals and the indigent aged tended to live in this area dependent upon the ministrations of public charity. This was Bronzeville's Bowery, with its missions, flophouses, cheap eating-joints, "floozies," and "bums."

The dominant household pattern for older, established families was the flat of three to six rooms in which family, boarders, lodgers, and impecunious relatives lived doubled up, overcrowded, and without privacy. There was continuous movement from building to building in search of lower rents, more adequate accommodations, or relief stations with a reputation for having sympathetic case-workers.

The bulk of the lower class, however, was getting used to "kitchenette" living. Fragments of families; young bachelors; girls and young women living alone, sharing apartments or maintaining transitory alliances with a succession of footloose men—these were scattered throughout the Black Belt, often living in the same building with more stable family aggregations. The trend toward kitchenette living was speeded up by the fact that between 1930 and 1938 houses in the "worst" areas were continuously disintegrating or being demolished. The lower classes were being gradually pressed southward into the better apartment-house areas. Building after building in these areas was cut up into "kitchenettes," for an enterprising landlord could take a six-room apartment renting for $50 a month and divide it into six kitchenettes renting at $8 a week, thus assuring a revenue of $192 a month! For each one-room household he provided an ice-box, a bed, and a gas hot-plate. A bathroom that once served a single family now served six. A building that formerly held sixty families might now have three hundred. The poorest and most unstable elements often inhabited the basements of the kitchenette buildings, where rents were lowest.

Into these kitchenettes drifting lower-class families moved, bringing a few clothes and buying a little furniture on time. There were no leases to sign. There was no necessity to cart coal and wood into these steam-heated buildings. They were crowded and inconvenient, but they were near the center of Bronzeville's activities. Thus once stable middle-class areas gradually became spotted with kitchenettes. The older residents, unable to expand into other neighborhoods because of restrictive covenants, were usually forced to remain against their will surrounded by—often within—these kitchenette buildings.

Middle-class neighborhoods in Bronzeville thus became the beach upon which broke the human flotsam which was tossed into the city streets by successive waves of migration from the South. There it mixed with the jetsam thrown off by lower-class families as they expanded within their restricted living quarters or disintegrated under the impact of economic crises or the explosions of family discord.

Flats and Houses: Smaller families, newly formed families, and broken families flocked to the kitchenettes. Large, older, or more stable families utilized "flats"—the larger apartments and the dilapidated houses on the margins of the Black Belt near the railroads and stockyards. Throughout the Depression years there was a continuous shifting about of these households in an unremitting search for a situation in which a relief or WPA check could be stretched farther, or where more lodgers and boarders could be accommodated. Under the impact of the Depression and wholesale demolitions, these lower-class households became a veritable mélange of lodgers, boarders, relatives, and friends. Among them were hundreds of newcomers from the South fleeing toward a city where relief was more continuous and WPA more lucrative.

Newcomers to the city, elderly couples who wanted to "live respectable," and those who had seen better days often preferred the ramshackle, frame, stove-heated houses on the fringes of the Black Belt near the stockyards, or in the old West Side ghetto near the famous Hull House settlement.[1]

Retreat to the White Ghetto: Throughout the Depression, a constant stream of Negroes filtered into the old West Side ghetto to escape the high rents and the rabbit-warren life of Black Belt kitchenettes. More sophisticated lower-class Bronzevillians looked down upon the West Side where lived Italians, Mexicans, and poorer Jews along with Negroes. But some Negroes, ever since the days of the Great Migration, had made their homes there. Recent migrants from the South often made it their first stop when they came to town. Here the educational level of the Negro population was lowest, and store-front churches predominated.

In 1938, when the West Side was thoroughly studied, there were some 15,000 Negroes living in the area, most of whom had moved in during the Depression years. Eight out of every ten of the family heads were either on WPA or receiving direct relief. Half of all persons who had any employment at all were "working for the relief" —usually at $55 a month. Of those who were not working on WPA, eight out of ten were unskilled laborers. Except for a score of preachers, two undertakers, and a dozen small storekeepers, there were no business or professional people. At least fifty per cent of the residents had never gone beyond the eighth grade. The pastor of one of the largest churches in the area apologized to an interviewer for the class level of his constituency: "Our people are poor and somewhat backward around here, but they are fine people."

One young WPA laborer recently arrived in Chicago apologized for living in the White Ghetto: "My people lived over here.* So when I came to Chicago I stayed here till I got straight and on my feet. Even after I got to know Chicago I stayed over here except for a year that I lived on the South Side. If everything wasn't so high I'da stayed over there. But I couldn't make it. I got five rooms over here with stove heat for $12. It's not so fine, but it's comfortable. I can pay that and not be hungry."

Most West Siders know what the South Siders think about them, and are on the defensive. Mrs. Smith, for instance, moved to the West Side in 1929, after having lived in a deteriorated and crowded area of the South Side. She didn't plan to stay, but in 1938 was still there. She has a ready rationalization of her extended residence:

"The people here don't have fine buildings, showy flats, and flashy cars . . . but they don't have to sleep in bath tubs or on ironing boards and let their insurance lapse to pay the rent. We need a lot over here, but we don't have to worry as much as they do over there."

* "Over here" as used in this section refers to the West Side ghetto; "over there," to the main Negro community—the South Side.

Mrs. Jones insists that "it's better over here" because "the people aren't as tough as they are over on the South Side":

"Over here they don't be in flats next to yours and they don't meddle you. Over there they have to do all sorts of things to pay rent and keep from dying of starvation. This neighborhood is for poor people that don't try to buy thousand-dollar cars on fifty-five a month. This house doesn't look so good, but it's good as any over there."

Mr. Williams resents the fact that "a lot of people think us West Side people ain't no good." He belabors those who have stayed in the Black Belt, accusing them of "trying to live like they make a hundred dollars a week and then owe everybody. . . . They have the nerve to look at us like we're some kind of animals they never saw before. Their flats are better than ours, but they pay three and four times as much as we do."

While housing is poor, it is cheap, and West Siders are continually referring to the fact that they "save on rent." Mrs. Duncan, however, supporting six people on $55 a month, feels that she can't make it:

"I came to Chicago in 1925. My husband came here a year before that. . . . He found work and sent for us. At that time work was plentiful, and he got a job as night man in a garage. He washed cars and his wages were $35 a week. We lived nicely off of that because it was much more than we had ever made at home. My husband worked at the garage until 1933. We find the WPA a great help, but it doesn't pay enough for the large number of people that have to get a living from it. There are my husband and myself, my mother, and our three children."

The current opinion seemed to be that living on the West Side was cheaper in terms of food as well as rent. One woman who paid $8 for three rooms indicated the technique of securing cheap food:

"It's easier to live over here. I've been over here for eight years and I wouldn't move over there [i.e., on the South Side] for anything unless I had a lot of money, because it takes more to live over there. One thing, over here you can always get something to eat at the market like a basket of beans or tomatoes and potatoes for a dime, before they are graded. If you get more than you can use yourself, you can always sell or trade what you don't want. . . . I've got sense enough to know that the houses out there are better, but they pay three or four times as much rent as we do."

Although there are cases of three people living in one room in a friend's apartment, or of ten people living in six rooms, the most frequent West Side pattern is of five or six people occupying three rooms. At the worst extreme is a house of the type described thus:

Entrance through the kitchen from the back porch of the building, the latter room equipped with an old-fashioned and battered coal range, a bare kitchen table, dirty sink, soiled shades, and dingy curtains . . . floor bare of any covering at all.

Off the kitchen an equally dirty bedroom with little in it but a bed swathed in dirty sheets and quilts. The room small and crowded, even with its single pieces of furniture. Second bedroom also crowded . . . combined living-room and dining-room barely affords space for standing when the day-bed is opened, since the rest of the space is taken by a dilapidated duofold, a small table, and two chairs. These four rooms house two parents and five children.

But a much more typical West Side house is described as follows:

The building is very old and has probably been condemned. The furnishings of this home are those of very poor people, but everything is clean and in order. The only new article in the living-room is a modern portable Zenith radio. Other furnishings include a large old-fashioned stove, a day-bed, three chairs, a trunk with a clean white towel spread over it, a Victrola, and a table. Apparently the walls and ceiling were papered many years ago. The plaster is falling from the ceiling in many places.

Within a physical framework of this type and limited by a meager income, these families had the South Sider's habit of taking in roomers, who usually pay from two to two dollars and a half a week for a room. Since steam heat is rare, the roomer usually had a stove which he used for both heat and cooking.

Even in this relatively stable lower-class neighborhood, the family units were predominantly broken families or fragments of families. They often included individuals who were just awaiting a chance to return to the more exciting and urbane Black Belt. Usually there was a nucleus maintaining the home while an ever-shifting circle was coming and going. Some were orthodox families: husband, wife, and children. Others were organized around a childless couple with several relatives "staying on." Occasionally a home had no married couples, but only brothers and sisters. In one such case, in 1938, a brother, aged thirty-five, unable to work because of a spinal disease, was getting relief for himself and a younger sister, while another brother worked for the WPA. The sister kept house for both.

Many of these families were actually mutual-aid societies, originated and maintained by economic necessity. A young person in his late teens or twenties might be irked at having to live with the "old folks" in the backwaters of the West Side. He might have no bonds of affection to keep him there. But if he had no job, no smart clothing, and no money, he might not only stay but even grudgingly co-operate. There would at least be meals and a place to sleep, even if food were scarce and his bed a pallet on the floor. A married couple might be displeased at the prospect of supporting relatives, but the larger the household the greater the chance that somebody might find a job. There was always, too, the possibility that the person with a job might lose it—and woe unto him who had once turned his relatives away!

The West Side had its share of people who were just staying around —often recent migrants from the South. Not unusual was the case of one young man, three months out of Mississippi, who had spent one month with a South Side cousin and two with a West Side relative. He commented: "I figure I'll stop with one awhile and then stop with the other awhile. They're both my cousins."

THE HAZARDS OF MARRIAGE

Maintaining any sort of home life at the lower-class level in Bronzeville has always been a problem because of low and fluctuating annual incomes and inadequate housing. The Depression simply intensified all the stresses and strains that had been present since the Great Migration. The Second World War, while it resulted in larger family incomes, even further disorganized these homes, owing to the absence of men in the armed forces and the increased use of women in industry.

For the ten years prior to the war families were never sure of either rent money or food money in sufficient quantities. There was little to fall back on when the Depression came; there was nothing to look forward to when it ended. Such people could set up no long-range goals of educating children, acquiring property, and "getting ahead," for organizing family effort; could maintain no family traditions. During the Depression years, too, old families were continuously being broken and fragmented. New household units also came into being as youngsters tried to "make a go of it" with or without benefit of clergy. Sometimes families came into being merely in order that the partners could qualify for more relief. Even illegitimate babies were an asset when confronting a case-worker.

In the parlance of the sociologist, Bronzeville was suffering from social disorganization. But lower-class family behavior is the product of more basic conditions than the Depression. The instability of Negro lower-class families throughout America was reflected in the high rates of desertion, illegitimacy, and divorce as well as in a great deal of violent conflict within the average lower-class household.*

Dependent Men and Forceful Women: Since Reconstruction days, America has stereotyped Negro lower-class men as "lazy" and "shiftless." This stereotype has been reinforced in our generation by the "Amos and Andy" and "Stepin Fetchit" characterizations of radio and screen. Side by side with this portrait is another conception of Negro lower-class men as "healthy bucks" who can stand the heat of blast furnaces and the weight of cotton bales and who can do the backbreaking work of farm and city. The latter picture is much closer to the truth, for when lower-class men can get jobs they work, as even a casual examination of the census or relief records will reveal. Historically, however, in Bronzeville as elsewhere in America, Negro men have suffered from irregularity of employment and from actual unemployment more than any other segment of America's lower class. They are the last to be hired and the first to be fired from the common labor jobs and servant jobs which they usually hold. In the cotton country, the fruits of labor are seldom realized in the form of cash, though the man may work the year around. Negroes have not been allowed to compete freely for the better jobs.

During slavery the master supported his Negro families. Since slavery, Negro men have never been able, in the mass, to obtain good jobs long enough to build a solid economic base for family support. Those who through the years have been able to accumulate something have formed the backbone of the Negro middle class. There has never been sufficient economic opportunity, however, to permit the mass of

---

* Between 1924 and 1928, 20 per cent of all the cases of desertion handled by the Chicago Court of Domestic Relations were Negro. For a full discussion of desertion as a lower-class trait in Chicago, see E. Franklin Frazier, *The Negro Family in the United States,* University of Chicago, 1939, pp. 336-341.

Negro workers to acquire the material goods—housing, furniture, clothing, savings—for laying the basis for a middle-class way of life. This lack of economic opportunity, coupled with denial of access to even a grade-school education, resulted very early in a peculiar pattern of restless wandering on the part of Negro men.

This notorious and widespread wandering has been primarily a search for better or supplementary jobs. Thousands of share-croppers have traditionally left their wives and children at home while they went to the cities or the lumber and turpentine camps during "laying-by time" to gain a supplementary income. Many of them never came back to the subordination of the cotton fields. Thousands flocked north during the Great Migration and through the Fat Years and the Lean. They are still coming. Some sent for their wives and sweethearts. Many didn't. Beginning with economic necessity, this pattern has become a custom which runs on its own steam. A wanderer's life is an exciting life.[2]

The roving of masses of Negro men has been an important factor, during the eighty years since slavery, in preventing the formation of stable, conventional, family units. It has shifted the responsibility for the maintenance of household units to the women of the lower class.

The economic weakness of Negro men was not confined to the plantation, however. In the southern cities and towns the masses of Negro men, ill paid and irregularly employed, have never succeeded in becoming the steady providers for their families. It has always been their wives and girl friends who, working as servants in white families, have "brought home the butter in the bag." Thus, both husband and children come to look to their women as the ultimate source of support. Even in Bronzeville during the last phases of the Depression, when hundreds of lower-class Negro men had WPA jobs, it was often the women who, through illegal and surreptitious employment as domestic servants, had the only ready cash for food, recreation, and clothes. Negro lower-class women almost always hold the purse strings.

Lower-class men are thus in a weak economic position *vis-à-vis* their women and children. Male control loosened, the woman becomes the dominant figure. Since she pays the piper, she usually feels justified in calling the tune. But while lower-class men are in a weak economic position, they are in a strategic position otherwise. Negro lower-class women, like all women, have their affectional and sexual needs. Being predominantly working women of limited education, unable to spend time or money in "prettifying" themselves, they cannot hope to get husbands from the middle and upper classes. They also face the sexual competition of the most attractive lower-class girls who can get men to support them, and of the prostitutes and semi-prostitutes. In a sense, therefore, most lower-class women have to take love on male terms. The men, on the other hand, are strongly tempted to take advantage of such a situation and to trade love for a living. The net result is an attitude of suspicion toward men blended with a woman's natural desire to be loved for herself alone.

It is no accident that Bronzeville's barbershop wags during the Depression used to say that the Negro National Anthem was "I Can't Give You Anything But Love, Baby." It is likewise no accident that one of the most popular juke-box songs was a woman's command: "Why don't you do right like other men do? Get outa here—get me some money, too."

The emotional dilemmas that arise from this awkward situation have developed a pattern of defensive hardness among lower-class Negro women alternating with moods of lavish tenderness; have developed, too, a glorification of emotional "independence" which is always belied by the facts. The men, insecure in their economic power, tend to exalt their sexual prowess. They cultivate an attitude of "love 'em and leave 'em." The women's pose is, "I'll let him love me (and I'll love him) until he doesn't act right. Then I'll kick him out."

Thus, an old southern pattern is intensified and strengthened in Bronzeville. Unstable common-law marriages of relatively short duration alternate with periods of bitter disillusionment on the women's part. The end result is often a "widow" and her children, caused either by a husband's desertion or by a wife's impetuous dismissal of him.

About three out of every five lower-class men and women in Bronzeville claim to be married. Census-takers do not ask to see marriage certificates, so the figure includes numerous common-law marriages. (Bronzeville's lower class has brought with it from the South a certain unconcern with the formalities of law and church as related to marriage.) Over half of the unmarried women claim to have been married at some period of their lives. The bulk of these have listed themselves as "widowed"—a term which Bronzeville's lower-class women use to include "desertion." Only one woman in five listed herself as single, and this term, too, probably includes some wives who have been deserted. The desertion rate is very high among the Negro lower class throughout the United States.

About forty out of every hundred lower-class women in Bronzeville before the war were "available" in the sense that they did not have husbands. About the same proportion of men were "available." Nearly all of these men, however, report themselves as "single," even though in many cases they may have been previously married.* The bulk of the "available" women, on the other hand, admit having once had some sort of "unfortunate" family life. Individuals from the ranks of the "sixty per cent married" are continuously dropping into the ranks of the "forty per cent available," and vice versa. Family tensions arising within the framework of the lower-class family are usually dissolved with violence, through arguing, fighting, and as a last resort, separation. While much of the instability of the family is due to desertion on the part of the males, a not inconsiderable proportion is due to the eviction of males by women who have decided not to "put up with foolishness" any longer.

One high school girl cited an instance where a husband finally wandered off after several years of internecine strife:

"My mother and father have been separated for two years. I don't miss my father at all. He was so unpleasant that I was glad to see him leave. He gambled and drank and didn't provide for the family. We had to go on relief because of the way he acted, so I hope I never see him again. He abused Mother, too. My mother has had a very hard life. She married young and he started mistreating her right after I was born—I'm the oldest; and he made her life so miserable that she had to leave him any number of times. But she always went back on account of us."

Sometimes a desertion is accompanied by a vindictive stealing of the other partner's personal effects, as in the case of a woman who reported that she had fought continually with her husband:

"One night he started an argument with me, and told me if I didn't treat him right I would not ever have the chance to treat him any way again. I wondered what he meant when he said that; I was afraid that he meant to kill me. It looked like I slept sounder than ever that night, for while I was sleeping he got up, packed all of his things and the best silks I had and left. I haven't seen him from that day unto this."

* Over half of the 2,000 unattached Negro men who sought aid from the shelters for transient men in Chicago during the Depression admitted that they had been married.

Another lower-class woman on the West Side came to Chicago with her husband, worked in a box factory ten years, and gave Saturday night parties to increase her income. After saving a large sum of money, she quit her job. The husband ordered her back to work and a razor altercation ensued, after which he ran away. He soon returned, and she agreed to go back to work! A few days later he absconded with all her savings. When he came back six years later she had another husband. The woman insists that when she discovered the loss of the money she got drunk and stayed drunk for eighteen days. (Desertions by wives under similar circumstances are not unknown, and in several cases a husband accused his wife of leaving with all of his savings.)

A family may also be broken by the enforced absence of the husband for a time. Thus the twenty-five-year-old woman quoted below lived with her parents, sister, brother-in-law, and niece. She had been separated for a year.

"He wouldn't do right and I worked to help him until I had to go to the hospital to have my baby. When I came out I left him, and he got in trouble and went to jail for twenty years. He didn't care enough about me to come out to County [hospital] to see me, and I all but died."

In this case, she and her mother and her father were all on relief; the brother-in-law worked, and he and his wife paid the entire rent and half the coal bill. Cases are frequent of daughters who have come back to live with their parents after a separation or desertion.

A Good Old Man Don't Live Sweet: Despite the instability and apparent disorder of sex and family relations, Bronzeville's lower class has its own standards for a "good" husband or a "good" wife. Lower-class women don't expect much from their husbands in terms of either complete sexual fidelity or economic security. Like most women in America they fantasy about romantic love and the ideal husband who has a steady job, brings his money home, and makes possible a life of leisure and comfort. In reality, however, a lower-class woman thinks she has a "good old man" if he will work when he can and if he does not spend all his money on gambling and drinking. If he does "run with other women," he will guard against emotional attachments and absolutely will not lavish his money on other women. A "good old man" may perhaps slap or curse his "old woman" if he's angry; he definitely will not "beat on her all the time" when he's sober, and will not endanger her life when drunk. If they have children, he will make some effort to feed and clothe them, and give them gifts. And, if she is to remain with him, she expects him to "satisfy" her sexually.

Inevitably, many a lower-class man tries to "live sweet" by depending entirely on a woman to provide him with money and clothes in exchange for companionship. But a woman who "pimps a man" is considered something of a "sucker" by other women. Although such "lucky men" may be looked upon with some envy by their fellows, it is generally considered unfair to "live on a woman." A "good old man don't live sweet."

A "good old woman" is sexually satisfying, will not "run around with other men," and will be loyal to her "old man" in arguments or fights. She'll divide up whatever money she garners from work or relief. If she's not a workingwoman, she'll keep other men out of the house during the day and will have supper ready on time when her husband gets home.* She will not try to "dog her husband around," nor will she be too demanding in terms of clothes and money. When the going gets too tough, she won't run off with another man or run home to her folks. Nor will she throw her husband into the street. And most important of all: she will not give his money to other men.

There is a good deal of tolerance for deviations from the pattern, but if a husband or wife flagrantly and too violently misbehaves, the spouse will issue the walking papers or else pack up and leave. Some couples manage to stick it out and maintain a stable, unbroken home, but this is not the typical lower-class pattern.†

✦

* This business of not having supper ready when the old man gets home was a frequent source of conflict in lower-class households during the Depression. The wives of men who worked on the WPA often took "day's work" to supplement the family income or spent time at the policy stations hoping for a lucky hit. When these activities interfered with the prompt preparation of meals, there was likely to be an explosion. The lower-class man seemed to view such "excuses" with suspicion, especially if the woman had no money to show in evidence. And even if she could show some money, how could he be sure where it came from? The atmosphere of mutual suspicion that characterizes lower-class family life is a dominant part of the *ethos* of Bronzeville.

† This generalization is based on the high desertion rate as well as on samplings within typical lower-class neighborhoods. In the study of the relatively stable West Side, for instance, over half the homes were broken, and in at least a third of the remaining families one partner had been previously married.

She Just Ain't Got the Stuff in Her to Be a Good Woman!: Often family fights and desertions result from breaking the "code." A case with many elements of a typical situation is cited below. Here a man has been arrested for beating his wife, and insists that he will never live with her again:

"I work for a junk yard. I'm the night watchman and I don't get home until seven o'clock in the daytime. I'm tired and I go to bed. Well, I woke up and called my wife one day; she wasn't home, so I dressed and went out looking for her. I found her at her friend's house with two other men. When I walked in on the four of them, there was a bottle of whisky on the table. I asked her what she was doing there. She looked at me and said, 'What do you think I'm doing?'

"We began to argue and a rap came to the door. A young man said, 'Is this the place that ordered the beer?' My wife said, 'Yes, bring it in.' She gave him a dollar bill and the boy was going to give her some change. She said, 'It's on John'—meaning me. I got mad and I punched her. I chased the two men out and I grabbed her again. I told her to put her clothes on and get home. She was half drunk and she took a long time to get ready.

"When we got down in front of the house she began to call me dirty names. I hit her on the face and she fell. She began to bleed, but I didn't care. I was so mad I could've killed her. Soon the police came, and here I am.

"That woman where she was—she ain't no friend of mine; she is a no-good bum, and I told my wife not to go up there. Who does she think she is, spending my money on other men! . . . This is the first trouble I had and the last. I won't live with a woman like that."

When asked if he planned a divorce he answered: "No, sir; I'll just go my way and tell her to go hers. I'm through with her. I should've known she was no good. She just ain't got the stuff in her to be a good woman." John didn't know why he had ever married her: "I've been asking myself that question quite a few times. I got a good job; I'll get me a good wife the next time."

The interviewer said: "That will be bigamy. They can send you to jail for a thing like that."

"I don't care what they do to me—I'm through with that bitch forever."

WILD CHILDREN

Most of Bronzeville lies within those areas of Chicago which the sociologists call "delinquency areas." Wherever neighborhoods have begun to "go down"—where there are waste tracts of land, dilapidated buildings, railroad sidings—here are the "delinquency areas," regardless of what nationality or race lives there. Yet, Negroes show an unusually high delinquency rate.

In 1930, 20 out of every hundred boys hailed before the juvenile court were colored boys. The rates for girls were almost as high. The Depression made a chronic condition acute. Parents were without money to give children for the shows, the dances, and the "zoot suits" which lower-class adolescent status required. There were few odd jobs. Purse-snatching became general in lower-class areas and even on main thoroughfares. Occasionally, too, a gang of youngsters would crowd some other child who had a little money into a doorway and rob him—at knife-point. Studies of delinquents show that their behavior is partly "rational" (e.g., desire to get money for a show) and partly the search for a thrill or excitement.

Bronzeville's wild children were not so numerous as the frightened upper and middle class thought, but there were enough of them roaming the streets during the Depression, stealing, fighting, and molesting pedestrians, to cause everyone—including lower-class parents—to talk about the "youth problem." Much more prevalent were the thousands of lower-class young men who were never arrested as delinquents but who skirted the borderline of crime. These were the "cats" who, clad in "zoot-suits," stood around and "jived" the women. "Sexual delinquency" was probably more widespread than petty thievery and violence.

BABIES WITHOUT FATHERS

Between 1928 and 1933 about 25,000 Negro babies were born in Chicago, and of these more than 2,000 were illegitimate.* The greater number of these "babies without fathers" were born of young lower-

* From 10 to 15 per cent of all Negro maternity cases at the Cook County Hospital between 1923 and 1928 were unmarried mothers. Virtually all of these were lower-class cases, since women of higher status do not go to the county hospital to have their babies delivered. (See E. Franklin Frazier, *The Negro Family in Chicago*, University of Chicago, 1932, pp. 179-83.)

class mothers, most of whom had been in the city less than five years. Such an "accident" rarely happens to girls in other social classes, or even to lower-class girls wise in the ways of the city. When it does happen to one of the latter, however, she is not "disgraced." Her friends may perhaps gossip about her, and her parents, if religious, will grieve over their daughter's sin; but she will hardly lose her friends, male or female, and will probably continue her activities in any organizations to which she belongs. The lower class, unlike the middle and the upper, not only tolerates illegitimacy, but actually seems almost indifferent toward it. As the illegitimate child grows up, it does not ordinarily suffer marked embarrassment or encounter many taunts.

This attitude toward illegitimacy is imported from the South, where on the plantations the masses of the Negro people have historically considered a child a welcome gift, another "hand" to help make a crop. It is only in the cities that children become "handicaps," and illegitimate ones, liabilities.

During the Depression years, a lower-class mother in Bronzeville with illegitimate children usually made an adjustment in one of the following ways :

   a. She would live with her parents and contribute to the support of the joint family.

   b. In a family without a male head, the mother would care for the illegitimate child while the daughter worked to support all three. If no work was available, relief provided for the family unit.

   c. She would rent a room for herself and the child, and depend upon relief for support.

   d. She would find a "boy friend" to support herself and the child.

One young woman with a three-year-old baby, commenting on this last arrangement, said: "I haven't got no husband. The boy was supposed to marry me, but he never did. I've got a new boy friend. He drives a cab and comes over here every day nearly."

Occasionally a woman with an illegitimate child is even fortunate enough to find a boy friend who may marry her, as in the case of this woman who detailed the circumstances of her two "slips":

"I was working, and he would meet me after work. I tried to avoid him but I couldn't. My mother told me fellows liked girls that were easy and not to have anything to do with him. I thought he was after my money. He was very nice to me. He would take me out and buy me anything I wanted to eat. He never gave me any money. One Sunday he met me after work and took me out and I didn't get home until Monday morning. We went from one tavern to another. He finally took me to a hotel. I was seventeen then, and he is the first man that I ever had. . . . The other baby's father wasn't any good either. Mother said that when I made one mistake, I shouldn't have made another one. I didn't know I would get caught so easily. What can you do? A woman has to have somebody. . . . I didn't love either of the children's daddies, but I love this man I go with now. We are engaged. He is crazy about the kids."

The girls' stories of these Bronzeville accidents usually follow the conventional boy-meets-girl pattern. Lucy, for instance, was living at home. Her boy-friend took the initiative:

"He used to stand on the corner of 49th Street, and when we girls would get out of school he and several other boys would follow us. So I liked him and I thought he liked me. He never would come out here to see me. I would meet him at another girl's home and we would go to shows. . . . He told me he loved me and asked me to go with him to a girl friend of his. I finally agreed to go with him. We went out there. The lady rented rooms. So he got a room, we went in, and he told me he wanted to be with me. I protested but he finally out-talked me. . . . I was then at a stage where I could not help myself; something just seemed to hold me in a spell. . . . I told him if anything happened to me he would have to marry me. He agreed. After that we had frequent dates. I just fell in love with him. I told him that Mother was very much upset, and I begged him to marry me. He told me he didn't want to marry. He said he couldn't swear the baby was his, so I began to hate him. He just left the city. I don't want him any more."

Since hundreds of Bronzeville's lower-class girls are "on their own" at an early age, the locale of their seduction is often their own kitchenettes:

"I met him through a girl friend of mine he used to go with. So one day he carried me to work and when I got out of his car I offered to pay him and he wouldn't take it. The next day he came around to my house and I gave him dinner. While we were eating he asked me if he could go with me. He said he and my friend had quit and he liked me, but I would have to stop all these men from hanging around me, that he didn't want anyone around where he went. The next night was my night off, and he called and said he would be over and didn't want anyone here when he got here, that he would be a little late—to have him something good to eat. So I fixed him a real good supper that night, and it was almost one o'clock when he got here. I was up with my gown on and he knocked on the door. I opened it and he wanted to know what I was doing up so late. I told him I was mad because he had waited so late to come and the supper was cold. He kissed me and said that was all right. Then he told me he had a dream about me the night before and I was as naked as when I was born. I said, 'Oh, that's a bad dream.' He said, 'No, it's a good dream' . . . and I got in a family way that night."

Though there is nothing distinctive about the way in which Bronzeville's babies without fathers originate, the attitudes of the mothers toward their own behavior is characteristically lower-class. Since lower-class men do not necessarily refuse to live with or even marry a girl who has had an illegitimate child, a girl has not necessarily "ruined herself." One woman, now married to a man who is not the child's father, said: "I had Petey before I was married. I was going to let his father marry me, but I didn't like him so well." Other women who have never married sometimes express both guilt and irritation, as in the case of a woman who shouted at an interviewer: "I ain't never had no husband. Haven't you heard of women having babies without a husband? Maybe I didn't want to get married."

One occasionally finds an older woman who has not only never married, but who boasts of the fact. The woman quoted below, though an extreme case, represents a type sometimes found in Bronzeville. A migrant from South Carolina, she exemplifies a pattern once widespread in the South but rare in Bronzeville—a woman with a large family of illegitimate children by a number of different men:

"I've been here eleven years, soon will be, and wouldn't be any place else I know of now. I was twenty-six years old when I came here. I didn't know where I was going when I came, but I had heard about Chicago and always said I was going up the country when I was older. None of my five children are whole sisters and brothers. One of my boys really has good blood in him—he is a white man's child and as bright as you are. He is really good-looking, even if I do say so. . . . Jack lived with me two years before he died. . . . No, we didn't live together all the time. I used to live on the place where I worked all the time, and when I had a day off I'd spend the night with him. I'm living with a boy friend now. He wants to marry, but I don't want to be bothered. I've been my boss too long now. I go and come and do what I want to do. I can't see when I can have anyone bossing me around now. . . . You see, I love the h—— out of him, but I don't need anybody to just

love. If he can't help me or pay me, I can't use him. I can love any-
where. . . . Sometimes I think of putting my kids in a home some place.
It is so hard on me to work and come home to see my children, but
I'd hate for them to leave me."

Most of Bronzeville's lower-class girls are neither "unspoiled children of Nature" nor defiant social rebels. They are aware of the fact
that the church-centered lower class and the entire middle-class world
does not approve of babies without fathers. Members of the more
stable lower-class families express frequent verbal disapproval. Some of
the other lower-class women, too, are responsive to the censure of the
church people on their own class level and of the entire middle-class
world. But the lower-class does not make a grave social or moral
issue of illegitimacy. Though a baby without a father may be an inconvenience to a lower-class mother, and most certainly a handicap to
upward social mobility, the mother is not ostracized and the child is
not ordinarily ridiculed. The interviewers on the Cayton-Warner Research reported several cases in which the mother felt that living
with a man other than the child's father was more reprehensible than
having an illegitimate child. One such woman was ashamed to move
her new boy friend into her home, although she thought he would
"do more" for her if she lived with him; but she'll starve, she says,
before she'll let her illegitimate daughter see her do anything wrong!
She wants to send the child to the country where "she can grow up
educated and be able to do more than scrub floors and wash clothes."

The high illegitimacy rate in Bronzeville is sometimes cited as evidence of the "immorality" of Negroes, and the particularly high rate
within the lower class as evidence of the special "immorality" of that
class. Lower-class Negroes are quick to counter with the assertion that
white people and higher-status Negroes "do everything they're big
enough to do, but they don't have the babies." There is some element
of truth in this if "immorality" means premarital or extramarital
sex-relations. Babies without fathers are primarily the consequence of
ignorance concerning birth-control and of a lack of concern for middle-
class proprieties and "front." The prevalence of illegitimacy among the
lower class is also a reflection of the incomplete urbanization of the
rural southern migrants; for, as E. Franklin Frazier has suggested,
illegitimacy in the rural South is not the social disaster it is considered
in the cities, but "where the rural folkways concerning unmarried
motherhood are in conflict with the legal requirements of the city, the

persistence of these folkways in the urban environment will create social problems."

IT'S HARD TO KEEP GIRLS STRAIGHT

As a rule, lower-class parents do not approve of abortions—"murdering babies they call it. If a girl is pregnant, they feel that she should "have the baby" and that the father (if they can find him) should contribute to its support. They seldom insist, however, that he marry the girl to "give the child a name" or to save their daughter's honor. The child may or may not assume its father's name. The daughter when able usually goes to work (or during the Depression, applied for relief). Older members of the family or relatives and friends help to care for the baby. Despite this acceptance of illegitimate children as "acts of God," parents do consider them unfortunate accidents. One West Side father hopes that his daughter won't have "bad luck," because "so many of the other girls have babies and have to get married." Yet he says, "If she has one, I don't want her to marry the boy unless she wants to." Another father has been wondering whether his eleven-year-old daughter is going to ."come up with a baby" because it's so hard to keep girls straight "over here." But he is not going to insist that she marry if she does have a child.

A middle-aged husband, a migrant from North Carolina, wants to take his children "back South" to raise them because "I don't want no children of mine to be like the children I see on the streets nowadays." He proceeds to describe "girls fourteen or fifteen carrying babies when they ought to be carrying books," and concludes bitterly, "People waste a lot of money trying to make something out of these little whores!" Another father has already sent his two daughters to Florida, because "Chicago is no place to raise girls if you want them to be something when they grow up." But such decisions are rare even among the respectable lower class.

Lower-class parents who have the ambition to "make something" out of their girls may be atypical, but they are bitterly articulate:

"That's one reason so many of our girls don't even get through high school. They get knocked up and have a baby before they are in their teens good. And the boys all want to be pimps and gangsters, so they quit school and buy clothes to look sharp."

One lower-class mother approves of her daughter's desire to be a stenographer because it will give her a chance to get a nice man for a husband. (Her oldest son was in the county jail at the time for disorderly conduct.) Her fears are revealed by her comment that

"you can't raise a girl right over here . . . This is a rotten neighborhood. . . . By the time they are fifteen they are no good. The boys are the same way. It's because the parents don't care and the schools don't teach them anything. If she'll only listen to me I'm sure she won't come up with a baby."

"Listening" does not mean learning the use of contraceptives—it means hearing a lecture on "staying away from men." But such parents often have daughters who don't "listen," like this girl who has already had one baby:

"I don't want to hurt Mother again. She provokes me. I am very much upset about all of it. We were always taught the right way. It's no fault of Mother's. I must say my mother has always been a real mother ever since our father died. . . . I'm sorry for all of it, but I really think Mother should not be so hard on me. I love the baby and Mother loves it too, but I'll never let another man get me like that. I'll do anything to make Mother forget. We still go to church. I feel so ashamed among my chums, but I guess it will be over. I promised I will go back to school and forget the past and be a good girl."

HUSTLING WOMEN

Not all of Bronzeville's lower-class women maintain family relations with men, or organize their lives in terms of romantic love. Instead, some of them "hustle." * "Hustling women," however, forfeit the respect of both men and women in their social stratum. To "live" with a man, even temporarily, is sanctioned, but women who promiscuously "turn tricks" for money are denounced by most lower-class women, and lower-class men do not consider them desirable for potential mates. The lower class does, however, distinguish between habitual, professional prostitutes (especially those who cater to white men and higher-status Negroes) and casual pick-ups available for a "good time" to lower-class men. Many women of the latter sort are regarded not as prostitutes but as "freebys"—the passing of money becomes not so

---

* I.e., engage in prostitution.

much a commercial transaction as a token of appreciation for a "good time"; but the line is a thin one.

During the Depression Bronzeville's reputation as a "vice area" was reinforced by the prevalence of street-walkers in certain areas. While "vice" was institutionalized to some extent—with madams, pimps, and call-houses—it was on the whole what tavern-touts called "two-bits business." A member of the Social Service Department of the Morals Court commented in the late Thirties on their pattern:

"The question of vice in the Negro district is mostly street-walking. That would be true in any district as poor as that, either white or colored. And this type of prostitution is more open to the possibility of arrest. Police arrest street-walkers rather than prostitutes in the higher-class vice resorts. In the Negro district, too, there is much prostitution practiced in the kitchenette apartments."

In fact, the unorganized nature of Bronzeville's prostitution means that any building in a lower-class area is likely to include some prostitutes. During the Depression years the boldness of their solicitation drew bitter comments from lower-class women who were trying to maintain stable relations with their men or "raise children right." Thus one lower-class housewife, when asked about the building in which she lived, replied: "Honey, this place is full of whores. They are the cheapest, nastiest set in Chicago. If I could get me another place I wouldn't be here."

Another person commented that the housekeeper did not attempt to keep prostitutes out of the building: "I think you'll find them in every kitchenette apartment. Nearly everybody in here is doing first one thing and then another."

One woman stated: "I have been here for eight months and there are lots of street-walkers here. It's terrible the things they do. The police used to run them out of the entrance. They'd stop in the entrance or any place and have a man." And another reported that "they almost knock you down if you are on the stairs. When you see 'em coming you'd better get out of the way."

There is rather general agreement among social workers and policemen that the Depression increased the amount of open solicitation in Bronzeville. One official of the vice squad who had a reputation of being none too friendly to Negroes stated in 1932:

"To talk fair about the situation, you must realize that the colored girl does not have the chance for work that the white girl has. Then the Depression has caused a lot more hardship among the Negroes than it has among the whites. Since the Depression prostitution has increased about 20 per cent. Recently our 12 P.M.-to-8 A.M. shift has picked up an average of a hundred girls a month.*

The captain of one Black Belt police station felt that the Depression not only increased the amount of street-walking in Bronzeville, but also gave the death-blow to organized vice in the area:

"There was at one time a bit of commercialized vice here, but the Depression hit this. The trade came almost altogether from white laborers around the stockyards district. They were mostly foreigners who were not married and came over here looking for women. Now these laborers have little money or aren't working at all. That's what has knocked out commercial prostitution in the district.

"In this community there is not much organized vice. There are a lot of women here who are trying to make a dollar and will take a chance and 'turn a trick.' But for the most part these people are just poor women who are out of a job and can't make it any other way. If they could just get a job scrubbing floors you wouldn't see them trying to be whores very long. They are for the most part just unfortunate women who have to do anything to get something to eat."

A judge of the Morals Court suggested an additional factor—the inability to maintain an expected standard of living:

"The idea has often been advanced lately that the Negroes are hit worse by the Depression, and that they, being in a much less prosperous community, have suffered greatly. There is something to this, even if it doesn't tell the whole story. We have Negro girls come in here who are high school girls. I ask them why they are prostitutes and they tell me that

* Another Morals Court official reported "a difference between prostitution and those who are arrested for prostitution. There are many prostitutes who are never arrested. For example, I don't know any of the keepers of resorts who have been brought into this court in the last six months. On the other hand, some of the people who are arrested for prostitution are not prostitutes. The race question enters in here. There are more accidental arrests for persons who are not prostitutes among the colored than would be true in the case of whites. Poor people often have to live around prostitutes because of cheap rent, and when the officers raid a place they usually bring in everybody in the house. They sometimes charge Negroes like that when they may not be prostitutes. . . . I think that Negro women as a class are dealt with more harshly here in the Court than the whites."

the only work they can get is housework, waitresses, and in hotels. It is true that many of these girls cannot get employment because of their race. The Negro girls who have better education want the better things of life. They are not satisfied to work for these small wages."

Prostitutes themselves, when in an analytical mood, sometimes make this same defense of their behavior. Thus, one young woman in a buffet flat exclaimed: "When I see the word *maid*—why, girl, let me tell you, it just runs through me! I think I'd sooner starve." Another, who lost her white-collar job during the Depression, first took work as a maid and then became a prostitute: "I didn't want to do housework. Here I had been in some kind of office since I was fourteen years old. Now why should I start scrubbing floors at this late date in life? I tried first one thing and then another, and I couldn't make a hit of it, so . . ."

Though economic factors alone cannot account for the high incidence of prostitution, inability to secure satisfying employment has played its part. Since not all poor girls become prostitutes, the reason why a given individual adopts this form of adjustment must be sought elsewhere.

In most cases there is evidence of an early social environment which tended to produce personal disorganization—such as unkind foster-parents, parent-child conflicts, a sense of inadequacy due to very dark or very light skin color, etc. Conspicuous also is the lack of an ordered life-plan, or of a well-integrated set of expectations or goals, or of means for achieving them. Given these conditions, a crisis situation— loss of job, an unwanted child, disillusionment with men, inability to get adequate clothing—will often lead to prostitution. There is certainly much in lower-class life that presents both the preconditions and the crisis. Many experiences that Negroes of other class levels share may also cause an unstable personality here and there to shift into a prostitute pattern.

The housing shortage in Bronzeville, and the intense competition for roomers and boarders, make it very hard for the "respectable" segment of the lower class to sort out the sheep from the goats. During the Depression years even "respectable" lower-class families were inclined to be indulgent toward prostitutes. Often their own relatives and acquaintances, or boarders and lodgers, were involved. The following interview reveals not only the hazards of the prostitute's life, but also the way respectable lower-class families are thrown into intimate contact with her when she is a lodger:

"That girl just lives in jail. She got arrested for soliciting and she got out and came home and went right out of here and started the same mess again. So she was arrested again, and now she's doing time. I think she needs to go to the doctor, too. I thought that was why you wanted to see her: I can't see why girls will lead such lives. She doesn't get anything out of it, especially her type. She has just got to have some no-good man to give her money to. It seems as if the law has her picked out. They run her backward and forward from 31st Street on out south. She won't ever talk about getting a job. She has been in jail now about a week. She may soon be out again.

"I have been in Chicago for fifteen years. I never did do anything like the girls do now. I figure they can find some kind of work. If they don't get such high salary, they can at least protect their bodies from all sort of diseases. I have a little niece, and I tell her if she ever starts doing the things these girls are doing, I will just give her such a beating she will never be able to get over it.

"I worked, and when a girl tries to help herself she is sure to win because someone is always ready to help. I just married about two years ago. I want one or two children, but I wouldn't try to keep no child of mine in this neighborhood. This is a rotten spot. Police don't seem to clear it up."

This woman's reaction is typical of church people who want to "live clean" and of the secular-minded who want to "live respectable" but who cannot escape from the physical framework of lower-class neighborhoods. To understand such people we must move beyond the family unit and examine the "lower-class world."

CHAPTER 21

The World of the Lower Class

WHEN LOWER-CLASS PARENTS WITH A CHURCH ORIENTATION OR MIDDLE-class aspirations for their children make a remark such as "It's hard to keep girls straight over here," they are referring to the general physical and social environment of lower-class neighborhoods.

The physical "world" of Bronzeville's lower class is the world of store-front churches, second-hand clothing stores, taverns, cheap movies, commercial dance halls, dilapidated houses, and overcrowded kitchenettes. Its people are the large masses of the poorly schooled and the economically insecure who cluster in the "worst" areas * or nestle in the interstices of middle-class communities. The lower-class world is complex. Basic to it is a large group of disorganized and broken families, whose style of life differs from that of the other social classes, but who are by no means "criminal" except so far as the children swell the ranks of the delinquents, or the elders occasionally run afoul of the law for minor misdemeanors. Existing side by side with these people is a smaller, more stable group made up of "church folks" and those families (church and non-church) who are trying to "advance themselves." In close contact with both these groups are the denizens of the underworld—the pimps and prostitutes, the thieves and pick-pockets, the dope addicts and reefer smokers, the professional gamblers, cutthroats, and murderers. The lines separating these three basic groups are fluid and shifting, and a given household may incorporate individuals of all three types, since, restricted by low incomes and inadequate housing, the so-called "respectable" lowers find it impossible to seal themselves off from "shady" neighbors among whom they find themselves. The "church folks," despite their verbal protests, must live in close contact with the world of "Sin."

Although the world of the lower class is not rigidly localized in space, its center lies close to the downtown business area (the Loop) and flanks the stockyards (Figure 32). The social scientist reveals the

* As defined on p. 384.

Figure 32

THE WORLD OF THE LOWER CLASS

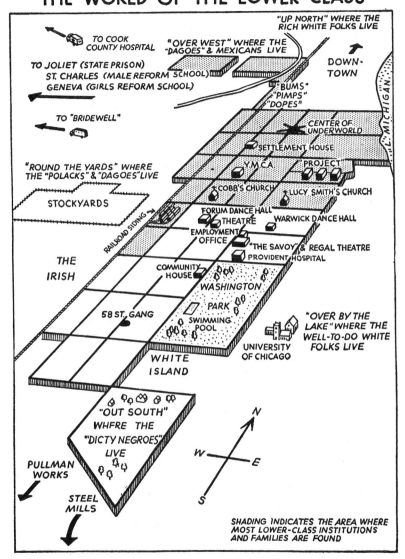

"UP NORTH" WHERE THE RICH WHITE FOLKS LIVE

"OVER WEST" WHERE THE "DAGOES" & MEXICANS LIVE

TO COOK COUNTY HOSPITAL

TO JOLIET (STATE PRISON)
ST. CHARLES (MALE REFORM SCHOOL)
GENEVA (GIRLS REFORM SCHOOL)

DOWN-TOWN

"BUMS"
"PIMPS"
"DOPES"

TO "BRIDEWELL"

L. MICHIGAN

CENTER OF UNDERWORLD

SETTLEMENT HOUSE

"ROUND THE YARDS" WHERE THE "POLACKS" & "DAGOES" LIVE

Y.M.C.A.

PROJECT

STOCKYARDS

COBB'S CHURCH

LUCY SMITH'S CHURCH

RAILROAD SIDING→

FORUM DANCE HALL
THEATRE

WARWICK DANCE HALL

EMPLOYMENT OFFICE

"THE SAVOY" & REGAL THEATRE
PROVIDENT HOSPITAL

THE IRISH

COMMUNITY HOUSE

WASHINGTON

PARK

58 ST. GANG

SWIMMING POOL

"OVER BY THE LAKE" WHERE THE WELL-TO-DO WHITE FOLKS LIVE

UNIVERSITY OF CHICAGO

WHITE ISLAND

"OUT SOUTH" WHERE THE "DICTY NEGROES" LIVE

N

W — E

S

PULLMAN WORKS

STEEL MILLS

SHADING INDICATES THE AREA WHERE MOST LOWER-CLASS INSTITUTIONS AND FAMILIES ARE FOUND

anatomy of the lower-class world by statistics. He can plot on the map those aspects of behavior which the upper and middle classes designate as characteristically lower class. (Figures 33-34.) Such a view indicates that, while lower-class traits are concentrated in the northern and western fringes of Bronzeville, they are by no means confined to them or to the areas immediately contiguous. Rather, they are scattered from one end of the community to the other. There are no restrictive covenants compelling the lower class to inhabit specified slum areas, and the restrictions of the white world and of poverty do not allow the Negro middle class to sort itself out as can the white middle class. There are *more* lower-class people in some areas than in others, but specific buildings (especially kitchenettes) and entire blocks may be found throughout Bronzeville occupied by lower-class household groups. Here and there, too, throughout Bronzeville, one finds taverns and other specific spots of congregation which have a lower-class reputation.

This world of the lower class, which the uppers and the middles sometimes visualize as a "problem" and always as an embarrassment, is, to lower-class people, the normal and familiar context of daily life. Bronzeville is small—eight square miles that Negroes call their own, an island in a big white sea. Outside of it—in the white man's world— are definite focal points of attention that loom large in the everyday conversation of lower-class people, but which are less important to persons of higher status. (Figure 32.) Among these areas are the places where they work—the steel mills and car shops, the factories and foundries, and the vast sprawling stockyards, and the white homes "up north" and "over by the lake" in which they clean and cook, fire furnaces, and take care of children, and which they leave when darkness falls. Toward the western edge of the city are two institutions where unlucky lowers sometimes find a temporary resting place—the Chicago Jail ("the Bridewell") and the Cook County Hospital. Miles away, on the outer rim of the metropolitan region, are Joliet (the state prison), St. Charles (the male reform school), and Geneva (the girls' reform school). To the lower class, the white world is the world of The Law and The Boss—a potentially hostile world, though an admittedly necessary one.

The center of their own world is the northern end of the Black Belt (heavily shaded in Figure 32). It is a world of old and decaying homes, and it contains three-fourths of all lower-class churches, and innumerable taverns and poolrooms and policy stations, where people of slender means and education may freely enjoy themselves. The two most spectacular lower-class churches, known familiarly as "Cobb's Church" and "Lucy Smith's Church," are also in this area. Within it, too, are a few middle-class islands—the YMCA, a couple of settlement houses, and a few exclusive blocks of homes. Dominating it since 1938 is "The Project," where 1,600 families inhabit the federally financed Ida B. Wells Homes.

When lower-class Bronzeville dresses up for an especially good time, however, it streams out of the northern end of the Black Belt bound for the center of the area. Here are the larger commercial dance halls, two very large and well-appointed theaters, and the Savoy—a large auditorium where boxing and wrestling are major attractions. Farthest from the lower-class area is the preserve of the "strivers" and "strainers" and "dicties" (unshaded area in Figure 32). Here and there in these neighborhoods a few lower-class institutions have taken root, and each year an increasingly large number of buildings are cut up into kitchenettes. But, in general, "out south" means away from lower-class neighborhoods.

Between the Negro strainers and strivers and the white middle class to the east is a two-square-mile plot of green—Washington Park. To this park in the summer, Bronzeville's teeming thousands swarm, lounging on the grass, frolicking in the Black Belt's one large swimming pool, fishing and rowing in the lagoon, playing softball, tennis, or baseball. Here, too, is Bronzeville's equivalent of Hyde Park where "jack-leg" preachers joust with curbstone atheists, and Black Zionists break a lance with sundry varieties of "Reds."

The world of the lower class is a public world; contacts are casual and direct with a minimum of formality. It is also a neat and compact world; mobility is quick and easy with dime jitneys always at hand and most places of congregation within walking distance. Conversation and rumor flow continuously—about policy, "politics," sports, and sex. Arguments (often on the "race problem"), while chronically short on fact, are animated and interesting. Emotional satisfactions in such situations are immediate. Physical gratifications are direct. There are status-bearers within this realm, but they are not the civic leaders and intellectuals. They are, rather, the "policy kings"; sportsmen, black and

Figure 33

DISTRIBUTION OF SELECTED CLASS INDICES

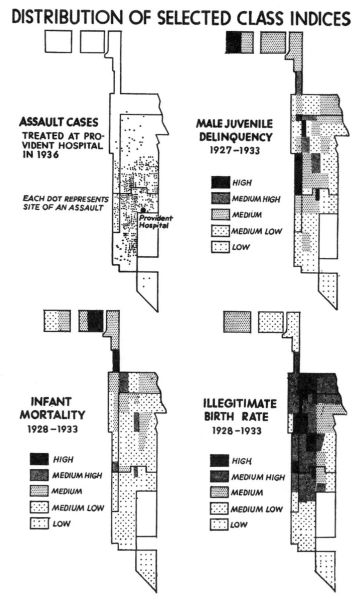

From Cayton-Warner Research maps.

Figure 34

DISTRIBUTION OF SELECTED CLASS INDICES

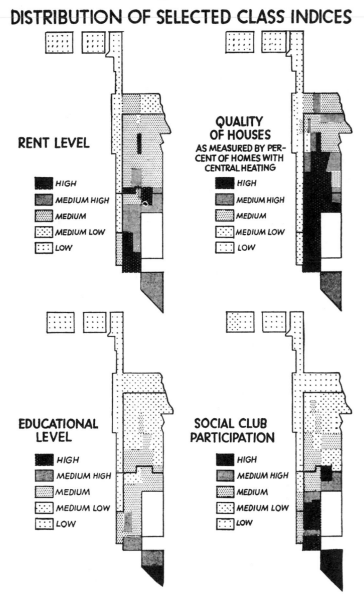

From Cayton-Warner Research maps.

white; the clever preachers and politicians; legendary "tough guys"; and the good fighters and roisterers.

Sitting Out the Depression: When Bronzeville's upper class is expressing its displeasure at lower-class behavior, it usually denounces the pattern of leisure-time activities that consume lower-class time and money. During the Depression years the lower class had plenty of time and little money. "Just sit at home," "listen to the radio," "foolin' aroun'," "playin' cards"—these were the repeated answers to the query, "What do you do most of the time?" "Foolin' aroun'" covered a variety of activities including card-playing and dancing in informal house groups; congregating on street corners, in taverns, barbershops and poolrooms; sex-play in kitchenettes, buffet-flats, and joints; and waiting tensely for the policy drawings three times a day.

Bronzeville's lower class participated in very few formally organized activities (except those of the church), and there is some evidence to indicate that economic factors were very important in limiting formal activities. Although accentuated by the Depression, this absence of formally organized recreational activity has been characteristic of Bronzeville's masses ever since the Great Migration. The following comments indicate, however, that some sections of the lower class felt that they "ought to belong to something":

"I am interested but I don't belong to any clubs. I don't have the money to join clubs. I think clubs are for people who can afford to join them and pay dues. I go to the Parent-Teacher meetings at Douglass School sometimes. I enjoy these meetings."

"I used to belong to a Baptist church, but I don't go there now. I can't go anywhere looking like this."

"I don't attend church as often as I used to. You know I am not fixed like I want to be—haven't the clothes I need."

"At one time I was active in church, but now I can't dress well, so I don't go to church, only at night, because I haven't got anything to wear."

"I'm a lone woman and I have a hard enough time keeping a roof over my head without paying dues here and there."

"I plan to join a whist club in the fall. I don't have the clothes or place to entertain."

"I have been asked to join a lodge, but not since I have been so down-and-out. When people see that you can't spend money and do things, then they don't bother with you so much. I have good clothes but they are not the very latest fashions, but I try to keep clean and look nice all the time."

There is some evidence to suggest that for some lower-class women the church became the one organized Depression activity. Statements such as the following were frequently made:

"I don't have the money to attend these things. All of my life I have enjoyed being around good people. I like to go to meetings, but when you are broke and having all kinds of trouble you are just not in the mood to go to anything unless it is church. There is something about church that lifts me up and that is why I go. I don't belong to any church clubs."

Even church, however, became a problem if there were several persons to be fed and clothed, as in this woman's case:

"I belong to a Baptist church. My husband doesn't belong. I have been trying to get him to make up his mind to join some church, but I haven't been able to get him to join.

"I don't belong to any church clubs. I haven't been to church in a long time. I let my children go to Sunday School. My children need shoes but they [the relief agency] won't give them any shoes for some reason or other, so I just have to do the best I can with the little money I get and buy second-hand shoes so that they can go to school and church. I received shoes the last time for my children year before last. It is hard to get second-hand shoes to fit the children. I tell you it is a shame the way we have to try to get along with the little money we get."

Men, too, sometimes cited their inability to keep up the dues and appearances necessary for club and church membership:

"I don't have any interest in any of those organizations now because I have no money to make the appearance and keep up the dues and what not. My wife is a member of a church and she goes quite often."

"I don't belong to anything. I don't have the money to keep up appearance in any club or organization. You need money for everything, you know."

"I used to belong to the Knights of Pythias, but when times got hard I had to get out."

✦

The Primacy of "Pleasure": During the periods when the lower class has had regular employment—the First World War, the Fat Years, and the present period—it has been more inclined to spend its money for commercial recreation than for voluntary organizations. Even during the Depression years when funds for recreation were very limited, the neighborhood movie-houses, the cheaper taverns, and the pool-rooms continued to do a flourishing business. Bank nights and souvenir nights attracted nickels and dimes with a promise of economic gain as well as fun and excitement. The crowds that frequented Bronzeville's commercial dance halls, its wrestling and boxing matches, and the city's baseball games were evidence that the lower class was able to garner enough from the relief, WPA, and odd jobs to have a good time. The pursuit of "pleasure"—direct and exciting—is a dominating feature of lower-class life.*

Rootless, ever-shifting from crowded kitchenette to crowded kitchenette, the Bronzeville masses necessarily took most of their pleasure outside of the home—though not all of it. An excerpt from the observer's journal gives us a glimpse of leisure-time pursuits within the household of Baby Chile and Mr. Ben during the latter years of the Depression.

"I arrived at six o'clock bringing twelve cents' worth of sausage and a ten-cent loaf of bread. Mr. Ben and Slick were both dozing in their chairs. I mentioned that I was tired and sat down. Ben and I passed a few words about the weather. Slick announced that he wanted to listen to 'Gang Busters' on the radio at nine o'clock. Finally, Baby Chile called us to the kitchen for supper—a platter of neckbones and cabbage, a saucer with five sausage cakes, a plate of six slices of bread, and a punchbowl of stewed prunes (very cold and delicious). Baby Chile placed some corn fritters on the table, remarking, 'This bread ain't got no milk in it. I did put some aig in it, but I had to make it widout any milk.'

"We played whist for about forty minutes after the meal, each side winning one game. Baby Chile was very noisy, but good-natured. She took great pleasure in 'cutting' Slick, crying 'Take him, Jick!' as she slapped down the joker, or 'Cut him, Ben!' She occasionally forgot to 'play back.'

---

* "Pleasure" is used by rural southern Negroes in a number of distinctive ways. "To pleasure yourself" is one way of saying "to have sexual intercourse." "To take my pleasure" means "to have a good time." In general, however, "pleasure" is synonymous with direct, exciting enjoyment whether it be watching a fight, enjoying a lively church service, or sexual gratification.

Mr. Ben seemed irritated at this display of *joie de vivre*. 'Hish up and play!' he'd roar. 'Why you gotta make so much noise? If you can't keep quiet I'm gonna quit.' But he enjoyed himself in his grumbling manner and actually tried to switch a trump on his opponents once or twice.

"During the game someone on the radio mentioned Memphis. Baby Chile said she loved Memphis and Beale Street and the 'quarter-boats.' * When I asked her if she was from Memphis she answered that she was born in Georgia, but was brought up in Tennessee."

Though this household represented extreme poverty and social disorganization, its members attempted to maintain a few family rituals to give both variety and order to their otherwise disordered existence. Everyone always said a Scripture verse before meals. Sometimes, Mr. Ben would playfully give as his verse, "Rise, Peter, slay and eat," or Slick would quote the shortest verse in the Bible—"Jesus wept." Less than a month after the Christmas stabbing, Baby Chile gave a birthday party for her daughter. Clothes were patched but clean; hair was oiled, ironed, and beribboned. Ten adults and five children came as guests. The children ate ice cream and cake, and the adults drank wine and whisky, after which the youngsters were sent into the street to play. The old folks then began a very noisy card game involving one or two heated arguments. Near midnight the children were rounded up and the guests departed. Christmas, Thanksgiving, Easter, birthdays, or a Joe Louis victory usually called for a special party of some sort.

The basic elements of a "party" are the same in most strata of American society: a deck of cards, a supply of diluted and disguised alcohol, and some "hot" music. Among the uppers, a party takes place in an atmosphere of ritualized restraint or exclusive hilarity, with elaborate preparation and setting. Among the lowers, a party tends to be casual and spontaneous. Informal groups of friends and acquaintances are always ready to "have a ball" on a moment's notice—sometimes a game of cards, occasionally a real "boogie-woogie."

Most of the time during the Depression years the masses of the lower class could not afford to pay for admission to commercial dance halls except on special occasions. When they wanted to dance they simply "pitched a boogie-woogie" at home, using the radio or a Vic-

---

* "Quarter-boats" are river boats with "living quarters" for men who work on the levees or as dredgers.

trola for music; or they congregated at a buffet-flat or tavern where the more affluent would feed nickels into a juke-box.*

Lower-class people will *publicly* drink and play cards in places where people of higher status would lose their "reputations"—in the rear of poolrooms, in the backrooms of taverns, in "buffet-flats," and sometimes on street corners and in alleys. They will "dance on the dime" and "grind" around the juke-box in taverns and joints, or "cut a rug" at the larger public dance halls. They will "clown" on a street corner or in public parks. It is this *public* behavior that outrages the sensibilities of Bronzeville's "dicties." "It gives The Race a bad name," they are quick to announce.

These centers of lower-class congregation and festivity often become points of contact between the purveyors of pleasure "on the illegit" and their clientele—casual prostitutes, bootleggers, reefer peddlers, "pimps," and "freaks." Some of these places are merely "fronts" and "blinds" for the organized underworld.

The Underworld: Policy is technically "on the illegit," but it is a protected business. Prostitution, bootlegging, "freak shows," "reefer dens," and "pads," however, must operate as an "underworld." They, too, are protected, but liquor, dope, and women are too "hot" for an open political "fix." Money passes, but in a very guarded fashion, and usually it is small change—to the cop on the beat or to the minor ward politicians. The big-shot politicians play the game safe.†

The primary institutions of the underworld are the tougher taverns, the reefer pads, the gambling dens, the liquor joints, and the call-houses and buffet-flats where professional prostitutes cater to the trade in an organized fashion.

Much of the petty gambling, bootlegging, and prostitution, however,

---

* Among the most popular juke-box numbers in Bronzeville on the eve of the war were the following: "Doggin' Around," "Truckin' Little Woman," "Jitter Bug," "Don't Make Me High," "Lazy Man Blues," "Loving Blues," "Champ Joe Louis," "He Caught That B. and O.," "Franklin D. Roosevelt Jones," "Stop Beatin' Round the Mulberry Bush," "A Tisket a Tasket," "The Mail Man Blues," "It's Your Time Now, Big Bill," "WPA Rag," "Wild Man Blues," and "Brown Gal."

† "On the illegit"—illegal.
  "Reefers"—marijuana cigarettes.
  "Reefer pad"—hangout for smokers of marijuana cigarettes.
  "Freak shows"—pornographic exhibitions by sexual perverts.
  "Pads"—houses of assignation where dope is available.

is carried on in apartment houses, particularly in kitchenette buildings whose owners and superintendents make little or no effort to control the tenants' activities. The denizens of the underworld operate on a much wider scale, and may be found drumming up business in cabarets, more or less respectable dance halls, and—in the case of prostitutes—on the streets.

Bronzeville has always had an "underworld" operating in intimate relationships with the city political machine. It has never had a highly organized gang world, however, dealing in alcohol, dope, robbery, murder, and women. Bronzeville's criminals tend to be lone wolves, and the Black Belt's reputation as a "vice area" today rests primarily on arrests for petty misdemeanors, crimes of passion, and streetwalking. A prominent police official remarked during the Depression:

"Most of the crimes in this district are robbery and vice. These are caused by the conditions. People are out of work and hungry and have to get a dollar the best way they can. I think it's wonderful the way these colored people stand up under these terrible conditions. It's much harder for them to keep work than it is for white people."

Occasionally, however,—on the eve of an election, when reformers become demanding, or when the payoff becomes too irregular—"the heat is turned on." Then (as one "tapper" expressed it), "Johnnie Nab comes through and takes every 'cat' and his brother to California [i.e., to the jail on California Avenue]." *

RELIGION AND THE CHURCH

There are about 500 policy stations in Bronzeville, 80 poolrooms, 200 taverns, and scores of buffet-flats and dives. But there are also about 500 churches, at least 300 of these being located in definitely lower-class neighborhoods. The evening hours of Bronzeville's lower-class areas are noisy with the cacophony of both hymns and blues, gospel songs and "low-down" music. It is obvious that some people in Bronzeville take their pleasure by "making a joyful noise unto the Lord." This complex that we have just described is to them "The World of Sin," and they claim to live "in it, but not of it."

* "Tapper"—tavern habitué.
"Johnnie Nab"—a policeman.
"Cat"—a zoot-suiter; sometimes used to refer to any man.

The church-oriented segment of the lower class is important because it represents an element of stability in a disordered milieu. The church world is a women's world, for less than a third of the lower-class church members are men. These lower-class church women are, on the whole, an influence for stable family relations within their social strata. As they phrase it, they are often "unequally yoked together" with men who are "sinners" and whose "sin" is reflected in a devotion to gambling, extra-marital sex relations, and "big-timing." "Respectable lowers"—male and female—are usually "church people," but they are a decided minority within the large lower class. The Negro "dicties" and the larger white world view lower-class religion with amused condescension. To some lower-class people, however, identification with the church is considered the "better" alternative of a forced option: complete personal disorganization or "serving the Lord." But, as we shall see later, certain secular organizations such as the labor unions and radical political sects have recently begun to pull a segment of the lower class into their orbits.

Slightly over half of Bronzeville's 100,000 lower-class adults *claim* to be church members. The majority of these identify themselves with the Baptist or Methodist denominations, and are therefore nominally committed to opposing gambling, card-playing, dancing, drinking, fornication, and similar derelictions. A small proportion of the lower-class church group claims membership in a score of other denominations, each having its own distinctive doctrinal emphasis. Although about half of the lower class claims church membership, a careful analysis of church records indicates that fewer than a third of the lower-class adults were actually dues-paying members of any church on the eve of the Second World War. An even smaller number organized the greater part of their leisure time and their emotional life around the church and religion.

It has been estimated that of the approximately 30,000 lower-class persons who were actually affiliated with churches, about a sixth belonged to three very large lower-class churches (each having more than 1,500 members); another sixth were distributed among a score of medium-sized lower-class churches (each with 200 to 500 members); about one-third of the total group were worshiping in remodeled stores, garages, theaters, houses, and halls; and another third were members of churches in which higher-status members predomi·

nated. Lower-class neighborhoods were plentifully supplied with small Baptist and Holiness churches. (Figure 35 and Table 26.)

Old Wine in New Bottles: The prevailing attitude of Bronzeville's lower-class church people is expressed in an old spiritual: "Gimme that old-time religion, it's good enough for me." Drawn into the Baptist and Methodist evangelical tradition by white missionaries during and immediately after slavery, Negroes have preserved on a large scale the religious behavior which was prevalent on the American frontier between 1800 and 1890. Since, however, the Negro church has evolved in isolation from the white church, certain distinctive modifications and colorations have grown up which give Negro religious services a flavor all their own.

The fountainhead of the old-time religion is the rural South—the Bible Belt. Urban life puts its stamp on this religion, and while the basic features of the old beliefs and rituals persist in Bronzeville they have been modified by contact with the complexities of a large northern city. "Sin," and the "Devil" too, are wilier adversaries in Chicago than in the less complicated world of the Deep South.

To most of Bronzeville's lower-class church people, "Sin" is a malevolent reality. It was responsible for Adam's fall. It is the cause of all our present woes, individual and collective. In defining "sin" there is much unanimity on the nature of the major sins, and much disagreement about the minor ones. One preacher at a lower-class revival took as his subject, "Look What Sin Has Done. Let's Get Rid of It." He named as the main derelictions adultery, anger, atheism, cheating, "acting stuck-up," covetousness, "being too critical," deceit, dishonesty, disloyalty, gambling, hypocrisy, "backbiting" and "spasmodic speaking to one another," lack of personal cleanliness, fighting in the home, drunkenness, and "sex immorality."

References to lower-class sex and family behavior are prevalent in sermons delivered before lower-class congregations. The following excerpt from a Sunday sermon in one of Bronzeville's largest churches illustrates the usual type of attack upon "sinful" family habits:

"Why, the people have lost all self-respect, and most of our children are brought up in homes where there is strife, anger, and viciousness all the time. Some of you people lie down mad and get up mad. Just cursing

Figure 35

DISTRIBUTION OF CHURCHES BY DESIRABILITY OF NEIGHBORHOOD IN BLACK METROPOLIS

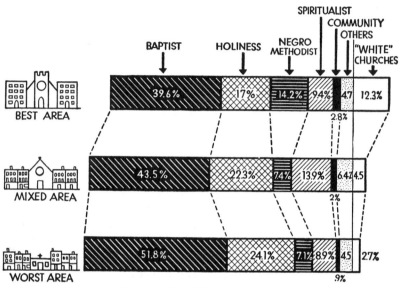

From table in St. Clair Drake, "Churches and Voluntary Associations in the Chicago Negro Community."

TABLE 26

PERCENTAGE DISTRIBUTION OF CHURCHES BY DENOMINATION AND
TYPE OF NEIGHBORHOOD: 1938

Worst Areas		*Mixed Areas*		*Best Areas*	
Baptist..........	51.8	Baptist........	43.5	Baptist..........	39.6
Holiness........	24.1	Holiness........	22.3	Holiness........	17.0
Spiritualist......	8.9	Spiritualist......	13.9	Negro Methodist	14.2
Negro Methodist	7.1	Negro Methodist	7.4	White denomina-	
Miscellaneous....	4.5	Miscellaneous...	6.4	tions..........	12.3
White denomina-		White denomina-		Spiritualist......	9.4
tions........	2.7	tions........	4.5	Miscellaneous....	4.7
Community.....	.9	Community.....	2.0	Community......	2.8
Total........	100.0	Total........	100.0	Total........	100.0

and swearing all the time over the children. I sometimes wonder can't you that live that sort of life find a place for Jesus in your homes. That's where to start a remedy, right in your home life. One thing I want to impress upon you—no couple should ever marry that don't have love and respect for each other."

The tone of such a sermon would imply that the pattern of sex and family behavior described in Chapter 20 as typically lower-class is characteristic of "church people" as well as "sinners." Interviews with a score of preachers in intimate contact with the lower class, as well as observation of families affiliated with lower-class churches, seem to indicate that where *both* heads of a family are "church people" the unit tends to have a pattern similar to that of the middle class. Most of the members of lower-class churches, however, are women married to husbands who are "unchurched" or women who have been deserted or divorced. In the latter case, sexual affairs outside of marriage, while frowned upon, do not ordinarily result in social ostracism so long as they do not involve open scandals or public fights. The influence of the church on lower-class sex and family life seems to be confined to moderating public brawling and to creating a group of women who try to make their children "respectable" and encourage them to assume a middle-class family pattern even though they themselves, due to "weakness of the flesh" or bitter experiences with men, do not maintain stable family relations. Children of such families are often torn between affection for a parent and contempt or disgust for the family behavior pattern. It is probable that juvenile delinquency is closely related to such conflicts. There are, of course, numerous lower-class women whose lives are so completely organized around the church and religion or middle-class ideology that sexual "delinquency" would never occur.

The pattern of lower-class family life thus finds its reflection in one definition which lower-class ministers give of "Sin." Most of them also include diatribes against card-playing and dancing, attendance at movies and baseball games on Sunday, and "putting the 'world' before Christ." A few denounce all forms of athletics.

Lower-class theology is Fundamentalist. The preachers paint vivid pictures of a stern Father "who gave His only begotten Son to save a sin-sick world!" They call upon sinners to seek salvation through the "Four-square Gospel"—confession, repentance, regeneration, and sanctification. They preach justification by faith, declaring that a man is not saved because he is good, but will act good because he's saved. Once saved, a Christian may backslide, but he can be "restored to fellowship" by repentance and prayer. The immediate rewards of salvation—the "fruits of the spirit"—are usually described as joy, peace, and "a clear conscience." The ultimate rewards, however, are reserved for Heaven, the final destination of the "saved." Conversion, baptism, and confirmation are assumed to be the high spots in the Christian's life, and the faithful meet periodically at testimonial meetings and prayer meetings to recount the circumstances of their conversion, to detail their "trials and tribulations," and to "tell their determination" to "press on." Preachers, too, sometimes relate the circumstances of their own conversions, as in the case of one Baptist minister who exhorted his congregation to "inquire about the path and follow it." He told them that "a long time ago, down in Arkansas, I found the path and I've tried to walk in it ever since. I've made mistakes just like anybody else, but I'm trying to keep on the path. God needs clean men!" Allusions to a conversion "back South" are common in testimonials, with some such statement as: "I know some of us found 'it' out down South after praying all night long. I got 'it' in Louisiana and am satisfied that I am saved by the blood of Jesus."

Prodigal Sons and Daughters: Most of Bronzeville's adults and a large proportion of the children have been exposed to the general outlines of this theological scheme and are familiar with the ritual requirements for salvation. Almost half of the adults claim to have been "converted" and immersed as Baptists. A very large proportion of them are "backsliders." Nevertheless, they (and many of the "sinners" too) continue to accept the church's estimate of their status as apostate or unsaved. Bronzeville's lower class seems to carry a heavy load of deeply buried guilt feelings. In Bronzeville's buffet-flats and dives it is not unusual to hear proprietors and patrons alike reminiscing when a religious song is sung on the radio—about their "Christian mothers" or their own religious experiences when young. The very vehemence with which these prodigal children sometimes denounce the preachers and "the church folks" reveals a latent uneasiness.

Bronzeville's lower class generally recognizes an area of the sacred and profane, a dichotomy evidenced by the comment of one tough woman: "My sister goes to the Holiness church. She's good. I went down there to her church once drunk and the usher put me out. *I shouldna done that.*"

But the acids of modernity are at work in Bronzeville as they are everywhere. Skepticism about the truth of the saga of salvation is general. Mistrust of the motives of the professional religionists is widespread. Often hungry and beset by family troubles, discriminated against by white people and more affluent Negroes, Bronzeville's lower class, during the Depression years, entertained serious doubts of either the necessity or the efficacy of religion. They demanded results in the "here and now" rather than in "the sweet by-and-by."

In the country and small towns of the South, the church and the preacher are often influential and powerful. In the city, the average preacher is shorn of his power. Except for one or two influential ministers, Bronzeville's preachers are not in a position to secure jobs, legal favors, and similar gains for their constituencies. The precinct captain or alderman tends to replace the preacher as the key person in time of crisis. It does not take long for a migrant Negro to recognize the wielders of power in the city; to discover who can secure relief for him; who can get him out of jail; or who can find him a job. (One does not even need a preacher for burial or marriage, and Baptist children, at least, do not need to be christened—it's "unscriptural.") Deprived of his power in this fashion, the minister is in a very precarious position indeed, and such criticisms as the following are common among lower-class persons. The first speaker is a church member; the second and third are not.

"There are too many churches in colored neighborhoods anyhow. What we need is something to put people to work."

"It's nice to have religion, and it's nice to go to church. But you've got to look after self first. Most of our people have got their minds too deep on religion and let everything else get away from them. If they'd stop so much religion and do a little more thinking, it would be better for us all. As far as I can see, half of these preachers ain't right. *They* do everything they're big enough to do, and then expect *you* to live holy. I don't believe half of them."

"Religion's all a lot of bunk."

Even those who believe that "God will reward the righteous according to their deeds" are quick to say: "I can be saved if I live right. I don't need to go to church and give no preacher my money," and for the backsliders there is always the old Baptist doctrine to comfort them: "Once in Christ you're never out" (i.e., if you have once been converted and baptized, nothing you do afterwards is really fatal). Despite repeated clerical warning that "you can't count on a death-bed repentance," plenty of Bronzeville's people are willing to take the chance.

Snatching Brands from the Burning: Lower-class preachers have long since despaired of saving the lower class *en masse*. They content themselves, as they phrase it, with "snatching a few brands from the burning." They offer their wares from their pulpits and gratefully accept a convert here and there. For a preacher to appear on the street, Salvation Army style, is a rare event. Most churches have annual revivals, widely advertised but poorly attended except by those already "saved." Dramatic conversion ceremonies, with prolonged praying and singing over the sinners and wild rejoicing over those who "come through," occur in a few churches, but they attract little attention and have none of the compelling fervor of such meetings in the South where many of Bronzeville's people originally "got religion."

The practical problem of recruiting and keeping members calls for numerous concessions to the secular urban world. Instead of demanding a period of praying and seeing visions, pastors of the larger churches merely require a perfunctory statement that the candidate for membership believes Jesus died to save him from his sins, whereupon he is voted into the church. (Among Baptists, the prospective member must subsequently be baptized by immersion.) Older members and most preachers speak with nostalgia of the passing of the "mourners' bench"—that conspicuous spot down in the front of the church where the sinner is supposed to sit and wait for the spirit to strike him.

The Time of the End: Realizing their impotence, lower-class ministers lean heavily upon "prophecy." They thunder away at "Sin," reminding their congregations of the destruction of Sodom and Gomorrah and of Noah's flood. Their choirs sing ominously that "God's gonna move this wicked race, and raise up a nation that will obey." Seizing upon the eschatological tradition in Christianity, they claim insight into God's "plan of the ages." They teach that we are living in the "last dispensation." After the Gospel has been preached throughout the world ("giving everybody a fair chance") "God's gonna close the books." Jesus will return "in clouds of glory," destroy the wicked and set up the millennial kingdom. Men will beat their swords into plowshares and their spears into pruning-hooks, and will study war no more. The "righteous dead" will arise to enjoy the new age, and the unsaved will be consigned to eternal torment.

We are living in "the time of the end." Men have been "growing weaker and wiser." This old world can't last much longer. Even now the Four Horsemen of the Apocalypse are riding. The impending battle of Armageddon is at hand. The persecution of the Jews, pestilences, earthquakes and famines, "wars and rumors of wars," are all signs of the end. Jesus will soon return. The sheep will be separated from the goats. And most important of all, they see the imminent fulfillment of a much-cherished Biblical prophecy: "Princes shall come out of Egypt, and Ethiopia shall stretch forth her hands unto God."

This is the "Gospel" as it is preached in Bronzeville's lower-class churches. Some sects concentrate on this apocalyptic note, while other ministers preach occasional "special sermons" on the Second Coming and weave the myth into their regular sermons. Even when it is not hammered home continuously, this world view colors the thinking of all the faithful and is shared by large numbers of people—in combination with divers other beliefs—who do not attend church. It is a paradoxical theology of despair and hope, mirroring the realities of life in a Black Ghetto.

THE COMMUNION OF THE SAINTS

Bronzeville's lower-class churches are sustained by what the ministers like to call "the faithful few." Probably less than 10,000 people (two-thirds of them women) form the core of Bronzeville's lower-class church life. These are the people who attend Sunday services regularly, who go to prayer meetings and special services, who contribute faithfully to the numerous collections, and spark-plug the rallies and financial drives. They beg and canvass and see that the preachers are housed and fed. Their lives revolve around religion and the church, and their emotional needs seem to be met primarily by active participation in the worship ceremonies.

Prayer meetings and communion services are the more significant

experiences in their common life, and such services are highly charged
with emotion. They involve group singing, individual prayers, and
"testifying." On the occasions when the "true believers" relate their
conversion experiences, they usually couch them in certain traditional
phrases similar to the following:

"I remember the day and the hour when Christ spoke peace to my
soul. He took my feet outa the miry clay and placed them on solid ground.
He put a new song in my mouth."

They also recite their "trials and tribulations," sometimes weeping as
they tell how they've been " 'buked and 'bused and scorned." They
confess, too, that they haven't always been able to "live clean," and
end by "telling their determination":

"I'm still pressing on up the King's Highway and I want you all to
pray for me that I may grow stronger and stronger."

In such services individuals also express themselves in prayer. Lower-
class church people look with scorn upon "book prayers," for praying
is an art, and a person who can lead his fellows to the throne of grace
with originality and eloquence gains high prestige. Praying sometimes
becomes a collective ritual characterized by a sort of weird beauty.
Rhythmic moans from the congregation, interjections of *Amen, Praise
the Lord,* and *Hallelujah* encourage the intercessor, and prayers may
be punctuated with the tapping of feet. Though each person makes
up his own prayer, there is a common stock of striking phrases and
images which are combined and recombined throughout the Negro
lower-class religious world. The following generalized prayer includes
phrases that may be heard in any place where the faithful meet to
pray: *

O Lord, we come this morning knee-bowed and body bent before thy
throne of grace. We come this morning, Lord, like empty pitchers before
a full fountain, realizing that many who are better by nature than we are

---

* Prayers of this type are often heard in churches which are not stratified as
lower-class. When dealing with church rituals "lower-class" in Bronzeville almost
becomes synonymous with "old-fashioned" or "southern" and in modern southern communities, or a generation ago everywhere, such prayers were common in
colored Baptist or Methodist churches of *all* status levels. Therefore, an elderly
person or an "old-fashioned" person in a Bronzeville middle-class congregation
may pray in a manner which is *typical* of Chicago's lower-class congregations. A
congregation cannot be stratified by any single item such as type of prayers or
sermons. It is the total configuration of the ceremonies that counts.

by practice have passed into the great beyond, and yet you have allowed us, your humble servants, to plod along just a few days longer here in this waste-howling wilderness. We thank thee, Lord, that when we 'woke this morning, our bed was not a cooling board, and our sheet was not a winding shroud.* We are not gathered here for form or fashion or for an outside show unto the world, but we come in our humble way to serve thee. We bring no merit of our own, and are nothing but filthy rags in thy sight. We thank thee, Lord, that we are clothed in our right mind and are not racked upon a bed of pain. Bless the sick and the afflicted and those who are absent through no fault of their own. And when I've done prayed my last prayer and done sung my last song; when I'm done climbing the rough side of the mountain; when I come down to tread the steep and prickly banks of Jordan, meet me with thy rod and staff and bear me safely over to the other side. All these things we ask in Jesus' name, world without end, *Amen.*

Under the stress of emotion, worshipers may "get happy" (in the vernacular, they "shout"), flailing their arms about, crying, running up and down the aisles, yelling *Amen* and *Hallelujah!* In fact, many churches have special attendants, dressed in white uniforms, to fan and calm the shouters. Shouting may be set off by a prayer or testimony, by singing or a sermon. Attitudes toward shouting are ambivalent, however, even among lower-class church people, and it is not unusual to hear a preacher, when stressing morality or money-raising, make some such remark as "You don't need to think you're going to Heaven by shoutin' an' knockin' over benches. Some of the biggest hypocrites in the world kin make more noise than anybody else." One minister of a lower-class congregation discussed shouting with an observer, inserting a characteristic defense of the practice:

"Some preachers think they haven't done a thing unless they get their congregation to shouting. I have gone to church with the intention of getting a shout and didn't get a one. On the other hand, I may prepare a sermon and say, 'I know there will be no shouting,' and I will get plenty of shouts. I know of a big preacher who had a peculiar sort of crying voice. He didn't realize it, but the minute he uttered a few words, only reading the Scripture, people would begin shouting. I don't believe people should be so critical. We should not try to delve too deeply into people's souls."

* A member of one small store-front church utilized some of these phrases in a variant form, expressing satisfaction that "when God woke me up this morning my bed was not my cooling board, my four walls were not the grave walls, and my cover was not my winding sheet."

The high rate of attendance at lower-class church services is partly due to the fact that a rousing service is an exciting show. The curious and skeptical enjoy the spectacle as much as the participants and the non-shouting church members. Younger people, particularly, often crowd the back benches to giggle and nudge each other surreptitiously. A few—very few—of those who come to scoff remain to pray.

A JOYFUL NOISE UNTO THE LORD

Participation in "the communion of saints" is restricted to those who "feel the spirit." These tend to be older women, though younger women and a few older men pray and shout. A regular preaching service, however, has a much wider appeal and seems to be enjoyed by many persons whose lives are by no means oriented around religious ecstasy. A lower-class Sunday morning service is seldom less than an hour in length and the singing, prayers, Scripture lesson, sermon, and numerous collections and announcements may stretch out to two and three hours. But large numbers of people enjoy it.

Sometimes spirited and lilting, often dragging and solemn, but always loud and vigorous, singing is an indispensable part of any Black Belt church service. Spirituals are seldom used for congregational singing in Bronzeville churches (gospel hymns and traditional Protestant hymns are more popular), but choirs, gospel choruses and quartets keep the folk music alive, often improvising and dramatizing as they sing. During the last five years gospel hymns, some written by Bronzeville's own song-writers, have been in vogue. They are sung with syncopated or blues effect. The names of these gospel hymns reflect traditional Christian theology with special trimmings: "Precious Lord, Take My Hand," "I Can Feel the Fire Burning," "Just a Little Talk With Jesus Sets It Right," "He's a Rock," "He's the Lily of the Valley." *

* Bronzeville's most popular gospel hymn was written during the Depression by a local Baptist choir-leader, a "converted" writer of popular songs. It has become known within the last two years in evangelical white church circles throughout the country:

> Precious Lord, take my hand,
> Lead me on, let me stand;
> I am tired, I am weak, I am worn;
> Through the night, through the storm,
> Take my hand, lead me on,
> Precious Lord, take my hand, lead me on.

The master of ceremonies and major performer in the lower-class church is the preacher. Only the "saved" pray and shout, but even the "sinners" enjoy a good preacher. In "breaking the bread of life" (a phrase referring to preaching), an uneducated minister has a distinct advantage over an educated preacher, for the typical lower-class sermon is an "unprepared message." The minister takes a subject and a text, neither of which necessarily bears any relation to the other or to the sermon that follows. While a sermon usually contains some moral advice and pious exhortation, it is primarily a vivid, pictorial, and imaginative recounting of Biblical lore. A sermon may have a modern application to stimulate "cheerful giving," to subordinate "educated fools," or to "warn a wicked world," but the important thing is to show familiarity with Bible stories and to tell them in an interesting fashion and in such a way as to stimulate shouting or admiring comments. A good preacher is a good raconteur of religious tales. His highly embroidered individual variations are accepted as pleasing modifications of an original story with which both preacher and audience are familiar. A good preacher must "know The Book." Among the most popular Bible stories are "The Prodigal Son," "The Three Hebrew Children in the Fiery Furnace," and "The Parable of the Virgins," together with the exploits of Moses, Samson, David, Esther, Solomon, and other Jewish heroes. A medley of parallels to the South, the Negro, Chicago life, and current events is often mixed in.

A typical performance is Rev. Jonah Goodfriend's revival sermon on "He is Able." The Reverend, dark, and with a voice to fit his 250-pound frame, was preaching in a small Baptist church from the text, "Our God whom we serve is able to deliver us." After announcing his subject he closed his Bible and began to preach to his hearers as follows: "You have faith in God, you know He won't let you down! . . . We need courage to run on! The Race needs courage to run on!" He ran across the rostrum, crying with rising inflection, "To run on, run on, run on!" He then began to discuss "the idols men serve"—women, whisky bottles, policy slips, declaring that "men are mixed up about which God to serve. They got so many idols." He dropped to his knees, pantomiming obeisance to an imaginary idol while the audience responded with shouts of *"Yes"* and *"It's the truth!"* He then lauded the three Hebrew captives who refused to bow before Nebuchadnezzar's idol: "The wicked king chunked 'em in a fiery furnace, heated seven times hotter than it ought to be. But they didn't care. They knew that my God was able to deliver His children." Coming down from the rostrum, he selected three young men in the congregation to represent the Hebrew children, and led them to the pulpit, where he placed them in a corner representing the furnace. He began to mimic the wicked king, saying, "I guess now you'll bow, won't you? When those flames begin to eat you, you'll bow." The minister then roared, "But my God-a-mighty, the king jumped back, crying, 'I put three men in there—now I see four.' My Jesus was in that furnace walking with those Hebrew children."

"Fear not, I am with thee, be not dismayed," he yelled triumphantly, while the audience shouted; "flames can't hurt you. Fire can't singe you. Bad names can't break you. Lo, I am your God. I will deliver you from *this* fiery furnace and *every* fiery furnace." Rev. Goodfriend was sweating from his exertion when he finished and the church was in an uproar. He then began to sing "Just a Little Talk With Jesus Sets It Right." A woman cried out, "That boy's really preaching." The church responded with a loud *Amen.* Such preaching will draw crowds, whether the performer be the Rev. Jonah Goodfriend or Billy Sunday.

Lower-class preachers also like to dwell upon the glories of Heaven. (The terrors of Hell are rarely depicted.) They place emphasis upon the great family reunions destined to take place "on the other side" and upon the opportunities for meeting famous Biblical characters. One minister detailed his prospective celestial activities very precisely:

"I want to walk down Hallelujah Avenue . . . go down and meet ol' Abraham, talk with ol' Isaac, and see ol' Jacob. I want to go down by the great white throne an' see my Jesus. I want to feel the nail-prints in his hands and feet an' put my han' in the spear hole in his side. Hallelujah! I wanta ask ol' Daniel 'bout how God stopped the lion's mouth, an' them Hebrew children how they felt in the fiery furnace. I'm gonna have a good time in Heaven!"

The sermon frequently becomes a recital of the Christian saga from the Creation to the ultimate triumph over death and hell and the establishment of the millennial kingdom on earth. (This is called "preachin' from Genesis to Revelation.")

Since the service often takes the form of a collective ritual, even the pictorial content in a sermon is unnecessary. It is possible to find preachers who merely repeat phrases over and over with a rising and falling inflection of the voice, or who take one word such as "Oh-h-h-h" and sing it as a chant, with the congregation shouting all the while. Certain key words and phrases may have the same effect. A preacher may "get a shout" by simply piling up familiar words in the following fashion:

"My God is a great God. He's a shelter in a time of storm. He's more than a mother in a time of need, the Prince of Glory, the everlasting rock; the Great Shekinah, the Lily of the Valley, the Rose of Sharon, the Bright and Morning Star. My God is a physician who never lost a case, a general who never lost a battle, the Great Jehovah's son, the seed of David and the rod of Jesse. Hear ye him!"

When a preacher is too cold, a "Come on up" or a "Preach it" from a member may remind him that he is losing his stride.

A good sermon is more, however, than "rousements." It contains pithy humor, scathing denunciations, ribaldry, and satire. A semi-humorous shaft is sometimes hurled at church members who are suspected of habits associated with the world of sin, as in the case of one preacher who denounced the men to the great satisfaction of the women:

"You lazy, kidney-kneed men are too lazy to work. You have these poor women out in some white person's kitchen or laundry, and you go out for your meals, and then stand around the corners the rest of the day being sissies."

When such oratorical display is accompanied by gestures and "shouting," it is particularly effective in evoking laughter to break the tension, or a reaction of awe and respect for the preacher's eloquence. (Persons will turn to each other and say, "He's preachin', ain't he?" or "That boy is tellin' 'em.") Eloquence is as highly praised as ability to shout a congregation, mimicking is particularly enjoyed, and a minister who can imitate "stuck-ups" and "sinners" voices both the class antagonism and the religious enthusiasm of his congregation.

Even "lifting the collection" is usually done with a high degree of showmanship. The traditional method of raising money involves "going down to the table" for the main collection and passing a basket for a "penny collection" to be used for "poor saints" or missionary work. The pastor usually tries to dissolve antagonism by joking;

"Now, here's where we can all do our part; here's where we can *all* serve God. Get your hands down in your pocket," or "I'm a preacher an' you know what *I* want," or "I may not be able to preach, but there's *one* thing I sure can do!" Spirited music is used while the members march to the front. The collection is then "blessed" and dedicated to the "service of God." Occasionally, a pastor will ostentatiously prime the pump (or have some official do so) by laying down a bill.

Where the basket method is used for the main collection, other devices must be utilized. In one large church, the pastor has the church to rise in sections and stand while the ushers wait on the congregation section by section. A technique that is growing in favor in some churches is to have each person in the audience hold a dime high in the air while the preacher "blesses" all who will give, threatening those who do not by implication and sometimes by direct statement. The members are then asked to hold the coin up in the air until the usher comes for it.

When the size of the collection is insufficient (a definite goal is usually set by the church officials who are raising the money) there is much cajoling and coaxing: "We need one more dime. Who's goin' to make this collection five dollars even? Who's gonna give Brother Brown that penny he needs?"

"After-collections" are frequently taken for a special purpose, and the church-goer knows that in most churches he will be expected to contribute to at least three collections during a single service.

The following statements designed to clear the air for raising money were all noted in lower-class churches:

"You pay your doctor bill, your grocer, and your bootlegger, and I'm giving you something far more valuable than these, and you're going to pay *me*." (Said jokingly.)

"You got 'something' for me? I'll come get it." (Said suggestively as a form of double-talk.)

"Look, man—get that money from that lady before she changes her mind." (Said jokingly.)

"Some of you people sit around here and say, 'It ain't none of my duty. Now it's your duty *and my* duty to get that $926." (To pay on mortgage.)

"Let us kinda loosen up. You know when you talk to Baptist folk about money they sorta draw up. The Methodists grumble about money, but they meet their obligations." (With appropriate gestures.)

TIES THAT BIND

The primary ceremonial in all churches is the regular weekly Sabbath service. All of Bronzeville's churches have such services, most of them presenting both morning and evening worship. A weekday prayer meeting, too, is a part of the regular program, as well as a Sunday School. On these fundamental core-services, each individual church elaborates a more or less complex group of other ceremonies. Monthly communions are the most frequent special occasions, and Easter, Thanksgiving, and Christmas services are also important parts of the yearly program. In addition to these Christian red-letter days, such events are celebrated as Mother's Day and Children's Day. Baptisms, anniversaries, installations, youth nights, and choir nights break the routine. The complexity of lower-class church programs varies with the size of the church, but something is always afoot in even the smallest.

Interchurch visiting is continuous, cutting across denominational lines. When the pastor goes to preach at another church his choir and congregation usually accompany him. Quartets and quintets with colorful names such as The Four Heavenly Trumpets, Righteous Four, Barons of Harmony, Overtone Five, Gospel Voices, and Jubilee Boys, travel from church to church and even city to city giving concerts. Junior choirs compete lustily with senior choirs. Popular soloists receive wide acclaim. Unknown to the upper-class and middle-class world, these lower-class performers have a wide and appreciative audience and occasionally break through to the radio and receive national attention.

Churches depend on many small contributions rather than on a few large ones. In addition to current expenses there are often mortgages to be amortized, special assessments to be raised for state and national bodies, and sometimes furniture and organs to be paid for. All this outlay calls for occasional "special efforts" in the form of rallies and drives. Competitive money-raising takes the form of elaborately organized campaigns with prizes bestowed upon the best workers. There are Queen's Rallies in which the winner is crowned; Election Rallies, where "Democrats" vie with "Republicans"; or a church may be divided into the Twelve Tribes of Israel or into States, with honors accorded to the group which raises the most money. Plays, concerts, suppers, teas, and even fashion shows are used to swell the coffers.

For those who participate, the lower-class church provides a core of meaningful activity, a stable point of orientation, amid the complexities of the urban world. In the predominantly lower-class West Side area, a careful study revealed that during the Depression a very large proportion of both adults and children took no part in any sort of organized recreation. Of the people who did express their preference in the matter of leisure-time pursuits, however, over half said that church work occupied all of their spare time.

There are few financial rewards for being a faithful church worker, but the prestige rewards are great. Precisely because the church provides an opportunity for a display of talent and initiative, it has a strong appeal to people of limited means and education. One lower-class minister, well aware of this function of the church in providing leadership positions, revealed his plans for exploiting the desire to "show off":

"One thing we plan to do is to get out a weekly reminder,* and we will mention all the good work done by all the good people. We know that this will stir the people who don't work so hard as others to do more, because we feel that our people are jealous of one another and will work hard to keep others from getting ahead of them."

Another pastor stated that:

"In a little church there is something for everybody to do. Every man in the church, as well as every woman, can have an office. You know people like to be called on so they can do things."

Laymen serve as delegates to associations and conventions, as members of trustee boards and deacon boards, and as officials in auxiliaries. In lower-class churches, no training is required for holding such positions, but persons with some ability as speakers, singers, and keepers of minutes are likely to become leaders. Training in leadership begins early, and it is not unusual in store-front churches to observe very small children reading the reports from their Sunday School classes while the older people look on with approval and the superintendent

---

* About a third of all churches have mimeographed or printed church newspapers.

or pastor gives them loud verbal encouragement. A child may learn early that he can secure approval by becoming a church leader. If he drops out of school before adolescence and remains oriented toward the church, he may end up as a "jack-leg" preacher, a Sunday School superintendent, or some similar functionary.

During the Lean Years even the inexpensive gratifications of the church were sometimes beyond the range of adults. "I belong to the Baptist Church. I'm not an officer. I useta belong to the Pastor's Aid Club, but I got unfinancial and got out." (Dues were ten cents a week.) Such comments were general throughout Bronzeville during the Depression. The comment of one church member suggests that church membership was sometimes a substitute for club membership, and also reveals the inability of the church alone to satisfy the emotional and recreational aspirations of the younger generation:

"I don't belong to any clubs, but I am a member of the Pentecostal Church. I stay home most of the time. It takes money to stay in clubs, and I am not able to make the proper appearance as far as clothes are concerned. My daughter is a member of some club—I don't know the name of it. She worries quite a bit when she can't get the things she wants most of the time. Young people worry about things more than we old people do. I don't worry because I have learned to take things the way they come."

SHEPHERDS OF THE SHEEP

The dominating figure in the lower-class religious world is the preacher, and most lower-class churches have not only a pastor but also a bevy of "jack-leg" preachers or "chair-backers," who sit on the platform at regular services, and visit other churches seeking a chance to preach. Most of them are ambitious to get a church of their own some day. One of the most persistent criticisms of churches on all class levels is directed at the splits that frequently occur, led by ambitious preachers without churches.

With over 700 preachers competing for 500 churches, the struggle is always keen. During the Depression it was intense, with ambitious individuals trying to escape from the WPA or the relief rolls by getting a church; with older preachers under attack by the younger ones; and with pastors who had prestige using it to subordinate new-

comers to the professional ranks. Such competition, while most intense in the Baptist Church, exists in all lower-class churches.

Most lower-class churches require no formal training for pastors,
and the alleged authenticity of the "call" is deemed more important
than any type of preparation. The gifts required for ministering to a
lower-class congregation are simple: a good voice, the ability to relate
the sacred myths vividly, and a certain amount of conviviality and
savoir faire. Illiteracy, while a handicap, can easily be compensated
by these gifts. The charge of a larger lower-class church, however,
requires some business and executive ability. The prestige gains of
preaching are immediate. The financial gains are usually small, but
the perquisites are not to be scorned, for churches lavish gifts of
food, money, and clothing on their preachers.

The prevalence of "jack-legs" probably reinforces the frequent charge
that preachers are "racketeers," and their churches, "rackets." The
following table indicates the reactions of 325 people who were asked
to give their opinion of "jack-leg" preachers:

TABLE 27

ATTITUDES EXPRESSED TOWARD "JACK-LEG" PREACHERS, BY STATUS OF INFORMANTS
(IN PERCENTAGES): 1938

	Like	Indifferent	Dislike	Total
High-status.........	3.0	67.0	30.0	100.0
Low-status..........	24.0	55.0	21.0	100.0
Store-front members..	46.0	38.0	16.0	100.0

(Such ministers were least popular with higher-status persons,
though most of the informants held no strong opinions. In another
sample of 77 persons, ages 25 to 35, of high school level, nearly
two-thirds expressed a dislike of "jack-legs.")

A few store-front ministers get their major income from property
or by their labor. Their chief gains from the church are prestige gains.
Some are proud of the fact that they earn their own living and take
no salaries from their churches; but these are in the minority.

Some ministers organize their own store-fronts and then try to
round up a congregation. One Baptist minister bought an apartment
building with his savings garnered from work in the stockyards,

rented out the upstairs, and turned the downstairs into a church. He erected a loud speaker on the outside, and then sent his wife to canvass the neighborhood for members. In 1938 he complained to an interviewer that he was having a hard time maintaining his membership. His theory was that it took three things to run a church: "grit, grace, and greenbacks," and defended the small church as follows: "All we want is the people to get their souls saved. It would be better to have a few members than a lot of members and all of them goin' to Hell."

A successful jack-leg minister can either build up a store-front or house church into a larger congregation, or else compete for the pastorate of a larger established church. The pastors of the larger lower-class congregations, however, are men who have had some formal theological training, and are sometimes apologetic about the tactics they must use to "hold the masses." They occasionally launch attacks upon the more unsophisticated "jack-legs," as in the case of one prominent minister who actually denounced the general run of lower-class ministers with withering sarcasm during a Baptist conference:

"Brothers, the day is past for untrained preachers. You can't hop around, whoop and holler and spit-at-a-bubble these days. You have to deliver the goods. Some of these preachers are ordained for a mere five-dollar bill. Some of you deacons get notions you ought to preach, so you go to your pastors and pay a few dollars and you are ordained. I remember an incident in Philadelphia. A huckster used to sell vegetables; he used to go down the alley shouting his wares. And one day his wife said to him, 'You sound just like a preacher.' He got the idea, and decided if he sounded that good to his wife he could preach; so he started a church."

Ambitious Baptist preachers will think twice, however, before alienating the "jack-legs," for the votes of small congregations count at denominational conventions when officers are being elected. A man may easily kill his influence if he gets too far out of line, and he can never hope to be the president of the state or national convention if he can't get the support of little preachers.

A Male Monopoly: Most of the lower-class ministers are men, for neither the Baptists nor the Methodists will ordain women preachers. One rather unorthodox Baptist minister was accused of encouraging women to preach, and was forced to explain his action at a district convention. He tried to mollify his fellow preachers without alienating the women in the audience: "I know somebody said I had the women down at my church preaching. If doing their Christian duty and talking about Christ is preaching, then I hope every woman in my church starts soon. But there is enough work for the women to do without them swinging around up here [i.e., in the pulpit]. You can do all of your preaching right down there [on the floor], but not up here."

The preachers jealously guard the pulpit against female infiltration, but they must depend upon women for the bulk of their regular attendance, financial support, and general church work. The preacher just quoted further rebuked his colleagues by saying: "We preachers think we have a monopoly on who can talk about Jesus. We play on the women's sentiment, while the men sit back and do nothing. I think the pulpits today are just full of lazy preachers who went off on a tangent, thinking they were called to preach when they weren't."

All churches do, however, provide opportunity for women to fill many types of positions. Spiritualist churches have female healers, mediums, and choir members; all lower-class churches (and indeed most churches of all classes) have deaconesses, stewardesses, mothers, and heads of missionary societies and clubs. The ban on women pastors in the regular churches has increased the popularity of the Pentecostal, Holiness, and Spiritualist churches where ambitious women may rise to the top. The general run of church women do not challenge or resent male dominance in the pulpit. They accept their place in a church pattern where the shepherds of the sheep are men.

WHEREVER TWO OR THREE ARE GATHERED

Of Bronzeville's nearly 500 religious congregations, only one in five worships in a regular church edifice. (Table 28.) The remainder praise the Lord in vacant stores and in houses, abandoned theaters, remodeled garages, and halls. These small churches tend to be concentrated on run-down, low-rent, business streets and in generally undesirable residential areas. (See Figure 36.) One street alone had 90 to a three-mile stretch, or 1.9 to a block. Their members tend to be drawn from areas relatively close to the church. On the whole, they show visible evidence of low social status—illiterate scrawls for bulletin boards, tasteless ornamentation, untrained ministers, a low-

TABLE 28

PERCENTAGE DISTRIBUTION OF BRONZEVILLE'S CHURCHES BY TYPE OF BUILDING
AND DENOMINATIONAL GROUP: 1938

Denominational Group	Total		Edifices	Store-Front	Other
	No.	Per Cent			
"White" Denominations	27	100.0	81.5	....	18.5
Negro Methodist.......	42	100.0	52.3	19.0	28.7
Community............	10	100.0	30.0	30.0	40.0
Baptist...............	215	100.0	22.8	49.7	27.5
Holiness..............	107	100.0	8.4	66.4	25.2
Miscellaneous.........	23	100.0	4.4	52.2	43.4
Spiritualist............	51	100.0	2.0	50.1	47.9
Total...............	475	100.0	22.5	47.6	29.9

income membership, "shouting" worshipers. The members have often drifted away from larger churches.

The ten or twelve thousand persons who have abandoned the larger churches cite arguments at length to justify the existence of store-front and house churches. The following reports are typical:

"I got religion in 1929. I was baptized at the Bright Star Baptist Church. I worked with the Pastor's Aid Club for three years, then I couldn't keep up with this group because the times got tough with us and I did not have the clothes like I wanted and all the people that go to that church have good clothes. So I dropped my membership with Bright Star and joined this church. This church had about fifty members when I joined. The reason that I joined a small church was because the people in this church don't pay so much attention to how you are dressed. All they want is that you be a Christian and attend church regularly. We have worked hard to build our church and we have done a fairly good job of recruiting and we have about one hundred members now that attend."

"You have to go to one of the large churches early on Sunday morning to get a seat, you have to be dressed in style or you feel out of place, and there is not as much friendship in a large church as in one of these store-fronts. In a big church the preacher don't know you unless you make big donations or you are an officer of some kind. With my church it is different. We are more like churches in the South—everybody is recognized."

Closely associated with this type of defense is the argument that large churches do not give the poorer and less well-educated members a chance to express themselves. An elderly woman, the mother of several children, explained the matter thus:

"I will say that some small churches give you more chance than a large one. Now our little boy is going to Sunday School at Mount Cyrene. He didn't seem to do anything or learn very much. So we started him at a small church. He is doing fine now, and I think it's because they can give more attention to each child."

Most frequent of all the criticisms, however, are those charging that the larger churches are "full of graft" (an interesting charge in view of the fact that many people accuse the store-front preachers of being somewhat less than disinterested). One sympathetic observer, not a store-front member, summed the matter up by observing: "Any church puts you out if you don't pay your dues. There is a bit of graft in all of them, but the bigger the church, the more the graft."

When store-front members are not charging larger churches with actual "graft," they are accusing them of "draining the pocketbook." High overhead expenses came in for condemnation by one man who said: "A lot of people make fun of store-front churches because they belong to some large church that owes fifty or sixty thousand for their church they bought from the Jews, for which they'll be paying the next hundred years. They are ignorant. All they want is to say 'I belong to so-and-so's church.'"

The informality of the ritual in these small churches is more attractive to some than the more formalized services of the larger churches. One woman who has been in Chicago for 17 years joined the largest church in the city when she came, but "couldn't understand the pastor and the words he used." She insists, too, that "I couldn't sing their way. The songs was proud-like. At my little church I enjoy the services." This antagonism toward a "citified ritual" also involves a criticism of the increasing secularization of the church worship service. Thus one man complains:

"The alderman or ward committeeman or whoever it may be will give the minister one or two hundred dollars and he will forget the sermon and preach politics, telling the members to vote for a certain man. Usually

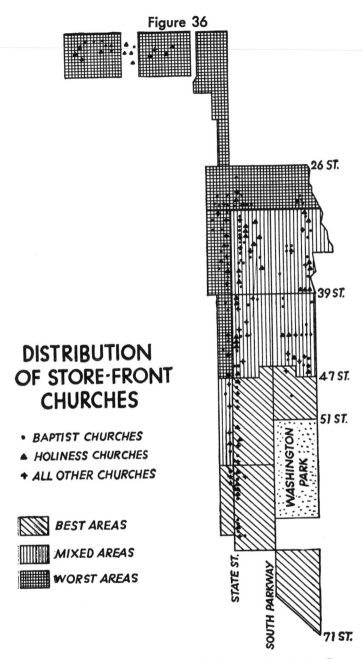

Figure 36

DISTRIBUTION
OF STORE·FRONT
CHURCHES

- • BAPTIST CHURCHES
- ▲ HOLINESS CHURCHES
- ✚ ALL OTHER CHURCHES

BEST AREAS
MIXED AREAS
WORST AREAS

26 ST.
39 ST.
47 ST.
51 ST.
71 ST.

WASHINGTON PARK

STATE ST.
SOUTH PARKWAY

From St. Clair Drake, "Churches and Voluntary Associations."

the candidate is no good. Understand me; we need churches, but they should be used as such."

Another member of a small church explains that he "visited around" when he first came to Chicago and then decided to join a small church. Of larger churches he said:

"They ain't no better than my little church. As a matter of fact, they ain't as good. They talk politics and prize fights and how much the church needs, instead of preaching."

If we examine the store-front pattern carefully, however, it seems evident that dissatisfaction with ritual alone would not account for their persistence, for there are at least three large churches with as many members as all store-fronts combined, which offer a rousing lower-class worship service. Probably the really important factor is the desire to belong to a small face-to-face group, to "know everybody."

Important, too, in the proliferation of store-fronts is the tendency toward splitting when would-be leaders in larger churches become disgruntled and strike out for themselves. Such "jack-legs" were defended in a homely manner by a WPA employee:

"Well, I tell you how I think about them. You've seen men working on a project. Well, one does this and one does that. Now one man may be holding a flag, and another may be down in the ditch digging. Well, the man who holds the flag is just as important to the superintendent as the man digging down in the ditch. His job may not look big, but it's just as important as any other."

DEFENDERS OF THE FAITH

About a quarter of Bronzeville's store-fronts and house churches are occupied by a group claiming to represent "the defenders of the faith as it was delivered to the saints." Most of these are missions established by a half-dozen large "mother churches" affiliated with one or another Holiness or Pentecostal group. Derided as "sancts" and "Holy Rollers," some six or seven thousand "Saints" represent the extreme reaction against "worldliness." Their theme song expresses their aspiration:

> "Singing Holy unto the Lord—
> And if I could, I surely would
> Stand on the Rock where Jesus stood."

Baptist and Methodist ministers may trim their theological sails and pep up their services to compete with "the world of sin," but for the "saints" and "precious ones" (as they call themselves) there must be no compromise. They profess to believe that it is not only possible, but obligatory, for Christians to "live free from all sin," "set apart," "sanctified." To do this requires a "second blessing," the "Gift of the Holy Spirit," for which one must "tarry" (i.e., wait). Once received, this "second work of grace" enables a person to live "holy." Holiness sermons constantly emphasize the necessity for living a "clean" life, devoid of tobacco, liquor, adultery, cursing and swearing, fighting.*

Thus, one preacher (also a WPA foreman) began with a tirade against the young people's recreational pattern: "All they think about is doing some kind of dance where they draw up like a cold cricket. The people are going astray. The world has so many attractions. They have the Grand Terrace, the Savoy, and all kinds of entertainment. People are even sending their children to dance schools to learn how to dance and kick up their heels. They should be teaching them how to sit down and keep quiet." The young men, he was certain, "all try to be pimps and meddle every girl or woman that passes." As to the young women, they "beat the men drinking, smoking and cursing. I don't know what the next generation will be if these are the mothers and fathers."

The audience shouted its approval when he assailed the "strainers" and "strivers":

"Some of our people just can't stand prosperity. If a lot of us would get fifty dollars tomorrow it would turn our heads. We get dignified too quick. Ninety per cent of the people in Chicago are from the South. When they get to Chicago they can't live anywhere on the other side of State Street [i.e., in a lower-class area]. When they were in the South they bathed in tin tubs and didn't have electric lights. Now they have to live on South Parkway, Drexel, or Oakwood Boulevard. We get puffed up too quick. We must remember that pride comes before destruction and a haughty spirit before a fall."

* One Holiness elder referred an observer to the first chapter of Romans when pressed for a list of "sins." This Biblical catalogue cites "carnal-mindedness," homosexuality, fornication, covetousness, maliciousness, murder, debate, deceit, envy, backbiting, spitefulness, disobedience to parents, boasting, pride, and idolatry. When the elders apply this list as a yardstick of contemporary behavior they emerge with a general attack upon Bronzeville and the white world surrounding it.

Racial sentiments, too, found their way into his attack on "Sin":

"We should remember our relatives and friends in the South. In the South people are working for seventy-five cents a day. White people are making twice as much for the same kind of work. We aren't classed as a race of people, but as animals. That's what makes me so mad with these northern Negroes. A white man will come in our neighborhood and get our women. Colored fellows will get women for white men for a dime. They consider themselves too slick to work. I would rather work my finger to the bone than lead that kind of life. One day I heard a colored fellow ask a white man for the quarter that he owed him. The white fellow said, 'I don't owe you a quarter.' The colored fellow said, 'You know you ran out on me when I got that woman for you.' "

His race pride had almost made him forget his Holiness for the moment:

"He made me so mad. I would have beat him up if I hadn't been saved. He should have somebody to hit him from four ways so he could have thought God knocked him out."

Such sermons are not the central feature of a Holiness service, however. In fact, the sermon is usually replaced by an expository talk in which the preacher designates a reader, selects a Bible passage, and comments on the "lesson," verse by verse as it is read. These are usually basic proof texts of the denomination and are used to prove that "holiness" is possible, or to reinforce the belief in "the plan of the ages." (All Holiness members have a reputation for being "good Scripture quoters.")

The primary activity of a Holiness service is "shouting," which tends to be a frenzied exhibition often accompanied by the noise of guitars, tambourines, and drums. Sometimes it takes the form of "holy dancing." Some of the Holiness sects also encourage "speaking in tongues"—an incoherent babbling supposed to indicate possession by the Spirit. The following "testimony" reveals something of the thought processes of the "precious ones."

"I have been a saint about three years," Mrs. Sadie Jones explained. "I been a member of the church about seven years, but you ain't a saint when you first get converted—not till you learn how to cut yourself loose from the world and follow Christ." She described her tutoring by older sisters, who advised her to "pray and forget everything but Jesus." Then one night, after "tarrying" three weeks for the

Holy Ghost, she received the "blessing": "I saw a large beautiful city upon a hill and at the gate stood an angel with a sword. A man came up beside me and said nobody but the saints could enter that city. He led me to a large stream of water and baptized me. Then he said, 'Your sins have been washed away.' When I awoke I was saying, 'Thank God, I'm free from sin.'"

Such professions of special purity evoke scornful and ribald sneers from those members of the lower class who are not "Saints"—sinners and orthodox church members alike. The precious ones tend to react to these "persecutions" as did Mrs. Jones, who declared, "I don't care what the world says about me—I'm living free from sin!"

Brother Martin Jones, quoted below, describes his own conversion and deals a blow in defense of the faith:

"One Sunday I had been drinking all day. I passed a church when they was singing and decided to go in. When they asked the unsaved people to come up to the altar and kneel, I did. I know they smelled the liquor on my breath, but they prayed with me and talked to me. I promised that I would come back the next Sunday. I decided to accept their faith. . . . I can't explain the feeling of getting the Holy Ghost. You feel light as a feather, and you find yourself speaking in tongues. You can't keep from saying the words that come in your mouth. . . . There is no such thing as what people say about 'rolling in sheets.' *
You see, we have an altar that other churches call the mourners' bench. We let those that will tarry for the Holy Ghost kneel there, and we will stay with them and help them pray and help them to get it. When the Holy Ghost strikes you, you will either jump up and shout, or you'll fall out and roll over and over on the floor. But nobody is supposed to touch you until you have fully come to yourself. Now there's where that saying about the 'Holy Rollers' comes from."

The pastor of the Apostolic Church of Jesus Only nerved his flock against contumely by stating:

"They criticize us for shouting and crying 'Glory to God.' Shouting is a thing expected from a church. Yes, shout. Say 'Amen.' Say 'Hallelujah.' Some people might say, 'Oh, I don't see no professional people or high-up people connected with that church.' But don't mind that saying. We are the common ordinary people that Jesus dwelt among."

* This is a reference to the popular charge that Holiness worshipers of both sexes not only roll on a floor covered with sheets, but sometimes actually engage in "sin" while so occupied, since "two clean sheets can't soil one another."

The path to Holiness is a rigorous one and not every novitiate "attains." One young man who boarded in a sanctified home tried it under his landlady's urging. He never "came through," and finally gave it up as a bad job:

"I asked how to get the Holy Ghost, and they told me to keep on praying. I did, but I didn't get anywhere, so I thought it was about time to confess. So I told the church that I was ready to join, although I wasn't converted, and I haven't been yet. But I stayed in the church over three years. I couldn't get the Holy Ghost, so I quit going to the church. I think the reason I didn't do so well was because I could not put aside all of my past life for the work of the church. That is, I would go to wild parties, and that calls for gambling and dancing, as well as drinking. Sometimes I would stay up all night and then I couldn't go to church the next day."

Most of Bronzeville declines to try for these high spiritual stakes.

The Holiness church exercises a high degree of control over its members through visiting committees and formal purges. The elders proudly contrast their denomination with others:

"The Baptist people preach a lot of things they don't do. I found out that there is a lot of hypocrisy in the Baptist churches. Our people really do live the life."

It seems certain that the sectarian nature of these groups and their willingness to expel errant members from the church does keep its membership living in closer conformity to its professions than in the case of the average lower-class Baptist or Methodist church. But their Holiness also effectively limits their appeal, for their air of self-righteousness makes them the continuous butt of jokes from the "unsaved" and the target of attacks by Baptist and Methodist preachers.

The rewards of Holiness are assumed to be certain "gifts"— "prophecy," "interpretation," "speaking in tongues," and "healing." Healing is a prized gift, and one elder carefully explained that:

"It's a true fact that you can't sin as long as the spirit of the Lord is in you. All that receive the Holy Ghost can heal if they continue to carry on and don't backslide."

Special healing services are usually held during the week, amid much singing and shouting. Holiness church newspapers carry pages of testimonials, of which the following are samples:

"The Lord surely is a healer. I had the toothache—my jaw was swollen so that I couldn't eat. I said, 'Lord, what will I do?' While sitting there suffering, the Lord anointed me. I put my two fingers into my mouth and pulled the tooth out. Thank the Lord!"

"Sister S. R. went to the doctor and he told her that she had to be operated on for the appendix. She came to the church and asked the saints to pray for her, which they did. When she went to the hospital the doctor said he didn't see any trace of the appendix. Now she is a well woman. See, dear friends, what the Lord will do for you if you only believe?"

The real ties that bind, however, are essentially the same as those in more orthodox churches—organized activity in an atmosphere of social approval. Mrs. Amanda Wilson, "very active in church," and president of the Sewing Circle, indicates the range of these meaningful activities:

"We meet once a week and sew things like pillow cases, men's work shirts, dresses, scarfs, ladies' handkerchiefs, and a lot of small things like that. We sell those things and put the money in our treasury and help with the expense of the church. Our sewing circle is giving a program this Sunday. There are four features to this play, as follows: Beauty, Fame, Wealth, Religion. The play is about a girl just entering womanhood and all of these things."

And, as in all other Bronzeville churches, the Holiness women despair of saving the men. Mrs. Amanda voices the complaint:

"We do not have many men in our church. They just won't join like women. My husband is the man that beats the drum. He used to beat the drum in an orchestra before he was sanctified. Now he plays for the church."

NEW GODS OF THE CITY

Bronzeville's "Saints" try diligently to recapture the spirit of the "old-time religion," while the orthodox churches seek to hold their own by streamlining their services. But a few "jack-legs" have broken with tradition and remade God in the image of Bronzeville's mercurial masses. Here and there among the store-front and house churches one can note a strange sign calling attention to an organization such as Bishop Morgan's Power House, Madame Williams'

Haven of Rest, the Truth Seekers' Liberal Temple, or the Preparatory Psychic Science Mission.

Among these cults are a few non-Christian groups—the Black Jews, two Temples of Islam, a Temple of Moorish Science, and a small kingdom of Father Divine's Peace Mission. Others represent variations within the Christian tradition—the Independent African Methodist Episcopal Church, Spiritual; the African Orthodox Church; the Liberal Catholics. All these cults have remained small and ineffective except the Spiritualists. In 1928 there were seventeen Spiritualist storefronts in Bronzeville; by 1938 there were 51 Spiritualist churches, including one congregation of over 2,000 members. In 1928 one church in twenty was Spiritualist; in 1938, one in ten.

The Spiritualist denomination seems to have been born in New Orleans and transplanted to Bronzeville, where it flourished, especially during the Depression. It borrows its hymns from the Baptists and Methodists, and appropriates altar, candles, and statues from the Catholics. It offers healing, advice, and "good luck" for a prayer and the price of a candle or holy flower.* It provides colorful robes for its preachers and "mediums," but despite its name it rarely offers messages from the dead. Its "mediums" claim direct contact with the *sources* of wisdom. And, most important, the Spiritualist church in Bronzeville has no unkind words for card-playing, dancing, policy, ward politics, or the "sporting life."

Only those Spiritualist establishments which actually held worship services were enumerated as churches. But more than a hundred individuals not affiliated with a church were operating as spiritual advisers and readers in Bronzeville on the eve of the war. Many of these persons had merely erected an altar in a front room of a house, and hung out a sign. To these "wayside shrines," daily during the Depression, came hundreds of Bronzeville's lower-class people, for counsel and advice on playing policy, getting or keeping a lover or mate, finding a job, or healing a disease. These spiritual advisers sometimes proved

---

* The altar is used not for the celebration of Mass, but as a place from which holy candles are sold; in some cases, too, flowers are blessed on it and sold as "luck charms." One observer counted 150 holy flowers sold at a regular Sunday evening service of a Spiritualist church. The church charged 25 cents each. They had allegedly been bought by the pastor for three cents each from a florist relative. At a subsequent meeting, members testified that the flowers had been efficacious in solving problems ranging from the renting of a room to the easing of pains from gallstones.

to be shrewd students of human nature, who mixed sound advice with their mystical rigamarole. One Spiritual reader stated frankly: "People around here are very insecure. There is nothing so upsetting as fear of losing your job. A lot of people are troubled and nervous, and I'm here to help them. . . . What I do is to advise people what to do to better themselves." Another reader had the habit of saying after selling a candle: "This candle won't do you a bit of good if you don't get out here and keep clean and fresh and stop looking like a bum and drinking yourself to death. You gotta help the spirits along. Now light your candle and put it on the altar."

Despite the obvious popularity of the Spiritualists, there was widespread skepticism of their motives among the lower class. "They turn out the lights and light a candle and have a lot of words to say about nothing," explained one down-and-out tavern tout; "that's a lot of bunk. Some people believe in it. Well, let them—it's nothing to me. But I think they're crazy." Another unbeliever compared the larger Spiritualist churches with the Holiness churches: "It's something like a Sanctified [Holiness] Church, singing and clapping hands. They say they are healers. Everybody who belongs there believes they've been healed and can heal. But I don't know—I think the same about them as I do about the Sanctified people, and that's that they are fakes."

The impact of the Depression on the polyglot Negro communities in the East produced a number of colorful evangelists and "prophets"— among them Father Divine.* No such messiahs arose from the basements and store-fronts of Bronzeville, but two striking personalities did emerge from the competitive struggle of the store-front world and within ten years had established themselves as Bronzeville's best-known lower-class preachers. One was a woman, Elder Lucy Smith, a black puritan preaching holiness. The other was a man, Reverend Clarence Cobb, a sepia latitudinarian dealing in spiritualism. Neither elaborated an economic program similar to Father Divine's heavens and farms; both succeeded in acquiring relatively large new churches, radio programs regularly broadcast, a large number of lower-class devotees and admirers, and the intense hostility of the higher-status members of the community.

Elder Lucy Smith, elderly, corpulent, dark-skinned and maternal,

---

* These religious movements have been described with rare insight by Arthur Huff Fauset in his *Black Gods of the Metropolis,* University of Pennsylvania, 1944.

began her ministry in 1930 in a Bronzeville store-front. Eight years later she moved her Church of All Nations into a modernistic build-ing on a fashionable boulevard. Like many other lower-class preachers, she attributes her initial success to the fact that she played a confessor's role to the lower class: "I started with giving advice to folks in my neighborhood. This made me realize how much a good talking does to many people. Very soon they started coming more and more, and so for the last seven years I've been preachin' to larger numbers. I'm building a new church; it will soon be finished. You should come to see my new place. You wouldn't believe that these folks with barely enough to live on are the very people who helped build my new large church."

She complained, "The established churches have never shown any interest in the work I'm doing," but dismissed them peremptorily: "I don't care much for those folks who are stuck up and live separated from the common people." In commenting on another woman preacher, more highly educated than herself but also a "healer," Elder Lucy elaborated this class point: "I don't think she's healing. Her kind of services are altogether different, an' my people couldn't understand her or feel comfortable there.* You have to understand a little more about the feelings of a lot of folks who enjoy my church services and need my help. Deep down in their hearts is pain and suffering, and I must bring them joy."

She constantly reiterated this theme to participant-observers, on one occasion stating: "The members of my church are troubled and need something to make them happy. My preaching is not about sad things, but always about being saved. The singing in my church has 'swing' to it, because I want my people to swing out of themselves all the mis'ry and troubles that is heavy on their hearts."

Elder Lucy is proud of her reputation as a healer. She spoke of her "rare power" and invited an observer to "come to my church more often and witness how many hundreds of men and women I heal—all kinds of sores and pains of the body and of the mind. I

---

* Class lines were very sharply drawn in evaluating these women. In a sample of 238 persons, not one of the higher-status informants expressed approval of Elder Smith, and nearly two-thirds were violently opposed to her. On the other hand, over half the persons of lower status approved of her activities. Only a fourth of the high-status informants objected to the higher-status woman preacher, but nine out of ten of the lower-status informants disliked her.

heal with prayers—jus' lay my hand on the troubled place and pray, and it all goes away."

To those who believe—and there are many in the lower class— there is awe-inspiring truth in the catalogue of cures published in the Elder's church newspaper: of the sister who was healed of heart trouble and broken veins; the white brother in the last stages of tuberculosis "who had got so offensive we had to hoist the windows while we prayed for him"; the woman "past talking or seeing—in a dying condition," whose "death demon" Elder Smith rebuked, and numerous others. "There is so much healing to be done," she explained, "that I had to give some of my healing power to two other women."

Elder Lucy also prides herself on not drawing the color-line: "My church is for all nations and my preachin' for all Christians. I distribute clothes and food to the poor and I make no distinction of color. Even poor whites come in and receive help." In fact, she professes to believe that white people appreciate her services more than higher-status Negroes do. She is the symbol of that old-time religion which most of Bronzeville rejects, but about whose demise it still seems uneasy. She is the mother-image of the drifting black masses.

Slight of build, medium-brown in color, dapper in manner, not yet thirty but wise in the ways of the world, the Reverend Cobb, unlike Elder Smith, is proud of his connections with politicians and policy kings, and does not attempt to conceal his love of good living, including attendance at the race track. Within eight years he not only attracted a large congregation, but also forced the community to recognize his influence. He has knocked the rough edges from his services and begun to support civic enterprises. One year his church made the largest single donation to the local branch of a national organization for racial advancement. Although this church, like other Spiritualist churches, is still considered lower-class by the "dicties" it was rising in status during the late Thirties, and had begun to attract middle-class members. It is probable that in a few years even upper middle-class people will not lose status by becoming members of it. Such mobility of an entire congregation demands the continuous evolution of the ritual in the direction of a more restrained ceremony and the participation of the pastor in civic activities.

The Reverend Cobb wears clothes of the latest cut, drives a flashy car, uses slang, and is considered a good sport. Such a preacher appeals to the younger lower-class people and to the "sporting world" —he's "regular." To the older people he offers the usual Spiritualist wares—advice in time of trouble, "healing," and good-luck charms —as well as a chance for self-expression in a highly organized congregation.*

At eleven o'clock every Sunday evening a large segment of lower-class Bronzeville listens for his radio theme song, "Jesus Is the Light of the World," sung by a well-trained but "swingy" choir to the accompaniment of two pianos, a pipe organ, an electrical guitar, and several violins. They like the universality of his appeal as he opens his radio program: "You in the taverns tonight; you on the dance floor; you in the poolrooms and policy stations; you on your bed of affliction—Jesus loves you all, and Reverend Cobb is thinking about you, and loves every one of you. It doesn't matter what you think about me, but it matters a lot what I think about you." Not a "good" preacher by lower-class standards, he rarely "shouts" his congregation, but depends on soothing words and music to put his program across.

The Reverend Cobb's power in the lower-class world has been demonstrated on several occasions. Once he gave a candlelight service at the White Sox ball park, charged for the candles, and attracted almost 3,000 visitors on a cold, rainy night. At another time, after he had been accused of some delinquency, he held a vindication service at a downtown auditorium and drew a crowd of nearly 10,000 persons. "Brother Cobb" symbolizes the New Gods of the Metropolis. He is the alter-ego of the urban sophisticate who does not wish to make the break with religion, but desires a streamlined church which allows him to take his pleasures undisturbed.

RELIGIOUS CROSS-CURRENTS

There is some evidence to indicate that the orthodox Baptist and Methodist churches felt the pressure of the Spiritualist and Holiness competition during the Depression years. This was reflected in their denunciations and in slight modifications of ritual. Concessions to

* An analysis of a 10 per cent sample of the 2,000 members of this church reveals that they were recruited largely from among former Baptists and Methodists, tend to be slightly above Bronzeville's average in education, and are considerably younger than most lower-class church members.

the Spiritualist appeal were difficult to make, and only one or two preachers had the temerity either to imitate or to establish professional relations with Spiritualists, but the doctrines of the "saints" were not too much out of line to be appropriated in part.

One or two ministers of larger orthodox churches have (perhaps unconsciously) met Holiness competition by claiming to have received a "second blessing." The pastor of one large Baptist church reports that he received the Holy Ghost while traveling across the Arizona desert in a Pullman car several years ago. The Holiness pastors were at first suspicious of his sincerity and refused to co-operate with him. Being looked down on in Bronzeville, however, they were ultimately pleased to have a prominent pastor inviting them to his church, and they finally accepted him as a friend. Flirting with the "sancts" earned him the hostility of the more conservative ministers, and he revealed his difficulties in a Sunday sermon: "Why, let me tell you, honey, the other day I went to the ministers' conference and two brothers were talking. One of them said, 'You know I hear Reverend Maxwell says he has the Holy Ghost now.' The other replied: 'Oh, ain't nothing the matter with Reverend Maxwell—he just got religion. He just now got what I got over thirty-four years ago.'

"I heard them and sat down right in front of them. But oh, bless God, I may have just got what he got thirty-five years ago, but I just got *another* bath and he only got one. I could tell him I got a bath over fifty years ago by my mother or somebody; I had another bath thirty years ago, another twenty years ago; another ten years ago; another three years ago; another this morning. You see what I mean? Let me tell you, some folks got converted and had a visitation from the Holy Ghost and they have become lazy, unconcerned, and dirty, and they haven't had a bath from the Holy Ghost since. That's what was wrong with that brother—he had one bath and stopped!"

The Spiritualists, Catholics, Christian Scientists, Holiness churches, and many independent groups offer divine therapy. Even most orthodox preachers sanction healing in theory, but few of them will go so far as to endorse it so wholeheartedly as the Baptist preacher who told the following story:

"He is able to conquer. He is able to cure diseases. Do you hear me? Now I know what I'm talking about. Let me tell you about my own experience out in Colorado. I don't mean that doctors aren't all right, for God placed them here to help keep our bodies working. But in 1926 out in Colorado, I was given up. My family had spent all of their money on medicine and doctors and X-rays, but they couldn't find the cause of my pain. The pain was so severe, until it took away the appetite and the bones began to show through the flesh. After all hope had been given up, I asked my mother and friends to leave me in the room by myself. I hadn't laid down in bed for six months, but that night I prayed to God and said, 'Now, God, I want to rest tonight, if I don't ever rest any more. I have spent sleepless nights and if I never live to get back to this place let me rest tonight. If it's your will that I preach again I want a change tonight.' Let me tell you, darling, at eleven o'clock I began to get drowsy. I eased down on my elbow and felt no pain."

Not even this minister, however, tried to establish healing as a part of his church ritual.

The orthodox churches have had to come to terms with the competition of the "Saints." But some of the "Saints," on their part, have had to make accommodation with sin. Thus Elder Lucy Smith observed in a conversation with an interviewer: "I don't hold it against the people if they play policy numbers, so long as they don't deny themselves the necessities of life. I know this is often unavoidable." She insisted that "it sets a bad example for the younger folks," but raised the query: "What can be done about it? Conditions here are not good. The opportunities for making a decent living are very small. People have to live and they must find ways and means." She claimed an attitude of avoidance: "I never talk about policy in my preachin'. What I like to see is to get them moving and singing so they'll forget their troubles."

That Holiness churches are responsive to the pull of what they call "the world" is also revealed in their modifications of ritual. Thus, at one small Church of God in Christ, after a session of shouting, the girls of the Sewing Circle presented a pageant stressing the folly of Beauty, Wealth, and Fame—but the pageant was introduced by a very literate paper praising "the part played by women in politics, schools, and clubs." Also, within a period of eight years, at least three Holiness congregations were observed in the process of streamlining their services, moving into more elaborate quarters, and emphasizing "community improvements." *

---

* The Negro unionist who was killed in the "Memorial Day Massacre" (see p. 323) belonged to a Holiness Church. This is an account of his funeral as provided by an observer who attended the services:

The Church of God in Christ is located in a large store-front building. The

The pastors of Bronzeville's medium-sized and large churches waste very little time on doctrinal disputes. They have to use their ingenuity to provide a service pleasing to the exponents of the old-time religion, to compete with the new Gods of the Metropolis, and to raise enough money to keep in business without driving their members away. Brother Brown, "Baptist-born and Baptist-bred," illustrates the prob- lem. He was talking to an interviewer:

"Young man, you won't find the churches of today like the churches of years ago. I have seen the time when a minister would walk ten or fifteen miles to preach and maybe get a dollar or maybe nothing. The church was a house of worship and not a money institution as it is today. I haven't enjoyed a good service since I left the Southland. The meetings down home was soul-stirring, and when the people would 'get happy' they were 'happy.'

windows are painted black half way up. The interior is quite plain, with bare, uneven, wooden flooring. . . . Plain white curtains hung at the windows. The attendance at the funeral was small. Altogether, about 250 persons were present, of which about 30 were white.

Several beautiful floral offerings were sent in before the service. Most of these came from union lodges. About 14 members of the family were present.

The minister, Rev. B—— introduced Mrs. J ——, who introduced L. K——, a Negro organizer. He made a short speech, paying tribute to the dead and his loyalty and willingness to make "the supreme sacrifice," along with the 9 others who were slain. He was particularly bitter in his statements concerning the police, whom he claimed were responsible for the deaths of the brothers in South Chicago.

The next union speaker was a white man, who was much calmer and who spoke very briefly on the intention of the union to see that these men should not have died in vain. The assemblage was noticeably cool in its response to this speaker.

Before the service began, several interesting comments were overheard reveal ing the reaction of the church membership to Mr. T—'s death. One elderly lady said, "The members ain' turnin' out so well, is they? Some of them done tole me they wa'n comin', 'cause he had no bizness out there with them unions. That was sinful groun' out there. God done punished him and the members don' inten' to flaunt God. I jes' came myse'f 'cause his wife's my frien', but I hope God will forgive me, 'cause I sure ain' got no bizness here either."

When a union member pointed out that since Christ had died for a cause, T—'s death might be interpreted similarly, one of the women present answered in sonorous tones, "Christ died that the world might live. Brother T—— and nine others died because they were on sinful ground. He had no bizness out there that day."

To many of the other members of this striker's church, union activity and the new solidarity between black and white, the conflict with the law, and the violence were all new and bewildering occurrences, that required reinterpretation within their own frame of reference.

"In Chicago, the preacher's subject is money. He must have an automobile, a swell flat and fine clothes before he can preach—and *then* he can't preach. They all want a big name and want to do everything on a big basis and don't have time to serve the people. They even have all high-class singing and not the old-time soul-stirring songs that furnish the soul with happiness. The whole truth is that the people of today don't have religion. They only join the church. The big pastors live in luxury, have fine cars, expensive clothing, and all the comfort of life. It is said that some of our pastors have yearly incomes of $3,000 to $4,000 a year. That's too much money for any preacher. The larger churches are too high-toned to serve God."

Brother Brown was equally censorious of the store-fronts and cults: "The trouble is that there are too many churches and too many different religions. Every little jack-leg preacher you see wants a church of his own, and if not his own denomination he will call it anything —just so he can exploit his people. First, he tells them of the beautiful church that he is going to build when 'we leave this store-front'— and the truth is he'll never leave the store-front." Brother Brown doesn't have any answers, but he hasn't yet abandoned the Baptists. He proudly states, "I am a Baptist and I think that the Baptist is good enough for any man." Less loyal critics either shift from church to church, join the "cults," go Catholic, or backslide.

REVOLT AGAINST HEAVEN

Bronzeville is in revolt against Heaven, and the rebellion centers in the lower class. It is reflected in continuous vitriolic attacks upon preachers and church members. It is a part of the general secularization of life in the urban, industrial society. In most cases, however, it is not a frank and open atheism. It is not even an attack upon the church *per se,* for Bronzeville's lower class seems to still feel that it ought to be religious. Rather, it takes the form of a protest against the alleged cupidity and hypocrisy of church functionaries and devotees.

The preachers bear the brunt of the attacks, and comments on ministers are sometimes violent. This was especially true during the Lean Years, when statements involving charges of clerical greed were commonplace:

"The Bible says we should not bring the price of a dog into the House of God, but these damn preachers don't care how the money is gotten; they take it."

"The average pastor is not studying the needs of his race. He's studying the ways to get more money out of people. He gives the little children cans to beg pennies with and has the older children give plays. He has the sisters and brothers go broke on rally days."

"Every time you see them [the preachers], they want money."

"I don't go to church. I need what the church needs—that's money."

"These preachers are sickening. They want you to work and bring them all of the money. That's worse than policy. They'll collect for their own benefit and then come around last for the sick collection. See, they know you've already given all of your money."

But the same sinners and backsliders who assail preachers in this fashion are likely to single out individuals as "good" preachers or "sincere" preachers, and to contrast them with "bad" preachers. Even in the disorganized atmosphere of the household of Baby Chile and Mr. Ben, there were sometimes discussions of religion. The following conversation illustrates a prevalent tendency to accept religion and the church as a necessary part of life while attacking specific ministers. Mr. Ben, who never went to church, asked one of the authors whether he had listened to Elder Lucy Smith the preceding Sunday night. He seemed disappointed when the reply was negative. The ensuing discussion, recorded from the observer's notebook, is revealing:

Ben said: "You oughta been here. We all pulled up to the radio and listened." (When I left Sunday night, four people were playing cards. One man had been laid out drunk. Another woman had already drunk three glasses of whisky. Bottles of port and muscatel were yet to be consumed. Probably they were all "high" by the time Elder Lucy Smith came on the air.)

Slick chimed in: "You should have heard them sing 'Precious Lord, Take My Hand'—and what was that other song they sang? 'He's a Rock'? They shore did sing, and Elder Lucy Smith preached a good sermon, too."

I asked explicitly what she preached about. No one remembered anything she had said. Baby Chile, commenting, said, "I can't jist remember what she said, but it was a good sermon."

Baby Chile's brother, already half-high, stopped begging for a quarter to buy more liquor and started to talk. "A lot of these preachers are just pimps nowadays," he said. "You see them walking around in pimpy clothes.* They ain't God-sent."

Slick asked, "Which would you rather be—a educated preacher who ain't God-sent, or a God-sent man who ain't got no education?"

The brother responded: "I don't like these preachers standing up saying things, and you don't know what they're talking about, all hifalutin'. I like the preaching like we had it down in Alabama. I remember when my mamma died. The preacher hadn't even seen her. He was an old preacher with his shoes all run down and wearing old clothes—he didn't have no pimpy clothes like *these* preachers. We handed him the writing. You know those things—what you call 'em?" (Slick volunteered "condolences," but that wasn't the word. So he tried "obituary"—that was the word.) "Yes, that's it. He took that obituary and he looked at it and then he begun to preach. He told all about how angels of death come down and called Sister Mag and took her on home to glory." He then moaned out the whole funeral sermon, which sounded very much like James Weldon Johnson's "Go Down Death."

I said: "You should have been a preacher. You missed your calling."

"Well, the Lord passed me by and got my brother," he answered.

The conversation then turned to the Reverend Byrnes, and somebody said: "Yeh, he's all mixed up in politics. He ain't like Reverend Simpson. That was a God-sent man. When he stepped out on the pulpit, you could tell what he was saying was coming from down inside. He wasn't pimpy either. Man, they sent Reverend Byrnes to the Holy Land."

Here Slick said: "Yea, I remember that. I was in St. Louis then and Reverend Wilson's congregation sent him too. And, man, he took up dollar bills and blessed them and told them he was going to bring them some sand from the Holy Land and some water from the Jordan river. And those folks just gave him dollars. He had a racket."

Sinners and backsliders level their attacks at the flock as well as at the shepherds of the sheep, the comment of one lower-class critic being typical: "I lost interest in churches because they are always preaching 'Don't smoke; don't drink; don't do anything that is pleasure.' Then, too, I've seen older people, who say they are good church members, smoking. I've seen them entering taverns, and in fact, I see no difference from those who are not in church."† Occasionally, too, a

---

* A reference to the flashy dressing of some ministers, i.e., "they dress like pimps."

† This is a widespread charge: "Church folks do everything they's big enough to do. Why join the church? They ain't no different from anybody else."

person will charge preachers with opposing "pleasure" from pecuniary motives:

"Theaters, cafés, policy, and dance halls? There's nothing wrong with these things; they are things that the Negroes enjoy. The preachers condemn them because they think if they can stop their people from going to these places they will put more money into the church."

It is interesting to note that, when a mass of these comments and criticisms were presented to a group of over a hundred Bronzeville preachers at a conference during "Go to Church Week" in 1938, they were almost unanimously dismissed as "just excuses." One minister said angrily: "The people ain't interested in church nohow. They just want to find some way to cover themselves before man. But they ain't fooling God!" This emotional explosion conceals some sound analysis, for it is not the "insincerity" of church people that accounts fundamentally for the prevalent antagonism toward church and for the general indifference to the religious way of life. Perhaps even the apostates realize only vaguely the source of their disaffection. The most important factor in weakening the influence of the churches is the centripetal pull of the urban milieu. There is a bewildering diversity of denominations and of types of churches within a denomination. The movies, ball games, social clubs, and policy stations offer competing forms of participation and throw doubt on all absolute conceptions of sin. The group controls of the small town are absent. The prosperous "wicked" are a perpetual challenge to the "poor saints." "Take the world and give me Jesus" may be the essence of the old-time religion. "What do I get out of it?" is Bronzeville's persistent query.

WHEN THE OLD GODS GO

In the face of this wide range of alternative interests, religion ceases to be the focus of lower-class life. The vast majority organize their behavior around "good-timing," fixing their attention on the cheaper forms of commercial recreation and gearing the rhythm of their daily life to the policy drawings. Some cling to the church as a subsidiary center of interest. Others drop their church connections entirely and become completely secularized except for fleeting moments of reverie or remorse.

Within the lower class are some individuals, however, who assume a pattern of serious secular interests. These are of four main types: (1) participation in "racial" movements; (2) identification with the Communist movement; (3) participation in trade union activities; (4) striving to "get ahead" in the traditional fashion of saving money, acquiring a middle-class consumption pattern, trying to get more education, and participating in ward politics. Occasionally an energetic or ambitious person may incorporate all these interests or shift from one to the other. Sometimes the individual may become a well-known "leader" on the lower-class level, and in specific crisis situations may attract a temporary following from the unorganized and undisciplined masses.

Getting Ahead: Lower-class "sinners" sometimes refer scornfully to the philosophy of "Take the world and give me Jesus," but even some church people also adopt a pattern of trying to emerge from lower-class status or to provide an opportunity for their children to do so. Numerous lower-class persons have become sensitized to the middle-class way of life as they see it portrayed in the movies and periodicals, or as they observe it in white homes where they work, or among higher-status Negroes. Sometimes a family has one partner—usually the wife—who is sensitized toward the middle class. In other cases both partners are middle-class individuals who have taken a social fall. The conflict within a family where one parent is oriented toward middle-class behavior patterns can sometimes result in considerable strain. There is, for instance, the case of Mrs. C—— whose husband, a common laborer on the WPA and a native of Chicago, had just made a derogatory remark about her southern origin:

"Yes, I'm from Mobile and proud of it. I lived better there than you will ever live in Chicago. My people are what we call 'good livers.' They've got a car and a home. What have you got? A raggedy bicycle and a WPA job. I have to do without everything so I won't be sleeping outdoors and starving to death. Do you buy me any clothes? Did you send me home to visit? If I didn't have a child I'd go back there to stay. Excuse me, Mister [to the observer], but this big bastard gets on my nerves, always making fun of me. . . . He's been in Chicago all his life and what's he got? A $55-a-month job—and he's too lazy to keep that. Yes, I'm going to leave him. I was planning to move so I can bring my girl up in a better environment. I'll take her home before I'll let her grow up among these trifling no-good people. These people are the lowest I ever heard of—some of them are too lazy to put on shoes. And do you think my daughter is not going to have a chance to associate with better children—or people like that?"

There are many such families within the lower class who wish to see their children get ahead. Another mother commented:

"I hate the fact that I am unable to keep my daughter in high school. I am willing right now to work my fingers to the bone if I could get work to do to be able to put my daughter back in school, and to be able to give her some of the things she would like to have in this world."

Emerging, too, from within the lower class are those young people who because of their contact with the middle-class world—at school, in the larger churches, social agencies, or community houses, and through their reading of the Negro press and a general awareness of "successful" Negroes—have psychologically repudiated their lower-class status. Some of these are able, by getting jobs of their own, joining social clubs, or moving away from their families, to begin mobility out of lower-class status. One lower-class woman whose daughter has middle-class aspirations indicated the influence which a mobility-minded child can have on a lower-class family:

"I like this neighborhood all right, but I don't like some of the people in it. I mean I don't like their ways. My daughter, Juanita, says that as soon as she finishes grammar school, she's going to move out of the neighborhood. She tells me, 'Mamma, if you stay, I'm going to leave you.' "

One high school girl revealed the content of these dreams of "getting ahead":

"I was going to high school up until last September. I had to drop out because of financial distress. I have had two jobs since I've been out of school. I've worked as a maid, and also have done a little factory work. Right now my main concern is where I can get a job. I would like to get away from that maid-and-nurse-girl type of job, but I would consider anything at present. I sit down and think of the pretty togs that I could buy if I could get a decent job."

For younger people, "getting ahead" usually means staying in school beyond the grades and then securing a non-menial job and moving out of definitely lower-class areas. Girls particularly seem sensitive to the "respectability" of their surroundings, and this is a serious matter if they want to make a "good match."

Girls with a mobility drive have to fight an almost physical battle against the lower-class world. Even those who reach the high school level do not always succeed in developing an integrated pattern of middle-class behavior. During the Depression years, there was a tendency for lower-class girls to stay in school since jobs were scarce. But increased schooling was sometimes associated with a lower-class pattern of sex behavior. Truancy was prevalent among girls at both of Bronzeville's high schools. One very articulate girl of a lower-class family, who likes school and "hopes to be somebody," described the activities of many of these truants:

"They take money from men to get themselves stockings and a little lunch money. Lots of those girls meet men after school and go to rooms with them. They tell me I am crazy and don't know what I am missing."

She admitted that she had thought of doing this when in her early teens, but said that

"after I got sixteen years old and began to see so much happen to girls, I just made up a solid mind I will never do a thing like that. My home is already a mess, and if I start to doing things and get pregnant or get a social disease it will be too bad. Men pick at me because I have large legs, but I tell them in a few words where to get off."

One seventeen-year-old lower-class girl who had gone as far as the first year of high school was definitely oriented toward "living decent." Her description of the world she hopes to reject is graphic:

"If I wanted to, I could be bad here on Calumet and never go to school. But I don't want to be a bad girl. I see so much here on Calumet. We have lived around here ever since I can remember, and this building has had lots of hustling girls in it, some of them younger than I am. Just the other night a man beat a girl nearly to death and wouldn't give her ten cents to get a sandwich. Men had been going to her room all day— white and colored. We counted ten men go in and out. When her pimp came home he told her she hadn't made him enough money. He made her get in the streets, and she cried and begged him for ten cents to get herself a hot dog, and he kicked her down the steps and told her she had better bring him some money, he didn't care how she got it. I have seen girls rob men and seen men stick up men and take off their clothes. That's why I hate that kind of stuff. We have lived among it and I have seen and heard of it since I was six years old."

When asked if she would like to move, she answered: "Yes, ma'am! But I guess we are so poor and down-and-out, we have to stay here."

CHAPTER 22

The Middle-class Way of Life

AS WE HAVE SEEN, THERE ARE WITHIN THE LOWER CLASS SOME INDIVIDUALS whose interests and aspirations are turned away from the physical and social milieu in which they live—the church-centered "respectables," the more secular "respectables," and some young people who want to get ahead. They often phrase their aspirations in terms of "moving out South" or getting "a decent place to live." This is a familiar pattern in the city, the desire of the ambitious in all ethnic groups to escape the slums. As we have mentioned several times, the lack of available housing has made it extremely difficult for such people to take this first step in upward social mobility even when they have the money. For the masses of the relief clients during the depression years it was next to impossible. Thus the constant complaint, "We can't raise children right around here," or "We're stuck here." Out of the search for better neighborhoods has arisen the ecological pattern of the Black Belt described on page 384, with its "best," "worst," and "mixed areas."

The map below and the table on page 659 reveal the limited measure of success that the people of Bronzeville have had in sorting themselves out into broad community areas which might be designated as "lower-class" and "middle-class." (Table 29 and Figure 37.)

Figure 37

COMMUNITY AREAS AND CENSUS TRACTS IN THE BLACK BELT

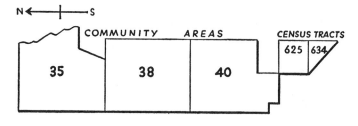

TABLE 29

COMPARISON OF SELECTED SOCIAL DATA FOR AREAS WITHIN BLACK BELT: 1934-1940

	Area 35 (L.C.)	Area 38 (L.C.-M.C.)	Area 40 (L.C.-M.C.)	Tract 625 (M.C.)	Tract 634 (M.C.)	Rates for City (Negroes and Whites)
Negro population...	50,000	90,000	45,000	8,000	2,000	
Families on relief	63.6%	52.3%	36.1%	*	*	14.0%
Adults with less than 5th grade education (M) (F)	9.0% 7.8%	5.6% 5.4%	3.5% 3.6%	6.4%	6.1%	3.6% 3.2%
Adults with more than 13 years of education (M) (F)	2.3% 1.9%	2.9% 2.8%	3.8% 3.4%	12.5%	11.4%	5.1% 3.7%
Illegitimate birth-rate (per thousand)	126.5	93.7	64.5	52.4	36.8	26.8
Syphilis rate (per 10,000)	304.5	285.2	243.8	*	*	*
TB death-rate (per 100,000)	67.7	53.9	54.8	*	*	*
Birth-rate (per 1,000)	17.5	16.7	16.0	15.8	21.3	15.4
Death-rate (per 1,000)	21.3	15.8	13.5	12.2	12.2	10.2
Infant mortality rate (per 1,000)	97.6	76.0	64.7	57.7	66.2	56.7

* Data available by local community areas only. (Data for community areas from Wirth and Furez, *Local Community Fact Book* and data for tracts from Cayton-Warner Research.)

Yet the "ambitious" Negroes are unable to keep their communities "middle-class" because the Black Ghetto is too small to accommodate its population and the less well-to-do must filter into these "best" areas. One woman bemoans the fate of her neighborhood:

"The spirit of the people around here seems to be broken. Some of them were buying their homes; then the Depression came and a lot of the property went into the hands of the receivers, and the receivers just won't make repairs on the houses. Then, too, many of the new people coming into the community are poor people looking for cheap rent."

Another woman describes her fears of what will happen to "the house next door":

"I hear that the people who are buying the place are going to cut it up into kitchenettes. This will be terrible, but what can we do? I wish that we could petition and protest against their making kitchenettes here. Kitchenettes usually bring a lower class of people into the neighborhood. So many fine houses have been ruined by cutting them up into kitchenettes."

Only one area of the Black Belt has that atmosphere of stability which America calls "middle-class"—two small census tracts (Figure 37) at the southern tip of the Black Belt. Instead of middle-class *areas* Bronzeville tends to have middle-class *buildings* in all areas, or a few middle-class blocks here and there.

Students of life in Bronzeville as well as some real-estate men have suggested that the problem of housing within the Black Ghetto might be partly solved by rebuilding *within* the area rather than by an expansion of the Black Belt or a scattering of the population. We have already indicated the economic factors that prevent the reclaiming of the area. But two attempts at providing model housing developments within the Black Ghetto have been realized: a privately financed project for higher income groups—the Michigan Garden Boulevard Apartments ("The Rosenwald Apartments") built in 1927; and a Federally financed low-cost housing project completed in 1938, the Ida B. Wells Homes—popularly known as "The Project." For seventeen years the former has been a symbol of good living on a relatively high income level; its waiting list is always very long. For five years during the Depression, "The Project" was the unrealized dream of respectable lowers who wanted to make the mobility step to lower middle class. Its 2,000 families are the envy of the whole South Side. By contrasting the occupational status of the residents in these two projects, we can see the upper and the lower limits of occupation within Bronzeville's middle class. (Table 30.)

When a common laborer or a relief client tried to "get in The Project" he was attempting to take the first step toward living middle-

TABLE 30

COMPARISON OF OCCUPATIONAL STATUS OF HEADS OF 2,141 FAMILIES IN
TWO BRONZEVILLE HOUSING PROJECTS: 1941

Occupational Group	Rosenwald Apartments (Upper-middle-class)			Ida B. Wells Houses (Lower-middle-class)		
	Number	Per Cent	Cumulative Per Cent	Number *	Per Cent	Cumulative Per Cent
Professional............	59	12.0	12.0	55 (44)	3.3	3.3
Independent business-men................	49	10.0	22.0	7 (0)	.4	3.7
Clerical and kindred .workers............	149	30.3	52.3	130 (50)	7.9	11.6
Craftsmen, operatives and kindred workers..	15	3.0	55.3	226 (167)	13.7	25.3
Laborers..............	8	1.6	56.9	431 (237)	22.2	47.5
Service (all types)......	179	36.4	93.3	365 (13)	26.1	73.6
Relief................	0	....	93.3	404 (0)	24.5	98.1
Miscellaneous, retired, etc................	33	6.7	100.0	31 (0)	1.9	100.0
Total............	492	100.0	....	1,649 (511)	100.0	....

* The numbers in parentheses indicate the number of family heads within each category who were employed by the WPA. Over half (52.3 per cent) of the family heads in the Rosenwald Apartments did "clean work"; only about an eighth (11.6 per cent) of the Federal housing project family heads had such high status jobs. Less than two per cent of the Rosenwald sample (1.6 per cent) were laborers; over a fifth (22.2 per cent) of "The Project" sample were laborers.

class. Those who got in had gone one rung up the ladder. When a post-office worker hopefully had his name put on the Garden Apartments waiting list, he too was trying to get into a middle-class atmosphere. Here are two extremes of occupation and income level; but, as we shall see, there is enough in common between the two groups to dub them both "middle-class," for neither occupation nor income is, in the final analysis, the decisive measuring rod. Rather, the middle class is marked off from the lower class by a pattern of behavior expressed in stable family and associational relationships, in great concern with "front" and "respectability," and in a drive for "getting ahead." All this finds an objective measure in standard of living—the way people spend their money, and in *public behavior*.

To be "poor but middle-class," a person must repudiate the pattern of behavior described in Chapter 20, and must display some actual effort to "better his condition"—which means anything from joining the right club or church to getting a better job. To be relatively well-to-do but *only* middle-class usually means that the person lacks certain symbols of education and influence which would put him in "at the top."

Throughout the world of the middle class "right connections" are stressed, and this otherwise sprawling group of people with diverse incomes and occupations is given cohesiveness by an intricate and complex web of voluntary associations. These constitute the "markers" by which individuals symbolize their aspirations and the position they have attained in the competitive struggle to get ahead. They provide occasions upon which a middle-class person can display his other symbols, such as clothing and correct public behavior, among people who, like himself, prize these. Middle-class organizations put the accent on "front," respectability, civic responsibility of a sort, and conventionalized recreation. Some of these organizations, too, become the means by which middle-class people "on the rise" come into contact with people "above" them socially and by which mobile lower-class individuals can rise from the class below. There is a recognized "middle-class way of life"; Bronzeville's Postal Clerk A on $2,400 a year knows that Stockyards Worker B on $1,200 a year has essentially the same goals, and A will not "snub" or "cut" him as he might Stockyards Worker C who has "a lower-class pattern." *

Given a common interest in "getting ahead" and "living respectable," the middle class is subdivided by effective income and (to a lesser extent) by occupation and education. Near the top are the

---

* E. Franklin Frazier, in his *Negro Family in the United States,* discusses "The Brown Middle Class." He uses a group of occupations in order to come to grips with the problem of describing the middle class. However, he states: "In limiting the new Negro middle class which has emerged in recent years to these four occupational classes, we have omitted representatives of other occupational classes who maintain similar standards of behavior and are sometimes accepted socially by members of the middle class. But here we are dealing with an economic class composed of certain occupational groups that may be identified statistically" (p. 421). We have started the other way around, by taking the similar standards of behavior as the independent variable, and relating occupation and income to the way of life. (See p. 704 for a statistical approach to this method.)

upper middles, oriented toward the upper class and very conscious of the "big shots" above them. Within the upper middle class are many persons who are anxious to strengthen their ties with the people above them or to so train their children as to push them into that set. At the other end are the people socially and financially much closer to the lower class. Life for these becomes a constant struggle to keep from falling back, and to maintain a middle-class standard of living and conduct against the pressure of the lower-class world.

ESTABLISHING A FAMILY

A Nice Home: For married people who are trying to live middle-class, "having a nice home" usually becomes a consuming passion—nearly always a primary interest. Though in a metropolitan area this does not necessarily mean owning a home, 10 per cent of the Negroes in Chicago owned some sort of home in 1930, and 8 per cent in 1940. To former sharecroppers and the descendants of chattel slaves, real estate is a potent symbol of stability and respectability. Most of the property bought by Negroes in Chicago was accumulated between the Great Migration and the Depression, although quite a few Negroes turned their savings into real estate soon after the Depression began. Most of the remarks about home ownership are significantly brief: "Of course we own our house." "Yes, we bought this place just as soon as we got married." "I'd never rent." All such remarks establish status quickly.

During the Depression years, the struggle to buy a home (or to save one from foreclosure) was often a painful process. One lower-middle-class woman discussed her situation as follows:

"I have lived here for ten years. We are buying this home. I have to work out in service all the time. I only have one day off and I take that in resting. I don't get a chance to socialize, and I don't even go to church any more. You see, my husband and I have quite a financial responsibility and jobs today don't pay much."

A widow stated that she was working for the first time in sixteen years: "You know my husband died last year and my home wasn't paid for, so I'm trying to carry on." Another woman, lamenting the loss of her property, said: "I've always been accustomed to having something, and I've had a mighty hard fall. You see I had such a fine home. I had to sell nearly all my fine furniture for almost nothing. I had my home under HOLC. That was my last chance to save it—and I lost it."

Some families solved their problem of hanging on to a house during the Depression as did the woman who said:

"We are buying this home. My husband has relatives and so do I. Well, we just made it a family affair. They all have pretty good jobs, so they live with us and pay just like any other roomers would. My mother keeps house for me and I work out. It gives me a lot of joy to know that my mother can rest from her toils and worries, and it releases me to get some money to help keep up the payments."

Those youngsters who came to their majority during the Lean Years had little incentive and less money with which to start buying homes. They used their money for other forms of display—clothes and a good time. The Second World War resulted in an increased interest in real estate, but there were few homes for sale and priority problems made it almost impossible to build.

For the majority of the families in Bronzeville's middle class, buying a home is seldom seriously visualized as a goal. The people are "cave-dwellers," paying high rents for apartments and forced to take in boarders and relatives to make ends meet. It is to such middle-class people that Bronzeville's overcrowding proves the greatest annoyance; they want space in which to live, but they rarely get it. People in Bronzeville are continually saying, "Boarders are a nuisance—but how else can we pay the rent?" As to relatives, one woman sums up a prevalent attitude: "I am glad to have them, and they all pay their way all right. But I do get tired of the crowd sometimes." Another, expressing a general American middle-class ideal, said: "On my wedding night when we returned to our new home we were so happy. I thought it was a dream instead of reality—I couldn't believe it. At last some peace and quiet, and above all some privacy—something neither of us had ever had the pleasure of before." In the Black Ghetto, privacy is one of the rarest of the good things of life.

Raising a Family: Established upper-middle-class families with an assured income are able to make long-range plans for their children. The wife of a postal clerk, after explaining to the interviewer that she had an education policy on her eleven-year-old daughter which could be cashed in when the girl was nineteen, called the child to "tell what she wanted to do when she grew up." The girl answered:

"Well, I'm going to finish grammar school next February. Then I'm going right on through high school, and after that I'm going to college. I want to go to the University of Chicago and study to be a medical social worker."

Prompted by her mother to "tell about her music," she went on:

"I take piano now, and when I'm in another recital at Kimball Hall I'd like for you to attend. I take dramatic art, too. I wanted to take dancing, but Daddy didn't like for me to take that; he thought I might want to go on the stage."

To the parents of children like these, "education" often means more than formal schooling, and this mother was already making plans for sending her daughter to a summer camp "to broaden her out" and teach her how to get along with other children of her age.

This same mother was a little worried about Junior, her nine-year-old son, because he didn't seem to be "learning as fast as he ought to." It would have to be summer school for him rather than camp. She was ashamed of not having a "bright boy": "I was talking with a lady the other day who had to send her son to summer school. I didn't tell her, but I had a shaky feeling that my son will have to go this summer." The children are closely supervised, have time for practicing music and for studying. Junior is also being taught that even though he is a boy he has to help with the dishes.

In the upper middle class, this planning of the child's life often begins before birth. One expectant mother explained that she and her Pullman porter husband had already looked over an educational policy and were studying *Parents' Magazine* and a book on infant care. They're hoping the baby will be "a pretty medium brown" and smart. One civil servant father of a three-day-old baby observed: "I'm already thinking about how to give my daughter all the best advantages. She's only three days old, but I'm thinking about how I want her to finish college and about all the things I'd like her to do. She's going to get music and dancing and everything else that'll help her to develop her personality." And so goes the preoccupation with children in this stratum:

"Children are a lot of trouble, but when they're sweet like mine they are worth all the trouble they give you. I pray that I'll live to see them grown and successful in something."

"I try to take my children to a variety of programs. I want them to be at ease at musicals and lectures so when they're old enough to understand these things they'll seek cultural entertainment."

"I want to give my children every opportunity to succeed in life. My husband and I try to be interested in all the things that'll help the children."

"My youngest boy is seven. All my kids are in school. I try to instill in their minds that the only sound way to succeed is by laying a good foundation of learning and then to get actual experience. I hope to be able to see them all through college. I own the property where I live and have a few dollars in the bank. I own a car, too. My greatest ambition is to see my children come along and keep this cleaning and pressing business of mine going, or else get into something they like better."

Making Something Out of the Children: Most parents in lower-middle-class families are people with a limited education and they earn their bread by hard .work when they can get it. During the Depression many of them were on relief. (See Table 29.) The backbone of the lower middle class during the Depression years was that group of semi-skilled and common laborers who had managed to retain their jobs. Most lower-middle-class adults, aware of the strata above them, feel that they have reached their limit in social mobility and place their hopes for family advancement in the children. They see the key to success in "education" *plus* hard work, and they drive this point home to their children. A domestic servant, talking about her ten-year-old son, says:

"He goes to Betsy Ross School now. He's in 3A and getting along fine. He's my greatest joy and happiness in the world. I'm going to do everything in my power to see that he gets the very best education so he'll be able to make a mark for himself in life. He'll be able to tell the world that his mother took an interest in him, and if he don't make good he'll have nobody to blame but himself. I do know how necessary it is to have a good education today."

A stockyards worker expresses faith in the success of the builders of better mousetraps:

"The laboring man's chance is slim. I'm trying to educate my children and bring them up so they won't have trouble finding work. I tell them all the time if they do what they're supposed to do *well,* they won't have to worry. Many Negroes have good chances these days, if they'll only grasp the opportunity—especially if they've had a good education."

Over and over again these sentiments are repeated by Bronzeville parents, usually accompanied by the statement that they are "sacrificing for the children." This whole philosophy was summed up by the mother of five girls and three boys, all under sixteen. Her husband was earning $30 a week in a mattress factory. She did not work, stating that "I have too many children to work. The Lord knows I need to—everything is so high. But I can't leave them to try to work. Raising them is a job that never ends. I have my children under pretty good control, though. I try to teach them to the best of my knowledge." This woman, a grammar-school graduate, says that she "constantly stresses the need for being prepared to be a good citizen" and feels that all mothers ought to "teach their children the need of more education and the difference it makes to be intelligent." If they did this, "the country wouldn't be so full of people no good to themselves or anyone else." She makes them all go to Sunday School, and the older ones to church also. She hopes they'll "choose the better things in life" but is going to "let them be what they want to be." She is very conscious of her "sacrifice" for the children, stating: "I do without almost everything myself in order for them to have what we can give them. I explain to them that I am doing my best and sacrificing my life that theirs can be better for them than mine has been for me." Children in lower-middle-class families very often get this kind of lecture.

For most of the children in these families, a "good education" means a high school education at the most, but a few go on beyond. One domestic servant said proudly:

"The eighth grade is as far as I got in school, but I wanted that son of mine to get a chance. So I sent him to Howard University in Washington. He graduated down there and now he's a doctor practicing in New York. He wants me to come there and live with him. But he's married and I don't want to be in the way."

Striving and Straining: The whole atmosphere of middle-class life is one of tension, particularly at upper-middle-class level, or among people on the way up, but not yet secure in their position. The drive to get ahead, to "lay a little something by," to prepare for the education of children, and at the same time to keep up "front" by wearing the right kind of clothes, having a "nice home," and belonging to the proper organizations—the pursuit of these goals brings into being definite social types which Bronzeville calls "strivers" and "strainers." With limited incomes, the problem of striking a balance between the conspicuous consumption necessary to maintain status, and long-range goals like buying property and educating children, becomes a difficult one. During the Depression years particularly, Bronzeville's middle-class families faced a continuous crisis.

Sometimes the family units break under the strain, particularly if one of the partners is oriented toward excessive conspicuous consumption. The testimony of the husband quoted below may be a rationalization in his individual case, but it does indicate a type of domestic tragedy that occurred often enough in upper-middle-class circles to excite widespread comment:

"One reason my wife and I couldn't make it was that she wanted to spend everything on good times and clothes. I wanted to have something some day. My wife makes good money as a schoolteacher, but she spends more than she makes all the time. Just about the time she gets out of debt she's back in again in a big way. Our paths are just two different ones. We'll never be able to make it. We've agreed to disagree, and my mother's here taking care of the child.

"I'm trying to raise my daughter to be a real substantial person. I try to talk to her about her future. My mother treats her just like she's her own child. I want to give her all the advantages and opportunities I'd have had if I hadn't married so soon."

The last comment is very general in middle-class circles. "I would have been farther ahead if I hadn't married so soon." And this attitude further weakens the stability of the family. But the need to maintain front and the concern for children are a counterweight to separation which does not operate generally at the lower-class level. The relative stability of the middle-class family is partly a function of long-time goals and of the desire to be "respectable" even if it means sacrificing personal happiness.

ORGANIZATIONAL LIFE OF THE MIDDLE CLASS

The dominating note of middle-class life is "getting ahead." This means "having the proper connections" as well as a stable pattern of sex and family life. The traditional bulwarks of organized middle-class life—the conservers of the traditions—have been the church and the lodge. The latter has within the last twenty years lost most of its influence, but the church is still a rather important element of middle-class social organization. Recreational clubs of all types—athletic, riding, musical, card-playing, and dancing—exist in Bronzeville, as well as the more serious "civic" organizations. Many people organize their spare time around one or several "centers of orientation." These numerous organizations express the middle-class standards of disciplined and ordered behavior as contrasted with the general disorganization at the lower-class level. Middle-class individuals are great "joiners" and "belongers," and these organizations assume a special importance in a community where family background is not too important. They are the organs by which aggressive individuals rise in the world and confirm their status. They also provide numerous positions of leadership for the ambitious and serve as an outlet for talent.

Though there is a church-centered middle-class group, the church seems to be giving way in importance to the more secular organizations. At the lower-class level the church is almost the only element of stable, organized life; but this is not true of the middle class. When a highly respected and popular businessman can answer "Hell, no!" to the question, "Do you belong to a church?" it is obvious that church membership is not a crucial or decisive middle-class trait. There is, in fact, a large secular-minded group within Bronzeville's middle class which believes that "Negroes have too much religion" and that "preachers aren't doing the race any good." There are many more, however, like the proprietor of a small business who said: "I pay my dues at church wherever I go, but I don't believe in neglecting my wife, home, and children's needs in order to make an impression at church. I'm buying a home and I believe that a man should pay his honest debts first before doing so much on the outside."

Occasionally a person turns up like the postal clerk who doesn't go to church because he thinks he's "unworthy": "I belong to the Methodist church but I don't go. I believe that church people ought to be aboveboard. I don't think that I ought to be active in the church until I change my way of living."

There are still others like the college-bred Red Cap who is a trustee of a Baptist church and who believes that "Christianity at its best is indispensable to the full flowering of human personality."

It is not necessary to be a church member to maintain middle-class status and to have friendly and close relations with the church-centered middle-class people. But if a person does belong to a church it must be "the right kind."

MIDDLE-CLASS RELIGION

When a person in Bronzeville says that he is "sanctified" or that he attends a Spiritualist church or one of the "cults," he is immediately marked down as "low-status." We have referred in the preceding chapter to the fact that the members and preachers of these churches are well aware that they are "looked down on." If a man says he's an Episcopalian or a Congregationalist, Bronzeville thinks of him as "dicty" or a "strainer" or "striver." But if he says he's Baptist or Methodist or Catholic he can't be "placed" until he tells what specific congregation he belongs to. Some entire denominations are "class-typed," but among the larger denominations there are "class-typed" congregations *within* the group. There are, for instance, one or two Methodist and Baptist churches that have the reputation of "catering to high-toned people," and there are scores of churches that are of very low status—usually store-fronts.

If we examine what the opponents of store-fronts have to say about them, we get some clues as to what makes a church low-status. A rather comfortably situated Catholic housewife comments on her religious preferences as follows:

"I like good music, but I don't like the songs that these gospel choirs in the store-fronts sing—these jazz tunes. I think it is heathen-like to jazz hymns. Another thing about these store-fronts is all these funny 'isms'— like giving a person a rose that's been blessed with the idea of bringing good luck. Some people actually believe these fool things."

A young high-school graduate who wants to go to college pays his respects to the store-fronts:

"I've stood outside these store-fronts a lot of times and listened to the people sing and dance. In my opinion that kind of service has done more than anything else to cheapen the feeling people once had for the church. When I stand and listen to them I say to myself, 'Why should I pay to see a show when these people are putting one on free?' "

A postal employee who is thinking of joining the Catholic Church comments:

"No wonder white people laugh at colored people and their peculiar ways of worship. Just look at these store-fronts. I don't believe in shouting and never did. I like a church that is quiet. I just can't appreciate clowning in any church."

Occasionally the store-front preachers are assailed:

"There's a store-front everywhere you turn. I think these people at the head of all these store-fronts are just in the churches for what they can get out of them. I know some of them may be in earnest, but since there is a church everywhere you turn, it makes me wonder if the people who are starting them are sincere."

"I don't know much myself, but I feel that people in the pulpit and schoolroom should be trained to lead other people. Some of these men and women take preaching for a racket—just to raise money in an easy way. Some of them preach one thing and live another."

A railroad porter, living in the high-status Rosenwald Apartments, was very definite in his opposition to store-fronts:

"I'm not in favor of these store-front churches. I think they give all churches a bad name. From what I know of them, the store-fronts are composed of people who have very little education, and their type of service is the kind that has made our people a laughing-stock for years. I may be too severe, but I think that everything people do ought to be done in an intelligent way."

Other persons interviewed were not so careful about being "severe." For instance, a young Presbyterian minister shelved his Christian charity to denounce them:

"I am certainly very much against store-fronts. They are demoralizing to our race. The field is overwhelmed with them. The lower class of people support them and I feel that they are just another place to go to express their pent-up emotions. They encourage 'jumping-jack' religion. I think those people are in the first stages of insanity."

A Congregational pastor, however, was somewhat more moderate in his appraisal:

"There is no doubt that some 'jack-leg' preachers are charlatans, but some aren't. A good many of them are ministering to folks that I just couldn't minister to. . . . The folks a 'jack-leg' preacher has to handle are in such a socio-economic and educational position that they just wouldn't understand me. They need an outlet for their embittered emotions. Their lives are pretty much disorganized. The 'jack-leg' preacher fills a need. He may be ignorant and utterly uninformed in the respects that we think a preacher should be trained, but he has a useful role."

Even while justifying the existence of the store-front, however, this minister reveals the class gulf between his upper-middle-class congregation and lower-class church people.

If we analyze the complaints which middle-class people make against store-fronts, it is obvious that it is not *size* alone that repels them. They are reacting against the type of religious *behavior* which goes on in most store-fronts—and this behavior is not confined to such churches. There are at least three Baptist churches seating over 2,000 members which have the reputation of being "shouting churches," as well as several Methodist churches. Two or three Holiness congregations and one Spiritualist church also have large edifices in which the members praise the Lord with gusto. One young lady, high-school-trained, belongs to one of these large Baptist churches:

"I belong to the —— Baptist Church. Rev. —— is my pastor. He is certainly a good man and a soul-stirring preacher. The only thing I dislike about the church is the shouting of its members. It seems like Rev. —— never wants to end a sermon until his flock gets happy. The men as well as the women have outbursts. They run up and down the aisles shaking and yelling, overcome as it were with emotion. I get happy to the point of wanting to cry and sometimes do, but I have known the sisters and brothers to become so happy that persons around them are in actual danger of getting knocked in the face. They might even get their glasses broken sometimes if the 'nurses' didn't watch out for them." *

The woman just quoted has remained in her church, but many people of her type either move to some other quieter denomination or to a quieter church within the denomination. The split between "shout-

* Some of these churches have a white-uniformed nursing corps to take care of the shouters.

ers" and "non-shouters" often reflects an age division as well as a class division. Both middle- and lower-class people in the older age groups lean toward the "old-time religion"; the younger people of both classes, toward "refined," "fashionable," or even "high-toned" religion.

One minister in a church where objections to shouting had been raised stated:

"I try to preach to the old as well as the young. You know most of the older people have worked hard to help us, and they just want a little consideration. I think every church should remember that the older people struggled to help get us where we are. Some preachers just push the older people out of the picture. I don't have much of a shouting crowd, but they know they can shout if they want to. You know young people are educated so far above the older people that the older people feel out of place in some of our churches."

Preachers of this type, concerned with holding the allegiance of "shouters" and "non-shouters," face a problem. Out of their attempts to meet it have arisen the "mixed-type" or "mass" churches, in which the tone is set by people with middle-class aspirations, but in which some concession is made to the "shouters." These churches, with memberships ranging from a thousand to five or six thousand, tie together people of all social levels into a functioning unit. This is done by having a variety of organizations and activities, and by modifying the ritual so as to put the older middle-class people and the lower-class members at ease. The pastor of such a church is usually a college-trained, middle-class man, who consciously manipulates the status system to get the maximum in co-operation. He even turns class divisions into an asset by organizing competition between groups of differing class levels in money-raising campaigns, always taking care, of course, to moderate and control the rivalry so that it does not flare into open antagonism. Occasionally, however, a church will "split" if the pastor is not skillful; some of his lower-class members may desert to the storefronts or to a large "shouting church," or some of his middle-class members may transfer to a "dicty" congregation or a high-status denomination.

The Mixed-type Church: Most of Bronzeville's middle-class church people belong to what one student has called the "mixed-type" congregation,[1] one that incorporates both lower-class and middle-class features in its ritual and its pattern of organization. Most of the very large

congregations and many of the medium-sized churches try to hold together in one congregation the people who like "rousements" and
"shouting," as well as those who prefer a more restrained service. The
pastor of a large church must cater to those who like the "old-time
religion" as well as to the more modern members. Such ministers become adept at keeping the allegiance of both groups.

To satisfy middle-class members, an astute pastor of a mixed-type
church will present a "prepared message" with moral and ethical exhortation and intelligent allusions to current affairs; but he will also
allow his lower-class members to shout a little. Such shouting is usually
rigidly controlled,* however, so that it does not dominate the service.
Since most of the pastors of the larger churches are seminary-trained
men with a middle-class orientation, and some are university men
with advanced degrees, they do not want to be classed as "ignorant"
or "uncultured," nor do they wish to alienate professional and businessmen, or younger people who reject the "old-time religion."

So a skillful pastor will rigorously control the emotional display by
changing the tone of his sermon at strategic points to stimulate shouting, shutting it off before it gets out of hand. Thus, one very astute
performer shouts his audience violently and then suddenly stops, with
a remark such as the following:

"My, I forgot where I was this morning. I musta thought I was still
down between the plow-handles and not here in a Chicago pulpit. Lemme
get back to this paper [manuscript]. I forgot I had these educated folks
in here.† But I'm not ashamed of my Jesus!" [There will be a chorus of
"Amens" and some laughter, and the shouting will be over for a while.]

* There are significant exceptions. In one of the largest Baptist churches in
Bronzeville, for instance, the pastor often lets his shouters get out of hand, with
people falling out and running up and down the aisles hysterically. Yet this
church has a large middle-class attendance. At the opposite extreme is a church
where the pastor has been known to stop when a member began to shout, commenting sarcastically: "We'll just wait until the confusion is over. God doesn't
like confusion."

† There is some evidence that, while the younger and the middle-aged persons
of higher-status levels belonging to "mass churches" do not shout, they are not
overcritical of shouters. They will ridicule them privately or smile superciliously
at each other when a shouting display begins in church, but will defend the
right of the shouters to "get happy." One interview study revealed that three-
fourths of a sample of professional people made statements such as the following: "There's no harm in shouting in church. White people shout . . . it is a
product of the environment." "I think . when it's sincerely done, it's all right.
On the whole, though, I regard it as a turning back toward slavery days." "The

When Baptist and Methodist conventions and conferences are in session, even a "dicty" middle-class church may become the scene of considerable shouting. On one occasion when the pastor of a local Methodist church shouted the congregation at the annual conference, a woman sitting next to the participant-observer remarked, "I declare, you would think we were in Reverend Cobb's [Spiritualist] church, the way these people are acting tonight." When asked, "Don't they shout at the regular services?", the woman answered, "No, but you know there are people here from 'all over' tonight." The preacher was aware of the possible criticisms that might be leveled at him by some of his members and tried to head it off. Clapping his hands and walking to and fro, he cried out pointedly: "We don't have conferences like this up here in the North. These are the kind we have down home!" An evangelist who followed him on the program also made a defensive statement:

"I don't know about you, but I feel all right. I don't believe in being a fool, but I *am* a fool *for God*. All over everywhere folks are fools for the Devil. A couple of years ago, at the annual conference, many men turned away from me because of my 'foolishness.' They said, 'You are going crazy.' But the spirit moved me. If you ever have 'it' really happen to you, you can't forget it. Sometimes, I like to turn loose. I want everyone to know I'm a fool for God."

Another familiar device for establishing rapport with the lower class in a mixed church is "talking down"—using dialect or broken English, or referring to aspects of lower-class life. Talking down ranges from quiet statements of sympathy with the trials and tribulations of the lower class to a very secular, and even joking, attitude toward lower-class "sins." Pastors of mixed-type congregations also occasionally play up to their lower-status members by putting the higher-status members in their places. This is usually done by direct allusions to the "sinfulness" of the proud or to the "pretensions" of the educated. The lower-class members of a congregation will always say *"Amen"* with fervor when a preacher modernizes a Bible story in the following manner:

church is surcease from six days of labor—after all, they can't go to universities and bridge parties. I think they need some emotional outlet."

One-fourth of the persons interviewed, however, were bitterly critical of such behavior: "I think such people are silly." "I think they're crazy." "I become very much disgusted." "It [shouting] seems entirely unnecessary to me." (Ethel Ramsey Harris, *op. cit.,* Appendix.)

"Jesus was standing by the temple, trying. to teach the people. Here come the scribes and the Pharisees in their long robes, trying to catch him, trying to set a trap for him. One of them says, 'Rabbi, is it right for us to pay taxes to Caesar?' They thought they had him in a hole. But my Jesus asked one of the disciples to give him some money; then he held it up and he asked them, 'Whose picture do you see on there?' One of them said, 'Caesar's.' 'Well,' my Lord said, 'render unto Caesar the things that are Caesar's and unto God the things that are God's.' That fixed 'em—all those Ph.D.'s in their long robes and mortarboard hats, all puffed up with their education. With all their degrees and learning, they couldn't trick the Son of the Living God!"

Higher-status members understand the necessity for this type of appeal to the uneducated, even if it is at their expense. Instead of being insulted, they are more likely to smile and say, "Rev. —— knows his psychology."

Other features of a Sunday worship service than the sermon have this dual class appeal. All of Bronzeville's churches have an adult or senior choir, and many have a junior choir. These present ordinary hymns and anthems. Some are highly trained choral groups. But, in addition to these choirs, most large Bronzeville churches also have one or two "gospel choruses"—a concession to lower-class tastes. A gospel chorus is not highly trained, but it is usually loud and spirited. The gospel chorus specializes in spirituals and revival songs. Chorus members often shout while they sing. In many lower-class churches there is no choir other than the gospel chorus. These choruses are very popular throughout Negro America and have an independent national organization known as The National Convention of Gospel Choruses and Choirs, the president of which is a Bronzeville musician. (In the course of his presidential address in 1939, he referred to the opposition that gospel choruses encounter from "high-toned" people who think that "God just wants to hear anthems and arias.")

The "Order of Sunday Worship Service" as printed in one Baptist church newspaper reveals the place assigned to the gospel chorus:

> 10:45 A.M.—*Organ Prelude*
> 11:00 A.M.—*Processional—All Hail the Power*
> *Chant—Congregation—Holy, Holy, Holy*
> *Scripture Reading*
> *Chant—"Let the Word of My Mouth"*
> *Morning Hymn—"Keep Me Every Day"*

Invocation
Song—Gospel Chorus
Consecration and Meditation
Anthem—Choir
Tithes and Offerings
Song—Choir
Sermon
Invitation—Gospel Chorus
Special Offering
Doxology—Benediction

The weekly calendar of this same church also indicates "concessions" to the lower-status members in the form of midweek vespers and a visit on Wednesday to a Spiritualist church:

SUNDAY:
9:15 A.M.—Church School—"Take my yoke, learn of me."
11:00 A.M.—Worship Service—O Come! Let us bow before Him.
3:00 P.M.—Pastor to preach at Morning Star, "Love ye one another."
6:00 P.M.—BYPU—A Christian Program for Young and Old.
8:00 P.M.—Holy Communion—"This do in remembrance of Me!"

MONDAY:
12:00 Noon—Housewives' Hour—"Church Women and Their Work."
2:00 P.M.—Missionary Society.
7:30 P.M.—Progressive Young Women Meeting.
8:00 P.M.—Calendar Social.

TUESDAY:
8:00 P.M.—Midweek Vespers—Meditation, Bible Study, Prayer, Song—Sermonette.

WEDNESDAY:
8:00 P.M.—Pastor to preach at 1st Deliverance, Spiritualist.

THURSDAY:
8:00 P.M.—Mortgage-Burning Meeting, Educational Movies Program, Christian Social.

FRIDAY:
12:00 Noon—Mothers' Annual Dinner.

The same issue of the church paper announced "PRIZES AWARDED FASHION-SHOW TICKET-SELLERS" and carried a half-page of ads from Negro businesses.

Faced with the competition of secular organizations, and constantly needled by businessmen and Race Leaders, the pastors of Bronzeville's larger churches can attract and hold middle-class members only by making some concessions to their standards, too. For the Baptist and Methodist churches there is always the competition of the Presbyterians, the Congregationalists, the Episcopalians, the Christian Scientists, and the Lutherans, who offer what is called colloquially a more "high-toned" service. Yet an appreciable number of people with a middle-class orientation (including a great many young people who have attended or finished high school) do not leave the churches in which they were raised for the less emotional denominations.

Appeals to middle-class members, as previously said, take the form of "good" music rendered by a well-trained choir singing anthems and other classical religious works. The ministers take some care, too, to prepare intelligent sermons and to deliver at least a part of the message in such a form as not to alienate the "educated" members. They refer frequently to "advancing The Race," and mention with praise individuals who are away at school and those who are Race Leaders. They also handle their services in such a way as to signify that they appreciate the "higher things of life." It is not at all unusual to hear a minister make a remark such as, "All this hollering and shouting isn't religion."

The large "mixed type" church is an institution with members of diverse class levels under the leadership of a middle-class preacher who skillfully attempts to gradually reshape lower-class behavior into a middle-class mold. Meanwhile, the institution provides meaningful activity for people of diverse social levels. The medium-sized and large churches are very complex institutions with a variety of sub-organizations and activities. This permits the voluntary segregation of persons within the church according to class lines. Individuals gravitate to those organizations in which people like themselves are in the majority. Thus, weekly prayer meetings tend to have a lower-class pattern and to attract the older people who wish to sing, pray, and shout. Missionary societies tend to organize middle-aged and older women who do not have a social-club pattern or civic interests. Here they may gain prestige from money-raising and from participation in the larger state and national conventions. Mothers' boards also function to make a place for the older woman of lower- or middle-class rank. There is a tendency for upper middle-class people to assume the positions of financial leadership within the larger churches and to take over all posts which require some training, such as the direction of the choral groups or the keeping of records. A large church duplicates the pattern of social stratification in the outer world.

The Preacher as a Race Leader: The ministry is not a very popular profession with Negro college graduates. Yet enough young Negro men enter the ministry to provide a group of well-trained ministers for the larger mass churches and for the few high-status churches. These ministers, on the whole, tend to be theologically conservative, at least in their public utterances. An interview-study of the 51 most prominent Bronzeville preachers made in 1935 indicated that on such matters as the Virgin Birth and orthodox conceptions of sin and salvation and Biblical authority, the majority claimed to be dispensers of "sound doctrine." (See Table 31.) This same group of ministers was sophisticated enough to have doubts about miracles and to profess an interest in squaring religion with science. (Answers to questions 5 and 6, top.) Yet, paradoxically, they were on the whole very conservative when asked about certain church procedures. The overwhelming majority believed that people needed "individual conversion" in order to be saved, and that "Christian education" (moral instruction) was no substitute for a "second birth." They thought, too, that preaching was the most important function of the church and that the Bible should be the center of Sunday School instruction. A surprisingly large number claimed to believe that church property was sacred and that preparing people for Heaven was the churches' main business.

The latter responses are interesting in view of the facts that Bronzeville's large churches are anything but other-worldly institutions, and that their pastors concern themselves with all sorts of community matters, including politics. It seems likely, however, that these ministers feel that they must stress religion as the *raison d'être* for their churches even while they make them community institutions. This is their sole claim to leadership as they face the competition of secular leaders.

These pastors of middle-class churches may say they believe that their primary job is "to prepare people for Heaven," but they are very this-worldly. The Negro church is a "Race institution" and the preachers, in their sermons and through their support of Negro politicians and professional and business men as well as in their connections with organizations like the NAACP and the Urban League, display a lively interest in "advancing The Race." In fact, not a few ministers

TABLE 31

SELECTED OPINIONS ON MATTERS OF FAITH AND CHURCH PROCEDURE OF
51 BRONZEVILLE PASTORS: 1935 *

	Conservatives (Answer: "True")	Liberals	
		Modernists (Answer: "False")	Doubtful
Matters of Faith			
1. The death of Jesus on the Cross is the one act that makes possible the remission of man's sin.	37	6	8
2. It was God's plan that Jesus should die on the Cross to save the world	34	11	6
3. Jesus was born of a Virgin without a natural father.	33	12	6
4. The Bible is the complete and final revelation.	29	16	6
5. God sometimes interferes with Nature to perform miracles.	16	28	7
6. Religious ideas cannot be interpreted in the light of the scientific interpretation of the universe.	7	30	14
Church Procedure			
1. Christian education can never be a substitute for conversion.	47	1	3
2. Preaching is the most important function of the church.	43	7	1
3. The main aim of Christian education should be to teach the Bible.	36	11	4
4. Nothing should be included in the church program which does not prepare for life after death.	33	12	6
5. The church should be reserved for worship only.	32	18	1
6. Modern Christian education undermines the authority of the Scriptures.	20	6	25

* Compiled by the authors from data in David Rice Hedgley, "The Attitude of Negro Pastors in Chicago toward Christian Education," Master's Thesis, University of Chicago, 1935.

dabble in business ventures or serve on boards of Negro business enterprises. The following life history of the pastor of a large Baptist church illustrates the type of preacher who is likely to get ahead as the pastor of a middle-class church. He is considered "a progressive young man," a "go-getter," and is interested in labor activities as well as in Negro business.

"I was born in 1904 on a farm in Mississippi. I went to a rural school until I was sixteen and had completed the fifth grade. I then left home to work on the railroad as a water boy, section hand, and track man. I made $21 a week, plus overtime. When I was nineteen, I returned home. Father gave me a horse which I immediately tried to sell, but I couldn't get enough money for him. Finally, I found a man who traded his mule colt for my horse. I then sold the colt for $50 and with this money decided to go to Jackson, Mississippi, and enter school: My father gave me $20 more. At this time I was a big, overgrown boy, countrified, nineteen years old and had only been to fifth grade. I enrolled in the public school, but the kids all laughed at me so I quit.

"I then went to Jackson College [a boarding school] and talked with the president. He was a very kind man and encouraged me to enter special classes for overgrown students. I studied hard and in two and a half years completed the eighth grade. While in school I worked at the best hotels as porter, elevator operator, bus boy, clothes-presser, and waiter. I am an expert waiter.

"I came to Chicago in April of 1926. My first job was as a waiter. I entered Wendell Phillips High School, graduating in three and a half years with an average of nearly 90. While attending high school, I worked at night at the stockyards and at a hotel. The white woman who ran the hotel was a good, understanding friend.

"In 1930, I registered at a law school. One day on my way to class I had what I term a mystical experience. I was led not to take law, but to register at the Moody Bible Institute and to prepare for the ministry. I graduated from there. I took a general course and a special course in archeology. In my class were 150 students, the largest ever to graduate. I was the only Negro in the class.

"For two years after finishing the Bible School, I worked at a law firm as an all-round man. I served warrants and was a general investigator. My average salary was $80 a week. In 1934 I entered the Baptist Theological Seminary, graduating with a Th.B. There were two Negroes in my class. I have since registered at Northwestern University and have done all my B.D. work except one year of Greek and the writing of a thesis. I hope to start work on my Master's in the fall.

"In 1930, while attending law school, I opened a grocery store and school supply store. I sold it in 1931 for $900 cash. I also worked for a while as a clothing salesman. I preached my first sermon on Easter in 1932. My subject was 'The New Birth.' That same year, I went into the undertaking business, and five months later was called as 'supply pastor' to the Solid Rock Baptist Church. After supplying for three months, they called me to the pastorate.

"I married in 1927. My wife is a preacher's daughter and has had two years of high school. She is now taking nursing. She is rather quiet and reserved, easy to get along with, and understands a minister's work; she's not jealous.

"Since I took this church we have enrolled 2,400 members. I have baptized 1,000 myself. We have an active membership of 700. We have built and paid for the first unit of our church. It was a storefront, at first, you know. It seats 500 now. We are only $400 in debt, and we hope to complete building next year.

"In our church we have adult education classes—sewing, business administration, and reading and writing—all sponsored by the WPA. We also have a benevolent society connected with the church, of which I am president. This society charges 10 cents to join and a 10 cents weekly fee. We give a $2 sick benefit and a $90 burial. We have a welfare center and a free employment agency. In the last two years we have placed 187 people on jobs. I also have assigned to my supervision a number of boys from the juvenile court, and six men from Pontiac and Joliet [state prisons].

"I am a part of every organization in the Baptist church and am secretary of my association, which consists of more than 70,000 members. I am secretary of the Apex Funeral Parlor, Inc., and I own a half-interest in the business and the funeral cars. I am a Mason, and also the sponsor of a Boy Scout troop.

"I own a three-flat building and a vacant lot. I also have a two-car garage. I might add that I carry $5,000 in straight life insurance and a $1,000 sick and accident policy. I own a good car.

"My salary from the church is $35 a week. They pay me, too—not *promise* to pay!"

.

Middle-class people (and Bronzeville in general) expect the ministers to be interested in "advancing The Race." Ministers accept this as one of their functions, and during the Depression years the pastors of all of the larger churches were active in campaigns for better housing, more adequate relief, and health programs.

The way in which "advancing The Race" becomes an integral part of church dogma may be illustrated by an excerpt from a pamphlet written just before the CIO drive in the late Thirties by the pastor of one of Bronzeville's highest status churches.[2]

THE GREAT OPPORTUNITY OF THE NEGRO CHURCH

Dr. George E. Haynes of the Federal Council of Churches [a Negro] advanced the idea that, inasmuch as the Negroes are not organized in labor unions, as 85 per cent of them are in industrial or domestic occupations, and as the Negro church is the largest organized unit of Negro life, the Negro Church today faces a most unusual opportunity to overcome an uneconomic and unsocial past. The building up of a moral reserve, the securing of Negro workmen's living standards, the saving of body along with the soul, is the big job for Christianity today. All interracial contacts must point to deep understanding of the problems of living which all must face, especially Negroes. The problem of Christianity among the 13,000,000 Americans of African descent is more or less contingent upon the Christian solution of the problem here. Chicago, one of the greatest racial laboratories of the world, faces, because of its very constitution and problem, an opportunity and a challenge that are unique.

Pastors of the larger mass-churches are less erudite in their formulation of the problem and are sometimes very blunt in their statement of what they think the Black Ghetto needs in the way of social reform. They have a tendency, too, to stress individual salvation as well as social service. The comments of the pastor of one very large church during Negro Health Week will illustrate this type of straight talk:

"I think it would be a good thing for everyone in this church—visitors, friends, and members alike—to go out and find a child and put him in the Bible Study School of this church. We have a certain definite program that we are going to carry out in an effort to try to save our race. Sometimes a good talk is better than a sermon. The world is laughing at us. Do you know that venereal diseases are eating us up? That a very large percentage of syphilis and gonorrhea is found among our little children of five, six, and ten years old? Out of a corrupted mess like that we cannot hope to do anything."

Anticipating middle-class resentment and embarrassment, and lower-class disapproval of injecting such worldly matters into a sermon, the minister continued:

"It may not sound right to speak about this on Sunday, but it is something that we suffer for on Monday. Unless the Negro churches will get busy and help to save them you—as a race—are damned forever. Get out in these alleys and get these children who need guidance and help."

Middle-class people seldom respond to these exhortations to do missionary work among the lowers, but they, as well as church-people of all social levels, are continually talking about "saving the youth" of Bronzeville.

"Saving the Youth": Bronzeville's devouter church people are almost unanimous in their belief that "our young people are on the road to Hell." They see the youngsters streaming to the movies and taverns and dance-halls—even on Sunday, for Sunday School and young people's societies are unable to compete with the city's more exciting leisure-time pursuits. They know that the lower-class world provides even more sinister enticements and that the preacher's pleas, the teacher's admonitions, and their own whipping and counseling do not hold the children in line. Older people in Bronzeville, like oldsters everywhere, spend a great deal of their time shaking their heads and denouncing the younger generation. Most of them feel that the church ought to do something about it.

In analyzing the problem of juvenile delinquency, Bronzeville's middle-class ministers usually exhibit an interesting blend of theology and sociology. One minister began a sermon by insisting that "we can't have peace until sin is conquered," and then proceeded to say that "Christian people must help to fight down some of the things in our community that cause our boys and girls to go astray." He gave his prescription as follows:

"I tell you I am getting quite alarmed about our young people. I was called into a private meeting with some of the city officials. They told me that the Negro youth of Chicago were committing more crimes than ever in the history of Chicago. They wanted to know just what is the cause. I could only give this solution—wipe out vice and give my people jobs!"

In the final analysis, all preachers blame the home. One minister did so before a statewide Baptist convention by saying:

"We must have Christian fellowship in the home. Boys don't want to be bad, but economic conditions compel them to be so. One parent has to get up at one hour; another at another hour; and one may work at night. There is no more of that 'set time' for devotion in the home. This has caused the home to be upset. What to do about it? Re-establish family altars. . . . Bring the young people into the church. . . . Make your children comrades. . . . The home has fallen short of what it should do. You can never have right homes unless they are built on this book [the Bible]."

He compared the Baptists and Methodists with the Catholics and Jews who "come closer to saving their young people by not letting outsiders get to them. Wherever you find a Jewish synagogue or Catholic Church, you find their school right along with it. If you can't make a program to interest them you can't hold the young people. If you can't hold the young people, what of the future?"

The large Baptist and Methodist denominations have their hands tied, however. In the first place, "sound doctrine" does not permit dancing and card-playing under secular auspices. It absolutely forbids any such activities under church control. Attempts to plan community recreational programs therefore do not have the wholehearted support of most older church people except among Congregationalists, Episcopalians, and Catholics.

The feeling that they are losing the youth leads many ministers to assail the Catholics and other churches that do not denounce card-playing and dancing. One minister commented: "You've got a proposition on your hands with the Catholics. They say these things are all right if you go to Mass afterwards." Several conferences have been held in Bronzeville during the last few years to discuss ways and means of saving Protestant youth from the Catholics. At one such conference a preacher advised, "Have a program so interesting that the Catholics will come *here*." But he had no practical suggestions. Another minister said, "If the Catholics encourage them with plays and parties, so can we." He then mentioned an attempt to poll some youngsters in his church as to what they did at the last party they had attended. They answered, "We talked a while, played cards, and danced." An elderly delegate to the conference shouted out, "That's all they want to do— play cards!" This particular meeting closed with another statement of generalities:

"You can't tell young people to come back to the church because your parents go to this church. Youth must have recreation. The church alone can't do the job, but there should be a set-up made of half adults and half youths to make a program for young people under the right direction where they can function at our own churches."

Some of the younger ministers venture timid suggestions, such as:

"Help them along by entertaining them. Don't say they can't dance, but occupy their time so they don't think of dancing."

The majority—the standpatters—continue to thunder away in the traditional theological vein, like one pastor who blamed *the home* ("There are so many broken homes among our race that are causing our boys and girls to go astray"); *the schools* ("they allow slot machines in their vicinity" and they "poison the mind against God"); the *recreational centers* (which "are not properly supervised"); *obscene literature* (which "is everywhere"); the *moving pictures* (some of which "are too suggestive for even older people to see"); *laziness* (on the part of youth); and *lack of patriotism*. He concluded with an attack on another group whose influence has been worrying the clergy:

"We owe all our patriotism to our country. One thing we can say for the Negro race in America: we have reduced our ignorance, created wealth, and educated our boys and girls, so I am telling you to be loyal to the country. Don't join no Reds, no time, nowhere! The battle isn't long. I am urging Christians to put on the whole armor of Faith and pray that our young people will overcome and the way will be clearer and clearer for them to lift up the banner of Jesus Christ."

The lower-class youngsters meanwhile continue to go to Sunday School (if sent) until they reach their teens. Then they begin to feed their nickels into the tavern jukeboxes and to cut rugs in the "jive-joints." When they have the money, they "tog down" and go to the cheaper dance halls. A few of them also continue to attend church. More of them do not attend, but laugh and joke at the antics of their elders who "shout" and denounce "the world."

Although unable to attract any large number of lower-class youth, the middle-class churches do manage to retain the loyalties of numerous young people from middle-class families. This is done by a sort of compromise. The young people ignore the injunctions against card-playing and dancing and meet their recreational needs by joining social clubs. The preacher on his part, while he may preach against card-playing and dancing, never embarrasses his members by "bringing them before the church" for trial and expulsion or "repentance." Hundreds of cases have been noted in which young people—"loyal church workers"—lead a double life from the standpoint of the religious die-hards. One young girl, for instance, who was quite active in her Sun day School told an interviewer that she liked her church but also her social club. She belonged to the Snappy Sophisticates and observed: "I like both, but it is natural for young folks to want to have some pleasure outside of the church." Another young lady stated: "I like the church, but of course there are certain things that you can't do in the church, and that is why there are so many social clubs." One girl said: "They're both important in their place. I like the church, but a young person in these days must have some place to go beside the church and the show." She has not become "church-centered" because as she phrased it:

"There are certain things you can do in a social club you might be criticized for doing in a church.* Really we organized the club so we could have some dances to attend. My mother is really peculiar about dances. She starts questioning you—Who is going to be there? So a group of us girls got together and organized us a club of our own."

On the other hand, a young member of a medium-sized Baptist church and an officer in Les Jolies Douze (a social club) reported that her club began with a church clique:

"The idea was mine. I suggested the idea of forming a club to some of my friends who are members of my church. Most of us attend the Stone of Moses Baptist Church. Most of us also belong to the Willing Workers, an organization in the church that raises money to help the sick members. Some of the members belong to the church's First Aid Society, too. I was president of the First Aid Society for three years, so I finally decided to give someone else a chance. . . . We play bridge one week, and whist the next. We have an annual invitational dance. . . . We also have two pay dances a year."

Few ministers of the larger churches wish to alienate this type of member by imposing drastic sanctions.

Since a large proportion of the middle-class church people attend movies and dances and play cards, verbal opposition to such "sins" has relaxed somewhat. A doctor or lawyer may be given a position of importance in a church, even though it is known that he is active in associations that give dances. And in one or two of the larger Baptist churches very prominent clubwomen whose names appear in the Bronzeville papers in connection with bridge parties and dances are

---

* Two pastors of high-status Baptist churches permit their young people's clubs to give dances. They are conspicuously "out of line," however.

considered valuable church workers. Hundreds of middle-class people like their church, but they like a good time too.

MIDDLE-CLASS "SOCIETY"

Glance at the placards in Bronzeville's store windows and you will see numerous notices of dances sponsored by this or that social club. Look through Bronzeville's newspapers and you will find columns devoted to the activities of such clubs—reports and pictures of dances, notices of club meetings to be held, and descriptions of those past. It is obvious that social clubs play an important part in community life. Most of them are middle-class organizations.

The names of some of the clubs reveal the light and gay spirit that characterizes them, as well as their average size. The mottoes that most of them have adopted suggest that the members feel constrained to stress a "serious" as well as a frivolous side. Social-club activity is confined to no one age-group or sex. Two-thirds of the clubs are composed of women only. The others are either all-male or mixed.*

The middle-class social-club world thrives on publicity. In the upper class, only the male dance clubs and the sororities and fraternities desire and receive publicity, but within this middle-class "Society" publicity is highly prized. Every social club has its reporter who must see

* The following are some typical club names:

Amicable Twelve	Ten Sweethearts	Twentieth Century
Loyal Twelve	Unique Twelve	Cavaliers
Don't Worry Twelve	Personality Eight	Women About Town
Duplex Nine	Midnight Twelve	Modern Maids
Eight Pals of Pleasure	Silent Eight	Avalon Bridge
Fourteen Orchids	Bronzettes	Bronzeville Debs
Original Sophisticated	Casanova Boys	Lovely Ladies
Eight	Duchesses	Aquamarian
Peppy Ten	Gayettes	Snappy Sorors
Ritzy Fifteen	Just Us Girls	Dawn Busters
Twelve Classyettes	Jolly Brownettes	Les Petite Chéries
Twelve Wonders	Leap Year Girls	Les Barons
Thrifty Twelve	Knock-Knock Club	Las Amigas Señoras
Busy Five	Moonlite Tippers	El Progresso Girls
Thirteen Congenial Girls	Orientalettes	Les Jolies Douze
Gracious Nine	Rialto Girls	Les Jolies Jeune Filles
Twelve Lucky Strikes	Starliteens	Semper Fidelis
Pepper Ten	Smart Debs	Les Invincibles
Octennettes	Twentieth Century Girls	Les Uniques Femmes
Merry Ten	Sophisticated Duchesses	

that notices of club meetings are inserted in the weekly press and that favorable accounts of dances and other special events, accompanied by pictures, will get into the papers. (Club news is reputed to be a great circulation-builder for Bronzeville weeklies.) Competition for favorable publicity is keen and a club always has its eye on what the *Defender* or some other paper will say about its affairs. Some eight or nine hundred small social clubs and their ten to twelve thousand members are thus bound together in a prestige system dependent upon newspaper publicity. Their rivalry for public attention makes them unusually responsive to the opinions of each other and to the attitude of the general public.

The typical social club is small, eleven members being the average. Such clubs usually begin as small cliques of friends who decide to "organize." Occasionally, everyone in the club is an officer, for there are usually a president, a vice president, a recording secretary, a corresponding secretary, a treasurer, and a reporter. Some clubs also have a parliamentarian, a social secretary, and a "sponsor" (usually a higher-status woman). All have a number of committees. In the average club the turnover in membership is high, but in 1938 at least a third of them had had a life-span of more than five years without a change in personnel. The others are constantly losing members and replacing them—a process that acquaints a wide circle of people with the correct behavior pattern for middle-class "Society."

These social clubs express and reinforce the middle-class ideals of restrained public deportment and "respectability." To be a Model Matron, for instance, one must be married, have over five years' residence in Midwest Metropolis, and a high school education. A member states: "Most of the ladies are housewives, and the character of a new member must always be vouched for by another member of the club." An officer of the Snappy Señoras describes her group: "We are all on the same level. We don't have any doctors' or lawyers' wives in the club. The girls who are married and are still with their husbands live good lives. Their husbands have good ordinary jobs, and of course some of the girls work." The constitution of the Modern Gaieties—organized "to socialize and do charitable work"—illustrates how elaborate the process of selecting new members may become. Only "young girls of good behavior and character" may belong, and

If a vacancy shall occur, any member may suggest a name and submit it to the chairman of the membership committee, who, in turn, submits it to the club to be considered before any mention of joining the club has been made to the girl in question.

When several girls' names are before the house for membership, the club will give a tea to which those girls will be invited. During the tea the members are given a chance to become acquainted with and observe the behavior of their guests.

The general run of clubs may not always have a tea to size up new members, but all of the middle-class social clubs do make some attempt to select new members who will not violate the general code of "respectability."

Club constitutions and by-laws also frequently provide for disciplining members who get out of line. The Modern Gaieties have a provision that "each member will be fined for violation of the following rules: talking out of turn or coming more than 15 minutes late—5¢." The Sepia Girls, somewhat lower in status, have similar rules incorporated in the by-laws:

Section 11: Any member or officer of this club who fails to report at business meetings shall be fined.

Section 12: Robert's *Rules of Order* and Congressional Rules and Regulations shall be the authority on all questions not covered by the constitution and by-laws.

There is a constant interchange of ideas on which breaches of decorum merit fines, and clubs revise their by-laws from time to time to embody provisions found in the regulations of Bronzeville's "good clubs." This voluntarily assumed discipline marks the great gap between lower-class and middle-class recreational behavior; such explicit statements of the code are never found in upper-class adult clubs, and they distinguish middle-class clubs from those "above" them socially.

Each middle-class club has a motto, a set of colors, and sometimes a flower. The Sepia Girls' constitution, for instance, reads as follows:

Article 1: This organization shall be known as the Sepia Girls Club; a social club consisting of not more than 15 matrons. The color scheme shall be carmine and silver.

Article 2: The object of this club is to bring about social contact between its members and the public, and to improve our standing.

Routine club activity involves a meeting twice monthly or oftener. Most of the adult clubs meet at the members' homes, rotating in alphabetical order, but at least a third of Bronzeville's younger clubs meet at the YWCA, the YMCA, the Federated Club House, or some similar public place. (In fact, some of the social agencies have attempted to organize the club pattern into their own institutional structure.) One factor that, perhaps, limits the size of clubs is the custom of home meetings, since, with the crowded living conditions in Bronzeville, entertaining a large group is usually impossible. A member of the Bronze Maidens described one proposed solution to the problem of finding space for meetings:

"We meet once a week at each member's house. We go alphabetically from A to Z. We are thinking of consolidating with a group of clubs, and we will all hold our meetings in some large hall. . . . We have a larger group now than we had three years ago, and it is hard for us to get into some of the members' homes, and we aren't able to rent a hall ourselves, so we decided to go in with some of the groups of clubs."

Behavior at club meetings varies little from club to club. The program consists of: (1) business, while visitors wait in another room; (2) card-playing; (3) eating; and (4) a period of rather general unorganized conversation and hilarity. There are wide variations, however, in the nature of the "business" discussed and in the amount of formality involved. Some of the clubs are very formal in their conduct of business, having a parliamentarian to correct the group on points of order, even when only four or five members are present. Since there is a great deal of interclub visiting, the clubs are careful about "doing things in an orderly manner" so that they will not get "a bad name." Some clubs play whist, but most play auction bridge and a few play contract. A few vary the procedure by the use of some currently popular game such as "Pick-up-sticks," "Lexicon," or "Pit."

It is customary for each club to give several "pay dances" during the year in order to raise money, and to present at least one elaborate formal a year to which only invited guests may come. Although various schemes are used for "building up a treasury," such as cabaret parties, plays, or teas, the most popular method is the pay dance. This involves extensive interclub co-operation. (Upper-class club people pay their dues and assessments but do not supplement their funds with "pay dances.")

A club deciding to give a dance requests other clubs to buy its tickets, and even to sell tickets; in turn, it feels obligated to do the same for other clubs. Such a system of reciprocal relationships, involving as it does several thousand people, is very complex, as was indicated by a prominent clubman who stated that he would be "going every night" if he went to every dance or affair for which somebody was trying to sell him a ticket.

These dances are an important agency for standardizing and disciplining public behavior within the middle class. Behavior at dances has been described by several band leaders as being very formal and correct, in significant contrast to dances at commercial halls frequented by the lower class:

"They are all 'on their behavior' when attending a club affair. If someone gets into a scrap, they know they are blacklisted from then on. So they keep on their P's and Q's. I think such things as fights are taboo at all types of dances now. They seem to realize that such things aren't to be tolerated any more and never start them."

As the above statement implies, and as is made explicit below, there was a time when fighting at club dances was not unknown. One prominent orchestra leader testified:

"But they broke that up years ago. In four years, in all my club playing, I haven't seen a fight. At a public dance one may see a fight or squabble, but it is soon quieted down by the floor walkers. Even at public dances, people go to enjoy themselves today, and they know they can't get away with it as they used to. As soon as a fight is started, someone with authority stops it. I am thankful for that!"

This opinion was shared by another orchestra leader who stated: "Why, say, man—the 'social affairs' are pretty nice now. But at a public dance, you may still run into a fight or squabble."

At a large pay dance many people will be present who are not club members, including some lower-class persons. All, however, are brought into a social situation which demands restraint and conformity to middle-class standards of decorum.

In the closing years of the Depression, the average profit from a "pay dance" was less than a hundred dollars, for an orchestra charged $30 or $40,* and $25 or $30 was required for rental of a hall; yet popu-

* In the fall of 1938, a group of clubs began to boycott the orchestras because they felt the union rate was too high. They threatened to use automatic phonographs, and they were powerful enough to make the union capitulate and reduce the fee.

lar clubs with energetic members often cleared considerably more than $100 from a single, well-worked-up dance.

One might ask: "What does a small club of ten or twelve members do with its money? Why does club life involve this extensive money-raising pattern?" In the first place, a club is expected to give at least one elaborate formal dance a year, to which it invites people it wishes to honor or gain prestige from, and entire clubs which it considers on its own social level. But not all the other clubs that sell its tickets are invited to its formal—only those whose members are liked or which must be impressed. At these formals, the club members are on display as a group, and usually wear some symbol such as a band across the breast in the case of men, or identical gowns in the case of women. As the high point of the occasion, the club members are introduced as a group to the assembled guests by a master of ceremonies. A formal, since it is an invitation affair, represents a considerable outlay of money. One popular club composed of nine upper-middle-class men spent $400 in 1938 for a formal, $100 going for invitations. Average expenditures are considerably lower, however.

Not all the social clubs spend all of their money for elaborate formals. Most of them contribute sparingly to various charities. Nearly a tenth of the clubs have a Christmas savings feature, several own or wish to buy clubhouses, and a few are saving money to go into business as a group. One large male club was functioning as a credit union in 1938. An officer described this club with much pride:

"Ours is the only club in the city, as far as I know, that makes loans. You noticed in our recommendations that from now on the loans are not to exceed $50. A member doesn't need to have any collateral to borrow money from the club, but other members have to sign with him, and if he doesn't pay, they have to pay his loan pro-rated among the members signing.

"We pay a sick benefit—$5 per week, but not to exceed six weeks. We've been chartered by the state for thirteen years as a social club—the 'Gay Counts'—you know, like in England, Counts? We're not chartered as a benevolent association or society, but as a social club.

"You remember the recommendation about the delinquent members? You know how it is—fellows get out of work and can't keep up their dues, and sometimes they hate to come to meetings. Well, we encourage them to keep on coming to meetings so they'll keep in touch with what's going on, but as long as they are delinquent, they are not allowed to vote or even enter in the discussion.

"Our membership is limited to fifty. We don't have fifty members now, though. Each member pays the doctor for the examination to become eligible for sick benefits, and the doctor is a club member. We get most of our revenue from dances. We give about four pay dances and two formals a year."

The status of a club within middle-class society depends on the elaborateness of entertaining and the orderliness of meetings, as well as on "giving a good formal." Within this close-knit social-club world there are certain popular clubs which set the pattern. Other clubs strive to imitate them and to win their approval. Among the most popular middle-class women's club on the eve of the Second World War was the "Amethyst Girls."

THE MODEL WOMEN'S CLUB

The eleven Amethyst Girls, women in their late thirties and early forties, light-brown-skinned to "very light," stylish dressers, and cultivated in manner, constitute one of the small group of clubs that set the pattern in the middle-class social-club world. These women are migrants from the South, but have lived in Bronzeville over fifteen years, and while none of them have had a college training they are all highly literate and deplore their "lack of education." One of them, in stating her own interests, reveals the conception of a life pattern which these women share:

"I would say that my hobbies are going places, doing things for others, and trying to use my time to the best of my advantage. I read, study, and go to lectures, movies, recitals, and plays, and I visit my friends and they visit me—and, of course, I attend quite a few dances. I enjoy teas quite a bit. They seem to have a fascination for people who like people."

All the women have been married, but six of the eleven are divorcées. None seem to have ever had employment as domestic servants, and at present the unmarried women are employed as seamstresses, maids, and attendants in downtown dress shops. They have acquired the reputation of being among the best-dressed women in Bronzeville. Although at the top of the middle-class social world, they have virtually no contact with the upper class except at very large dances.

Because their activities are highly publicized in Bronzeville's press, and because of the elaborate formal dances and fashion shows which they sponsor, the Amethyst Girls are well known in middle-class club circles. They are active church workers as well as clubwomen, and occasionally a notice of their elaborate cocktail parties will appear in the same edition of a paper which is publicizing their money-raising activities for one of the larger Baptist churches. They are also tied into the entire web of middle-class activities by their relations with other social clubs.

A single club meeting of the Amethyst Girls suggests the wide range of relationships which the members and the club sustain with other community groups, a factor which lends them increased prestige. At this meeting, the conversation over the bridge table and luncheon reflected the varied contacts and interests of the members.

There was a prolonged discussion about hold-ups on the South Side. Individual women recited their "harrowing experiences," one boasting that her husband had been "furious," and that he wanted to whip every man he saw who wore a leatherette lumber jacket, because the man who had been so brutal to her wore this type of jacket. Two of the women castigated the police, charging that "they are too busy wasting their time talking and drinking beer in such popular spots as the Apex Grill instead of keeping their eyes open and trying to do their duty as they should." "The cops on the North Side [white neighborhood] are more interested in the protection of their women and children than the cops are on the South and West Sides," one woman observed. The president and senior member felt that "clubwomen and Parent-Teachers Associations should co-operate and demand that womanhood be better protected. Something could be done if we forced action!"

There was a flurry of discussion on "policy," with some disagreement as to whether it should be sanctioned—a subject that is no doubt perplexing to these women, who on one hand are active church workers and "civic-minded," and on the other hand have intimate and friendly relations with the relatives of several policy kings.

An Amethyst Girl who had joined a newly organized Girls' Saddle Club described her club to the participant observer, mentioned some of the prominent members, boasted of the success of a cocktail party they had given, and spoke of "some persons excluded from the Saddle Club, because they dressed in their riding habits and just played around on the bridle path instead of learning to ride well." The Saddle Club girls, however, were "really riding" and they were "enjoying themselves," she said.

Throughout the evening there were references to various charitable enterprises in which the members were engaged. They discussed the Queens' Contest being given by the Matrons of Zenith Baptist Church in which two Amethyst Girls were entered (their club sisters were selling tickets to aid them). Several members congratulated one of their number who had recently organized a club at a Congregational church, the group having raised $55 by using "gleaners" (small cans for collecting coins). There was some discussion about a gift to a church Community Center Fund, and after the business meeting the treasurer announced that they were presenting the hostess with $12 for this charity.

An emissary from the Lions' Social Club (a young men's group of the same general class level) was present to announce a benefit dance which his club was giving for the Boys' Court work. Thirteen tickets had already been distributed among the Amethyst Girls. The president thanked the young man for coming, and stated that the club would "co-operate with the Lions in every way by trying to attend the affair themselves, and by telling others about it." One Amethyst Girl spoke of how much the Boys' Court work needed help, and urged every person to co-operate.

The luncheon was elaborate, as at all of their meetings. Their "repasts" are sometimes complete dinners from cocktails to mints.

The Annual Fashion Shows: The Amethyst Girls usually give two fashion shows a year, one for themselves and one for a Baptist church. In 1938 a newspaper headlined the latter in glowing terms: SPECTACULAR STYLE SHOW PACKS GLAMOROUS WALLOP IN FASHIONABLE CHURCH AND SOCIAL CIRCLES. A group picture of members of the Amethyst Girls who modeled gowns from their personal wardrobes appeared on the society page, with pictures of other participants. Individuals and their clothing were described in detail, with references to "the modiste wearing her own creation, a black chiffon evening gown, and a dinner gown of lovely passion-flowered matelassé"; another member, "striking in twenty yards of peach net, rhinestone-trimmed, over a lustrous slip"; and a third clad in "brown derby, brown coat, and brown boots, man-tailored gabardine suit and gray blouse."

The *Defender* in reporting the affair called it "one of the most spectacular style shows ever staged and directed down church aisles. . . . The church, newly decorated, flanked with palm, fern, and massive flower groups, offered something unique in the way of background for the pretty models who stepped blithely down the aisles of capacity-packed pews exhibiting to hundreds what the well-dressed maid, matron, and man of 1938 will wear." The show netted $1,173. A member commented on the club's fashion shows, the day after the church affair:

"I wore a violet dinner dress with a darker shawl to match. I also wore a veil and a flower in my hair. I have held the office of score-keeper in the club, and I was interested in the fashion show, but I wasn't particular about appearing. I thought that most of the officers should appear in the show. But I was a little tired of fashion reviews since we worked so hard to put over the big affair at Bacon's Casino this year. I think we made around $400 on the show there. That wasn't bad at all. Everybody in the club really worked."

Another member remarked:

"We look forward to our fashion show every year. We always model our personal wardrobes at our own show. We make money on the fashion shows every year. Now we don't have to worry about selling tickets. They sell themselves without very much sales talk."

The Annual Formal: The Amethyst Girls not only win prestige by serving as authorities on clothing styles. They also lead the social season with their formal dances given (according to the newspaper account) "amid splendor, gaiety, and congeniality." At one formal in the closing years of the Depression, the published guest list of about four hundred persons included a sprinkling of upper-class people, including the editor of the Chicago *Defender;* the only Negro member of the Civil Service Commission; several of the upper "shadies," including two policy kings and their wives; the Mayor of Bronzeville; several upper-middle-class businessmen; a popular orchestra leader; and a few doctors and other professional men. The year before this, the eight hundred guests had the same class range, and prominent among the names mentioned was Colonel John C. Robinson, recently returned from Ethiopia, where he had been the personal pilot of Haile Selassie the Emperor.

A member expressed her pride in the club formals when she invited a participant-observer to attend: "Hope you will attend our formal Monday evening. You will be able to get an insight then into practically everything you want to know about the Amethyst Girls' Club. I wish that you could be there about one o'clock to see us when we are introduced." This ritual of presentation, important in middle-class clubs (though never a part of upper-class events), was thus described by a reporter: "After the grand march, introduction of club members was made by the master of ceremonies. . . . Softly, Roberts' orchestra played *Roses in Bloom*, and through the crowd walked beautifully gowned club women to the center of the ballroom." There they received the applause of their guests and were presented with baskets of roses.

The Amethyst Girls, although they enjoy their dances and fashion shows, their bridge parties and elaborate dinners, are anxious to earn a reputation for an interest in civic problems and racial advancement. They contribute to charity, and hope some day to open a store in order to "make jobs for our boys and girls." They are as proud of their civic work as of their elaborate formal dances. The social mistress of the club remarked to an interviewer:

"I know that you have been told by some of the other members of the club about some of the outstanding things we have done, such as donating to the flood relief in Kentucky last year, and buying dining-room furniture for the Children's Home. We bought outfits for those children from head to foot for Christmas, for which we paid $50 after the discount was given us. We even included sleepers in the Christmas gifts for the children.

"We buy tickets to the Chicago *Defender* Christmas Basket Fund every year, and we usually purchase an extra ticket through the club for each club member's escort. The club is responsible for about 24 to 26 tickets. The *Defender* can depend on us because we never come up short. We were always prepared to attend.

"I suppose you have heard about the bedding supply that we gave to the Nursery this last Christmas? I would like you to make a visit to see just what we have done at these various places I have named."

Giving to charity has its material rewards, too, for one member stated:

"No, we don't have to spend as much money as some clubs who do not contribute as much as we do to charity. We get our orchestra a little cheaper, usually; also the hall. They accommodate us in this way because of our hard struggle to do worth-while things to help those who are less fortunate—especially children."

For teen-age girls of Bronzeville's middle-class, as well as for older women, the Amethyst Girls represent the ideal toward which a club should work—skill in entertaining, co-operative relations with other clubs, and some civic work. There are men's clubs, too, that set the pattern, and we shall now examine the Kool Kustomers.

THE MODEL MEN'S CLUB

The Kool Kustomers are among the half-dozen men's clubs that set the social pace for the male clubs in middle-class "Society." There are only thirteen members, but their invitation affairs rival the dances of the much larger upper-class sororities and fraternities, both in size and in expenditure. One of the best-informed middle-class clubmen in Chicago (a barbershop porter), after stating that he hadn't missed a Kool Kustomer dance in ten years, said: "Their affairs are so swanky until other club members ask, six months in advance, 'Please send me a ticket to your next formal.' Their guests are just as elated over attendance at a Kool Kustomer affair as a hungry man is over a banquet. . . . Without a doubt they receive more invitations to formals during the year than any other club in Chicago, because every club wants to receive an invitation from them."

The Kool Kustomers are able to set the pattern primarily because they manage to do, with skill and lavishness, what all male clubs of comparable size would like to do—namely, "throw" a colorful annual formal with hundreds of guests, free drinks, and favorable newspaper publicity. Important, too, is the fact that they manage to stay in the news throughout the year. They always co-operate with other clubs in ticket sales; their members dress fashionably; and, when other clubs give special affairs, they are always ready to spring a sensational surprise. For instance, when the Lions gave a European Ball, all the Kool Kustomers were on hand dressed as members of Louis XIV's court. One Kool Kustomer stated with pride: "We represented the whole court from the King on down. We really stole the show. We were the most correctly attired, in strict accordance with the history books." Bronzeville's band leaders testify that Kool Kustomer formals are "swank affairs."

The Kool Kustomers are willing to spend money for prestige. A few years ago one of the members boasted to an interviewer: "Our entire dance is going to cost about $500. The invitations will cost over $100. I've never seen any invitations like ours before, with all the members' pictures in their full-dress suits. We are the only club which serves wines and drinks. When the guests go to the bar, the drinks are on the house."

The Chicago *Defender* reported the event in glowing terms: "Twelfth annual formal. . . . Comments have been pouring in since then from over 2,000 of the élite of Chicago and out-of-town visitors. . . . Grand march . . . hostess perfectly gowned . . . members re splendent in their white ties, top hats, and tails. . . . Wines and liquors served without cost." A bystander commented on the neon sign outside the dance hall, the chauffeured limousines, and women with ermine shoulder wraps. Dazzled by the display, he was sure that "this is a club composed of members of the upper crust of Negroes." Yet an upper-middle-class girl who was present and who also attends upperclass affairs was lively in her ridicule of the Kool Kustomers' affair: "Well, to begin with, the place was too crowded. Every dog and his mammy was there. I told George [a member], 'You had from schoolteachers to housemen excusing all the in-betweens. . . . There was every style, color and what-not of a dress imaginable.'" She criticized the behavior of the women ("throwing up their legs—publicly hugging the men") and dubbed the free wine "junk." "I told them about their wine," she said, "and one of the members answered, 'Since we're giving it away it's good enough. Beggars can't be choosers. Come and take a drink from the private reserve.'" She concluded with a final thrust of class-conscious criticism: "I don't think the affair was worth the expense. They could have spent that money, if they wanted to throw it to the winds, by having several small invitational affairs. They would have had a large attendance of fairly decent people, and not a mob of a little bit of everything." They could have—but only at the price of losing prestige in that vast club world that has come to look upon the Kool Kustomers as the men who set the pattern.

The three original Kool Kustomers began to "run together" in high school during the Twenties. Two of them were migrants from Alabama, one from New Orleans. They met on Sunday afternoons with a few other boys, and their parents would "serve a repast." They were first formally organized as the Good Fellows Uplift under the sponsorship of a city truant officer. This venture in adolescent reform was short-lived, however, and the group reorganized in 1928 as a social club with a membership limited to twelve. The dues have increased over a ten-year period from $5 a year to $25 a year, with a $10 joining fee!

The eight regular members of the club and the five honorary members are middle-class men in their late twenties and early thirties with a drive for "getting ahead." Thirteen years before, all of them (except one) were children in the deep South—three in Alabama, three in Louisiana, one in Texas. In 1938 they were distributed throughout Chicago's occupational hierarchy—two as hotel porters in Loop hotels, one as an independent clothes salesman, one as an interior decorator, and three as owners of small businesses: real estate, taxi, and liquor. All had finished high school; none had gone to college.

This lack of formal education and professional occupation had definitely kept them out of the upper class, and while it has not hindered their rising to the top of the middle class, it has resulted in a definite social gulf between them and the fraternity and upper-class clubmen of their own age. This social gulf is recognized within the club by the fact that some of their early associates who went on to college have been accorded the status of *honorary* members. When asked whether club members ever received bids to upper-class affairs, one member replied that he had received such an invitation but hadn't gone. He mentioned that upper-class clubs invited individuals and not entire clubs, and brushed the matter off by saying, "One thing—the Snakes and the Forty Club and the Assembly are all much older groups than we are." (The names are those of upper-class clubs.)

The Kool Kustomers do not think of themselves as frivolous. While the club is dubbed "purely social," organized "to have clean fun," the constitution insists that any prospective member must (1) have high morals; (2) be a good citizen; (3) be a high school graduate; (4) be a good sportsman. Each member is enjoined to "pledge himself whatever he can afford to give for that year toward charity." Meetings open with the Lord's Prayer and close with the club creed. They take pride in aiding any member who suffers financial distress. They also contribute to charity.

"Society," Status, and Racial Advancement: During 1937, almost 800 social clubs reported their activities in the Chicago *Defender*,

totaling between 10,000 and 11,000 members. If we plot on a map the addresses of all homes at which clubs met during that year, we find a very revealing distribution. (Figure 38.) In the "best areas" of Bronzeville we find over seven times as much social-club activity as in the "worst" areas, and the amount of social-club activity rises as we move from the lower-class northern end of the Black Belt toward the more well-to-do southern tip. A statistical correlation with the indices upon which the "best" and "worst" areas were defined suggests that social-club activity is associated with an above-average educational and economic status. (Table 32.)

TABLE 32

CORRELATION BETWEEN INCIDENCE OF SOCIAL CLUB PARTICIPATION AND SELECTED SOCIAL FACTORS *

Social Factors	Coefficient of Correlation	Standard Error
Median grade completed......................	.74	±.05
Median rental..............................	.62	±.07
Insanity rate...............................	.59	±.08
Illegitimate births..........................	.49	±.09
Infant mortality............................	.37	±.10
Juvenile delinquency........................	.30	±.11

* Over 4,000 addresses at which social clubs met in 1937 were tabulated by census tract and district and then related to the six factors which were used to define "best," "mixed," "worst" areas. In tracts where there were over 35 addresses per 1,000 Negro adults at which clubs met participation was classified as "very wide"; 25-34, "wide"; 15-24, "average"; 5-14, "limited"; less than 5, "very limited."

If we turn from these gross statistics to an examination of the social characteristics of a group of club members, we find additional evidence that the members come neither from Bronzeville's top group nor from the lower class. (Table 33.)

Though some of the younger members of the middle class are not club-centered, even these often think of club membership as "normal" for people of their status. Fay, for instance, did not join any clubs when she was in high school, but now, at the age of 22, married and with two small children, she looks forward to joining a club some time in the future. She is probably typical of many of the more quiet,

Figure 38

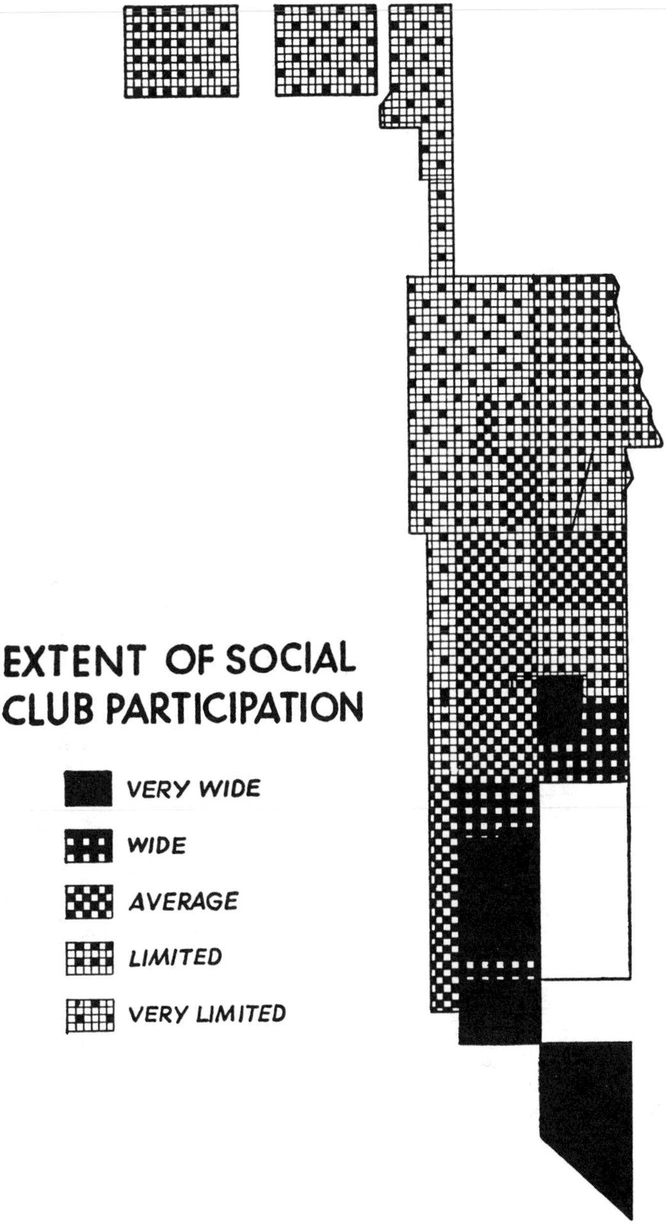

EXTENT OF SOCIAL CLUB PARTICIPATION

■ VERY WIDE

▓ WIDE

▓ AVERAGE

▓ LIMITED

▓ VERY LIMITED

From St. Clair Drake, "Churches and Voluntary Associations."

TABLE 33

SOCIAL CHARACTERISTICS OF 133 MEMBERS OF 13 TYPICAL ADULT FEMALE SOCIAL CLUBS DURING THE DEPRESSION PERIOD *

Case	Size of Club	Number of Officers	Marital Status a	Age Range	Mean Monthly Wage of Employed Members	Occupation b									Education c				Church Membership d						
						1	2	3	4	5	6	HBP	HO	Total	C	H	E	Total	1	2	3	4	5	6	Total
1	13	8	M	30-40	$67			6	4				2	12	4	5		9	5	4	1				10
2	9	6	4M, 5D	25-30	64			2	1		3		3	9		2	6	8		5	2				7
3	7	6	M	25-35	64			1	2		1		3	7	2	5		7		1	2	2			5
4	13	7	6M, 4S, 1D, 2W	20-30	52				1	3	7		1	12		11	2	13	4		1				5
5	12	10	9S	25-35	50					12				12		7	1	8		3		1			4
6	12	8	2M	24-30	50			6	2				1	9		10		10	5	2		4			11
7	16	8	5S	15-25	50				5		6		1	12		16		16			2				2
8	9		3S, 1M, 3W, 1D	25-35	50						5			5	1	2	5	8	3						3
9	13	8	8M, 2S, 3D	20-25	50				3		4		2	9	1	7	2	10	8			2			10
10	18	5	10M, 3W		36			1			1		11	13			17	17			3	6			9
11	10		5M, 5D	25-35					5	1	4			10	1	1	8	10	2	1	2				5
12	7	7	M	20-30			1	2			1		3	7	3	4		7			4				4
13	9	7	6M, 2S, 1D			1	2				1		2	6		9		9			4	2			6
Tots. & avs.	133	7				1	3	18	23	16	33		29	123	12	79	41	132	27	16	21	17			81

a M—Married; S—Single; D—Divorced; W—Widowed.

b Occupation: 1—Professional; 2—Proprietors, managers, and officials; 3—Clerks and kindred workers; 4—Skilled workers; 5—Semi-skilled workers; 6—Unskilled workers and servants; HBP—Housewives, business or professional husband; HO—Housewives, others.

c Education: C—Some college training; H—some high school training; E—some elementary school training.

d Church Attendance: 1—Baptist; 2—Negro Methodist; 3—White-controlled bodies; 4—Community Church; 5—Holiness; 6—Spiritualist.
(Of the 133 women, 52 were not church members.)

* Complete data for every member in each club were not available.

home-centered girls who married upon finishing high school and settled down. When she was approached by an interviewer, the conversation proceeded as follows:

Interviewer: "Do you think if you had time now you would join some social club?"

Fay: "Oh, I think so! I really think clubs are very nice, and sometimes I wish I had joined one of them back in my high school days. But then, I was having a good time without belonging to a club, and now that I don't have the time, I want to join some club. Isn't it funny how you look back and see the things that you really should have done?"

Interviewer: "That's the way it always is. What are the names of the clubs which asked you to join?"

Fay: "Let's see. There was the Les Chic Chères, and you know that club out at Englewood High School—the Circle Saroines, and some club called the Smart Dames. I think that the Les Chic Chères and the Smart Dames have just about broken up. At that time I knew quite a few girls in Les Chic Chères, but I haven't seen any of them for a long time. I knew one girl in the Smart Dames. She wanted me to join so bad, but I just didn't care much for that group as a whole—sort of a 'ratty' bunch to me.* Did you ever hear of the club?"

Interviewer: "Les Chic Chères gave a lovely formal two years ago."

Fay: "Yes, it was a lovely affair. They served a dinner, too. Well, it was right after that affair that I was asked to join the club. I remember commenting to one of the officers about how nice the affair was, and we talked a long time about the club. Finally she asked me why I wouldn't join, that several members had said that they thought that I would be a good member. But I just didn't bother. I didn't have anything against any of the members or the club as a whole, but you know how you just put things off. Then I got married and of course you know what happened then—just lost all interest. Now I couldn't join if I wanted to."

Interviewer: "Well, why didn't you join the school club? Same reason?"

Fay: "No, I just didn't care much for that bunch of kids. They were always gossiping and meddling in your business. And I just didn't want to be mixed up with them. They tell me now the club is full of real young kids and that the dances are a mess!"

Interviewer: "I know a girl who went, and she said this last dance was the best. Just a difference of opinion, I guess. Some have a good time and others don't. What would you say makes a fairly good club?"

Fay: "You know something? I don't think there *are* any real good clubs.

---

* "Ratty" is a term denoting loose sexual behavior. The tendency of club life is to ritualize sex-behavior and to make flirtation less obvious and public. This is in significant contrast with lower-class sex behavior.

These kids get two or three of their friends and 'stick together' and talk about other members and try to take their boy friends—you know, all that stuff. I just can't stand that. I really think members should try to be loyal and co-operate and help keep a club together. Clubs should be careful about taking in members. Look at some clubs that have been organized for years because the members were loyal and kept together. You know, in these Negro clubs everybody wants to be president; two or three want to run the club. A club can't last long at that rate. I think that after the children get older I might join some nice bridge club, or just a plain social club. It keeps you in contact with your friends and gives you something to look forward to."

There are a few clubs in Bronzeville which do not follow the entire pattern of conventional behavior which is typical of middle-class club life. Recent migrants who form clubs in imitation of the pattern they see displayed in the *Defender,* and rising lower-class people who have never belonged to a "good club," sometimes form groups which display a mixture of lower-class and middle-class behavior. Over a period of time, however, as they begin to compete for prestige by attending the pay dances of other clubs, and through interclub visiting, as well as the desire to get bids to formals, they are likely to knock off the rough edges. The drift toward conformity is in the direction of middle-classness.

Sometimes, however, a group of older people will have a behavior pattern that incorporates both middle-class and lower-class elements. The Tremont Social Club, for instance, was composed of thirty lower-middle-class men and women similar in age-range to the Amethyst Girls. On the participant-observer's first visit she noted that one member's comments concerning an old boy friend who had fought in the First World War revealed an approach to sex and family life which was essentially lower-class:

"That was when the boys were going to war in 1917. My man was sure good to me. But, girl, I was having one swell time. I was stopping everywhere on my way to Brooklyn to see him off on the boat. I stopped off in Cleveland, Detroit, and everywhere. Girl, when I got there, the boat was pulling out! I was too high to even care at the time, but I believe he was hot about it! When he came back I was here in Chicago and he married some gal in Detroit and had a baby. When they broke up, do you know what he did? He sent that boy of his here and told me to dress him up!

"I did it, too, and didn't spend no $2 nor $3, either. I spent plenty!

That guy used to give me all kinds of money and he sent me money all the time he was overseas. I wasn't fixing to have him come here and cut my head!"

The business session of one meeting of this club also revealed a mixture of lower-class and middle-class traits. There was much horse-play throughout the meeting, with considerable "broad" joking and petty gambling. One woman blurted out to a man with whom she was playing cards: "Well, you'd better lay your money on the table. I don't want to have to take your pants off."

At this point in the conversation, the secretary entered and, over-hearing her, said: "Uh-huh—gone to taking off pants already!"

A few moments later a male member warned the woman: "You know if you lose, Mr. P. will take *your* pants off—that's what he told me."

But the woman was equal to the occasion and flashed back: "No, he won't—I haven't got any on!"

Yet, except for this playful interlude, business was conducted in a dignified manner. It was followed by a luncheon of frankfurters, spaghetti, chopped egg and lettuce salad, bread and beer. Each member gave the hostess a "charity gift" of twenty-five cents. One member explained to the observer, "We believe that charity begins at home, so we pay the hostess for her house and each member pays for his luncheon."

The participant-observer reported that the meeting ended with "a bit of wrestling" and "liquor-throwing." One member referred to this liquor-throwing as follows:

"I don't let these folks come up here and drink and spill liquor all over everything. Now, when they come, I take them right back to the dining room. You know they don't care a thing about your furniture. I've seen women drink so much they couldn't hold any more, and then—just be-cause somebody would buy it for them—pour liquor in the corner of the davenport. Yes! I've seen 'em do it."

The youthful club president apologized to the obviously middle-class observer and tried to disassociate himself from the group:

"Well, I guess you wonder how I came to be president of a club like this. You see, I have my bachelor's from Michigan and I started taking law. I have a couple of cousins practicing law here, *but I like to study these people, too, just to see how they act.* They wanted a young president and so made me president. I live on the near North Side."

Despite the fact that this club indulged in conduct very unusual in the middle-class club world, its members were aware of its position in the social-club hierarchy and of the differences between it and the clubs that set the pattern. One of the members remarked to the participant-observer:

"You know there are some clubs that think they're better than we are— you know, look down on us; but there are some that look up to us, too."

There were clubs "above them" which were trying to draw them into the pattern of reciprocal ticket sales for pay dances. At this meeting, for instance, a representative of the Snappy Twelve (a higher-status club) came to solicit such support. He announced that 500 tickets were out, with four "ladies' clubs" selling for the Snappy Twelve, as well as two men's clubs. He appealed to the Tremont, as a mixed club, to join with them, and assured them that he would line up the other six clubs to help sell Tremont tickets in the future.

The club voted to assist. Before the visitor left, one of the women members (possibly with her mind on a future bid to a formal) apologized for the disorderly conduct: "Don't think we carry on like this all the time, Mr. S——. You know sometimes we just get a little too much under the belt."

Typical middle-class club members in the middle age-group don't cut up quite this way at club meetings, even when they "have too much." In fact, they wouldn't take too much—at a business meeting.

In order to assure wide ticket sales for pay dances, a system of interclub co-operation has come into being in which groups of clubs definitely pledge themselves to sell each other's tickets and to invite each other to their formal dances. Usually an informal arrangement, this is sometimes formalized in a "pact." *

Several ambitious persons have even tried to establish ticket exchanges and to organize the club world on a more "efficient" basis. One such promoter told his story as follows:

"I started to organize the Amalgamated Clubs in 1932 and at the start found the clubs very cold to the idea, but I kept on after them and finally got a few of them to join with me.

* Some clubs also function as "brother" and "sister" groups, helping each other to sell tickets, inviting to each other's affairs, etc., as for instance the Rexall Boys and Rexall Girls.

"We required a joining fee of $5 per club and monthly dues of $1. The money collected was for the expense of a hall for meetings. We met at a hall on Forty-third Street. Also we had a small paper printed each month, giving the names of the clubs that were members, their addresses, and meeting nights. We announced the affairs in advance, and in every way tried to make the clubs realize that they should be more friendly to one another, and instead of only visiting when tickets were involved they should visit each other as a friendly gesture.

"The officers reserved the right to give two dances each year, the money from these two affairs to go to the Association. Member clubs were supposed to take tickets, and also help to advertise these two affairs. As there was no large amount of money in the treasury, we would borrow five dollars each from some of the clubs to help finance the affair; after the affair we would pay them the amount of the loan back.

"This money raised was for the expenses of the Association, but the clubs that loaned us the money thought that they should share in the proceeds. This caused ill feelings, but we knew nothing of it until the members began to drop out of the Association. Of course, the general opinion was that us officers were using the money for ourselves.

"When we learned of the displeasure of the Association members, we told them that they could put a person from the membership on the Association committee and let them report on the use of the money; but even that did no good. It seemed that they were determined to quit anyway and were glad of any excuse."

He then proceeded to the familiar Bronzeville "race" theory of failure: "Sorry to say that it is extremely hard to get people of 'our group' to stick together."

But the Associated Clubs were interested in more than merely facilitating the sale of tickets, and sought to serve as an agency for enforcing more formal party behavior:

"We had in one of our by-laws the demand of more respect for the women of our race. At many affairs the men would start drinking and become a little too loud, often using language that was objectionable. For anyone caught doing that, there was a fine on the first offense, and if the offense was repeated, the person had to be expelled from the club.

"There is a general tendency for men to wear tuxedos to formals, and we approved of this. But some of the clubs were so slack about rules that they allowed men to attend their formal dances dressed only in a street suit. This we thought was an insult to the women, and it was a rule of the Association that all clubs must enforce the rule that men wear at least a tuxedo."

In addition to these "standardizing" functions, the organization shared Bronzeville's ever-present ambition that some day it might "go into business." The founder of the Association described its plans in this connection:

"For a while it looked as if we might get to be a large organization, and we had plans where each club would deposit a certain amount of money each year. This fund would be used to open a business of some kind, so that the members would feel that membership would turn into a paying proposition."

ADVANCING THE RACE

When upper-class and middle-class people speak of "advancing The Race," what they really mean is creating conditions under which lower-class traits will eventually disappear and something approaching the middle-class way of life will prevail in Bronzeville. Middle-class people want to remake the Black Ghetto in their own image. Because the upper class and the upper middle class control the press, the schools, and the pulpits of the larger churches, they are in a position to bombard the lower class with their conceptions of "success," "correct behavior," and "morality"—which are in general the ideals of the white middle-class. Bronzeville's lower-class people, on the whole, accepts this definition of what "ought to be." This accounts both for their display of antagonism and defensiveness *vis à vis* the higher-status groups, and for the fact that some lower-class people try to "get ahead." In seeking to advance The Race by transforming the lower class, Bronzeville's Race Leaders do not rely on moral exhortation alone. In fact, they are almost economic determinists, nothing being mentioned more often in public speeches than the necessity for raising the general economic level of Negroes. Even the preachers, despite their penchant for theology, make this kind of analysis. Education and a good job—these are thought to be the keys to racial advancement; and, as we shall see in the next chapter, Race Leaders believe in vigorous action to secure equality of opportunity.

The process of differentiation among Negroes in Bronzeville has given rise to a loose system of social classes which allows for mobility upward and downward. This class structure operates as a system of social controls by which the higher-status groups "protect" their way of life, but admit "strainers" and "strivers" who can make the grade. Individuals and organizations on the higher-status levels become models for imitation and also serve as an incentive toward social mobility.

In Figure 39 we have a schematic representation of the class system as it operates in Bronzeville today. At the top are the uppers, oriented

Figure 39

THE STRENGTH OF CLASS CONTROLS

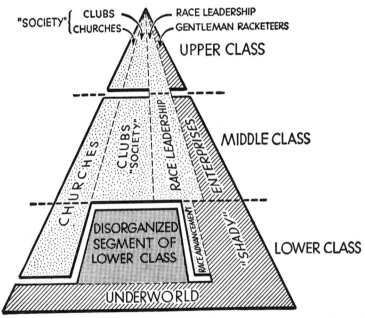

The wide spaces indicate absence of "social" participation between individuals in the adjacent segments. Broken lines indicate some "social" contact between the groups.

predominantly around "Society" and Race Leadership, and with a small group of Gentleman Racketeers who have gained some status as Race Leaders but who are not accepted socially. Below them is the middle class with four "centers of orientation"—church, social club, "racial advancement" (including *individual* advancement), and "policy." At the bottom is the lower class with a large "disorganized segment," but also with a "church-centered" group and a small group of "secular respectables" interested in "getting ahead." Underlying the whole structure is the "underworld" of the Black Ghetto.

Class lines are drawn most sharply between upper-class "Society" and middle-class "Society," and almost as rigidly between middle-class "Society" and the disorganized segment of the lower class. The church and civic organizations throw some lower-class people into contact with the middle class and make it possible for them to rise through a display of talent, "decorum" and "front." They can then move "across" and find *social* acceptance, ultimately becoming middle class. Middle-class people may rise through talent, race leadership, and the acquisition of education, and then move "across" to *social* acceptance. Within the middle class world itself there are no sharp breaks between church people and others, although in the lower class the line is sharp. "Shadies" can become "respectable" if they acquire middle-class public behavior and show an interest in racial advancement.

The bases of status within the middle class are gradually shifting. Among older people, church and lodge have been very important, but among younger people (and many older folks) social clubs and civic clubs are assuming increasing importance as an index to status. Two examples of stable older middle-class "models" will illustrate the traditional bases of status. The first is the death notice (in the *Defender*) of an upper-middle-class woman. The second is a profile of a lower-middle-class family.

Mrs. B—— J——, a leader in church, fraternal and social circles, died at her home on Tuesday evening, April 4, at 7:45 after a prolonged illness.

For many years Mrs. J—— was a member of the Woman's Board of the Provident Hospital; worked ardently for the Douglass League of Women Voters, and was a member of the Department of Education and Foreign Policy. She was Past Worthy Matron of Princess Bernice Chapter, Order of the Eastern Star, and of the choir of St. Edmund's Episcopal Church.

"A Great Deal for Which to Be Truly Thankful": The Davises are typical of the older and "more settled" lower-class families. Jim, 43

years of age and eleven years out of Alabama, has worked at the same Chicago soap factory ever since he came to Midwest Metropolis. Near the end of the Depression he was making $37.50 a week and maintaining a four-room apartment which, according to the interviewer, was "neatly arranged and very nice and clean." Sarah, his wife, hadn't worked since her small dress shop "folded up when the Depression began." For the thirteen years that Jim and his Georgia-born Sarah have been married they've always tried to save some money. They lost a few hundred dollars when "the bottom fell out" of the dress shop. For years now they have both been church-centered. Sarah spends most of her spare time working for the Methodist church that they both attend. Jim is also a Mason, but thinks that "lodges don't mean much any more." He likes to spend his evenings at home reading the newspaper and the Bible. They both go to bed early and rise early.

Jim claims to have "come from a good family" and insists that all his brothers and sisters "got themselves a good education." He is sorry that he had to go to work early and only got to the eighth grade. He is a little ashamed of his lack of education and very seldom visits his sister, who is a social worker in Bronzeville. He and Sarah refer quite often to "our little girl" who died ten years ago at the age of four. They had planned to give her "everything within reason"; they had wanted her to have "the best of everything"; they were going to see that she "got a good education." Now, without a child to plan for, they have concentrated on "keeping a nice house." They like the neighborhood in which they live because "it is quiet and the children aren't wild." Jim is proud that he's able to rent from a Negro doctor, although he feels that the rent is too high. "A white man would be worse, though," he observes.

Jim's grievances against his world are usually stated in terms of Bronzeville's high rent and bad children. He doesn't worry much about civil liberties and such abstract matters, but he has been heard to say, "I like a nice place to live in just like any other man in the world, but I don't see why I have to pay $42.50 a month for four rooms" (actually a low figure for the Black Ghetto). He doesn't blame the Negro doctor from whom he rents, because he believes that all rents in Bronzeville are "rigged." He wonders why the Government doesn't build more projects, "because if anybody's gonna be fair to colored people you'd think it would be the Government." Jim is not too articulate about such matters. He tells the interviewer: "I don't know how to say just what I want to say, but it does look to me like something for our betterment could be done in Chicago. I don't think it's quite right that we are called true American citizens and then have to get the worst of everything all the time."

But Jim is essentially an optimist, as his concluding statement indicates. After all, he once lived in Alabama, and coming to Midwest Metropolis was a big step ahead. He states:

"When I think of the conditions that colored people are confronted with in Chicago, I want to tell you the truth—it's a mystery to me that we are as good as we are and as far advanced as we are today. However, I'm certainly proud to say that we've had some of the greatest men in the world in our race. After all, taking everything into consideration we do have a great deal for which to be truly thankful. I have the greatest hope for the Negro some day in the far future. I do believe we are progressing slowly but surely."

BRONZEVILLE'S "NEW NEGRO"

From the standpoint of "racial advancement," the "middle-class way of life" is perhaps the most significant pattern of living in Bronzeville. It represents a relatively stable pattern that has been emerging since the Flight to Freedom, and has already been defined here as a "model" that emphasizes a type of disciplined public behavior which will distinguish a segment of the population from the "crude" and "unpolished" masses.

These are people interested in maintaining a stable home life, who want to marry and raise a family, who take steady employment when they find it. The older Negro middle class was church-centered; not so the "New Negro." During his leisure time he sees nothing wrong in enjoying life, in playing cards, dancing, smoking, and drinking. At the same time he often maintains membership in a church, attends its services regularly, and helps to raise money for it; but he takes its theology with a grain of salt or ignores it completely, and puts pressure on his minister to work for "racial advancement." He believes in "Negro business" and admires a Race Man.

Because of the narrow occupational base in the Negro community, he has adjusted his thinking to the rise of the labor union movement, which embraces many of the occupations in which Negroes of the middle class are employed. It is not unusual, therefore, to find a person who, though he has finished high school, still works as a laborer in the steel mills and belongs to a CIO union as well as a social club and a church; indeed, membership in some left-wing organization is sometimes added to this pattern.

This is Bronzeville's "New Negro"—usually a fairly well-educated working man or woman who knows the ropes of the urban world, wants to get ahead, and is determined to be "decent." He is likely to be somewhat skeptical of the good intentions of most white people, and suspicious of the disinterestedness of Race Leaders. He is keenly aware that Negroes don't have "their rights," but sees no hope in the extremists of either the racialistic Right or the revolutionary Left, although he may opportunistically support both. If married, he is raising his family and educating his children with the hope that they will "get a break" in the future. The number of such "New Negroes" is set, however, by the iron bands of the Black Ghetto and the pressure of the Job Ceiling. Their future and the future of their children is largely beyond their control.

CHAPTER 23

Advancing the Race

WHEN NEGROES SPEAK OF "ADVANCING THE RACE" THEY MAY BE REFERRING to either of two things: (1) individual achievement which "reflects credit on the race," or (2) organized social activities which are consciously designed to raise the status of the group as a whole. Thus, while Negroes measure the progress of The Race since slavery in terms of the number of people who have become middle class, and of the writers, artists, soldiers, scientists, musicians, prize-fighters, etc., who have won recognition from the white group, they also measure progress in such terms as legislative victories over Jim-Crowism, or breaks in the Job Ceiling.

With memories of slavery less than a hundred years behind them, Negroes are prone, in their conversation and formal pronouncements, to echo Booker Washington's words, "Do not judge us by the heights we have attained, but by the depths from which we've come." But this is only one side of the coin. In a society that preaches equality of opportunity, Negroes inevitably resent the existence of *any* restrictions that hamper their continued progress. They are thoroughly American in their acceptance of the optimistic dogmas of progress and in their insistent demand that they be given a fair chance to demonstrate as individuals, and as a group, what they have in them. The presence of a Job Ceiling, the existence of a Black Ghetto, the denial of certain civil liberties, constantly generate widespread discontent. Sometimes, especially during periods of economic crisis or war, this discontent explodes, for under such circumstances, the separate-subordinate status of the Negro becomes most sharply delineated.

THE DISPERSAL OF DISCONTENT

Faith, Hope and Charity: Discontent is widespread in Bronzeville. It is most articulate, of course, among individuals of the higher status groups, for the Negro newspapers, the politicians, and the Race Leaders are the spokesmen for The Race. Even a cursory observation of a political rally or a barbershop discussion, however, would convince the most skeptical that these spokesmen are expressing the attitudes and desires of the Negro masses when they assail the Job Ceiling, the Black Ghetto, and the denial of civil liberties. Yet this discontent rarely flares forth in the form of spontaneous violence, and only occasionally in the form of organized social movements. That the resentments and discontent do not explode more often is partially due to the existence of a class system within the Negro community.

The fact that *some* Negroes have secured wealth and an education is a powerful argument for "patience." An upper-class or upper-middle-class Negro is bound to have some faith in the promises of American democracy, for, after all, he and his family *did* get ahead. But even the lower status groups, perceiving the individuals above them, can see some hope for themselves or their children. Like all successful people, Bronzeville's uppers see their own achievement in terms of their having displayed "individual initiative" and "ambition." They feel that others, too, can rise if they try hard enough. And this estimate of their success is widespread throughout all classes. The system is thus stabilized by the general American belief in the ultimate triumph of individual initiative. The upper status groups tend to visualize their function as one of "uplifting the masses"—of urging them to get an education and to be thrifty, thereby advancing themselves, and in so doing, also "advancing The Race."

The existence of a small élite group and a considerably larger number of comfortably situated people would not stabilize the Negro community, however, were it not for the fact that the large lower class is normally able to secure food, clothing and shelter, albeit in meager measure. Faith and hope play some part in dispersing the discontent of the masses, but "charity" is probably far more important. The masses of Negroes during the Twenties and Thirties had the jobs nobody else wanted or "public assistance." They also had access to the county hospital and various clinics when they were sick. On this restricted economic base the lower-class way of life as it has been described in Chapters 20 and 21, persists from decade to decade. A few individuals, here and there, emerge into the middle class, and the general educational level rises from year to year; but the lower class continually recruits new members from the rural South. Lower-class people are not unaware of their status position in the society, but there has, so far, been no way for them to advance as a group, and the number who can rise as individuals remains extremely limited.

Unable to alter their social status by becoming middle class, and unable to escape the exclusion and subordination of the white world, the people in the Negro lower class half consciously express their frustrations in many devious forms. The vigor with which they shout or dance; the rapt attention that they fix on the policy wheel; the floods of liquor they consume; the "clowning"; the hero-worship—all look suspiciously like unconscious ways of escape from the double subordination of caste and class.*

The tormenting devils of poverty, ignorance, and racial discrimination are never completely exorcised by prayer nor drowned by rotgut liquor. They are not banished by hot music or gospel hymns, nor danced away by jitterbugging or shouting. They lie slumbering in the nether soul of every man, woman, and child in the Black Ghetto, and they emerge at unsuspected times and places.

Taking It Out in Talk: Negroes of all class levels have a habit of "taking it out in talk." If we examine the random comments, the unprompted conversations, the discussions and arguments, that go on among Bronzeville's lower class, we will find that they, no less than the more literate higher status groups, are not satisfied with things as they are.

Blaming white folks is the most prevalent form of "ritual condemnation." "The Jews," "the crackers," "the unions," "the politicians," "the bosses," "the landlords," "the foreigners"—all are verbally flayed on street corner and in barbershop, poolroom, and church. A newspaper headline, a radio comment, a chance remark or gesture, can convert a gambling den into a forum on the race problem, or a group of street-corner jitterbugs into a conspiracy of verbal revolt. An inadvertent shove by a white person may unleash a torrent of invective and sometimes a violent blow. Bronzeville's lower class knows that it is black and poor, and it definitely doesn't like America's attitude toward either trait.

The tendency to "take it out in talk" was frequently observed dur-

---

* It has been suggested that the extreme disorganization within the lower-class family, the extreme violence in personal relationships, is a form of in-caste aggression. Negroes can't hurt the larger white world, so they take it out on each other. (See John Dollard, *Caste and Class in a Southern Town*, p. 214.)

ing the study of Bronzeville. On one occasion near the close of the Depression, one of the authors casually mentioned, while visiting a lower-class home, that the anti-lynching bill was under discussion again in Congress. The response he got could be duplicated in any Bronzeville tavern, barbershop, or poolroom.

"High Pocket," a native of Mississippi, began to describe a lynching he had seen. "Sandy" outdid him by reciting the details of an even more gruesome lynching in Aiken, S. C., including a tale that while the mob was "cutting the baby out of a pregnant woman," all the Negroes went to church and sang spirituals.

"Hot Lips," twenty-five years of age and a native of St. Louis, burst out defiantly: "I bet all the colored folks was afraid to walk around. If I'da been there they'da had to kill *me!*"

"Gate-Mouth" cut in: "Yeah, me too. I believe when we go we oughta take one of 'em with us!"

"Big Sam," an elderly man from Georgia, was the conservative in the group. He chided them: "Well, I'll tell ya, it's disaway. If ya reely b'lieve tha Lord'll holp ya, yuh'll go to chu'ch an' git on ya knees an' stay there till ya starve."

The conversation drifted away from lynching to the imminence of war. "Big Sam" said: "Las' time I was down home it looked like war. Mens was goin' roun' buyin' up all the scrap iron they could git. That means a war's comin' soon."

"High Pocket" said: "Yeah, this time nex' year I guess they'll have us all in the war."

"Sandy" began to tell tales about his experiences in the last war: "I went to France last time—in the medical section. I useta drive them white officers up to Paris so they could raise hell. That was the mos' beautiful place I ever see. But they'll have to kill me next time. I see plenty to fight for here, but I don't see nuthin' to go over *there* to fight for!"

"Gate Mouth" chimed in: "Well, you gotta die, an' you jus' as well die a quick death as a slow death. You jus' as well die quick in a war as to starve to death here." Everybody laughed a sort of embarrassed laugh.

At this point Ida Mae, "Big Sam's" wife, called in from the other room, "Here's that lynchin' bill on the radio agin."

"Big Sam" said "Shhh," and everyone listened to the commentator recite the details of a southern Senator's filibuster against the anti-lynching bill.

"Gate Mouth" asked bitterly, "Do those white folks jus' *lak* to kill colored folks?"

"Big Sam," the elderly conservative, explained very slowly and authoritatively: "Oh, yeah, they gits sport outa it. In a way of speakin', we's still in slav'ry. The only diffunce is they cain't shackle an' sell us, an' we ain't driv'. We been out 'bout seventy years an' we ain't got nowhere yit."

This same verbal condemnation of white people *in toto* may also be illustrated by an incident in 1939 at a city-wide meeting of lower-class preachers. A highly trained minister, who was nevertheless very popular with the store-front preachers, proposed a motion calling on President Roosevelt to convene an international conference to head off war. It was passed in a perfunctory manner without debate. At the close of the meeting an almost illiterate woman missionary, recently returned from Africa, was granted three minutes in which to speak. She immediately began to condemn the peace vote:

"No, we don' want no peace. God's punishin' the white folks by lettin' 'em kill each other off. Look at ol' Leopol' an' his Beljuns now! Look what ol' Mussaleeny did to Ethiopia! My God! Naw, don' vote for no peace. God don' want no peace!" *

She was interrupted with cries of "Amen" and "That's right, sister!" Bronzeville's lower-class preachers had voted for the peace resolution, but their hearts were with the woman who interpreted war as the fateful lightning of a terrible swift sword. Within two years all of these people were deeply involved in what they called "the white man's war."

Panning "Big Negroes": The double subordination of the Negro lower class means that some of their ritual condemnation will be focused upon the Negroes above them. Whenever a lower-class Negro confronts a Negro of higher status in the role of patient being treated

---

* References to King Leopold are occasionally encountered in the speeches of the older Race Leaders. They have not forgotten the international scandal created during the Nineties when it was discovered that Leopold's agents in the Congo had several times cut off the hands of recalcitrant natives who refused to work on rubber plantations.

by doctor or dentist; of client receiving relief; of domestic servant waiting on a colored employer; of student taking directions from a teacher; or even of club member receiving orders from an officer, the atmosphere is surcharged with latent class antagonism. These antagonisms are often moderated in the interests of the co-operative task or dissolved in a glow of race pride, but underneath they remain. And when lower-class folk are participating with one another, they are likely to emerge in violent denunciation, ribald joking, or compensatory scorn. The Negro lower class is as cynical in its appraisal of Negro "big shots" as it is of white folks. This tendency to deride Negro leaders is illustrated in a snatch of conversation taken down by one of the authors in a lower-class home. An elderly Negro was talking to a younger group that had not known Binga the Banker before his fall:

Older Man: "When Binga had that bank down there at 35th and State, I had fifteen hundred dollars in there that I had saved from working in the stockyards. I went down there when the Depression started to draw it out an' move it up to the Lincoln Bank. Well, when I went in, ol' Binga come a-walkin' ovah, lookin' up ovah his glasses, and sez, 'Well, Mistah Johnson, I heah you's goin' to make a little wifdrawal.' I sez, 'Yassuh, Mistah Binga, I'se plannin' to investigate [invest] a little of my money, so I'se drawin' it out.' He says, 'Well, I wouldn' try to investigate it all if'n I was you. You oughta be careful.' Well, I jus' draws all my money out an' takes it up to the Lincoln Bank."

Younger Man #1: "Was the Lincoln Bank a colored bank?"

Older Man: "Naw."

Younger Man #1: "Well, the white bank failed too, didn't it?"

Older Man: "Yeah—that's where my fifteen hundred dollars went down."

Younger Man #2: "You'd just as wella let it stayed at Binga's."

Older Man: "Yeah, mebbe so. But *they* sho knows what to do [meaning the "Big Negroes"]. That Binga had put all his propity in his wife's name. An' he'd investigated his money in propity all ovah town. When the folks come for their money, he jus' didn't have none to give 'em. But the Lawd knows how to handle folks like dat. He's up there now doin' hahd labuh for messin' with the folkses' money."

Younger Man #1: "Yeah, he's doin' hahd work now all right."

Younger Man #2: "He knew all along that bank was goin' down."

Older Man: "Co'se he knew it! An' that lawyer of his—he looks like a white man—well, he's got an office now up on 47th Street. Well, he was

Binga's treasureman, an' now he's got propity all over the city an' he rides aroun' in a big automobile. I went up to him one day an' said, 'Mr. ——, heah you are a-ridin' 'roun in a big automobile, an' Mista Binga's up there in the pen. You used yo' head!' He laughed an' said, 'I know you folks all think I got the money.'"

Younger Man #1: "He musta been playin' Binga's wife."

Older Man: "Naw, I don' think he was doin' that. He was playin' Binga's money!"

This is the way Bronzeville's lower class gossips about Race Leaders. But lower-class people also berate themselves, thus accepting the upper-class definition of one cause of their plight—lack of thrift and initiative. The following conversation occurred in the Baby Chile-Mr. Ben household:

Slick: "Ya know if I'da just had one more dollar, I coulda got a room here in this building on the third floor, kitchen an' all."

Interviewer: "Well, you didn't need a kitchen, did you?"

Slick: "Naw, that's right since we're eatin' here. You know rent sho is high—four and five dollars for a room with nothin' in it."

Interviewer: "Well, we're not going to get low rents until the government steps in and controls rents."

Mr. Ben: "You wrong there! I'll tell you what. These rents ain't gonna come down till people stops crowding up in these kitchenettes and moves back into flats. Two families sleepin' in a room; it's a shame. The Board o' Health was aroun' today lookin' in at kitchenettes. They done figured it down that so many people kin live in a room, an' the others gonna have to git out an' git themselves rooms or flats."

Slick: "Some folks lives two family in a room 'cause they wants to save they relief rent money to buy food an' things."

Mr. Ben: "That ain't it. Folks are spendin' their money in these taverns —spendin' it for rotgut when they oughta be spendin' it for somethin' else. You know, you oughta divide ya money into three departments— you gotta eat, you gotta have a roof on ya head, an' ya' cain't run aroun' nekked. But these folks are gittin' drunk instead o' usin' their money right; an' they's runnin' roun' with pawnshop suits on, an' good shoes, an' ain't got nowhere ta lay their heads."

Thus ritual condemnation completes the circle: lower-class people condemn whites, higher-status Negroes, and themselves. But ritual condemnation is not confined to these specific groups. People of all social levels are continually flaying "The Race" itself.

THE DEMAND FOR SOLIDARITY

Although Negroes of all class levels stress individual initiative as a factor in "racial advancement" they are keenly aware that as a separate-subordinate group in American life, the dice are loaded against the individual. Everybody knows that "no matter how high a Negro gets he's still just a Negro." Race consciousness breeds a demand for "racial solidarity," and as Negroes contemplate their existence as a minority in a white world which spurns them, they see their ultimate hope in presenting some sort of united front against that world. As individuals move about in the Black Ghetto among a quarter of a million people like themselves, and as they think of the 13,000,000 Negroes in America, they fantasy about what Negroes *might* do "if they'd just stick together." But the Negro group is divided into social classes. There are numerous organizations within these social strata, as well as some that cut across class lines. Negroes are not just Negroes: they are upper-class and lower-class Negroes; Baptist, Methodist and Holiness Negroes; shady and respectable; ambitious and lackadaisical. Such divisions along the axes of life other than "racial advancement" impede the development of solidarity. Bronzeville is inclined to blame its woes on lack of unity and to indulge in ritual condemnation of The Race itself. This Negroes of all social strata do continually.

Sometimes a Negro will deride The Race with a touch of humor,* such as: "I can't say that I don't like a 'jig,' because I'm one myself. But they sure won't help one another." More often one hears a spate of simple, serious observations, such as this comment of a hotel waitress: "I know this much—we are divided against one another more than any race in the world." This tendency to compare Negroes with other groups is very widespread: "Dagoes will help

* Not all of the denunciation of white people is done with venom. It often takes the form of a joke that cuts two ways—at the Negro's plight and the white man's meanness or susceptibility to flattery. A typical double-edged joke is the following: A Negro drives through a red light in a Mississippi town. The sheriff yells, "Hey, boy, where you think you going?" The Negro thinks fast and answers: "Well, boss, when I see that green light come on an' all them white folks' cars goin' through, I says to myself, 'That's the white folks' light!' So I don' move. Then when that ol' red light comes on, I jus' steps on the gas. I says, 'That mus' be us niggers' light!'" The sheriff replies, "You're a good boy, Sam, but next time you kin go on the white folks' light." Such jokes are told continually in all sections of Negro society. Joking, too, is one way of dispersing discontent.

one another; Japs'll help one another—everything but a nigger"; "The Negroes might be able to do something if they would stick together"; "The Jews stick together, and that's how they get the better of the Negroes." A housewife whose husband works in the stockyards reports that "there is a Polish movement here that is very strong because they stick together." "We don't," she adds; "and I think Negroes would be better off if they did everything as a body." One prominent Negro politician, speaking to a group of preachers in 1938, actually said: "Look what Hitler's done! *We* need leadership!"

Closely allied to this tendency to idealize the solidarity of other people is the tendency to idealize Negroes in other communities, to feel that they have accomplished more than Bronzeville Negroes. Thus the proprietor of a tavern, after a trip to New York, compared Harlem with Bronzeville. "The Negroes in New York," he said, "are united and do things for each other not with their hand out for a pay-off, but just because they are of the same race. These Chicago Negroes have not learned that." One unemployed laborer contrasted American Negroes with Negroes in other countries: "You know, I've seen colored people in many countries, but ain't none of them like the American Negro. He won't co-operate for nothing. In Cuba, the Negroes stick right together, and in Puerto Rico the same. See, I've been in the army and I've traveled plenty. I'm fifty-four years old now, and when a Negro walks up to me, I can more or less figure out what kind of fellow he is. This is the only country where Negroes don't stick together. Instead of Negroes trying to help each other here—they cut each other's heads off. The American Negro ain't no good!"

Many of the less sophisticated people are likely to express this plea for unity in semi-religious or mystical terms. Thus, a number of lower-class women were heard to make the following comments:

"They [the Negroes] will never amount to very much unless they learn to love each other more and more as the days and years go by—then things will be better for us some sweet day."

"If the time will ever come when we colored people will feel that when one of us is in trouble all of us are in trouble, and when we learn to have more confidence in one another, and feel that after all we are just one great big family, then we will be able to go places and do things."

"Well, I think the whole thing wrong with the Negro is he just doesn't have brotherly love—just plain brotherly love."

"We ought to love one another like brothers and sisters."

The majority of the people, however, are very matter-of-fact about it—they just think Negroes need to "stick together more." They will say:

"I believe that the thing that holds us back most is the fact that we are given to being jealous of one another. If one seems to be making a success, the others try to stop his progress. We lack the one quality that will make us a great people, and that is unity and co-operation."

"I have made a study of the Negro problem, and I find that up to the present time there is no real solution. The one thing that holds us back more than anything else is lack of unity. It seems that we hate to see each other get ahead, and instead of helping we always hinder."

Sometimes it is the class system that Negroes denounce as the source of disunity. Thus a Pullman porter complains: "The greatest trouble is Negro against Negro. The Negro don't believe in the future. The educated Negro in this city comes first, the laborer last. That's bad."

Criticism of "leaders" is particularly widespread. Most frequently they are assailed for not "getting together," for not presenting a united front and a program to the white majority. Sometimes the criticism is a calm statement, such as:

"I believe our leaders should get together. Social club leaders and leaders of our race in all walks of life should get together and fight for our rights and the things we are entitled to in general."

". . . It does look like to me that our leaders could get together and do something for the colored people in Chicago."

". . . If our supposed-to-be leaders would get together, they could change many present conditions in Chicago and teach many of us that don't know how to live what to do, and why to want to live."

"I don't feel the Negroes are grasping every opportunity. I feel this is because the leaders are, in a way, betraying the race. They are not interested in the race as a group but only so far as the race can help them as individuals."

A housewife who "would like to see the Negro race, as a whole, check up on themselves and see if they could not live a little better as a race," criticized the leaders for not setting an example: "I think many of our supposed-to-be leaders in Chicago first of all should live better lives and do more than most of them do for The Race in general."

Bronzeville from top to bottom sees its salvation bound up with the development of Bigger and Better Negro Business. The people often denounce their leaders for not having provided The Race with flourishing business enterprises. One hotel maid, after belaboring the white people for rent-gouging, turned on the "respectable uppers," contrasting them unfavorably with the shadies:

"Take a big business like the Jones Brothers. Dr. —— and others could unite and put people to work instead of spending their money going to Europe. The majority spend their money going to the old country. The Jones Brothers are doing wonderful putting people to work. Colored are as capable as the whites if they had the chance."

Another representative of "the man in the street" had the same theme:

"Colored should do like the Jones boys—put people to work. They got a Food Store at 43rd Street and the El. If we had more men like that we would get somewhere. Joe Louis should go into some kind of business. The men with money should open up business and put people to work."

The businessmen themselves heartily concur, but throw the blame back on the people as a whole and on other leaders:

"One of the things that may tend to help the public in getting some race solidarity lies in the attitude of the ministers, who, among our people, are looked upon as leaders. A talk from the minister on Sunday when all of the people are assembled together would do untold good, for most of those who buy from white merchants do so as a natural course of action, and do not stop to think of the benefit they would gain by patronizing their own merchant."

The verbatim record of an important meeting called to discuss the housing problem reveals the way the leaders themselves sometimes denounce each other. First, one of the preachers intimated that politics should be kept out of the organization. A prominent politician rose to answer: "You say keep the politician out? After all, politics is very necessary. Yes, I am a politician. Somebody's got to be a politician. Every politician should be at this meeting. The quicker we get away from factional differences, the quicker The Race will progress. . . . We need leadership. . . . We have an inferiority complex. . . . Let's form a clearing house to invite all committees from various organizations and get behind the job that is to be done. This housing question is sapping our lives. Instead of worrying about whose church the meeting is taking place at, you ministers should *all* come out!" Then a preacher rose to release a diatribe at the businessmen, none of whom were present at this noonday meeting, and at some of his fellow ministers: "That's why we don't get any place as a race. There is so much confusion and criticism which always breaks up Negro organizations. This is a meeting for *all* Negroes, and how many are present? The businessmen need to come in—not only preachers. We're going to be Negroes until Doomsday, so we might as well pull together as Negroes. While we are thinking, the white man is acting. We should have united forces and a leadership that all the ministers will support."

Bronzeville's leaders are acutely aware of the fact that they are continually under fire. Some shrug it off as inevitable. Some react by denouncing "the people" themselves. And often this ritual condemnation by leaders takes the form of denouncing other leaders. One minister, speaking before a large church audience, was very blunt about the matter: "The Negroes have never been able to produce a leader. Why? *Every* Negro wants to lead!" Articles occasionally appear in the Negro press in this same vein of racial self-criticism. The former president of one important women's organization wrote the following lines:

"Charges have been made that the Association has been exploited by a few women who wished to perpetuate themselves and their friends in office. It has been asserted that the Association has been honeycombed with jealousies and torn with the selfish aims of individuals who cared nothing for its objectives but merely used whatever opportunities they possessed as leaders to climb, climb, climb.

"The meshes of hatred and disabilities of caste that hamper the forward and upward going of our millions cannot be overcome or broken by any selfish, vain-glorious leadership. We cannot triumph over obstacles unless we have law-governed organizations to fight our battles and help us onward.

Emphasis upon "race pride" and "race solidarity" is sometimes coupled with an expression of contempt and scorn for people who tell all their business to white folks. Bronzeville feels that, as a minority existing within a Black Ghetto, "protective secrecy" is necessary if their solidarity is not to be broken. One woman, after stating her belief that "the only thing that holds us back is our behavior in public," was saying in the next breath: "Negroes are always ready to knock and run to the white folks about something."

A woman who stated of herself, "I don't have much education . . . but I know that I have a mind of my own," said: "I do know that we need the help of the good white man, but at the same time we should be very careful just what we let him know about us."

A prominent Negro minister from New York speaking to a Bronzeville audience was vehement in his condemnation of people who "run to white folks":

"The thing that is most damning to Negroes is the diabolical jealousy among themselves. When Negroes learn to respect themselves, then the whites and the entire world will respect them also. Some say there is envy among other races, but listen: narrow-minded, hide-bound, two-by-four 'Negro strife' among the white people stays among the white people. If they get to arguing about who is who, or who is to get a certain office, when it's settled it still goes to a white man; but when Negroes get to fighting, it goes from The Race to another race."

This dislike for the "white folks' Negro" was decisively expressed by a lower-class woman who was being interviewed by a Negro girl for a WPA research study:*

"I have heard all about you folks picking on the colored churches. Why don't you go and ask the white people? You let the white folks *use* you. . . . White folks are doing everything they can to find out how the colored people are thinking. If God keeps *His* spirit in *me*, I'll keep *that* knowledge out of *their* heads."

All this ritual condemnation adds up to a demand for "a program" and for action. Even the very otherworldly church people who advise "trust in God" also advocate dry powder and big battalions. Typical of this attitude is the expression of the lower-class housewife who first

---

* Works like "Black Metropolis" are likely to draw the fire of very race-conscious Negroes who feel that the authors are betraying secrets that should stay within The Race.

insists: "When the advancement of The Race starts, it won't be by politics at all. It must be started by Christ Himself." In the very next breath she adds that Negroes should *vote* independently, concluding on the usual note: "Why, there are enough Negroes in Chicago to get anything they want. If our people would learn to stick together and trust each other, there are enough to do wonders for The Race. . . . You know, 'United we stand'—but ours is a house divided against itself."

This same mixture of theology and realism is implicit in a Holiness minister's statement:

"Men have strayed so far from God they can't find their way back. . . . I think that a good neighborhood club would go far in helping to solve our problems, but we colored people will not do that. The church could do much. Suppose every church member was asked to contribute one dollar. Some would give more. Then we could pool all the money and open up any kind of store and tell all our members to trade at that store. If such a thing was done inside of a year we would have a lot of money and maybe we could open up a factory and employ a lot of colored people. Look at the children that are coming outa school nowadays. They have no place to go and look for a job. We don't think about the future at all!"

When Bronzeville becomes concrete about this "unity" and "love" and "co-operation," it calls for *organized* action by Negroes. A post-office clerk complains that "our people are hit hard because they don't organize and try to work out their own salvation." A hotel maid feels that "the solution of the race problem rests with the race itself. The Negro as a whole must become more race-conscious, and form organizations that will bring the race issue before the public." A businessman favors increased organization: "There are several kinds of organizations, yet there is plenty of room for more. Each one will do some good, and we are badly in need of all the good we can get —more, if possible." A store clerk expresses this prevalent feeling in a few forceful words: "There is a remedy! Co-operate! Build up Negro organization."

Some of Bronzeville's business people have an almost naïve faith in the spoken word. One very articulate proprietor of a barbecue stand stated his belief that "every social organization, every Negro newspaper, all churches and fraternal organizations should constantly keep pounding at the people that the only way we will ever make any great success is to stand together and learn how to co-operate. Business, social, fraternal, or spiritual success depends on the amount of unity we present to the world."

Another man urged "proper leadership by church and politicians." The Negro, he held, *must* patronize Negro business. "Negroes can take positive action if they would. It is hard for them to develop solidarity. . . . The Negro . . . has not suffered like the Jew. He needs religious and racial solidarity—then he will begin to go places, I think."

The overwhelming majority of the people had no "program." They probably just felt like the middle-class housewife who replied when asked what her solution to the race problem was:

"The Negro problem, as a whole, is too much for me, and I do not know just what to say. But I would like to see the Negro race come closer together as a whole, to have more confidence in one another."

A hotel waitress, also stumped by the problem, echoed these sentiments: "I don't know just what I would like to see happen for the Negro in Chicago above everything else, but I do know that I would like to see many changes *in* the Negro as well as *for* the Negro."

A businessman summed it up thus: "The problem that we face today is: Can we cement ourselves together so that it will really be a case of 'all for one, and one for all'?"

But a lot of people in Bronzeville felt like the woman on relief who told an interviewer: "The people is the cause of things staying the way they is today. They never think for themselves. But if they ever do wake up, the big shots will never get them to listen to them again. That is my hope."

THE ORGANIZATION OF DISCONTENT

Any objective estimate of the success of Race Leaders in organizing discontent would probably reveal that there has been a lot more unity displayed than the people give themselves credit for. This was especially true during the four years immediately preceding the Second World War. The successful struggle for a housing project in Bronzeville; a suit against the real estate interests that was carried to the Supreme Court; the opening up of jobs here and there; the appointment of Negroes to the Library Board and the School Board—all were concrete gains. In winning these victories the decisive factor has been the Negro's *political* power implemented by the threat of mass action, and even of violence. Paradoxically enough, they have come not from a monolithic unity but from a diversity of competing leaders stimulating each other to win gains for the Negro people. There has been a kind of informal and even unplanned division of labor, with the "accepted leaders" negotiating and pleading for the Negroes, while the "radicals" turned on the heat. A shrewd leader can always remind the white folks that he's trying to control the unruly Negro masses, but that he doesn't know whether he can continue to do so if some concessions aren't made right away. This—coupled with the power of the Negro vote, desired by both major parties—is an effective minority technique. It hasn't broken the Job Ceiling nor abolished restrictive covenants, but it has won numerous isolated victories here and there.

Negroes are a minority in the midst of a white majority. They can win concessions only because certain sections of the white society need their votes or their labor, and because white America "respects the rights of minorities." An ethnic minority has to learn how to maneuver, to play balance-of-power politics, and to appeal to the conscience of the majority. Negroes have to learn how much the traffic will bear, and not to exceed this maximum. Race Leaders grow astute in measuring the factional alignments of the white community and in throwing, in just the right manner, the weight of the economic and political power they control.

Leaders must present a program of racial advancement and win enough support to put it through. Race Leaders of all class levels are agreed upon the necessity for cultivating a set of attitudes built on the basic fact of widespread "race consciousness." As they see it, "race consciousness" should be transformed into "race pride," replacing shame and lack of confidence. "Race pride," they feel, should then be made the basis of "race loyalty"—and all these should produce "race solidarity": a solid front facing the white world. From this point on, however, there is wide divergence on a program of action. (See analysis on page 732.)

"Accepted" Leadership: It has been evident in the story of Black Metropolis as we have traced it from the time of the Flight to Free-

THE ORGANIZATION OF DISCONTENT

Basic Attitudes	Basic Activity	Types of Leadership in Bronzeville and Typical Action Patterns	
		Non-violent	Violent
Race consciousness ↓ Race pride ↓ Race loyalty	Race solidarity	ACCEPTED LEADERSHIP 1. Encouraging individual achievement 2. Cleaning up the Black Ghetto 3. Supporting Negro business 4. "Wise" use of ballot 5. Court cases in defense of civil liberties 6. Cooperation with "best whites" 7. Occasional cooperation with more "radical" whites and Negroes	Defensive violence only, e.g., in case of attacks upon individual Negroes or groups
		RACE RADICALS 1. Demonstrations 2. Boycotts 3. Very limited cooperation with "white allies"	"Squeeze plays" and isolated, sporadic acts of violence
		ECONOMIC RADICALS 1. Demonstrations 2. Boycotts 3. Close cooperation with "white allies"	
		LABOR LEADERS 1. Joint action with whites on specific issues 2. Manipulation of Negro blocs within unions	

dom up to the First World War, that there were certain Negroes who were looked upon by the white people of power and influence as the "accepted leaders" of the Negro community. These were usually the more successful businessmen, the more prominent preachers, the outstanding Negro politicians, and here and there a professional man. These Negro leaders could always count upon a small group of whites—"the friends of the Negro"—to lend financial and moral support to colored churches and community institutions. Among "the friends of the Negro" were prominent white political leaders, socially conscious and not-so-socially conscious businessmen, and white liberals and radicals of varied hue. Negroes were not a "problem" to Chicago in those days and leaders seldom found it necessary to lead any dramatic protests against flagrant injustices. They concentrated upon trying to widen economic opportunity so that Negroes as individuals and families could "advance themselves," and they constantly urged Negroes to "take advantage of every opportunity."

The Great Migration created the "Negro problem." Numerous Negroes smarting from the rebuffs of a white community that did not seem to want them, took refuge in a kind of defensive racialism. Individuals arose on the lower and lower-middle-class level who fervently preached "race pride" and "race solidarity." We have already noted that the Commission on Race Relations in 1922 appealed to the "accepted leaders" to curb "agitators." A distinction emerged in the minds of white people between "safe leaders" and "radicals." The former were those who counseled thrift, patience, education and "wise" political action as the key to racial advancement. They were expected to throw their weight against violence and the blandishments of radicals—both economic and racial—and the enticements of labor unions. Many of the older Race Leaders accepted this role of "safe leaders," but numerous Negroes in the growing professional and business class were far less docile than a "safe leader" was supposed to be. They did not hesitate to voice their disapproval of any attempts to infringe upon the rights of Negroes or to deny them equal opportunity. Most of the community leaders had their hands full, however, maintaining Bronzeville's institutional life. They were the people who knew how to organize fund-raising drives and to make a budget and stay within it. They were people who were "uplifting the masses"—not leading them. Discontent was well dispersed in the prosperous Twenties.

The Challenge of the Racial Radicals: With the outbreak of the Depression, a small group of militant Race Men began to organize discontent into a "Spend Your Money Where You Can Work" Campaign, and this involved a new weapon, the boycott. The "intellectuals" of the movement were upper-middle-class businessmen and newspapermen; but the "leg work" was done by young high-school-trained Negroes who needed white-collar jobs, and by a few aspiring Negro labor leaders and "jack-leg" preachers. They expressed the sentiments, however, of the Negro masses, who loyally rallied around them. The idea of the boycott as a weapon persisted throughout the Depression and was supported by some Negro businessmen, a few politicians, and a group of militant young men and women organized into a Negro Labor Relations League. Inevitably, these activities involved sporadic violence, for the less disciplined hangers-on about such a movement often think in terms of a "squeeze play." A convenient brick tossed through a recalcitrant merchant's window may make him decide to negotiate with the leaders of the boycott.

The "accepted leaders" had to adjust to the threat of the Racial Radicals. The Chicago Urban League, for instance, had always been considered the citadel of "safe leadership" but when the Bronzeville masses began to picket for jobs, the Urban League ". . . not only gave its sanction to the movement, but also placed the facilities of its offices at the disposal of the leaders. . . . Beyond this whole-hearted support and encouragement, however, the League took no active part in the campaign. Its organization was such that it could not co-operate directly in the use of coercive methods." Yet, on October 9, 1930, a prominent official of the Chicago League wrote the national office in the following vein: [1]

"The time has come for a more aggressive attitude on the part of Negroes. We, of the Chicago Urban League, realize that fact, and our future programs will be far more aggressive than they have been in the past."

Throughout the Depression, the Urban League gave its moral support to the younger radicals who were channelizing the discontent of Black Metropolis into non-violent patterns of aggressive action.

Thunder on the Left: The accepted leaders not only had to maintain their ties with the sources of white economic and political power in Midwest Metropolis. They also had to adjust to the moods of racial radicalism, and were forced to take cognizance of pressure from the Left. Prior to the Depression, interracial co-operation had meant the contact between Race Leaders and the "best white people" or between Negro and white politicians. Now something new was added.

During the early Thirties, marchers in left-wing demonstrations in Midwest Metropolis frequently carried placards bearing the slogan BLACK AND WHITE UNITE! Close interracial co-operation became associated in the popular mind with "the Reds." Of course Negroes and a few whites, as we have seen, have always "co-operated" in Midwest Metropolis—but usually in white employer-Negro employee relations, or as Negro leader-white patron. These Communist slogans, however, signified something that was new to the city: a small band of white men proclaiming as a goal complete unity of Negro and white workers in a joint struggle to build a new society. Not even the Abolitionists had stood for that!

True, the old Industrial Workers of the World (IWW) and the various Socialist groups had made some feeble attempts to recruit Negro members in the period preceding the First World War, but not until 1924 did any left-wing group seriously begin exploiting the revolutionary potential latent in Negro America. The success of the Communist Revolution in Russia had inspired an international upsurge among the working classes of Europe and the colonial peoples of the East and of Africa. It was inevitable that the revolutionary wave would at least lap the shores of America. Under the ideological guidance of the Communist International, the American Communists, some time around 1924, began to think of the Negro group in America as an important section of the population which had nothing to lose but its chains. But those were the days when Black America had no use for anything led by white people—its memory of the race riots and of the wartime jobs now lost was too fresh.

This period of disillusionment in the early Twenties was followed by the Boom Years, and—though Negroes did not get their proportionate share of the good jobs—like their fellow white Americans, they were better off than they had ever been before. Yet throughout the Twenties small groups of white Communists worked diligently in the Black Ghetto handing out copies of the *Daily Worker,* staging interracial dances, and leading a few protests against high rents and "fire-traps."

With the Depression, "the Reds" emerged as leaders—fighting against evictions, leading demonstrations for more adequate relief, campaigning to free the Scottsboro Boys. Their reservoir of good will was filled to overflowing, with even the *Defender* writing an editorial on WHY WE CANNOT HATE REDS.

There has been much loose talk about Negroes going Red. A few hundred Negroes in Midwest Metropolis did "join the Party," some of them becoming prominent officials in the American Communist movement. They studied Marxism and became ideologically committed to the extension of World Socialism. But the Negro masses who "could not hate Reds" were not Marxian Socialists dreaming of a Socialist society—they were hungry, frustrated, angry people looking for a program of action. And the Reds had a plan. So Negroes joined the parades, attended the picnics, and fought bailiffs and policemen. As they did so they found white men marching and fighting beside them. Together they carried the signs, BLACK AND WHITE

UNITE, and demonstrated for more relief and better houses; but most of them were attracted to the Communists primarily because the "Reds" fought for Negroes *as* Negroes. Thousands of Negro preachers and doctors and lawyers, as well as quiet housewives, gave their money and verbal support to the struggle for freeing the Scottsboro Boys and for releasing Angelo Herndon. Hundreds, too, voted for Foster *and* Ford, Browder *and* Ford, for what other party since Reconstruction days had ever run a Negro for vice president of the United States? And who had ever put Negroes in a position where they led white men as well as black? Every time a black Communist appeared on the platform, or his picture appeared in a newspaper, Negroes were proud; and no stories of "atheistic Reds" or "alien Communists" could nullify the fact that here were people who accepted Negroes as complete equals and asked other white men to do so. Some of the preachers opposed the Reds publicly, but remarked privately, "If the Reds can feed the people, let 'em." Politicians dutifully denounced them, but privately admired their spunk. A few Negroes sincerely hated them.

"The Reds" won the admiration of the Negro masses by default. They were the only white people who seemed to really care what happened to the Negro. Yet few Negro sympathizers were without reservations. Some thought Communists were "using Negroes." Others felt that "if they ever gain power they'll be just like the other crackers." Many regarded the interracial picnics and dances as "bait." But Negroes are realists. They take "friends" and allies where they can find them.

BRONZEVILLE'S UNITED FRONT

After 1935, Communist emphasis shifted from revolution to building a "united front" against Fascism. During this period a significant number of the "best people" in Bronzeville followed Communist leadership on specific issues. They helped to raise money for the Spanish Loyalists and honored the Negroes who fought in the Abraham Lincoln Brigade. They put their names on petitions denouncing Hitler, Hirohito, and Mussolini. They gave financial and moral support to delegations seeking more adequate relief and better housing. A few well-known college-bred Negroes generally reputed to be Communists circulated freely among the upper class, stimulating discussion and winning a member here and there. This acceptance of Communists by Bronzeville was well illustrated in the Chicago *Defender's* 1938 "Bud Billiken" parade. Among nearly two hundred floats was one representing the Young Communist League. It bore the slogans BLACK AND WHITE UNITE and FREE THE SCOTTSBORO BOYS. On it rode a group of Negro and white youngsters. A student connected with the Cayton-Warner Research followed the float for five miles up Bronzeville's main boulevard, mingling with the crowd as he walked. He reported that a wave of applause followed the float along the whole route. Old women shouted, "Yes, free the boys!" People commented: "Them's the Communists. They don't believe in no differences. All's alike to them." Here and there a 100 per cent Negro-American would begin to denounce "the Reds," and a little knot would gather around him to argue. A few skeptics sneered: "Them trashy white women on that car don't mean the Negro no good." And some of the teen-age boys whistled and shouted "Hello, honey" at the white girls on the float. In general, however, Bronzeville demonstrated that it approved of whatever the Communists stood for in its mind. This widespread approval of "the Reds" was not only associated with the fight of American Communists; it was also grounded upon admiration for the Soviet Union which, to thousands of Negroes, was the one "white" nation that "treated darker folks right."

The Passing of the "Safe Leader": The old style "safe leader" has virtually disappeared from Bronzeville. Challenged on one hand by the Communists and on the other by the racial radicals, the "accepted leaders" have had either to accommodate themselves to new techniques or give way to men who could do so. The major community institutions (exclusive of the churches) are now in the hands of people who know how to steal a little of the radical's thunder, and "when they can't lick 'em, to jine 'em." In 1936, when the left-wingers announced that the newly organized National Negro Congress planned to federate all existing community organizations into one body to "struggle for Negro rights," the "accepted leadership" countered by organizing a Council of Negro Organizations.* By 1938, this organi-

* The first national conference of the National Negro Congress met in Chicago on February 14, 1936. It drew 817 delegates from 28 states; of these, 353 represented Black Metropolis. The Congress at first tried to federate all the

zation, led by upper and upper-middle-class, middle-aged men and women, was itself organizing demonstrations in the proletarian style. One protest march included 200 marchers and a motorcade bearing the following signs:

WE FEEL LOYAL AND PATRIOTIC? WHY?

WE DEMAND BETTER HOUSING CONDITIONS ON THE SOUTH SIDE

WE WANT SCHOOL BOARD MEMBERS: WE WANT A NEGRO POLICE CAPTAIN

CHRISTIAN AMERICA—YOUR BLACK SAINTS WANT BREAD AND SHELTER

OPEN DOORS OF ALL AFL TRADE UNIONS TO NEGROES

DOWN WITH FEINBERG
[a judge who favored restrictive covenants]

TB KILLS OUR CHILDREN

BUILD MORE BUSINESSES OF OUR OWN

ABSENTEE LANDLORDS HAVE NO INTEREST IN THE SOUTH SIDE

MR. MONEYBAGS, WE DRIVE YOUR CAR; WHY CAN'T WE DRIVE STREETCARS?

By 1938 it had become respectable to support a demonstration or a boycott in the struggle for Negro rights.

With the outbreak of the Second World War, many very "respectable" Negroes began to appear on picket lines and in demonstrations for jobs sponsored by the relatively conservative Council of

major Negro organizations in Bronzeville. Many of these groups, however, considered the Congress a "Red" organization and therefore hesitated to formally affiliate. The Congress was forced to concentrate on maintaining a solid labor union base for its financial support. At no time did it have more than 500 dues-paying members. It did, however, have energetic leaders, and on several occasions was able to organize broad community action.

The Council of Negro Organizations by the late Thirties listed as its affiliates some 57 organizations representing over 100,000 people. Only 19 of these were civic organizations; there were 10 social clubs, 6 fraternities and sororities, 10 church groups, 6 labor unions and 5 technical and professional societies. The Council "carried weight."

Negro Organizations, the NAACP, and the new militant March on Washington Movement, as well as by spur-of-the-moment committees. Between 1938 and the outbreak of the Second World War, the Communists were playing an active part as Bronzeville's extreme left wing in a "united front" that included even Catholic lay leadership.

National Unity? With the opening of the defense program, a decided shift took place in Bronzeville's attitude toward the Communists. It was obvious that America sympathized with Britain. But the Communists were beginning actively to preach opposition to "the imperialist war." There were plenty of people in Bronzeville who opposed the war, but among the upper and the upper-middle classes a split was taking place between "interventionists" and "non-interventionists." Even the non-interventionists didn't think it politic to be too closely allied to a group that was getting out on a limb. Coincident with the program of opposing the imperialist war, the Communists stepped up their "Negro work," particularly the fight for jobs in defense plants. At this point a curious thing happened: the "accepted" leadership took the ball away from the Reds, and Bronzeville's biggest demonstrations and picket lines were organized by non-Communist leaders—the younger "race pride intellectuals." Though the Communists remained in the united front they had created, they were pushed somewhat into the background. This tendency to take the leadership away from the Reds sprang partly from an increased racialism, but it was also related to the fact that the Communists insisted upon linking opposition to "the imperialist war" with every demonstration for jobs or better housing. Many Negroes felt that they should hew to the line of "Negro rights" since the broadest unity could be secured by ignoring the war controversy.

During this period, the Communists were placed in a very awkward position. Their national leader was jailed, President Roosevelt denounced them, strikes in defense plants were being blamed upon them. Negroes began to shy off. But even so, numerous Bronzeville people signed petitions to free Earl Browder, and not all of them were from the proletariat. It was during this period that the March-on-Washington Movement sponsored by non-Communist Negroes took the spotlight in the struggle for Negro rights.

When the Soviet Union was attacked by the Germans, the Communists felt that the character of the war had changed—that it was now a "war of national liberation," a "reversal of Munich." They began gradually to preach "intervention." At first this shift did not weaken their position among Negroes; indeed, it made co-operation with them easier because the slogans now coincided with the temper of the nation. Then the first great wave of dissatisfaction with the Communists swept through the ranks of Negro intellectuals and Race Leaders, for the Communists began to preach "national unity." After Pearl Harbor, many Negroes felt that the Communists were advising the Negroes to moderate their demands for full equality, and charges were hurled that "the Reds are selling out the Negroes." What actually took place seems to be this: The Communists insisted that defeating Hitler came first (some Negroes put defeating Fascism *at home* on the same plane). The Reds felt that Negro demands should be couched in "win the war" terms (Race Leaders preferred couching demands in terms of straight democratic rights). The Communists feared that mass demonstration by Negroes during the war might hurt the morale of the Negro soldiers fighting in a coalition war beside the Soviet Union (many Negroes felt that Communists should take the lead in fighting discrimination by organizing mass protests as they had done in the early Thirties).

This dissatisfaction with the Communists seemed to be centered among intellectuals and some professional labor leaders. Many rank and file Negroes in the labor movement were familiar with another aspect of Communist strategy: they saw that while "the Reds" played down mass action they continued to fight for Negro rights *within* the labor unions, and tried to inject the issue of Negro rights into the political coalitions they formed with liberals and the Democratic machine. Throughout the period of the war, although the Communists *as Communists* lost some of their prestige among Negroes in Bronzeville, Communists as politicians and labor leaders probably strengthened their position. The Communists were still preaching BLACK AND WHITE UNITE, but in a more quiet fashion than during the stormy Thirties, and with less emphasis upon Negro mass action.

MOBILIZING THE COMMUNITY

Raising Money: The primary activity of most "accepted" leaders centers around raising money to finance such organizations as the

NAACP, the Urban League, Provident Hospital, the YMCA, the YWCA, the Federated Women's Clubs, and a number of other institutions. The leaders of these groups are upper-class and upper-middle-class men and women who "have the confidence of the community" and who can also secure donations from white philanthropists and funds such as the Community Chest, the Community Trust, the Rosenwald Fund, etc. In raising money from Bronzeville itself, the procedures are highly ritualized with annual drives, accompanied by high pressure salesmanship, banquets and victory celebrations.

Speaking for the Race: Accepted leaders are the people who "speak for the race," acquainting the white political and business leaders and heads of social agencies with Bronzeville's needs. They also help to give form and direction to movements which arise from below, and make use of petition, protest, demonstrations, and "campaigns" to further the cause. Because they are primarily administrators and not mass leaders, they have worked out informal patterns of co-operation with those leaders who are "close to the masses."

The Urban League, particularly, has built up a reputation of being able to say a word for The Race in places where it counts. Typical of its activity was a drive, during the Second World War, to get employment for colored women in downtown stores. During 1944 and 45, the League took the leadership in the drive. Here was a hard nut to crack. The Women's Division of the League set up a campaign on an interracial basis and proceeded to secure the indorsement of a number of liberal organizations black and white.* Subcommittees were set up to arrange for meetings with department store officials, to recruit and train well-qualified girls for possible new openings, and to start a widespread educational campaign including petitions from shoppers and leaflets with favorable comment from the buying public.

The NAACP works in slightly different fashion, concentrating on court cases where the Civil Rights Law has been violated. It has far

* Among the organizations listed as "interested and lending support" were: Association for Family Living; Women's City Club; Hyde Park Co-operative Society; Council of Social Agencies; Chicago Round Table of Christians and Jews; Business and Professional Department of the YWCA; Friendship House (Catholic); Chicago Council on Racial and Religious Discrimination; Neighborhood Improvement Association, South Center Project; American Jewish Congress; Chicago's Women's Aid, Kansas Women's Club; Chicago Branch of the National Association of College Women.

less close contacts with the white world and gets its major financial support from the upper and middle classes in Bronzeville.*

The Balance Sheet: Despite the claim that Bronzeville "cannot be organized," the record shows that during the Depression years, a number of concrete gains came from organized pressure. Where actual gains were not recorded, the very activity of fighting for something probably helped to keep the morale of the community up. A few of the campaigns for "advancing the race" are analyzed on pages 743 and 744.

In addition to the housing problem and employment problems, community leaders all through the Depression organized public sentiment against double-shift, overcrowded schools, attempted to work on the problem of eliminating juvenile delinquency, and agitated for increased representation in important political appointive positions. Some of these were chronic problems whose ultimate solutions were beyond the control of any local leaders.

In all of these activities Bronzeville's leaders work with whatever white allies are at hand. One type of interracial co-operation may be illustrated by a mass meeting called to celebrate Lincoln's Birthday in 1939. The meeting was held in the DuSaible High School in the center of the Black Belt. It was sponsored by the predominantly white Chicago Civil Liberties Committee and the predominantly Negro Chicago City-wide Forum. The South Side was flooded with leaflets upon which appeared the following slogans: CIVIL RIGHTS MEAN NEGRO RIGHTS! REMEMBER JOHN ROBINSON! (a Negro who had been a victim of police brutality); OUTLAW RESTRICTIVE COVENANTS! PASS THE ANTI-LYNCHING BILL! A FULL SCHOOL DAY FOR NEGRO CHILDREN!

The sponsoring committee included 137 persons, 67 white and 70 Negro. The extremists of the right and left were in the decided minority, less than a dozen Communists and Socialists were on the list

---

* The NAACP is a "fighting organization" but it has developed the technique of organizing the social club world. In 1944, for instance, that organization offered a trophy to the club raising the most money. The Silent Eight won the trophy which was presented at a tea. In addition to school clubs, fraternal orders, fraternities and sororities and one or two state clubs, the following social clubs sponsored tables at the tea: Silent Cylindricals, Valencia Bridge, Old Tymers, Trail Blazers, Bronze Duchesses, Original Peter Pan Bridge and Civic Club, Nine Joyettes, and Twelve Lucky Strikes.

and not more than 6 racial radicals. Over a hundred prominent liberals (38 Negro and 62 whites) were listed and 19 Negroes of a general liberal orientation but only "ordinary citizens." The chairman of

MAKING JOBS FOR THE RACE

Campaigns	Date	Groups Involved	Technique	Outcome
"Spend Your Money Where You Can Work" Campaign (directed at white stores in the Black Belt)	1929	Sponsored by *Negro Proessionals and Business men.* (Led by Race Radicals, with broad community support)	Boycott; picketing	Successful: 2,000 jobs in Black Belt stores
51st Street Riot (directed at white laborers)	1930	Spontaneous outburst by laborers	Violence	Successful
Fight for Skilled Jobs on Construction in Black Belt (directed at AFL building trades unions)	1929-38	*Consolidated Trades Council*—group of Negro artisans	Picketing; political pressure; some violence	Partial success with advent of New Deal
Fight for Branch Managers with *Daily Times*	1937		Threat of boycott	Six managers appointed after one week campaign
Fight for Branch Managers, *Evening American*	1937	*Negro Labor Relations League*—group of young men and women; some co-operation from Urban League and politicians	Conference; implied threat of boycott	Eight managers appointed
Campaign for Motion Picture Operators in Black Belt (directed against AFL Unions)	1938		Picketing; threat of boycott	Ten operators appointed after short campaign
Campaign for Telephone Operators (directed against phone company)	1937-39		Threat that all Negroes would remove telephones	Unsuccessful; threat not carried out fully
Drive for Negro Milkmen (directed against major dairies and the AFL unions)	1929-39	Fight begun by *Whip;* revived in 1937 by *Council of Negro Organizations* and *Negro Labor Relations League*	Threat of boycott; attempt to organize "Milkless Sundays"	Unsuccessful due to lack of community support
Campaign for bus drivers and motormen on transit lines	1930-44	*"United front"* with strong left-wing influence; campaign aided by FEPC.	Demonstrations; threat of boycott; strong political pressure	Successful in securing a few positions

HOUSING STRUGGLES

Campaigns	Date	Groups Involved	Technique	Outcome
Fight against Restrictive Covenants (directed against Chicago Real Estate Board, Chicago Title and Trust Company, and neighborhood property owners' associations)	1925-present	Led by Negro business and professional men with *NAACP* as the spearhead and politicians co-operating; specific drives sponsored by *Urban League* and *Council of Negro Organizations*	Court cases including one carried to Supreme Court; attempts to have bill passed in state legislature; mass meetings	Partial success in winning more living space; no success in securing clear-cut decision against restrictive covenants
Agitation for Federal Housing Projects	1935-38	Community-wide pressure led by *Urban League* and *Council of Negro Organizations*	Mass meetings, petition, demonstrations and political pressure	Success after 3 year campaign
Fight against High Rents	1929-42	*National Negro Congress; Consolidated Tenants League*	Tenant strikes; petition and protest	Sporadic and isolated successes

the meeting was the lone Negro member of the Chicago Housing Authority. On the platform with him were: a Negro member of the CIO National Executive Council; a vice-president of the National Lawyers Guild, the Chief Counsel of the NAACP and a leading lawyer from the American Civil Liberties Union. (Only 7 ministers, four white and three colored, were listed as sponsors. Ninety per cent of the sponsors were secular professionals.)

WAR COMES TO BRONZEVILLE

After Pearl Harbor: To most of white America, Pearl Harbor was a national tragedy. To Bronzeville, however, the event had a somewhat different meaning. The average Negro knew little about Japanese militarism and its brutal history. He did know that Japan was the one "colored" nation which was a great power—that it had steamships and large factories, and that it was breathing defiance at the white powers which had heretofore dominated the East. When the Japanese took Singapore and bombed Pearl Harbor, many American Negroes experienced a kind of vicarious (and vindictive) pleasure. On numerous occasions in the early days of the war, people in Bronzeville were heard to make comments like the following: "I see where the papers are complaining 'cause some Jap slapped a white woman. Well, they been slappin' colored women all these years. Now, they gettin' it back." * Even some of the more politically conscious Negroes betrayed ambivalence about the Japanese. One man whose loyalty to America and to the left-liberal movement is beyond question, made the following "confession" to one of the authors:

"I was really ashamed of myself the day Pearl Harbor was hit. When I heard the news I jumped up and laughed. 'Well, sir,' I said, 'I don't guess the white folks will say colored people can't fly airplanes from now on. They sure slammed hell outa Pearl Harbor.' Then I caught myself. I know the Japanese are a bunch of Fascists; and I've been raisin' money for China relief for years. I know this isn't a race war. I shouldn't have been pleased at anything the Japs did. But I suppose I just see it this way—we're bound to win this war in the long run, and a few tactical defeats like Singapore and Pearl Harbor, in the framework of a strategy for total victory, may help democracy in the long run. They may make the white man wake up to the fact that he can't shove darker people around forever. Of course, we've got to lick the Japs. I'm not for a negotiated peace or anything like that."

There were a few Negroes in Bronzeville, however, who were really pro-Japanese. Among them were the members of a small nationalistic sect—"The Moors"—composed of Negroes who had psychologically rejected their allegiance to America. They called themselves "Asiatics," assumed names with some Arabic flourish like "Bey," and often wore the red fez. They called upon all "Asiatics" to present a solid front against the "Europeans." There are not over a couple of hundred Moors in Chicago, but a score of them were tried for resisting the draft and for sedition. One rather well-known Bronzeville woman, leader of the Peace Movement to Ethiopia, was also sentenced to the Federal penitentiary for advising Negroes to resist the draft and for propagating pro-Japanese sentiments.

* The authors have not had access to the confidential interviews and polls made in Bronzeville and other urban areas by the OWI and similar government agencies. It is their guess, however, that when these findings are eventually released, they will show a rather general tendency for Negroes to identify emotionally with Japan in the early days of the war, especially since epithets such as "yellow bastards" were used. A preliminary report states, however, that less than a fifth of the Negroes interviewed throughout the country admitted pro-Japanese sentiments (Myrdal, *op. cit.*, p. 1400).

For most Negroes, however, any admiration for Japan as a "colored fighting power" tended to be a fleeting mood rather than an organized creed. As the war progressed and their friends and relatives began to fight in the Pacific, Negroes, like other Americans, began to visualize the Japanese as "the enemy." There is no evidence that Negroes facing the Japanese have been any less loyal than those facing the Nazis. So long, however, as a world-wide color-line is drawn, there is always a tendency for Negroes to see a "colored" enemy nation from a slightly different perspective than a white man would view it.

The Race Leaders and the Negro press constantly tried to clarify the Negro rank and file as to the issues involved in the Second World War. Their position was essentially that of Joe Louis who said upon one occasion, "There's a lot wrong with this country, but Hitler can't fix it."

The Sources of Patriotism: Although resentful about discrimination and injustices, Bronzeville "supported the war." The sources of their patriotism were essentially those which operate in the general society.

Colored men, like white men, were called upon to fight and die. No matter what an individual thought about the aims and objectives of the war, or about his grievances, if he, or those close to him, was in the service, he had an emotional investment in the war. Bronzeville was caught up in the general mood of the nation and swept along with it. It developed the normal interest in its men and boys who were overseas. And the men and women who entered the service developed those loyalties to their units which are the basic elements in morale.

Patriotism also received powerful reinforcement from the social ritual. In peacetime, Bronzeville had its unit of the National Guard, its Veterans of Foreign Wars and American Legion post which kept alive an interest in military affairs. To these were added a number of new patriotic organizations, the middle-aged Women's Army of National Defense, the young women's Joe Louis Service Guild, and numerous committees for special activities such as preparing medical supplies, selling bonds, and entertaining service men.

The whole community was organized in support of a Service Men's Center, and an analysis of the organizations that contributed time, money and gifts reads like a roster of all the voluntary associations in Bronzeville. College fraternities and sororities, fraternal orders, gospel choruses, choirs, churches, alumni associations, and social clubs vied with one another in making the boys feel at home in Bronzeville. Whether they were the Gay Girls or the Romping Earls presenting cigarettes to the soldiers, or an older women's group cooking Thanksgiving turkeys for the Center, Bronzeville's club world made war work a part of the social ritual.

The war also affected the social ritual itself. The annual dances often became Victory Balls. At the climax of the grand march in middle-class clubs, a ceremony was sometimes held in which a bond was presented to the most popular member. During the winter social season of 1944-45, one upper-class fraternity reported its dance as follows:

Discarding the traditional formal tone in favor of wartime simplicity, guests wore informal clothes and the sole decoration was a huge service flag hung at the far end of the ballroom in front of the bandstand. The flag was dedicated to our men in the armed forces.

The masses who had been drifting, unorganized and aimless, during the Depression years were now drawn into meaningful activity. Men and women who were nobodies became heroes overnight, with their names mentioned in the press and with higher status people honoring them. One of the largest department stores in Bronzeville set up a Hall of Heroes and invited everyone to contribute "a picture of your favorite service-man or woman . . . to show to the world the heroic Americans from the South Side now fighting for our country."

But patriotism received its strongest reinforcement from the widespread belief that the war might help to "advance The Race." When the country needs men to work and fight, Negroes have a chance to prove—in a fashion they do not always have in times of peace—that they, too, are Americans. Bronzeville followed the Negro fighting units with rapt attention, and always with the hope that the white world would see and appreciate their services. It was just as proud too of victories on the home front. The same issue of a Bronzeville paper that praised "the first Negro member of the Army Nurse corps to hold the rank of captain" also gave a big display to "the first Negro cashier employed in the downtown office of the Bell Telephone Company."

Negroes were also getting a chance to tell their story to America, to remind it of historic heroes like Crispus Attucks, first man to die in the Boston Massacre as well as the young men scattered around the world in the Second World War.

Proving Patriotism: Negroes see in war an opportunity to prove their patriotism and to thus lay the nation under obligation to them. It has become traditional for leaders to boast that "No American Negro has ever been shot as a spy or a traitor," and to call the roll of great Negro soldiers beginning with Crispus Attucks, and including the exploits of Negro individuals and units in every war America has fought. Black Metropolis guards jealously the memory of Negroes who fought in previous wars. At one end of South Parkway, the main thoroughfare, there is an equestrian statue of George Washington. At the other end is a monument to Negro soldiers who died in the First World War. It took a prolonged legislative to get such a statue on a boulevard.

Bronzeville is proud, too, of its Illinois Eighth Regiment, which in peacetime had several thousand members, a large armory, and each year paraded impressively through the South Side on its return from spring maneuvers. This regiment, officered mainly by professional and business men, became an artillery unit in the Second World War. Bronzeville was furious when the unit was reduced to a labor battalion. This was regarded as an insult to The Race and patent evidence of discrimination in the armed forces.

Bronzeville has no doubt of its patriotism. It knows the record. It feels, however, that it must prove its patriotism with each new war. Therefore, war activities, such as bond selling, are more than patriotic duties—they are also one more way of advancing The Race.

"Proving patriotism" became a powerful stimulus for community organization during the war. Bronzeville, in one bond drive in 1944, had a $5,000,000 quota. The drive was under the direction of one of the community's most energetic businessmen, a former Major in the Illinois Eighth Regiment. The committee sponsored several midnight shows at a large theater and set up a community-wide sales program. On one occasion, shortly after the $2,000,000 mark had been reached, the *Defender* cited by name some 25 upper- and middle-class leaders who were heading the group of 3,000 canvassers. Individuals who made large bond purchases were in the news throughout the campaign, such as the postal employee, "veteran of World War I, having won a Purple Heart for wounds he received in France." He and his wife bought a one thousand dollar bond. One issue of the *Defender* displayed the pictures of three Black Belt businessmen, TOP BOND BUYERS IN $1,000 PLATE DINNER. Prominent businessmen presented checks running into three figures to purchase bonds for their companies and business associations at rallies in the big Loop hotels. At one bond rally and banquet, the Beauty Shop Owners Association reported $3,900 in sales and awarded a prize of a $25 bond to a woman who had sold over a thousand dollars' worth. A resourceful Bronzeville school held three rallies in the assembly hall and raised $10,000, "enough to buy two jeeps, two amphibian jeeps, one flying jeep, one motor scooter, one lifeboat and a parachute for the air corps."

The high point of the 1944 bond drive came when the United States Maritime Commission launched the Liberty ship, U.S.S. *Robert S. Abbott,* "purchased" by Bronzeville with $2,000,000 in bonds. Bronzeville's bigwigs journeyed to San Francisco where the wife of the publisher of the *Defender* broke the champagne bottle on the prow, and the publisher proudly announced that this was "the first time in history that such a plan has been adopted by Negroes."

Without fanfare, thousands of Negroes also bought bonds through the payroll-checkoff in the factories of Midwest Metropolis. Bronzeville was investing in its future. A newspaper columnist contemplating the millions which Black Metropolis was saving could not refrain from commenting, "Suppose all this money could be corralled for a Negro business enterprise."

A *Defender* editorial published during the 1944 bond drive expresses the general attitude of the "accepted" leaders toward the Second World War:

> Regardless of how deeply we may resent numerous injustices perpetrated against us and how hard we may fight against them, we must admit that this is our war too. Our boys are fighting overseas, facing a dangerous, murderous enemy who will destroy them and us as quickly as he will our white brother. . . .

> Participation in this Fourth War Loan drive is not only a patriotic act, but is a matter of self-interest. It offers a splendid opportunity for wage-earners to save some of the money they now earn as a result of high salaries in war industries. It is the best safeguard against their dissipating every penny of it on non-essentials during the present boom. These bonds can become a "nest egg" which will act as a cushion during the post-war

period for the persons who own them. They may well form the nucleus of capital for business enterprises which Negroes desire to organize. . . .

The quicker the war is over, the sooner this danger will be passed, and our strong virile youths can return to help buttress the fight for our full rights.

This mixed philosophy of patriotism and self-interest is typically American. But for Negroes in America both patriotism and self-interest are seen as aids to "racial advancement," and the "fight for our full rights"—in time of war as in time of peace—is considered one aspect of the struggle for democracy.

Post-war Prospects: Despite its enthusiastic participation in the common struggle, a note of anxiety ran through all of Bronzeville's war activity. It was reflected not only in newspaper discussion, but also at the grass roots—in churches, at social club meetings, on the street corners. One of the questions that bothered Bronzeville was a source of anxiety to other Americans also, "Will there be a depression after the war?" But another question was a special one, "Will 'our people' be any better off after this war?"

A conference of the Colored Methodist Episcopal Church meets in Bronzeville. Its theme is "The World We Want."

When 27 midwestern chapters of the Delta Sigma Theta Sorority convene for a regional conclave, the theme is "Delta Participation in Post-war Plans."

When the city Pan-Hellenic Council, representing all the college Greek-letter societies, meets, it ponders the question, "How to Retain Wartime Gains in the Post-war Period."

The National Association of College Women meets to discuss "The War, the World and the College Woman."

A small Methodist church sponsors a debate, "Should a Negro Sit at the Peace Table?"

A wealthy real-estate man organizes the National Negro Progress Association and tries to amass capital so "we can have some *real* businesses after the war."

And preachers, Sunday after Sunday, advise The Race to save its money so that they can face the difficulties which are likely to follow.

Bronzeville was living in fear of another ten years on the WPA and was not too sure that the gains in the fight against the Job Ceiling would last.

On May 26, 1944, Bronzeville's Congressman, William L. Dawson, made a speech on the floor of the House in support of a permanent Fair Employment Practices Committee. His words reveal this deep concern about post-war prospects:

Mr. Chairman, I, too, am an American and in making my claim to that I apologize to no man. By every rule that you may measure men, apply it to me and see if I measure up to the test. This mark on my brow coming down here is the burn of mustard gas in the last war. This left arm of mine is a slip joint today, from raiding German trenches in the last war. I volunteered then because I was an American. So when we stand here today and talk about our country, I can speak for more than a million Negro Americans fighting today with our armed forces and more than 13,000,000 here at home—all Americans. They, too, have a part in this country.

. . . We might as well face this situation. Thirteen million people compose one-tenth of the population of this great Nation of ours. What shall be the attitude of America toward those 13,000,000? Are you going to deny to them the opportunities that you proclaim to the world should be given to all men?

ONE NATION INDIVISIBLE?

Out of the bitterness and frustration following the First World War, almost a million Negroes in America embraced a peculiar form of Black Zionism—a "Back to Africa" movement led by a West Indian Negro, Marcus Garvey. There had been colonization movements in America ever since the early nineteenth century but none had ever been popular. The Republic of Liberia, for instance, languished for want of Negro emigrants returning "home to Africa." Then, in the Twenties, Marcus Garvey, eloquent and black, burst upon the scene—a real Race Man.

One God, One Aim, One Destiny: The official Garvey organization was called the Universal Negro Improvement Association, and had as its satellites the Royal African Legions, the Black Star Line, and the Black Cross Nurses. Africa was divided up on paper into a number of principalities and Garvey assumed the title of Provisional President. He dreamed of transporting several million American Negroes back home to redeem Africa from the imperialists and of having the remaining Negroes in America and the West Indies keep up a brisk and lively trade with the Motherland. For his pains he was sentenced to five years in the Atlanta Penitentiary, and was ultimately deported to Jamaica. In 1940 he died in London, still dreaming of the day when all Negroes would have "One God, One Aim, One Destiny." Several million American Negroes were once dues-paying members in the UNIA.

Garveyism was never very popular in Chicago, but the UNIA did recruit several thousand fanatical members from the lower class and lower middle class, who spread its influence far beyond the small circle of its membership. With his emphasis upon the "proud tradition of the African past," upon "race pride," and particularly upon the virtue of "blackness," Garvey put steel in the spine of many Negroes who had previously been ashamed of their color and of their identification with the Negro group. Before his time, such things as colored dolls or calendars with colored families and heroes were a rarity; today they are commonplace. Garvey didn't get many Negroes back to Africa, but he helped to destroy their inferiority complex, and made them conscious of their power.

By 1938, Bronzeville had almost forgot Garvey and Black Zionism. Only a corporal's guard of the faithful were still meeting in their dilapidated Liberty Hall beneath the dusty and fly-specked portraits of The Leader. The more capable and realistic Garveyite leaders had long since become successful Bronzeville politicians and businessmen or had gone over to the Communists. But here and there were a few individuals such as the domestic servant who was vague about the UNIA but who said:

"All I know about Garvey is that he wanted to form the colored people into some kind of union and have us all go back to Africa and form a country of our own. That was a good idea. A union like that would make a strong nation. I'd like to try something like that."

Or the successful merchant who, slurring over the "Back to Africa" emphasis, sees Garvey as "one of the few great leaders who taught the people to open places of business."

Most Negroes, however, tended to ridicule Black Zionism as did one relief client: "Why should the colored people go back to Africa? There ain't nothin' for them to do over there." Or the WPA employee who said, "I don't see why I should return to Africa to get all the things I need." One barbershop lounger said flatly, "There ain't no boulevards in Africa!" An upper-middle-class businessman expressed the general temper of Bronzeville when he said:

"There never was a more foolish movement than the Garvey movement. I think Garvey has just about lost his influence in the United States, but there are still quite a few Garveyites in America who want to run away from the situation here and who are not willing to fight. I hope the younger people will have more fight in them than the older people had."

No counterpart of Garvey Zionism is likely to sweep Bronzeville in the post-war years, but a "racial radicalism" of gigantic proportions may well up in Black Metropolis if Negroes feel that the Second World War liberated the world, but did not "advance The Race."

The people are rather definite about what they want: the abolition of the Job Ceiling; adequate housing; equal, unsegregated access to all places of public accommodation; the protection of the rights of those Negroes and whites who may desire to associate together socially. And they want to see this pattern extended to all of America—including the South.*

The Fifth Freedom: Sometimes Negroes in Bronzeville picked up their weeklies and read that colored troops were forced to eat in the kitchen at some southern railway station, while Nazi prisoners traveling on the same train ate in the dining room. Occasionally a mother received a letter from a son who had been beaten by a bus driver because he didn't Jim-Crow himself fast enough. Such incidents aroused hot resentment, and the off-the-record comments at such moments would certainly "give comfort to the enemy." For the average person these were bitter moods that left their mark, but did not "unbalance" him. Some people, however, reached the breaking point, for there were

---

* This national outlook is understandable when we remember that most of the people in Bronzeville are migrants from the South. This broad perspective was illustrated at the 28th annual conclave of the Phi Beta Sigma Fraternity, meeting in Chicago in 1944—"A War Emergency Meeting." There were the usual social activities—a smoker, a tea and luncheon for the ladies, a dance, and the dedication of the fraternity service flag at a Baptist church. But the fraternity also went on record as favoring the immediate passage of a permanent Fair Employment Practices Act, and an anti-poll tax bill. It pledged to help raise $1,500,000 for the Negro College Fund, and to establish a fund for the post-war education of men in the armed forces.

those who could not adjust themselves to fighting for other people's freedom while they were themselves subordinated.

There were at least 10 young men in Bronzeville who formed an organization, "C.O.'s Against Jim-Crow," and asked that conscientious objector's privileges be extended them since they did not believe in a segregated army.

A half dozen Bronzeville men stationed in Arkansas, when abused by civilians and their own officers, went AWOL and reported to a Michigan camp saying that they would not serve in an area where they were not treated as men.

When a half hundred Negro sailors mutinied on the West Coast because they felt they were being discriminated against, there were Bronzeville names among the men court-martialed.

One Bronzeville soldier actually tried to commit suicide on the Capitol steps in Washington as a protest against Jim-Crow and discrimination in the armed forces.

There were only a few such extremists in Bronzeville, but they reveal sharply what was going on at least some of the time in most Negro's minds. They were prototypes of what may conceivably happen on a larger scale in some future war, if Negroes are not fully "liberated" in the post-war years.

The Negroes who went to fight in the Second World War, unlike those who fought in the First, were not masses of illiterate cotton-field hands dragooned into battle, never asking, "Why?" At least half of the Negro soldiers—and Bronzeville's men fall in this class—were city people who had lived through a Depression in America's Black Ghettoes, and who had been exposed to unions, the Communist movement, and to the moods of "racial radicalism" that occasionally swept American cities. Even the rural southern Negroes were different this time—for the thirty years between the First and Second World Wars had seen a great expansion of school facilities in the South and the wide distribution of newspapers and radios.

All Negroes were aware, however vaguely in some cases, that they were participating in a titanic struggle fought under the banner of the Four Freedoms. They were liberating people from Fascism abroad and they were expecting to be liberated from Jim-Crow at home. For them, this was a Fifth Freedom as precious as the other four.

PART IV

CHAPTER 24

Of Things to Come

We are now constructing the baby figure of the giant mass of things to come

THE NEGRO COMES TO TOWN

THE NEGRO COMMUNITY IN CHICAGO BEGAN AS A HAVEN OF REFUGE FOR escaped slaves. It emerged a century later as Black Metropolis inhabited by the grandchildren and great-grandchildren of slaves. In the years between, it had become a citadel of economic and political power in the midst of Midwest Metropolis—an integral part of the city political machine and a reservoir for industrial labor and personal and domestic servants. The story of the growth of Black Metropolis between the Civil War and the Depression is, with minor variations, the story of the Negro in New York, Detroit, Philadelphia, Pittsburgh, and a number of other cities in America's northeastern and east-central industrial areas. During the Second World War it became the story, too, of San Francisco and Los Angeles as Negroes streamed to the West Coast to help man the arsenal of democracy. Negroes in America are becoming a city people, and it is in the cities that the problem of the Negro in American life appears in its sharpest and most dramatic forms.* It may be, too, that the cities will be the arena in which the "Negro problem" will be finally settled. A study of Negro life in Chicago is

---

* Much of the material in this chapter is based on the following articles: Horace R. Cayton, "Fighting for White Folks?" *Nation,* Sept. 26, 1942; "The Negro's Challenge," *ibid.,* July 3, 1943; "The American Negro—A World Problem," *Social Education,* May 1944; St. Clair Drake, "Chicago," *Journal of Educational Sociology,* January 1944; and Elaine Ogden McNeil and Horace R. Cayton, "Research on the Urban Negro," *American Journal of Sociology,* September 1941. We are especially indebted to Mrs. McNeil, having used without quotation marks much of the material from the article that she wrote with Horace Cayton.

important not only because it is typical of northern urban communities, but also because it involves one of the cities in which change is taking place most rapidly and where in the next decade friction, and even conflict, between capital and labor, Negroes and whites, will probably reach its most intense form, and where a new pattern of race relations is most likely to evolve.

The progressive urbanization of the Negro has not been confined to cities of the North and the West, however. Even before the Civil War southern cities were "havens of refuge" for a significant segment of the Negro population—"free persons of color." In Charleston, Savannah, Richmond, New Orleans, and even smaller centers like Natchez, those Negroes congregated who had been able to buy their freedom or who had been freed by their masters. Except in New Orleans their status was precarious and in no southern cities were they allowed full freedom. In the cities of the pre-Civil War North, on the other hand, free Negroes (and escaped slaves) were able to develop in a more favorable social environment. These differences between urban North and urban South have persisted to the present day, and thus, while Negroes in the South are *more free* than those in the small towns and on the plantations, they are *less free* than Negroes in Black Metropolis and cities like it. These differences have been summarized by one Negro scholar, Dr. L. D. Reddick, who lists four basic things which distinguish the Negro's status in the North from his position in the South: the law is on his side in the fight for equal rights; he is not disfranchised; there is no tradition of slavery, a "lost cause," and the crime of Reconstruction; and the general social and intellectual development of both whites and Negroes is higher.*

The difference between Negro and white is the basic social division in the Deep South and in most of the border states. *The very existence of social order is believed to depend upon "keeping the Negro in his place."* The stability of the economy, the political system, the educational system, and church, family, and associational life are all passionately believed to require the subordination of Negroes. Even when modifications are made because of economic necessity, political expediency, and democratic idealism, they must never challenge the funda-

---

* Dr. Reddick edited the January 1944 issue of *The Journal of Educational Sociology* (New York University), entitled "The Negro in the North During Wartime." The list above appears in his summary article, "What the Northern Negro Thinks About Democracy."

mental rule of *segregation* in most aspects of community life. And concessions must not place Negroes in competition with whites for power and prestige. So all-embracing is this view of life and so rigid are the controls that some scholars refer to the system of Negro-white relations in the Deep South as a "caste system." Northern institutions, on the other hand, as they evolved did not have "keeping the Negro in his place" as one of their primary objectives.

In many ways, the position of Negroes in northern urban communities has been similar to that of foreign-born immigrants. The masses of both come into the city's economic life at the bottom and find their first homes in the slum areas. Both are looked down upon by those who got there first. As time passes individual immigrants and their ethnic groups as a whole rise in status. Many of them are "assimilated" and become socially accepted. People eventually forget the foreign antecedents of successful Americans. In the case of Negroes, however, the process stops short of complete assimilation. A Job Ceiling limits them to unskilled and semi-skilled work and condemns them to the relief rolls during depressions. Residential segregation results in a Black Ghetto. The color-line preserves social segregation and sets the limits of advancement in politics and other non-economic hierarchies. But few people feel that Negroes should have or will have a *permanently* fixed status. Negroes are expected to complain and to use the ballot, their economic power, and the courts to alter their status if they can. When Negroes "demand their rights" Midwest Metropolis may resist their claims, but it does not usually do so on the ground that they are "niggers getting out of their place."

Negro-white relations in Midwest Metropolis always involve two contradictory principles of social organization: *free competition* and *fixed status*. In industry, politics, and the use of public services the principle of *free competition* is dominant but is checked and limited by the principle of *fixed status*. In the realm of housing, on the other hand, the principle of *fixed status* predominates but is challenged by the principle of *free competition*. In "social" affairs the principle of *fixed status* operates almost unchecked. At the present time, Negroes on a mass scale are concerned with establishing the principle of *free competition* throughout the economic and political life of the city and in the realm of competition for housing. They absolutely refuse to accept the principle of *fixed status* in these areas.

Unlike the South, Midwest Metropolis does not attempt to cow

Negroes when they raise such demands. A tradition of native-American white supremacy is absent. The expediencies of city life, the characteristic mobility and anonymity, the wide range of relationships which are interpreted as impersonal, the complex division of labor—all present a favorable setting for the operation of the principle of *free competition*. The principle of *fixed status* is alien to urban life as well as to American idealism. Race conflict in northern urban areas arises when competition is particularly keen—for jobs, houses, political power, or prestige—and when Negroes are regarded (with or without foundation) as a threat to those who already have these things or who are competing for them. The typical form of Negro-white conflict in the North is the riot; in the South, lynching.

ALONG THE COLOR-LINE

Negroes and whites in Chicago are consciously competing for space, for jobs, for political power, and for status. Underlying this conscious competition, of course, is the struggle for existence, a basic and unconscious biological process which is modified by economic factors as well as by the demographic characteristics of the various ethnic groups—for example, age-sex distribution and marital status. Competition for space is a basic ecological process which, in a city where race and ethnic segregation occurs, is interpreted by nearly everyone as competition between the ethnic groups. Negroes are limited in their competition for jobs by lack of training as well as by unfair employment practices; and probably only in times of acute labor shortage do they compete with whites on anything approaching equal terms, and even then not for jobs in the highest occupational brackets. Yet some few Negroes have obtained positions of economic power in the city. Since the political power of Negroes, although circumscribed, is fully appreciated by Chicago politicians and by Chicago Negroes themselves, Negroes have made occupational gains which they could not have attained through other means.

In "social" matters the principle of fixed status operates. Negroes do not belong to white churches or social clubs, nor do they generally marry into white families; and there is a system of social classes among Negroes which is distinct from that of the whites. The rise of a separate Negro social structure is a response to the fixed status of Negroes as enforced by whites wherever intimate contacts prevail.

The Negro is ever attempting to widen the sphere of opportunity within the areas of life where he is already competing. Each new achievement of a Negro—whether it be the winning of a world's title in sports or a new appointive position in the city government—is hailed by the Negro press as a "step forward." New migrants are amazed and delighted to see Negro policemen, to have a Negro alderman, to be served by a Negro employee at the public library. After a time the "gains" of the Negro in the North are taken for granted, and the Negro loses more and more of the "caste mentality" which he could not avoid developing in the South, and comes to think of himself as being able to advance to a status beyond any allowed him there. Social distance fixes the role of the Negro in certain spheres of social life; yet competition allows him to widen the other areas in which he participates. It is the interaction of these two processes—competition and fixed status—which determines his position in the social structure at any given moment.

This conflict between the Negro's fixed status in some areas and his right to compete in others is reflected in the individual personality. In a northern city such as Chicago, influenced by the democratic ideology and the freedom of city life, the Negro lives in two worlds—the white world and the Negro world. He becomes aware of the contradiction between the ideology of democracy which emphasizes free competition and the efforts of the white world to fix his status. While in the South there is little doubt how he is expected to act, in a city like Chicago he is often not at all sure. He may work for a white man and receive recognition for his skill and capabilities, but he must not "marry the boss's daughter." He may be awarded a degree from a university, but he cannot expect to practice medicine in a white hospital, or to be pledged to a white fraternity, or attend the senior formal dance—at least under ordinary circumstances. But there is no strict rule to guide him. White northerners, too, are themselves often uncertain as to how they should act toward Negroes, what to expect from them, and how far to treat them as equals.

What has been termed the marginal personality (and all Negroes in Chicago are to some degree marginal) results from this dual position in society. The fact that in a supposedly democratic society they are allowed to compete for some values but not for others sets up a conflict in most Negroes' minds. If their status were unalterably fixed and explicitly defined in all aspects of community life—to an extent that has not existed even in the South—Negroes would perhaps, over a period of time, become accommodated to this situation or else be exterminated. If, on the other hand, Negroes could compete fully and equally in all spheres of life, they would develop a mentality no different from that of other persons in the society. In either case the marginal man would disappear, since his personality arises out of the confusion that exists in the minds of persons in a society which countenances the principles of fixed status *and* of free competition.

This, then, is a statement of "the Negro problem" as it has existed through time and in Midwest Metropolis during the Depression and the Second World War. But although this statement may describe the Negro problem as it has existed, it does not show the total impact of the crisis in race relations which faced Black Metropolis, the United States, and the world during the Second World War.

THE DYNAMICS OF RACE RELATIONS

The war changed the entire course of race relations and brought America face to face with the contradictions in our culture in a manner and to an extent which made it impossible for either Negroes or whites to evade them longer. *Life* Magazine summed up the problem in a sentence: "The dilemma, of course, is this: the basic tenets of the American creed make all men free and equal in rights. Yet in fact we deny equal rights to our largest minority, and observe a caste system which we not only criticize in other nations but refuse to defend in ourselves. This makes us living liars—a psychotic case among the nations." [1]

The war operated to change the Negro problem, almost overnight, from a chronic social difficulty which the hopeful thought time and education would solve to a crisis in our national life. As a result of the conflict of ideologies the Negro problem became a world problem; and the problem of all the common peoples of the earth—especially the nonwhite peoples—came to include the problem of the American Negro.

The United States was fighting a yellow nation that challenged white imperialism and ridiculed the "democracies" for clinging to the notion of white superiority. We had another yellow nation as an ally, and were also allied with a white power desperately trying to hold in check the brown people of Africa and Asia. Japanese references to our treatment of the American Negro embarrassed our attempts at psychological warfare. Every time a Negro was lynched here, the Japanese broadcast the event to China, India, and South America. The stupid racial policy of the Anglo-Saxon nations was an important factor in their early setbacks in the Pacific. The United Nations had the task of setting up a new balance of power based on a moral order which, to be workable, must include yellow, brown, and black people. How could America share in this when it did not include its own black citizens in the moral order prevailing within its boundaries?

But there were also internal complications accompanying the war, which broke down to an astonishing extent the conventional patterns of race relations. It was impossible to maintain the old and established racial etiquette when the entire world order was in flux. New situations for which a new racial etiquette had not been devised arose in the factories, on the farms, and in the overcrowded boom cities. There were attempts to maintain the old pattern or to improvise a new pattern; but the expansion of industry was so rapid, the need for productivity so great, that the society did not have sufficient time and energy to devote to developing and maintaining a rigid color-line. War always shuffles and reshuffles people, distributing and redistributing them throughout the country to such an extent that sectional prejudices and local customs often lose much of their meaning. Technological changes were so swift and the assembly-line method of production was so involved that it was difficult for new patterns to develop before the situation had again changed, owing to further mechanical innovations.

The simple fact was that to develop its maximum striking power in the factories, the fields, and the armed forces, the nation could not entirely ignore one-tenth of its people. The sheer need for manpower opened more and more opportunities to Negroes. But though many advances were made, as late as 1942 there were millions of Negroes still idle or working in nonessential industries because northern farmers refused to employ them, many defense plants limited their participation by a quota system, and the armed forces relegated them to limited services.

POLITICAL EXPEDIENCY AND ECONOMIC NECESSITY

Political expediency and the pressure of economic necessity brought about many changes. Reinforcing the changes in the mores were the ideologies that gave moral justification to the war itself. Probably at no other time in the history of the country had there been so much concern for the institution of democracy—perhaps because it was in such danger both at home and abroad. Certainly not since the period of the abolitionists had so many important and articulate people concerned themselves with the problem of the American Negro. Even such groups as the army, noted for anti-Negro bias, were active in breaking several strikes against employment of skilled Negroes. The most effective arguments were that Negroes had a right to work in any position and that it was unpatriotic to refuse to work with a Negro when the country was in such a desperate need for war material. The principle occasionally articulated by army officials, that Negroes have a right to work any place in a plant, was indeed new, and illustrates how fundamental and rapid was the change in the Negro's role in the United States. But this rapid change in the Negro's status caused great confusion, racial tension, and in some places violence.

THE NEW NEGRO MENTALITY

Accompanying and indeed constituting the subjective aspect of the change in the social structure was the attitude of the Negro himself. He found the problems of the Chinese, the Indians, and the Burmese strangely analogous to his own. In this sense the Negro became more international-minded than the rest of the population. His sympathy with other colored peoples had been aroused long before the general population had begun to question America's policy of isolationism, especially during the Italo-Ethiopian war. He even had a certain amount of admiration for the Japanese because they had successfully fought white nations. Many Negroes, however, placed their hope for the representation of the dark people among the Great Powers with the Chinese and the Soviet Union. Realizing more acutely than whites the global significance of a guaranty of democratic rights and privileges to all people of the world, the Negro broke out of his caste-bound mentality, transcended his purely racial point of view—which led him only to despair—and began to see his position in world society as identified with that of all the "disinherited." Negro leaders were forced to sharpen their thinking and define for The Race the role that Negroes wished to play in American civilization. The conflict between the pressure that was forcing the Negro into a caste position and the slogans for democracy that raised his expectation of complete citizenship developed in the leaders a new critical consideration of the Negro's position in the society and a new attitude toward the theory and practice of democracy. At first this new capacity for critical analysis seemed to be expressed only in a series of complaints. Brought up sharply against the paradoxes of democracy, the Negro in this initial stage of the development of a line of action could do little more than articulate his discontent. But in the crucible of frustration and despair a new and positive line of thought was forged, which, if it could be implemented, would hold hope for black people and for the institution of democracy. This philosophy of a struggle for complete equality was not at variance with the expressed aims of the United Nations.

The change in the Negro's mentality came about so rapidly that few people, even Negroes, realized its extent. It often took the form of continued and intensified demands for better housing, better schools, and health programs. More fundamentally, it was expressed in the Negro's refusal to accept segregation without complaint even in the armed forces (numbers of Negroes went to prison rather than fight in a Jim-Crow army), in impetuous individual defiance of cultural patterns of racial subordination, and in the hysterical oratory of excited speakers for Negro rights. But underneath all this was the Negro's determination to become a full citizen, to plan and think for himself regardless of past friends and old leaders. He began to make demands, not for concessions, not for small gains, but for *equality*.

In trying to assess the situation, white people did not realize that in measuring "gains" for the Negro they were using an obsolete yardstick. At a time when entire peoples were being liquidated or given equality over night, the theory of "gradual gains" for Negroes had little meaning. With a world revolution in progress, Negroes refused to be held apart from the stream of thought and to be told to have faith in the long-time processes of education and goodwill. To ask the American Negro to go slowly was to attempt either to slacken the international pace of social change or to isolate the Negro from the world forces in which he was engulfed.

In refusing to accept a philosophy of contentment with gradual gains, the Negro was in many respects making a more rational analysis of contemporary events than were those who attempted to give him counsel. The war was one against oppression—whether the tyrannical forces of Hitler and Hirohito, the colonial imperialism of the British Empire, or the racial imperialism of the United States. To win a military victory over the Axis and then to continue the exploitation of subject peoples under the Western European colonial system and the subordination of Negroes in the United States was to set the stage for the next world war—possibly a war of color. Negroes knew, though many of them could not articulate or formulate the problem, that two worlds were at war—the world of Fascism and the world of democracy—and that any hope for "the brotherhood of man" could arise only out of the struggle of all people united for a common end— liberty, equality, and fraternity. To insure a victory for the common man—including the American Negro—who had too often been mobilized to fight for a noble objective only to find himself cheated by selfish interests when a military victory was won, the essential elements of "brotherhood" must be achieved during the struggle itself, for "brotherhood" was both the means and the end of the struggle. To Negroes this was more rational than the theory of "gradual gains." Although he could not enforce his demands, the Negro refused to accept gradualism as a philosophy.

THE MORAL PROBLEM

The problem which faced America was essentially a moral problem. It cut deeply into the cultural contradictions of the society. America was not prepared to meet it, having neither the moral stamina nor the psychological background to deal with it. While there were a few white people who demanded that Negroes be granted complete equality at once, the response of many white "liberals" was to tell Negroes to be patient, to adopt an optimism unwarranted by reality; for the intellectual maturity and the moral integrity which would make possible the unification of collective aims for a solution of the problem did not exist. Other white people reacted either with fear or hate. In the South, and often in other parts of the country too, they feared that their prerogatives as white people were being challenged. They were infuriated by the Negro press and were in terror of the emotions which they sensed behind the masklike countenances of their once humble black servants. There was no background of understanding or even sympathy with which they could interpret the upsurge of feeling on the part of Negroes, nor did their stereotyped notion of the Negro and his "place" allow them to envisage with tolerance or understanding his new demands. They could explain his behavior only as the result of a plot of Communist agitators, Fascist agents, and the "subversive" Negro press.

America was not mentally equipped to deal with this demand for democracy, equality, and fair play raised by its largest minority even though it was constantly repeating that the nation was founded on these very principles. As Gunnar Myrdal has stated: "Trying to defend their behavior to others, and primarily to themselves, people will attempt to conceal the conflict between their different valuations of what is desirable and undesirable, right or wrong, by keeping some valuations from awareness and by focusing attention on others. For the same opportune purpose, people will twist and mutilate their beliefs of how social reality actually is." [2] When Negro maids quit their jobs in domestic service to take positions in war industries to produce for the arsenal of democracy, many white housewives discovered a "plot" and an "organization" whose purpose was simply to annoy them. Like wildfire rumors spread—and many people firmly believed them—that elaborately financed "bumping" and "pushing" campaigns had been organized, although for seventy-five years their leaders had been unable to organize Negroes on any such scale for any purpose.

Unable to deal with or even face the moral issue involved, America stood frozen and paralyzed before its Negro problem. The divergent and contradictory streams of thought in its culture, and its inability even to envisage a different pattern of race relations, prevented it from conceiving a rational approach to a solution. Faced with the problem in its most acute state, it was unable to plan action to meet the impending crisis. Nothing illustrates better the confusion and impotence that existed in race relations than the Detroit riot. The government knew, as did all the reading public, that it was just a question of time before racial violence would break out in Detroit. All the evidence was before the people, but the government, the labor unions, the churches, and the solid citizens were powerless to do anything about it. So a society convulsed by fear found itself not only unable to act rationally but unable to act at all. Again America resorted to artificial techniques—to magic—in trying to meet the problem. Rather than face the moral issue, society placed its reliance in "planning"—in frantically organized committees to prevent race riots, in anything that would allow it to escape the reality of its confusion and impotence.

OF THINGS TO COME

Let us return to Bronzeville. It is conceivable that the Negro question—given the moral flabbiness of America—is incapable of solution. Perhaps not all social problems are soluble. Indeed it is only in America that one finds the imperative to assume that all social problems *can* be solved without conflict. To feel that a social problem cannot be solved peacefully is considered almost immoral. Americans are required to appear cheerful and optimistic about a solution, regardless of evidence to the contrary. This is particularly difficult for Negroes, who at the same time must endure all the disadvantages of the Job Ceiling and the Black Ghetto, as well as other forms of subordination.

So far, most Chicagoans view Negro-white relations negatively—solely in terms of preventing a riot. *While all responsible Negroes try to prevent violent conflict, their primary interest is in the complete abolition of political and economic subordination and enforced segregation.*

Chicago's last riot came after the First World War. There is still danger that in the critical years following the Second World War it might happen again. Any attempts to effect a moving equilibrium which will prevent racial outbursts must involve the following processes: (1) the continuous interpretation of the Negro's aspirations and demands to all sections of the white community; (2) the actual progressive relaxation of discrimination and segregation, beginning immediately; (3) the inclusion of Negroes in all postwar plans on an equitable basis; (4) the strengthening of social controls—familial, associational, and governmental—within the Black Belt; (5) the constructive channelizing of the Negro's mass resentment into successful action-patterns of nonviolent protest. Whether at this time Chicago, America, or the world can take such progressive steps in relation to their subject people, even to avert violence, is questionable.

But the problem of Bronzeville and of the American Negro is not an isolated problem. The fate of Black Metropolis is dependent on the fate of Midwest Metropolis, of the country, and of the world. Forces which are in no sense local will in the final analysis determine the movement of this drama of human relations toward hope or tragedy. "The Negro problem is an integral part of, or a special phase of, the whole complex of problems in the larger American civilization," states Myrdal; "it cannot be treated in isolation." [3] The fate of the people of Black Metropolis—whether they will remain the marginal workers to be called in only at times of great economic activity, or will become an integral part of the American economy and thus lay the basis for complete social and political integration—depends not so much on what happens locally as on what happens in America and the world. Given widespread postwar unemployment, for instance, the Negro may again become a chronic relief client, despised by the majority of white citizens who have to support him from taxes and the symbol around which the aggressions of a frustrated society can be organized, so that he may fill the role of whipping boy for an emerging American Fascism. This, too, depends not so much upon Chicago as upon the possibility of America's achieving full employment in the postwar world and on the development of a world program for emancipating the Common Man.

So it is really only "One World." The problems that arise on Bronzeville's Forty-seventh Street encircle the globe. But the people of Black Metropolis and of Midwest Metropolis do not feel that this relieves them from maintaining their own constant struggle for a complete democracy as the only way to attain the world we say we want to build. The people of Black Metropolis and of Midwest Metropolis and of all their counterparts are intertwined and interdependent. What happens to one affects all. A blow struck for freedom in Bronzeville finds its echo in Chungking and Moscow, in Paris and Senegal. A victory for Fascism in Midwest Metropolis will sound the knell of doom for the Common Man everywhere.

A Methodological Note

by W. LLOYD WARNER

THE CONFLICT IN AMERICAN IDEOLOGIES

WE PEOPLE OF THE UNITED STATES ARE A MIXED BREED. WE HAVE COME from all parts of the world; all races of men compose our biological aggregate. We have created an official ideology to fit this condition which declares that men of all races and all cultures are equally precious in the eyes of God and are, therefore, equal,—and here we pause for a long afterthought—"At least, they should be equal, in the thoughts and actions of men." In the second thought we see the ever-present basic conflict that permeates our way of life: a deep faith in the principles of equality which we proudly proclaim, and a fundamental, unofficial, unacknowledged, and almost guilty belief that certain Americans are the "real" ones and superior, while all others are second-class citizens and inferior. Our communities' social systems reflect this conflict when attempting to organize the lives of men who hold these opposing beliefs. Commonsense observation of these communities, buttressed by the more exact findings of social science, demonstrates that despite our equalitarian credo two types of separate and subordinate groups have emerged in the United States. All dark-skinned races with Mongoloid or Negroid ancestry are placed by our social system in subordinate groups, and all deviant cultural groups, speaking different languages, professing different faiths, and exhibiting exotic manners and customs are set apart and classed as inferior.

These groups develop subsystems of their own. For the cultural, or ethnic, groups such systems for a time maintain the way of life of the Motherland while preparing the people for, and fitting them into, American society where they can compete with everyone for the prizes our culture has to offer. Not so for the dark-skinned people. Until now we have not permitted the Negro or Asiatic to live as other men live. He cannot shed his symbols of "inferiority" and pass over to the larger life all others enjoy, for his symbols are racial: they are kinky hair, dark skin, or epicanthic fold which our society recognizes as badges of "inferiority." Such groups, and the Negro in particular, have built social systems of their own which order their community life and relate them to the dominant white group.

This significant study by Mr. Drake and Mr. Cayton of Black Metropolis presents us with a clear analysis of the social system existing among northern urban Negroes. It is the first study of a northern Negro community which combines the research approaches of sociology and social anthropology. As such it is a real contribution to science and further proof that the two disciplines are essentially one. The authors' results, being of scientific importance, will be of inevitable significance in the practical world of affairs. Our plans for the immediate future must take account of their knowledge of the urban adjustments of whites and Negroes.

Since I helped organize and plan the research and served as co-director for the study, the authors have invited me to tell what we had in mind when we planned the research and carried it to completion. To do this adequately, it will be necessary to present a brief theoretical background and short history of the recent development of this type of community research to explain the kind of interest which took us into the research on Black Metropolis.

COMMUNITY RESEARCH AND THE COMPARATIVE METHOD

Early in 1930, a few months after my return to the United States, to a position in the Department of Anthropology at Harvard University, from a field study among the Murngin tribes in Australia,[1] I began a series of studies of contemporary communities for the purpose of acquiring an understanding of modern life comparable in meaning and method to the knowledge of the social anthropologists about many non-European civilizations and cultures. The social anthropologist characteristically studies literate and non-literate communities as wholes and as systems whose various parts are interconnected in time and space. He investigates all aspects of the life of a people to learn how the parts fit together and to understand how each of the interconnected parts functions in maintaining a social system as an ongoing way of life. For example, field investigators of the African Bantu have reported how the family life, the social roles of men and women, the political order, and status system mutually influence each other and form a web of

---

[1] W. Lloyd Warner, *A Black Civilization*, Harper, 1937.

interdependent relations which largely controls the sacred and secular ideologies of the group and is the basic matrix of the Bantu individual's personality structure. Similar studies have been done for hundreds of non-European peoples.

Since the social anthropologist's science is by nature comparative, his purposes are not satisfied with learning about separate social groups as ultimate units of investigation. His goal is to fit the tribes, communities, their institutions, and their ideological systems into a comparative framework which includes the social systems of all men and permits basic generalizations about the social life of man which cannot be derived from the data of one culture or the study of one nation or tribe. The use of the comparative method in social science for the study of contemporary communities is similar to that used in the biological sciences where man is viewed as but one of many contemporary living species. Man is compared with and contrasted to other species in order better to understand the nature of living things. Once this conception of the human species was advanced some of the most significant knowledge about ourselves was discovered.

Comparative social science is beginning to make similar gains. Nieboer in his comparative study, *Slavery as an Industrial System*,[2] developed a series of hypotheses on the nature of slavery which could not have been achieved had he studied only European and American slavery. Hobhouse, Wheeler and Ginsberg [3] examined the relation of social stratification to certain economic forms. A. L. Kroeber [4] has made similar studies of kinship, Westermarck,[5] of the family, and Margaret Mead,[6] of sexual roles.

For adequate knowledge about ourselves to be acquired and validated it is necessary to make detailed field studies of American group life which embody in their methodology these two basic ideas of (1) examining communities as wholes where the several interconnected social institutions are seen functioning in the total social economy and

[2] H. J. Nieboer, *Slavery as an Industrial System,* Second edition, The Hague: M. Nijhoff, 1910.

[3] L. T. Hobhouse, G. C. Wheeler, and M. Ginsberg, *The Material Culture and Social Institutions of the Simpler Peoples,* London: Chapman and Hall, 1915.

[4] A. L. Kroeber, "Classificatory Systems of Relationship," *J. Royal Anth. Inst.,* 39:77-84, 1909.

[5] E. A. Westermarck, *The History of Human Marriage,* Allerton, 1922.

[6] Margaret Mead, *Sex and Temperament in Three Primitive Societies,* Morrow, 1935.

(2) subjecting the results of the field studies to the hypotheses developed from the study of other social systems in order to determine what our social world is like when viewed from the detached and broader generalizations of the comparative sociologist.[7] It was with these thoughts in mind that I began studying contemporary communities.

SOCIAL CLASS AND COLOR-CASTE

When a community is studied, not as an atomic sand pile of separate individuals, but as a set of interconnected human beings living in a vast web of vital relations, it is necessary to learn what the relations are which bind people together and maintain their interactions in cohesive union. This necessitates living with the people being studied, interviewing them, and observing what they do. The first community we studied was in New England; we call it *Yankee City*.[8] After a short time in the field it became evident that one of the most significant and important set of relations which we were studying was a form of social stratification which placed the population at varying levels of prestige and power according to the evaluation of the members of the community. This evaluated order superordinated some individuals and subordinated others. We called the several levels social classes. By this term we meant "two or more orders of people who are believed to be, and are accordingly ranked by the members of the community, in socially superior and inferior positions. Members of a class tend to marry within their own order, but the values of the society permit marriage up and down. A class system also provides that children are born into the same status as their parents. A class society distributes rights and privileges, duties and obligations, unequally among its inferior and superior grades. A system of classes, unlike a system of castes, provides by its own values for movement up and down the social ladder. In common parlance, this is social climbing, or in technical terms, social mobility."[9]

The emphasis for class placement is not on socio-economic catego-

[7] It does not follow that because the scientist is detached in his research he is necessarily detached *as a citizen* when he considers the social implications, the application, or the significance, of the social facts he examines.

[8] W. Lloyd Warner and Paul S. Lunt, Yankee City, Volume II, *The Status System of a Modern Community*, Yale University Press, 1942.

[9] W. Lloyd Warner and Paul S. Lunt, Yankee City, Volume I, *The Social Life of a Modern Community*, Yale University Press, 1941, p. 82.

ries, although they are powerful factors in determining status, but on the evaluated participation of individuals and families. To understand how these social classes were derived it might be well to add, "a 'social class' is to be thought of as the largest group of people whose members have intimate access to one another. A class is composed of families and social cliques. The interrelationships between these families and cliques, in such informal activities as visiting, dances, receptions, teas, and larger informal affairs, constitute the structure of a social class. A person is a member of that social class with which most of his participation, of this intimate kind, occurs." [10]

There were a large number of ethnic groups in *Yankee City* Series. Each of them had had members who had climbed up the class ladder and out of the group entirely. The cultural stigmata of the ethnic origin rapidly disappeared and left the members of the group free to try to move to higher levels.[11]

When the research on community and status was extended to the Deep South it became apparent that another form of social stratification existed alongside the social-class order. Everyone knows about "race prejudice" and how white "prejudice" prevents the Negro race from competing on a basis of equality with the white race. The research staff of *Deep South* believed the terms "prejudice" and "race," as used in America, to be very often misleading since they inadequately refer to the social realities of American life.

The reason for this belief needs explanation. The interconnected relations composing the social system which holds people together consist of evaluated acts and beliefs which are learned by all the members of each new generation. As participants in the society in which they grow up they internalize the prevailing way of life of the community and make it part of themselves to the extent that, by the time they have reached adolescence, much of the basic beliefs and values of the total group become a part of the emotional structure of each individual. Social systems notoriously are not composed entirely of rational beliefs. Much of any system is non-rational and, it might be argued, must be. For example, it is difficult to subject the love of husbands and wives, of parents and children, to the rules of cold reason. The individual's

[10] Allison Davis, Burleigh B. Gardner, and Mary R. Gardner, *Deep South*, The University of Chicago Press, 1941, p. 59.

[11] W. Lloyd Warner and Leo Srole, *Yankee City*, Volume III, *The Social Systems of American Ethnic Groups*, Yale University Press, 1945.

personality is a product of his organic experiences in his social system; his mind, character, and emotional structure are organized residues of what he has learned from living in his social world. His evaluated beliefs, personal values, and social outlook are maintained and continuously reinforced by the constant contemporary pressure from the social system which originally formed him as a person. "Race prejudice" is much more than "prejudice." In the individual it is an organized system that has been deposited into his personality structure by the society; in the group, it is a status system which maintains such beliefs and values in the culture.[12]

These considerations about status and learning led us to the next question: "What is the type of social system in *Deep South* which organizes the lives of Negroes into a subordinate level and of whites into a superordinate level?" Simple tests of the class hypothesis easily convinced us it did not fit the facts. Negroes and whites cannot intermarry; members of two classes can. Negroes cannot rise out of the lower to the higher white levels; members of a lower white class are able to do this. Unlike the ethnic individual, the Negro individual's symbols of inferiority cannot be removed; they stay with him until death.

As the research progressed we saw it was not by chance that rules of endogamy held for each of the two levels, that rules of descent existed for the offspring of intergroup mating which made them *all* members of the "punished" lower group and that rules expressing social distance kept whites and Negroes in separate political, social, and economic groups. It was obvious that all these social phenomena formed an interdependent whole where each part functioned to maintain the entire status system. When we used the comparative method to identify this rank order, applying the same scientific rules observed by the biologist in identifying a species, we found it possessed all the critical characteristics of what social anthropologists call a caste system. It was so designated because ". . . caste may be defined as a rank order of superior-superordinate orders with inferior-subordinate orders which practice endogamy, prevent vertical mobility, and unequally distribute

[12] I should like to say these considerations should not discourage reform efforts. It is the function and duty of white liberals and Negro militant groups, interested in destroying this system, to seize upon every opportunity in this changing society to direct change in a direction where individuals have experiences which teach them the virtues of equality and make it painful for them to accept our present status order.

the desirable and undesirable social symbols. Class may be defined as a rank order of superior and inferior orders which allows both exogamy and endogamy, permits movement either up or down the system, or allows an individual to remain in the status to which he was born; it also unequally distributes the lower and higher evaluated symbols." [13] It should be added: "The rule of once a caste member always a caste member holds throughout the lifetime of an individual and throughout the lives of his descendants. In a caste system there are no positive sanctions for changing a person's caste status and there are a large number of negative sanctions or punishments which function to prevent intercaste movements. When functioning fully, caste tends to maintain a stable equilibrium in the outward lives of the generations which occupy the system at any given time and permits little disturbance when members of the generations enter and leave the system by birth and death." [14]

By the use of the term caste I do not imply that caste is a permanent part of our society. Since our society is a changing one, it is clear that this system must change too. My intent is to identify it accurately and, to improve our theoretical insight—to place it in its proper scientific classification. By implication we see more clearly why men capable of reason and endowed with the traditions which produced such manifestations of equality and freedom as the Declaration of Independence and the Bill of Rights continue to maintain a social world where reason and justice are often conspicuously absent.

In each of the two castes, a system of classes was found which permitted social mobility within the caste. The Negro class order, being new and subject to white restrictions, was less well developed than the white.

Once the *Deep South* research had developed the class-caste hypothesis the question arose whether this caste system was present elsewhere in the United States, particularly in the northern cities where there are large concentrations of Negro populations. If present, how was it modified under urban and northern conditions? Furthermore, what happens to the Negro community and to the social classes of the Negro under these circumstances? These questions were germinating when I met Mr. Cayton in the mid-Thirties on his return to Chicago

[13] Edgar T. Thompson, ed., *Race Relations and the Race Problem,* Durham: Duke University Press, 1939, p. 229.
[14] *Ibid.,* p. 228.

from Fisk University where he had been teaching in the Department of Social Sciences. Mr. Cayton shared a similar interest in the problem of American status systems as they affected the Negro. He had already given considerable thought to this problem, and·in the process of writing his *Black Workers and the New Unions*,[15] he had devoted a chapter to the internal structure of the Negro community and a discussion of class. Mr. Cayton was particularly interested in the effect of subordination and exclusion upon the personality of Negroes and upon the development of Negro institutional life.

Out of numerous discussions between Mr. Cayton and myself the outlines of a large-scale research project on the Negro in Chicago emerged. The leading problem of this research shaped itself into the following question: *"To what degree is the Negro subordinated and excluded in relation to white people in the society, what are the mechanisms by which the system is maintained, and how do the lives of Negroes reflect this subordination and exclusion?"*[16] In order to answer this question it was necessary to examine every aspect of institutional life and to study life histories of numerous individuals.

PURPOSES AND METHOD OF THE STUDY

The criteria we fashioned for the kind of Negro community which would answer our questions were largely satisfied by *Black Metropolis*. These criteria were designed to insure that we would have a community which contrasted sharply with *Deep South* and would thereby tell us something about the diversity of Negro-white relations in the United States. Let us review a few of them.

In contrast to *Deep South* we wanted a metropolitan area with great social complexity and a very large Negro population which was founded on an industrial, rather than an agricultural, base. We wanted the community in a region where a tradition of slavery had not had direct opportunity to mold the Negro-white relations which followed Emancipation. We sought a place where a great variety of basic industries permitted absorption of Negro labor into the elaborate industrial hierarchies in contrast to the plantation system with its simple system of control. We hoped to find a community where rapid social change

[15] Horace R. Cayton and George S. Mitchell, University of North Carolina Press, 1939.
[16] From a research memorandum prepared by the authors.

prevailed, since change in *Deep South* was comparatively slow. We wanted a community with a number of ethnic groups to compare them with the Negro community and to contrast them with Deep South, which had very few ethnics. Chicago fitted each of these criteria; moreover, it had the great advantage of having been studied by the Chicago school of sociologists. A large body of valuable published research was present, including *The Negro in Chicago,*[17] prepared by social scientists after the Race Riot at the conclusion of World War I. Furthermore, WPA funds were available which made possible the employment of the large field and clerical staff necessary for the study of the quarter of million Negroes in Chicago.[18]

The field work continued for three years under Mr. Cayton's direction and with my advice. He was trained by Professor Robert E. Park at the University of Chicago and was well equipped with the techniques of the ecologists and with the sociological methods used by Professors Park and Burgess in the study of community life. These techniques were added to those used in the study of *Yankee City* and *Deep South.*

When Mr. Drake joined the research he had just completed two years' work in the study of *Deep South,* six months of which included field work. He had been trained in research techniques by Professor Allison Davis at Dillard University and was continuing his studies in anthropology at the University of Chicago. Mr. Drake supervised the work on the churches and associations for *Black Metropolis*[19] and was a participant observer at various levels of community life. He and Mr. Cayton planned and wrote the final manuscript.

Since it was practically impossible to study both the Negro and the white community as had been done in *Deep South,* the research was concentrated in the Negro community itself. "The basic task has been to describe the actual position of the Negro in the various hierarchies and to explore the mechanisms by which he is kept 'in his place' and by which he changes his social position. White attitudes toward the Negro may be inferred from the Negro's position in the society. By describing minutely the position of the Negro in the spatial, eco-

---

[17] Chicago Commission on Race Relations, *The Negro in Chicago,* A Study of Race Relations and a Race Riot, The University of Chicago Press, 1922.

[18] In 1941 the Rosenwald Fund gave a grant to aid in the preparation of the manuscript.

[19] See Drake, St. Clair, *Churches and Voluntary Associations in the Chicago Negro Community* (mimeographed), W.P.A., 1941.

nomic, political, 'social,' and other structures of Chicago (and knowing the Negro's reaction to his position) we are able to infer the attitudes of various segments of the white population without making an extensive study of white people's *verbalizations*." [20]

SOCIAL CLASS, COLOR-CASTE, AND SOCIAL CHANGE

The results of the research, reported in this book, further demonstrate the paradox of an American ideology which entwines the democratic faith of "equality and freedom for everyone" with the caste beliefs and practices which exclude dark Americans from their rights as fellow citizens. Reasonable men, unconsciously, hold and practice these opposing beliefs at the same time. This has been as true in Chicago as in *Deep South*: "From the earliest history of Chicago up to the present time there has been a great deal of uncertainty among white people as to what the 'place' of the Negro 'should be.' On the one hand there has been a tendency to 'fix his status'; on the other hand there has been the tendency to allow him to 'compete freely.'" [21] The authors conclude that the structural organization of the Negro-white ranking can be summarized somewhat as follows: that the Negro in Black Metropolis more often than not is subordinated to menial tasks but, nevertheless, has some chance for job advancement; that the Negro has made real political gains both in voting and political power; that in his social relations with whites there is "a high degree of exclusion"; and that while intermarriage is legally sanctioned it is generally discouraged.

For purposes of brevity and to sharpen the focus of our analysis let us examine the accompanying chart which summarizes the basic social similarities and differences existing between Deep South and Black Metropolis. The details of the social relations in each major area should be carefully examined.

Real gains are found in the governmental and economic areas (see chart), important advances have been made in the field of education, very moderate gains have been achieved in spatial and family relations, but little has been accomplished in the area of "social" equality. Each of these major areas has been separated into subdivisions to permit the analytical reader to assess my interpretation.

[20] From a research manuscript prepared by the authors.
[21] *Ibid*.

	Deep South	*Black Metropolis*
I. THE FAMILY *Sex relations outside marriage:*		
Negro men and white women	Highly disapproved of; violent sanctions applied; very infrequent.	Disapproved; frequently ostracized except in liberal circles; more frequent than in *Deep South*.
White men and Negro women	Disapproved; less frequent than formerly.	Disapproved but no rigorous sanctions; participants ostracized except in very liberal circles if relations are open.
Marriage	Legally impossible; a very few common-law unions of white men and Negro women.	Legally possible; but socially disapproved; informal sanctions applied.
Descent of children of mixed matings	Children are always defined as Negroes.	Children are always defined as Negroes.
II. SOCIAL RELATIONS *Associations:* Professional	Negroes always excluded.	Negro membership very limited except in liberal groups.
Lodges and secret societies	Negroes always excluded.	Negroes very rarely (if ever) included.
Social	Always excluded.	Exclusion except in liberal groups.
Reform	Very rarely included.	Almost always included.
Cliques: Social	Negroes always excluded.	Negroes excluded except in a few liberal groups.
Occupational	Negroes completely excluded.	Negroes sometimes included but not usually.
III. GOVERNMENTAL *Voting*	Not generally permitted.	Permitted and encouraged.
Office holding: Appointive	Not general; a few traditional posts.	Appointed to high and low levels but less frequently than proportion in population.

	Deep South	Black Metropolis
III. GOVERNMENTAL (*continued*)		
Elective	Impossible in the system.	Elected to high and low but not the very top places, and are usually from Negro election districts.
Political power within the city party system	Excluded from the "one party system."	Powerful, sometimes beyond their voting strength.
State	No power.	Sometimes greater than voting strength through organized pressure groups.
National	Very little power, but some in Republican Party.	Very effective through organized pressure groups as well as strength of vote.
IV. EDUCATIONAL		
School segregation	Legal; children always separate.	Segregation not legal but usually results from residential segregation. Some mixing.
Pay of teachers	Much less than whites.	Same as whites.
Length of time Negro children stay in school	Very short; many Negroes almost illiterate.	Period in school compares with whites of same socio-economic level.
V. SPATIAL RELATIONS		
Segregation of dwelling areas	Less than in Black Metropolis.	Very great (the "Black Belt").
Public recreational areas	No mixing.	Some mixing, but residential segregation results in segregated facilities.
VI. SOCIAL MOBILITY		
From Negro to white group	Not permitted.	Not permitted.
Within Negro caste	Difficult; few places at higher levels.	Mobility easier with more movement and more places at the top; greater range.
VII. ECONOMIC		
Occupation in skilled jobs	Decreasing for Negroes (1930's); largely laborers today.	Slowly increasing for Negroes (1940). More Negroes in such jobs but disproportionate percentage of unskilled jobs.

	Deep South	Black Metropolis
VII. ECONOMIC (continued) Chances for advancement when competing with whites Ownership of large production enterprises Retail ownership, merchants, etc.	Very difficult. A few large plantation owners. Small, but not important.	"First fired and last hired"; few cases of successful competition. No owners of large industrial enterprises. A few Negro medium-sized enterprises. Negro business shows some development but is at a competitive disadvantage.
VIII. FREEDOM OF MOVEMENT Public conveyances Theaters Eating places	Complete segregation; "Jim-Crowism." Complete segregation. Complete segregation; separate eating places.	No segregation. No formal segregation; but occasional informal efforts in a few theaters to do so. Moderate degree of segregation.
IX. INTENSITY OF WHITE CASTE ATTITUDES TOWARD NEGROES	Very great consciousness of Negroes as a "problem."	Less clearly defined.

This evidence strongly supports the hypothesis that, while there is a noticeable difference between *Deep South* and *Black Metropolis,* a great improvement in the status of the Negro, and an increasing assurance that he will continue to advance, nevertheless, the *type* of status relations controlling Negroes and whites remains the same and continues to keep the Negro in an inferior and restricted position. He cannot climb into the higher group although he can climb higher in his own group. Legally, he is permitted to marry across the color line but there is very little intermarriage. The children of such marriages are always Negro and suffer, as do their parents, the "restrictions" and deprivations of the Negro caste. The rewards and punishments, the rights and duties, knowledges and advantages are unequally distributed. In short, there is still a status system of the caste type. It is of small consequence what we call it if we remember that it is a status system which organizes and controls the lives of our people and "educates" the oncoming generations to learn its ways and conform to its precepts.

Despite the many encouraging signs of betterment already indicated in this excellent study, the most important is yet to be mentioned. At the present time there are indications throughout the United States and throughout the world that important changes are on their way and that the present system may reform into something quite different which will give Negroes many—if not all—the opportunities now denied them. It must be emphasized that such miracles do not come by themselves, they must be worked for. A system as deeply implanted in the lives of all of us as this one needs more than the trumpets of equality to be sounded for its walls to tumble down. It is my belief that the next generation's principal task will be the hard and painful one of destroying color-caste in the United States.

Notes and Documentation

INTRODUCTION

1. The Chicago *Tribune*, Oct. 29, 1893, as quoted in Claudius O. Johnson, *Carter Henry Harrison I*, University of Chicago, 1928, p. 44.
2. The percentages for 1890-1930 and for 1940 are based upon the U. S. Census. The figures for 1934 were calculated from Charles S. Newcomb and Richard C. Lang, *Census Data of the City of Chicago: 1934*, University of Chicago. The 1944 percentages are estimates made by the Mayor's Committee on Race Relations, 1944.
3. Adapted from Ernest W. Burgess and Charles S. Newcomb, *Census Data of the City of Chicago, 1930*, University of Chicago, 1933, p. xv.
4. Claudius O. Johnson, *op. cit.*, p. 31.
5. Eugene Staley, *History of the Illinois State Federation of Labor*, University of Chicago, 1930, p. 40.

PART I

CHAPTER I

1. From the diary of Colonel Arent Schuyler de Peyster, British commander at Michilimackinac, July 4, 1779, as quoted in A. T. Andreas, *History of Chicago from the Earliest Period to the Present Time*, Chicago, 1884, Vol. I, pp. 70-71.
2. Milo Milton Quaife, *Checagou*, University of Chicago, 1933, p. 46.
3. For a full account of the Underground Railroad, see Henrietta Buckmaster, *Let My People Go*, Harper, 1941.
4. As quoted in L. D. Reddick, "The Negro in Chicago, 1790-1860," unpublished manuscript, Schomburg Collection, New York, p. 73.
5. Shawneetown *Gazette*, as quoted in Reddick, *op. cit.*, p. 68.
6. *Weekly Chicago Democrat*, Nov. 3, 1846, as quoted in Bessie Pierce, *A History of Chicago*, Knopf, 1937, Vol. I, p. 253.
7. *Watchman of the Prairies*, n.d., quoted in Pierce, *op. cit.*, Vol. II, pp. 382-83.
8. Chicago *Daily Journal*, Oct. 3, 1850.
9. J. S. Currey, *Chicago: Its History and Its Builders*, Clarke, 1912, Vol. I, pp. 415-16. See also C. W. Mann, *The Chicago Common Council and the Fugitive Slave Law of 1850*, Chicago Historical Society, pp. 73 ff.
10. Pierce, *op. cit.*, Vol. II, pp. 195-97.
11. *Western Citizen*, as quoted in Reddick, *op. cit.*, p. 73. The reference was not to the earlier Fugitive Slave Law of 1793 but to the fugitive-slave act embodied in the Compromise of 1850.
12. Chicago *Daily Journal*, Aug. 5, 1853.
13. *Democratic Press*, March 29, 1855, as quoted in Reddick, *op. cit.*, p. 106.
14. Cairo (Ill.) *Weekly Times*, Sept. 9, 1857. For another famous case, see Pierce, *op. cit.*, Vol. II, p. 198. See also Chicago *Democrat*, Feb. 7, 1848; and Chicago *Daily Journal*, Feb. 5, 1848, Oct. 3, 1850, June 26, 1857, Nov. 12, 1861, and April 4, 1861.

15. Chicago *Journal*, April 5, 1861.
16. *Ibid.*, April 8, 1861.
17. Pierce, *op. cit.*, Vol. II, pp. 228-35.
18. Lloyd Lewis and H. J. Smith, *Chicago: The History of Its Reputation*, Harcourt, Brace, 1929, p. 89. See also Pierce, *op. cit.*, Vol. II, pp. 255-58.
19. *Christian Times*, Sept. 2, 1857.
20. Chicago *Journal*, July 29, 1850.
21. *Ibid.*, August 5, 1853. Probably this thrust was directed at the large Irish population. "As in other American cities, clannishness, religion, poverty, and a distinguishing dialect held them aloof from the rest of the population. In the eyes of other groups the proportion arrested for disorderliness and roistering tended further to set them apart." (Pierce, *op. cit.*, Vol. I, p. 180.)
22. *Ibid.*, February 1, 1860.
23. *Ibid.*
24. *Ibid.*, Nov. 1, 1860.
25. Charles L. Wilson, editor of the Chicago *Journal*, quoted in Pierce, *op. cit.*, Vol. II, p. 231.
26. Chicago *Tribune*, July 15, 1864.
27. Chicago *Times*, Oct. 5, 1869.

CHAPTER 2

1. Chicago *Daily Tribune*, Sept. 10, 1871, quoted in Lewis and Smith, *op. cit.*, p. 119.
2. Rushville (Ind.) *Democrat*, quoted in Lewis and Smith, *op. cit.*, p. 135.
3. Quoted in Ralph Davis, "The Negro Newspaper in Chicago," unpublished manuscript, Parkway Community House, Chicago, 1939, p. 30.
4. Davis, *op. cit.*, p. 34.
5. Davis, *op. cit.*, p. 62.
6. Harold F. Gosnell, *Negro Politicians* (University of Chicago, 1935, pp. 198 and 247), mentions the following persons: J. W. E. Thomas, state representative, 1876; John Jones, elected county commissioner in 1871 and 1872. The first colored police officer was appointed in the same year by the Republican mayor.
7. For a colorful description of this period, see Lewis and Smith, *op. cit.*, pp. 138-67.
8. Staley, *op. cit.*, pp. 159-60.
9. A newspaper account of this minister's difficulties appeared in the Chicago *Daily Tribune*, Sept. 16, 1887.
10. Quoted in Davis, *op. cit.*, p. 13.
11. *Ibid.*, p. 46.
12. J. C. Ridpath, cited in Lewis and Smith, *op. cit.*, p. 172.
13. Chicago *Daily Tribune*, Jan. 2, 1894, as quoted in St. Clair Drake, *Churches and Voluntary Associations in the Chicago Negro Community*, WPA (mimeographed), 1940, p. 89.
14. *Ibid.*
15. For a detailed account of this strike, see Alma Herbst, *The Negro in the Slaughtering and Meat Packing Industry in Chicago*, Houghton Mifflin, 1932, pp. 12-27.
16. The literature on this period is voluminous, but one of the best studies of the mechanisms by which Negroes were "put in their place" is W. E. B. Du Bois, *Black Reconstruction*, Harcourt, Brace, 1935.

17. C. G. Woodson, *A Century of Negro Migration,* Association for the Study of Negro Life and History, 1918, Chapter VIII, "The Migration of the Talented Tenth."

CHAPTER 3

1. Chicago Commission on Race Relations, *The Negro in Chicago,* University of Chicago, 1922, Chap. III (hereafter referred to as *The Negro in Chicago.*)
2. E. J. Scott, *Negro Migration During the War,* Oxford, 1920, pp. 72-85.
3. Allison Davis, B. R. Gardner, and Mary R. Gardner, *Deep South,* University of Chicago, 1941, pp. 422-82.
4. Chicago *Defender,* editorial, Oct. 7, 1916.
5. Chicago *Defender,* January 9, 1915.
6. *The Negro in Chicago,* pp. 529-30.
7. *Ibid.,* Chap. IV.
8. P. J. Stackhouse, *Chicago and the Baptists,* University of Chicago, 1933, pp. 200-207.
9. *The Negro in Chicago,* pp. 122-33.
10. *Ibid.,* Chap. VI, "Racial Contacts."
11. *Ibid.,* pp. 108-13.

CHAPTER 4

1. *The Negro in Chicago,* pp. 12-20.
2. Chicago *Tribune,* July 4, 1917.
3. Quoted from a manuscript document, Cayton-Warner Research.
4. Annual Report of Provident Hospital and Training School, 1919, *Provident Hospital in the Race Riot of July, 1919,* Issued by Authority of the Board of Trustees.
5. Quoted in *The Negro in Chicago,* p. 45.
6. Chicago *Daily News,* Aug. 5, 1919.
7. *The Negro in Chicago,* pp. 595-651.
8. This term is used by Robert Redfield in his vivid account of Yucatan, *Tepotzlan.*

CHAPTER 5

1. Smith and Lewis, *op. cit.,* Part II, p. 411.
2. *Ibid.,* p. 422.
3. Chicago *Whip,* May 14, 1921.
4. Hyde Park *Herald,* March 30, 1928.
5. Chicago *Defender,* January 29, 1929.
6. *Ibid.,* March 10, 1929.
7. *Ibid.*
8. Lewis and Smith, *op. cit.,* p. 502.
9. O. C. Cox, "The Negroes' Use of Their Buying Power in Chicago as a Means of Securing Employment," unpublished manuscript, 1932, quoted from an article in the *Crisis,* July, 1931.
10. Quoted from the Chicago *Whip,* July 25, 1931, in Gosnell, *op. cit.,* pp. 329-330.

PART II

CHAPTER 6

1. *The Negro in Chicago*, pp. 100-103.
2. For a comprehensive analysis of such practices consult Charles S. Johnson's *Patterns of Negro Segregation*, Harper, 1943.
3. Quoted from the Chicago *Tribune* in *The Negro in Chicago*, p. 551.
4. Gosnell, Harold F., *Negro Politicians*, University of Chicago, 1935, pp. 18-19.
5. Gosnell, *op. cit.*, p. 11.
6. Quoted from the Chicago *Tribune* in *The Negro in Chicago*, p. 551.
7. Mayor's Conference on Race Relations, *City Planning in Race Relations*, 1944, p. 31 (hereafter referred to as *City Planning in Race Relations*).
8. *The Negro in Chicago*, p. 552.
9. *The Negro in Chicago*, p. 122.
10. Quoted from the *Property Owners' Journal*, in *The Negro in Chicago*, pp. 590-591.
11. Gunnar Myrdal, *An American Dilemma*, Harper, 1944, p. 601.

CHAPTER 7

1. Chicago *Defender*, September 26, 1914.
2. Wirth and Goldhamer, "The Hybrid and the Problem of Miscegenation," in Otto Klineberg, *Characteristics of the American Negro*, Harper, 1944, pp. 301-02.
3. Wirth and Goldhamer, *op. cit.*, p. 253.
4. Edward M. East, *Heredity and Human Affairs*, 1929, p. 100. (See also, E. A. Hooton, "The Anthropometry of Some Small Samples of American Negroes and Negroids," in C. B. Day, *A Study of Some Negro-White Families in the United States*, 1932, p. 108.

CHAPTER 8

1. The scale of "desirability" of various ethnic groups, as well as this estimate of the influence of the racial factor on property and land values, is from Homer Hoyt, *One Hundred Years of Land Values in Chicago*, University of Chicago, 1933, p. 317.
2. Quoted in *The Negro in Chicago*, p. 12.
3. Chicago *Tribune*, January 10, 1920.
4. *Ibid.*, May 21, 1921.
5. The quotations on pp. 185-87 are from a leaflet circulated by the Small Property Owners, Associated, Inc.
6. From a copy of the brief in the files of the Illinois State Commission on the Condition of the Urban Colored Population, Parkway Community House, Chicago.
7. Howard Hazlett, "The Lee-Hansberry Case Indicts . . .", in *Real Estate*, Dec. 7, 1940.
8. Myrdal, *op. cit.*, p. 623.
9. Gosnell, *op. cit.*, pp. 288-291.
10. *City Planning in Race Relations*, p. 21.
11. Chicago *Defender*, July 22, 1944.
12. *City Planning in Race Relations*, p. 60.

CHAPTER 9

1. E. Franklin Frazier, *The Negro Family in Chicago*, University of Chicago, 1932, p. 88.
2. Quoted in *The Negro in American Life*, Washington Intercollegiate Club of Chicago, Inc., 1929, from article in New York *Age*, June 15, 1885.
3. Chicago *Defender*, January 17, 1925.

CHAPTER 10

1. For a definitive study of the development of racial ideologies and their apologia in America, consult Myrdal, *op. cit.*, Part II.
2. *The Negro in Chicago*, p. 453.
3. *Ibid.*, pp. 460-73 (summarized).
4. *City Planning in Race Relations*, p. 14.

CHAPTER 11

1. See H. F. Gosnell, *op. cit.*, Table VIII, p. 239, and discussion, pp. 236-40.
2. Quoted in *The Negro in Chicago*, p. 423.
3. Herbst, *op. cit.*, p. 42.
4. *New Majority*, August 2, 1919, as quoted in Herbst, *op. cit.*, pp. 48-49.
5. Chicago *Defender*, March 26, 1921.
6. *City Planning in Race Relations*, p. 37.
7. *Ibid.*, p. 42.

CHAPTER 12

1. Quoted in the Chicago *Defender*, December 4, 1944.

CHAPTER 13

1. H. F. Gosnell, *Negro Politicians*, University of Chicago, 1935, p. 39.
2. *Ibid.*, p. 46.
3. *Ibid.*, p. 147.

PART III

CHAPTER 14

1. E. Franklin Frazier, *The Negro Family in Chicago*, University of Chicago, 1932, pp. 91-116.

CHAPTER 15

1. Quoted from the January 14, 1933, issue of the Chicago *Defender* by Gosnell, *op. cit.*, p. 341.

CHAPTER 16

1. Chicago *Defender*, February 6, 1937.
2. The quotations here given for the *Defender* are from the issue of March 7, 1931.
3. Chicago *Daily News*, July 12, 1931.

CHAPTER 18

1. In 1899, Dr. W. E. B. Du Bois published the first important sociological study of a Negro community in the United States—*The Philadelphia Negro* (University of Pennsylvania). At the outset, he presented an ecological map

detailing the distribution of the Negro population by "social condition," and divided his subjects into four "grades": (1) the "middle classes" and those above; (2) the working people—fair to comfortable; (3) the poor; (4) vicious and criminal classes. Despite the economic emphasis in this classification and his extensive presentation of data on physical surroundings, Du Bois concluded that ". . . there is a far mightier influence to mold and make the citizen, and that is the social atmosphere which surrounds him; first his daily companionship, the thoughts and whims of his class; then his recreations and amusements; finally the surrounding world of American civilization . . ." (p. 309). This emphasis upon the *social* relations—in family, clique, church, voluntary associations, school, and job—as the decisive elements in personality formation is generally accepted. The authors feel that it should also be the guiding thread in a study of "class" rather than the more arbitrary approach of defining classes by looking for "breaks" in a statistical distribution of incomes, or rents.

All serious students of Negro communities since Du Bois have been concerned with the nature of social stratification among Negroes and with the relative importance of the various factors upon which power and prestige within Negro communities are based. In the Thirties this interest was given added stimulus by the suggestive hypotheses thrown out by Professor W. Lloyd Warner (cf. pp. 772-76) and by a general concern in anthropological and sociological circles with social stratification in America. When, in the Forties, a series of studies on Negro youth sponsored by the American Council on Education appeared, a number of scholars who had been working independently on the problem of "class" for years, organized their materials in a frame of reference that utilized various conceptions of "class." (Note List of References, pp. 793-96.)

Throughout the late Thirties and early Forties, there was widespread discussion (sometimes acrimonious) in academic circles over the "class concept"—its meaning and the techniques of empirical research required for studying social stratification. Gunnar Myrdal, in his monumental study, *An American Dilemma* (Harper, 1941) made a thorough critique of the concepts and of the empirical research on the Negro in America, in his chapters on "Caste and Class" and "The Negro Class Structure," and his note on "Research on Caste and Class in a Negro Community." The latter discussion lays down a set of criteria by which an "ideal study" of a Negro community should be judged. The authors are in general agreement with Myrdal's "practical proposals" and with his description of "what a study of a Negro community should be." The research for *Black Metropolis* had been concluded and the first draft of the book made before Myrdal's study appeared, but the authors have been interested in judging their own work by Myrdal's criteria. *Black Metropolis* is far from being the "ideal study" as he defines it. From the beginning of their research, however, the authors have been conscious of one problem which Myrdal raises about the nature of social classes. They are not entirely in agreement with his conclusion that "our class concepts have no other reality than as a conceptual framework" (see Ch. 18 of this book and Figure 39) although they are aware of the dangers of reification. Yet, in contradistinction to some of the previous studies, the authors have concentrated not upon defining and describing classes as "natural" groups on one hand nor "a series of continua" on the other; rather, they have tried to define *those patterns of behavior and attributes that various segments of the community look upon as having high or low social status.* Such a conception presents a number of research problems, for it not only involves taking cues from interview material and the notes of participant-observers, but also necessitates trying to mediate the *ethos* of various groups within the community, with all of the consequent dangers of falling into subjectivism. (Cf. Kurt H. Wolff, "A Methodological Note on the Empirical Establishment of Culture Patterns," *American Sociological Review,* 10:2, April, 1945.)

In using this approach to a study of class, the first procedure has been to define the "measures of the man" as they are derived from interviews and observation. (This step is amenable to statistical controls through the use of social distance scales and questionnaires administered on a sampling basis to various sections of the population, once the student has ascertained "what questions to ask" from his intimate knowledge of the community.)

The next step has been to estimate the number of people at various levels in several different hierarchies. (See Note 2, p. 790.)

The research techniques used for ascertaining patterns and stratifying them are implicit in Chapters 18-23. The task is least difficult at the highest status-levels, for the population aggregate is small and the patterns are highly standardized and are closely related to the controls imposed by membership in professions or by business careers or the demands of "Society." At this level the class is definitely a "natural" group.

The lower-class patterns were studied as, and are presented as, "polar opposites" to the upper-class style of living. There are definite advantages in using a modification of Voegelin's "contrast conception" or "counter conception" in studying social stratification. (Cf. Lewis Copeland, "The Negro as a Contrast Conception," Edgar T. Thompson [ed.], *Race Relations and the Race Problem,* Duke University Press, 1939.) In taking a point of departure from the upper-class conception of the lower class, however, one ends up with a "stereotype." It is possible to take this "stereotype" as a research lead and by studying those people who actually approximate the stereotype to reshape it closer to reality. Then, on the basis of the stereotype and the empirical data, one can construct an "ideal type" of lower-class behavior, against which an individual, a family, or an institutional increment can be studied.

Since the lower-class pattern exists in a context made up of upper- and middle-class patterns, some clues to the nature of these are picked up from a study of the lower class. For instance, "typical" lower-class people are not dominated by mobility aspirations, but most lower-class people fantasy at some time about "getting ahead," and some, *in their overt behavior* try to be mobile. By studying the fantasies of the larger group, and the overt behavior of the "exceptions" it is possible to arrive at the meaning of "middle-classness" to lower-class people.

Groups of people exist in the community who are dominated by a drive to "get ahead"—to shake off lower-class traits, to place social distance between themselves and others "below" them. There are others, who have made this mobility step, or who were born in families that had made it in the past. By studying such people, we arrive at the conclusion that actual bonds of social solidarity exist between them—objectified in clique, associational and church life, and that in numerous instances these social bonds override wide differences in occupation and income—and even education. Thus, the drive for "respectability" and "right connections" and "front" is isolated as the dominant motif of what we call "the middle-class way of life." Type of ritual and public behavior become the touchstone for stratifying churches and institutions rather than the economic or occupational status of the members. The latter are stated as dependent variables in terms of ranges and modal averages.

Such an approach to class makes it difficult to estimate "how many" individuals or families share a fully integrated pattern approaching the "ideal typical," for in a dynamic society, a given individual or family may incorporate parts of several patterns from various status levels. The patterns exist, however, both subjectively in the consciousness of the community and objectively in the loose linkage of families and voluntary associations, churches, and cliques which make up the social organization of Black Metropolis. (It is possible, by using rating scales to classify a statistically adequate sample of families and individuals in terms of their approximation to an "ideal type" for each class pattern.)

2. In arriving at some rough estimate of the proportion of the Negro population on each class level, the Cayton-Warner Research selected three class-indices for which census data were available. (See table below.)

PER CENT OF ADULTS OR FAMILY GROUPS * CLASSIFIED AS UPPER, MIDDLE, AND LOWER CLASS

Approximate range of educational status †, occupation ‡ and standard of living § at various class levels	Per Cent	
	Total Population	Negro Population
1. UPPER CLASS:	10.0	5.0
(a) Education beyond high school........................	8.7	4.9
(b) All professionals, and half of the proprietors, managers and officials..	10.4	3.9
(c) All rentals of over $75 per month and half of the rentals between $50 and $75.	13.5	4.6
2. MIDDLE CLASS:.......................................	40.0	30.0
(a) Some high school education..........................	29.9	24.4
(b) All clerical and skilled workers; half of the semi-skilled workers...	59.9	26.0
(c) All rentals of $30-49 per month and half of the rentals between $50 and $75.................................	40.6	32.5
3. LOWER CLASS:.......................................	50.0	65.0
(a) Grammar school education or less.....................	60.6	69.5
(b) All unskilled workers and half of the semi-skilled workers	30.1	70.2
(c) All rentals of $29 per month and less..................	45.9	62.9

* The percentages for education and occupation are based on total persons, 18 years of age and over. The percentages for rental groups are based on number of families.

† Percentages based on 2,300,000 persons in total population and 175,000 Negroes. Data from Charles S. Newcomb and Richard O. Lang, *Census Data of the City of Chicago,* 1934, University of Chicago Press, 1934.

‡ Percentages based on 1,500,000 persons in total population and 130,000 Negroes. Census data as retabulated from 1930 Census by Cayton-Warner Research.

§ Percentages based on 830,000 families in total population and 53,000 Negro families Data from Newcomb and Lang.

In striking a rough average per cent of the three indices for each class level (note bold-face figures), the middle-class figure was weighted at the expense of the lower-class figure since some people with very low educational level and occupational status are middle class if judged by standard of living, public behavior, and associational ties. The concept of class used in this study makes the latter pattern decisive in establishing the social stratification of an individual or family in Bronzeville. The approximate class range for each index was arrived at from a study of interview material and an analysis of the social characteristics of the members of social clubs, churches and families that had been previously stratified on the basis of their behavior pattern.

3. The schematic representation of "The System of Social Classes" in Figure 31 embodies the results of extensive empirical research. In studying social stratification among some 175,000 adults and 50,000 families, a number of approaches must be used. The first tentative studies by the Cayton-Warner Research involved an attempt at "stratifying" institutional units. It was a relatively simple matter to identify individual churches and social clubs which had very high or very low social status. It was then possible for participant-observers to isolate the individuals and families within these groups who had the highest or lowest prestige, subjecting them to detailed study. In the meantime, the clerical staff, using data supplied by the participant-observers, analyzed membership lists to determine the occupational and educational ranges, and the extent of membership in other clubs, churches and cliques. Members were interviewed to find their attitudes toward other individuals and institutional units and toward the criteria of stratification. (See Albert Blumenthal, *Small Town Stuff,* Allison Davis, Burleigh Gardner, and Mary Gardner, *Deep South,* and W. Lloyd Warner's *Yankee City Series* for detailed discussions of these procedures as applied to other communities.) Eventually, the research staff was able to arrange numerous clubs and churches in a rough hierarchy and to define status levels within larger groups that were not themselves class-typed. From a study of the people who belonged to these organizations it was possible to find other individuals of similar occupational and educational status with whom they had "social" relations but who did not belong to any organizations or who belonged to others.

It soon became clear that between a thousand and two thousand families of high educational status and relatively high economic status constituted some sort of "upper class." Most of these people were not "church-centered," although a few did organize their leisure time pattern around church activities. This group was acutely conscious of the social competition of a small wealthy group—mostly policy kings—"the upper shadies."

In studying the lower class the research staff began with a study of several groups that ranked "lowest" in a number of prestige hierarchies—those with the least education, the least money, the poorest housing in the worst neighborhoods, and the members of store-front churches. Here again it was possible to state ranges and modal averages of traits within groups, e.g., most store-front church members were poor and uneducated; most, but not all, of the poor and uneducated who belonged to churches belonged to those with low-status rituals; there were very few social clubs in the areas of poorest housing. It was also evident that low-status church people were censorious of other families of similar socio-economic status who had no associational ties and who were characterized by extreme social disorganization—the "lower shadies." There were few stable family groups which were not "church-centered" at this level. By active participation in this stratum, it was possible to describe the pattern of lower-class life as portrayed in Chapters 20 and 21.

Both the lower class and the upper class recognize people with another extensive "center of interest" in the community—those who stress "getting ahead." By studying individuals who were "getting ahead," "improving themselves," "advancing," it was possible to identify the churches, clubs, and neighborhoods which were looked upon as "respectable" or "good connections." Further study of these institutions and neighborhoods in terms of uniformities and ranges of education, occupation, overlapping memberships, etc., resulted in a gradual building up of the pattern of the middle-class way of life.

Once the criteria for social stratification had been ascertained some 8,000 individuals were "stratified" on the basis of education, occupation, church and associational memberships, number of years in Chicago, skin-color, area of residence in the city, positions held in the political hierachy and in community organizations. Marginal and borderline cases were studied in order to arrive at the crucial criteria; e.g., a Red Cap found associating socially with professional people or a professional man who attended a very low status church. These "exceptions" threw additional light upon the bases of prestige in the community.

CHAPTER 19

1. Ethel Ramsey Harris, *Voluntary Social Activities Among Negro Professional People in Chicago,* Unpublished Master's Thesis, University of Chicago, 1937, Appendix.
2. *Ibid.*

CHAPTER 20

1. The material used in this section is based on a monograph now on file at the Parkway Community House, Chicago.
2. E. Franklin Frazier, *The Negro Family in the United States,* University of Chicago, 1939, Chapter XIII, "Roving Men and Homeless Women."

CHAPTER 22

1. Robert L. Sutherland, *An Analysis of Negro Churches in Chicago* (Ph.D. Dissertation, University of Chicago, 1930).
2. Harold M. Kingsley, *The Negro in Chicago,* Chicago Congregational Missionary Extension Society, 1933.

CHAPTER 23

1. O. C. Cox, *op. cit.,* p. 126.

CHAPTER 24

1. Editorial, *Life,* April 24, 1944, p. 32.
2. Myrdal, *op. cit.,* Vol. I, p. xlv.
3. *Ibid.,* p. xlix.

Bronzeville 1961

IN COMMENTING UPON THE CONTENTS OF THIS VOLUME, THE AUTHORS WROTE,
in 1945: "The picture of life in Bronzeville that emerges from these
chapters is a candid-camera shot of the community in the final stages
of the Depression and in the midst of the Second World War." Depression and war have passed; peace and prosperity prevail. The
reader will, no doubt, want to know, "To what extent has the community changed during the past 16 years?" Bronzeville, as a compact
and self-conscious community, still exists. There has been very little
change in the fundamental values of its people or in the basic social
structure and cultural patterns of the community.

If we compare the content of the Chicago *Defender* as described in
Black Metropolis, for instance, with that in the "World's Greatest
Weekly" of today, we find that the basic themes and orientations
persist, although details have changed. Church and club news is still
reported in elaborate detail, and Race Heroes and Race Leaders are
still "big news," although Joe Louis has been replaced by Rafer Johnson and Archie Moore, and Haile Selassie by the New African leaders.[1]
Stories about Martin Luther King now compete for space with those
about old-line politicians and Race Leaders; and there is an increasing
number of "Firsts" and a diminishing number of "Onlies." [2]

Even a cursory tour of Bronzeville will reveal that "The Measure of the
Man" [3] remains the same, and that much of life still revolves around those
"axes of life" originally selected for discussion: "staying alive," "getting
ahead," 'having fun," "praising god," and "advancing the Race."

The changes which have occurred are related primarily to two crucial
facts of the 1960's; namely, that America is experiencing a period of
prosperity and that Negroes are living in the Era of Integration. By
1950, the lean years had gone. Just staying alive had ceased to be the
problem for most people. Negroes were beginning to sing "Happy
Days Are Here Again" instead of moaning "I've Been Down So Long

---

[1] See pp. 401–412 and especially pp. 403–408, Tables 15 and 16.
[2] See page 391 for the significance of these terms.
[3] Cf. Ch. 18, "The Measure of the Man."

Down Don't Bother Me." By 1961 money had been circulating freely and rapidly for over a decade. Credit had been made easy through budget plans and wage assignments and, in 1961, it was even possible to find an ad like this in the Negro press: *EVERYONE RIDES. WE GUARANTEE YOU A CAR EVEN IF YOU'VE HAD A REPOSSESSION, GARNISHEE OR JUDGMENT. NO CO-MAKERS NEEDED.* Fine clothes, new furniture and household gadgets, ubiquitous TV and radio sets, as well as a plethora of cars, give visible evidence of Bronzeville's participation in the abundance of the "Affluent Society."

The Negro population of Chicago doubled between 1950 and 1960. Bronzeville's doctors, dentists, lawyers, preachers and businessmen captured a sizeable share of the dollars circulating in the expanded and, to some extent, "captive" Black Belt market. Their offices, churches, and homes reflect the new prosperity as do newspaper notices of frequent continental and occasional intercontinental travels, and the elaboration of social rituals. The addition of new neighborhoods to the Black Belt has increased the number of Negro aldermen in City Hall, and has resulted in more precinct captains, ward officials, and "jobs for the boys," as well as symbolic appointments to high office.

The business center of Bronzeville has shifted two miles southward as the community has grown in size—from 47th Street to 63rd Street.[4] Negro entrepreneurs have opened up numerous new restaurants, taverns, liquor stores, hotels, barber shops and beauty parlors. Some Negroes have also made a "killing" in real estate. Negro cab owners have not only expanded their illegal (but protected) business of running jitney cabs on Bronzeville's main thoroughfares, but they have also won the fight to operate their metered cabs throughout the city. Negro insurance companies have held their own and some have prospered greatly, although they are still pygmies beside giants like Metropolitan and Prudential. (Morticians, too, have profited from the population increase.) A highly successful sausage company and a $2,000,000 cosmetics enterprise are both selling to the broader white market, but these are the exceptions which prove the rule that Negro business still caters to a predominantly Negro market.

The most spectacular business successes during the past decade have been scored in the publishing field. One enterprising Bronzeville publisher has nurtured his magazines, *Ebony, Jet, Tan, Hue,* and *Negro Digest* to the point where they not only attract a high volume of

[4] Cf. pp. 379–382.

national advertising, but are also sold on newsstands throughout the country and overseas. A *Daily Defender* has been in existence for almost five years to supplement the weekly Chicago *Defender*. Both publishers have purchased property in downtown Chicago and moved their businesses there. A Bronzeville businessman has bought the *Pittsburgh Courier* and now publishes a *Chicago Courier* as well for the benefit of readers in Black Metropolis. The *New Crusader* has replaced *Dynamite* as a sensational, race conscious, agitational organ carrying the slogan "Negroes Must Control Their Own Community."

The preachers have taken full advantage of the Fat Years to pay off mortgages and to build new churches and remodel old ones. Attractive modernistic edifices have sprung up and several church community centers, planned and dreamed of during the Depression years, have now materialized. Also, as in the past, Negro congregations have been buying the churches and synagogues abandoned by white congregations as they retreat in the face of Negro settlement in new neighborhoods.

What was once Bronzeville's most spectacular Negro business— policy—has been taken over by "The Mob." "Policy shops" no longer operate openly as "Negro Businesses." The Jones Brothers, the "Gentlemen Racketeers" who were described as Race Heroes in the first edition of *Black Metropolis,* have now gone into legitimate business in Mexico City.[5] They fled Chicago after one of them was kidnapped by white racketeers and held for ransom. The "front man" whom they left to look after their business in Chicago was eventually gunned down on a street in Bronzeville, thus making the "takeover" of the once black "syndicate" complete.[6] While some successful Negro policy operators still remain, they are really only "small fry" and none of them exhibit social pretensions. The policy racket lost its functional utility when prosperity came to Brônzeville and its glamor when it ceased to be a *Negro* controlled business. Few Race Leaders feel called upon to defend it now, as they did during the Depression.

Change is most immediately evident in the physical setting within which community activities take place. The Black Belt has grown enormously in size, and thousands of Negroes are now living in fine apartment buildings and in relatively new, attractive homes vacated during the last ten years by white people who were "getting ahead"

[5] See pp. 486–490.
[6] Note diagram on p. 483.

(and who symbolized the fact by increasing the physical distance between themselves and Negroes). With money in the bank and G.I. and F.H.A. loans available, Bronzeville's home owners have been lavishing attention upon their newly acquired properties, partly because of intrinsic satisfaction in so doing, pride of possession, and also because it is part of the ritual of "advancing the race." They feel impelled to stamp out the stereotype that "Negroes always run neighborhoods down."

Even the older parts of the Black Belt have a new look. Extensive slum-clearance and rebuilding have changed the face of the Black Belt's northern section while "elbow grease," paint and grass, storm windows and flowers, have eliminated much of the drab, run-down, depression look of yesteryears. But unkempt neighborhoods and litter-laden alleys and streets have by no means disappeared; and Bronzeville's *masses* are still piled up on top of each other in cramped quarters to a greater extent than in any other part of Midwest Metropolis. To them the Black Ghetto has become a gilded ghetto, but a ghetto all the same.

The economic and ecological changes have inevitably affected what was referred to as "the system of social classes" in Bronzeville, although the basic pattern has not been altered. Figure 39 on page 711 still describes the contemporary scene, with one significant difference. The departure of the "Gentlemen Racketeers" from the city and the tendency of members of what was described as the "Upper Shady" group to concentrate their investments in legitimate enterprises has been accompanied by the disappearance of an upper-class sector that was important during the Depression years. It might now be more accurate to define a center of orientation at the upper-class level called "The Unconventional Uppers" or "The Sporting Set" and to drop the term "Upper Shadies."

The style of life of the "Upper Respectables" or the "Conventional Uppers" has not changed. It has simply become more elaborate. The same exclusive male clubs originally described in *Black Metropolis*[7] set the tone of upper-class social life, but the civic activity and social ritual of the upper-class, and the activities of the Greek letter fraternities and sororities, are now functioning to weld together a new and larger upper-class stratum based upon a core of younger college graduates recruited from all social levels—those who have made money during the Period of Prosperity and who want to live the upper-class

[7] See pp. 532–536.

style of life. (Not all of the successful professional men strive to become upper-class, however. Some settle for a less expansive upper-middle-class existence.)

The upper and upper-middle strata continue to supply leadership for the National Association for the Advancement of Colored People, the Urban League, the Y.M.C.A., the Y.W.C.A., Provident Hospital, and a wide range of other civic organizations in Bronzeville. Members of these strata, too, are beginning to appear in greater numbers upon the city-wide boards of charitable and civic organizations, thus linking Bronzeville to influential sectors of the white community through membership in a variety of interracial organizations upon whose boards they serve, at whose meetings they frequently speak, and with whose members they now sustain, to an increasing extent, more intimate social participation. But the major professional organizations do not yet welcome their Negro counterparts as members, and parallel structures to those organizations still exist in Bronzeville. The members of the upper stratum also continue to link Bronzeville's elite to the Negro elite in cities throughout the country by membership in national Negro organizations and clubs, and by frequent intervisiting.

The "black proletariat," divided into middle-class and lower-class segments, and sharing the fruits of the Period of Prosperity, is even less inclined than in the past to think of itself as a part of some interracial "working-class" in the Marxian sense—except during an occasional strike. Many of its members do, however, like their white counterparts, belong to unions by check-off if not by choice.

Middle-class status, now as in the past, demands respectable public behavior, relatively conventional family life, and some concern for getting ahead. The fact that recent migrants from the south are better educated than those of the past has probably augmented the size of Bronzeville's middle class.

The "World of the Lower Class" is no longer neatly patterned, in a physical sense, as it was sixteen years ago. (Figure 32, p. 601). Slum clearance and urban redevelopment programs have wiped out the concentrated cluster of lower-class institutions and scattered the population. But as a sub-culture, the "World of the Lower Class" still exists. Store-front churches flourish, but illiterate and semi-literate individuals who feel that they are "called to preach" find it increasingly difficult to rent stores, since run-down business streets are being eliminated by slum clearance, and low-cost housing projects make no provision for such spiritual entrepreneurs. There has been a substantial increase, however, in the number of conventional churches catering to lower-class religious tastes. The two large churches which were popular in these religious circles when *Black Metropolis* first appeared are still in existence,[8] but Elder Lucy is dead and when she "passed" her body was paraded through Bronzeville's streets "in state" with coach and horses. New churches appealing to recent immigrants from the South are now far more popular than either of these two. Churches still constitute a center of stability amid the constant flux and disorder of the world of the lower class.

Bronzeville's upper class continues to worry about the Negro "image" created among outsiders by lower class activities, but they have had to resign themselves to what they consider the "loud" and "unrepresentative" radio programs for which the lower status churches easily find sponsors. They are particularly concerned over the high degree of social disorganization which persists at the lower-class level, for the Slicks, the Mr. Bens, the Baby Chiles and their circle of associates are still prevalent. How prevalent we really do not know, but because their plight is so dramatic and their activities so unconventional, they receive continuous publicity, and thus help to fix an image in the popular mind. Within the disorganized segment of the lower class are the highly publicized unwed and deserted mothers, some of whom draw a regular income from welfare sources, as well as the women and men who have formed loose and shifting common-law alliances; the recalcitrant and sometimes violent school children; the teen-age gangsters; the dope users and pushers; and the small hard core of habitual criminals.

Urban renewal tends to make the entire city more aware of Bronzeville's *lumpen-proletariat,* for as the slums are cleared, and the physical locus of the lower class is shattered, individuals and families are forced to scatter into middle-class neighborhoods and onto the margins of these areas, since public "relocation housing" has never kept pace with demolition. Enterprising realtors in middle-class neighborhoods are always ready to convert houses and apartment buildings in order to accommodate new tenants in crowded discomfort, while the most marginal families huddle in dilapidated buildings awaiting demolition within clearance areas. An occasional tragedy, as when a firetrap burns or a baby is bitten by a rat, excites a spate of excited newspaper com-

[8] See pp. 641–646.

ment and sometimes an exposé. (The Urban League refers to members of this group as "Chicago's D.P.s.") Bigger Thomases, as Richard Wright described them in *Native Son,* keep on being bred, and the frying pan is still useful against the rodents.[9]

Most of the people in Midwest Metropolis are now aware that "all Negroes are not that way." But many people, Negro and white, feel that "too many of them are." The middle classes insist upon increased police protection, but realize that arrest and punishment solve no problems. There is a general feeling that all social work efforts are merely "holding operations" until complete job equality and adequate housing provide a new physical and economic framework of existence and new incentives for young people, out of which it is hoped new patterns of behavior will grow.

The lower-class churches do not speak to the condition of the disorganized masses and very few brands are snatched from the burning despite continuous praying and singing, preaching and revivals.

In recent years new "Black Gods of the Metropolis" have appeared. "The Leader and Teacher, the Honorable Elijah Mohammed, who was taught by the God whose proper name is Allah" has bought a Jewish synagogue near the University of Chicago and converted it into Mr. Mohammed's Temple No. 2, with its affiliated University of Islam. Here (and through his newspaper and over the radio), he exhorts the "so-called Negroes" to repudiate the white man's religion, to cast off the names inherited from slavery, to eschew pork, drinking, smoking, and gambling, and to help "build a Nation in this Wilderness of North America." He encourages his followers to go into business; but the attempts of the Muslims to erect a business center in a new Negro middle-class neighborhood created such vigorous opposition that the venture was blocked. (The "Moors" referred to on p. 745 were operating in Chicago as early as the 20's, but it is only since the Second World War that Black Muslims have attracted a substantial following.) The female faithful in their colorful pseudo-Arabic gowns and the fanatical males, including the judo-trained Fruit of Islam, can fill the Chicago Stadium at nationwide conventions of the Black Muslims, but the number of people in Bronzeville who have actually joined the movement would hardly fill the auditoriums of the two largest Baptist churches. The rise of the Black Muslims is one index to the deep resentment among lower-class Negroes, but is no more likely to have

[9] See Richard Wright, *Native Son* (Harper & Brothers, 1940), pp. 3–6.

a significanct impact upon Bronzeville than did the Communist Party during the Depression years. Neither the Christian churches nor Mr. Mohammed are able to influence that large segment of the lower-class whose resentment is expressed in apathy, cynicism and aggression, and whose primary mode of escape is through "having a good time."

It is the hope of most middle-class social workers and educators that, as increasing numbers of migrants find regular employment— as they "settle in"—and as the educational level of Bronzeville's population rises, more and more people will adopt "the middle-class way of life." In addition to conventional family patterns this would involve widespread acceptance of church oriented and "society" oriented behavior. The middle-class way of life thus takes on a degree of significance which justifies detailed consideration by sociologists. It represents a realistic goal toward which younger people in the lower-class can aspire. It provides patterns which can be acquired without a great deal of self denial and with only a moderate amount of schooling. (A regular income is the main prerequisite.) It is a pattern which is attractive to the masses, and which can motivate people to strive for it. Judged by intellectual standards it represents devotion to trivia. Judged by functional standards, it provides stability amidst disorder, consensus instead of *anomie*.

Middle-class "society" is very much as it was sixteen years ago. The same "clubs which set the pattern" when *Black Metropolis* was originally written are still "going strong." The Kool Kustomers' dances are even more elaborate in this Era of Integration, and they are sometimes held in Loop hotels.[10] But scores of new clubs have also come into being, some of them perhaps more popular than the Amethyst Girls [11] and the Kool Kustomers. The emergence of new clubs is sometimes mentioned in *Defender* "club notes" in such announcements as "a capacity crowd frolicked with the Dapper Dans . . . when the club marked its first anniversary in clubdom's ranks" or when it was stated that the Contessas were busily preparing for their debut in a "first annual Dance." [12]

---

[10] See pp. 699–701.

[11] See pp. 694–698.

[12] Occasionally a new club has a utilitarian aspect as when the wives of the salesmen who form the Bottle and Cork Club organized the Corkettes and had a "wine sip" for their first annual affair. The guests were regaled with the specific products sold by their husbands! The general pattern of club activity is the same as in the past, and so are the types of names chosen. In recent years the King of Clubs has emerged along with its Queens; The Lords of Charm

Fashion shows have become one of the most popular money-raising activities throughout Bronzeville. Prosperity has made possible an extreme elaboration of the "cult of clothes" which serves to integrate the world of "Society" and the world of the Church in upper-class and middle-class circles. Style shows and fashion revues are a fixture of the Bronzeville sub-culture, and no one sees anything incongruous about the guild of a Catholic church sponsoring a "Pert and Pretty Fashion Show," or a Baptist church presenting "Excelsiors in Fashion Review" at its thirty-third anniversary services.

At the center of the "cult of clothes" is a group of amateur and professional models, male and female, some of whom are graduates of, or students at, charm and model schools. The pace is still set by the group of women referred to in *Black Metropolis* as being the "fashion setters" sixteen years ago,[13] along with their younger admirers. These women have connections with downtown department stores, and some of them occasionally travel to Paris in order to familiarize themselves with the latest styles. These models move about Bronzeville continuously, appearing at events sponsored by clubs and churches, or giving their own revues.[14]

and their Ladies now give their "gala affairs"; and we find references to The Regular Fellows, The Gay Lords, the Juggs, the Blue Dragons, the Tan Tappers, the Silent Twelve, the Six O'Clock Girls, the Twelve Keys, the Exclusive Chics, the Purple Orchids, the Blue Gladiolas Coterie, the Valencia, the Stars of Fashion, and the Up-to-Daters. Those who have had some high school education tend to be attracted to clubs such as these as are also upwardly mobile adults with less education than those in the clubs setting the pattern.

[13] See p. 547.

[14] Members of social clubs often give their own style shows, as when the Eight Sophisticates presented a "Black and White Fantasy" for their fifth annual fashion revue, or when the Sapphire Girls presented "chic fashions" at their annual affair under the title "Paris in the Fall." Church clubs sometimes adopt a similar pattern of giving their own shows. Nearly every issue of the weekly *Defender* carries photographs of women displaying their clothes at money raising events. This preoccupation with clothes even leads to the formation of associations based upon an interest in stylish dressing as in the case of The Toggettes. (This club, incidentally, borrowed the higher status pattern of "pledging" potential members as sororities do.) To secure funds for building a new edifice, one middle-class church presented a "foursome" from the Academy Models Guild which was lucky enough to persuade Joe Louis' wife to come to New York to model her furs, formal gowns, and sportswear. The Decorators Club upon occasion showed their "many minks" for the benefit of a Baptist Church.

One of the more unusual recent fashion shows was that of the Chicago Musical Association built around the theme "What the Musician Should Wear and When." (Male models were included.) Another special event was the Blue

Despite the conspicuous consumption characteristic of Bronzeville's people during the past decade, considerable anxiety and apprehension exist beneath the surface, for the bubble could burst as it once did in 1929. Also, despite gains in living space, the middle classes still have the problems posed by Lorraine Hansberry in her play *A Raisin in the Sun*.

Uneasiness exists, also, over certain dilemmas presented by the Era of Integration. All Race Leaders must express full commitment to the ultimate goal of complete and total integration, but they find themselves involved in contradictions which result in inconsistencies of attitude and behavior. There are problems and questions such as the following:

> Bronzeville's political power is based upon the existence of a segregated community. What kind of political influence and rewards could Negroes hope to expect if the Black Belt were to disappear?
>
> Some middle-class Negroes are living in integrated communities. The pressure of an overcrowded Black Belt is likely to transform such communities into sections of the Black Ghetto. Should Negroes co-operate with whites in using various devices to maintain "a realistic racial balance" in these neighborhoods? Given the fact that their fellow black citizens need more housing, should they help to keep the proportion of Negro residents down in such areas?
>
> The prosperity of Negro business and professional men rests upon the existence of a Black Belt. Could they survive under conditions of general competition?
>
> If the church is desegregated will mixed congregations ever accept Negro ministers?
>
> Are there values and cultural products which have developed among Negroes that will be lost if full integration ever becomes a reality?

Such questions do not, of course, have the same urgency for those whose incomes do not depend upon the existence of a Negro market or a Negro electorate. (The Negro masses, for instance, applaud the new

---

Eagles' "Easter Extravaganza" where professional models appeared alongside amateurs from the High Society Club and the Sapphire Girls. One year, the ten best dressed women in Bronzeville were selected by the Association of Mannequins for awards which were presented to them downtown at "Le Petit Gourmet": "In recognition of the millions of dollars which Negro women spend annually" and "to bring acclamation and honor to those women of the Race who have achieved an appearance that is fashionable and appropriate."

Race Heroes on the White Sox and Cubs teams without giving a thought to the effect of this "draining away of talent" from the Negro baseball leagues.) Younger people, too, seem to be gaining a greater sense of confidence in their ability to face competition in an integrated America.

Bronzeville's institutions keep alive the myth of "salvation *via* Negro business," but the fact remains that despite the multiplication of small capitalists and the greater affluence of some large ones, Negroes have not broken into the industrial and commercial "big time," and the bulk of the Negro market's money goes to white banks and loan companies, the supermarkets, the downtown department stores, and to white insurance companies—not to Negro enterprises. Occasionally, integrationist trends are viewed with alarm as a threat to Negro business. In mid-April of 1961, for instance, the Chicago Negro Chamber of Commerce met to discuss "How Does Integration Affect Negro Business" and the *New Crusader* reported expressions of grave concern.[15] The Negro masses, on the whole, have shown no inclination to "sacrifice" in order to build co-operatives, nor to "earmark" a part of their income for supporting Negro private ventures. Enough have shown "racial loyalty," however, to support two very successful savings and loan companies and one cooperative store and credit union.

The goal of a self-contained Negro economy has always been considered a defensive measure and not an ideal solution to Bronzeville's problems. Now some of Bronzeville's capable and alert older-generation businessmen are talking of selling to the *American* market, not just to the *Negro* market.[16] And at least one is proving that it can be done

[15] These apprehensions revolve mainly around the new fashion of using downtown hotels for high status events. A typical *Defender* headline about such an event reads: *Fashionable Crowd Dances With Kappas* (a male fraternity) *in the Beautiful and Exclusive Crystal Ballroom of the Sheraton Blackstone.* Upon another occasion, an event by an exclusive male club was headlined: *Elite Makes Merry at Snakes Club Installation.* The caption under the picture indicated that the affair was held "in the exclusive Kungsholm Restaurant . . . in the atmosphere of old world charm." One picture noted that guests were "exchanging gay repartee between smorgasbord courses." In the past discrimination made such downtown events impossible.

[16] In 1955, the president of a leading Negro insurance company was honored at a banquet in a downtown hotel which brought together distinguished businessmen of both races, including a high official of the Chicago Association of Commerce and Industry. The Negro businessman who was being honored said that a "major move" of his insurance company "into the white insurance field" was "predicted." He stated that "limitations of race should be removed from the field of commerce and industry."

—he has developed a cosmetics business which sells one line of goods to Negroes and another to whites. Operating on a national scale, his annual conventions of executives and salesmen are held at downtown Chicago hotels, and the *Defender* refers not only to the "lush setting," but also to the fact that these conferences are an example of integration in action.[17]

The competitive situation in this period of highly developed capitalism makes it very difficult for Negroes to enter business with sufficient capital and enough influential contacts to ensure a successful building up of impressive manufacturing or commercial concerns. Most Negro businessmen find it much safer to invest in real estate or businesses within the Negro community than to risk their capital in businesses oriented toward the general American market. In recent years, too, there has been increased interest within the Negro middle class in conventional stocks and bonds investments.

Grumbling about Jim Crow is still one of Bronzeville's major indoor sports. "Taking the white man apart" remains a routine conversational activity. But full-time fighting against discrimination and segregation is considered a specialist activity—the job for Race Leaders and Race Heroes, for a certain kind of white person, for job holders in the newer race relations organizations, and for college kids who go Freedom Riding in the South or take part in sit-ins and swim-ins in Midwest Metropolis. Everybody feels, however, that such people should be backed up. Raising money for Freedom Riders became a part of church ritual during the height of the movement just as campaigns for the Scottsboro Boys, Emmett Till's Defense Fund, or the Montgomery Bus Boycotters had been in the past. People also generally feel that they should contribute to the NAACP and Urban League, even when they may not do so. But, for most people, wearing their dark skin color is like living with a chronic disease. One learns to "take it" and not to let it unduly cramp one's style of life. And anodynes are always present: religion, the social ritual, whiskey, dope—and for those who can afford

[17] Upon one occasion, the *Defender* carried a picture of white and Negro members of this firm at an annual banquet, citing this as evidence that "integration is the keynote" of the company's employment policy. A number of other pictures portrayed Negroes and whites fraternizing rather ostentatiously at the meeting.

There have been businesses run by Negroes in the past which catered to both races, including that of John Jones who was referred to on p. 41. Thus, some race leaders speak of reviving an old tradition rather than of starting something new when they think of selling to the general market.

it, an occasional trip to Europe, Latin America, or Africa as a kind of play therapy. From the Black Muslim's point of view, Negroes should deliberately accept segregation. They assert that Negroes of all social classes are losing their self-respect by pursuing an integrationist will-o'-the-wisp. The Muslims continuously assail Martin Luther King, the Freedom Riders, the NAACP, and the Urban League, and call for the building of a Black Nation upon land to be secured from the government as compensation for back wages "stolen" during several centuries of slavery. One member writes:

> There are at least three things that we must do in order to lift the heel of Satan (i.e., the white man) from our necks and that is to, one, separate our people from the Caucasian race, which means putting an end to integration; second, return the white man's religion of Christianity which is the mental chain that is rusting and destroying our people's minds; and third, we must come together—this means dissolving our very foolish and false class system. Doctors, professors, lawyers, college students, mothers and fathers, the young and old, should take up the banner of Islam and build a righteous nation on this earth.

Most Negroes reject the Muslim's racism and separatism while admiring their militancy and successful business enterprises.

During the 1960's there has been a marked increase of interest in Africa among the people of Black Metropolis—a fascination with the rise of the new African states, coupled with some resentment over the fact that special treatment is reserved for African diplomats so that they are less subject to discrimination. At the upper and upper-middle-class levels this interest is reflected in occasional parties for prominent African visitors, in vacation trips to Africa by the few who can afford it, by investment in a few African business projects, and by the frequent programming of lectures and discussions about Africa before church groups and clubs.[18] At lower status levels there is considerable vicarious identification with leaders like Jomo Kenyatta and Lumumba,

[18] In 1955, one group of lower-middle-class men revived the Ancient Order of Ethiopia, a lodge which once existed in Chicago and which had as one of its stated goals "to bring to the world the ancient achievements, grandeur and glory of a lost culture—the Ethiopian." Negro History Week is celebrated annually by speeches and concerts under the auspices of an organization called the Afro-American Heritage Foundation. But very few individuals are involved in these groups. The members of the Ethiopian World Federation also meet regularly to discuss their plans for emigration to the Emperor's domains.

who symbolize violent assault upon the ramparts of white supremacy. Yet, Bronzeville rejects neo-Garveyism with its Back-to-Africa emphasis as decisively as it rejects Mr. Mohammed's "Nation in This Wilderness."

Identification with emergent Africa, while providing reinforcement for the sentiment of Race Pride, is not diverting Bronzeville's leadership from the primary goal of full integration into American life. This blending of interest in the New Africa with the American struggle for equality was reflected in the activities of those Race Leaders who, in 1962, were preparing for an Exposition to celebrate the Centennial of the Emancipation Proclamation. Their lobbying had secured financial support from both the Federal and State Governments. Most of the exhibits were to deal with the progress of the Negro in America since slavery, but considerable time and money was also being expended upon preparing an attractive display of "our African background" and of development in modern Africa.

Life in Bronzeville is interesting, often exciting, and always "meaningful"—though usually not in terms of values Richard Wright would have respected or admired. (Yet, like most "intellectuals," he underemphasized the extent to which a serious interest in art, literature, music, and ideas has always existed side by side with the social ritual in the upper and upper-middle classes.) The system is paying off, and occasionally someone "hits the jackpot". Opportunities and money are present for "having a ball" when people want to. The mass culture provides a very wide range of satisfactions. Negro-sparked race riots or mass demonstrations; emigration to "Mother Africa," to the "Soviet Motherland" or to Mr. Mohammed's Utopia have no appeal, for they do not make sense in a Period of Prosperity and the Era of Integration. And the big questions, such as "What of The Bomb?," are seldom asked in Bronzeville.

Negroes in Bronzeville are very much Americans. And this means, too, that if the masses are driven too far they are likely to fight back, despite their sometimes seemingly indifferent reactions to discrimination and segregation. A potential for future violence within Black Metropolis exists that should not and cannot be ignored.

APPENDIX

Black Metropolis 1961

BLACK METROPOLIS WAS ORIGINALLY PUBLISHED DURING THE LAST YEAR OF the second World War. The final chapter, "Of Things to Come," was followed by "A Methodological Note" by Professor W. L. Warner (See Volume II). Both statements reflect the extent to which sociologists and anthropologists were then stepping out of their professional roles to discuss the implications of their findings for a democratic society, and to state their own values.

Remembering the situation after the First World War, the authors expressed their fear that unless full employment was maintained, there was danger of interracial violence after the Second World War. They listed a number of preventive measures which they felt were essential, including the progressive elimination of discrimination and segregation, and a constant interpretation of the Negro's needs to the wider community. Their view of the future was tinged with pessimism.

Professor Warner, on the other hand, was optimistic. He was convinced that ". . . there are indications throughout the world that important changes are on the way . . . the next generation's principal task will be the hard and painful one of destroying color-caste in the United States."

The period between 1950 and 1960 was one of great prosperity for Midwest Metropolis, and although the Negro unemployment rate tends to be three times that of white workers, Negroes have shared in this prosperity. On the national scene, the decade has marked the opening of the Era of Integration. It is relevant to ask how Black Metropolis has fared during this period.

MIDWEST METROPOLIS—POST WAR BOOM

Midwest Metropolis, still "Hog Butcher for the World," is gradually relinquishing its role as "Meat Packer." Still "Player With Railroads and Freight Handler to the Nation," it prefers now to boast of its Midway Airport which handles a larger volume of traffic than any in the nation, and of the larger airport being built. There is hope, too, that the opening of the St. Lawrence Seaway will make Midwest Metropolis a major port. Chicago's metropolitan region is still a top producer of steel (1955 was a peak production year). But the Midwest Metropolis of today is proudest of its new diversified light manufacturing industries, especially in the electrical equipment field. Dreams for the city's future revolve around the prospect of its becoming a major supplier of industrial products to the markets of Asia, Africa, Latin America and Europe. Leaders in Black Metropolis are deeply concerned over the question of where the Negro fits into this vision of the future.

During the past decade, Midwest Metropolis has placed very heavy emphasis upon "urban renewal." Acres of slums have been cleared and gleaming structures of glass and stone and steel have grown from the rubble. The city has taken full advantage of Federal aid for such improvements. New skyscrapers have sprouted on the skyline. Thousands of new homes have sprung up on vacant prairie lots. A web of new highways and super-highways has been woven across the city's vast expanse to handle the terrifying glut of traffic. These highly visible symbols of unprecedented prosperity have sustained and increased the boastful mood of optimism which has always been characteristic of the city. But there has been apprehension in Black Metropolis.

MIDWEST METROPOLIS HAS BECOME "MORE COLORED"

Rapid expansion and diversification of industry, as well as vast public and private programs of building construction during the 1950–60 decade, demanded a constant influx of new workers. As in the past, Negro Americans came to Chicago to meet that need. The Negro population doubled between 1950 and 1960.

In 1840, when the Flight to Freedom was just beginning and Chicago stood as a City of Refuge for runaway slaves, there were only 53 Negroes in the city. Today there are over 800,000. In 1840, there were only 4,470 people in Midwest Metropolis, and of these only about one in a hundred was a Negro. Today, there are over 3,000,000 residents, and almost one out of every four is a Negro.

The Negro population increased from 492,000 to 813,000 between 1950 and 1960. At least 60,000 were migrants from the South. But not all of the increase in Negro population has come by immigration, for the more Negroes in the city the more the population increases through the excess of births over deaths.

While the Negro population has been increasing, the white population within the city limits of Midwest Metropolis has been decreasing. There were 3,112,000 white residents in 1950. In 1960 there were only 2,713,000. The main factor in this population decline has been the flight to the suburbs. If we take the entire Midwest Metropolitan Region into consideration as a unit we will find that the proportion of people who live in the city, as opposed to the "ring" around it, was about 70 per cent in 1940 and 65 per cent in 1950. It was even less in 1960, about one half of the total population of city and suburbs. Most of the people who moved to the suburbs were white. On the whole, Negroes are decidedly not welcome in Suburbia.

THE JOB CEILING STILL EXISTS

Black Metropolis emphasizes the fact that the occupational distribution of Negroes in Midwest Metropolis has never been so fixed and rigid as in the South, and that through the years several factors have operated to widen the range of jobs available to Negroes.[1] As groups of whites move up into the best jobs, Negroes sometimes get better ones. Constant pressure by Negro and interracial organizations occasionally results in categories of work, formerly earmarked as "white" jobs, being thrown open to free competition. The continuing acquisition of higher levels of education and skill by Negroes makes it less easy to bar them from posts for which they are fitted. The whole process of change is sped up by periodic labor shortages and by the operation of "law as a lever" (e.g., the new Illinois state FEPC law); "profit as a prod" (use of Negro salesmen to entice more Negro customers); "government as an example," (a wide range of federal, state, and municipal jobs are open to Negroes, and political appointments of Negroes have been made to new types of posts); and "catastrophe as a catalyst" (the Korean War and the threat of a Third World War).

---

[1] Professor Warner, in his Methodological Note (see Volume II), stressed similarities between the social systems of the South and the North. The authors were more impressed by the differences. The theoretical framework which guided their analysis of Negro-white relations in Chicago (as opposed to the internal structure of the Negro community) has been stated in an article by Horace Cayton and Elaine Ogden, "Research on the Urban Negro," in *The American Journal of Sociology* for September, 1941.

It is relevant to ask how effective these forces have been during the past decade in effecting changes in the Job Ceiling.[2]

An examination of the occupational pyramids in Figure 21a reveals that Negroes found new opportunities in commerce and industry between 1940 and 1950.[3] The proportion of employed Negro men doing various kinds of "service" work (e.g., cleaning, carrying and cooking) dropped from about one person in three to about one in five. The proportion employed in industry rose. But there was no significant change in the category of skilled labor (craftsmen, mechanics, foremen). One out of every five white men were doing such work in 1950, but only one out of every ten Negro men were. The proportions were relatively about the same in 1960.

The most dramatic and significant change has involved the status of employed Negro women. Between 1940 and 1950, the proportion of Negro women in service occupations dropped from almost two out of three to *one* in three. The proportion employed as semi-skilled operatives in industry increased greatly, while at the same time the proportion of Negro women doing clerical work doubled. But despite these very substantial changes, less than 15 per cent of colored women were employed in clerical and sales work in 1950, while over half of all employed white women worked in these fields. By 1960, the proportion of Negro women doing clerical and sales work had risen to about 24 per cent, but at this slow rate it would take almost thirty years for Negro women to "catch up" with white women in these fields! Differences in degree of training and experience may account, in part, for this striking contrast, but such a wide gap is certainly related also to the fact that the city's offices and stores, by 1950, were not

---

[2] The concept of the "Job Ceiling" is developed in Chapter 9. See Figures 15 and 16 on pages 227 and 228, in which the proportions of Negroes and whites holding jobs above and below the skilled labor level are compared by means of bar graphs. The Job Ceiling was just below the skilled labor level in both 1940 and 1950. Figure 19 on page 253 attempts to make graphic the fact that there was wider opportunity for rising above the ceiling in government employment than in other fields.

[3] The data upon which the occupational pyramids are based may be found in publications by Otis D. and Beverly Duncan, *The Negro Population of Chicago* (University of Chicago Press, 1957), and a report prepared by these two scholars for the Office of the Housing and Redevelopment Co-ordinator and the Chicago Plan Commission, *Chicago's Negro Population*, 1956. The 1960 census data were not available in time to permit presentation of comparable occupational pyramids, but the text has been revised to include some statistics figured from *U.S. Census of Population: 1960, Illinois General Social and Economic Characteristics, Tables 74 and 78.*

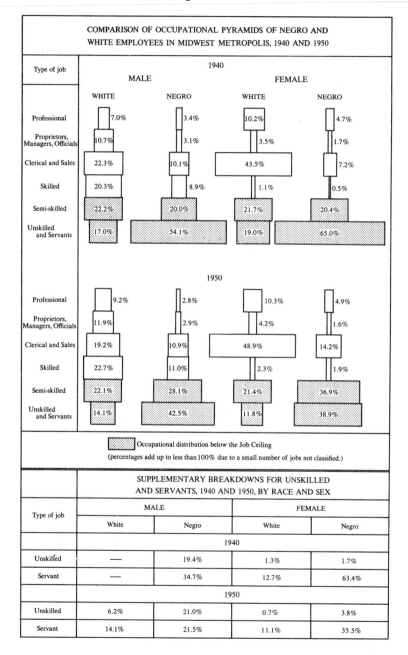

COMPARISON OF OCCUPATIONAL PYRAMIDS OF NEGRO AND
WHITE EMPLOYEES IN MIDWEST METROPOLIS, 1940 AND 1950

1940

MALE FEMALE

WHITE NEGRO WHITE NEGRO

Type of job	WHITE	NEGRO	WHITE	NEGRO
Professional	7.0%	3.4%	10.2%	4.7%
Proprietors, Managers, Officials	10.7%	3.1%	3.5%	1.7%
Clerical and Sales	22.3%	10.1%	43.5%	7.2%
Skilled	20.3%	8.9%	1.1%	0.5%
Semi-skilled	22.2%	20.0%	21.7%	20.4%
Unskilled and Servants	17.0%	54.1%	19.0%	65.0%

1950

	WHITE	NEGRO	WHITE	NEGRO
Professional	9.2%	2.8%	10.3%	4.9%
Proprietors, Managers, Officials	11.9%	2.9%	4.2%	1.6%
Clerical and Sales	19.2%	10.9%	48.9%	14.2%
Skilled	22.7%	11.0%	2.3%	1.9%
Semi-skilled	22.1%	28.1%	21.4%	36.9%
Unskilled and Servants	14.1%	42.5%	11.8%	38.9%

Occupational distribution below the Job Ceiling

(percentages add up to less than 100% due to a small number of jobs not classified.)

SUPPLEMENTARY BREAKDOWNS FOR UNSKILLED
AND SERVANTS, 1940 AND 1950, BY RACE AND SEX

Type of job	MALE		FEMALE	
	White	Negro	White	Negro
1940				
Unskilled	—	19.4%	1.3%	1.7%
Servant	—	34.7%	12.7%	63.4%
1950				
Unskilled	6.2%	21.0%	0.7%	3.8%
Servant	14.1%	21.5%	11.1%	35.5%

willing to accept colored women and girls freely as competitors for jobs, and the barrier against them still existed in 1960.[4]

The Duncans, upon whose study Figure 21a is based, were impressed by the changes in the Job Ceiling and stated that "As a result of the occupational changes of the decade, the non-white was more like the white occupational distribution in 1950 than in 1940."[5] This was true, but the Negro distribution was more *unlike* the white distribution than like it! So long as 70 per cent of Negro men held jobs below the skilled level while only 36 per cent of white men were in these less desirable jobs; and, as long as 75 per cent of Negro women were below this level while only 33 per cent of white women were in the lower status, lower paid jobs, nobody in Midwest Metropolis who was interested in free competition in the field of employment, unrestricted by considerations of race, could be satisfied. There has been constant pressure during the 1950–60 decade for raising the Job Ceiling and, eventually, breaking through it.

But in 1960, about two-thirds of the non-white men were still below the skilled labor level (67.3 per cent) while the same proportion of white men were above it (67.9 per cent). Of whites, 23.6 per cent were employed as craftsmen and foremen, while only 12.3 per cent of non-whites were. In the case of proprietors, managers, and officials, the ratio was even steeper—12.8 per cent of whites were employed in these capacities as compared to 2.6 per cent of non-whites. The Urban League reported in 1961 that "Almost two-thirds of all employed non-whites in the Chicago area work as semi-skilled operatives, service workers, or general laborers. These are the occupations that are least desirable, lowest paid, most often affected by extended periods of unemployment and that have the smallest promotion potential in all industrial classifications. . . . Within the industries employing large numbers of non-whites, the types of jobs they are allowed to perform are severely restricted."[6] It was noted that a survey by the Bureau of Jewish Em-

---

[4] There is some evidence to indicate that a point has been reached where the demand for highly skilled stenographers and typists is such that qualified Negro girls and women could now find jobs in this area. Lack of such opportunity in the past has meant that Negro girls, on the whole, did not deem it worthwhile to prepare for non-existent jobs. Thus, when posts become available, there are few qualified applicants.

[5] Duncan and Duncan (1957), *op. cit.*, p. 74.

[6] The quotations in this paragraph are from a pamphlet, "Equal Rights—Greater Responsibility, the Challenge to Community Leadership in 1961" prepared by the Research Department of the Chicago Urban League for use by participants in a Leadership Conference for Fair Employment practices.

ployment Problems of Chicago revealed that "98 per cent of the white collar job orders received from over 5,000 companies were not available to qualified Negroes." The following industries were cited as those which "seriously limit" the employment of non-whites: banking and finance, insurance, airlines, electrical equipment manufacturing, printing and publishing, chemicals and petroleum, railroads and trucking, medical and health services and construction. These are Chicago's most rapidly expanding industries.[7]

Even in those areas where Negroes have secured a sure foothold and some mobility their position is precarious. A fifth of all Negro workers are concentrated in the metal and food production industries and the Urban League reported in 1961 that "both of these industry groups have declined substantially as a proportion of total employment in the Chicago area since 1950. The shift of large packing plants to other cities in the mid-west, the increase in automation, and lack of opportunity for apprenticeship and for retraining, is creating a situation which during periods of unemployment over the past decade has resulted in a Negro unemployment rate three times that of white workers." Some observers feel that unemployment among Negroes may become chronic during the next decade unless pressures from the Federal and State government open up new areas of opportunity.

By 1960, it was almost impossible to find any leading or responsible citizen in Midwest Metropolis who would defend discrimination in employment on the basis of race or creed. There was a widespread tendency to speak of "the high cost of discrimination" as measured in terms of potential skills not utilized[8] and the exacerbation of social

[7] The Urban League, while taking note of the social pressures within Bronzeville to drop out of school early in order to secure the consumption goods necessary for status, as well as to help add to already low family incomes, feels that there is evidence from studies made of high school drop-outs and junior college students to support the conclusion that Negro students "feel little drive to prepare for occupations in which there is little hope of obtaining employment." They state further, that "Many trainee and apprenticeship programs of companies and unions do not admit non-white youths" and that work-study programs under the auspices of the Chicago Board of Education "cannot be extended in any meaningful way to schools with predominantly non-white students because business and industry will not accept these students." (*"Equal Rights Greater Responsibility,"* Urban League, 1961.) The process becomes circular because when students feel they cannot get jobs they will not prepare and thus when jobs do open up there are few Negro applicants who are qualified.

[8] The most militant fighters against discrimination have conceded the fact that individuals are "piercing the ceiling" at an increased rate, but the Urban League stated its belief that the "progress" often referred to with respect to economic opportunities for non-whites reflects placement of a "select few" or "window dressing placement" in the "non-traditional" employment of Negroes.

problems due to low incomes and uncertain employment among Negroes.[9] There was a general feeling, too, that the whole problem should be redefined in *individual* terms, that no one should be denied the opportunity to work at the highest level of his skill and training no matter what people might think of the Negro group as a whole. The result has been some token employment as well as support for legislation to ensure equality of economic opportunity.

A STATE FEPC NOW OPERATES

By 1961, Negro leaders and white liberals in Midwest Metropolis had succeeded in convincing Illinois' powerful Democratic politicians that the Job Ceiling could never be broken without the aid of a state Fair Employment Practices law and that the Negro voters wanted it. FEPC legislation had passed the House of the Illinois State Legislature in 1947, 1949, 1951, 1953, 1955, 1957, and 1959. However, it had always been "killed" in the Senate. But in 1961, a bill passed the Senate as well as the House and added a new weapon to the arsenal of those fighting discrimination.

The campaign for FEPC legislation was led by a statewide committee with an official of a major steel manufacturing company as its chairman. Businessmen's fears were assuaged by pointing out that

[9] Probably no aspect of the life of Black Metropolis has received more publicity in recent years than the small group of unmarried and deserted women who are receiving Aid to Dependent Children funds. It was alleged that these women were making a racket out of "having more and more babies at public expense" and were "supporting lazy boy friends," etc. Eventually a committee headed by a leading white businessman was set up to investigate the problem; its report has emphasized the extent to which the plight of these broken families is bound up with the existence of the Job Ceiling and the Black Ghetto. The report stated in part:

> Racial discrimination in employment was found to be one of the most serious direct and indirect causes of family disorganization, desertion and illegitimacy. . . . Racial discrimination is one of the most serious causes of family breakdown, desertion and ADC dependency. . . . The great majority had unskilled jobs. The last job for 50 per cent of the grantees was in domestic service. . . . 54 per cent were on the last job more than one year and 18 per cent more than 3 years. The median monthly earning on the last job was rather small for these mothers: $162.22. . . . ADC families live in generally substandard housing at high rentals. The rent allowance is the most generous part of the ADC budget, yet ADC families usually live in over-crowded, rundown buildings. Many are ingenious in making the inside attractive, but the outside is most often slum. The rent paid by non-white families for poorer housing is considerably more than that paid by white families. (Summarized from *Equal Rights—Greater Responsibilities*, Chicago Urban League publication, 1961.)

where FEPC legislation did exist in the United States the emphasis was upon "education, co-operation, conciliation, and full hearings" rather than lawsuits and punitive measures. It was pointed out, too, that nineteen states had passed such legislation without any disastrous effects upon business. There was widespread surprise when, in April, 1961, the Chicago *Daily News* carried an editorial, *FEPC GAINING IN ACCEPTANCE*, which advocated passage of the bill. The editorial referred to a very significant fact, namely, that the board of the Chicago Association of Commerce and Industry had "accepted FEPC in principle, although rejecting some provisions of the pending legislation."

Employers who had already opened the door wider to Negroes felt that their more reluctant colleagues deserved a legislative prod. Employers who were inclined to employ Negroes welcomed the FEPC as a stick with which to beat recalcitrant unions. While no one believed that the passage of the bill would work an overnight revolution many hoped that it might be the beginning of the end of the Job Ceiling in Midwest Metropolis.

NEGRO PURCHASING POWER INCREASES

Although the Job Ceiling did not disappear between 1945 and 1960, large-scale Negro unemployment did, and there was also a significant amount of upgrading below the skilled labor level. *Negro family income increased by 50 per cent between 1950 and 1956 while white family income increased by only 28 per cent.* But even with this increase, the median income for Negroes was only $4,200 per year while that for whites was $5,900. The significance of these increases can be measured in the Negro's improved standard of living since *Black Metropolis* first appeared, and in the wider base presented for living the middle-class way of life. Figure 21b suggests the far-reaching implications of changes-in-income levels for the Negro social class structure.[10] By 1960 the median family income for Midwest Metropolis had increased to $7,342; for Black Metropolis to $4,786.

There is evidence that Negroes spend a disproportionately high amount of this income for inadequate housing. One reliable source reports that:

[10] The increase in purchasing power also strengthened Negro publications in their appeal for advertising, and groups bargaining for better job opportunities for Negroes. As early as 1953, a study was published for the benefit of the general business world, Nickolas L. Barnes', *Some Potentialities and Limitations of the Negro Market* ·· *Chicago* (T and T Publishing Company, Chicago).

. . . it is clear that non-white families receive less "quality" per dollar spent on housing than do white families; and the relatively high proportion of non-white families in substandard housing can be attributed only in small part to their relative economic disadvantage (i.e., they are able to pay for better housing than they can secure). Non-white families apparently obtain no more space per housing dollar than do white families, but the space which they obtain is likely to be of poorer quality. In Chicago, non-whites are more than twice as likely as whites to be living in substandard housing if they are renters, six times as likely if they are home owners.[11]

Figure 21b

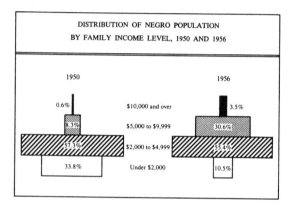

DISTRIBUTION OF NEGRO POPULATION
BY FAMILY INCOME LEVEL, 1950 AND 1956

1950   1956

0.6% $10,000 and over   3.5%

8.3% $5,000 to $9,999   30.6%

57.3% $2,000 to $4,999   55.4%

33.8%   Under $2,000   10.5%

The fact that a much larger proportion of Negroes than whites is still in lower status occupations and in lower income groups tends to perpetuate the image of *The Negro* as being "below" or "inferior to" whites. It also makes much much harder the assemblying by Negro families and community organizations of resources for coping effectively with problems such as crime, juvenile delinquency and family disorganization. The total situation forces whites in Black Metropolis to think of Negroes as "undesirable neighbors." Thus, the Job Ceiling is one factor in creating conditions which lead to the persistence of a Black Ghetto.

THE BLACK GHETTO EXPANDS

Chapter 8 of *Black Metropolis* tells the story of how a "Black Belt" came into existence, and how Negroes were kept within it by the operation of restrictive covenants. Less than three years after the book was published, the Supreme Court of the United States declared re-

[11] Duncan, Beverly and Hauser, Philip M., *Housing a Metropolis* (The Free Press, 1960), pp. 193, 196 and 207.

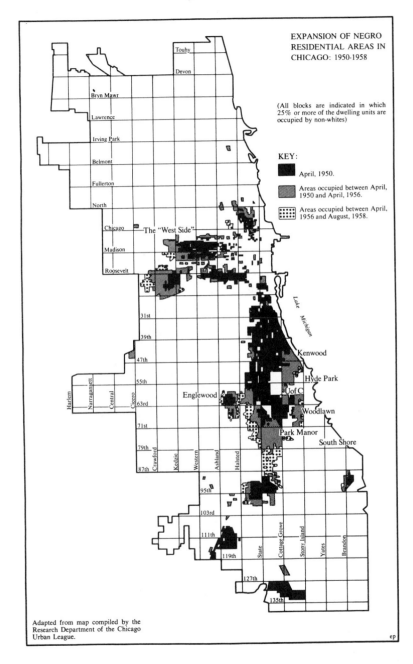

EXPANSION OF NEGRO
RESIDENTIAL AREAS IN
CHICAGO: 1950-1958

(All blocks are indicated in which
25% or more of the dwelling units are
occupied by non-whites)

KEY:

April, 1950.

Areas occupied between April,
1950 and April, 1956.

Areas occupied between April,
1956 and August, 1958.

Adapted from map compiled by the
Research Department of the Chicago
Urban League.

Figure 21d

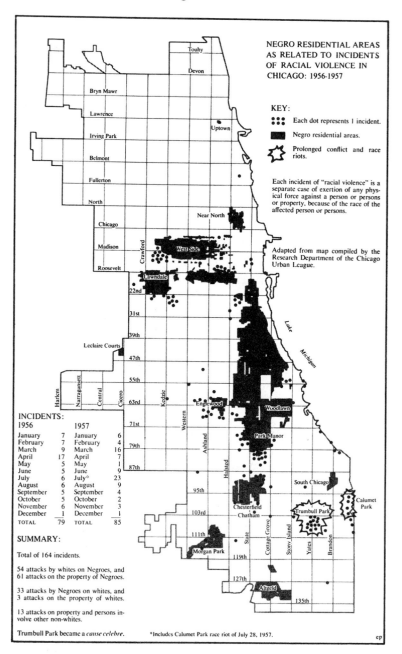

strictive covenants unenforceable in the courts. Covenants were still legal but now had to be enforced by private action. In some areas of Midwest Metropolis the action was violent, but neither frantic appeals to "Keep This Neighborhood White" nor violence prevented the expansion of the Black Belt. Figure 21c shows how the Negro population spread out between April of 1950 and August of 1958.[12]

The expansion took place in three main directions: (a) on the West Side where a small Negro settlement grew rapidly as Negroes of all social classes began to occupy houses and apartments relinquished by a predominantly Jewish population which moved northward and to the suburbs. Scattered violence accompanied this shift; (b) toward Lake Michigan to the east and south, as the Negro population filtered into Kenwood and Hyde Park and then made a jump around the University of Chicago into Woodlawn. Here, there was very little violent resistance; and (c) directly southward from the tip of the 1950 "Black Belt" and west into Englewood. Here the white population fought a bitter rearguard action with fire and bomb as the main weapons, and gang and mob harassment as a supporting measure. Figure 21d indicates the extent of the violence during a two-year period, 1956 and 1957.[13] There were 36 additional attacks upon Negro property in 1958, but the amount of violence began to diminish after that year.

Rapid expansion of the Black Belt after 1948 was due to the Negro's willingness—and ability—to pay inflated prices for property and to the awareness of real estate men (Negro and white) that larger profits per unit could be made from renting to Negroes than from renting to whites.[14] Many white owners were willing to sell or to move away

[12] Cf. pp. 62–64, "Black Lebensraum."

[13] Cf. with map on p. 63. Note that the patterning of violence against Negroes remains the same after 40 years.

[14] The Duncans (1956) state that ". . . there is some evidence that non-whites are forced to pay higher prices than whites for comparable dwellings. For example, in 1947 and 1948 in the Woodlawn area, it has been estimated that Negro buyers paid 28 to 51 per cent more than white buyers for one and two unit structures." It is now rather generally agreed that there is an upward movement of prices in Chicago when Negroes move in. See E.F. Schietinger, "Racial Succession and Value of Small Residential Properties," *The American Sociological Review*, 16, December, 1951. This knowledge is based upon detailed research by various individuals and groups connected with the University of Chicago. As the reader will note, this matter had not been cleared up when *Black Metropolis* was originally published and the authors accepted the view which was then general that property values were depressed by the moving in of Negroes. (Cf. *Black Metropolis*, pp. 174–175.)

and rent their property to Negroes. Needing living space as they did, plenty of Negroes were willing to run the risk of violence to themselves and their property by entering white neighborhoods. Some enterprising white realtors discovered that they could make a profit at both ends of the transaction—by promising to secure property for whites on the edge of the city or in the suburbs where they would be "safe from Negroes," and by promising to get Negroes into areas formerly barred to them. The expansion would not, however, have been possible had there not been a large amount of new building available to whites but denied to Negroes. (See Figure 21e for an analysis of new construction during the single year, 1956).

The story of the expansion of the Black Belt eastward toward Lake Michigan has historic significance. Here, for the first time, a group of white people in Midwest Metropolis made a deliberate attempt to create "interracial neighborhoods with high community standards," that is, to accept Negroes as neighbors on the basis of their social class position rather than on the basis of race. Very soon after the Supreme Court decision of 1948, the Oakland-Kenwood Association, one of the first groups to introduce restrictive covenants in Chicago, decided to reverse its stand and to substitute "occupancy standard" agreements for racial covenants. But the pressure of the housing shortage doomed this experiment.

Higher status residents directly to the south in Kenwood lived in an area zoned for single family occupancy. As members of the Negro upper and upper-middle class began to buy into this area, a basis was laid for interracial cooperation between Negroes and whites of similar status. Faced with an "invasion" by Negroes, the residents of Hyde Park, just south of Kenwood, organized the Hyde Park-Kenwood Community Conference to prevent the precipitous flight of white people and to form block organizations of whites, Negroes, and Orientals to keep the neighborhood safe, clean, and orderly. Eventually, with support from several philanthropic organizations, they proceeded to draw up a plan for urban renewal and redevelopment in the area.

The University of Chicago, which had been viewing its "encirclement" by Negroes with alarm, took independent action to "protect" its neighborhood by sponsoring the organization of a South-East Chicago Commission, which at first concerned itself primarily with crime prevention. Later, a plan for demolishing substandard structures eliminated both poor housing and congregation points of lower-class Negroes, poor whites and Puerto Ricans. It encouraged rebuilding at

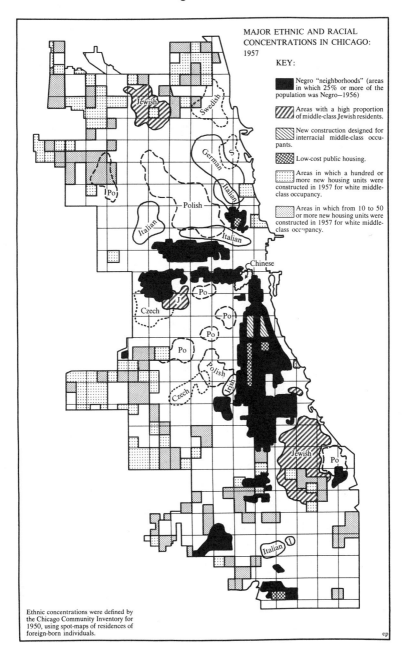

MAJOR ETHNIC AND RACIAL
CONCENTRATIONS IN CHICAGO:
1957

KEY:

Negro "neighborhoods" (areas
in which 25% or more of the
population was Negro—1956)

Areas with a high proportion
of middle-class Jewish residents.

New construction designed for
interracial middle-class occupants.

Low-cost public housing.

Areas in which a hundred or
more new housing units were
constructed in 1957 for white middle-
class occupancy.

Areas in which from 10 to 50
or more new housing units were
constructed in 1957 for white middle-
class occupancy.

Ethnic concentrations were defined by
the Chicago Community Inventory for
1950, using spot-maps of residences of
foreign-born individuals.

ep

higher income levels which automatically limited the proportion of Negroes who could live in the area. Eventually the University and the Hyde Park-Kenwood Community Conference began to co-operate in implementing a comprehensive plan for the whole lakeside area from 47th Street to 63rd Street. Many Negroes, as well as the Chicago *Defender* criticized these organizations for erecting what they called a "middle-class island" while the masses of Negroes had inadequate housing. The interracial groups in the area defended themselves on the grounds that they were setting a pattern for integrated living which could be emulated in other parts of the city.[15]

URBAN REDEVELOPMENT REINFORCES
THE BLACK GHETTO

The expansion of the Black Belt has taken place within the context of Chicago's elaborate plans for urban renewal and redevelopment. The question raised by Negroes in 1945 as to their future under such plans was still being raised in 1961. By 1951, the reclamation of the inner city was under way. A bond issue had made it possible to assemble land for resale to private developers at a generous write-down. Federal funds were also available. The New York Life Insurance Company was willing to erect a group of high-rise apartment buildings where the Negro slums stood. Thanks to federal regulations and the co-operation of the more enlightened real estate circles, a housing development, Lake Meadows, emerged where today white and colored middle-class residents live side by side and share the common facilities of supermart, clubhouse and schools. Nearby, the Michael Reese Hospital has erected a similar development, Prairie Shores. The colorline has thus been breached in dramatic fashion, although very few Negroes profit by it. To carry out this massive project of renewal, many of the lower-class Negro residents were moved westward about a mile into a group of high-rise low-income public housing projects. Others are scattered throughout middle-class communities to the horror of both white and Negro residents.

Persistent protest from white communities throughout Chicago has

---

[15] Julia Abrahamson, *A Neighborhood Finds Itself* (Harper, 1959) and Peter Rossi, *The Politics of Urban Renewal* (The Free Press, 1961) tell the story of the Hyde Park-Kenwood urban renewal effort and its repercussions.

led the Chicago Housing Authority to adopt a pattern of building most of its new low-cost housing along the western margin of the Black Belt in an undesirable area near the railroad tracks. A five-mile rim of high-rise public housing is gradually going up as a monument to Midwest Metropolis' insistence upon residential segregation. Even this adjustment to the demolition of slums in the Black Belt is resisted in some quarters on the grounds that it is "creeping socialism."

IS THERE ANY PROSPECT OF OPEN OCCUPANCY?

Chicago stands near the top of the list of American cities in the extent to which Negroes are segregated. There is widespread concern over the fact that the Black Belt is now reaching the limits of its expansion without danger of generating wholesale violence or the taking over of the high-income area, Lake Shore, just south of the University of Chicago. Liberals in integrated communities are demanding that other sections of the city "take their share of Negroes." Some realtors, most sociologists, and many social workers feel that unless the Black Belt is thinned out and overcrowding eliminated, and unless its block-by-block expansion is stopped, there will be incessant violence around its periphery as well as increased social disorganization within. These groups have been supporting an "open occupancy bill."

In 1961 when an open occupancy bill was laid before the city council, Negro politicians as well as white "ducked it," for they did not wish to embarrass aldermen loyal to the machine but living in wards where it would be political suicide to vote for open occupancy. The City Council voted to recommend to the State Legislature that it pass such a bill. Although the Chicago *Daily News* had supported FEPC legislation, it now drew the line at residential desegregation by law in an editorial "Discriminating Landlords."[16] The bill did not pass.

THE LINE OF COLOR IS STILL SHIFTING—BUT SLOWLY

The processes by which the Midwest Metropolis color-line has shifted over the years were discussed in detail in Chapter 10. There is still a *"shifting* line of color." Change in Chicago race relations has been hastened by the national trend toward desegregation and "integration," and by subtle, though nevertheless real, pressures emanating

[16] The editorial read, in part, as follows: We do not believe that the 38–7 vote (of the City Council) really reflects the convictions of the citizens of

from the dramatic postwar rise in the power and prestige of the Asian and African nations. On the local scene, considerations of political expediency and economic necessity have also continued to reinforce the efforts of those people, white and colored, who fight against segregation and discrimination because they believe in The American Dream.[17]

The beginning of the ideological assault upon the color-line during the closing years of the Second World War has been described in Chapter 10. The pressure has never been relaxed. The Mayor's Commission on Human Relations eventually became an institutionalized increment of the city government—The Chicago Commission on Human Relations. A coalition between trade union leaders and middle-class liberals functions on the race-relations front through a complex network of voluntary associations and committees in alliance with Negro pressure groups. The Communists are no longer an active component of this "united front." Resistance to change also finds institutional expression through numerous "neighborhood improvement associations" and "white property owners' associations," sometimes operating in a loose alliance with the not-too-respectable groups of the "radical right," such as the now inactive White Circle League. The anti-Negro organizations create a permissive atmosphere within neighborhoods for teen-age violence to express itself. Retaliatory aggression on the part of young Negroes sometimes brings a community to the verge of race riots. But careful police work has prevented the

---

Chicago on such a law, although it is true, and most people know it, that the inability of Negroes to find homes readily outside of a few areas creates one of the city's most serious problems.

We said the other day that the time had come to accept a fair employment practices law. It does not follow however that the case for compulsion in other fields is equally meritorious. . . .

The standards for choosing an employee and for choosing a tenant are not the same. In one, the test is can he do the work? In the other a landlord is rightly interested in obtaining a harmonious group. If he does not achieve it he is creating for himself not only trouble, but possible expense in turnover. . . .

The problem of racial discrimination in housing can and must be solved. We urge the agencies concerned with education in this field to redouble their zeal. And property owners should take note of the strength of the sentiment for compulsion and accelerate their efforts to make it unnecessary while they still have a free choice.

[17] The trends of the past decade confirm the general propositions about the type of social system which organizes Negro-white relations in northern cities, as they were stated in the first edition of Black Metropolis (pp. 756–757).

spread of violence throughout the city, and a press which stands firm for law and order 'and for racial equality, as well as crusading radio and TV commentators, have helped to create a "climate of opinion" in which the balance is tipped, at present, toward progressive social change in race relations.

Although the Job Ceiling and the Black Ghetto still persist, the color-line is now drawn less tightly in some areas of the city's life. The vigilance of The Chicago Commission on Human Relations and its quiet work of education have almost eliminated discrimination in downtown hotels and restaurants. Negroes now move about in the central business district with a confidence that they have not shown since the Great Migration shattered the structure of the pre-World War I "Golden Age" of race relations in Chicago. Fraternization across the color-line in homes and public places probably occurs with greater frequency and creates less adverse comment than it did fifteen years ago, and mixed couples report that they find people less likely to stare at them in public and more inclined to treat them merely as facts of urban life, while reprisals on the part of parents and relatives seem to be somewhat less severe. The most significant change involves an increase in the proportion of mixed marriages in which the husband is white. Yet, there are still areas of the city where Negroes do not find it safe to walk after dark and where a mixed couple would be risking assault and battery. Beaches are still major tension points.

"Token representation" of Negroes on various boards and committees, and in churches, schools, and business enterprises is becoming fashionable. The seeds of the future seem to be sprouting in a few integrated apartment buildings and interracial churches that have come into being during the last decade. The ritualization of equality at civic banquets and "brotherhood" ceremonies has become routine, and ever-widening circles of white people continuously reaffirm their loyalty to the ideal of eventual complete and total integration.

But Negroes still express impatience with the rate of change. Early in 1962 the NAACP and the Urban League were demanding transfer of children from overcrowded Black Belt schools into vacant classrooms in adjacent white areas. Middle-class Negro mothers were being arrested for conducting "sit-ins" at schools, while college students, colored and white, were sleeping in front of the office of the Chancellor of the University of Chicago in protest against "controlled integration" in Hyde Park. Negroes are taking seriously the *Defender's* slogan, "Race prejudice must be destroyed."

69 70 71 72 73   12 11 10 9 8 7 6

Postscript 1969

DURING THE PAST EIGHT YEARS, MIDWEST METROPOLIS, LIKE A NUMBER OF other large American cities, has continued to grow more "colored" and more segregated.[1] In 1960, there were somewhat more than 800,000 Negroes in Chicago; by 1969, almost a million. The proportion of Negro to white residents had risen from 14 per cent in 1950 to 23 per cent in 1960 to 28 per cent in 1965. Some demographers predict that the 50 per cent level will be reached by 1984.[2] Awareness of these trends has affected attitudes and collective behavior of both Negroes and whites in Chicago profoundly.

Open occupancy was no closer to realization in 1969 than it had been in 1961, when the City Council passed the buck for fair housing legislation to the State Legislature (cf. p. lvii). Since 1966, however, the Chicago Commission on Human Relations has been able to secure the co-operation of some of the most influential individuals in the metropolitan area real estate business in a program to break down discrimination in rental and sales. Their efforts have resulted not in increased residential integration, however, but rather in enlargement of the existing ghettos and genesis of some new ones. Middle-class Chicagoans still have a tendency to flee to the suburbs to avoid Negro neighbors.

Black Metropolis has become ecologically more compact and socially more differentiated as it grows. The three concentrations of Negro population northwest of the downtown business area (The Loop) have fused into one large West Side ghetto (cf. Figs. 21c and 21d, pp. li and lii). The gaps between the main South Side concentration (referred to

[1] The U.S. Bureau of Labor Report No. 332, *Social and Economic Conditions of Negroes in the United States*, October, 1967, points out (p. 12) that "In most of the 12 large cities where special censuses were taken in the mid-1960s the per cent of Negroes living in neighborhoods of greatest Negro concentration has increased since 1960."

[2] A list of cities and the year in which they are likely to reach the 50 per cent Negro point is given in *Report of the National Advisory Committee on Civil Disorders* (Bantam Books, 1968), p. 391. See also Philip Hauser, *Projections for the City of Chicago and the Chicago Standard Metropolitan Statistical Area, 1970–1980* (Chicago Community Inventory, 1963).

as "Bronzeville" in Vol. II) and Englewood to the west, and Chesterfield and Chatham to the south, have closed up. There has been a massive population drift eastward toward Lake Michigan from Woodlawn and Park Manor into the former relatively high status South Shore, whose white leaders have tried to use the Hyde Park–Kenwood approach to what the residents perceive as an "invasion" (cf. pp. liv-lvi). The lower-middle-class white ethnic-group areas to the northwest and southwest of the expanding ghettos have used violence and threat of violence to prevent either block-by-block expansion or what they define as "infiltration," as similar neighborhoods have done in the past (cf. Figs. 21d and 21e, pp. lii and lv). Today, however, they insist that a desire to preserve neighborhood stability, not bigotry or racial bias, motivates them.

The South Side ghetto has become more "gilded" as a large amount of property in good condition has been turned over to middle-class Negroes; a low-income black population has inherited the deteriorating structures of the West Side, some of which a few years ago were occupied by middle-class Negroes who had acquired them during the 1950s from the whites. The West Side was the scene of violent outbursts during the summer of 1966 and in April, 1968.

SOCIAL CLASS AND RELATIVE DEPRIVATION

The boom in Midwest Metropolis continues, accelerated by the escalation of the Vietnam war after 1965 (cf. xli-xlii). The median income of the black residents is higher than it was in 1961 but is still lower than that of whites. The shapes of the occupational pyramids for blacks and whites are still essentially the same (cf. Fig. 21a). However, the upward tilting of the Job Ceiling, described in 1961, has continued (see pp. xliii-xlviii), and in absolute numbers the size of the Negro white-collar class has increased greatly. An Urban League study in 1966 reported, "Relative to white workers of similar backgrounds, Negro managers, professionals, operatives, and clericals have been able to maintain their relative income positions while experiencing substantial increases in living standards resulting from the current economic prosperity."[3] The era of integration is still paying off for this stratum of

[3] Bennett Hymer, *The Negro Labor Market in Chicago, 1966*, A Chicago Urban League Report, 1967, p. 3.

the population—about a fifth of all black adults. Another group, too, were reaping substantial rewards from the expanding economy: *". . . skilled and semi-skilled workers, who together, form from 40 to 50 percent of the total Negro labor force, have been the major beneficiaries of recent changes in hiring policies."*[4] They, with the salaried white-collar group, form the stable core of a middle-class that differs little in its aspirations from its white counterpart.

About 40 per cent of the black labor force, however, had little reason to be enthusiastic over talk about either "integration" or "prosperity." The Urban League report of 1966 pointed out that there were between 190,000 and 225,000 unskilled Negro workers employed in factory jobs or service industries where not only was the pay low, but also ". . . relative to unskilled white workers, the earnings of unskilled Negroes remains as far behind as in 1957."[5] The passage of three years did little to alter this situation.

About one-fifth of the entire black labor force, in 1966, a peak prosperity year in Midwest Metropolis, was employed at incomes below the poverty line (set at $3,000 a year for a family of four in 1966). Many of these inadequately paid workers were also from time to time forced into the ranks of the unemployed by temporary lay-offs or closure and relocation of businesses. The Urban League assessment was that these workers formed ". . . a black urban peasantry that constitutes a pool of redundant surplus labor . . ." used only when white labor was not available or to take up the slack during periods of expansion in specific industries or business enterprises. They were competing in a dual labor market that persisted as one aspect of what Professor Warner calls "caste" and some sociologists today call "institutionalized racism." There was general agreement that these victims of sub-employment, along with the small group of chronically unemployed and women receiving Aid to Dependent Children (cf. p. xlviii, n.), could only break out of this submerged position by being trained for employment in those types of occupations above the Job Ceiling that had recently been opened up to Negroes because of a tight labor market as well as deliberate changes in hiring policy. Job-training programs have loomed large in the strategy for changing the status of the Negro in Midwest

[4] *Ibid.*, p. 3.
[5] *Ibid.*, pp. 3–4.

Metropolis since 1966. Implementation of such programs received widespread support after events in the summer of that year shook up the complacent.

The Urban League report of 1966 concluded with the comment that, "The conditions under which this urban peasantry work and live are responsible for the outbreaks of racial violence that occurred during the past year." The reference was to disorders on the West Side that led to 533 arrests, (including 155 juveniles), and three fatalities. Scores of civilians and police were injured during the rock-throwing, firebombing, and looting. Over 4,000 National Guardsmen were summoned to aid the police.

After this outburst in the West Side ghetto, there was increased sensitivity to the fact that the fuse that touches off such explosions is to be found among the group of unemployed youths between the ages of sixteen and nineteen, over 25 per cent of whom remain unemployed year after year, as compared with only about 12 per cent of white youth in the same age-bracket. Grossly inadequate ghetto schools have left them unprepared for the job market, outright discrimination against them is prevalent, job specifications have been set unrealistically high, and records of arrests for misdemeanors have constituted a barrier for many of them. In the years following the 1966 violence, some attempt was made to attack these problems, but with very limited success.

The major insight derived from reflection on the 1966 incident has been the realization that in a society that stresses the maximizing of consumption through the hard sell over TV and radio, by mail, and in newspapers and magazines, as well as through door-to-door sales, the black poor are continuously measuring their standard of living against that of the white majority that surrounds them, and against that of the Negroes who have got ahead and left them behind. The poor in American ghettos may not walk the streets in rags or collapse from hunger as the poor do in the slums of Calcutta (or as some of their kinsmen in the rural South do), but they have a burning sense of resentment over what they define as an unjust distribution of material goods and of opportunities to acquire money to buy them. "Liberating" a TV set is one way of expressing it. Their behavior is to be understood in terms of the principle of *relative* deprivation.

VIOLENCE — SPECTRE AND SPUR

Black Metropolis emerged as a self-conscious collectivity as a result of the Race Riot of 1919. The white Establishment as well as class-conscious radicals have been haunted, since then, by the spectre of another such conflict occurring in the future.[6] During the forty-eight years between 1919 and 1966, isolated episodes of small-scale violence were endemic in Midwest Metropolis but there were no major "race riots," even though other large cities experienced them. Nor did the pattern of widespread attacks on white property and policemen in the ghetto emerge as early in Chicago as it did elsewhere. The reasons are complex (including a large measure of good luck), but are due in part to measures taken immediately after World War II to prevent large-scale interracial violence, and continuing preoccupation with this problem.[7] But Chicago, like the rest of the United States, has not yet been willing to pay the price, in the money and inconvenience that massive structural transformations require, to abolish poverty and to assure full equality of opportunity to Negroes. Therefore, black attitudes toward violence cannot be the same as those of white people. What was true of Black Metropolis in 1945 was true when this book was updated in 1961 and is still true today: *"While all responsible Negroes try to prevent violent conflicts, their primary interest is in the complete abolition of political and economic subordination and enforced segregation."*[8]

Ghetto outbursts in Harlem, Rochester, and Philadelphia in 1964 signaled the beginning of an urban black revolt, spontaneous and ele-mental, not planned and organized. After Watts in 1965, civic leaders and ministers in Black Metropolis moved quickly to try to provide *non-violent* action alternatives. They organized a broadly based "Freedom Movement" and invited Martin Luther King to come to the city to lead in the organization of tenant unions on the West Side and to spearhead an open-occupancy campaign in white neighborhoods. Mean-

[6] A discussion of riots in the early nineteenth century arising from the im-portation of Negro strikebreakers is presented in Allan H. Spear's definitive work, *Black Chicago: The Making of a Negro Ghetto, 1890–1920* (University of Chicago Press, 1967), pp. 47–48. The impact of the 1919 riot is analyzed in *Black Metropolis*, Vol. I, Ch. 4, "Race Riot and Aftermath."

[7] Efforts to prevent a riot after World War II are described in detail in *Black Metropolis*, Vol. I, pp. 89–96.

[8] *Ibid.*, Vol. II, Ch. 24, "Of Things to Come," p. 766 (italics in original).

while, the pace of job-training and placement programs was stepped up. Although the leaders of the major West Side gangs—the Vice Lords and the Satans—gave Dr. King a pledge of non-violence for the summer of 1966, a serious disturbance broke out in July. It had overtones of reprisal for the violence being visited upon Dr. King and his nonviolent marchers in white neighborhoods. He suggested to the Mayor that instead of denouncing the perpetrators of the violence, he call upon the city to remove the conditions that breed interracial violence.

The Chicago Conference on Religion and Race, composed predominantly of white liberals, convened a "summit conference" to bring the leaders of the Freedom Movement and the economic and political leaders of the Chicago metropolitan area together. Mayor Daley was primarily concerned with extracting a promise from the protest leaders not to march into white neighborhoods any more. The Freedom Movement gave a pledge in return for one from the Chicago Real Estate Board and a group of prominent businessmen to begin immediately a series of moves to abolish the dual market in real estate. Other committees of prominent citizens were established to attack the Job Ceiling and to prevent police brutality. The Freedom Movement then adopted a wait-and-see attitude.

Two years before the events of summer 1966, the National Opinion Research Center of the University of Chicago (NORC) found that over two-thirds of the Negro respondents in the city agreed with the statement, "Violence will never help Negroes get equal rights." But there was a significant ambivalence in the reactions of the black community, since 55 per cent also said that they believed "riots do some good"![9] The hasty convening of the "summit conference," after the Mayor and Congressman Dawson had been denouncing Dr. King for months as an "outside agitator," undoubtedly confirmed them in their opinion that what was a spectre to whites was also a spur to action. No decisive action was taken until after the "riot."

Chicago was spared a serious outburst in 1967, a very "hot" summer nationally, which led President Johnson to appoint the National Advisory Committee on Civil Disorders. But in April, 1968, when Martin

---

[9] Gary T. Marx, *Protest and Prejudice: A Study of Belief in the Black Community* (Harper and Row, 1967), Ch. 1, "The Climate of Opinion on Civil Rights Issues." Tables 1–26, pp. 6–45, give comparative data for Negroes in Chicago, New York, Atlanta, and Birmingham.

Luther King was assassinated, the West Side exploded again. Chicago was one of the three cities in the nation where the ghetto outburst was most costly.[10] A middle-aged woman, resenting a term used by an interviewer, said: *"I* don't think there was any *riot* over here. This was an *insurrection."* Having burned out blocks of white-owned stores, many people now felt as did the man who said, "Stores should put something back into the community. We should have 50 per cent of the stores. We need some co-operatives. We want political control and we want black policemen."[11] Some people wanted black ownership of *all* the stores. A demand for Black Power welled up after the 1968 West Side outburst. It was generated by a pattern of Negro-white relations *within* the ghetto that has not changed appreciably in half a century (cf. p. 197, "White People in Negro Communities").

THE QUEST FOR BLACK POWER

The slogan "Black Power" gained wide currency nationally during the summer of 1966. Those who used it meant "defining ourselves for ourselves," organizing black pressure groups separately from white ("getting ourselves together"), but forming coalitions with selected groups of whites in order to "T.C.B.," (i.e., take care of business)— social and economic as well as political. Young militants, devotees of Frantz Fanon and Malcolm X, insisted that "any means necessary" to realize Black Power were legitimate.[12] More conservative groups retained their devotion to non-violence while adopting the Black Power concept, either implicitly or explicitly. The events in Chicago during

---

[10] Between April 4 and April 11, 9 persons were killed, 500 injured, and 2,931 arrested. Nearly 12,000 National Guardsmen and Federal Troops were involved. Property damage was assessed at $11,000,000 from arson, breakage, and pillage. Both Washington, D. C., and Baltimore had more arrests and greater property damage. Fatalities for Washington were 11 and for Baltimore 6. Casualties were low owing to policy decisions taken not to shoot looters. Mayor Daley subsequently alienated large segments of Negro opinion by an off-the-cuff statement that he thought looters should be shot. He softened it later.

[11] The quotations are from comments made to interviewers for a study carried out by a group of black community leaders organized as the Greater Chicago Citizens Riot Probe Commission.

[12] Stokely Carmichael, who first popularized the phrase, published a very moderate statement of goals and means in collaboration with a professor of political science, Charles V. Hamilton, in their *Black Power: The Politics of Liberation in America* (A Vintage Book, 1967).

the summer of 1966 were an expression of Black Power in both its violent and non-violent dimensions.

The argument still goes on in Black Metropolis as to whether or not it was a wise decision to call off the demonstrations during the summer of 1966 in exchange for promises from the white Establishment. By the end of the following year West Siders, particularly, were convinced that they got nothing from the deal. The Urban League Research Department had made a careful assessment in 1965 of the extent to which Negro leaders were in a position to influence basic decisions in the Chicago metropolitan region and had stated that *"The conclusions are simple and stark, that Negroes are virtually excluded from the major established positions of power and influence in all sectors of metropolitan life."*[13]

The people of Black Metropolis did not need an Urban League study to tell them this. They have always relied upon mass pressure to provide leverage for their leaders.[14] In the 1964 NORC survey, over two-thirds of the respondents reported that they believed that demonstrations had "helped a great deal" and another fifth thought that they had "helped a little." About 95 per cent thought that Martin Luther King was the leader who had "done most" for Negroes. The Freedom Movement knew what it was doing when it brought him to the city two years later. But just as in the 1930s, when they supported the Communists in order to generate some pressure but continued to vote Democratic, so, now, they did not break away from the Daley political machine. When he made his unprecedented bid for a fourth term during the year after the Freedom Movement campaign, and asked for the black vote, they gave him 85 per cent of it. At the same time, new leaders were organizing for new goals—Black Power—at the neighborhood level.

The West Side, in the wake of the destructive 1968 outburst, began

---

[13] Harold Baron, *Negroes in Policy-Making Positions in Chicago: A Study in Black Powerlessness,* An Urban League Research Report, released in 1968 with a covering letter that contains the quotation. Almost 11,000 policy-making positions in both public and private sectors were examined in 1965, *before* the Black Power upsurge began among the militants.

[14] For a case in the 1880s, see Vol. I, p. 44, and for the period of the 1930s and 1940s, pp. 83–96 and 340–341. For an analysis of strategies of "Advancing the Race," see Vol. II, "The Organization of Discontent," "Bronzeville's United Front," and "Mobilizing the Community," pp. 730–744.

to mobilize its resources to insist that rebuilding take place only on terms set by the residents—black ownership and control of most of the businesses and rental property. Several agencies became involved in the politics of planning and in trying to compose differences between themselves in order to present a "united black front." Some national church organizations and philanthropic foundations threw their weight behind attempts to strengthen "black capitalism" in the area. One of the significant events was a split in the ranks of one of the most notorious gangs, a faction of which, calling itself the *Conservative* Vice Lords, began to receive widespread commendation for its newly opened business enterprises, established with foundation support. This concept of Black Power did not go unchallenged.[15] By 1969, the West Side had become the Chicago turf of the Black Panthers, who insisted that only revolutionary reconstruction of the entire society could solve the problems of the black "internal colony." Assailing both the "black capitalists" and the "cultural nationalists" as incipient racists, they began to try to cement an alliance with an organization of Appalachian whites—the Young Patriots—and with Spanish-speaking minorities through the Young Lords. Highly disciplined and neatly uniformed, with black berets and guns in hand, serving breakfasts to school children, the small group of Panthers had a potential influence that was not to be underestimated. When Crane Community College installed a black president, Panthers were on the platform along with the wife of Malcolm X, whose name the college is to bear in the future. In the summer of 1969, shoot-outs began as the F.B.I. and the Chicago police attempted to destroy the Black Panther headquarters and to arrest their leaders.

On the South Side, which was only slightly affected by the rioting after Dr. King's death, the Blackstone Rangers, core unit in a gang

[15] Large segments of the population of Black Metropolis have clung persistently to the very old myth, supported by leaders as diverse as Booker T. Washington, Marcus Garvey, and W. E. B. Du Bois of, "salvation via Negro business." The white Establishment in the United States has thrown its weight behind an interpretation of Black Power that has aroused new hopes that black business will play a primary role in solving ghetto problems—once it has secured the capital to grow strong. (See E. Franklin Frazier, *Black Bourgeoisie,* Free Press paperback, 1965, Ch. VII, "Negro Business: A Social Myth"; *Black Metropolis,* Vol. II, Ch. 16, "Negro Business: Myth and Fact," and Allan H. Spear, *op. cit.,* Ch. 6, "Business and Politics—The Quest for Self Sufficiency," and Ch. 10, "The Impact of the Migration: Business and Politics.")

federation known as the Black P. (Power? Peace? Pride?) Stone Nation, claimed the credit for having kept the South Side "cool" when the West Side went up in flames. They began to reap the reward in increased moral and financial support for several businesses they had already embarked upon. Their leaders, when removed from O.E.O. project payrolls after the McClellan hearings, found other Establishment-sponsored posts. The Daley machine has blown hot and cold on the Rangers. Officially, the Gang Intelligence Unit (G.I.U.) of the Police Department has the assignment to infiltrate and dismantle the B.P. Stone Nation as well as other Chicago gangs. On the other hand, the willingness of the Rangers to oppose the Panthers (who were wooing the Disciples, traditional enemies of "the Stones"), and thus to help save the South Side from "Communist" influence, made the Blackstone Rangers useful to the Democratic political machine. The Rangers were reputed to be receiving a cut on gambling and prostitution for their patriotic services. Yet by the fall of 1969, some of their most prominent leaders were jailed and the Mayor was saying that gangs must be wiped out.

One South Side leader during 1969 was trying to involve both the Panthers and the B.P. Stone Nation in constructive activity as supporters of his own organization—Operation Breadbasket. The organization uses picketing and boycotts to wrest jobs from reluctant white employers, to pressure contractors to employ Negroes on work done in black communities, and to give sub-contracts to black contractors. Chicago in 1969 was the testing ground for what might grow into a national movement under Jesse Jackson's leadership.

The Black Power upsurge affected the Dawson-Daley machine. While no one believed that, even if black people secured their "expected" 28 per cent of the crucial political posts, it would mean any real power to affect their lives, the fact that so few Negroes held such posts was an embarrassing index to their powerlessness.[16] But, concur-

---

[16] The Urban League report on "powerlessness" revealed how small a share of these posts black people had, despite their loyalty to the machine. Of 59 city councilmen only seven were Negroes, 12 per cent, although blacks were over 25 per cent of the electorate. There was only one Congressman out of 13—8 per cent. Of Cook County judicial posts, blacks held eight of 138 policy-making positions—6 per cent, and of non-judicial posts, three out of 34—9 per cent. There were 72 policy-making positions with the Board of Education; Negroes held seven, or 9 per cent.

ring with Carmichael and Hamilton that "Black visibility is not Black Power," the electorate has not been greatly concerned about putting on pressure for a few more top posts. "Firsts" and "onlies" don't impress Black Metropolis any more.[17] Despite the all-out support given Daley in the 1967 mayoral election, it was obvious that many voters were dissatisfied with the representatives of the machine in their local areas. "Taking care of business" meant taking care of *them*. While they were giving their votes to the Mayor, the electorate in the Sixth Ward on the South Side defeated the machine-backed candidate for alderman and elected a very liberal independent who had once had the temerity to run against Congressman Dawson himself.

There are now four black independents in City Hall. With the black electorate approaching a third of the total, these manifestations of independent political action, not revolutionary rhetoric, may be the most significant expression of Black Power in Midwest Metropolis.

[17] See Vol. II, "The Cult of Race," "The Race Man," and "The Race Hero," pp. 390–395.

A List of Selected Books
Dealing with the American Negro

Bond, Horace Mann, *The Education of the Negro in the American Social Order.* New York: Prentice-Hall, Inc., 1934.

Bontemps, Arna, and Jack Conroy, *They Seek a City.* Garden City, N. Y.: Doubleday, Doran and Company, Inc., 1945.

Cayton, Horace R., and George S. Mitchell, *Black Workers and the New Unions.* Chapel Hill: The University of North Carolina Press, 1939.

The Chicago Commission on Race Relations, *The Negro in Chicago.* Chicago: The University of Chicago Press, 1922.

Davis, Allison, and John Dollard, *Children of Bondage:* the personality development of Negro youth in the urban South. Washington, D. C.: American Council on Education, 1940. (Prepared for the American Youth Commission.)

Davis, Allison, Burleigh B. Gardner, and Mary R. Gardner, *Deep South:* a social anthropological study of caste and class. Chicago: The University of Chicago Press, 1941.

Day, Caroline Bond, *A Study of Some Negro-White Families in the United States.* Cambridge: Peabody Museum of Harvard University, 1932.

Detweiler, Frederick G., *The Negro Press in the United States.* Chicago: The University of Chicago Press, 1922.

Dollard, John, *Caste and Class in a Southern Town.* New Haven: Yale University Press, 1937. (Published for the Yale Institute of Human Relations.)

Doyle, Bertram Wilbur, *The Etiquette of Race Relations in the South.* Chicago: The University of Chicago Press, 1937.

Du Bois, W. E. Burghardt, *The Philadelphia Negro:* a social study. Philadelphia: The University of Pennsylvania Press, 1899.

Embree, Edwin R., *Brown America:* the story of a new race. New York: The Viking Press, 1931.

Frazier, E. Franklin, *The Negro Family in Chicago.* Chicago: The University of Chicago Press, 1932.

Frazier, E. Franklin, *The Negro Family in the United States*. Chicago: The University of Chicago Press, 1939.

Frazier, E. Franklin, *Negro Youth at the Crossways,* their personality development in the middle states. Washington, D. C.: American Council on Education, 1940. (Prepared for the American Youth Commission.)

Gallagher, Buell G., *American Caste and the Negro College*. New York: Columbia University Press, 1938.

Gosnell, Harold F., *Negro Politicians,* the rise of Negro politics in Chicago. Chicago: The University of Chicago Press, 1935.

Harris, Abram L., *The Negro as Capitalist*. Philadelphia: The American Academy of Political and Social Science, 1936.

Herskovitz, Melville J., *The American Negro,* a study in racial crossing. New York: Alfred A. Knopf, 1928.

Holmes, Samuel J., *The Negro's Struggle for Survival*. Berkeley, California: University of California Press, 1937.

Johnson, Charles S., *The Negro College Graduate*. Chapel Hill: The University of North Carolina Press, 1938.

Johnson, Charles S., *Growing Up in the Black Belt*. Washington, D. C.: American Council on Education, 1941. (Prepared for the American Youth Commission.)

Johnson, Charles S., *Shadow of the Plantation*. Chicago: The University of Chicago Press, 1934.

Johnson, James W., *Black Manhattan*. New York: Alfred A. Knopf, 1930.

Kennedy, Louise V., *The Negro Peasant Turns Cityward*. New York: Columbia University Press, 1930.

Klineberg, Otto (ed.), *Characteristics of the American Negro,* New York: Harper, 1944.

Lewis, Julian H., *The Biology of the Negro*. Chicago: The University of Chicago Press, 1942.

Logan, Rayford W., and others, *What the Negro Wants*. Chapel Hill: The University of North Carolina Press, 1944.

Mays, Benjamin E., and Joseph W. Nicholson, *The Negro's Church*. New York: Institute of Social and Religious Research, 1933.

McKay, Claude, *Harlem: Negro Metropolis*. New York: E. P. Dutton and Co., 1940.

McWilliams, Carey, *Brothers Under the Skin*. New York: Little, Brown and Co., 1944.

Moton, Robert Russa, *What the Negro Thinks.* Garden City, N. Y.: Doubleday, Doran and Company, Inc., 1929.

Myrdal, Gunnar, *An American Dilemma,* the Negro problem and modern democracy. New York: Harper, 1944.

Northrup, Herbert R., *Organized Labor and the Negro.* New York: Harper, 1944.

Ottley, Roi, *New World A'Coming,* inside black America. N. Y.: Houghton Mifflin.

Powdermaker, Hortense, *After Freedom,* a cultural study in the Deep South. New York: The Viking Press, 1939.

Raper, Arthur F., *Preface to Peasantry,* a tale of two black belt counties. Chapel Hill: The University of North Carolina Press, 1936.

Reid, Ira DeA., *Social Conditions of the Negro in the Hill District of Pittsburgh.* Pittsburgh: General Committee on the Hill Survey, 1930.

Reuter, E. B., *Race Mixture,* studies in intermarriage and miscegenation. New York: Whittlesey House, McGraw-Hill Book Co., 1931.

Schrieke, B., *Alien Americans,* New York: Viking Press, 1936.

Spero, Sterling D., and Abram L. Harris, *The Black Worker;* the Negro and the labor movement. New York: Columbia University Press, 1931.

Sutherland, Robert L., *Color, Class, and Personality.* Washington, D. C.: American Council on Education, 1942. (Prepared for the American Youth Commission.)

Sterner, Richard, *The Negro's Share.* New York: Harper, 1944.

Thompson, Edgar T. (ed.), *Race Relations and the Race Problem.* Durham: Duke University Press, 1939.

Warner, Robert Austin, *New Haven Negroes,* a social history. New Haven: Yale University Press, 1940.

Warner, W. Lloyd, Buford H. Junker, and Walter A. Adams, *Color and Human Nature,* Negro personality development in a northern city. Washington, D. C.: American Council on Education, 1941. (Prepared for the American Youth Commission.)

Wesley, Charles H., *Negro Labor in the United States, 1850-1925;* a study in American Economic History. New York: Vanguard Press, 1927.

Woodson, Carter G., *A Century of Negro Migration.* Washington, D. C.: The Association for the Study of Negro Life and History, 1918.

Woodson, Carter G., *The Negro Professional Man*. Washington, D. C.: The Association for the Study of Negro Life and History, 1934.

Woofter, Thomas J., Jr., and Associates, *Negro Problems in Cities*. Garden City, New York: Doubleday, Doran and Company, Inc., 1928.

Wright, Richard, *12 Million Black Voices;* a folk history of the Negro in the United States. New York: The Viking Press, 1941.

Young, Donald R., *American Minority Peoples*. New York: Harper, 1932.

Suggestions for Collateral Reading
1962

The original edition of *Black Metropolis* presented *A List of Selected Readings Dealing with the American Negro*. The most important of these was Gunnar Myrdal's monumental study, *An American Dilemma* (Harper & Brothers, 1944). It is as relevant for understanding race relations in America today as it was when first written. Most readable of all the fifty-two items, perhaps, was Richard Wright's *12 Million Black Voices* (The Viking Press, 1941), a useful supplement to Myrdal's work.

During the past fifteen years a voluminous amount of literature has appeared dealing with race relations. Some of the works having the most relevance to problems raised in *Black Metropolis* are: Charles Abrams, *Race Bias in Housing* (ACLW, NAACP, ACRR, 1947); Frank H. Loescher, *The Protestant Church and the Negro* (Philadelphia, 1948); Wilson Record, *The Negro and the Communist Party* (University of North Carolina Press, 1951); and a Public Affairs pamphlet published in 1951, Crosby Alexander's *In These Cities*. An evaluative summary is available in an article by St. Clair Drake, "Recent Trends in Research on the Negro in the United States," *International Social Science Bulletin,* UNESCO, Vol. IX, No. 4, 1957.

Some of the more significant works dealing with aspects of American Negro community life are: Maxwell R. Brooks, *The Negro Press Re-examined* (Christopher Publishing House, 1959); G. F. Edwards, *The Negro Professional Class* (Free Press, 1959); and Charles Eric Lincoln's important study, *The Black Muslims in America* (Beacon Press, 1961). E. Essien-Udom relates the Black Muslim movement to a broader context in *Black Nationalism* (University of Chicago Press, 1962). A definitive work on a crucial subject is Luigi Laurenti's *Property Values and Race* (University of California Press, Berkeley, 1960).

A number of books have been published during the past sixteen years which illuminate various facets of Negro life in Chicago. Two novels are significant: *The Policy King* by Louis A. H. Caldwell (New Vistas Publishing House, 1945) and *Trumbull Park* by Frank L. Brown (Regnery, 1959); the latter captures the mood of tragic tension that surrounded a public housing project which remained the scene of racial conflict over a long period of time. Roi Ottley has memorialized the founder of the Chicago *Defender* in *The Lonely Warrior* (Regnery, 1955); Julia Abrahamson has described the struggle to build an integrated middle-class residential area in *A Neighborhood Finds Itself* (Harper, 1959); and James Q. Wilson brings the political saga up to date in *Negro Politics: The Search for Leadership* (Free Press, 1960). The Southside Community Committee describes a successful effort to deal with some phases of juvenile delinquency in an attractive little book, *Bright Shadows in Bronzeville* (1949). *Bronzeville Boys and Girls* (Harper, 1956) by Gwendolyn Brooks mediates the authentic flavor of community life in a charming group of poems.

For readers who want to learn about activities in Bronzeville from time to time, the weekly Chicago *Defender* is always available (2410 S. Michigan Avenue). For those desiring to study Black Metropolis and its current problems, publications may be secured without charge from the Chicago Urban League (2410 S. Michigan Avenue), the Chicago Commission on Human Relations and the Mayor's Committee on New Residents (54 West Hubbard Street). The May, 1947 issue of *Holiday* magazine carried a set of colored photographs of Bronzeville life in 1946, which illustrated a summary article, *Black Metropolis,* written by the authors. In March, 1962, *Fortune* magazine carried an article by Charles E. Silberman, "The City and the Negro," which discusses the Temporary Woodlawn Organization (TWO), a controversial new Negro movement.

The first serious research on Negro-white relations in Chicago was sponsored and financed by a governmental agency, the Chicago Commission on Race Relations. The findings were published by the University of Chicago Press in 1922 as *The Negro in Chicago.* The book reflected the influence of Dr. Robert E. Park who was, at the time, developing a theory of race relations, and to whose memory *Black Metropolis* is dedicated. One of his students, Dr. E. Franklin Frazier, published *The Negro Family in Chicago* in 1932 (University of Chicago Press), and this book remained for many years the only full scale sociological study dealing with Bronzeville.

Research on the Negro in Chicago during the Depression years reflected the influence of Professor W. Lloyd Warner and of Dr. Louis Wirth (a student of Park). Four years before *Black Metropolis* appeared, a study of the problems of Negro youth in Chicago was published by the American Council on Education: W. L. Warner, W. A. Adams, and Buford Junker, *Color and Human Nature* (Washington, D. C., 1941). Harold F. Gosnell's *Negro Politicians* (University of Chicago Press, 1935) also appeared during this period.

During the Second World War, emphasis was upon policy-related research sponsored by various government agencies and dealing with problems of housing, employment, recreation, etc. An American Council on Race Relations was established in Chicago under the direction of Dr. Robert C. Weaver, and devoted attention to local as well as national problems. Important research on race relations in industry was begun by Professor Everett C. Hughes,[1] and research on the effect of Negro population movements on property values by Dr. Louis Wirth. Dr. Wirth's students made pioneering studies on the effect of Negroes on property values.

After the Second World War, the most important theoretical work produced upon the Negro in Chicago was Allison Davis and Robert J. Havighurst, *The Father of the Man* (Houghton Mifflin Co., 1947). Combining social psychology and a socio-anthropoligical approach in the study of child-rearing practices among Negroes and whites at the lower-class and middle-class level in Chicago, this work might well be read as a follow up to *Black Metropolis.*

Since 1950, large-scale research on race relations in Chicago has proceeded as an adjunct to studies of problems of urban redevelopment. The Chicago Community Inventory of the University of Chicago has carried out a number of systematic studies of its own as well as those done for the Chicago Plan Commission and the South-East Chicago Commission. The literature is voluminous and much of it is highly technical. The work of Otis and Beverley Duncan cited in this edition of *Black Metropolis* would, however, interest the layman, as would also Peter Rossi's *The Politics of Urban Renewal* (The Free Press, 1961).

[1] See Everett C. Hughes, "The Knitting of Racial Groups in Industry," *American Sociological Review,* vol. XI, 1946, and his article written with B. Speroff, "Problems and Approaches in Integrating Minority Group Work Forces," *Journal of Social Psychology,* Vol. 37, 1953.

1969

Emphasis upon policy-related and action-oriented research, rather than the production of theoretical studies similar to *Deep South, Black Metropolis,* and *The Father of the Man,* has continued (cf. W. L. Warner, "A Methodological Note," pp. 769–782 and comments on p. 798). The best study of a black community to emerge from this trend during the 1960s was Kenneth Clark's perceptive analysis, *Dark Ghetto: Dilemmas of Social Power* (Harper and Row, 1965), which drew heavily upon the author's disillusioning experiences as chairman of Harlem Youth Opportunities Unlimited (HARYOU). A succinct summary of some of the most crucial problems facing many black communities was provided in 1965 by Robert C. Weaver, then administrator of the Housing and Home Finance Agency and later Secretary for Urban Affairs, as part of a more general discussion in *Dilemmas of Urban America* (Harvard University Press).

With respect to Negroes in Chicago, numerous special studies of employment, housing, and educational problems, discussions of crime and juvenile delinquency, and analyses of the impact of urban redevelopment and renewal have been published since 1962 by the Research Division of the Urban League, the Chicago Commission on Human Relations, and individuals and research groups connected with the University of Chicago and various city agencies. (Some of these have been utilized in the 1969 Postscripts to Vol. I.) A Pentecostal minister who supplied effective leadership to The Woodlawn Organization (TWO)[1] has published a personal document that reveals significant details about the first successful drive for "Black Power" at the neighborhood level: Arthur Brazier and Robert DeHaan, *Self-Determination: The Story of the Woodlawn Organization.* A young black scholar who was actively involved in community organization in the area where rioting was most intense in 1966 and 1968 has analyzed the attempt of residents there to assume control of their own affairs: William W. Ellis, *White Ethics and Black Power: The Emergence of the West Side Organization* (Aldine Press, 1969).

Of the two most significant works dealing with the Negro community as a whole, one is an excellent in-depth study of the period described in Chs. 2–4 of *Black Metropolis*—Allan H. Spear's *Black Chicago: The Making of a Negro Ghetto, 1800–1920* (University of Chicago Press, 1967). His discussion of pre–World War I race riots and of the roots of the myth of "salvation via Negro business" provide an invaluable background for understanding crucial aspects of current racial tensions and the appeal of black capitalism. The other book, published during the same year by the same press, Charles Keil's *Urban Blues,* is a fascinating report of field work by an anthropologist on one aspect of what is now widely referred to as "soul." He presents vivid illustrative material on the manner in which two "axes of life" in Bronzeville—"having fun" and "praising God"—interpenetrate, thus laying bare the roots of Gospel and various forms of secular music that have had their origin in the Chicago ghettos.[2]

---

[1] Charles Silberman writes with enthusiasm of TWO in *Crisis in Black and White* (Random House, 1964).

[2] The structural-functional approach of *Black Metropolis* so narrows the focus that events between the world wars related to jazz, theater, sports, and literature are not discussed. However, *Anyplace but Here* by Arna Bontemps and Jack Conroy (Hill and Wang, 1966) supplies the background needed for a full appreciation of Keil's work.

The emergence of new social types in American ghettos has been studied in Watts, Oakland, and Houston and reported upon in William McCord, John Howard, Bernard Friedberg, and Edward Harwood in *Life Styles in the Black Ghetto* (Norton, 1969). These social types can be found in Bronzeville, too, though they have not been carefully studied there—"The Stoic," "The Defeated," "The Achiever," "The Exploiter," "The Rebel Without a Cause," "The Activist," "The Revolutionary." (They exist alongside older types described in Vol. II, pp. 730–736.) One investigator has suggested that, for some purposes, this type of analysis is more satisfactory than studies of social stratification.[3] Analysis of "life styles" associated with social types is a valuable tool for studying black communities, but *social class* remains the basic key to understanding the dynamics of American ghetto life and the relation of Negroes to the larger society. Refinements of the class concept have been suggested in an article by one of the authors, St. Clair Drake, "Economic and Social Status of the Negro in the United States," *Daedalus,* (Fall 1965). A thoroughgoing reappraisal of the class concept as applied to black communities appears in one of the most important recent contributions to the literature on the Negro in the United States, Andrew Billingsley's *Black Families in White America* (Prentice-Hall, 1968).

The reformulations of the social class concept take into account one of the most important developments in black communities during the 1960s—the great increase in the number of white-collar workers, skilled laborers, and high-school and college students and graduates. They are made necessary, too, by the effects of rapid upward social mobility of thousands of individuals on the structure of individual families and institutions. *In Bronzeville, the life styles of the upper and middle classes have changed little since 1962, but the number of people living them has, as well as the availability of economic resources to undergird them. Also the families along the margin between the middle and lower class have taken on a very mixed class character.*

The most dramatic changes in black ghettos, however, have been occurring at the lower-class level, owing to the impact of new experiences made possible through VISTA, Head Start, and the "poverty program" with its emphasis upon "maximum feasible participation," as well as to a growing disillusionment with the payoff given by the system, intensified by the catalytic influence of young black militants. The widespread favorable publicity given to "soul," which is basically a lower-class phenomenon, has resulted in a tendency to ask, "Why is the middle-class way the best way anyhow?"

Concern for involving lower-class individuals in self-help activities and motivating them to "achieve" has led some scholars to design research that emphasizes the *diversity* of family types and value-orientations within the lower class. The research of Hylan Lewis on family life and child-rearing practices in the Washington, D.C., ghettos reveals not only diversity of family types but also elements of strength, even in the much-criticized matrifocal families, that have been ignored by social workers and planners, including Daniel P. Moynihan, whose controversial report (*The Negro Family: The Case for National Action,* U.S. Department of Labor, March, 1965) stressed family disorganization and defined the ghetto as a "tangle of pathology." *Black Metropolis* recognized the diversity

---

[3] Ulf Hannerz, *Soulside* (Columbia University Press, 1969). In trying to systematize his data on relationships within a single slum block in Washington, D.C., this anthropologist isolated out four life styles: "mainstreamers," "swingers," "street families," and "streetcorner men."

of lower-class family types in Chicago (pp. 710–715), but presented the disorganized family as typical for the late depression years. Interviews with social workers suggest that during the 1960s a higher proportion of lower-class families were succeeding in the attempt to achieve a greater degree of stability.

Index

Abbott, Robert S., 59, 60, 399, 400, 401, 404, 749

"Advancing the Race," 51, 385, 390-95, 710-15, 731; programs for, 716-64; see also "Race leadership," "Race Man," "Race Woman"

African Orthodox Church, 122, 414

Afro-American, 124 n.

Amalgamated Meat Cutters and Butcher Workmen, policy of toward Negroes, 304-07

Amalgamation, white attitudes toward, 41, 276, 279, 280 n.

American Council on Race Relations, 281

American Dream, The, content of, 25, 26, 385; as a factor in European immigration, 7, 18; Negroes' substitute for, 81

American Federation of Labor, policy toward Negroes, 96, 236, 238, 240, 260, 265, 271, 298-99, 304, 312, 315, 326, 327, 329; 743; and CIO competition, influence of, 299, 337, 340-41; liberal policy of some locals in, 327 n.; warning of leaders on postwar reconversion, 112

American Medical Association, policy of toward Negroes, 552, 566

Americanization, process of, and spatial mobility, 13

Anderson, Louis B., 349

Anti-semitism, evidences of among Negroes, 197, 213, 249, 432 n., 435-56 *passim,* 635

Antislavery movement, in early Chicago, 32-39; and the freedmen, 40-43

Armour, P. D., 20, 57

Associations, voluntary: in Negro community, effect of migration on, 75; importance of to middle class, 662, 669-70; see also "Churches, Negro," "Lodges," "Social clubs"

"Axes of Life, The," 385-95

Bahai, and intermarriage, 139, 146, 148, 152-53, 530

Barnett, Ferdinand L., 345, 346, 399

Benedict, Ruth, 269 n.

Bethune, Mary McLeod, 395 n.

Bilbo, Theodore, as symbol of southern attitude toward Negroes, 355

Binga, Jesse, bombing of his property, 178; collapse of his bank, 84, 465-66; his philosophy of success, 467; as a symbol of Negro achievement, 82, 465

Birth-rates, in urban areas, 7, 659

"Black Baby Bugaboo," 171-73

Black Belt, density within, 176; evolution of, 47-48, 53, 78-79; pattern of growth, 382-83; proportion of Chicago's Negroes living within, 12, 175, 176 n.; reputation of, 209-11; white residents in, 197; see also "Black Ghetto," "Residential segregation"

Black Code, Illinois, 32, 44, 50, 69

Black Ghetto, 113, 198-213; congestion in, 203; as an index to subordinate status of Negroes, 114; neglect of social services within, 113; see also "Black Belt," "Residential segregation"